STREET ATLAS
Somerset

First published in 2002 by

Philip's, a division of
Octopus Publishing Group Ltd
2-4 Heron Quays, London E14 4JP

First edition 2002
Fourth impression with revisions 2005

ISBN-10   0-540-08220-1 (spiral)
ISBN-13   978-0-540-08220-9 (spiral)

© Philip's 2005

Ordnance Survey®

This product includes mapping data licensed
from Ordnance Survey® with the permission of
the Controller of Her Majesty's Stationery Office.
© Crown copyright 2005. All rights reserved.
Licence number 100011710.

Ordnance Survey and the OS Symbol are
registered trademarks of Ordnance Survey, the
national mapping agency of Great Britain.

Printed and bound in Spain
by Cayfosa-Quebecor

Contents

Digital Data

The exceptionally high-quality mapping found in this atlas is available as digital data in TIFF format, which is easily convertible to other bitmapped (raster) image formats.

The index is also available in digital form as a standard database table. It contains all the details found in the printed index together with the National Grid reference for the map square in which each entry is named.

For further information and to discuss your requirements, please contact Philip's on 020 7644 6932 or james.mann@philips-maps.co.uk

D0326196

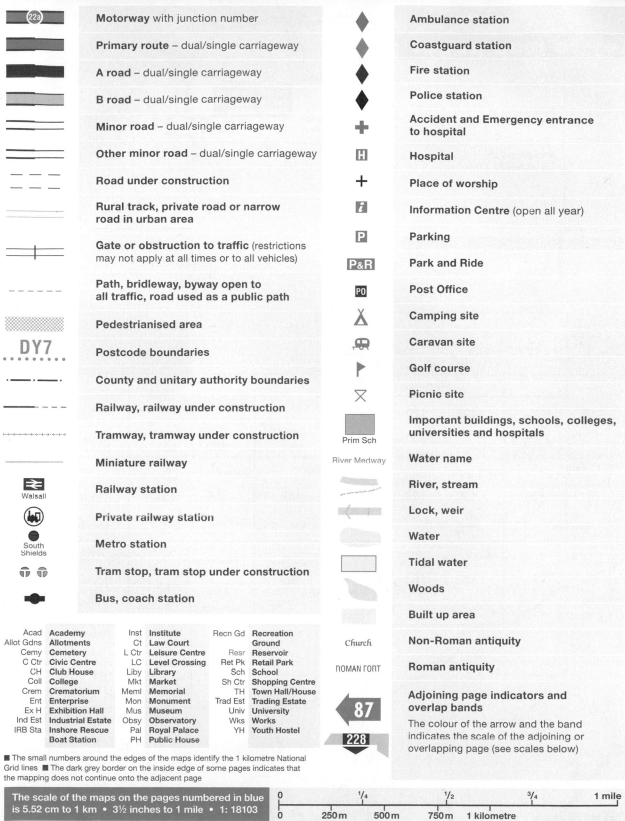

Motorway with junction number (22a)	
Primary route – dual/single carriageway	
A road – dual/single carriageway	
B road – dual/single carriageway	
Minor road – dual/single carriageway	
Other minor road – dual/single carriageway	
Road under construction	
Rural track, private road or narrow road in urban area	
Gate or obstruction to traffic (restrictions may not apply at all times or to all vehicles)	
Path, bridleway, byway open to all traffic, road used as a public path	
Pedestrianised area	
DY7 Postcode boundaries	
County and unitary authority boundaries	
Railway, railway under construction	
Tramway, tramway under construction	
Miniature railway	
Railway station (Walsall)	
Private railway station	
Metro station (South Shields)	
Tram stop, tram stop under construction	
Bus, coach station	

Ambulance station	
Coastguard station	
Fire station	
Police station	
Accident and Emergency entrance to hospital	
H Hospital	
Place of worship	
i Information Centre (open all year)	
P Parking	
P&R Park and Ride	
PO Post Office	
Camping site	
Caravan site	
Golf course	
Picnic site	
Prim Sch Important buildings, schools, colleges, universities and hospitals	
River Medway Water name	
River, stream	
Lock, weir	
Water	
Tidal water	
Woods	
Built up area	
Church Non-Roman antiquity	
ROMAN FONT Roman antiquity	
87 / 228 Adjoining page indicators and overlap bands	

The colour of the arrow and the band indicates the scale of the adjoining or overlapping page (see scales below)

Acad	Academy	Inst	Institute	Recn Gd	Recreation
Allot Gdns	Allotments	Ct	Law Court		Ground
Cemy	Cemetery	L Ctr	Leisure Centre	Resr	Reservoir
C Ctr	Civic Centre	LC	Level Crossing	Ret Pk	Retail Park
CH	Club House	Liby	Library	Sch	School
Coll	College	Mkt	Market	Sh Ctr	Shopping Centre
Crem	Crematorium	Meml	Memorial	TH	Town Hall/House
Ent	Enterprise	Mon	Monument	Trad Est	Trading Estate
Ex H	Exhibition Hall	Mus	Museum	Univ	University
Ind Est	Industrial Estate	Obsy	Observatory	Wks	Works
IRB Sta	Inshore Rescue	Pal	Royal Palace	YH	Youth Hostel
	Boat Station	PH	Public House		

■ The small numbers around the edges of the maps identify the 1 kilometre National Grid lines ■ The dark grey border on the inside edge of some pages indicates that the mapping does not continue onto the adjacent page

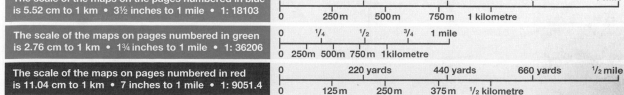

The scale of the maps on the pages numbered in blue is 5.52 cm to 1 km • 3½ inches to 1 mile • 1: 18103

| 0 | | ¼ | | ½ | | ¾ | | 1 mile |
| 0 | 250m | | 500m | | 750m | | 1 kilometre | |

The scale of the maps on pages numbered in green is 2.76 cm to 1 km • 1¾ inches to 1 mile • 1: 36206

| 0 | | ¼ | | ½ | | ¾ | 1 mile |
| 0 | 250m | 500m | 750m | 1kilometre | | | |

The scale of the maps on pages numbered in red is 11.04 cm to 1 km • 7 inches to 1 mile • 1: 9051.4

| 0 | | 220 yards | | 440 yards | | 660 yards | | ½ mile |
| 0 | 125m | | 250m | | 375m | | ½ kilometre | |

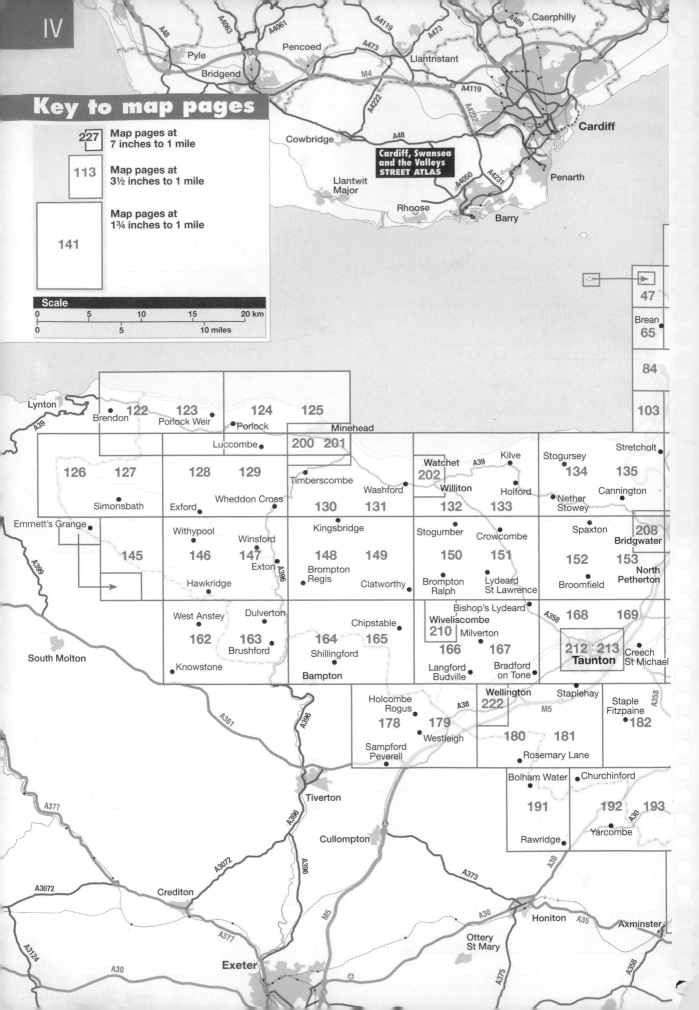

IV

Key to map pages

227	Map pages at 7 inches to 1 mile
113	Map pages at 3½ inches to 1 mile
141	Map pages at 1¾ inches to 1 mile

Scale

0   5   10   15   20 km
0   5   10 miles

Cardiff, Swansea and the Valleys STREET ATLAS

Caerphilly
Pyle
Pencoed
Llantristant
Bridgend
M4
A4119
Cardiff
Cowbridge
A48
Penarth
Llantwit Major
Rhoose
Barry

47
Brean 65
84
103

Lynton
Brendon 122   123 Porlock Weir   124   125
Porlock
Luccombe   200 201   Minehead
126   127   128   129   Timberscombe   Washford   Watchet 202   Kilve   Stogursey 134   Stretcholt 135
Williton   Holford   Cannington
Simonsbath   Exford   Wheddon Cross   130   131   132   133   Nether Stowey
Emmett's Grange   Withypool   Winsford   Kingsbridge   Stogumber   Crowcombe   Spaxton   208 Bridgwater
145   146   147   148   149   150   151   152   153 North Petherton
Exton   Brompton Regis   Lydeard St Lawrence   Broomfield
Hawkridge   Clatworthy   Brompton Ralph
West Anstey   Dulverton   Chipstable   Bishop's Lydeard   168   169
162   163   Brushford   164   165   Wiveliscombe 210   Milverton   A358   212 213   Creech St Michael
Knowstone   Shillingford   166   167   Taunton
Bampton   Langford Budville   Bradford on Tone   Wellington   Staplehay   Staple Fitzpaine
Holcombe Rogus   A38   222   M5   182
178   179   Westleigh   180   181
South Molton   Sampford Peverell   Rosemary Lane
Bolham Water   Churchinford
Tiverton   191   192   193
Cullompton   Rawridge   Yarcombe
Crediton
Honiton   Axminster
Exeter   Ottery St Mary

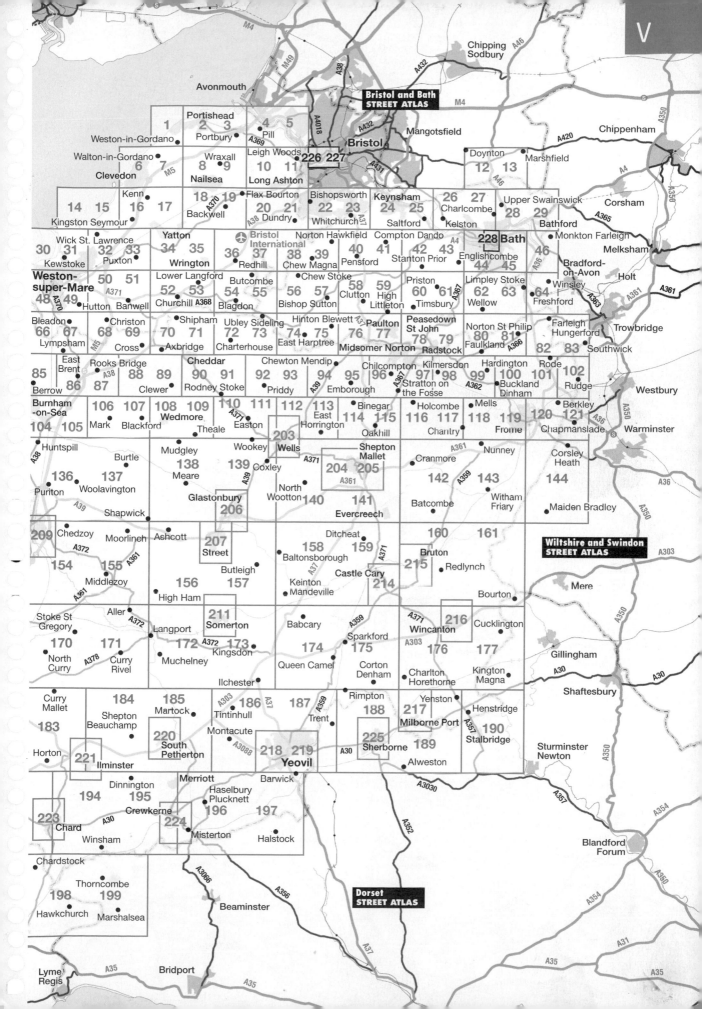

Route planning

Scale

0 1 2 3 4 5 6 7 8 km

0 1 2 3 4 5 miles

BRISTOL CHANNEL

BRIDGWATER BAY

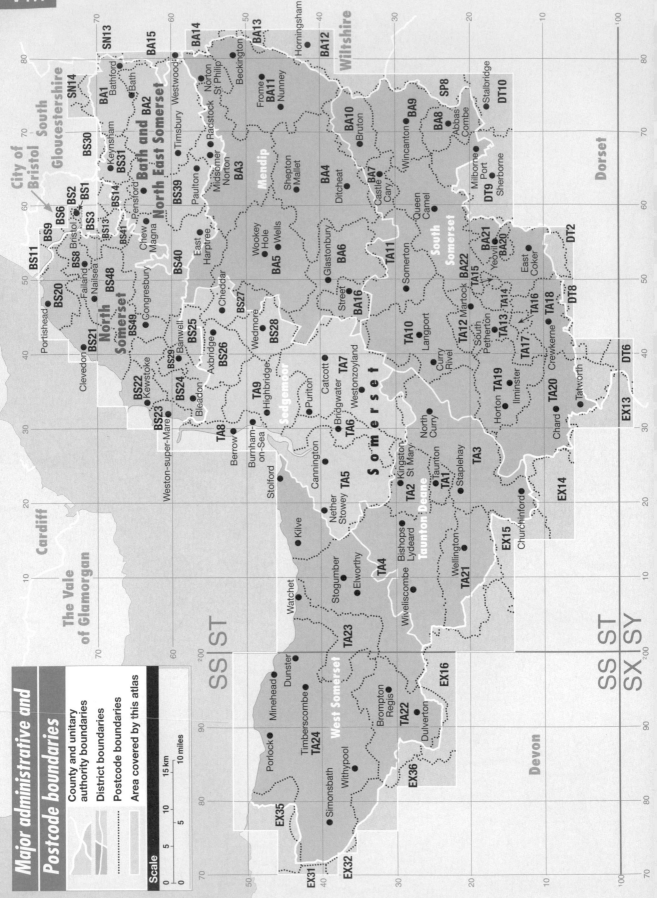

Major administrative and
Postcode boundaries

County and unitary authority boundaries

District boundaries

Postcode boundaries

Area covered by this atlas

Scale

0 5 10 15 km
0 5 10 miles

The Vale of Glamorgan

Cardiff

City of Bristol

South Gloucestershire

Wiltshire

Dorset

Devon

North Somerset

Bath and North East Somerset

Mendip

Sedgemoor

Somerset

South Somerset

West Somerset

Taunton Deane

SN13
SN14
BA15
BA14
BA13
BA12
BS30
BA1 Bathford
Keynsham Bath
BA2
BS31
BS14
Pensford
BS11
BS9 BS6 BS2 BS1
BS8 Bristol BS3
BS41 BS13
Chew Magna
BS40
BS20 Portishead
BS48
BS21 Clevedon
BS49
BS22 Kewstoke
BS23 Weston-super-Mare
BS24 Bleadon
BS29 Banwell
BS25
BS26 Axbridge
BS27 Cheddar
BS28 Wedmore
East Harptree
BA5 Wookey Hole
Wells
BA6 Glastonbury
Street
BA16
TA8 Berrow
TA9 Highbridge
Puriton
Catcott
Westonzoyland
TA7
Bridgwater
TA6
TA5 Nether Stowey
Cannington
Stolford
Kilve
Watchet
TA23
Stogumber
Elworthy
TA4
Bishops Lydeard
TA2
Kingston St Mary
TA1 Taunton
Staplehay
Wiveliscombe
TA21 Wellington
EX16
EX15
Churchinford
TA3
North Curry
TA10 Langport
TA19
Horton
Ilminster
TA18
Crewkerne
Chard
TA20
TA17
Tatworth
EX14
EX13
DT6
DT8
DT2
EX36
TA22 Dulverton
Brompton Regis
TA24 Timbercombe
Minehead
Porlock
Dunster
Simonsbath
Withypool
EX35
EX31
EX32

Norton St Philip
Beckington
Frome
BA11 Nunney
Radstock
Midsomer Norton
Paulton
BA3
BA39
Timsbury
Westwood
Horningsham
Shepton Mallet
BA4
Ditcheat
BA7
Castle Cary
BA10 Bruton
BA9 Wincanton
SP8
Abbas Combe
BA8
DT10 Stalbridge
Milborne Port
DT9 Sherborne
Queen Camel
BA21
BA20 Yeovil
East Coker
BA15
Somerton
BA22
Martock
TA12
South Petherton
TA13 TA14
TA16
TA11
Curry Rivel

SS ST
SX SY

SS ST
SX SY

Congresbury
Failand
Nailsea
Falaland

A B C D E F

8

7

77

6

Black
Nore

5

Severnmeade

Feddon
Village

Brackenwood
Gdns

76

Hang
Rock

Redcliffe
Bay

Redcliff
Bay

Mast

4

Little Halt

Mast

Police
HQ

BRANSCOMBE
WLK

3

Mast

PH

Nightingale
Valley

Charlcombe
Bay

Charlcombe
Wood

75

PORTISHEAD

Weston
Down

BS20

2

Walton
Bay

Black
Strip

Weston
Lodge

Seven Acre
Wood

Culver
Cliff

TWO ACRES
CVN PK

The
Ripple

The
Conygar

B3124

Pigeon House
Bay

WALTON BAY
HOUSE PARK
HOMES

BS21

Farley

Weston
Wood

1

Signal
Station

Walton
Down

Common Hill
Wood

PH

Weston in
Gordano

Canon's
Wood

B3124

74

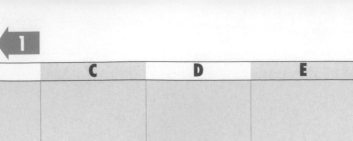

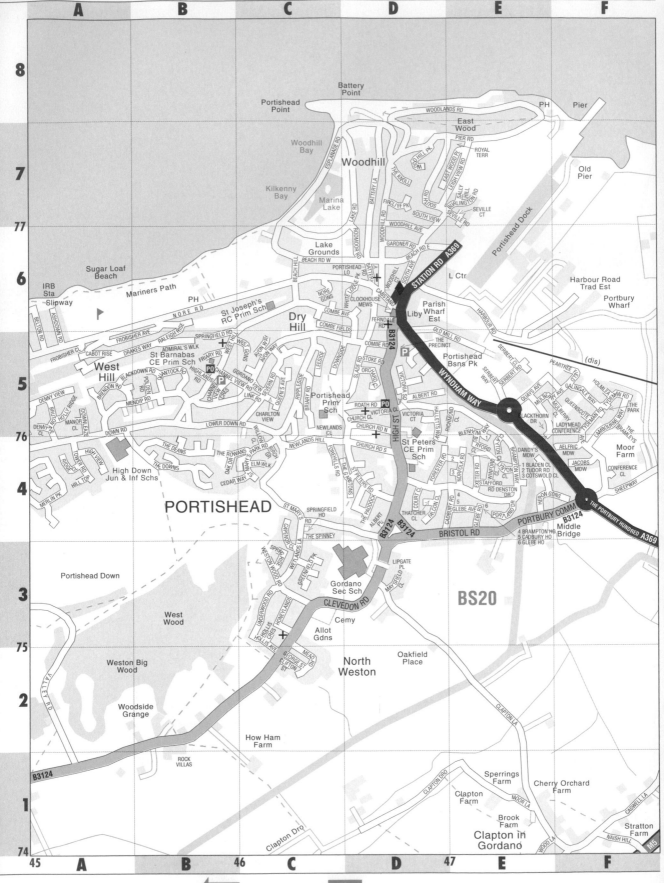

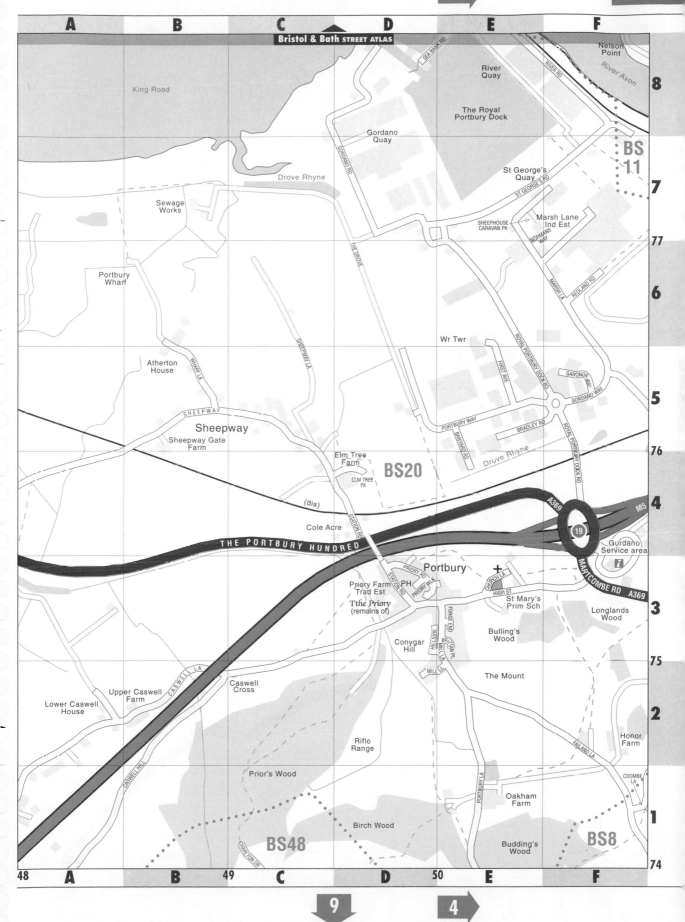

4

A   B   C   D   E   F

River Quay

Nelson Point

River Avon

8

King Road

SEA BANK RD

River Quay

RIVER RD

The Royal Portbury Dock

BS 11

Gordano Quay

GORDANO RD

Drove Rhyne

St George's Quay

ST GEORGE'S RD

7

Sewage Works

SHEEPHOUSE CARAVAN PK

Marsh Lane Ind Est

NORMANS WAY

77

Portbury Wharf

THE DROVE

MARSH LA

REDLAND RD

6

WHARF LA

SHEEPWAY LA

Wr Twr

ROYAL PORTBURY DOCK RD

GARONOR WAY

Atherton House

FIRST AVE

GORDANO WAY

5

SHEEPWAY

Sheepway

Sheepway Gate Farm

Portbury Way

BRADLEY RD

Drove Rhyne

ROYAL PORTBURY DOCK RD

76

Elm Tree Farm

BANYARD RD

BS20

ELM TREE PK

(dis)

A369

M5

4

STATION RD

Cole Acre

19

Gordano Service area

THE PORTBURY HUNDRED

Portbury

MARTCOMBE RD   A369

Priory Farm Trad Est

PRIORY RD

PH

PRIORY WLK

CHURCH LA

HIGH ST

St Mary's Prim Sch

Longlands Wood

3

Tthe Priory (remains of)

STATION RD

FORGE END

BRISTON PL

Bulling's Wood

Conygar Hill

HILLSIDE

MILL LA

MILL LA

The Mount

75

CASWELL LA

Caswell Cross

Upper Caswell Farm

Honor Farm

2

Lower Caswell House

FAILAND LA

Rifle Range

COOMBE LA

CASWELL HILL

Prior's Wood

PORTBURY LA

Oakham Farm

1

Birch Wood

CHARLTON DR

BS48

Budding's Wood

BS8

74

48   A   B   49   C   D   50   E   F

9

4

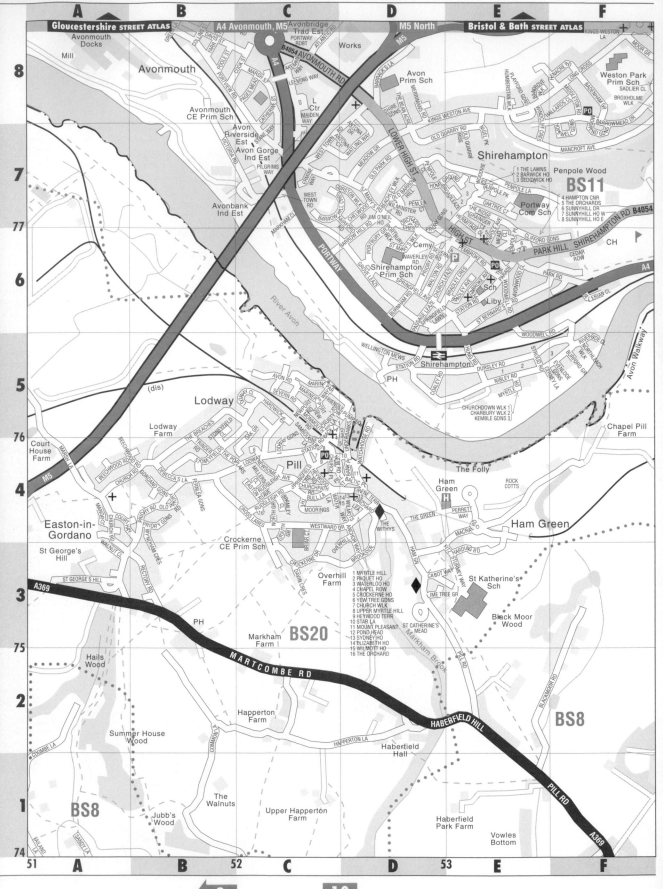

Gloucestershire STREET ATLAS   Bristol & Bath STREET ATLAS

Avonmouth Docks
Mill

Avonmouth

A4 Avonmouth, M5
Avonbridge Trad Est
PORTWAY ROBT
B4054 AVONMOUTH RD
Works

M5 North

Kings Weston La

8

Avonmouth CE Prim Sch

L Ctr
MAIDEN WAY

Avon Prim Sch

Weston Park Prim Sch

Broxholme WLK

Avon Riverside Est
Avon Gorge Ind Est
PILGRIMS WAY

Shirehampton

BS11

Penpole Wood

Portway Com Sch

7

West Town Rd

Avonbank Ind Est

HIGH ST

PARK HILL   SHIREHAMPTON RD B4054

CH

77

A4

6

PORTWAY

River Avon

Shirehampton Prim Sch

P

PO

Sch

Liby

Shirehampton

PH

WELLINGTON MEWS

Avon Walkway

Chapel Pill Farm

5

(dis)

Lodway

Lodway Farm

The Breaches

Pill

PO

The Folly

Ham Green
H

ROCK COTTS

76

Court House Farm

M5

Easton-in-Gordano

Crockerne CE Prim Sch

The Withys

The Green

Ham Green

PERRETT WAY

St Katherine's Sch

Black Moor Wood

4

St George's Hill

St George's Hill

PH

Overhill Farm

1 MYRTLE HILL
2 PAQUET HO
3 WATERLOO HO
4 CHAPEL ROW
5 CROCKERNE HO
6 YEW TREE GDNS
7 CHURCH WLK
8 UPPER MYRTLE HILL
9 HEYWOOD TERR
10 STAR LA
11 MOUNT PLEASANT
12 POND HEAD
13 SYDNEY HO
14 ELIZABETH HO
15 WILLMOTT HO
16 THE ORCHARD

ST CATHERINE'S MEAD

CABOT WAY

3

A369

PH

Markham Farm

BS20

Markham Brook

PILL RD

75

Hails Wood

MARTCOMBE RD

Haberfield Hill

BS8

2

Summer House Wood

Happerton Farm

HAPPERTON LA

Haberfield Hall

1

BS8

Jubb's Wood

The Walnuts

Upper Happerton Farm

Haberfield Park Farm

Vowles Bottom

PILL RD

A369

74

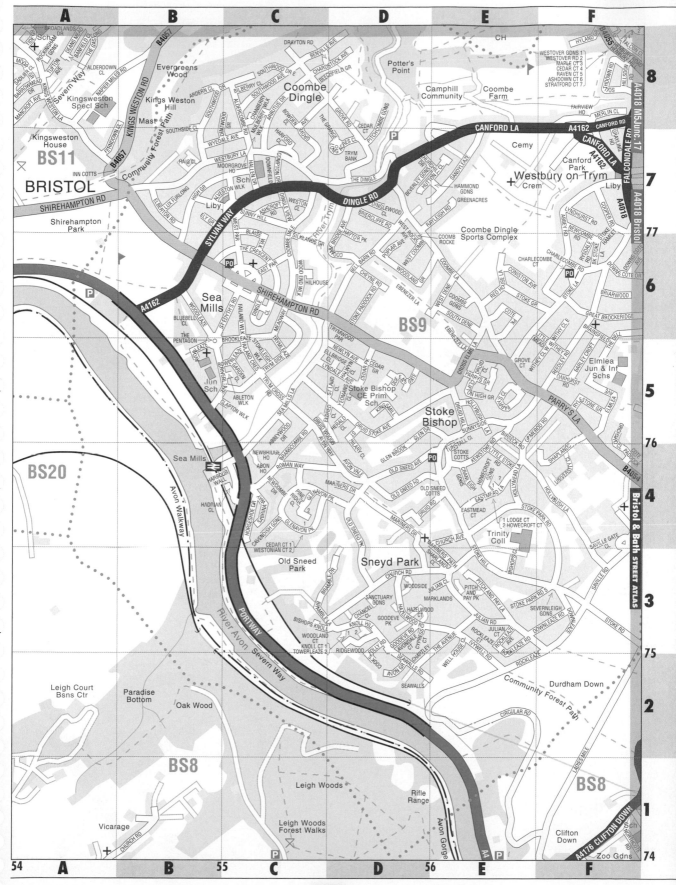

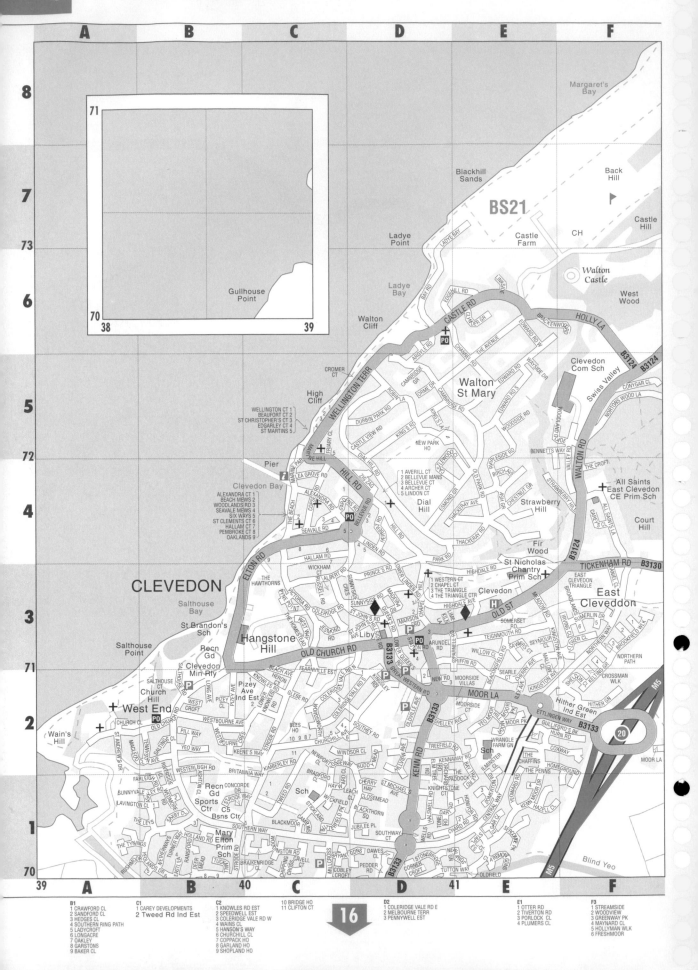

6

A B C D E F

8

7

73

6

72

5

4

71

3

2

1

70

BS21

Margaret's Bay

Blackhill Sands

Back Hill

Castle Hill

CH

Walton Castle

West Wood

Ladye Point

Castle Farm

Ladye Bay

Walton Cliff

Swiss Valley

Clevedon Com Sch

High Cliff

Walton St Mary

New Park Ho

All Saints East Clevedon CE Prim Sch

Pier

Clevedon Bay

Dial Hill

Strawberry Hill

Court Hill

Fir Wood

St Nicholas Chantry Prim Sch

East Cleveddon

CLEVEDON

Salthouse Bay

St Brandon's Sch

Clevedon

East Clevedon Triangle

TICKENHAM RD

Salthouse Point

Hangstone Hill

Recn Gd

Clevedon Min Rly

Moorside Villas

Church Hill

West End

Wain's Hill

Pizey Ave Ind Est

Moorside Ct

Hither Green Ind Est

Moor La

20

Mary Elton Prim Sch

Recn Gd Sports Ctr

Bsns Ctr

Wrangle Farm Gn

The Chaffins

The Penns

Homeground

Blind Yeo

39 A B 40 C 16 D 41 E F

71 70 38 39

B1
1 CRAWFORD CL
2 SANDFORD CL
3 HEDGES CL
4 SOUTHERN RING PATH
6 LADYCROFT
7 OAKLEY
8 GARSTONS
9 BAKER CL

C1
1 CAREY DEVELOPMENTS
2 Tweed Rd Ind Est

C2
1 KNOWLES RD EST
2 SPEEDWELL EST
3 COLERIDGE VALE RD W
4 WAINS CL
5 HANSON'S WAY
6 CHURCHILL CL
7 COPPACK HO
8 GARLAND HO
9 SHOPLAND HO

10 BRIDGE HO
11 CLIFTON CT

D2
1 COLERIDGE VALE RD E
2 MELBOURNE TERR
3 PENNYWELL CL

E1
1 OTTER RD
2 TIVERTON RD
3 PORLOCK CL
4 PLUMERS CL

F3
1 STREAMSIDE
2 WOODVIEW
3 GREENWAY PK
4 MAYNARD CL
5 HOLLYMAN WLK
6 FRESHMOOR

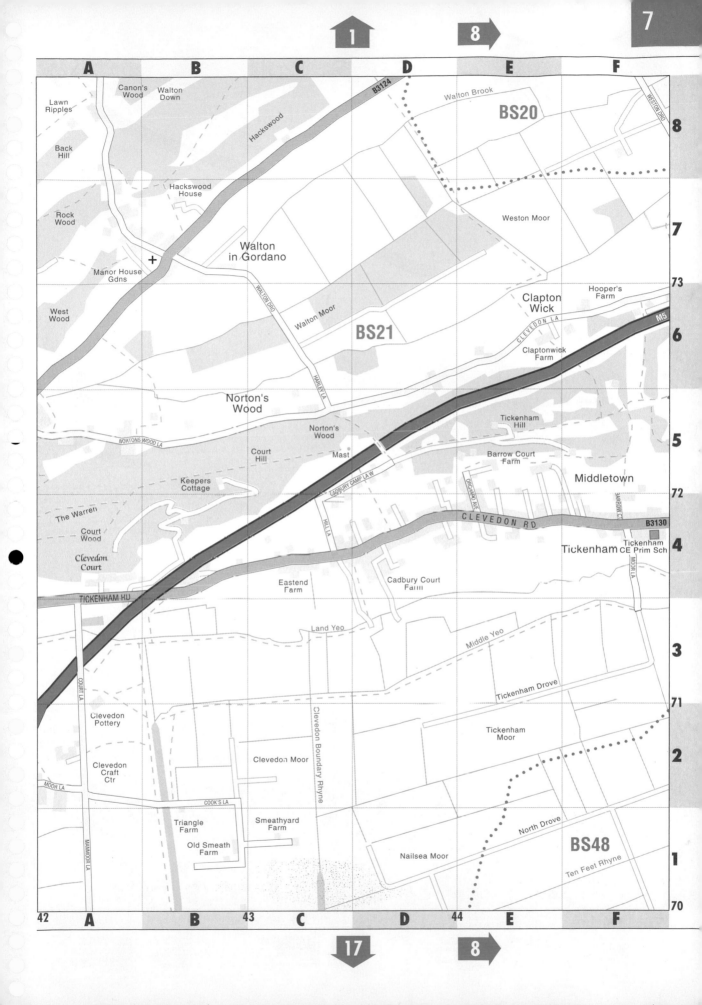

A B C D E F

8

7

73

6

5

72

4

3

71

2

1

70

45 A B 46 C D 47 E F

Clapton in Gordano

THE CAUSEWAY
SWANCOMBE
MORGANS BLDGS
M5
NAISH HILL

Hillcrest

Nicholas Wood

Clapton Court

WOOD LA

Morgans Buildings

The Old Rectory

Naish House

BS20

Clapton Moor

Parsonage Wood

Naish Farm

New Farm

Cockheap Wood

Dunhill Wood

Clevedon Lane Farm

CLEVEDON LA

West Park Wood

West Park Wood

Upper Sidelands

CADBURY CAMP LA

Chummock Wood

M5

Lime Breach Wood

Cadbury Camp

Abbot's Horn

Mogg's Wood

Baye's Wood

High Wood

Little Valley Farm

Round Wood

Hale's Farm

Longwood

CLEVEDON RD

B3128

Summerhouse Wood

CH

BS21

Folly Farm House

Luggard's Cross

OLD LA

PH

Batch Farm

SUMMERHOUSE

TICKENHAM HILL

STONEHENGE LA

Towerhouse Wood

Birdcombe Court Farm

B3103

PO

CLEVEDON RD

Luggard's Cross Farm

B3128

THE RIPPLE

Wellhouse Farm

LOWER HOUSE LA

WASHING POUND LA

CHURCH LA

Stone-edge Batch

Jacklands Bridge

Jacklands Farm

BS48

Tickenham Court

CAUSEWAY

Milton's Farm

NAILSEA

Southfield Rd Trad Est

Causeway Bridge

Tickenham Boundary Rhyne

LIMEBREACH WOOD 1
MIDDLE YEO GN 2

Ravenswood Special Sch

Greenslade Inf Sch

BIRDCOMBE CL

GREENFIELD CRES

MEADOW CL

VALLEY WAY RD

WOOD RD

Coates Est

3 VIEWS

WOODHILL

B3130

POUND LA

GREENSLADE GDNS

Kinghill CE Prim Sch

SUNNYMEDE RD

EASTWAY

Southfield Rd

TAVENERS CL

FRENCH CL

THE WILLOWS

WITHY CL

NAILSEA PK

HIGH ST

GODWIN DR

FRYTH WAY

NIGHTINGALE GDNS

MOOR LANDS CL

ABBOTS HORN

DROVE CT

EASTWAY SQ

SOUTHFIELD RD

HEATHGATE

HEATHFIELD WAY

FRIENDSHIP RD

WOODVIEW TERR

STOCK WAY N

North Dro

SILVER CT

FOSSE CL

SILVERLOW RD

BEECHWOOD RD

ERLOW GN

CRICKET FIELD GN

WESTWAY

Four Oaks Inf Sch

P

CHAPEL LA

P

STOCK WAY N

HIGH ST

1 HOBBS CT
2 FRIENDSHIP GR
3 SOUTHFIELD RD
4 SCOTS PINE AVE
5 HAWTHORN WAY
6 SCOTCH HORN CL

KINGSHEAD

FOSSE BARTON

FOSSE WAY

SILVER ST

Liby

SYCAMORE CL

P

PO

SCOTCH HORN WAY

P

North Dro

KINGSHILL

MOORFIELDS CT

GREENHILL CL

CAMP RD

MEADWAY AVE

P

STATION RD

WINDSOR DR

BROADMEAD

Golden Valley Prim Sch

PO

GILL CK

MOORFIELDS HO

ROCK AVE

LION CL

WHITESFIELD RD

WYATT'S CL

VALLEY GDNS

LAUREL CL

Poplar Farm

Parish Brook

WATERY LA

CHAPEL BARTON

ORCHARD RD

CHERRY CL

IVY CL

RIDGEWAY

THE DELL

HAZELBURY RD

STILL CL

BARNS CL

HILLCREST

HILLCREST

STATION RD

MORWOOD

RICHMOND RD

Nailsea Com Sch

PARISH BROOK RD

BRUNEL WAY

FIR LEAZE

KINGSHILL

YEW TREE CL

YEW TREE GDNS

GOSS LA

GOSS VIEW

GOSS CL

UNION ST

MIZZY CL

Allot Gdns

WAREHAM CL

BROOKE RD

CLARKEN CL

POLDEN

COOMBE

DUNKERY CL

POLLOCK GDNS

BRICKFORD WAY

CHARTERHOUSE

St Frances Prim Sch

LEIGHWOOD DR

BARNWOOD RD

NORTH ST

HANNAH MORE RD

CHAPEL LA

YEW TREE CL

EMS CL

GOSS CL

TRINITY RD

QUEENS RD

STRAWBERRY CL

CORFE CL

PORTLAND

BLAGDON

CLEVEDEN CL

HOLFORD CL

THE PERRINGS

MENDIP

BURRINGTON

MAYFAIR AVE

ASH HAYES DR

RICHMOND RD

West End Trad Est

ENGINE LA

WEST END LA

PYE CROFT

BLACKFRIARS RD

TRINITY CT

1 AVALON HO
2 CROWN HO

WHITESFIELD RD

CHANCEL CL

PLOUGHED PADDOCK

CHURCH LA

TRINITY RD

6

STRAWBERRY CL

ROWBERROW

ROWBERROW WAY

MAYFAIR AVE

D1
1 MIZZYMEAD CL
2 BEAUFORT GDNS
3 AMBERLEY GDNS
4 CLAREMONT GDNS
5 DOWNLAND CL
6 DORCHESTER CL

E1
1 FARMHOUSE CT
2 BRENDON GDNS
3 MENDIP CL
4 SELWORTHY GDNS
5 DUNSTER GDNS
6 BIDDISHAM CL

E2
1 CHRISTCHURCH CL
2 CLEVEDON WLK
3 SOMERSET SQ
4 COLLIERS WLK
5 CROWN GLASS PL
6 VALLEY CL
7 FARMHOUSE CL

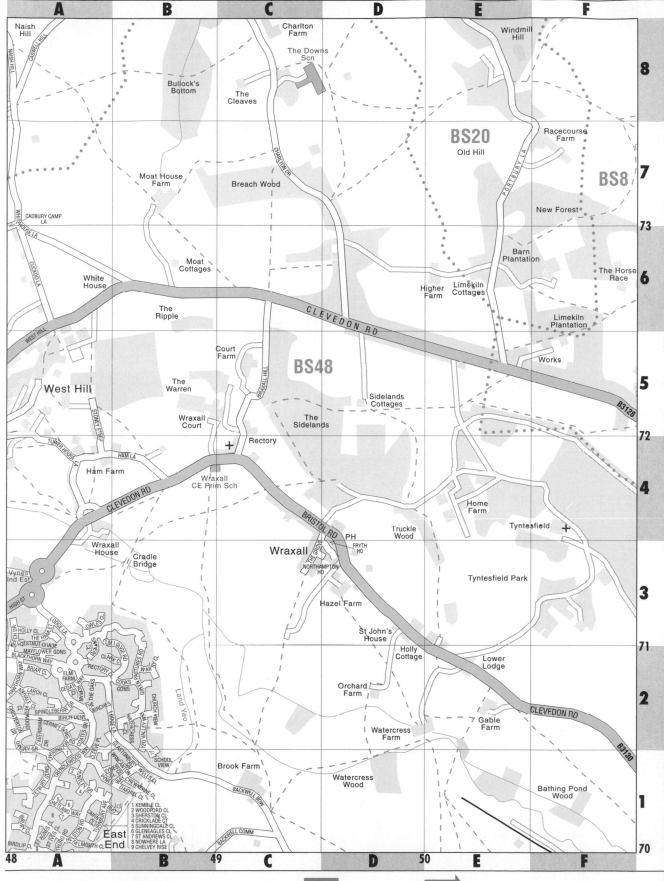

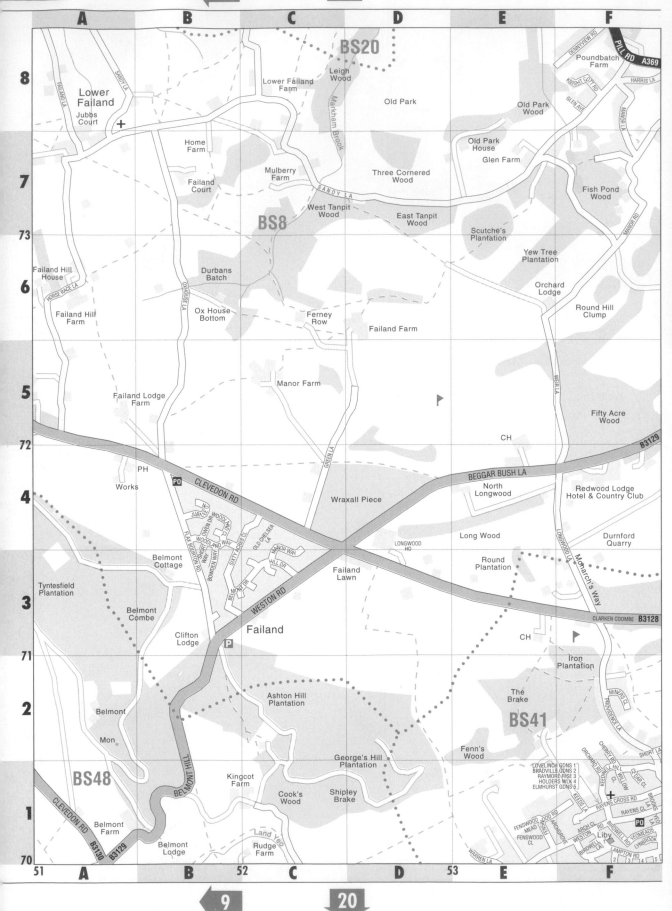

9
4

A   B   C   D   E   F

8   BS20
Lower Failand Farm   Leigh Wood   Old Park
Lower Failand   Poundbatch Farm
DENNY VIEW RD   PILL RD A369
KNIGHT COTT RD   HARRIS LA
Jubbs Court   Old Park Wood   GLEN AVE   MANOR LA
Home Farm   Old Park House
7   Mulberry Farm   Three Cornered Wood   Glen Farm   Fish Pond Wood
Failand Court   SANDY LA   MANOR RD
73   West Tanpit Wood   East Tanpit Wood   Scutche's Plantation
BS8   Yew Tree Plantation
Failand Hill House   Durbans Batch   Orchard Lodge
6   HORSE RACE LA   Ferney Row   Round Hill Clump
Failand Hill Farm   Ox House Bottom   OXHOUSE LA   Failand Farm   WEIR LA
5   Manor Farm   Fifty Acre Wood
Failand Lodge Farm   GREEN LA   CH
72   B3129
PH   BEGGAR BUSH LA   Redwood Lodge Hotel & Country Club
Works   PO   CLEVEDON RD   North Longwood
4   Wraxall Piece   Durnford Quarry
JUBILEE CL   WOODLAND DR   WOODLAND WAY   Long Wood   LONGWOOD LA
Belmont Cottage   LONGWOOD HO   Round Plantation   MONARCH'S WAY
Tyntesfield Plantation   BOWDEN WAY   SIXTY ACRES CL   OLD CHELSEA LA   MANOR WAY   Failand Lawn
3   BELMONT DR   WILL DR   CLARKEN COOMBE B3128
Belmont Combe   WESTON RD   CH
Clifton Lodge   Failand   Iron Plantation
71   P   The Brake   MINERS CL
2   Ashton Hill Plantation   BS41   PROVIDENCE LA
Belmont   Fenn's Wood
Mon   BELMONT HILL   LOVELINCH GDNS 1   CHERRY RD   SHORT LA
George's Hill Plantation   BRADVILLE GDNS 2   ORCHARD RD   WILLOW
BS48   Kingcot Farm   RAYMORE RISE 3   KEENELL HILL   CEDAR CL
CLEVEDON RD   Cook's Wood   Shipley Brake   HOLDERS WLK 4   KEEDS LA   BROOKS CL
ELMHURST GDNS 5   RAYENS CL   RAYENS CROSS RD   YEO
1   FENSWOOD RD   WOOD RD   RAYENS   PO   YEOMEADS
Belmont Farm   MEAD RD   ARCH CL   ARCHGROVE   WESTON   BIDWELL RD   Liby   LYNBROOK
B3130   B3129   Land Yeo   FENSWOOD CL   BIRDWELL LA
70   Belmont Lodge   Rudge Farm   WARREN LA   LAMPTON RD   2 3 4 5

A   B   52   C   D   53   E   F

51

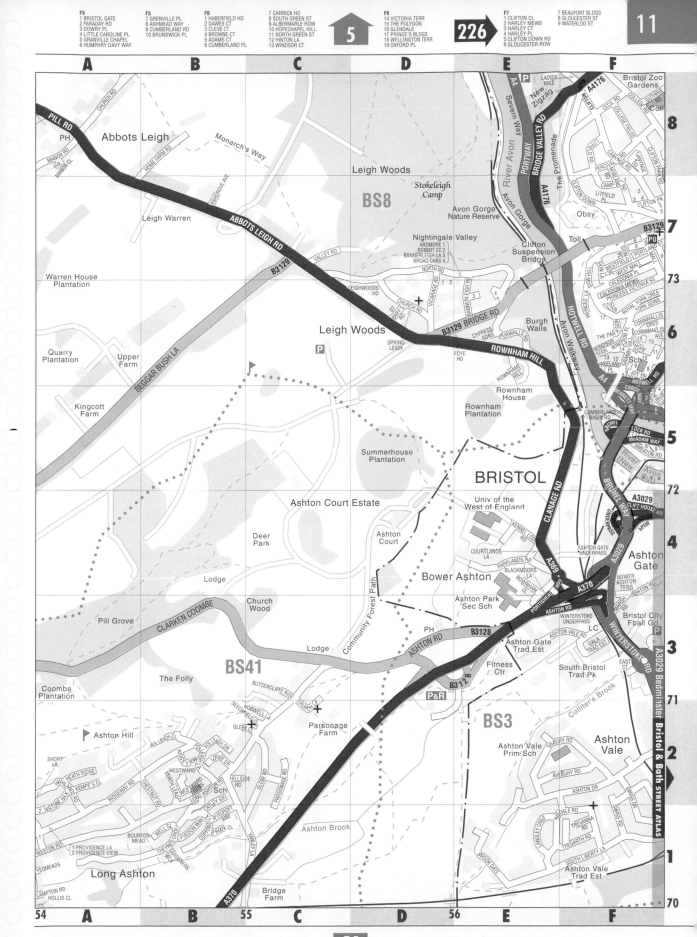

F5
1 BRISTOL GATE
2 FARADAY RD
3 DOWRY PL
4 LITTLE CAROLINE PL
5 GRANVILLE CHAPEL
6 HUMPHRY DAVY WAY

F5
7 GRENVILLE PL
8 ASHMEAD WAY
9 CUMBERLAND RD
10 BRUNSWICK PL

F6
1 HABERFIELD HO
2 DAWES CT
3 CLEVE CT
4 BROWNE CT
5 ADAMS CT
6 CUMBERLAND PL

7 CARRICK HO
8 SOUTH GREEN ST
9 ALBERMARLE ROW
10 HOPECHAPEL HILL
11 NORTH GREEN ST
12 HINTON LA
13 WINDSOR CT

F6
14 VICTORIA TERR
15 THE POLYGON
16 GLENDALE
17 PRINCE'S BLDGS
18 WELLINGTON TERR
19 OXFORD PL

F7
1 CLIFTON CL
2 HARLEY MEWS
3 HARLEY CT
4 HARLEY PL
5 CLIFTON DOWN RD
6 GLOUCESTER ROW

7 BEAUFORT BLDGS
8 GLOUCESTER ST
9 WATERLOO ST

11

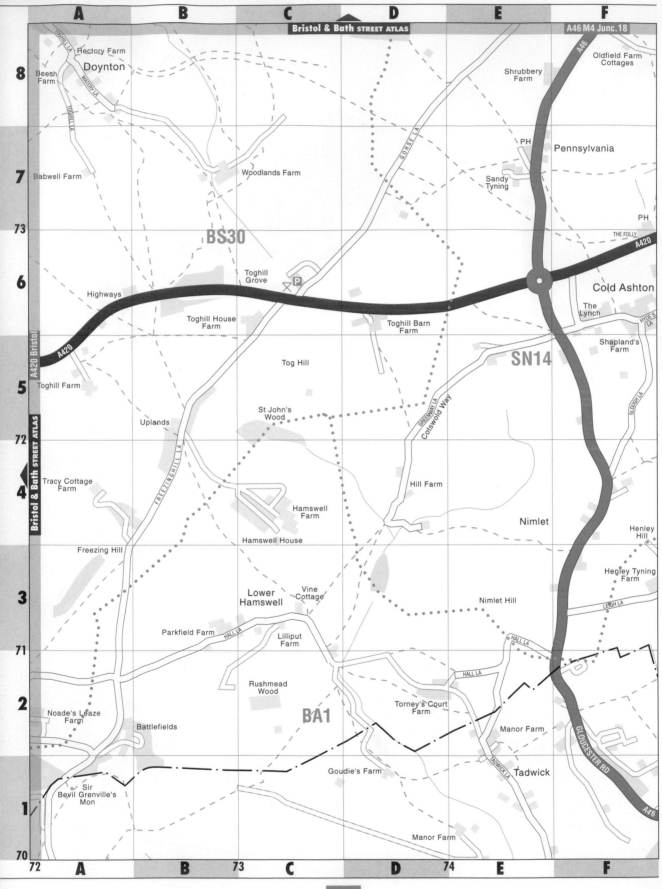

A46 M4 Junc.18

A   B   C   D   E   F

8

Rectory Farm

Doynton

Beech
Farm

Babwell Farm

Shrubbery
Farm

Oldfield Farm
Cottages

7

Woodlands Farm

PH

Pennsylvania

Sandy
Tyning

PH

73

BS30

THE FOLLY

A420

6

Highways

Toghill
Grove

P

Toghill Barn
Farm

Cold Ashton

The
Lynch

HYDE'S LA

Toghill House
Farm

Shapland's
Farm

A420 Bristol

A420

SN14

5

Toghill Farm

Tog Hill

GREENWAY LA

SLOUGH LA

Uplands

St John's
Wood

72

Cotswold Way

FREEZINGHILL LA

Bristol & Bath STREET ATLAS

4

Tracy Cottage
Farm

Hill Farm

Hamswell
Farm

Nimlet

Henley
Hill

Hamswell House

Freezing Hill

Hegley Tyning
Farm

3

Lower
Hamswell

Vine
Cottage

Nimlet Hill

LEIGH LA

Parkfield Farm

HALL LA

Lilliput
Farm

HALL LA

71

HALL LA

Rushmead
Wood

Torney's Court
Farm

GLOUCESTER RD

2

Noade's Leaze
Farm

BA1

Manor Farm

Battlefields

Goudie's Farm

TADWICK LA

Tadwick

Sir
Bevil Grenville's
Mon

A46

1

Manor Farm

70

72   A   B   73   C   D   74   E   F

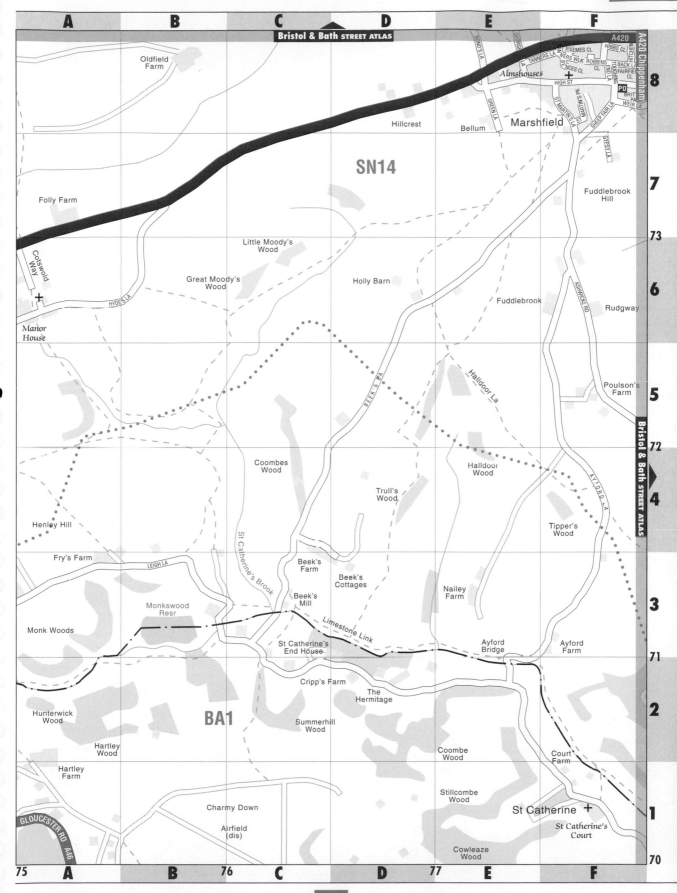

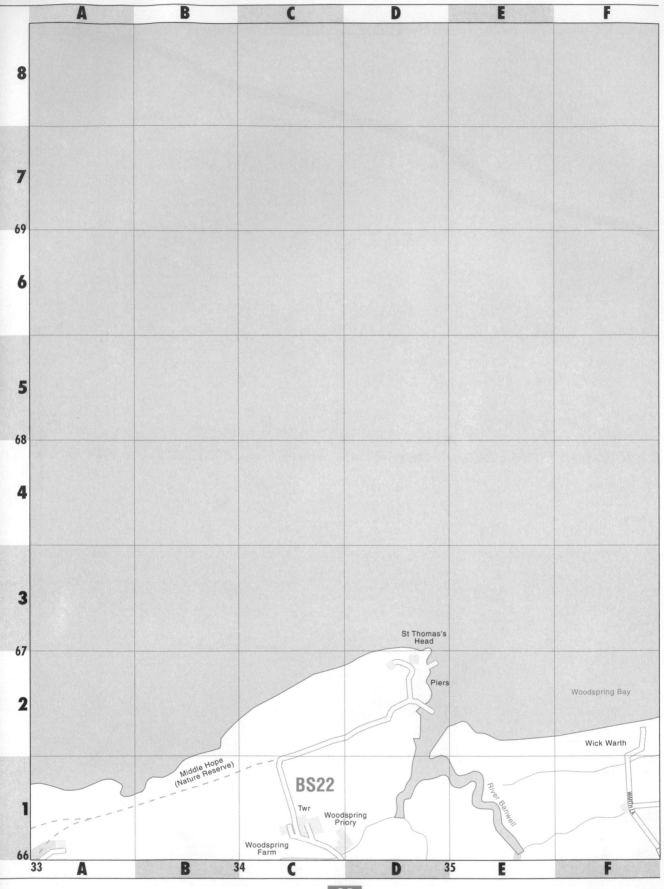

A B C D E F

8

7

69

6

5

68

4

3

St Thomas's
Head

67

Piers

2

Woodspring Bay

Wick Warth

Middle Hope
(Nature Reserve)

BS22

WARTH LA

River Banwell

1

Twr

Woodspring
Priory

Woodspring
Farm

66

33 A B 34 C D 35 E F

A B C D E F

Dowlais Ditch

8

7

Kingston Pill

69

Seawall Farm

6

Hook's Ear

Treble House Farm

BACK LA

5

Sewage Works

68

Channel View Farm

4

BS21

Broadstone Rhyne

MIDDLE LA

MIDDLE LA

Broadstone Farm

BROADSTONE LA

3

Wharf Farm

67

New House Farm

HAM LA

Ham Farm

Pool Farm

2

Ham Rhyne

Sewage Works

Mendip View Farm

YEO BANK LA

Yeo Bank Farm

1

MIDDLE LA

BS22

Mill Leaze Rhyne

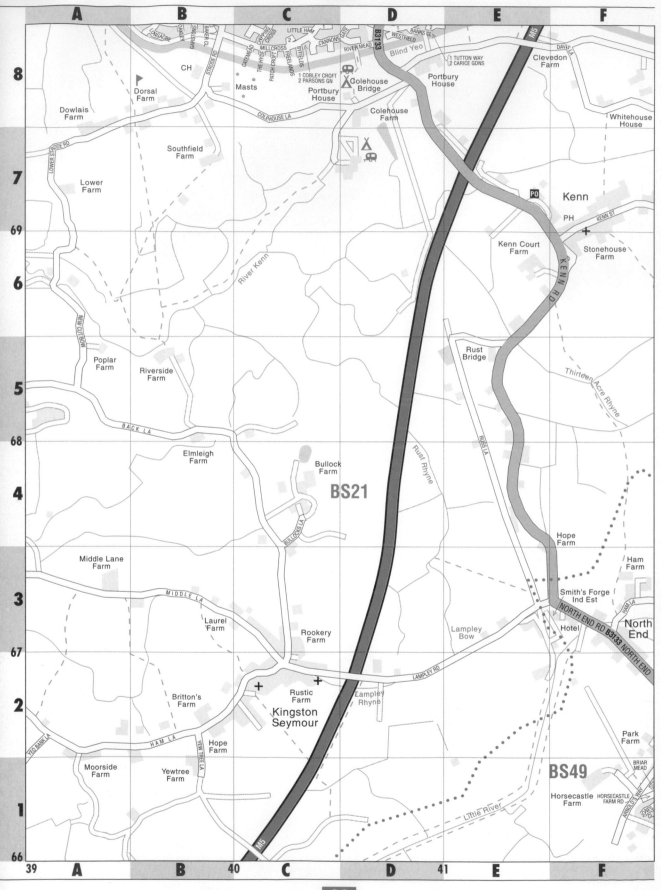

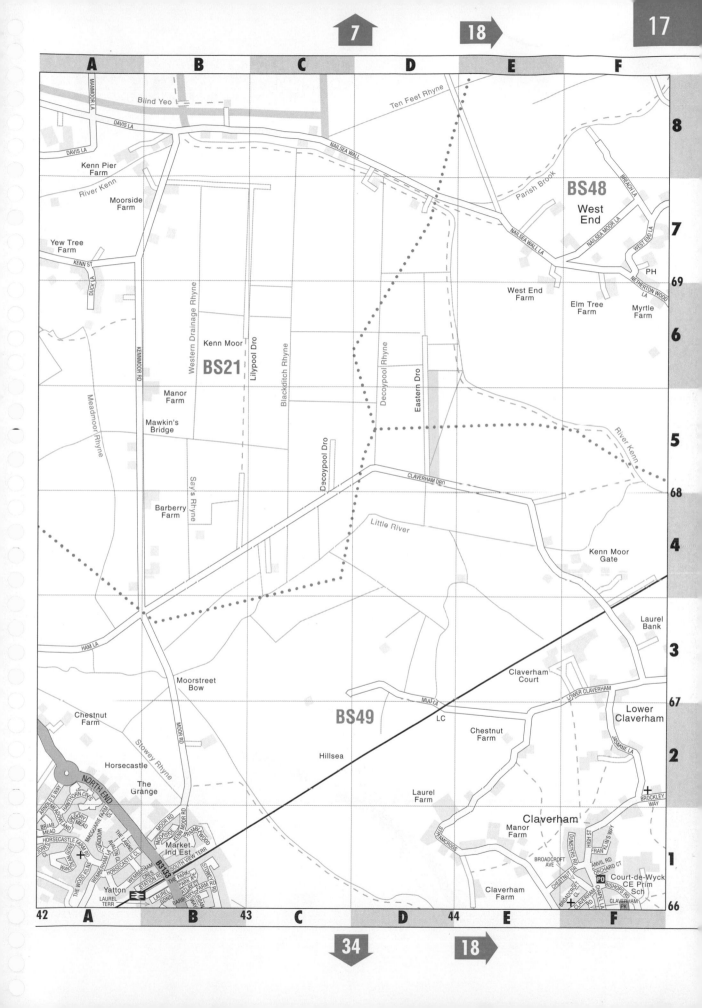

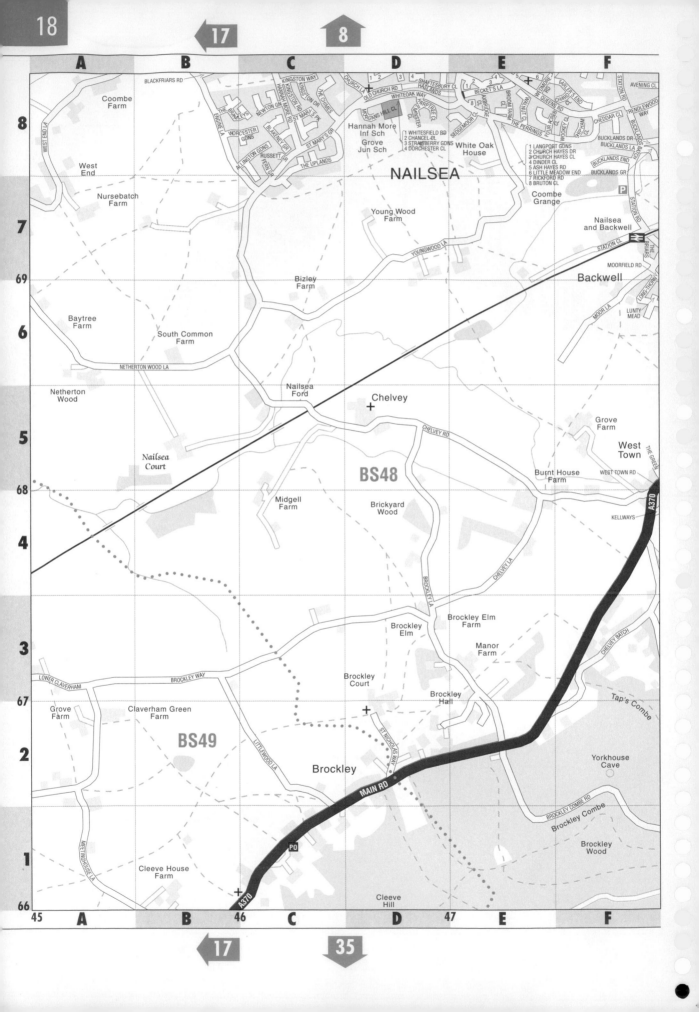

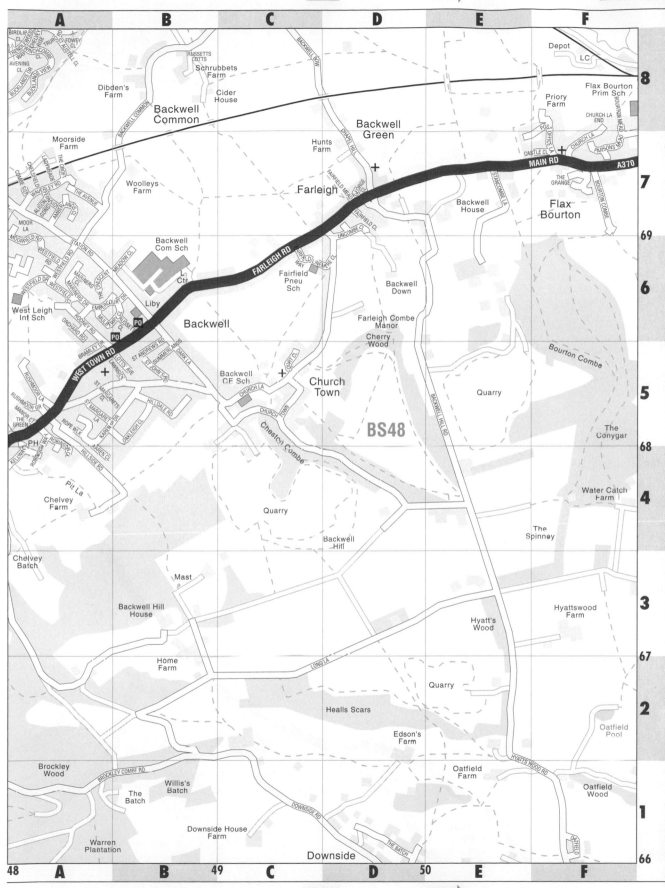

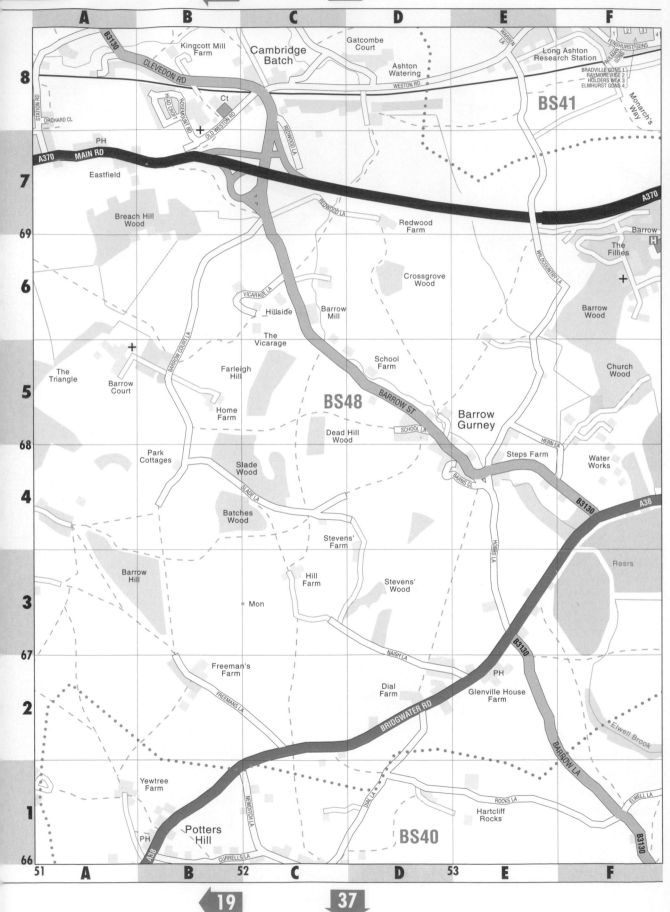

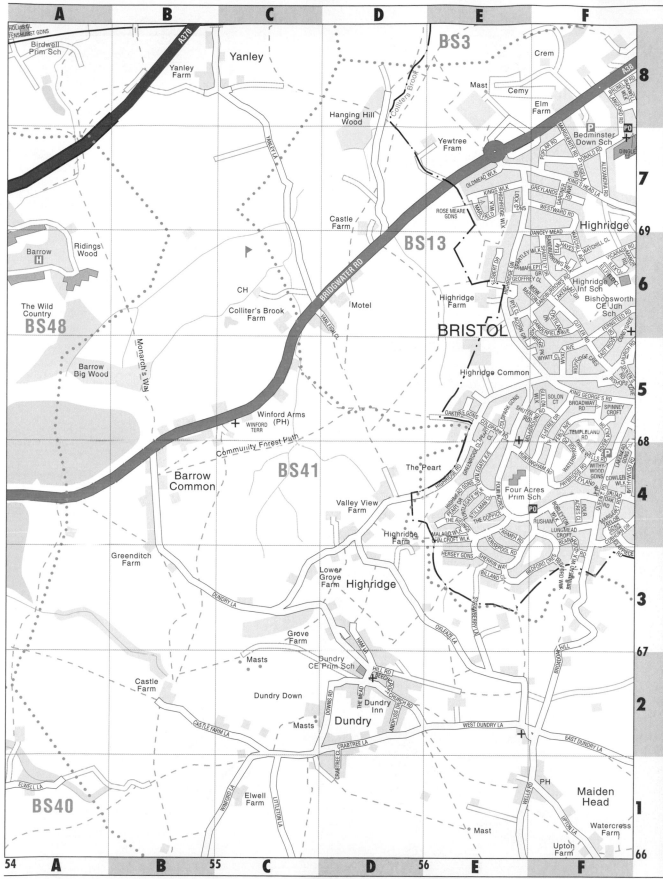

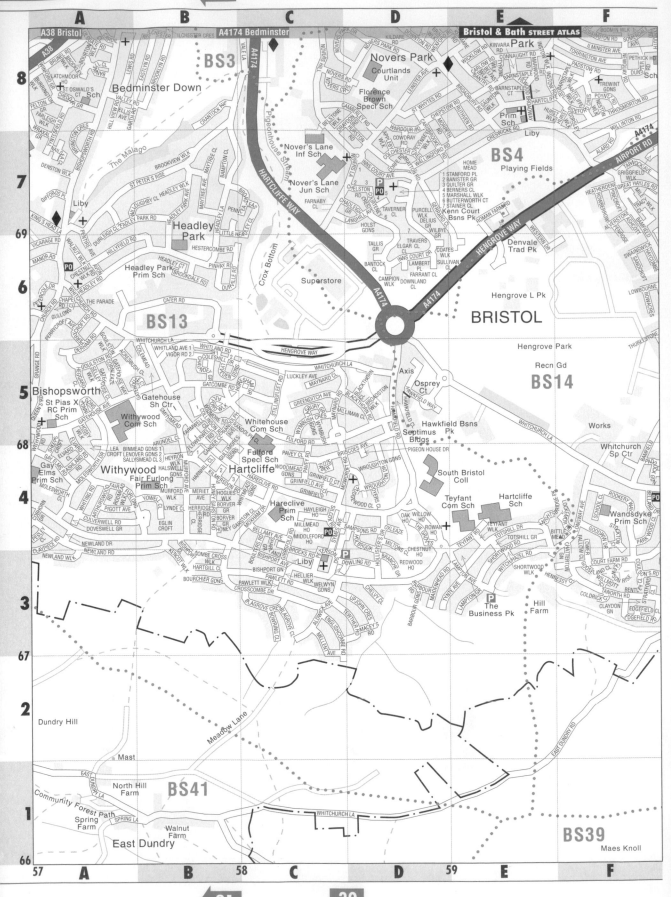

A38 Bristol   A4174 Bedminster

BS3

Bedminster Down

Novers Park

Courtlands Unit

Florence Brown Specl Sch

Nover's Lane Inf Sch

Nover's Lane Jun Sch

Prim Sch

Liby

BS4

Playing Fields

The Malago

Brookview Wlk

St Peter's Rise

HOME MEAD

1 STANFORD PL
2 BANISTER GR
3 QUILTER GR
4 BERNERS CL
5 MARSHALL WLK
6 BUTTERWORTH CT
7 STAINER CL

Kenn Court Bsns Pk

Liby

Headley Park

Hestercombe Rd

Crox Bottom

Denvale Trad Pk

Headley Park Prim Sch

Superstore

Hengrove L Pk

BS13

BRISTOL

Hengrove Way

Hengrove Park

Bishopsworth

Axis

Osprey Ct

Recn Gd

BS14

St Pias X RC Prim Sch

Gatehouse Sh Ctr

Withywood Com Sch

Whitehouse Com Sch

Septimus Bldgs

Hawkfield Bsns Pk

Works

Whitchurch Sp Ctr

Gay Elms Prim Sch

Withywood

Fulford Specl Sch

Fulford Rd

South Bristol Coll

Fair Furlong Prim Sch

Hartcliffe

Hareclive Prim Sch

Teyfant Com Sch

Hartcliffe Sch

Wandsdyke Prim Sch

Liby

The Business Pk

Hill Farm

Dundry Hill

Meadow Lane

Mast

North Hill Farm

BS41

Community Forest Path

Spring Farm

Walnut Farm

BS39

East Dundry

Maes Knoll

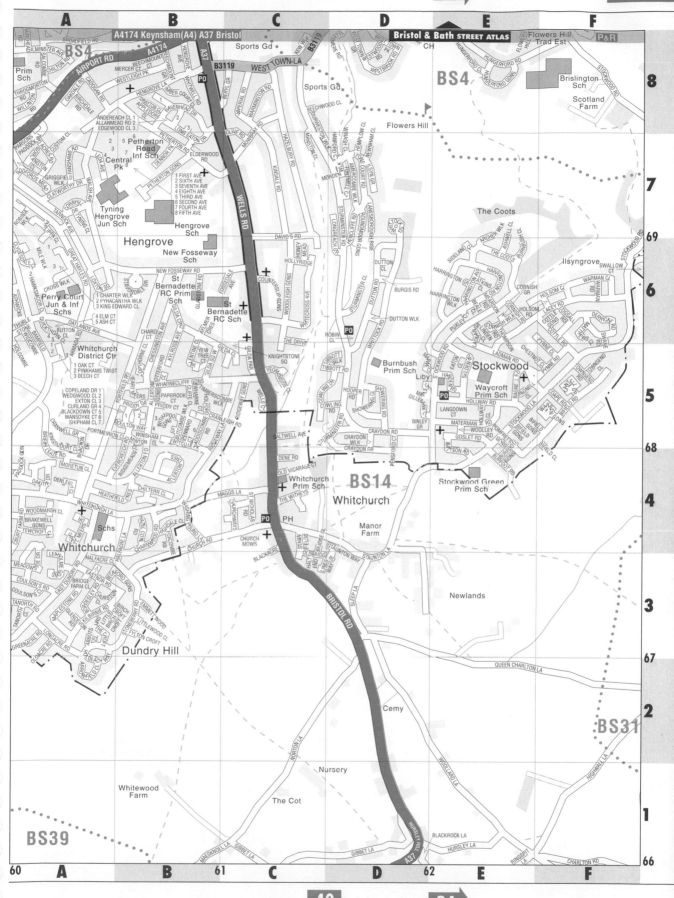

Bristol & Bath STREET ATLAS

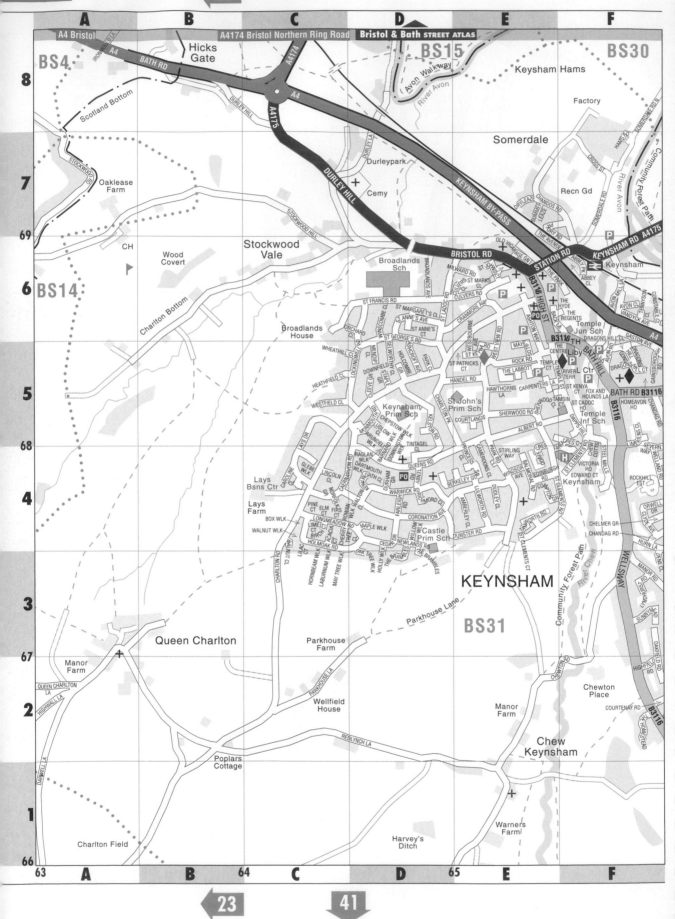

Bristol & Bath STREET ATLAS

A4 Bristol
A4174 Bristol Northern Ring Road
BS15
BS30

BS4

Hicks Gate

BATH RD

Keysham Hams

Avon Walkway

River Avon

8

Scotland Bottom

Somerdale

Factory

DURLEY HILL

A4175

7

Oaklease Farm

Durleypark

Cemy

KEYNSHAM BY-PASS

Recn Gd

River Avon

Community Forest Path

69

CH

Wood Covert

Stockwood Vale

BRISTOL RD

Keynsham

STATION RD

KEYNSHAM RD A4175

6

BS14

Charlton Bottom

Broadlands Sch

Broadlands House

B3116 HIGH ST

Temple Jun Sch

BATH HILL

Temple

The Centre

Liby

BATH RD B3116

5

Keynsham Prim Sch

St John's Prim Sch

Courtlands

Temple Inf Sch

B3116

68

Lays Bsns Ctr

Lays Farm

Windsor Ave

Victoria Ho

Keynsham

ROCKHILL EST

4

WELLSWAY

3

Queen Charlton

Parkhouse Farm

KEYNSHAM

Community Forest Path

River Chew

Chewton Place

67

Manor Farm

Parkhouse Lane

BS31

Castle Prim Sch

2

Wellfield House

REDLYNCH LA

Manor Farm

Chew Keynsham

B3116

Poplars Cottage

1

Harvey's Ditch

Warners Farm

66

Charlton Field

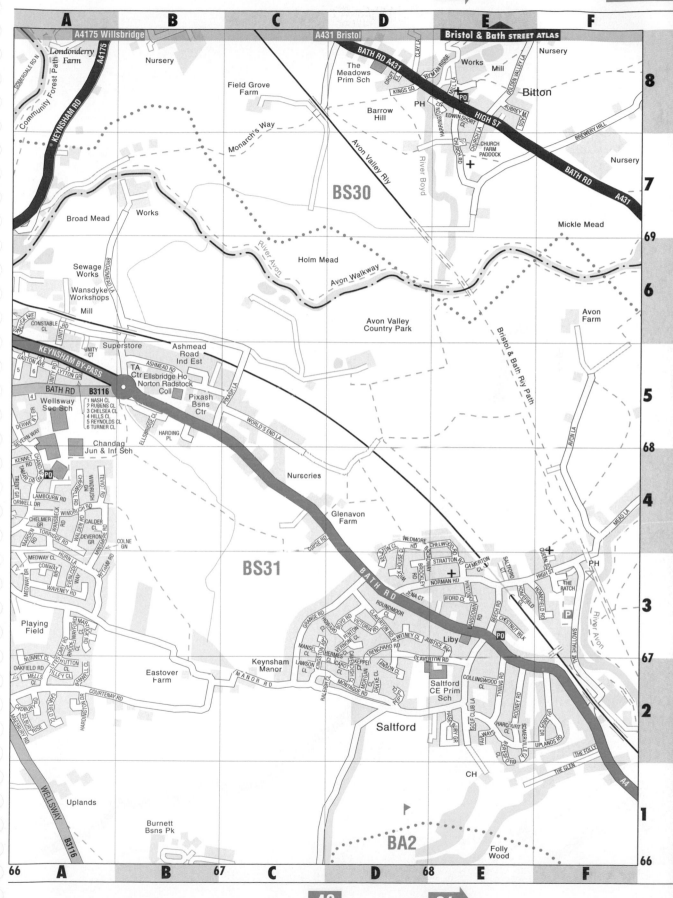

26

A   B   C   D   E   F

A4175 Willsbridge

A431 Bristol

BATH RD A431

Londonderry Farm

Nursery

SOMERDALE RD N

Community Forest Path

KEYNSHAM RD

A4175

Field Grove Farm

The Meadows Prim Sch

CLAY LA

WYMAN RIDGE

Works

Mill

Nursery

Bitton

8

GOLDEN VALLEY LA

Monarch's Way

Barrow Hill

Avon Valley Rly

River Boyd

CROFT

KINGS SQ

PH

EDWIN SHORT

PO

AUBREY M

HARRINGTON

CHURCH RD

CHURCHILL

CHURCH LA

CHURCH FARM PADDOCK

HIGH ST

BREWERY HILL

BATH RD

A431

Nursery

7

BS30

Broad Mead

Works

River Avon

Holm Mead

Avon Walkway

Mickle Mead

69

Sewage Works

BROADMEAD LA

Wansdyke Workshops

Mill

Avon Valley Country Park

Bristol & Bath Rly Path

Avon Farm

6

Superstore

Ashmead Road Ind Est

KEYNSHAM BY-PASS

CONSTABLE CL

UNITY CT

UNITY RD

UNITY WY

GASTON AVE

LYTTON GR

5

BATH RD

B3116

4

TA Ctr Ellsbridge Ho Norton Radstock Coll

Pixash Bsns Ctr

PIXASH LA

AVON LA

68

1 NASH CL
2 RUBENS CL
3 CHELSEA CL
4 HILLS CL
5 REYNOLDS CL
6 TURNER CL

Wellsway Sec Sch

DERWENT GR

SEVERN WAY

ASHMEAD RD

ELLSBRIDGE CL

HARDING PL

WORLD'S END LA

Nurseries

5

Chandag Jun & Inf Sch

PO

KENNET RD

TAMAR DR

CHANDOS RD

CHERITON PL

WINDRUSH RD

TEVIOT RD

Glenavon Farm

COPSE RD

MEAD LA

68

LAMBOURN RD

ORWELL DR

WINDRUSH GR

WINDRUSH RD

BS31

BATH RD

WEDMORE HO

CHELWOOD RD

BROADWAY

STRATTON

QUEEN SQ

PH

THE BATCH

4

CHELMER GR

MARDEN RD

TORRIDGE RD

CALDER GR

DEVERON GR

COLNE GN

CA MERTON CL

STONE CL

WICKHOUSE CL

NORMAN HO

JENA CT

SALTFORD CL

HIGH ST

IFORD CL

HOMEFIELD RD

HOMEFIELD CL

P

River Avon

THE SHALLOWS

3

MEDWAY CL

CONWAY RD

EDEN GR

HURN LA

WAY

WITHAM RD

ROUNDMOOR

GRANGE RD

BOYD RD

VICTORIA

FENTON

VERNON

WHITNEY CL

FRENCHARD RD

CLAVERTON RD

BEECH RD

CHESTNUT WLK

LANSDOWN

PO

Liby

JUSTICE AVE

COLLINGWOOD CL

67

Playing Field

MEDWAY DR

WAVENEY RD

MAR

WAYFORD

RHODE CL

MYTTON

MANSEL CL

HERMES CL

KEPPEL

ICARO T

MORGAN

KINGS CL

ANSON CL

DRAKE CL

Saltford CE Prim Sch

GOLF CLUB LA

DYRHAM CL

UPLANDS RD

HARCOURT CL

SOMERVILLE CL

2

NUNNEY CL

MYTTON CL

TILLEY CL

MELLS CL

OAKFIELD RD

BANWELL CL

LAWSON CL

MONTAGUE RD

RALEIGH CT

MANOR RD

Keynsham Manor

Eastover Farm

Courtenay Rd

Saltford

FAIRWAYS

BERESFORD CL

UPLANDS DR

THE GLEN

THE FOLLY

A4

WELLSWAY

COBURY

SILBURY RISE

MAESBURY RD

HARDINGTON CL

Uplands

CH

Folly Wood

1

B3116

Burnett Bsns Pk

BA2

66   A   B   67   C   D   68   E   F   66

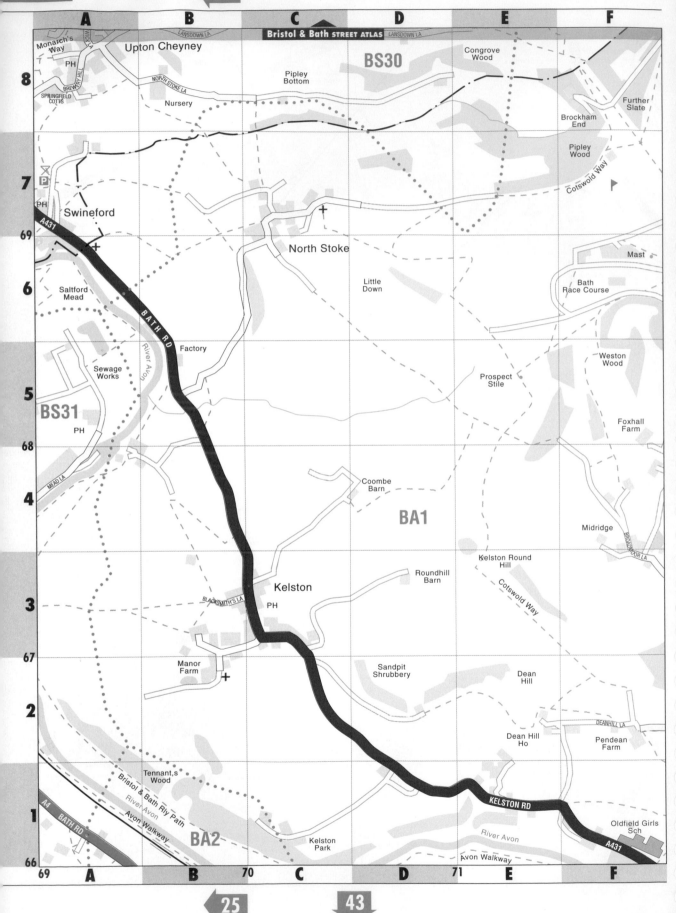

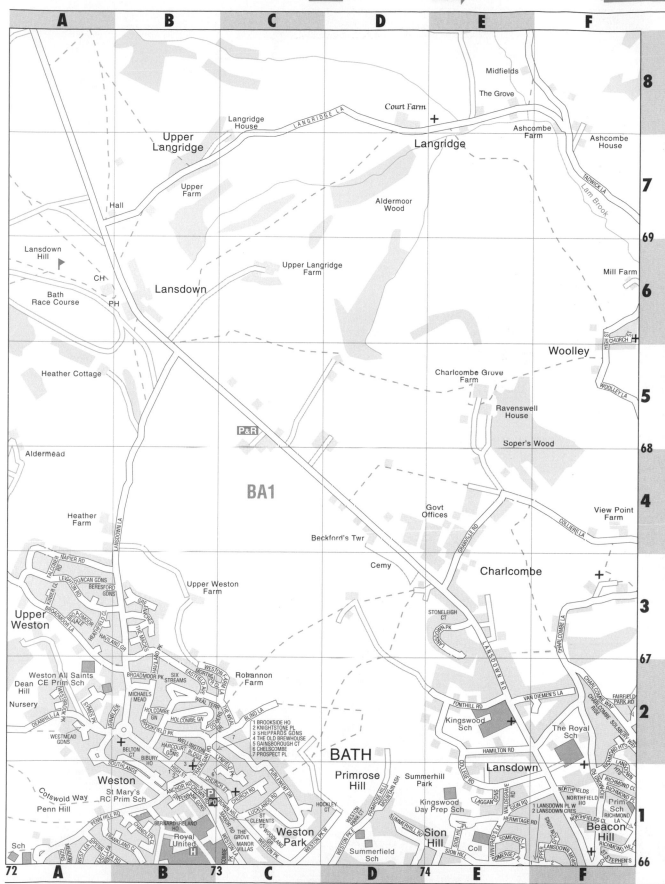

8

7

69

6

5

68

4

3

67

2

1

66

Midfields

The Grove

Court Farm

Langridge
House

LANGRIDGE LA

Langridge

Ashcombe
Farm

Ashcombe
House

TADWICK LA

Lam Brook

Upper
Langridge

Upper
Farm

Aldermoor
Wood

Mill Farm

HIGH ST

CHURCH

Lansdown
Hill

CH

Bath
Race Course

PH

Lansdown

Upper Langridge
Farm

Woolley

WOOLLEY LA

Heather Cottage

Charlcombe Grove
Farm

Ravenswell
House

Soper's Wood

Aldermead

P&R

BA1

Govt
Offices

View Point
Farm

COLLIERS LA

Heather
Farm

Beckford's Twr

Cemy

Charlcombe

LANSDOWN LA

GRANVILLE RD

STONELEIGH
CT

LANSDOWN PK

CHARLCOMBE LA

LANSDOWN RD

67

Upper Weston
Farm

Upper
Weston

NAPIER RD
FALCONER RD
LEIGH RD
KINDER GN
DUNCAN GDNS
BERESFORD
GDNS
BROADMOOR LA
HEATHFIELD CL
HAVILAND GR
THE NACLES
GREENACRES
HAVILAND PK

BROADMOOR PK

WESTON
AVE
MORRIS LA
EASTFIELD AVE

Rohannon
Farm

SIX
STREAMS

THE WEST

BLIND LA

Weston All Saints
CE Prim Sch

Dean
Hill

Nursery

MICHAELS
MEAD

WESTBROOK PK

SYKES RD

VERNH'A DE

HOLCOMBE
GN

HOLCOMBE GN

BROOKFIELD PK

WEAL TERR

PODGER

THE WAY

DEANHILL LA

WEGTMEAD
GDNS

BELTON
CT

HARCOURT
GDNS

WELLINGTON
BLDGS

LYNFIELD CT

1 BROOKSIDE HO
2 KNIGHTSTONE PL
3 SHEPPARDS GDNS
4 THE OLD BREWHOUSE
5 GAINSBOROUGH CT
6 CHELSCOMBE
7 PROSPECT PL

BATH

FONTHILL RD

VAN DIEMEN'S LA

Kingswood
Sch

The Royal
Sch

FAIRFIELD
PARK RD

CHARLCOMBE
SO, SALBURY
RISE

CHARLCOMBE WAY

Weston

SOUTHLANDS

St Mary's
RC Prim Sch

HIGH ST

ANCHOR RD

CROWN RD

GREENWAY GDNS

CHURCH RD

PURLEWENT DR

LUCKLANDS RD

ST
CLEMENTS
CT

Primrose
Hill

WESTON
PARK CT

PRIMROSE HILL

MOUNTAIN ASH

Summerhill
Park

Kingswood
Day Prep Sch

HAMILTON RD

COLLEGE RD

WALDEGRAVE

LAGGAN

Lansdown

NORTHFIELDS

HERMITAGE RD

NORTHFIELDS
HO

NORTHFIELDS LA

RICHMOND HTS

LANSDOWN
CL

RICHMOND
RD

The Royal
Sch

The
Royal
Sch

Beacon
Hill

Prim
Sch

RICHMOND
PL

Cotswold Way

Penn Hill

PENN HILL RD

WEST LEA RD

WEST LEA RD

CHANDLER CL

BERNARD IRELAND
HO

Royal
United
H

MANOR RD

WESTON RD

COOMBE PK

THE
GROVE

MANOR
VILLAS

Weston
Park

WESTON PK W

WESTON PKW

HOCKLEY
CT

WESTON PKE

Summerfield
Sch

SUMMERHILL RD

SION HILL PL

Sion
Hill

WINIFRED'S LA

SOMERSET LA

Coll

SION HILL

SOMERSET PL

1 LANSDOWN PL W
2 LANSDOWN CRES

SNUG NO 7

UPPER LANSDOWN MEWS

RICHMOND

ST STEPHEN'S

Sch

MEADWAY

FRANKLAND CL

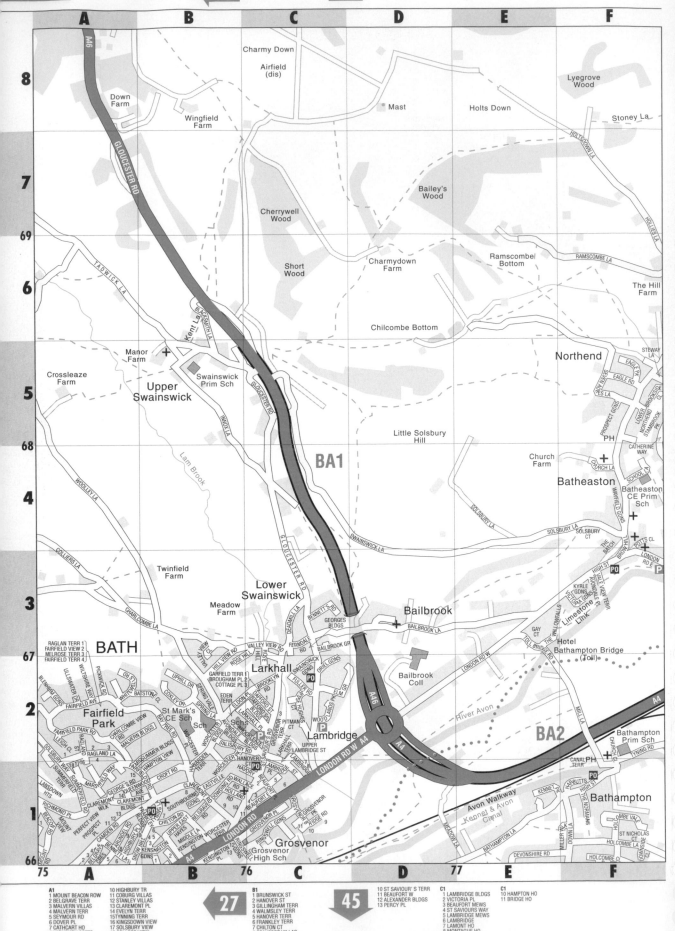

A B C D E F

8

7

69

6

5

68

4

3

67

2

1

66

75 A B 76 C D 77 E F

Charmy Down
Airfield (dis)

Lyegrove Wood

Down Farm

Wingfield Farm

Mast

Holts Down

Stoney La

Cherrywell Wood

Bailey's Wood

Short Wood

Charmydown Farm

Ramscombe Bottom

Ramscombe La

The Hill Farm

Chilcombe Bottom

Northend

Crossleaze Farm

Manor Farm

Swainswick Prim Sch

Upper Swainswick

Little Solsbury Hill

Church Farm

Batheaston

Batheaston CE Prim Sch

BA1

Twinfield Farm

Lower Swainswick

Meadow Farm

Bailbrook

BATH

Larkhall

Georges Bldgs

Bailbrook La

Hotel
Bathampton Bridge (Toll)

Fairfield Park

St Mark's CE Sch

Bailbrook Coll

River Avon

Lambridge

BA2

Bathampton Prim Sch

Bathampton

Avon Walkway
Kennet & Avon Canal

Grosvenor

Grosvenor High Sch

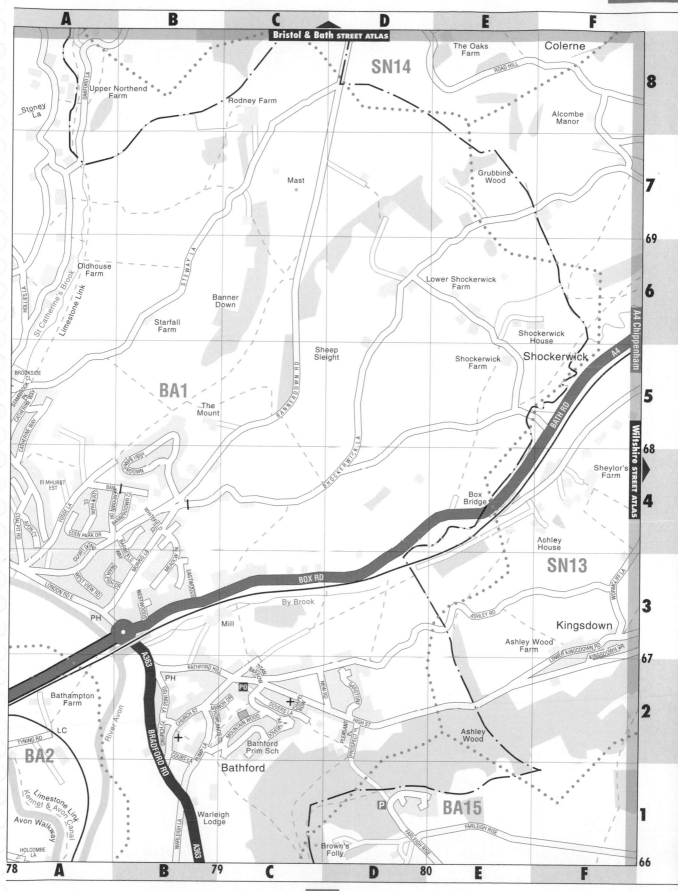

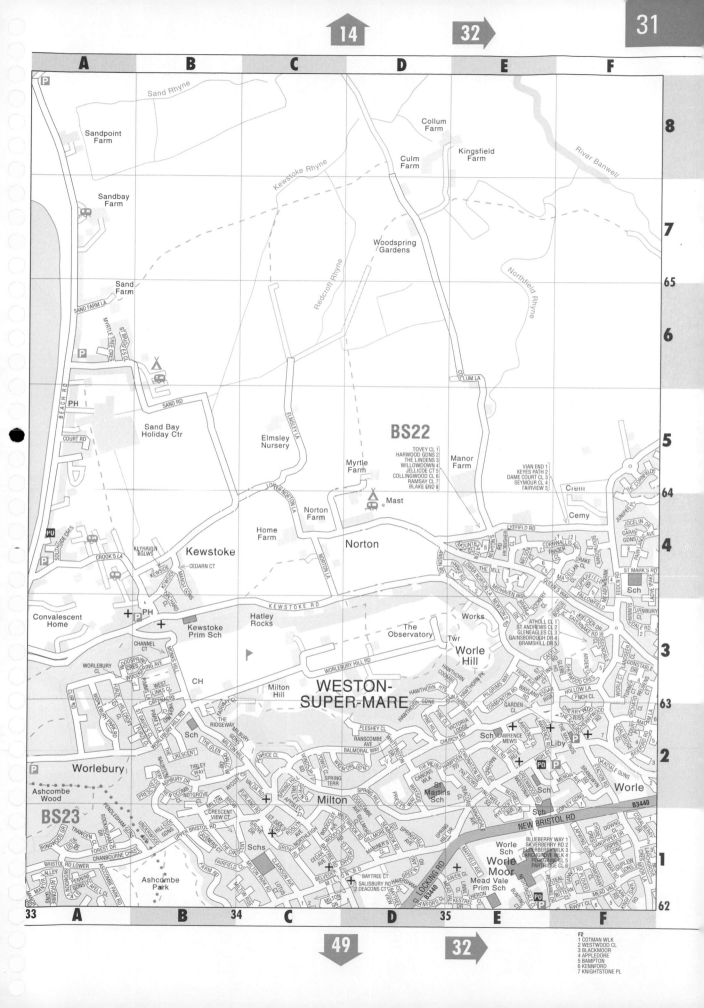

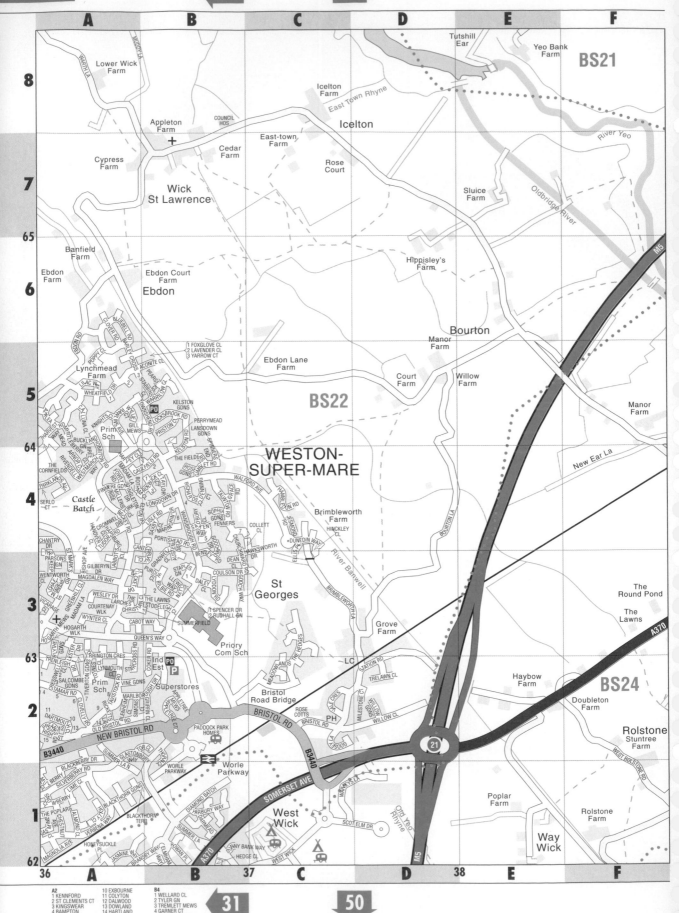

BS21

BS22

WESTON-SUPER-MARE

BS24

A2
1 KENNFORD
2 ST CLEMENTS CT
3 KINGSWEAR
4 BAMPTON
5 CREDITON
6 FENITON
7 INSTOW
8 IVYBRIDGE
9 HONITON
10 EXBOURNE
11 COLYTON
12 DALWOOD
13 DOWLAND
14 HARTLAND
15 EBDEN LO

B4
1 WELLARD CL
2 TYLER GN
3 TREMLETT MEWS
4 GARNER CT
5 WAINWRIGHT CL
6 EMLYN CL
7 THE SAFFRONS

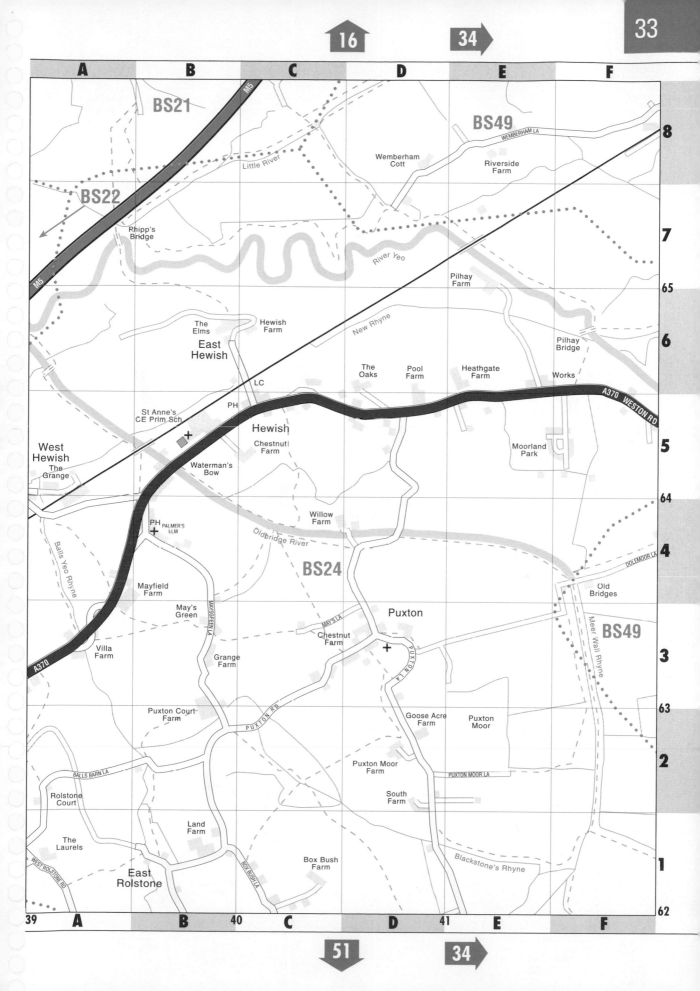

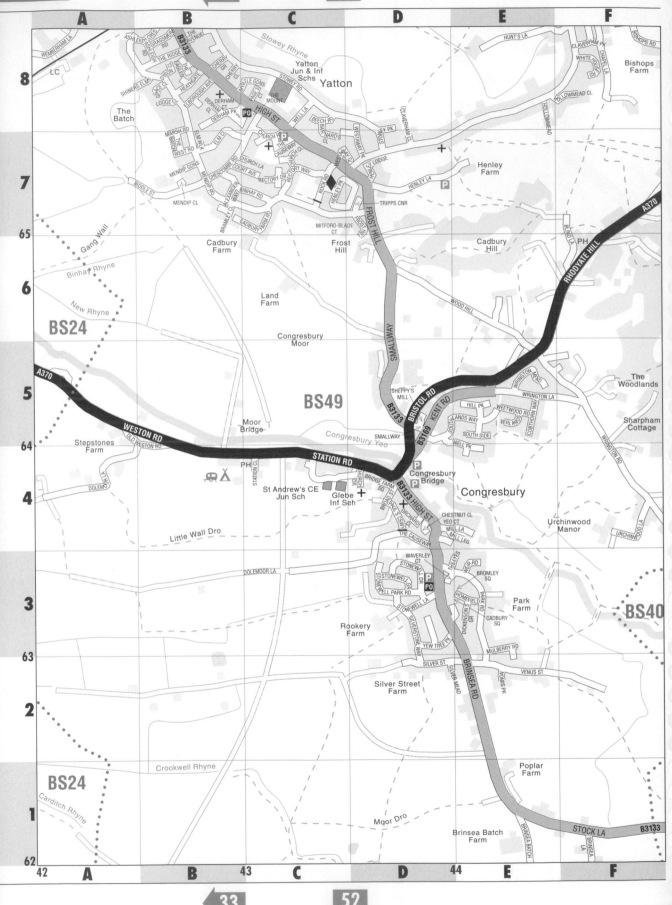

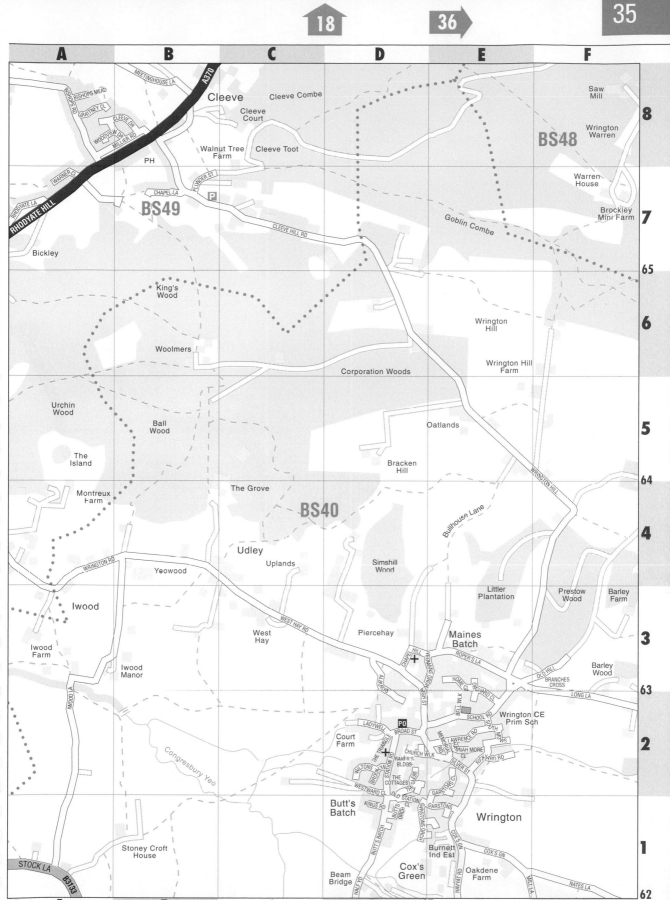

35
19

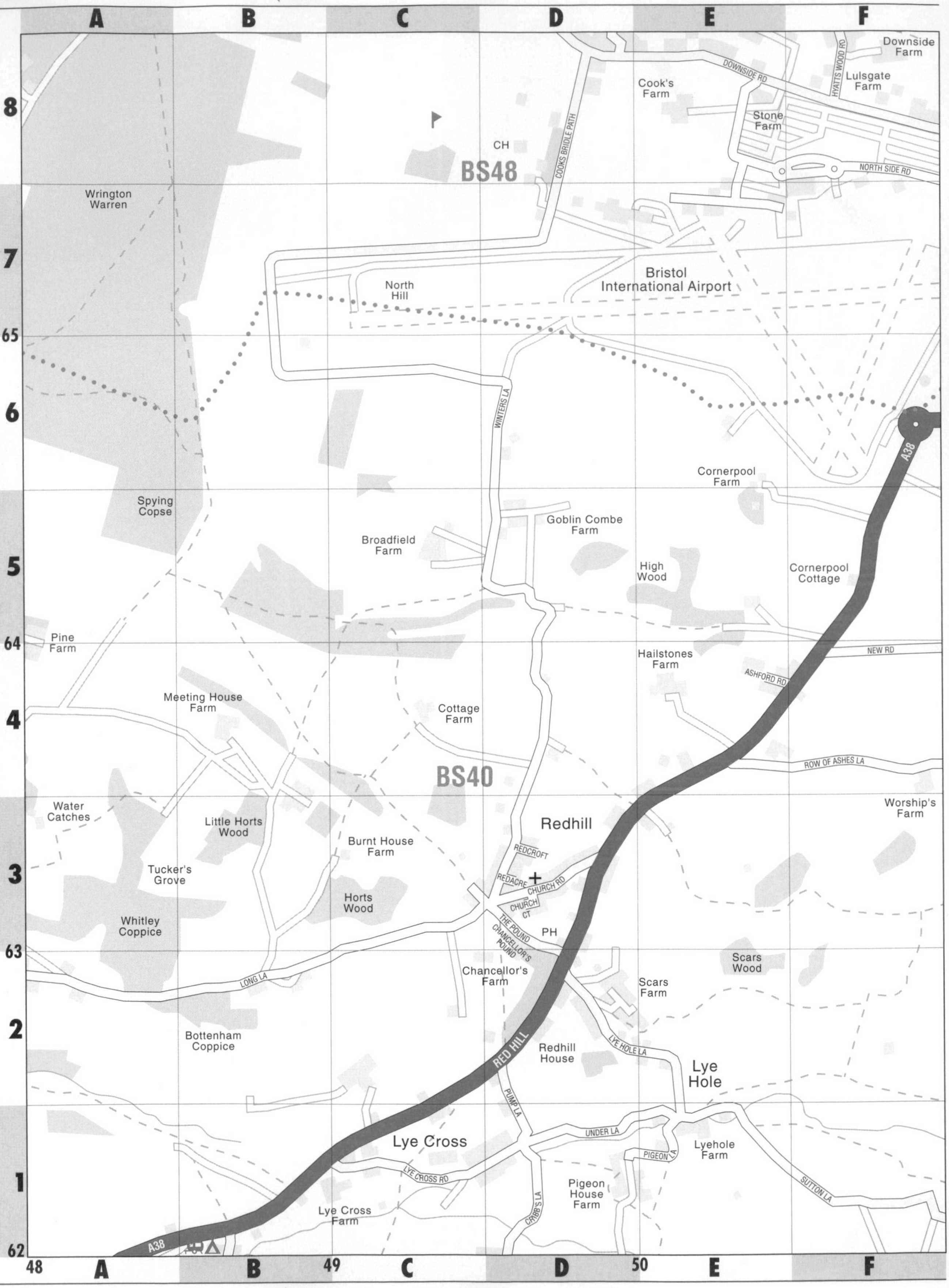

A   B   C   D   E   F

8

7

65

6

5

64

4

3

63

2

1

62

48   A   B   49   C   D   50   E   F

35
54

Wrington Warren

BS48

CH

Cook's Farm

Downside Farm

Lulsgate Farm

Stone Farm

DOWNSIDE RD

HYATTS WOOD RD

NORTH SIDE RD

Bristol International Airport

North Hill

COOKS BRIDLE PATH

WINTERS LA

A38

Spying Copse

Cornerpool Farm

Broadfield Farm

Goblin Combe Farm

High Wood

Cornerpool Cottage

Pine Farm

Hailstones Farm

NEW RD

ASHFORD RD

Meeting House Farm

Cottage Farm

ROW OF ASHES LA

BS40

Water Catches

Little Horts Wood

Burnt House Farm

Worship's Farm

Tucker's Grove

Horts Wood

Redhill

REDCROFT

REDACRE

CHURCH RD

CHURCH CT

Whitley Coppice

THE POUND

CHANCELLOR'S POUND

PH

Scars Wood

Long La

Chancellor's Farm

Scars Farm

LYE HOLE LA

Bottenham Coppice

RED HILL

Redhill House

Lye Hole

PIMPLA

UNDER LA

Lyehole Farm

SUTTON LA

Lye Cross

LYE CROSS RD

CRABS LA

PIGEON LA

Pigeon House Farm

Lyehole Farm

A38

Lye Cross Farm

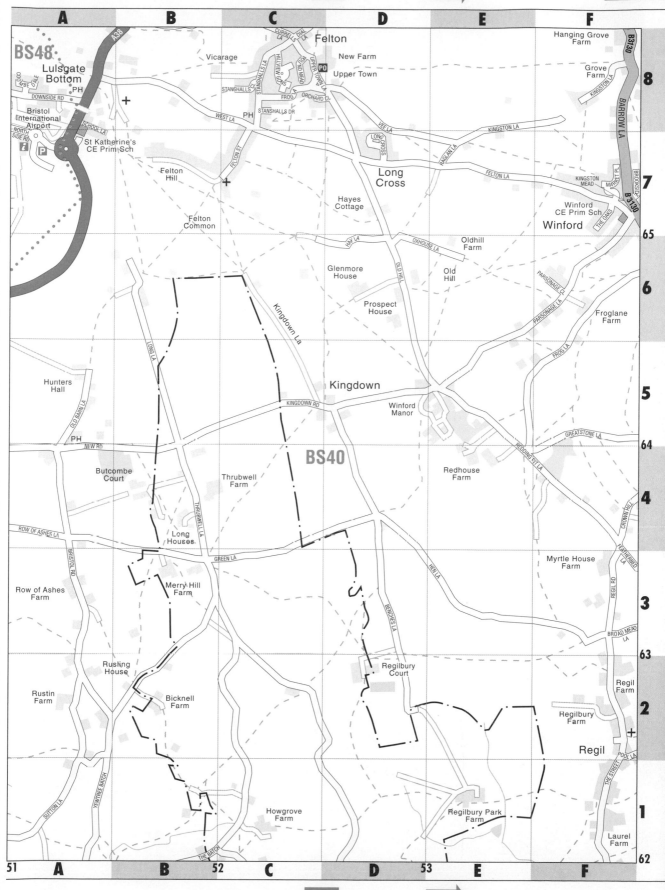

BS48

Lulsgate
Bottom

Bristol International
Airport

Felton

Vicarage

New Farm

Upper Town

Hanging Grove
Farm

Grove
Farm

8

St Katherine's
CE Prim Sch

DOWNSIDE RD

PH

WEST LA

PH

STANSHALLS DR

CURRELLS LA

DIAL LA

HILLVIEW GDNS

STANSHALLS LA

ORCHARD CL

FROG LA

PO

VEE LA

LONG CROSS

RAGLAN LA

KINGSTON LA

FELTON LA

KINGSTON LA

KINGSTON MEAD

MARSH LA

MARSH PL

BARROW LA

B3130

B3130

BROOKSIDE

THE OAKS

Felton
Hill

FELTON ST

Long
Cross

Winford
CE Prim Sch

Winford

7

Felton
Common

Hayes
Cottage

HAY LA

OXHOUSE LA

OLD HILL

Oldhill
Farm

Old
Hill

PARSONAGE CL

PARSONAGE LA

Winford

65

Glenmore
House

Prospect
House

FROG LA

Froglane
Farm

6

Hunters
Hall

Kingdown

Winford
Manor

GREATSTONE LA

REDDING ST LA

5

OLD BARN LA

LONG LA

KINGDOWN LA

KINGDOWN RD

BS40

Redhouse
Farm

CROWN HILL

64

PH

NEW RD

Butcombe
Court

THRUBWELL LA

Thrubwell
Farm

FEATHERBED LA

4

ROW OF ASHES LA

BRISTOL RD

Long
Houses

GREEN LA

HEN LA

Myrtle House
Farm

REGIL RD

BROAD MEAD LA

63

Row of Ashes
Farm

Merry Hill
Farm

BENCHES LA

Regilbury
Court

Regil
Farm

Regilbury
Farm

3

Rusling
House

Regil

2

Rustin
Farm

Bicknell
Farm

SUTTON LA

YEWTREE BATCH

Howgrove
Farm

Regilbury Park
Farm

THE STREET

POOL LA

Laurel
Farm

1

THE BATCH

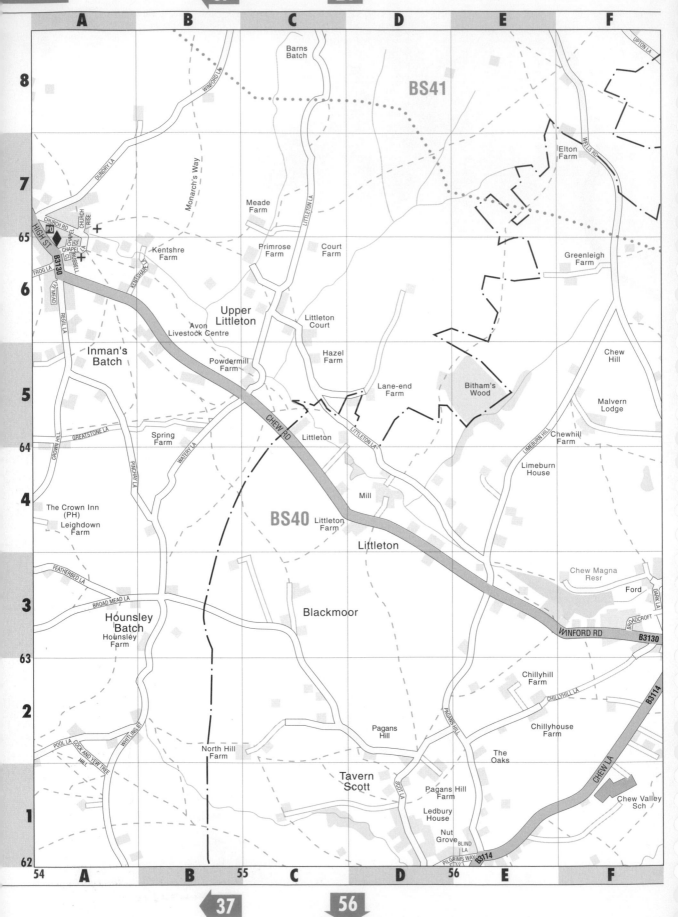

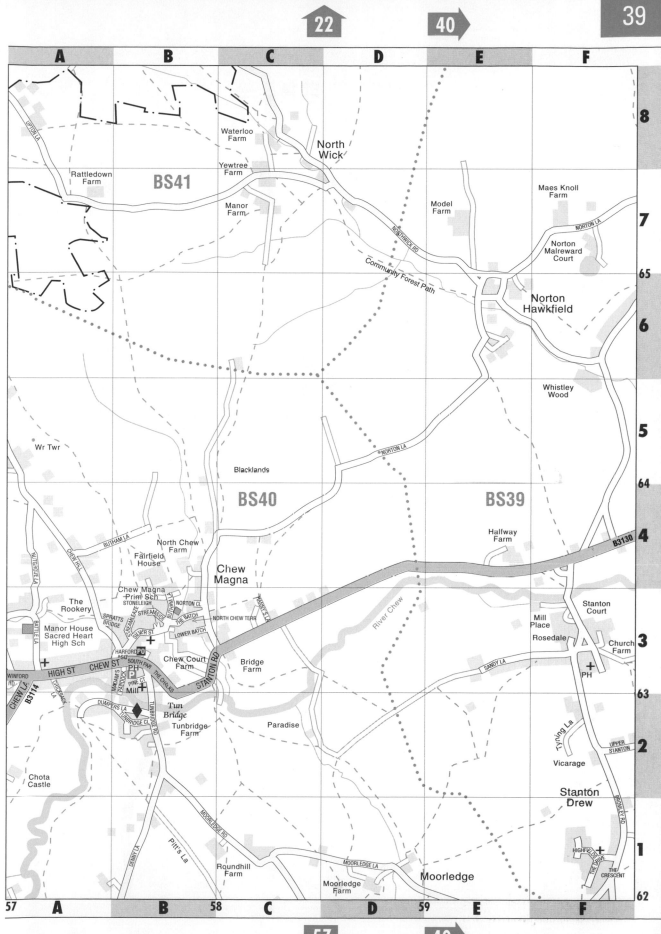

A B C D E F

8
7
65
6
5
64
4
3
63
2
1
62

Rattledown Farm

BS41

Waterloo Farm

Yewtree Farm

North Wick

Manor Farm

Maes Knoll Farm

NORTON LA

Model Farm

Norton Malreward Court

Community Forest Path

NORTHWICK RD

Norton Hawkfield

Whistley Wood

Wr Twr

Blacklands

BS40

NORTON LA

BS39

Halfway Farm

B3130

North Chew Farm

BUTHAM LA

CHEW HILL

NUTGROVE LA

Fairfield House

Chew Magna

Chew Magna Prim Sch

STONELEIGH

HT TWITHIN

NORTON CL

PARSON'S LA

River Chew

Mill Place

Stanton Court

The Rookery

SPRATTS BRIDGE

STREAM'S SIDE

CREAM EAZE

THE BATCH

NORTH CHEW TERR

Rosedale

Church Farm

Manor House Sacred Heart High Sch

BATTLE LA

SILVER ST

LOWER BATCH

PO

Chew Court Farm

Bridge Farm

SANDY LA

PH

WINFORD RD

HIGH ST

CHEW ST

HARFORD SQ

SOUTH PAR

STANTON RD

B3114

CHEW LA

CRICKBACK LA

MADAM'S PADDOCK

PINE CT

THE CHALKS

Mill

Tun Bridge

DUMPERS LA

TUNBRIDGE CL

TUNBRIDGE RD

Tunbridge Farm

Paradise

TYNING LA

UPPER STANTON

Vicarage

BROMLEY RD

Chota Castle

DENNY LA

MOORLEDGE RD

Pitt's La

Stanton Drew

Roundhill Farm

MOORLEDGE LA

Moorledge Farm

Moorledge

HIGHFIELDS

THE SPIVE

THE CRESCENT

39
23

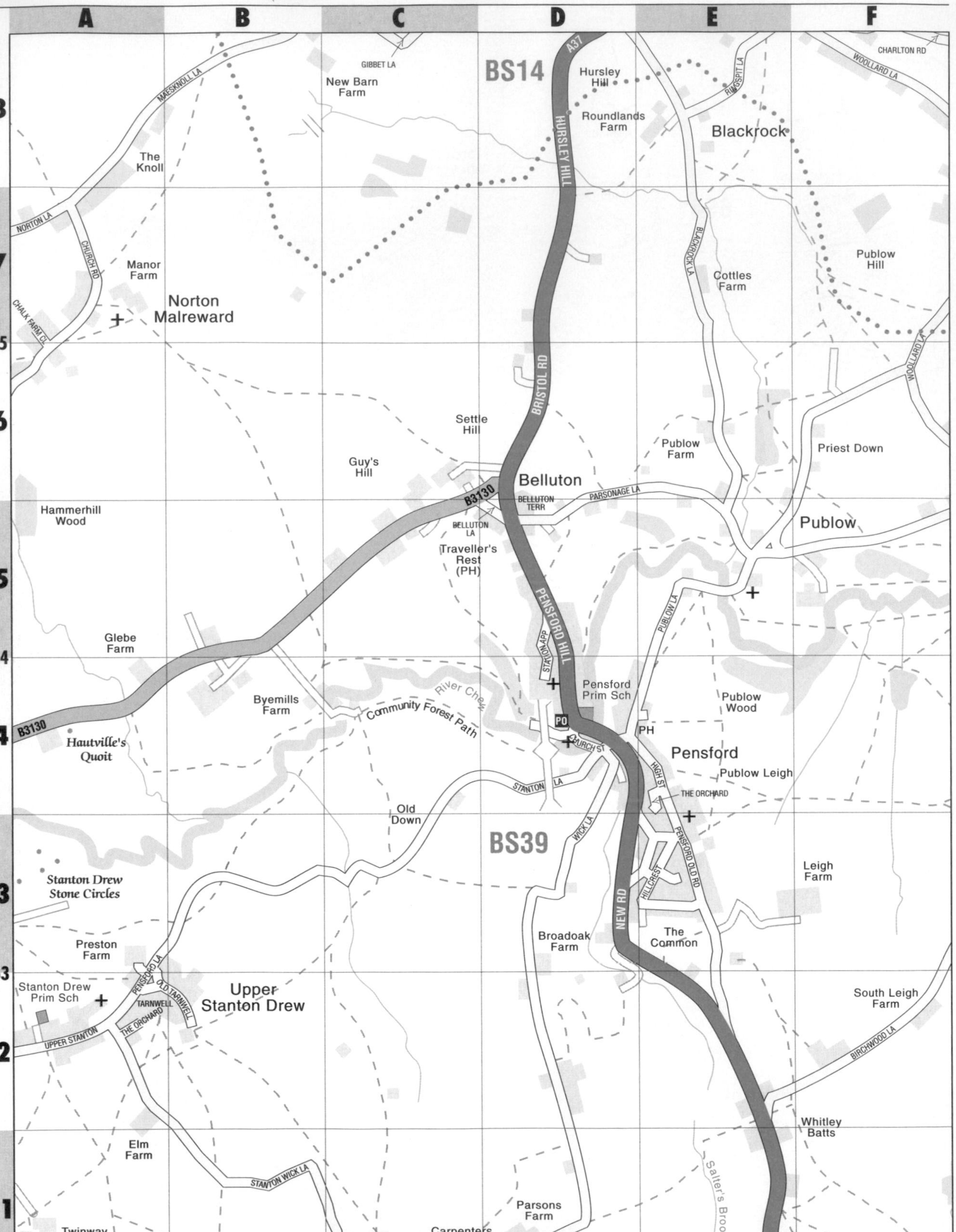

A B C D E F

8

BS14

CHARLTON RD

WOOLLARD LA

GIBBET LA

New Barn Farm

Hursley Hill

Roundlands Farm

Blackrock

RINGSPIT LA

The Knoll

NORTON LA

7

Manor Farm

CHURCH RD

Norton Malreward

Cottles Farm

Publow Hill

BLACKROCK LA

WOOLLARD LA

CHALK FARM CL

65

BRISTOL RD

6

Settle Hill

Publow Farm

Priest Down

Hammerhill Wood

Guy's Hill

Belluton

BELLUTON TERR

PARSONAGE LA

Publow

B3130

BELLUTON LA

Traveller's Rest (PH)

5

Glebe Farm

PENSFORD HILL

PUBLOW LA

64

River Chew

Byemills Farm

Community Forest Path

STONEY LAPP

Pensford Prim Sch

Publow Wood

4

B3130

Hautville's Quoit

CHURCH ST

PO

PH

Pensford

Publow Leigh

STANTON LA

THE ORCHARD

Old Down

HIGH ST

Leigh Farm

3

Stanton Drew Stone Circles

WICK LA

BS39

HILLCREST

PENSFORD OLD RD

Preston Farm

PENSFORD LA

Upper Stanton Drew

Broadoak Farm

The Common

63

Stanton Drew Prim Sch

OLD TARNWELL

TARNWELL

THE ORCHARD

NEW RD

South Leigh Farm

BIRCHWOOD LA

2

UPPER STANTON

Elm Farm

Whitley Batts

STANTON WICK LA

Salter's Brook

1

Twinway Farm

Parsons Farm

Carpenters Arms (PH)

A37

62

60 A B 61 C D 62 E F

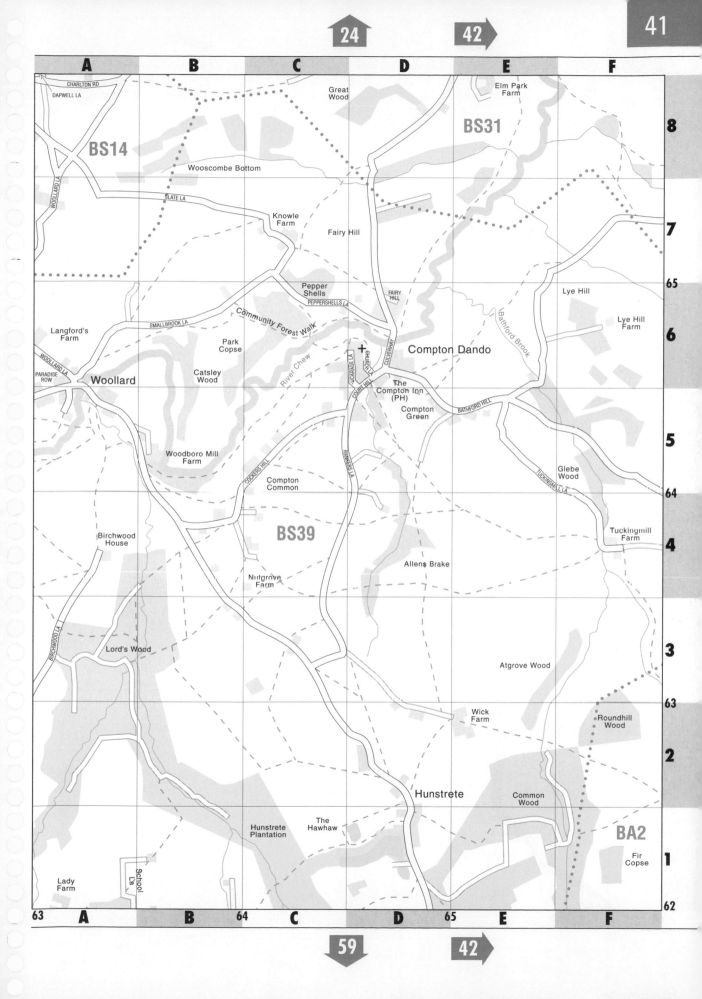

A   B   C   D   E   F

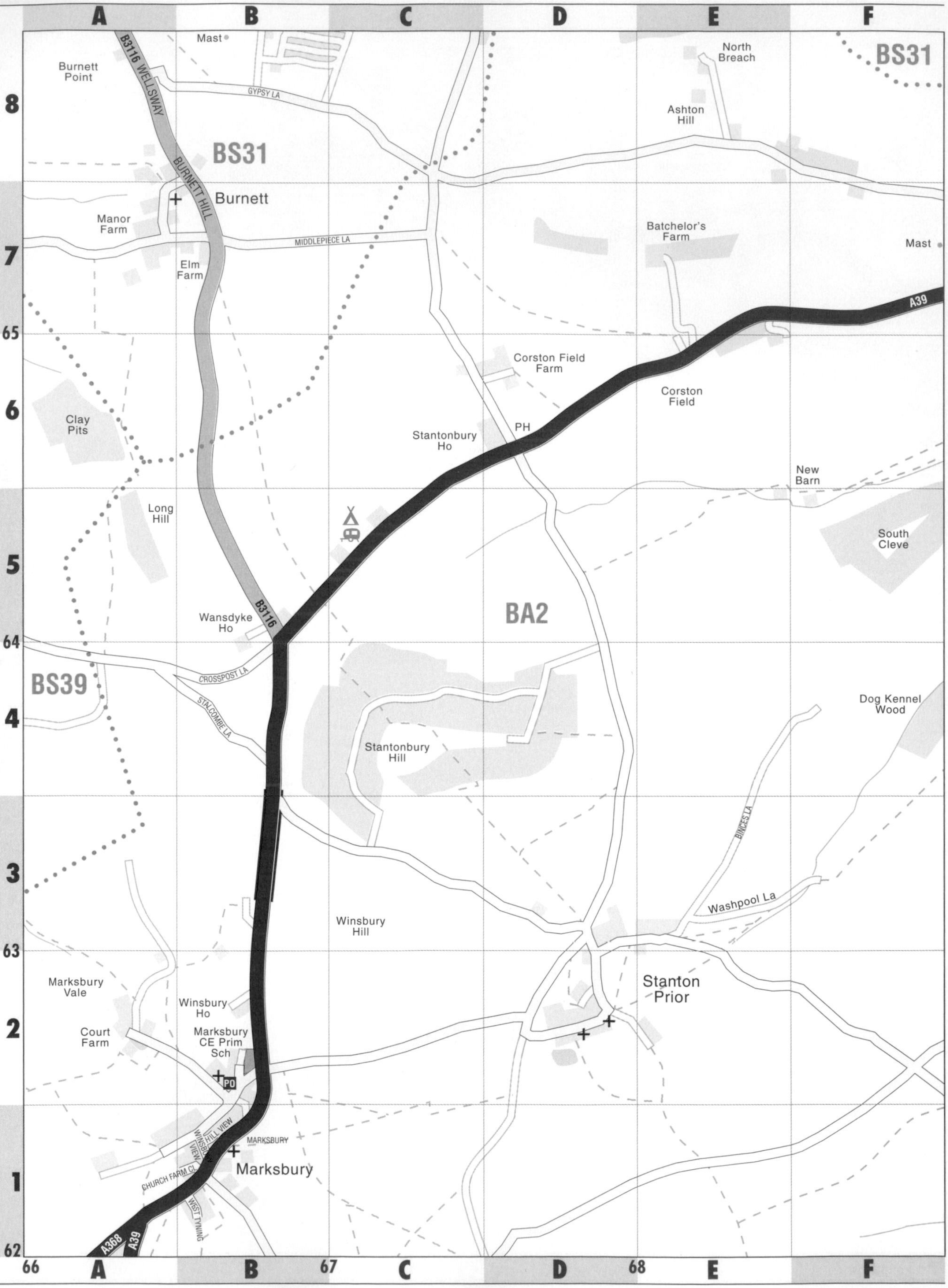

BS31

8

B3116 WELLSWAY

Burnett Point

Mast

GYPSY LA

North Breach

Ashton Hill

BS31

BURNETT HILL

Burnett

BS31

Manor Farm

7

MIDDLEPIECE LA

Batchelor's Farm

Mast

Elm Farm

A39

65

Clay Pits

6

Corston Field Farm

Corston Field

Stantonbury Ho

PH

New Barn

Long Hill

South Cleve

BA2

5

B3116

Wansdyke Ho

64

BS39

CROSSPOST LA

Dog Kennel Wood

4

STALCOMBE LA

Stantonbury Hill

BINCES LA

3

WASHPOOL LA

Winsbury Hill

63

Marksbury Vale

Stanton Prior

2

Winsbury Ho

Court Farm

Marksbury CE Prim Sch

PO

WINSHILL VIEW

MARKSBURY

CHURCH FARM CL

WEST TYNING

1

Marksbury

A368   A39

62

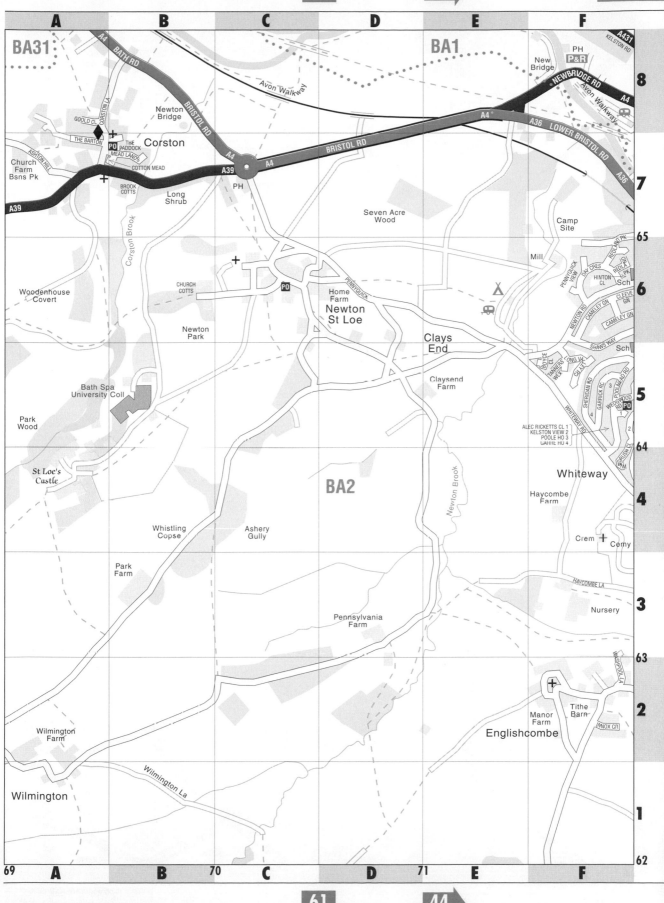

A B C D E F

BA31

BATH RD
BRISTOL RD
A4
Avon Walkway
Newton Bridge
Corston
GOOLD CL
CORSTON LA
THE BARTON
PO
THE PADDOCK
MEAD LANDS
COTTON MEAD
ASHTON HILL
Church Farm Bsns Pk
A39
BROOK COTTS
Long Shrub
A39
A4
A4
PH
Corston Brook

BA1
New Bridge
PH
P&R
KELSTON RD
A431
NEWBRIDGE RD
Avon Walkway
A4
A4
A36
LOWER BRISTOL RD
A36

8

7

Seven Acre Wood
Camp Site
Mill
PENNYQUICK VIEW
REDLAND PK
REDLA
PK
PK
HINTON CL
Sch
65

6
Woodenhouse Covert
CHURCH COTTS
PO
Home Farm
Newton St Loe
NEWTON RD
DAY CRES
CAMELEY GN
CLEEVE GN
CAMELEY GN

Newton Park
Clays End
Claysend Farm
SHAWS WAY
BOYCE CL
YANNERS CL
LONG VA
CL EST
SHERIDAN RD
GARRICK RD
POOLMEAD RD
WEDGWOOD RD
PO
Sch
5
Bath Spa University Coll

Park Wood
St Loe's Castle

BA2
Newton Brook
ALEC RICKETTS CL 1
KELSTON VIEW 2
POOLE HO 3
GARRE HO 4
BURUSH H
64
Whiteway

Haycombe Farm
4

Whistling Copse
Ashery Gully
Crem
Cem
HAYCOMBE LA

Park Farm
Nursery
3

Pennsylvania Farm
WASHPOOL LA
63

Wilmington Farm
Manor Farm
Tithe Barn
LNNOX CR
Englishcombe
2

Wilmington
Wilmington La
1

62

69 A B 70 C D 71 E F

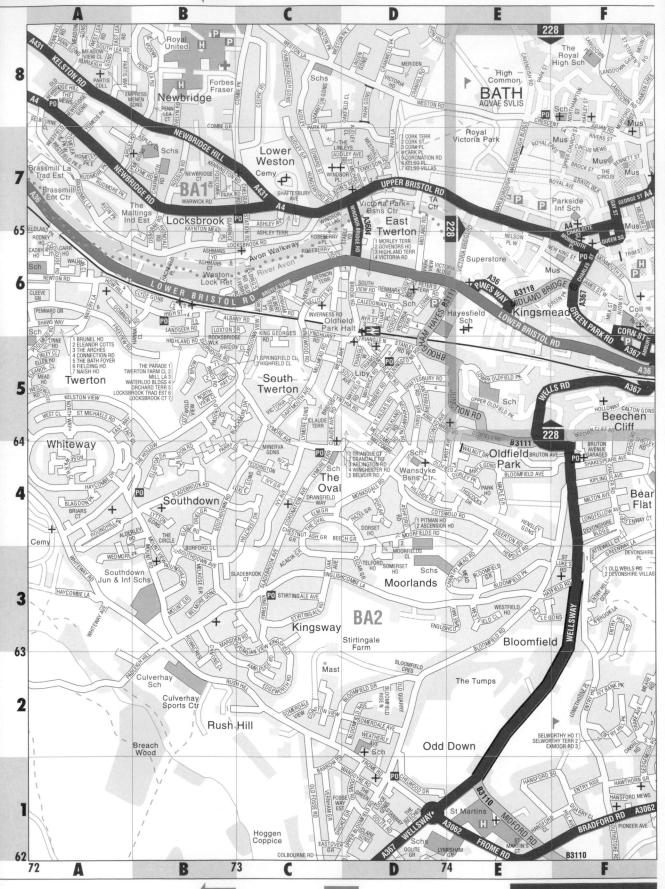

For full street detail of the highlighted area see page 228.

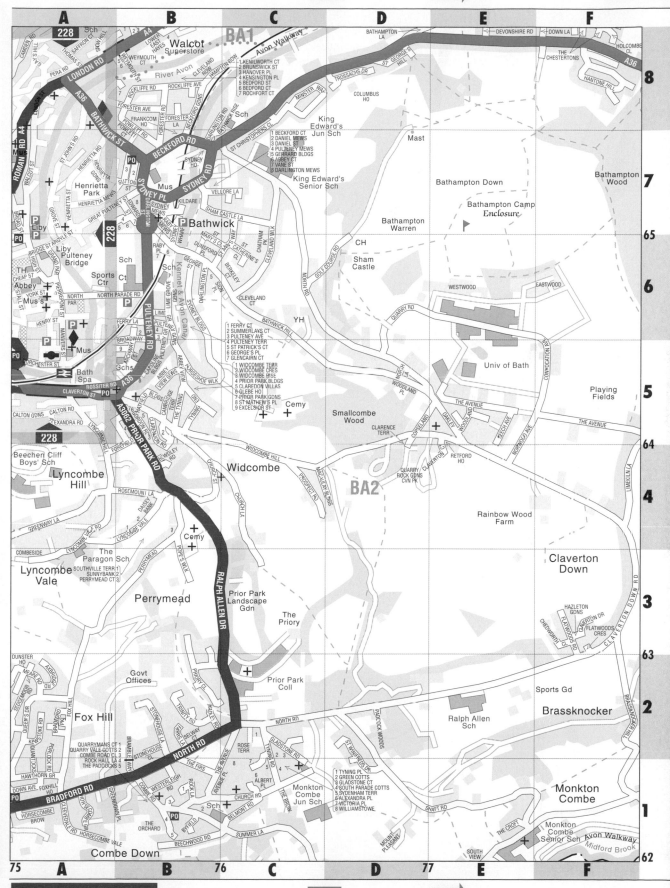

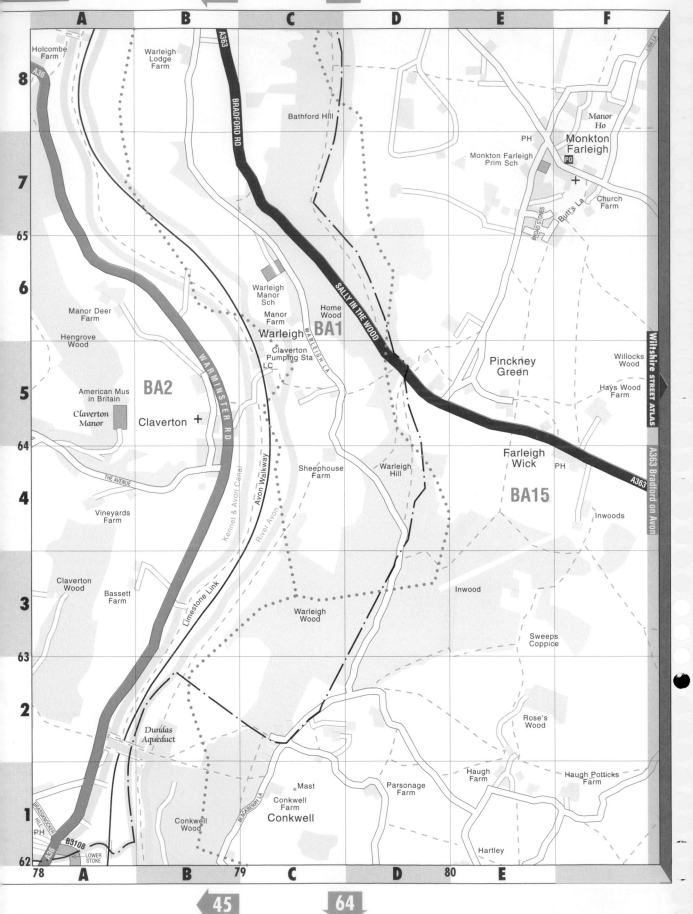

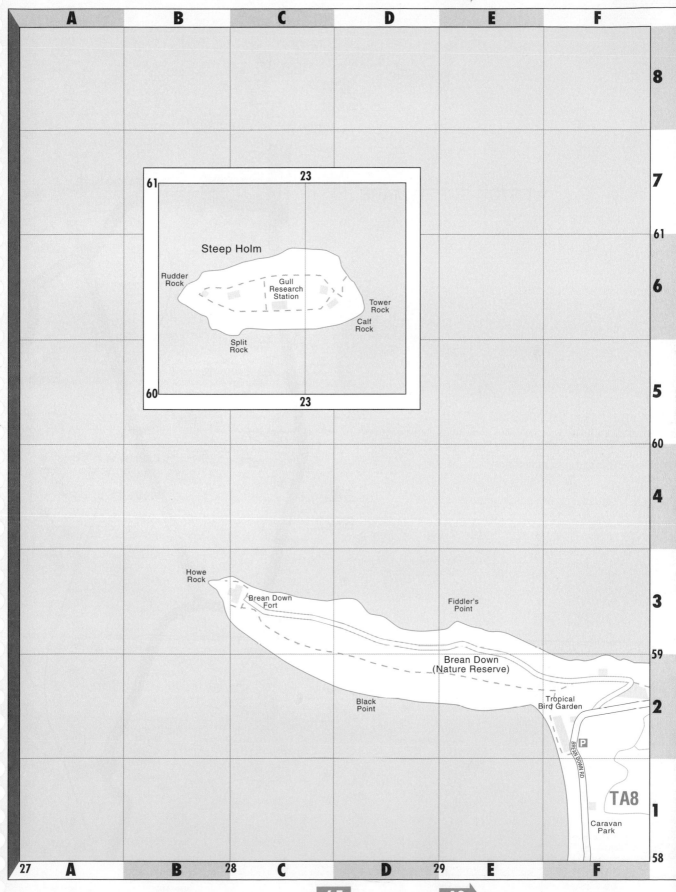

Steep Holm

Rudder
Rock

Gull
Research
Station

Tower
Rock

Calf
Rock

Split
Rock

Howe
Rock

Brean Down
Fort

Fiddler's
Point

Brean Down
(Nature Reserve)

Black
Point

Tropical
Bird Garden

BREAN DOWN RD

P

TA8

Caravan
Park

E7
1 ORCHARD PL
2 NORTH LA
3 CROSS ST
4 ALFRED CT
5 ALEXANDER MEWS
6 THE MART

E7
7 FRANCIS FOX RD
8 STATION LODGE
9 HILDESHIEM CT
10 THE CENTRE
11 WALLISCOTE GROVE RD

E8
1 EDINBURGH PL
2 LANDEMANN PATH
3 LONGTON GROVE RD
4 WORTHY PL
5 WORTHY LA
6 KING'S LA

7 PALMER ROW
8 JASMINE CT
9 PROSPECT PL
10 SAFFRON HO
11 HENRY BUTT HO
12 CHRISTCHURCH PATH S
13 HANS PRICE HO

14 MEADOW VILLAS
15 BURLINGTON ST
16 POPLAR PL

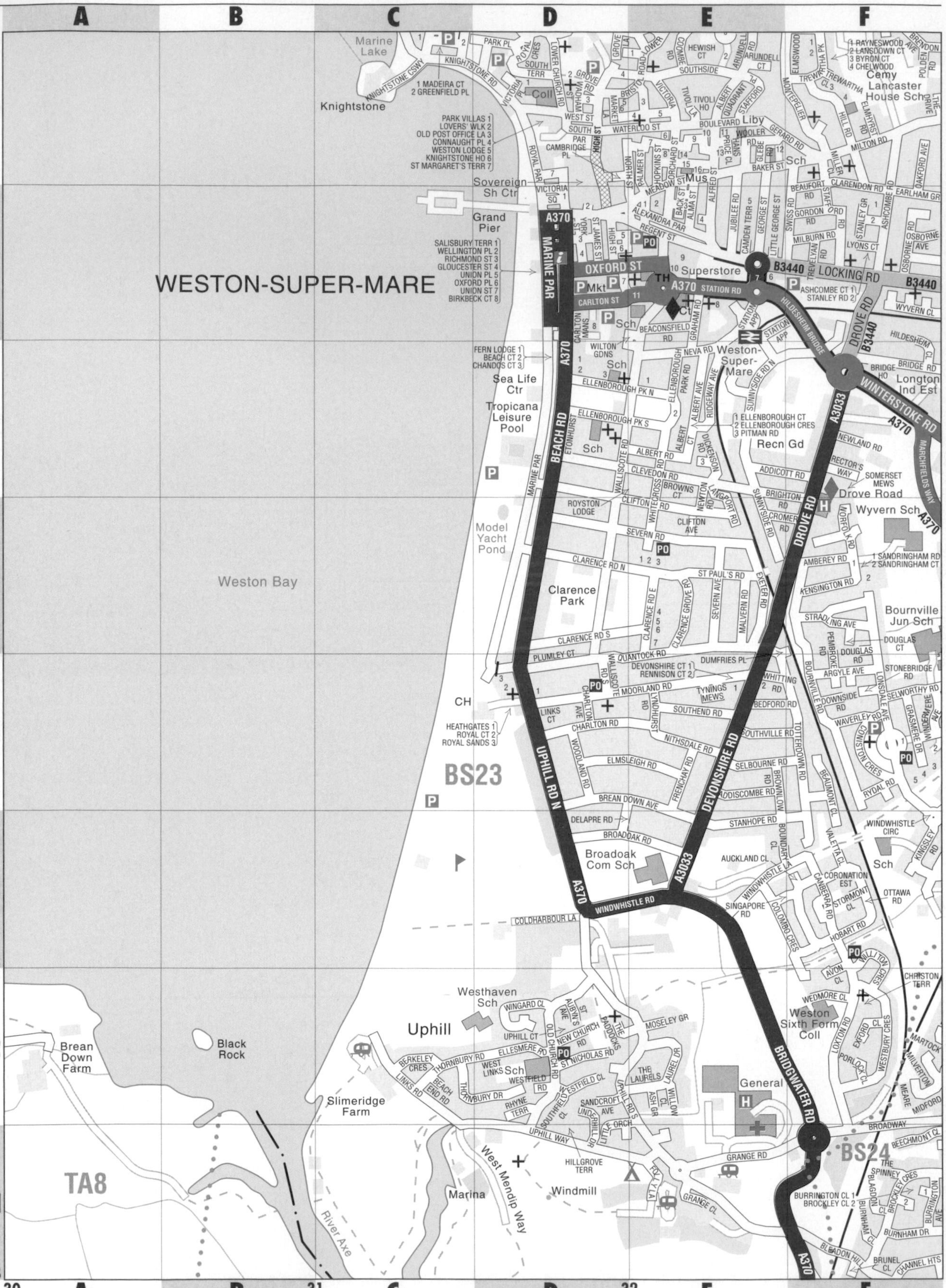

A B C D E F

8 7 61 6 5 60 4 3 59 2 1 58

WESTON-SUPER-MARE

Weston Bay

Knightstone

Marine Lake

Grand Pier

Sea Life Ctr

Tropicana Leisure Pool

Model Yacht Pond

BEACH RD MARINE PAR A370 UPHILL RD N

BS23

Clarence Park

Brean Down Farm

Black Rock

Slimeridge Farm

Uphill

Marina

Windmill

West Mendip Way

River Axe

TA8

BS24

DEVONSHIRE RD A3033 BRIDGWATER RD A370 WINTERSTOKE RD

LOCKING RD DROVE RD B3440

Weston-Super-Mare

Lancaster House Sch

Bournville Jun Sch

Wyvern Sch

Drove Road

Westhaven Sch

Weston Sixth Form Coll

General Hospital

Broadoak Com Sch

Windwhistle Rd

E5
1 SILVERCOMBE
2 WOODFORD CT
3 RALEIGH CT
4 KNIGHTSTONE PK
5 PARK CT
6 WINGARD CT
7 BERROW LODGE

F4
1 ST ANDREW'S PAR
2 BAILDON CT
3 MARLOWE HO
4 KEATS HO
5 ALEXANDER HO

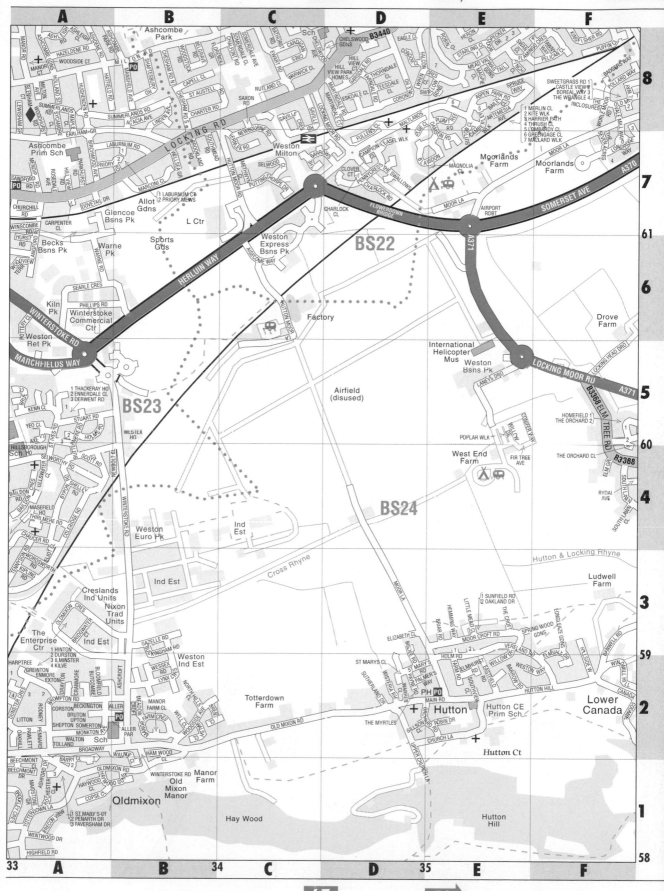

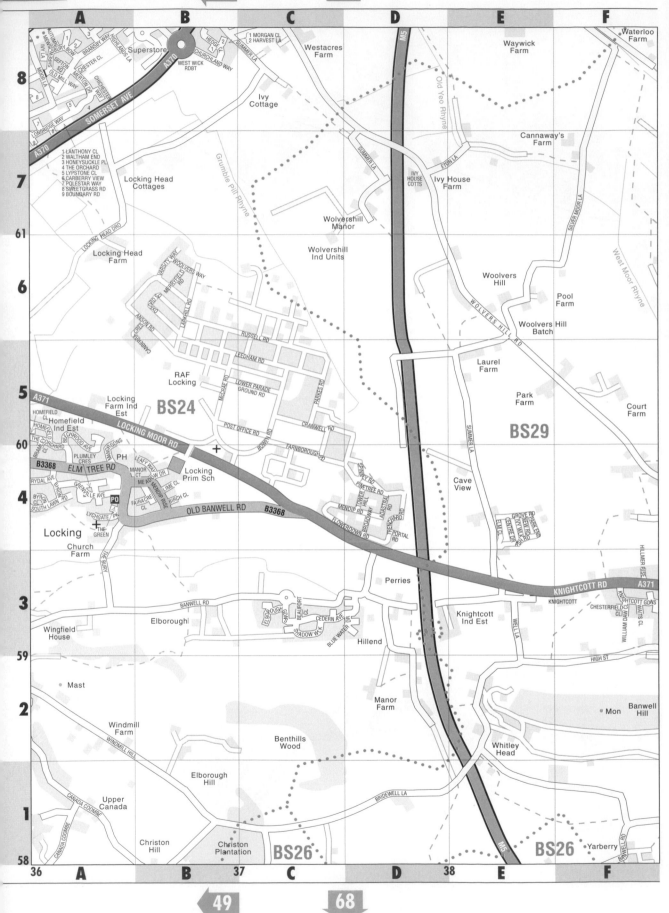

A B C D E F

8
7
61
6
5
60
4
59
3
2
1
58

Superstore

WEST WICK RDBT

SOMERSET AVE

A370

1 MORGAN CL
2 HARVEST LA

Westacres
Farm

Waywick
Farm

Waterloo
Farm

Ivy
Cottage

Cannaway's
Farm

1 LANTHONY CL
2 WALTHAM END
3 HONEYSUCKLE PL
4 THE ORCHARD
5 LYPSTONE CL
6 CARBERRY VIEW
7 POLESTAR WAY
8 SWEETGRASS RD
9 BOUNDARY RD

Locking Head
Cottages

Ivy
House
Cotts

Ivy House
Farm

Grumble Pill Rhyne

SUMMER LA

ETON LA

Old Yeo Rhyne

Wolvershill
Manor

Wolvershill
Ind Units

Woolvers
Hill

Pool
Farm

SILVER MOOR LA

West Moor Rhyne

Locking Head
Farm

LOCKING HEAD DRO

VARSITY WAY

WOOLVERS WAY

MERRYFIELD RD

LARKHILL RD

RUSSELL RD

LEEDHAM RD

MCRAE RD

LOWER PARADE

GROUND RD

PARKES RD

RAF
Locking

Woolvers Hill
Batch

WOLVERS HILL RD

Laurel
Farm

Park
Farm

Court
Farm

BS24

A371

LOCKING MOOR RD

CRANWELL RD

SUMMER LA

BS29

HOMEFIELD
CL

Homefield
Ind Est

BEECHWOOD AVE

PLUMLEY
CRES

POST OFFICE RD

BENCH RD

FARNBOROUGH RD

Cave
View

THE ORCHARD

B3368

ELM TREE RD

PH

MANOR
CT

LEAFY WAY

MENDIP RISE

LIME CL

BIRCH CL

Locking
Prim Sch

STINKY RD

PINETREE CL

LOWER
HILL

LADASTRAL

GROVE RD

PARK END

VIEW RD

IVY WLK

ASH RD

CENTRE DR

ELM CL

RYDAL AVE

GRENVILLE AVE

FAIRACRE
CL

MEADOW DR

Locking

OLD BANWELL RD

B3368

MENDIP RD

BROADLYN

TREVENARD RD

THE PORTAL

FLOWERDOWN RD

BYR
CL

SOUTH LAWN

PO

LYCHGATE
CL

THE
GREEN

Church
Farm

THE BURY

HILLMER RISE

Perries

Knightcott
Ind Est

WELL LA

KNIGHTCOTT RD

A371

Knightcott

CHESTERFIELD CL

WHITCOMBE CL

WATTS CL

KNIGHTCOTT GDNS

Wingfield
House

BANWELL RD

Elborough

ELBOROUGH

SAINS

BEAUFORT CL

CEDERN AVE

BLUE WATER DR

MEADOW WY

Hillend

Hillend

HIGH ST

Mast

Windmill
Farm

WINDMILL HILL

Benthills
Wood

Manor
Farm

Whitley
Head

Mon

Banwell
Hill

Upper
Canada

CANADA COOMBE

Elborough
Hill

BRIDEWELL LA

M5

Christon
Hill

Christon
Plantation

BS26

BS26

Yarberry

BANWELL RD

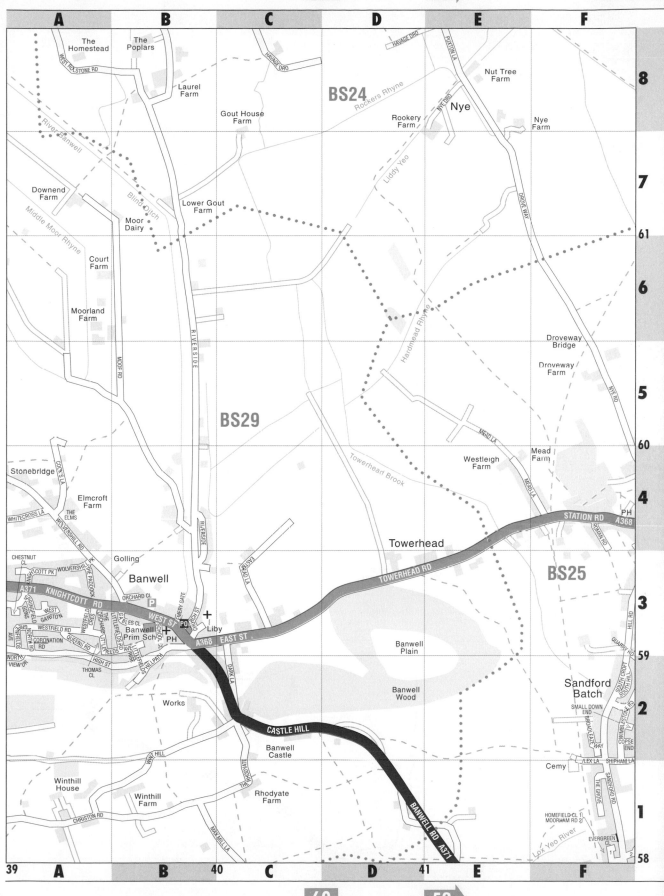

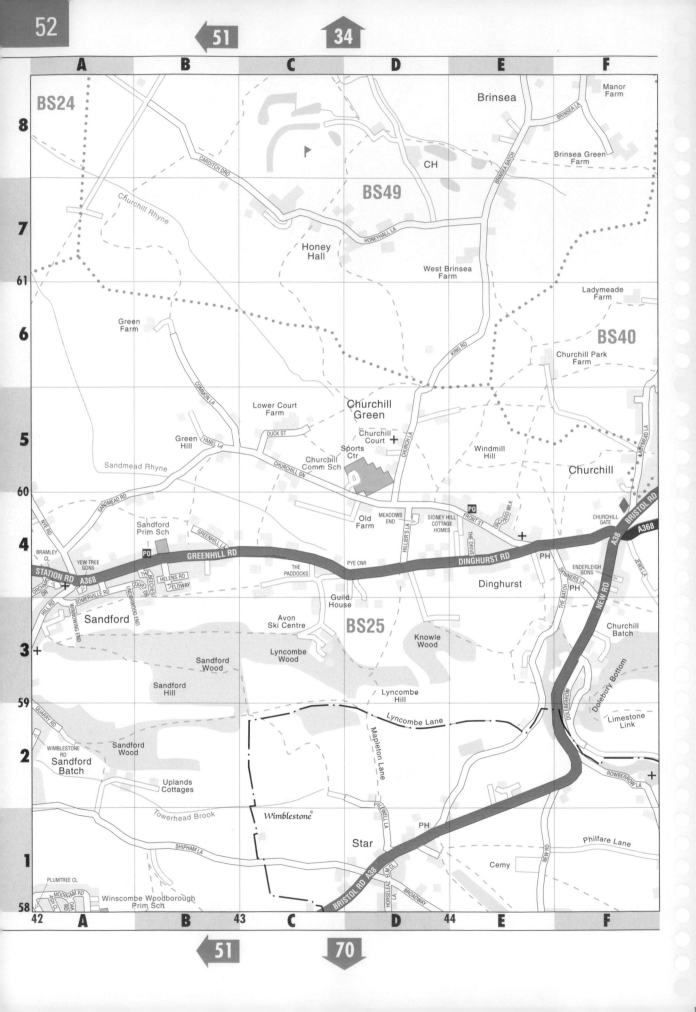

51
34

A   B   C   D   E   F

8

BS24

Manor Farm

Brinsea

CARDITCH DRO

CH

BS49

7

Churchill Rhyne

Brinsea Green Farm

BRINSEA LA

BRINSEA BATCH

HONEYHALL LA

Honey Hall

West Brinsea Farm

61

Ladymeade Farm

6

Green Farm

BS40

COMMON LA

KING RD

Churchill Park Farm

5

Lower Court Farm

Churchill Green

Green Hill

YANEL LA

DUCK ST

CHURCHILL GN

Churchill Court

Windmill Hill

Churchill

Sandmead Rhyne

Churchill Comm Sch

Sports Ctr

CHURCHILL LA

LADYMEAD LA

60

BRISTOL RD

PYE RD

SANDMEAD RD

Old Farm

MEADOWS END

Sidney Hill Cottage Homes

FRONT ST

PO

ORCHARD WLK

CHURCHILL GATE

A368

A38

4

BRAMLEY CL

YEW TREE GDNS

PO

GREENHILL RD

GREENHILL LA

HILLER'S LA

THE DRIVE

PH

ENDERLEIGH GDNS

DINGHURST RD

PYE CNR

LEWIS LA

STATION RD

A368

THE BEECHES

HELENS RD

COURT DR

FIELDWAY

THE PADDOCKS

PH

NEW RD

SOMERVILLE RD

UNDERWOOD END

Dinghurst

SKINNERS LA

THE BATCH

ORCHARD DR

HILL RD

WINNOWING END

Sandford

Guild House

Avon Ski Centre

BS25

Knowle Wood

Churchill Batch

3

Sandford Wood

Lyncombe Wood

Sandford Hill

Lyncombe Hill

Doleberry Bottom

DOLEBERROW

59

QUARRY RD

Lyncombe Lane

Limestone Link

2

WIMBLESTONE RD

Sandford Wood

Sandford Batch

Uplands Cottages

MAPLETON LANE

ROWBERROW LA

Towerhead Brook

Wimblestone

PYLENELL LA

Star

PH

NEW RD

Philfare Lane

1

SHIPHAM LA

BRISTOL RD A38

HORSELEAZ LA

ELM CL

BROADWAY

Cemy

PLUMTREE CL

MOORHAM RD

ASH CL

OAK

Winscombe Woodborough Prim Sch

58

42   A   B   43   C   D   44   E   F

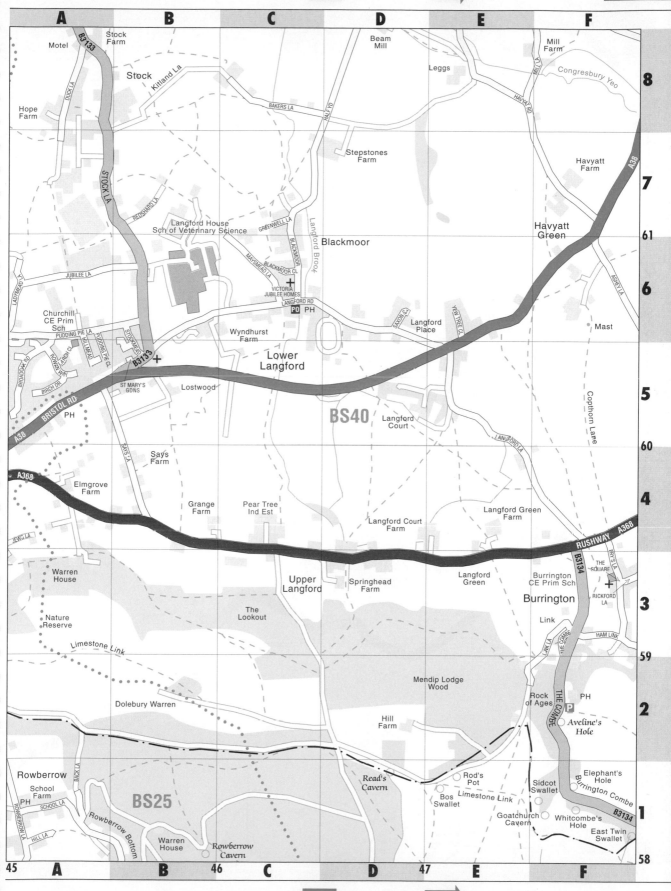

A   B   C   D   E   F

8

7

61

6

5

60

4

59

3

2

1

58

Motel
B3133
Stock Farm
Stock
Kitland La
Hope Farm
DUCK LA
STOCK LA
Beam Mill
Leggs
Mill Farm
Congresbury Yeo
MILL LA
HAVYATT RD
Bakers La
Half Yd
Stepstones Farm
Havyatt Farm
A38
Redshard La
Langford House Sch of Veterinary Science
Greenwell La
Langford Brook
Blackmoor
Havyatt Green
Jubilee La
Maysmead La
Blackmoor Cl
BLACKMOOR
Victoria Jubilee Homes
Langford Rd
PO PH
Saxon Cl
Langford Place
Yew Tree Cl
ASH LA
Mast
Churchill CE Prim Sch
Pudding Pie La
HILLMEAD
PUDDING PIE CL
Wyndhurst Farm
Langford
ROWAN DR
PYCROFT CL
STOCKMEAD
B3133
Lower Langford
Langford Court
Copthorn Lane
BROADAW RD
LADYMEAD RD
BIRCH DR
BRISTOL RD
A38
St Mary's Gdns
PH
Lostwood
BS40
LANGFORD LA
60
A368
SAYS LA
Says Farm
JEWGL LA
Elmgrove Farm
Grange Farm
Pear Tree Ind Est
Langford Court Farm
Langford Green Farm
RUSHWAY A368
B3134
THE SQUARE
FRY'S LA
Warren House
Nature Reserve
Limestone Link
The Lookout
Upper Langford
Springhead Farm
Langford Green
Burrington CE Prim Sch
Burrington
RICKFORD LA
LINK LA
Link
THE COMBE
HAM LINK
59
Dolebury Warren
Mendip Lodge Wood
Rock of Ages
P
PH
Aveline's Hole
Hill Farm
Rowberrow
School Farm
PH
BACK LA
SCHOOL LA
BS25
Rowberrow Bottom
Warren House
Rowberrow Cavern
HILL LA
ROWBERROW LA
Read's Cavern
Rod's Pot
Bos Swallet
Limestone Link
Sidcot Swallet
Goatchurch Cavern
Whitcombe's Hole
Elephant's Hole
Burrington Combe
B3134
East Twin Swallet

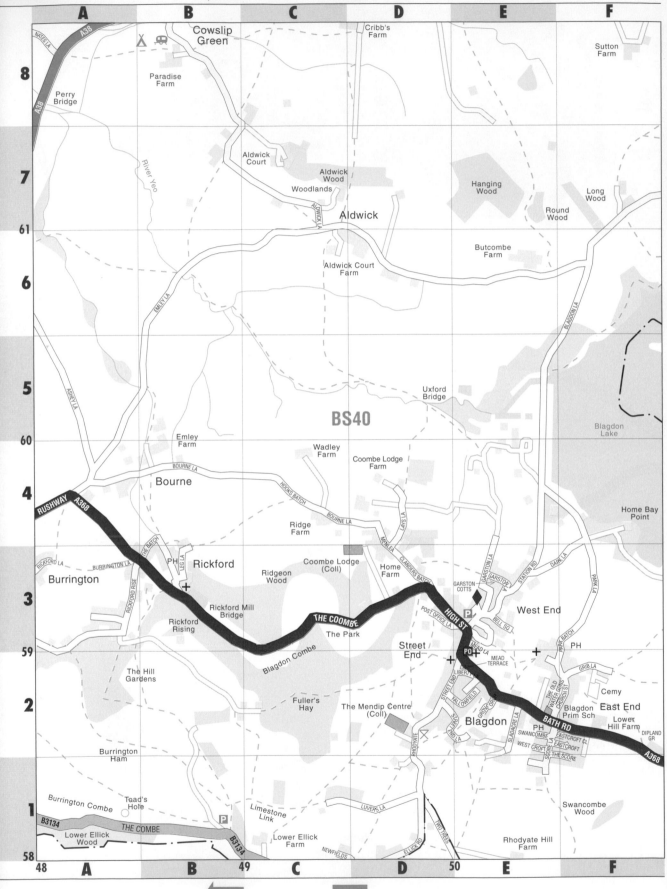

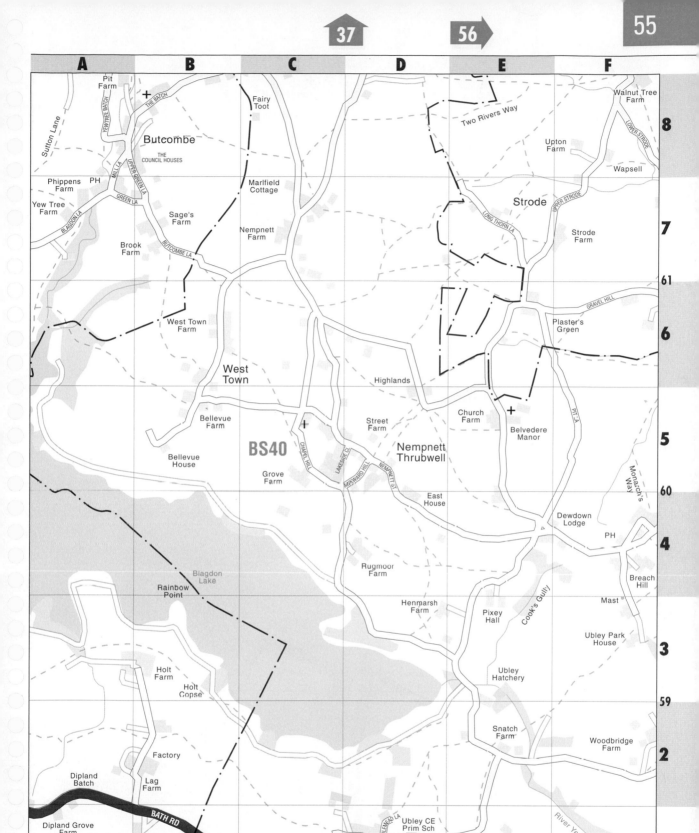

8
7
61
6
5
60
4
3
59
2
1
58

Pit Farm
Sutton Lane
THE BATCH
Fairy Toot
Butcombe
THE COUNCIL HOUSES
YEWTREE BATCH
Phippens Farm
PH
MILL LA
UPPER GREEN LA
Marlfield Cottage
Yew Tree Farm
GREEN LA
Sage's Farm
Nempnett Farm
BLAGDON LA
Brook Farm
BUTCOMBE LA
Two Rivers Way
Walnut Tree Farm
Upton Farm
Wapsell
Strode
LONG THORN LA
UPPER STRODE
LOWER STRODE
Strode Farm
Gravel Hill
Plaster's Green
West Town Farm
West Town
Bellevue Farm
Highlands
Church Farm
Belvedere Manor
PIT LA
BS40
Bellevue House
Street Farm
Nempnett Thrubwell
Monarch's Way
Grove Farm
CHAPEL HILL
LAKESIDE CL
MILKWARD HILL
NEMPNETT ST
East House
Dewdown Lodge
PH
Blagdon Lake
Rainbow Point
Rugmoor Farm
Henmarsh Farm
Breach Hill
Mast
Cook's Gully
Pixey Hall
Ubley Park House
Holt Farm
Holt Copse
Ubley Hatchery
Factory
Snatch Farm
Woodbridge Farm
Dipland Batch
Lag Farm
Dipland Grove Farm
Merecombe Farm
BATH RD
Ubley Farm
FROG LA
STILEMEAD LA
Ubley CE Prim Sch
INNICKS CL
SQUIRE LA
THE STREET
Park Farm
Ubley
River Yeo
Rookery Farm
A368
TUCKER'S LA

55 38

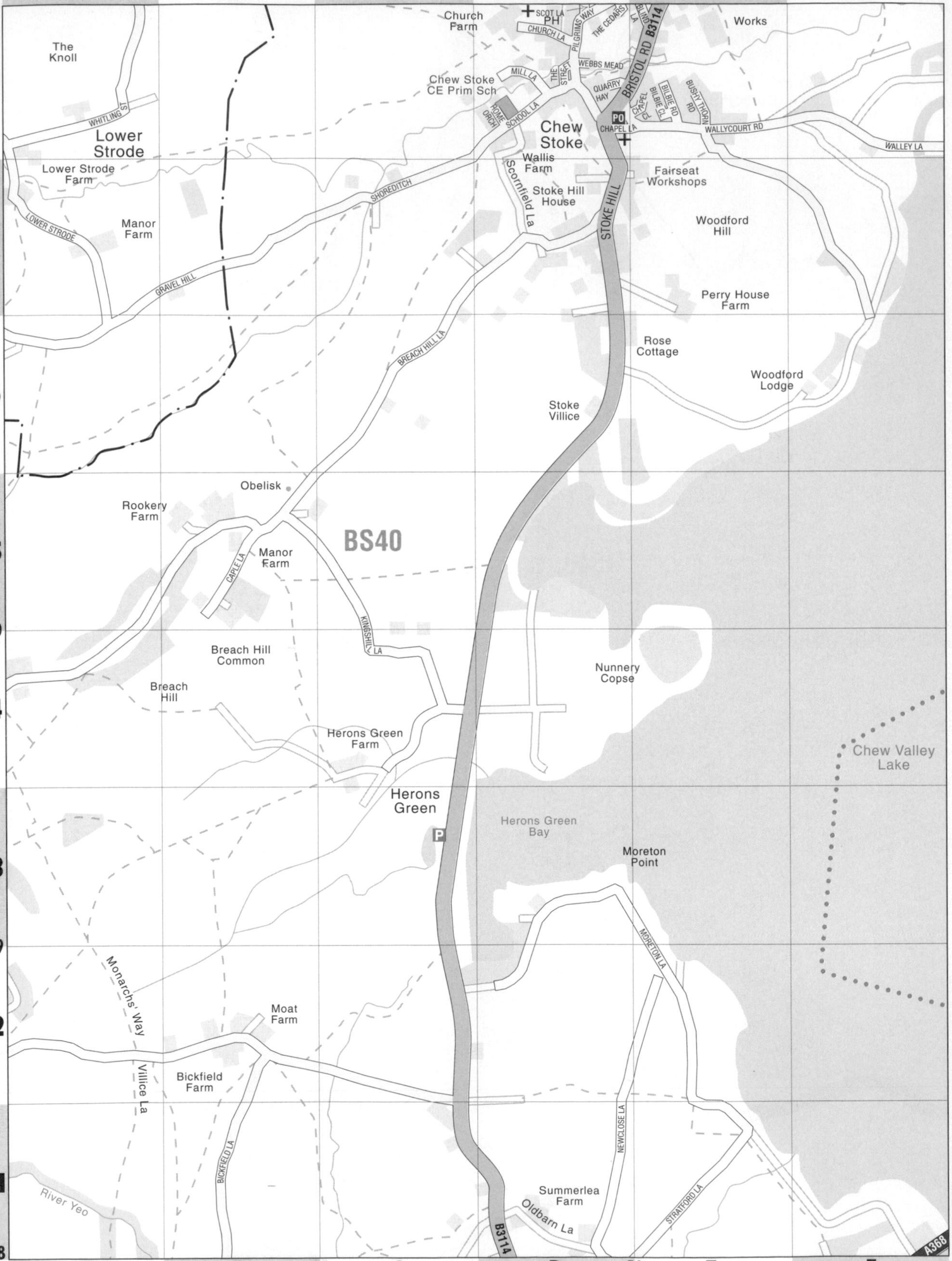

A B C D E F

8

The Knoll

WHITLING

Lower
Strode

Lower Strode
Farm

7

LOWER STRODE

Manor
Farm

GRAVEL HILL

61

SHOREDITCH

Church
Farm

SCOT LA
PH
CHURCH LA

THE STREET

PILGRIMS WAY

THE CEDARS

Works

BRISTOL RD B3114

WEBBS MEAD

Chew Stoke
CE Prim Sch

MILL LA

QUARRY
HAY

ACME

SCHOOL LA

SCORNFIELD LA

BREACH HILL LA

Chew
Stoke

Wallis
Farm

Stoke Hill
House

STOKE HILL

PO
CHAPEL LA

CHAPEL LA

BILBIE LA

BUSHY THORN

WALLYCOURT RD

WALLEY LA

Fairseat
Workshops

Woodford
Hill

Perry House
Farm

6

Rose
Cottage

Woodford
Lodge

Stoke
Villice

Obelisk

Rookery
Farm

CAPLE LA

Manor
Farm

BS40

5

60

Breach Hill
Common

KINGSHILL LA

Nunnery
Copse

Chew Valley
Lake

Breach
Hill

4

Herons Green
Farm

Herons
Green

P

Herons Green
Bay

Moreton
Point

3

MORETON LA

59

Monarchs' Way

VILLICE LA

Moat
Farm

2

Bickfield
Farm

BICKFIELD LA

NEWCLOSE LA

STRATFORD LA

1

River Yeo

Summerlea
Farm

Oldbarn La

B3114

A368

58

54 A B 55 C D 56 E F

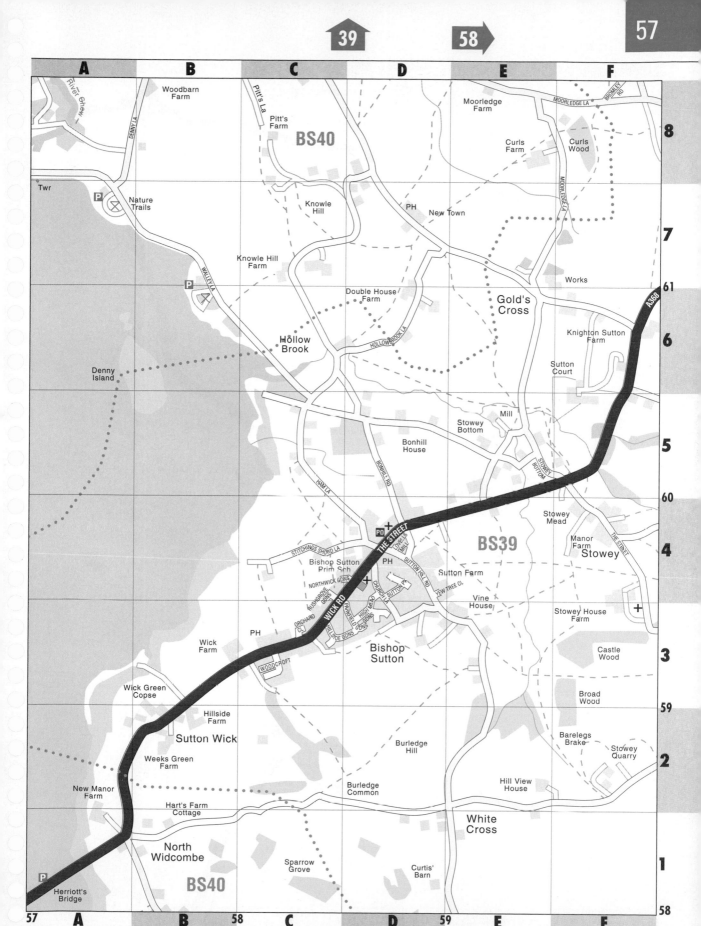

57
40

A B C D E F

8

Bromley Farm

Curl's Farm

STANTON WICK LA

Stanton Wick

Chelwood RDBT

A37

A368

Utcombe Farm

Chelwood House Hotel

7

A368

Stanton Wick Farm

Park Farm

Fry's Bottom

61

Round Hill

Salter's Brook

FEATHERED LA

Red Hill

Breach

6

Folly Wood

Honey Gaston

THE FLAT

North End Farm

BS39

5

Folly Farm Nature Reserve

North End

KING LA

60

Dowling's Wood

Taylor's Farm

LOWER BRISTOL RD

4

Cinderlands Brake

Tynemoor Wood

Hill Farm

A37

Warwick Arms (PH)

UPPER BRISTOL RD

WARWICK GDNS

TWYNINGS WAY

TWYNINGS

ROGERS CL

THE MEAD

FURN EAZE LA

BROOMHILL LA

Clutton Prim Sch

MAYPOLE

BURCHILL CL

BATCH LA

GREENRIDGE

CLUTTON HILL

3

Tynemore Farm

STATION RD

PO

Clutton

CHURCH LA

VALLEY VIEW

VENUS LA

CARLTON

MAYNARD TERR

59

Cholwell Farm

Church Farm

MISS OAK MDW

CHURCH SQ

Willow Farm

MARSH LA

2

Sleight Farm

Cholwell House

Cholwell

New Cholwell Farm

Bendalls Bridge

Temple Cloud

THE SQUARE

GOODNEY

GREYFIELD VIEW

NANNY HURN'S LA

1

Limestone Link

Paul Wood

Paulwood RD

PAULMONT RISE

FAIRVIEW

ELM VIEW

PO

PH

OAKLANDS

CHARBANK

TELE DOWN

ASHMEAD

TEMPLE INN LA

MEADWAY

GOLDEN VALLEY

NEG GARDENS

GOLDEN WAY

HARTCL

Cameley CE Prim Sch

A37

58

60 A B 61 C D 62 E F

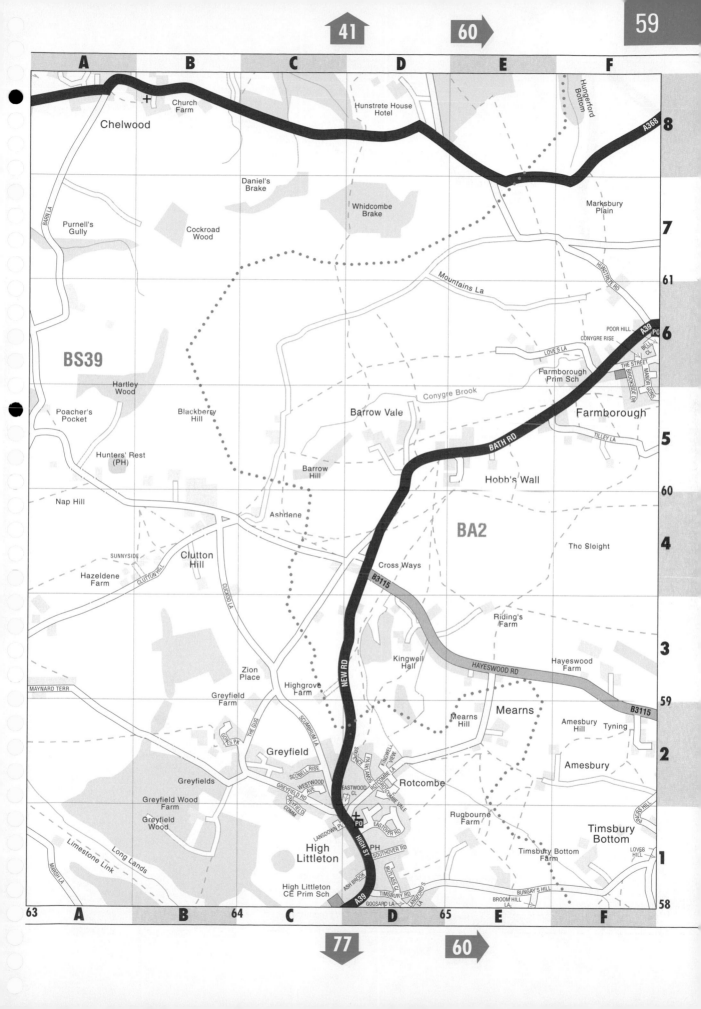

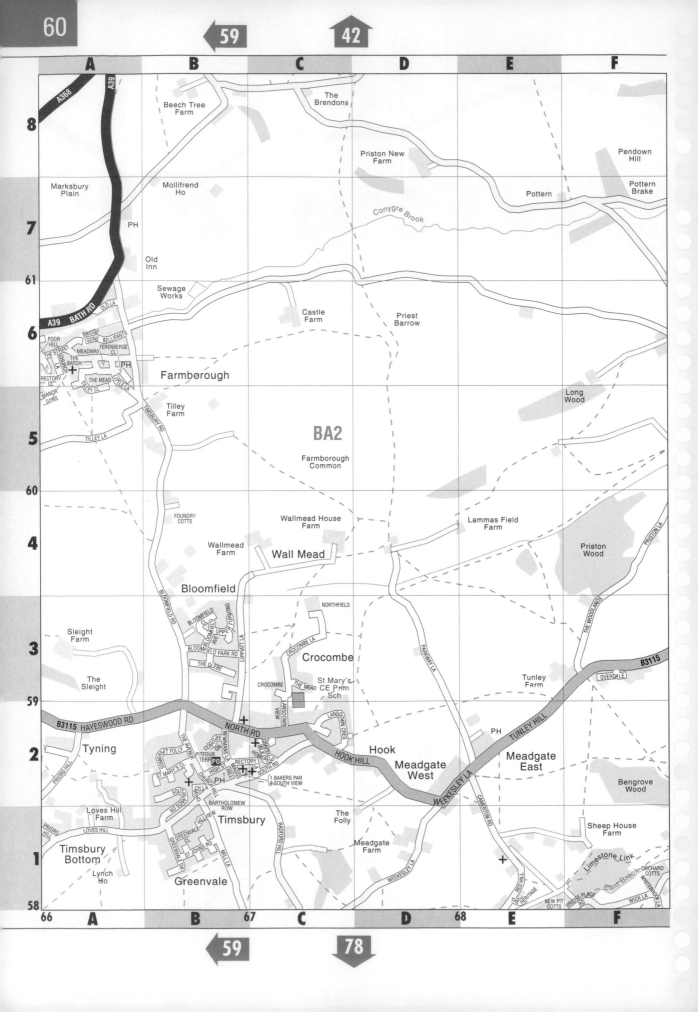

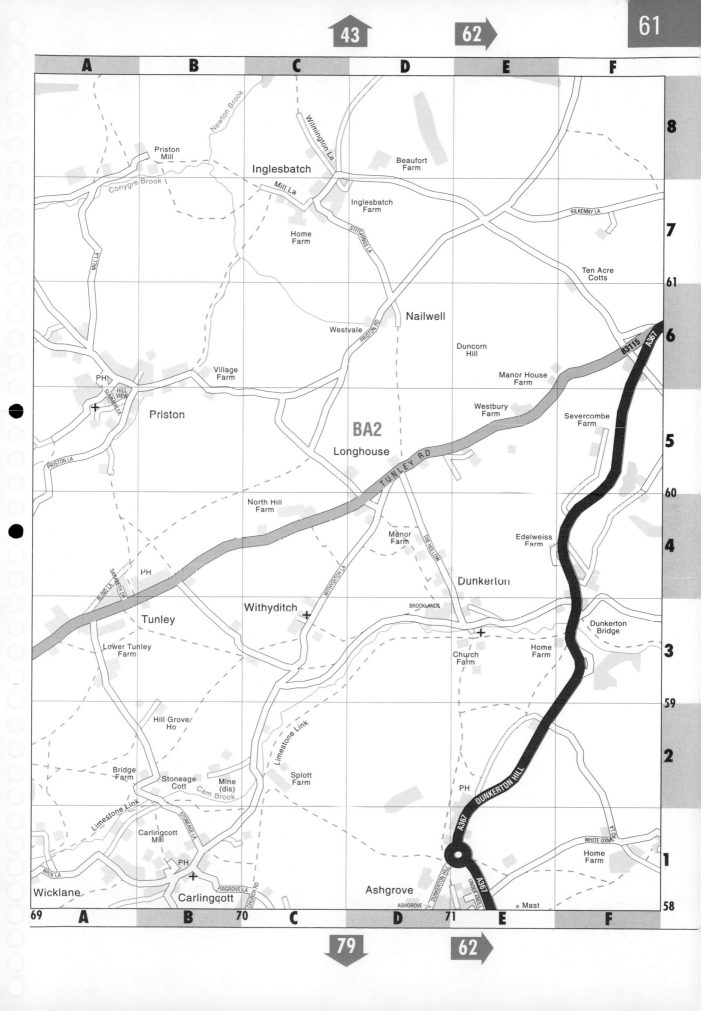

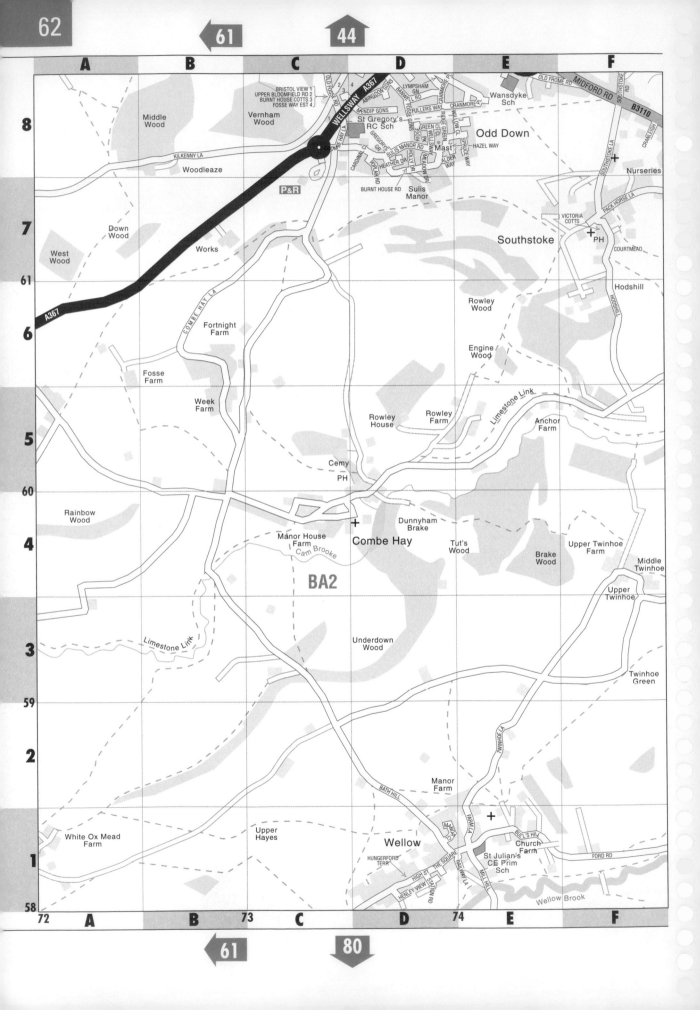

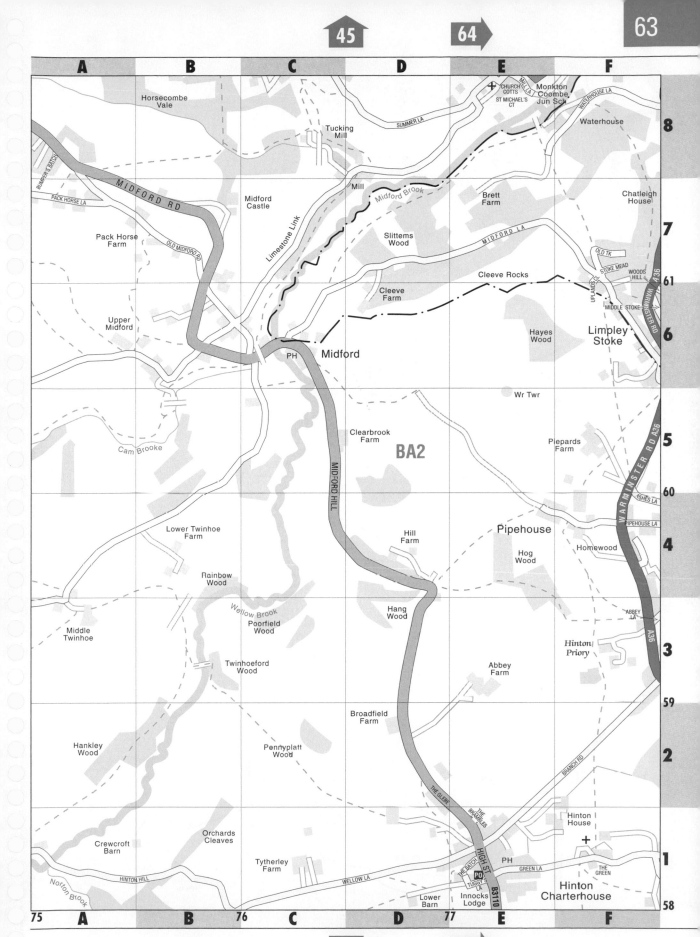

A B C D E F

8

Horsecombe
Vale

SUMMER LA

Tucking
Mill

Monkton
Coombe
Jun Sch

CHURCH
COTTS
ST MICHAEL'S
CT

Waterhouse

WATERHOUSE LA

MILL LA

PACK HORSE LA

MIDFORD RD

OLD MIDFORD RD

Midford
Castle

Mill

Midford Brook

Brett
Farm

Chatleigh
House

7

Pack Horse
Farm

Limestone Link

Slittems
Wood

MIDFORD LA

OLD TK

A36

WARMINSTER RD

61

BUMPER'S BATCH

Cleeve Rocks

STOKE MEAD

WOODS
HILL

UPLANDS CL

MIDDLE STOKE

Upper
Midford

Cleeve
Farm

6

Limpley
Stoke

PH

Midford

Hayes
Wood

Wr Twr

Cam Brooke

Clearbrook
Farm

BA2

Piepards
Farm

5

MIDFORD HILL

ASHES LA

60

PIPEHOUSE LA

WARMINSTER RD A36

Lower Twinhoe
Farm

Hill
Farm

Pipehouse

Homewood

4

Hog
Wood

Rainbow
Wood

Wellow Brook

Poorfield
Wood

Hang
Wood

ABBEY
LA

A36

Middle
Twinhoe

Hinton
Priory

3

Twinhoeford
Wood

Abbey
Farm

59

Hankley
Wood

Pennyplatt
Wood

Broadfield
Farm

BRANCH RD

2

THE GLEBE

Hinton
House

Crewcroft
Barn

Orchards
Cleaves

THE BRAMBLES

PH

GREEN LA

THE
GREEN

1

Tytherley
Farm

WELLOW LA

HINTON HILL

HIGH ST

THE BATCH

TUGGY'S

PO

Hinton
Charterhouse

B3110

Norton Brook

Lower
Barn

Innocks
Lodge

58

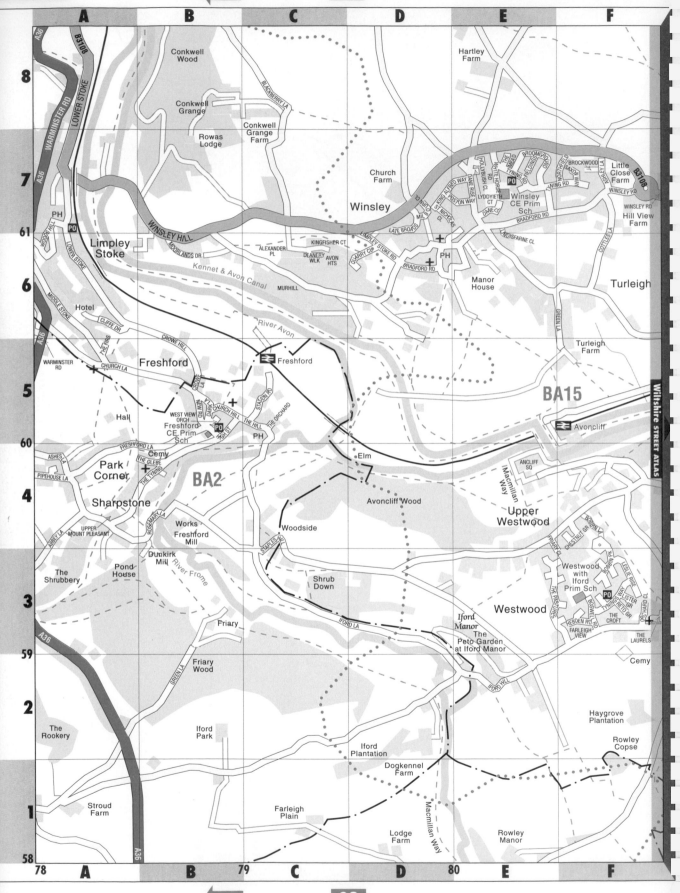

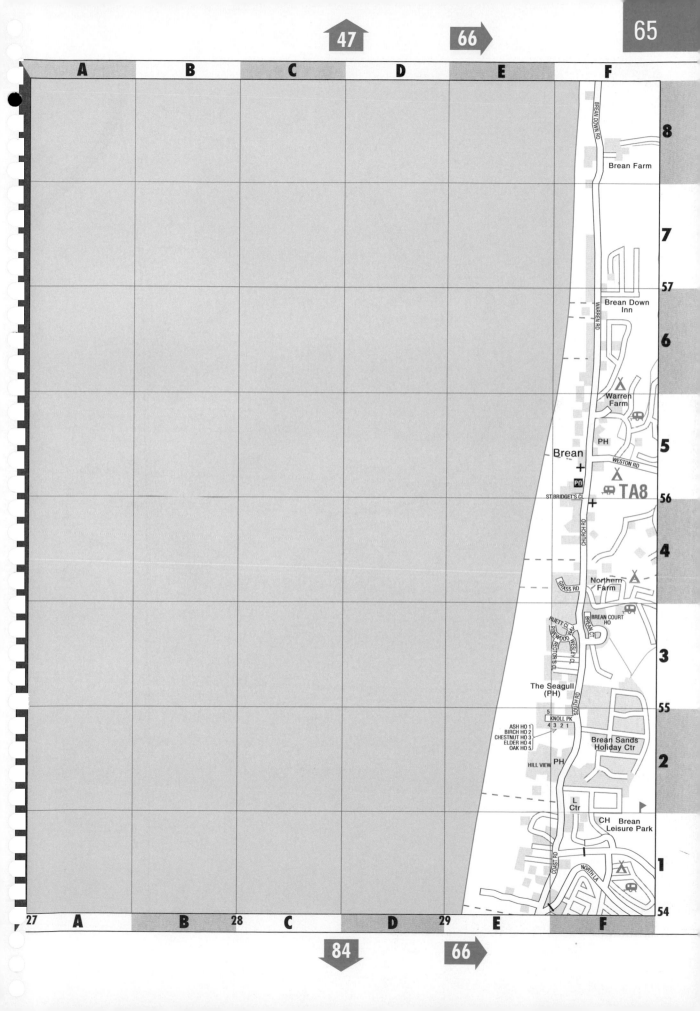

Brean Down Rd

Brean Farm

Brean Down Inn

Warren Rd

Warren Farm

PH

Brean

Weston Rd

P O

St Bridget's Cl

TA8

Church Rd

Grass Rd

Northern Farm

Brean Court Ho

Pruett Cl

Wm Wesley Cl

Pinewood

Rector's Cl

Brean Ct

The Seagull (PH)

South Rd

Knoll Pk

ASH HO 1
BIRCH HO 2
CHESTNUT HO 3
ELDER HO 4
OAK HO 5

Brean Sands Holiday Ctr

HILL VIEW

PH

L Ctr

CH Brean Leisure Park

Coast Rd

North La

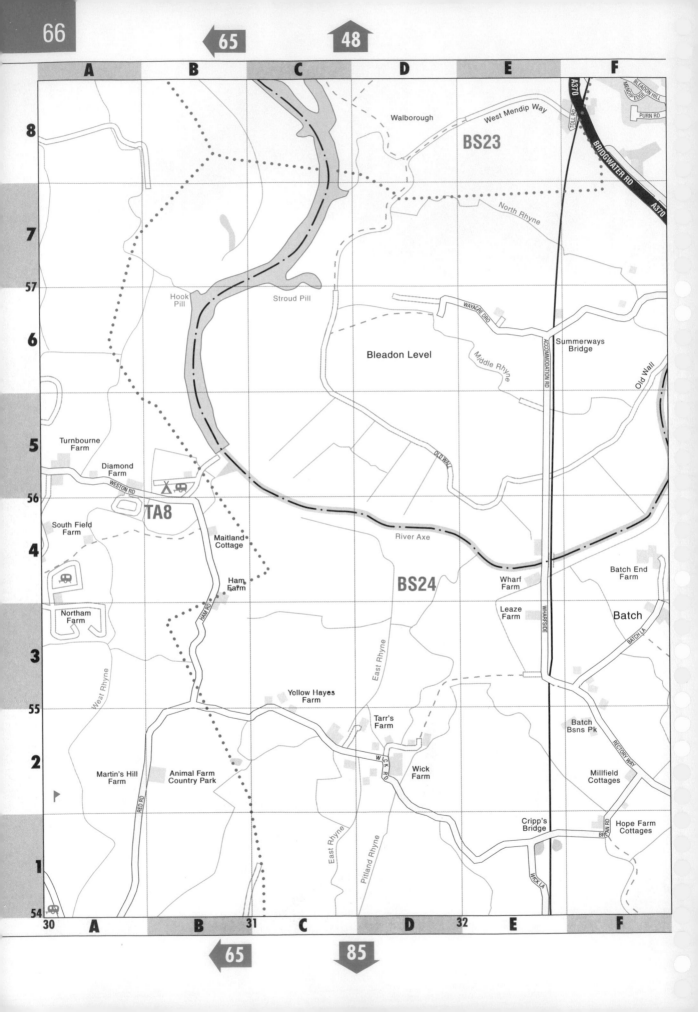

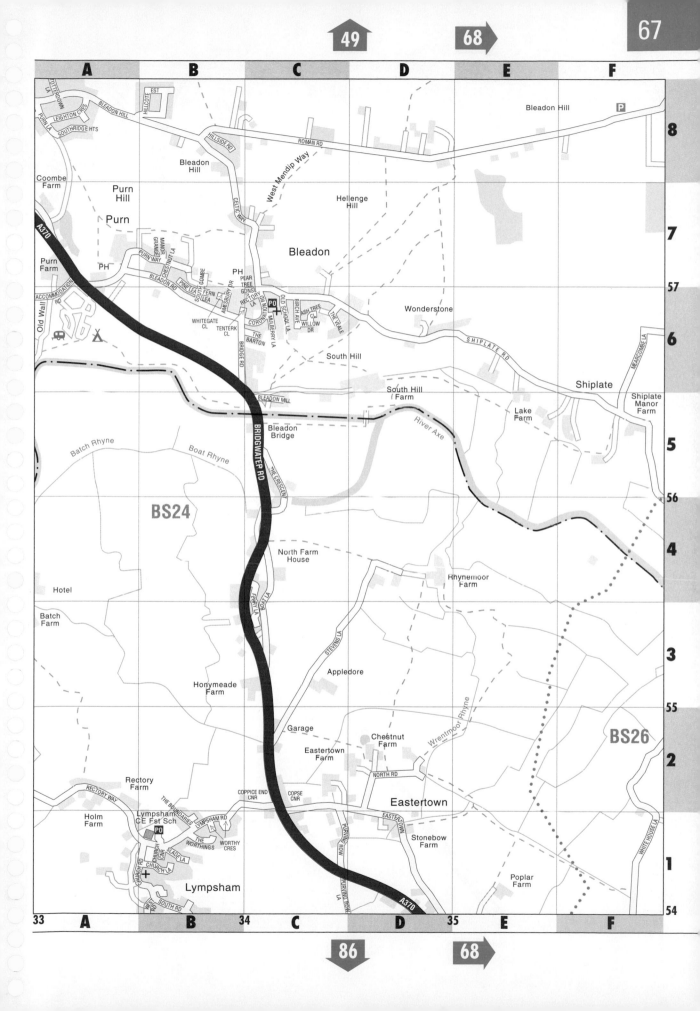

A B C D E F

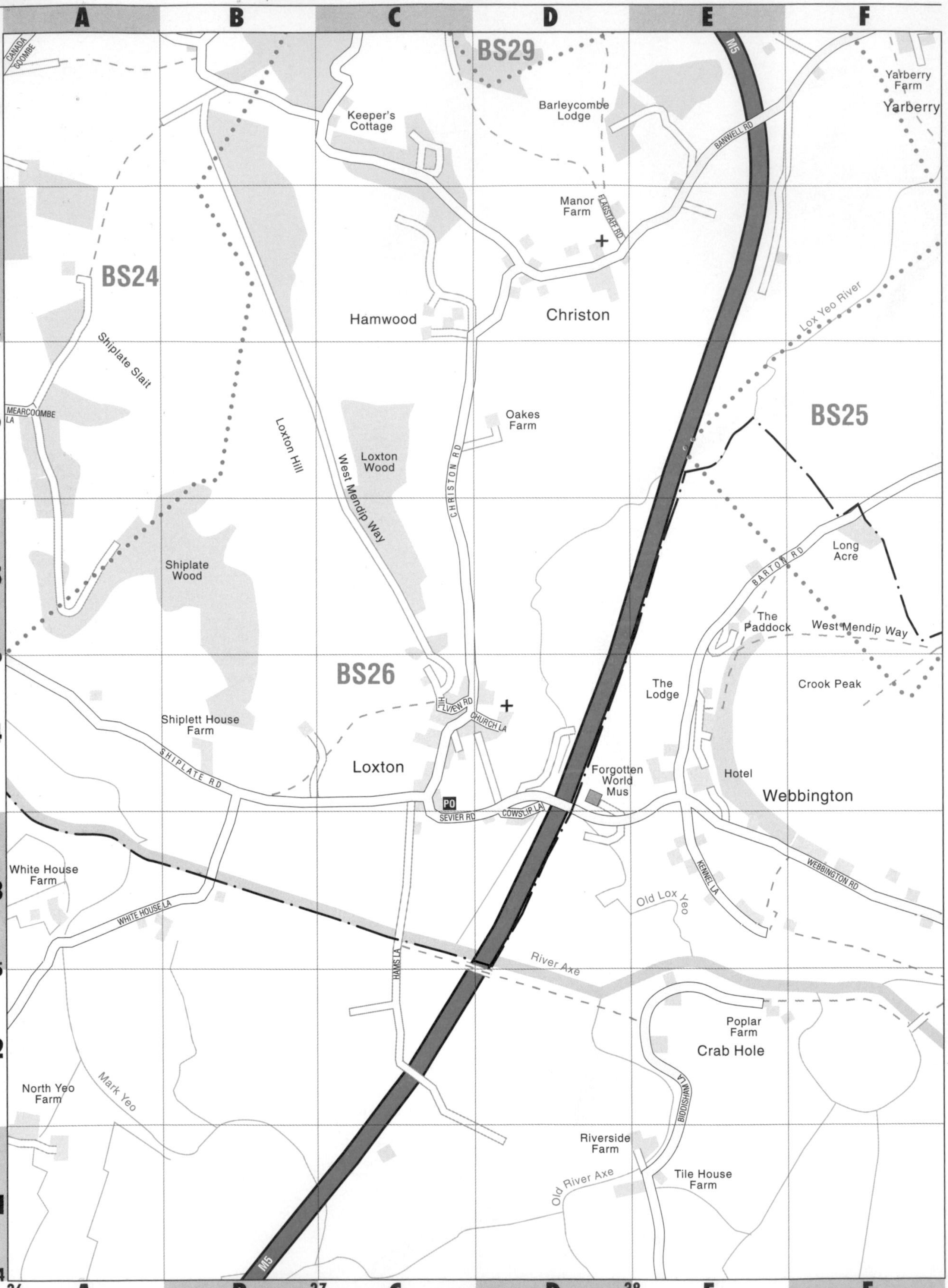

8

CANADA COOMBE LA

BS29

Barleycombe Lodge

Yarberry Farm

Yarberry

Keeper's Cottage

Manor Farm

BANWELL RD

M5

7

BS24

Shiplate Slait

Hamwood

FLAGSTAFF RD

Christon

Lox Yeo River

57

6

MEARCOOMBE LA

Loxton Hill

Loxton Wood

Loxton Wood

CHRISTON RD

Oakes Farm

BS25

West Mendip Way

5

Shiplate Wood

BARTON RD

Long Acre

The Paddock

West Mendip Way

56

BS26

HILL VIEW RD

CHURCH LA

The Lodge

Crook Peak

4

Shiplett House Farm

SHIPLATE RD

Loxton

PO

SEVIER RD

COWSLIP LA

Forgotten World Mus

Hotel

Webbington

3

White House Farm

WHITE HOUSE LA

HAMS LA

Old Lox Yeo

River Axe

KENNEL LA

WEBBINGTON RD

55

2

North Yeo Farm

Mark Yeo

Poplar Farm

Crab Hole

BIDDISHAM LA

1

Riverside Farm

Old River Axe

Tile House Farm

M5

54

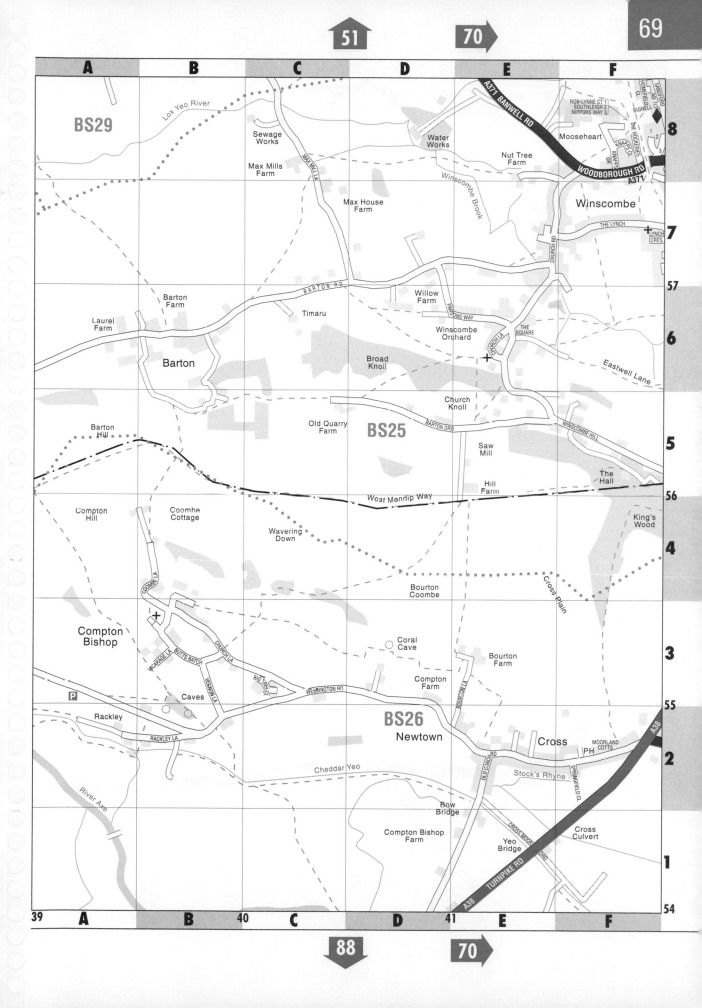

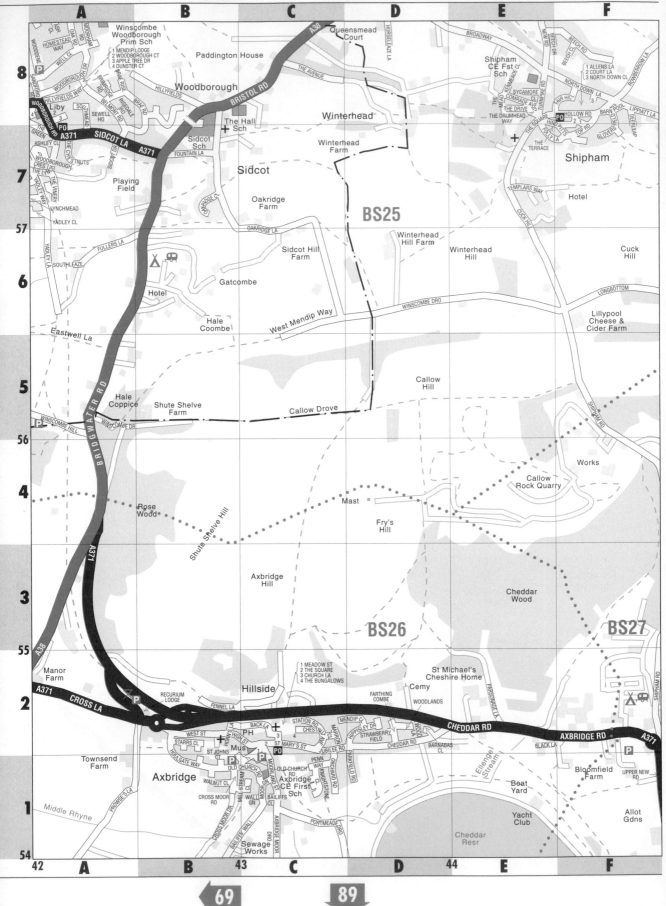

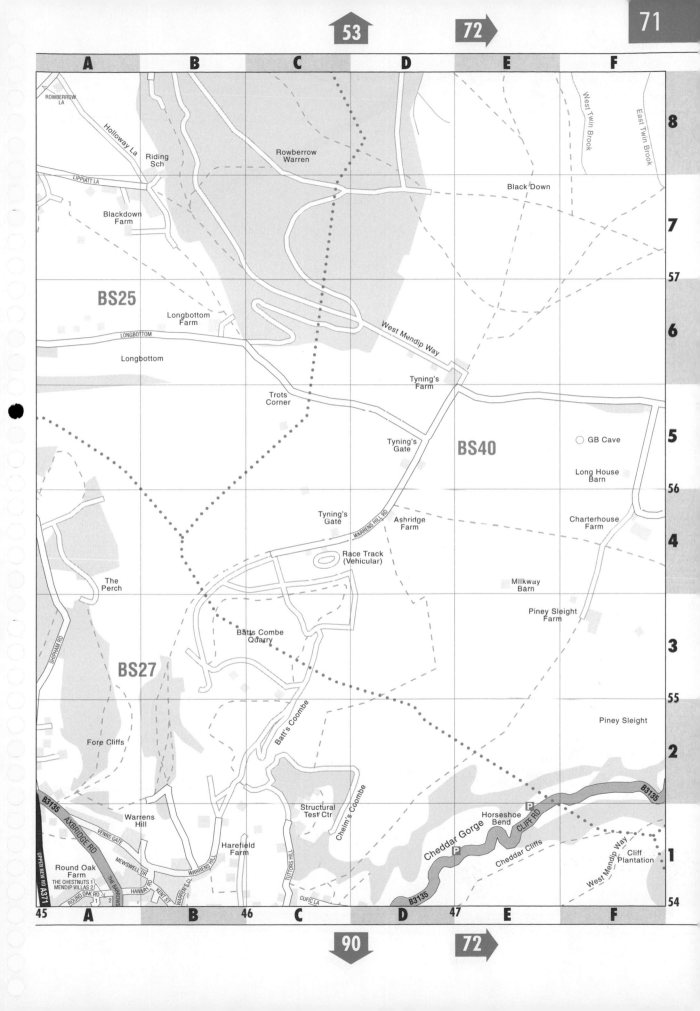

53
72

A B C D E F

8

ROWBERROW LA

Holloway La

Riding Sch

LIPPIATT LA

Blackdown Farm

West Twin Brook

East Twin Brook

Black Down

Rowberrow Warren

7

57

BS25

Longbottom Farm

LONGBOTTOM

West Mendip Way

6

Longbottom

Tyning's Farm

Trots Corner

Tyning's Gate

BS40

GB Cave

5

Tyning's Gate

WARRENS HILL RD

Ashridge Farm

Long House Barn

56

Charterhouse Farm

Race Track (Vehicular)

Milkway Barn

4

The Perch

Piney Sleight Farm

BS27

Batts Combe Quarry

3

55

Batt's Coombe

Fore Cliffs

Piney Sleight

2

SHIPHAM RD

Warrens Hill

Chelm's Coombe

Structural Test Ctr

Cheddar Gorge

Horseshoe Bend

CLIFF RD

B3135

P

P

B3135

Harefield Farm

TUTTORS HILL

Cheddar Cliffs

West Mendip Way

Cliff Plantation

1

AXBRIDGE RD

VENNIS GATE

MEWSWELL DR

WARRENS HILL

CUFIC LA

B3135

Round Oak Farm

THE CHESTNUTS 1
MENDIP VILLAS 2

HANNA RD

KENT ST

WARREN'S CL

THE BARROWS

UPPER NEW RD

A371

ROUND OAK RD

1 2

54

45 A B 46 C D 47 E F

90
72

A B C D E F

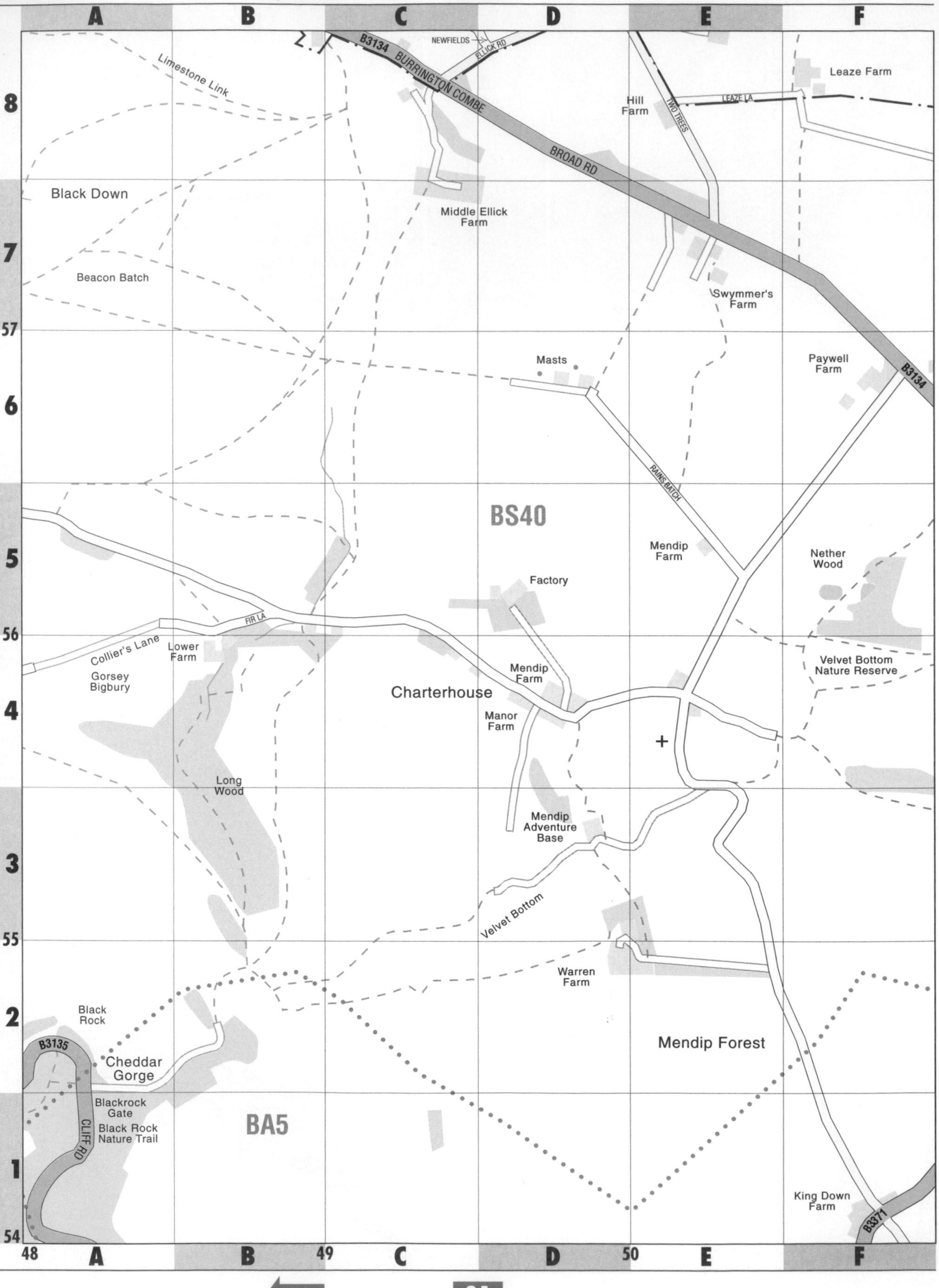

8

7

57

6

Black Down

Beacon Batch

Limestone Link

B3134
NEWFIELDS
BURRINGTON COMBE
ELLICK RD
BROAD RD

Middle Ellick Farm

Hill Farm

TWO TREES

Leaze Farm

LEAZE LA

Swymmer's Farm

Masts

RAINS BATCH

Paywell Farm

B3134

BS40

Mendip Farm

Nether Wood

5

56

Collier's Lane
Gorsey Bigbury

Lower Farm

FIR LA

Factory

Mendip Farm

Charterhouse

Manor Farm

Mendip Farm

+

Velvet Bottom Nature Reserve

4

Long Wood

Mendip Adventure Base

3

55

Velvet Bottom

Warren Farm

Mendip Forest

2

Black Rock

B3135

Cheddar Gorge

Blackrock Gate

CLIFF RD

Black Rock Nature Trail

BA5

King Down Farm

B3371

1

54

48 A B 49 C D 50 E F

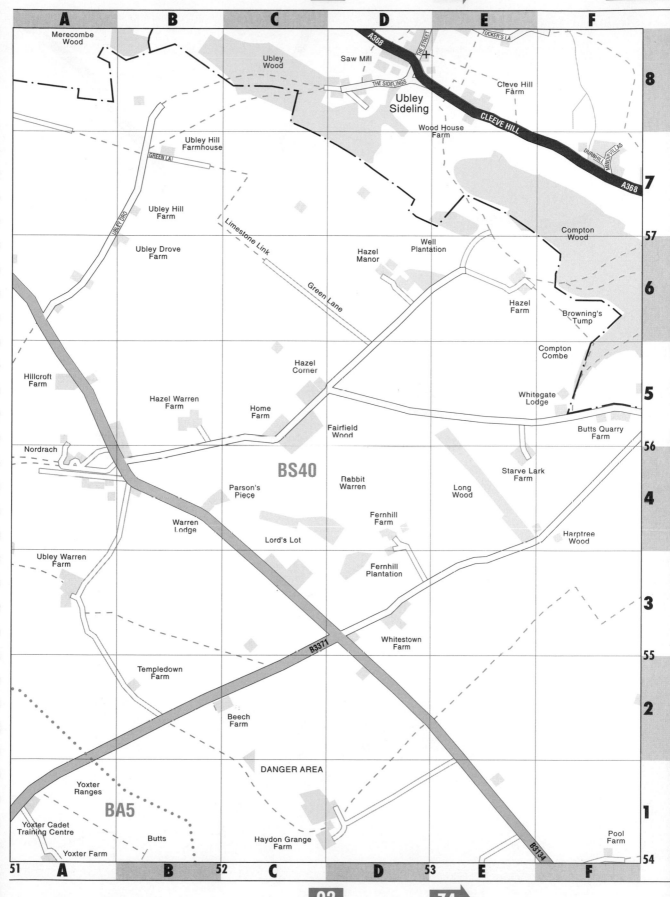

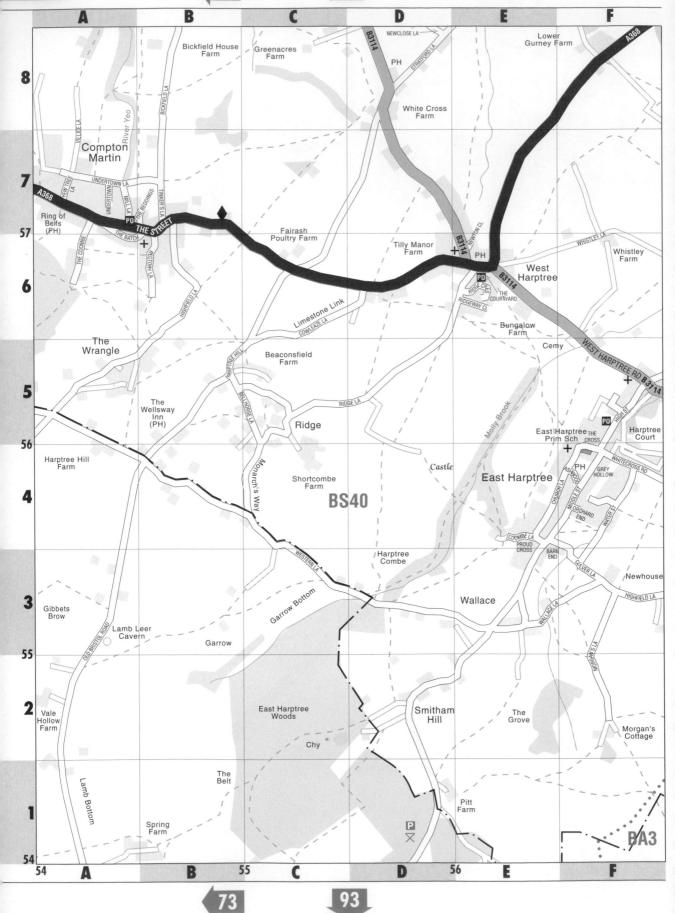

A B C D E F

8

NEWCLOSE LA
B3114
STRATFORD LA
PH
Lower
Gurney Farm
A368

Bickfield House
Farm
Greenacres
Farm

White Cross
Farm

Compton
Martin

7

VILLOE LA
YEW TREE LA
UNDERTOWN LA
River Yeo
BICKFIELD LA
UNDERTOWN LA
MILL LA
TINKER'S LA
TREE REDDINGS
THE BATCH
PO
THE STREET
A368
Ring of
Bells
(PH)
THE COOMBE
RECTORY LA
HIGHFIELD LA

57

Fairash
Poultry Farm

Tilly Manor
Farm
B3114
NEWTON CL
PH
PO
B3114
RYDE CRES
THE
COURTYARD
RIDGEWAY CL
West
Harptree

WHISTLEY LA
Whistley
Farm

WEST HARPTREE RD B3114

6

The
Wrangle

Limestone Link
COWLEAZE LA

Beaconsfield
Farm

HARPTREE HILL
BELL HORSE LA
RIDGE LA
Ridge

Bungalow
Farm
Cemy

5

The
Wellsway
Inn
(PH)

Monarch's Way

Molly Brook

HIGH ST
PO
Harptree
Court

56

Harptree Hill
Farm

Shortcombe
Farm

Castle

East Harptree
Prim Sch
THE
CROSS
East Harptree

WHITECROSS RD

4

BS40

Harptree
Combe

East Harptree

PH
GREY
HOLLOW
ASH CROFT
CHURCH LA
MIDDLE ST
WATER ST
ORCHARD
END

Newhouse
HIGHFIELD LA

3

Gibbets
Brow
OLD BRISTOL ROAD
Lamb Leer
Cavern

Garrow Bottom

WESTERN LA

Wallace

COOMBE LA
PROUD
CROSS
BARN
END
CALVER LA
WALLACE LA
MINE LA

55

Garrow

2

Vale
Hollow
Farm

East Harptree
Woods

Chy

Smitham
Hill

The
Grove

Morgan's
Cottage

1

Lamb Bottom

The
Belt

Spring
Farm

P
Pitt
Farm

BA3

54

54 A B 55 C D 56 E F

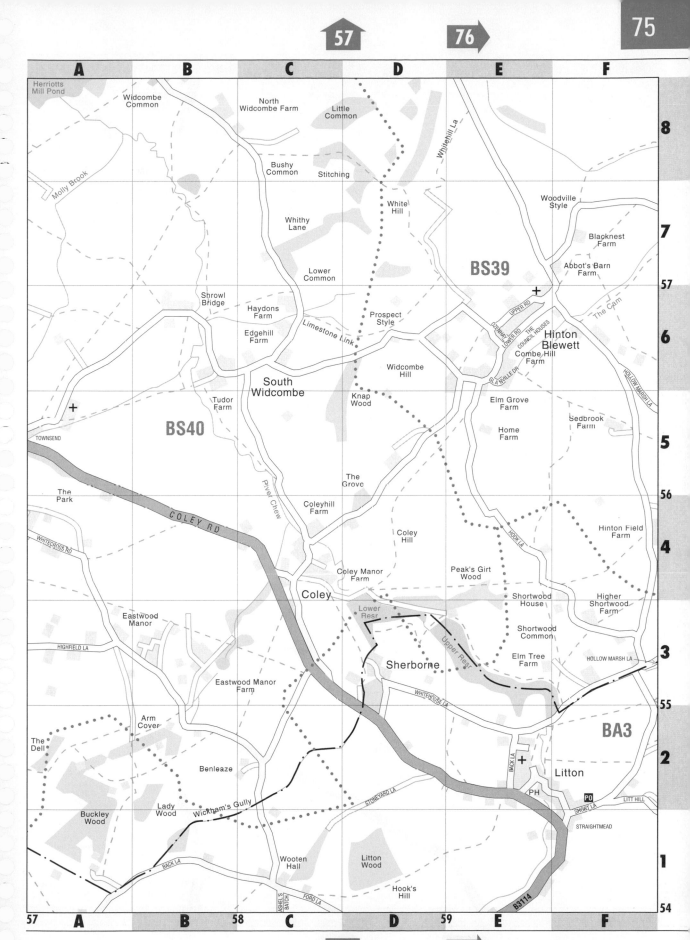

A B C D E F

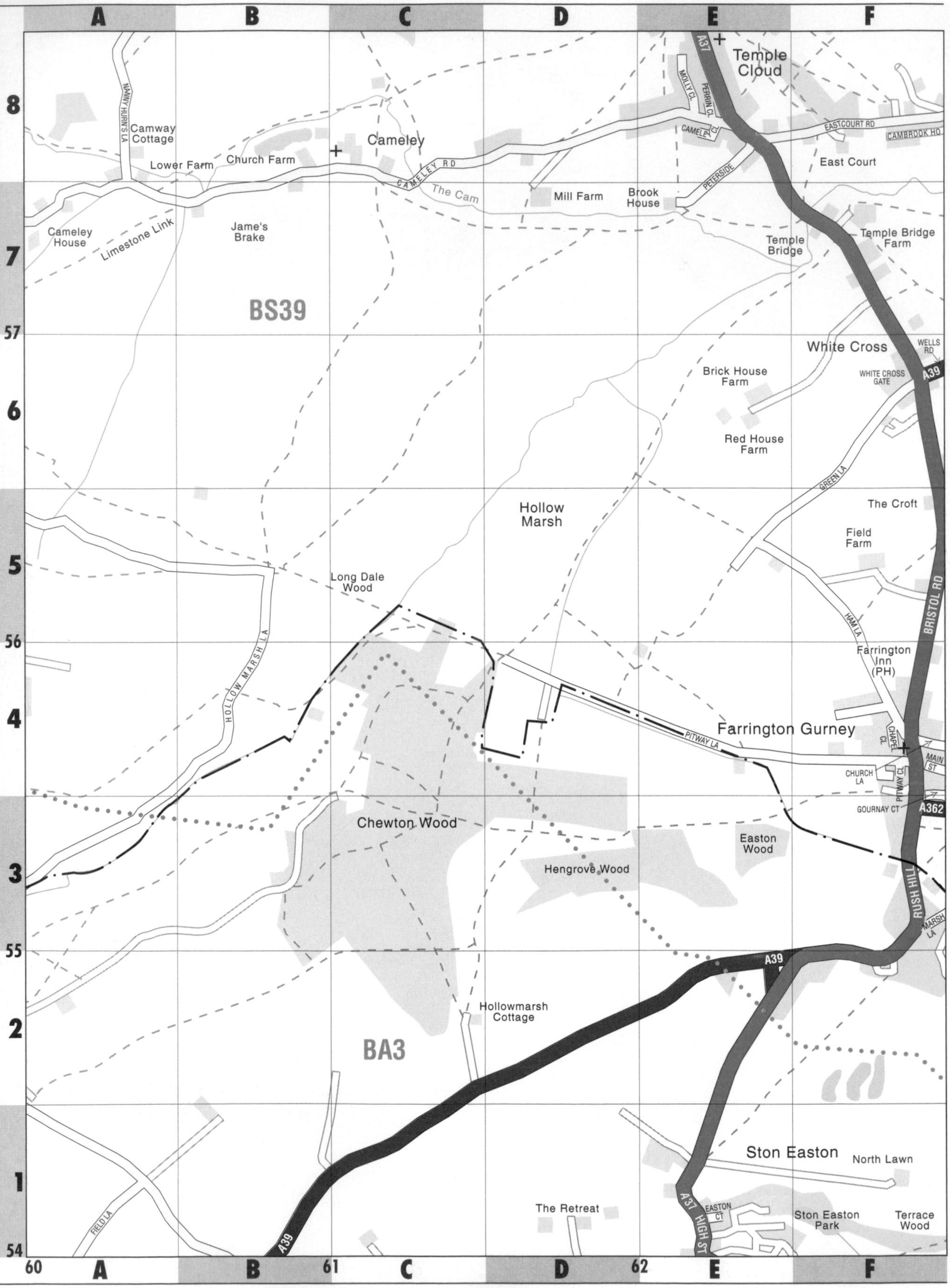

8

Camway
Cottage
Camley
Lower Farm Church Farm
Cameley

CAMELEY RD
The Cam

Mill Farm
Brook
House

A37
Temple
Cloud
MOLLY CL
PERRIN CL
CAMEL CT
EASTCOURT RD
CAMBROOK HO
East Court
PETERSIDE

7

Cameley
House
Limestone Link
HAWY HURN'S LA
Jame's
Brake

Temple
Bridge

Temple Bridge
Farm

57

BS39

White Cross
WELLS RD
A39

6

Brick House
Farm

Red House
Farm

WHITE CROSS
GATE

GREEN LA
The Croft

Field
Farm

5

Long Dale
Wood

Hollow
Marsh

HAM LA
Farrington
Inn
(PH)

56

HOLLOW MARSH LA

BRISTOL RD

4

Chewton Wood

PITWAY LA
Farrington Gurney
CHAPEL CL
MAIN ST
CHURCH LA
PITWAY CL
GOURNAY CT
A362

3

Hengrove Wood

Easton
Wood

RUSH HILL
MARSH LA

55

A39
A39

2

Hollowmarsh
Cottage

BA3

Ston Easton
North Lawn

1

The Retreat

A37
A39
EASTON CT
A37 HIGH ST
Ston Easton
Park
Terrace
Wood

FIELD LA

54

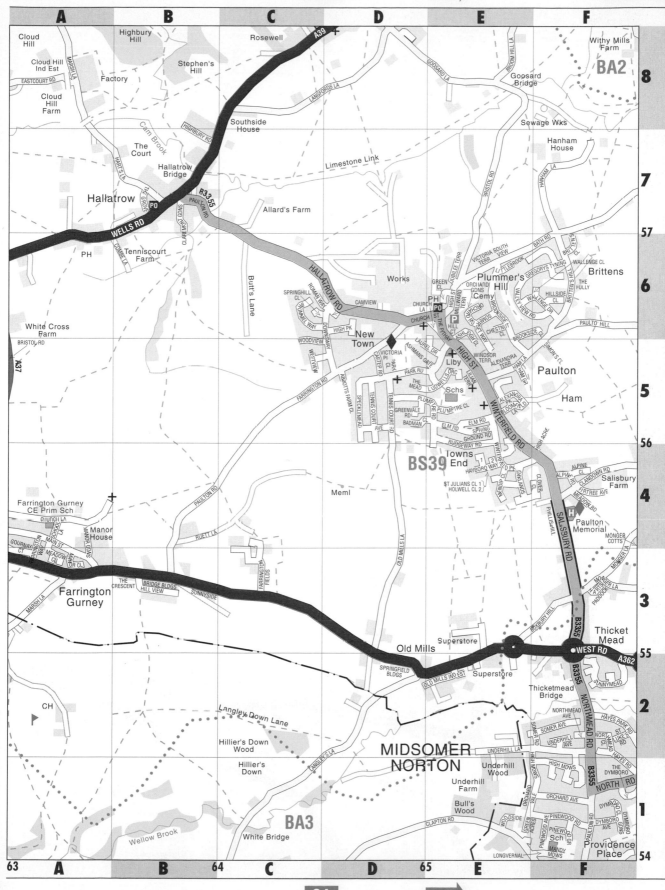

A B C D E F

8

Dunford Farm

Limestone Link

Upper Radford

Red House Farm

New Barn Farm

MILL LA

RADFORD HILL

WEEKESLEY LA

DURCOTT RD

Radford Hotel

Radford

Cam Brook

BA2

COLLIERS HILL

SUNNY VALE

OLD HILL

CANAL VIEW

THE HERITAGE

BRIDGE PLACE RD

WHITEBROOK LA

Cameron

CAMERTON HILL

Abbey Farm

Cameron CE Prim Sch

Cameron Court

Cameron Park

P

7

Withymills Farm

Withy Mills

RADFORD HILL

Old Hayes

PAULTON LA

Glebe Cottage

SKINNER'S HILL

Well Head Wood

57 BS39

PAULTO HILL

Cameron Farm

6

5 Broadway Cottages

BROADWAY LA

LOVERS LA

Clandown Bottom

Clan Down

EASTDOWN RD

BA3

Starvelark Wood

A367

56 Clandown Rd

WATER LA

Bowlditch Farm

POW'S HILL

NORTHDOWN RD

OVERDALE

DUCHY RD

PRINCE ST

SOUTH VIEW

DUCHY CL

SMALLCOMBE RD

SMALLCOMBE CL

FOSSE WAY

4 MONGER LA

BOWLDITCH LA

CRAWL LA

Kitley Hill

KITLEY HILL

Clandown Farm

Clandown CE Prim Sch

CHAPEL CT 1 HIGHFIELDS 2

SPRINGFIELD HTS

SPRINGFIELD PL

CHAPEL LAWNS

FOSSE GN

OLD PIT TERR

CHAPEL RD 1 2

PO

COOMB END

BATH NEW RD

BRISTOL RD

MENDIP WAY

BATH OLD RD

Monger

BINCE'S LODGE LA

Welton Hill

FOSSE LA

Clandown

3 MONGER LA

GREENHILL PL

GREENHILL RD

Greenhill

HILLSIDE VIEW

WELTON GR

ST BARNABAS CL

GREEN TREE RD

BELLE VIEW

Belle Vue

MILLARD'S HILL

OLD MILL LA

Manor Farm

COOMBAND HO

MIDSOMER NORTON

THICKET MEAD

GREENHILL RD

SPENCE DR

GELDOF DR

BEAUFORT AVE

LONG BARN

BARNABY

ST THOMAS RD

EAST MEAD

GLADSTONE ST

MILLARDS CT

WELLOW BROOK

WELTON VALE

ROCK RD

Welton Hollow

WATERLOO RD

55 A362

WEST RD

VALLEY WLK

Works

Welton

Welton Prim Sch

Midsomer Ent Pk

Sewage Works

SOMERVALE RD

WELTON RD

BATH OLD RD

Mus

P

A362

FROME RD

2 Hayes Park

ST VIVIEN AVE

GRACE DR 1 ST CHARLES CL 2 ST ANTHONY'S CL 3

STATION RD

STONES CROSS

BURLINGTON ST

Wheeler's Hill

RADSTOCK RD

FIVE ARCHES

FOSSE WAY COTTS

WELTON RD

ST CHURCH ST

Liby

P

St Nicholas' Inf Sch

Sch

HAYES PARK RD

N'S CRES

BERKELEY AVE

CLEVETON RD

ELM VIEW

RAILWAY MEW

SOUTH VIEW RD

LILAC TERR

FLORIDA TERR

WHEELERS

WEST HILL GDNS

WELLS RD

THE ORCHARD

WILLIAM

NORTON RADSTOCK COLL

PINE WLK

KILMERSDON RD

1 B3355 CHURCH LA

THE DYMBORO

POW'S ORCH

PRIOR

Midsomer Norton Prim Sch

THE HOLLIES

HIGH ST

Liby

STANLEY CT

RACKVERNAL RD

GULLOCK TYNING

CHESTERFIELD HO

PIT RD

Sp Ctr

1 HOPE TERR 2 RACKVERNAL CT 3 SOMER CT

HIGHFIELDS

River Somer

KESPEARE RD

WEST HILL GDNS

WELLS SQ

OAK TERR

SHAKESPEARE RD

FOSSEWAY

HOLLY RD

JUBILEE RD

BRYANT AVE

ELM TREE CL

MAPLE TERR

BIRCH RD

ACACIA RD

RADSTOCK

West Hill Gardens

KILMERSDON RD

54 66

SOMER RD

Sch

REDFIELD GR

TH

B3355

PRIMROSE HILL

IVY WLK

SHELLEY RD

LONGFELLOW RD

KINSKY RD

WATERSIDE CRES

INNER ELM TERR

A367

PO

Waterside

WATERSIDE RD

ELM TREE RD

MAGNOLIA RD

ASH TREE RD

MAY TREE RD

CHESTNUT RD

CHERRY TREE CL

ROWAN RD

GROVE WOOD RD

A B 67 C D 68 E F

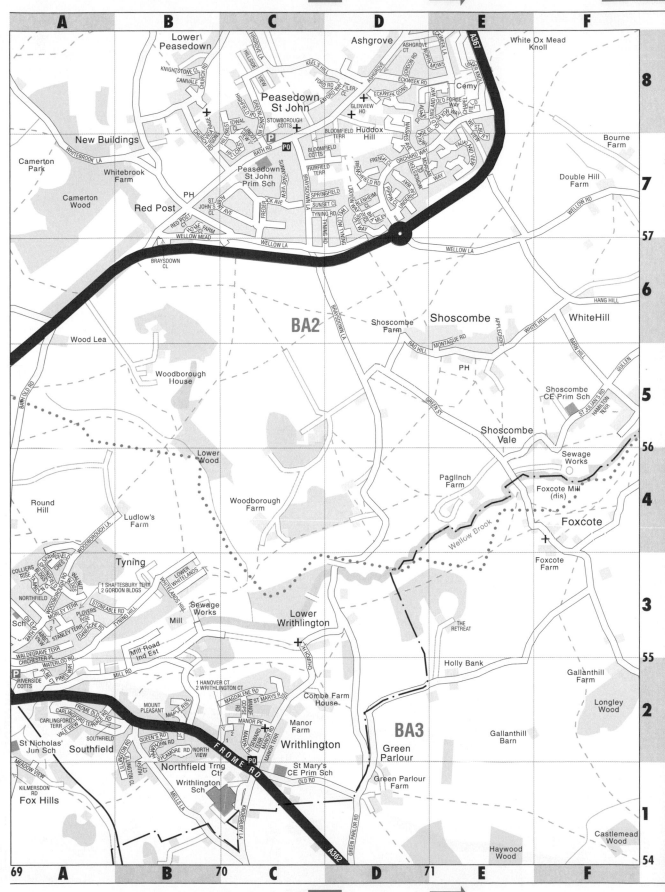

79
62

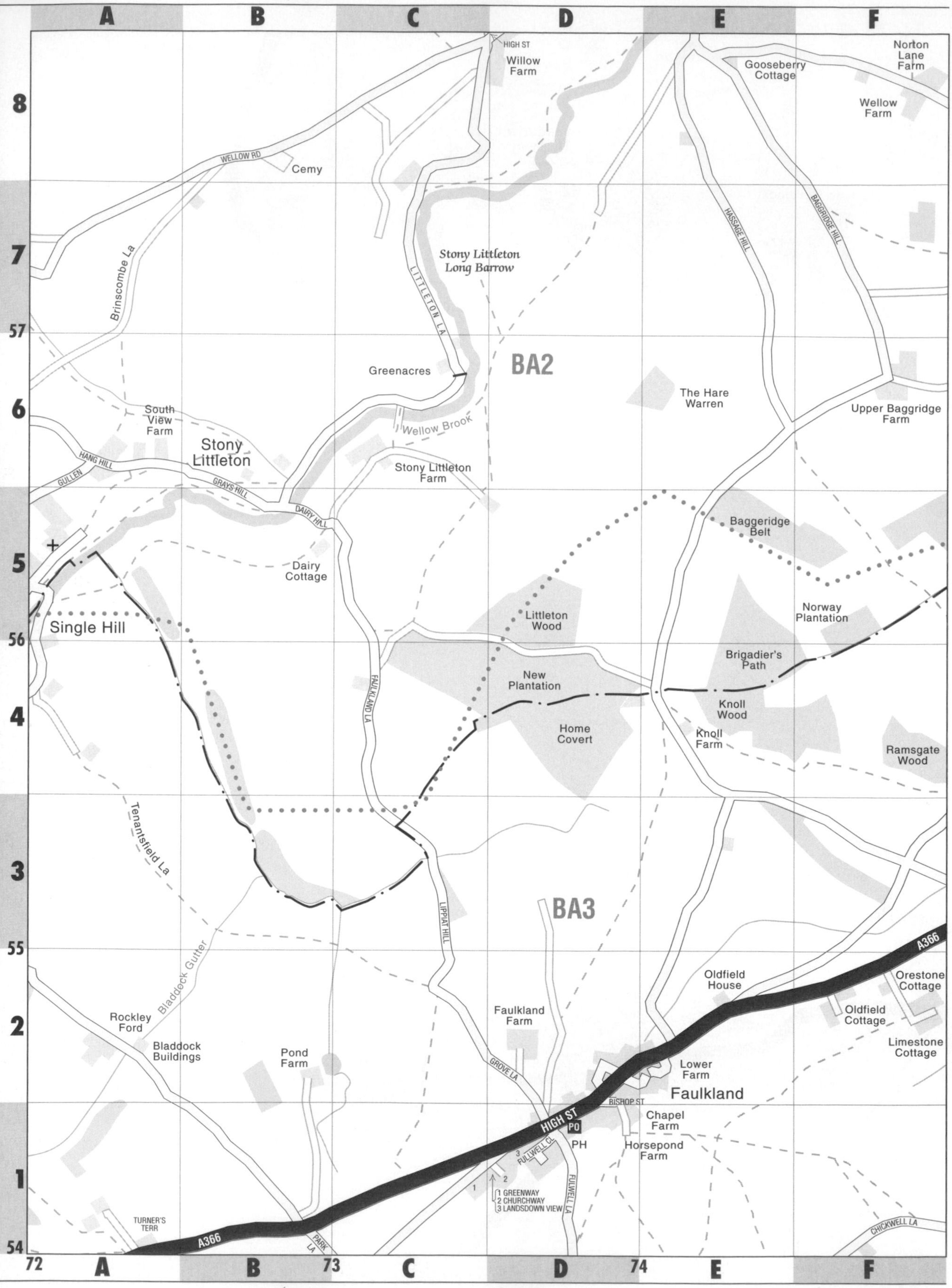

A B C D E F

8

7

57

6

BA2

5

56

4

3

55

2

1

54

72 A B 73 C D 74 E F

79
99

Willow Farm

HIGH ST

Norton Lane Farm

Gooseberry Cottage

Wellow Farm

WELLOW RD

Cemy

Stony Littleton Long Barrow

LITTLETON LA

HASSAGE HILL

BAGGRIDGE HILL

Brinscombe La

Greenacres

The Hare Warren

Upper Baggridge Farm

South View Farm

Wellow Brook

Stony Littleton

HANG HILL

GULLEN

GRAYS HILL

DAIRY HILL

Stony Littleton Farm

Baggeridge Belt

+

Dairy Cottage

Littleton Wood

Norway Plantation

Single Hill

Brigadier's Path

New Plantation

Knoll Wood

FAULKLAND LA

Home Covert

Knoll Farm

Ramsgate Wood

Tenantsfield La

Bladdock Gutter

BA3

LIPPIAT HILL

A366

Oldfield House

Orestone Cottage

Oldfield Cottage

Rockley Ford

Faulkland Farm

Limestone Cottage

Bladdock Buildings

Pond Farm

GROVE LA

Lower Farm

Faulkland

BISHOP ST

Chapel Farm

HIGH ST

PO

PH

Horsepond Farm

FULWELL CL

FULWELL LA

1 GREENWAY
2 CHURCHWAY
3 LANDSDOWN VIEW

TURNER'S TERR

A366

PARK LA

CHICKWELL LA

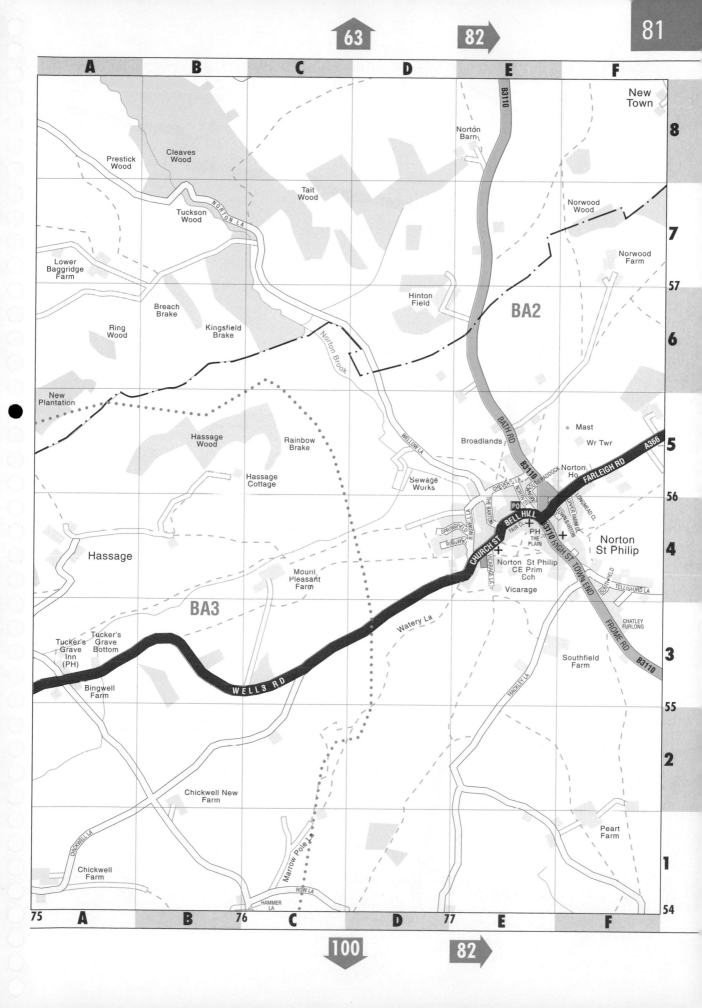

A B C D E F

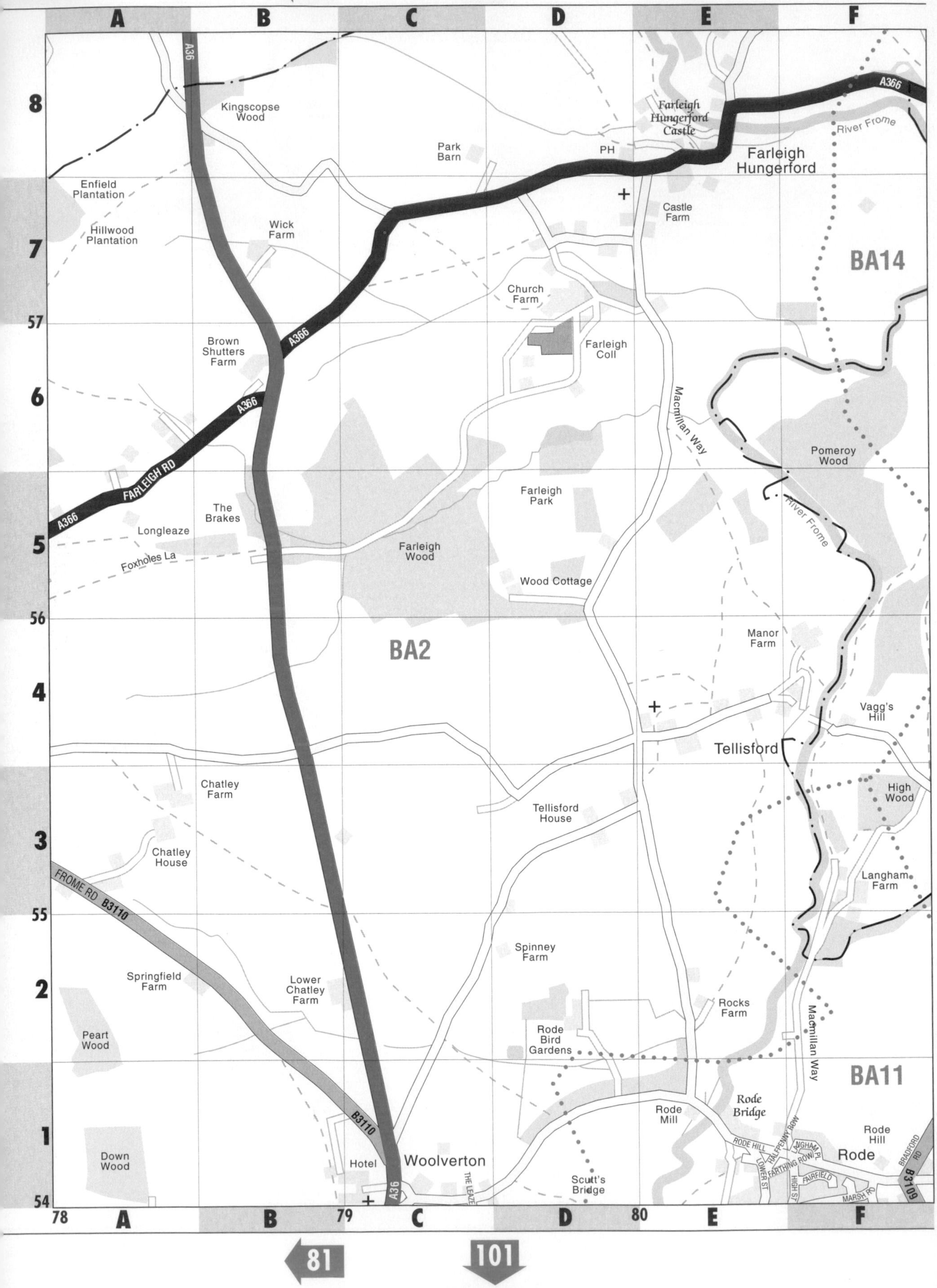

8

Kingscose Wood

Farleigh Hungerford Castle

Park Barn

PH

Farleigh Hungerford

River Frome

A36

Enfield Plantation

Hillwood Plantation

Wick Farm

Castle Farm

BA14

7

Church Farm

57

Brown Shutters Farm

A366

Farleigh Coll

6

A366

Pomeroy Wood

FARLEIGH RD

A366

Macmillan Way

River Frome

A366

The Brakes

Farleigh Park

5

Longleaze

Foxholes La

Farleigh Wood

Wood Cottage

Manor Farm

56

BA2

Vagg's Hill

4

Tellisford

+

Chatley Farm

High Wood

3

Chatley House

Tellisford House

Langham Farm

55

Spinney Farm

Rocks Farm

Macmillan Way

2

Springfield Farm

Lower Chatley Farm

Rode Bird Gardens

BA11

Peart Wood

Rode Mill

Rode Bridge

Rode Hill

FROME RD B3110

B3110

Down Wood

Hotel

Woolverton

Scutt's Bridge

Rode Hill

Rode

1

A36

THE LEAZE

RODE HILL

LOWER ST

TRAPPENIN ROW

FARTHING ROW

NGHAM PL

HIGH ST

FAIRFIELD

MARSH RD

BRADFORD RD

B3109

+

54

78 A 79 B C 80 D E 81 F

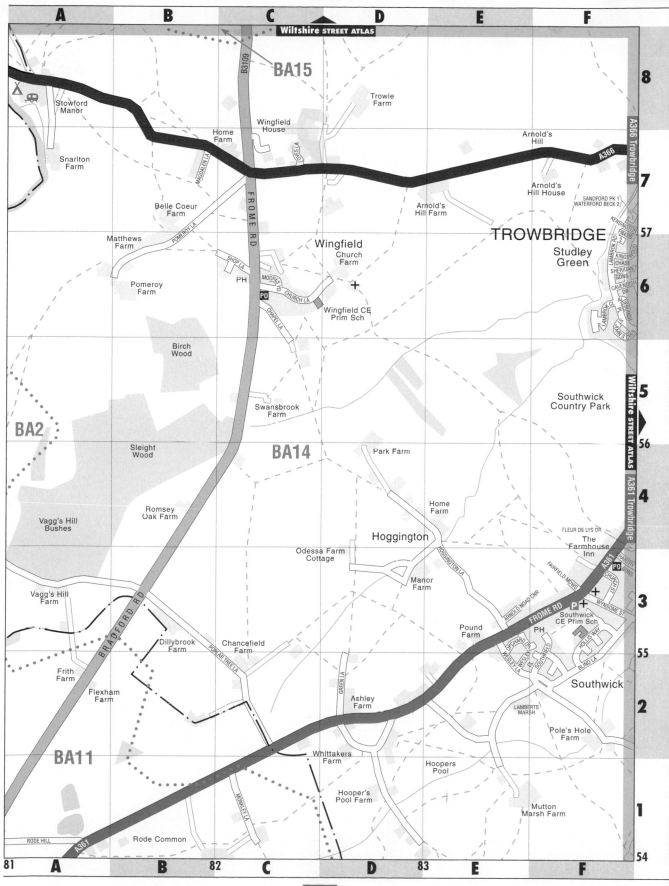

BA15

Stowford Manor

Snarlton Farm

Home Farm

Wingfield House

Trowle Farm

Arnold's Hill

A366

A366 Trowbridge

Arnold's Hill House

Belle Coeur Farm

MAGDALEN LA

FROME RD

Arnold's Hill Farm

SANDFORD PK 1
WATERFORD BECK 2

TROWBRIDGE

Matthews Farm

POMEROY LA

SHOP LA

PH

Wingfield
Church Farm

Studley Green

KENSINGTON FIELDS

LAMBROK RD

KINGS CHASE

SHERIDAN GDNS

CAVENDISH DR

Pomeroy Farm

MOORS YD

CHURCH LA

PO

CHAPEL LA

Wingfield CE
Prim Sch

57

6

LAMBROK CL

ST JOHN'S CRES

Birch Wood

Swansbrook Farm

Southwick
Country Park

Wiltshire STREET ATLAS

5

56

BA2

Sleight Wood

BA14

Park Farm

A361 Trowbridge

Vagg's Hill Bushes

Romsey Oak Farm

Home Farm

4

FLEUR DE LYS DR

The Farmhouse Inn

FAIRFIELD MDWS

Hoggington

HOGGINGTON LA

GANTRY GDNS

PO

CHURCH ST

Vagg's Hill Farm

BRADFORD RD

Odessa Farm Cottage

Manor Farm

ARNOLD ROAD CNR

A361

FROME RD

Southwick CE Prim Sch

WYNSOME ST

Frith Farm

Dillybrook Farm

POPLAR TREE LA

Chancefield Farm

Pound Farm

PH

HOLLIS WAY

3

55

Flexham Farm

GREEN LA

Ashley Farm

ORCHARD CL

WESLEY LA

SOUTHFIELD

BLIND LA

Southwick

LAMBERTS MARSH

Pole's Hole Farm

2

BA11

Whittakers Farm

Hoopers Pool

Mutton Marsh Farm

MONKLEY LA

Hooper's Pool Farm

1

RODE HILL

A361

Rode Common

54

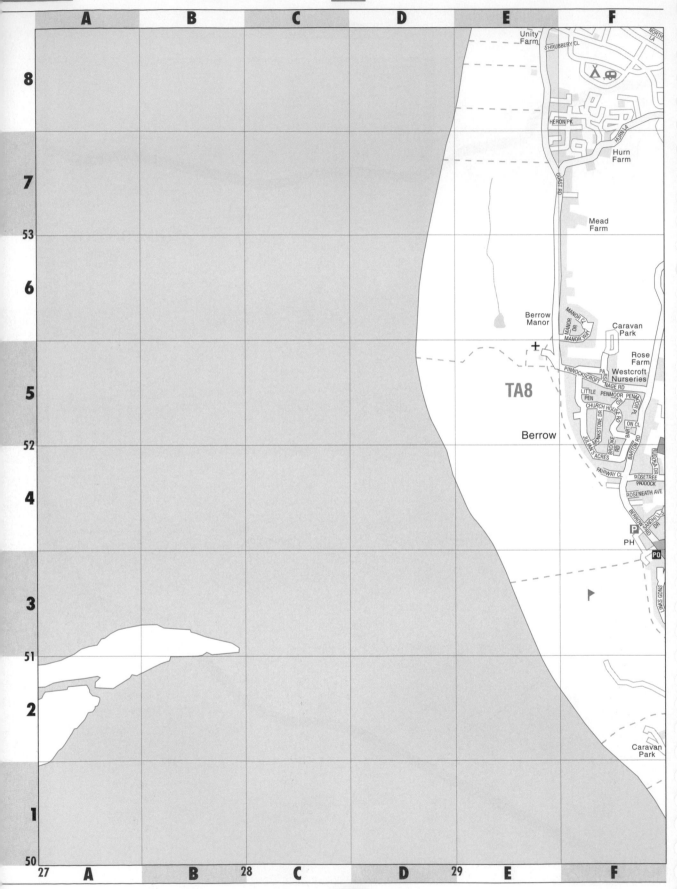

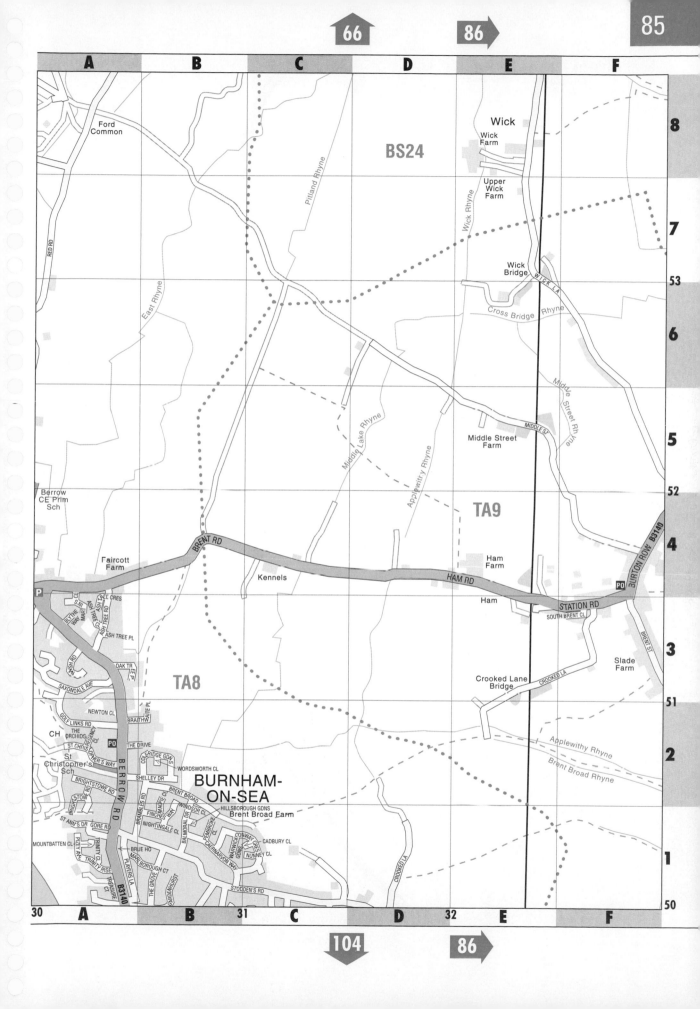

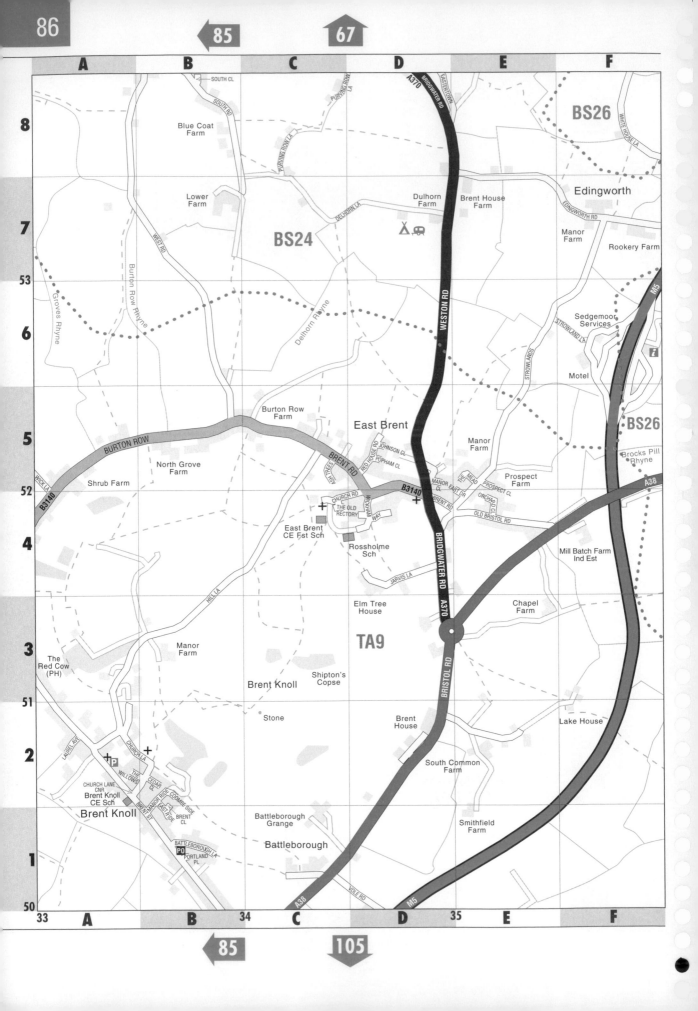

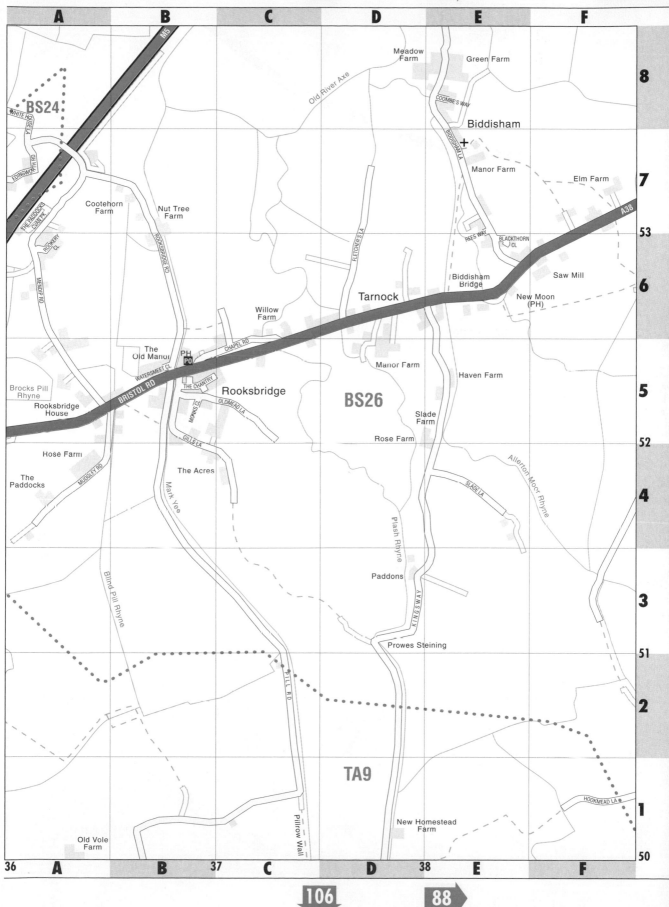

← 87   69

A B C D E F

8

The Lamb
at Weare
(PH)

Weare
Bridge

Lower
Weare

TURNPIKE RD

OLD COACH RD

A38

Weare
Culvert

Tanyard Farm
Nurseries

EAST END

River Axe

Badgworth Bow
Farm

7

A38

The Downs

Weare
CE Fst Sch

PIPERS CL

Weare

53

Kirklea
Farm

Upper
Weare
Farm

SPARROW HILL WAY

KENMORE LA

SPLOTT

Stream
Farm

6

CHURCH LA

Badgworth

Combe La

Hill House
Farm

BRINSCOMBE LA

Sparrow
Hill
Farm

BS26

5

Home
Farm

Cedar Tree
Farm

Badgworth
Court

BADGWORTH
BARNS

Notting Hill
Farm

NOTTING HILL WAY

Greenhill
Farm

GREENHILL LA

Ashlyn
Farm

52

Long Acre

BADGWORTH LA

Alston
Batch

Alston
Farm

ALSTON SUTTON RD

Alston Sutton
Farm

Field House
Farm

4

QUARRYLANDS LA

MILL LA

DUNKERRY RD

Alston
Sutton

Maltfield La

3

Stone
Allerton

PO

Fieldhouse
Farm

QUAB LA

51

STONE ALLERTON DRO

Mendip Hill
Farm

COPSEWOOD LA

SHORT LA

Wheatsheaf Inn
(PH)

RECTORY HILL

Fairview
Farm

Mount Pleasant
Farm

2

Bishop's Bow

Allerton Moor Dro

Brookland
Farm

NEW RD

COPSEWOOD LA

Chapel
Allerton

RAWLINGS LA

HOOREMEAD LA

Allerton Moor Rhyne (Drain)

Cribnell La

Brook House
Farm

Manor
Farm

BACK LA

FRONT ST

Ashton
Windmill

Little Orchard
Farm

1

Allerton Moor

Southview
Farm

SCOTLAND LA

Ashton Mill
Farm

BS28

50

39 A   B 40 C   D 41 E   F

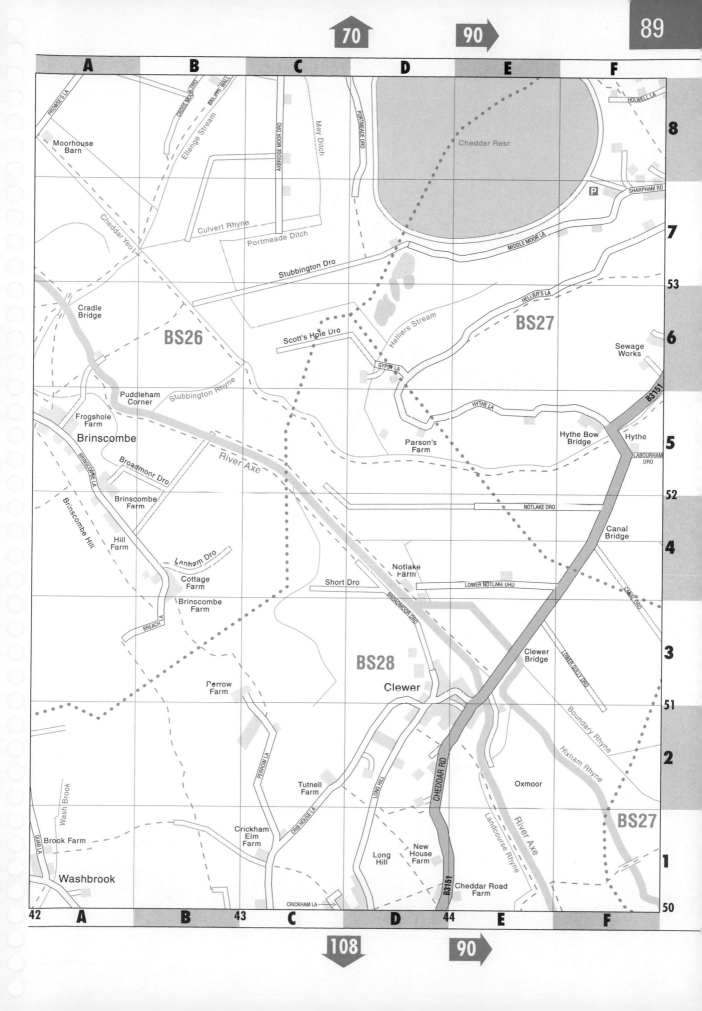

A B C D E F

PROWSE'S LA

Moorhouse Barn

CROSS MOOR DRO

BRUMPS WALL

Ellenge Stream

Culvert Rhyne

AXBRIDGE MOOR DRO

May Ditch

PORTMEADE DRO

Cheddar Resr

HOLWELL LA

P

SHARPHAM RD

8

Cheddar Yeo

Portmeade Ditch

Stubbington Dro

MIDDLE MOOR LA

7

53

Cradle Bridge

BS26

Scott's Hole Dro

Helliers Stream

HELLIER'S LA

BS27

Sewage Works

6

Puddleham Corner

Stubbington Rhyne

GYPSY LA

HYTHE LA

B3151

Frogshole Farm

Brinscombe

River Axe

Parson's Farm

Hythe Bow Bridge

Hythe

5

BRINSCOMBE LA

Broadmoor Dro

Brinscombe Farm

LABOURHAM DRO

52

Brinscombe Hill

Hill Farm

Lanham Dro

NOTLAKE DRO

Canal Bridge

4

Cottage Farm

Short Dro

Notlake Farm

LOWER NOTLAKE DRO

CANAL DRO

Brinscombe Farm

BREACH LA

BROADMOOR DRO

BS28

Clewer Bridge

LOWER GULLY DRO

3

51

Perrow Farm

Clewer

Boundary Rhyne

Hixham Rhyne

2

Wash Brook

PERROW LA

Tutnell Farm

CRIB HOUSE LA

LONG HILL

CHEDDAR RD

Oxmoor

Landcourse Rhyne

River Axe

BS27

QUAB LA

Brook Farm

Crickham Elm Farm

Long Hill

New House Farm

B3151

Cheddar Road Farm

1

Washbrook

CRICKHAM LA

50

89
71

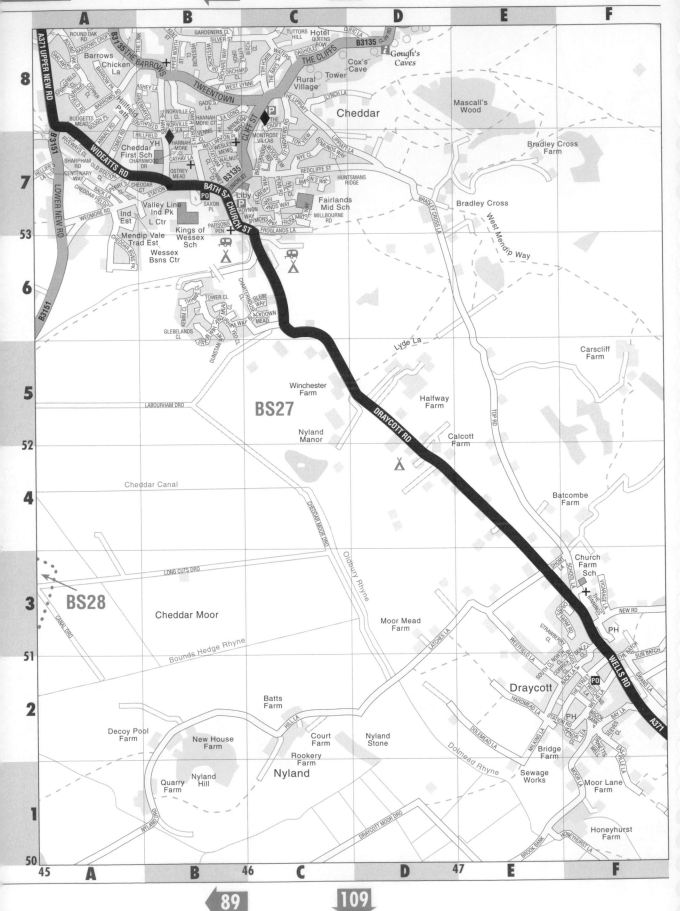

72
92

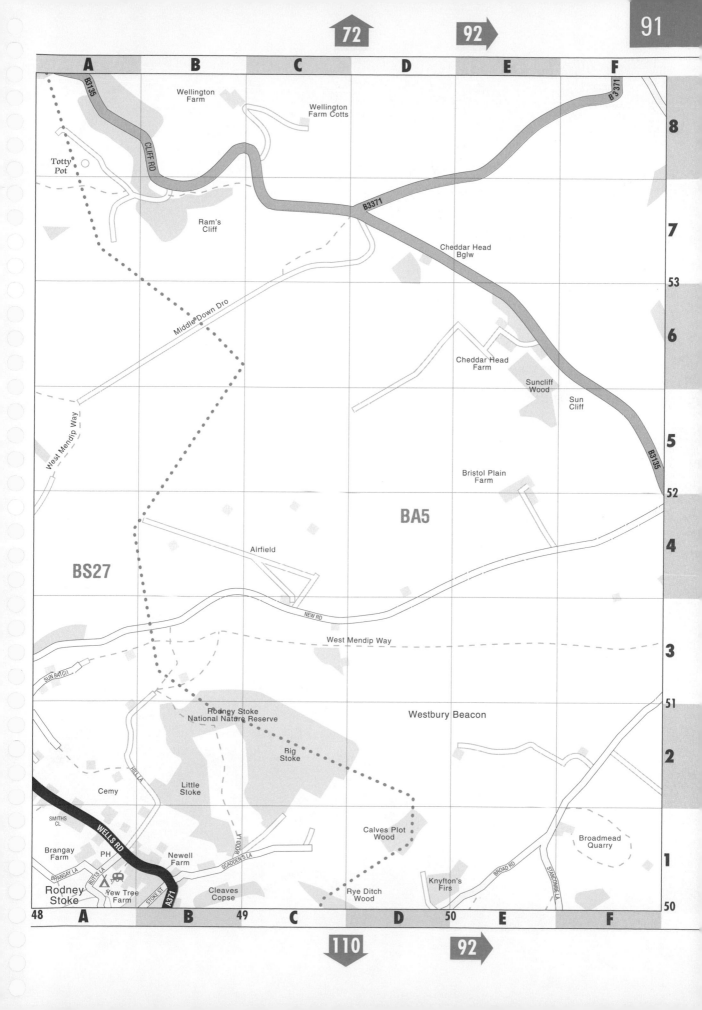

A B C D E F

8
7
53
6
5
52
4
51
2
1
50

Wellington Farm
Wellington Farm Cotts

B3135
CLIFF RD

Totty Pot

Ram's Cliff

B3371

B3371

Cheddar Head Bglw

Cheddar Head Farm

Suncliff Wood

Sun Cliff

B3135

Middle Down Dro

West Mendip Way

BA5

Bristol Plain Farm

BS27

Airfield

NEW RD

West Mendip Way

SUN BATCH

Rodney Stoke National Nature Reserve

Westbury Beacon

Big Stoke

Little Stoke

Cemy

HILL LA

WOOD LA

Calves Plot Wood

Broadmead Quarry

SMITHS CL

WELLS RD

Brangay Farm

PH

Newell Farm

SCADDEN'S LA

Knyfton's Firs

BROAD RD

STANCOMBE LA

BRANGAY LA

BUTTS LA

Yew Tree Farm

Rodney Stoke

STOKE ST

A371

Cleaves Copse

Rye Ditch Wood

48 A B 49 C D 50 E F

91
73

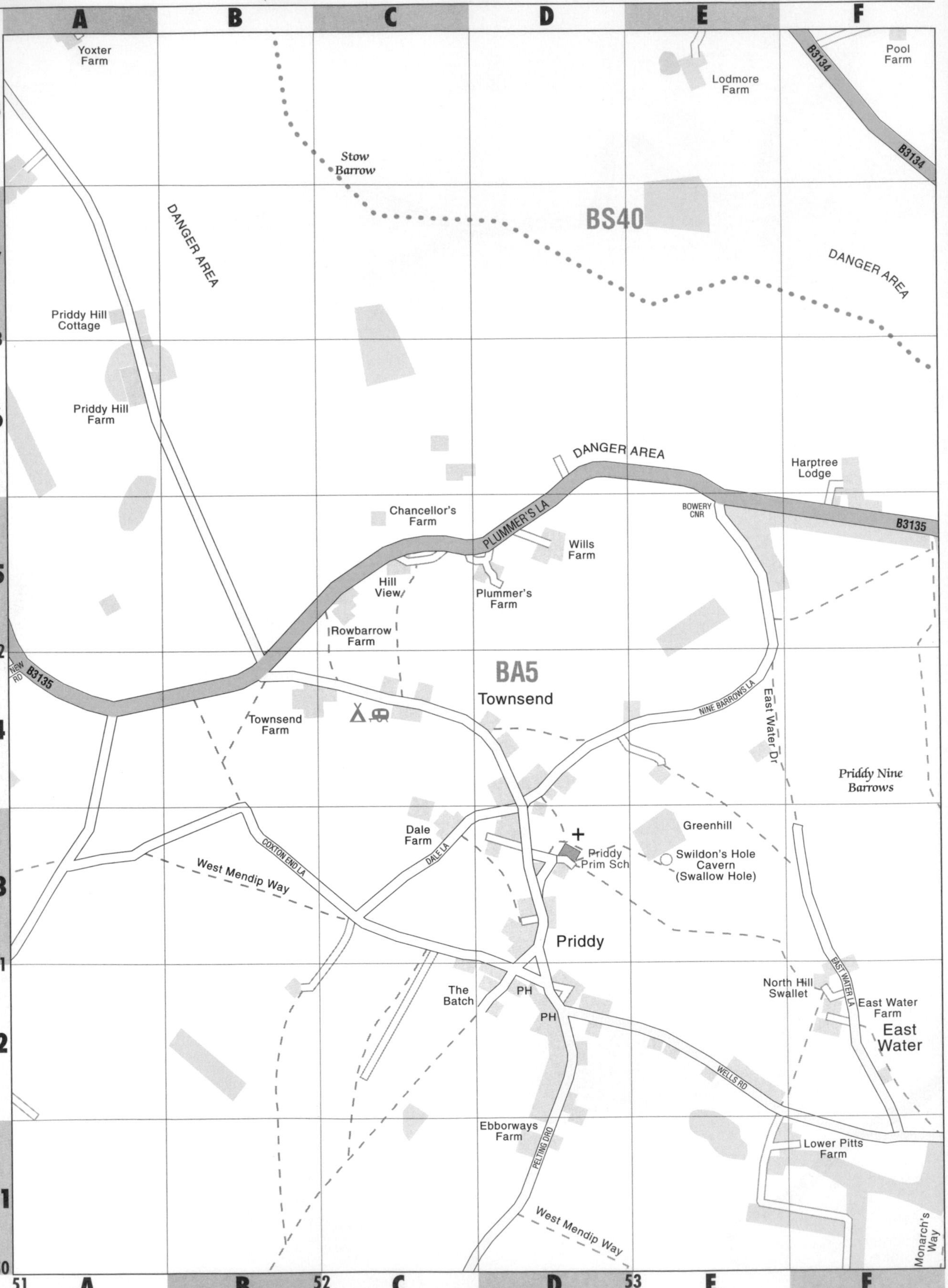

A **B** **C** **D** **E** **F**

8

Yoxter
Farm

*Stow
Barrow*

Lodmore
Farm

Pool
Farm

B3134

B3134

7

DANGER AREA

BS40

DANGER AREA

53

Priddy Hill
Cottage

6

Priddy Hill
Farm

Harptree
Lodge

DANGER AREA

BOWERY
CNR

B3135

5

Chancellor's
Farm

PLUMMER'S LA

Wills
Farm

Hill
View

Plummer's
Farm

52

Rowbarrow
Farm

BA5
Townsend

NINE BARROWS LA

East Water Dr

NEW RD

B3135

4

Townsend
Farm

Priddy Nine
Barrows

3

West Mendip Way

COXTON END LA

Dale
Farm

DALE LA

Priddy
Prim Sch

Greenhill

Swildon's Hole
Cavern
(Swallow Hole)

+

51

Priddy

EAST WATER LA

North Hill
Swallet

East Water
Farm

**East
Water**

2

The
Batch

PH

PH

WELLS RD

1

Ebborways
Farm

PELTING DRO

Lower Pitts
Farm

Monarch's Way

West Mendip Way

50

51 **A** **B** 52 **C** **D** 53 **E** **F**

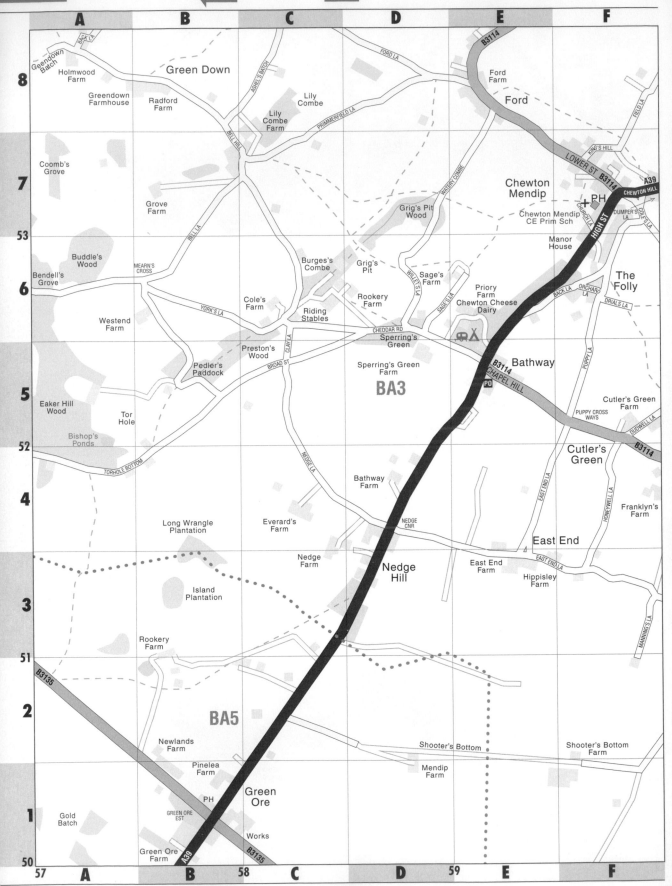

A B C D E F

8 Geendown Batch
Holmwood Farm
Greendown Farmhouse
BACK LA
Radford Farm
ASHEL'S BATCH
Green Down
Lily Combe
Lily Combe Farm
FORD LA
Ford Farm
B3114
Ford
KING'S HILL
FIELD LA

7 Coomb's Grove
BELL HILL
PRIMMERFIELD LA
WATERY COMBE
Grove Farm
Grig's Pit Wood
LOWER ST
B3114
Chewton Mendip
Chewton Mendip CE Prim Sch
A39
CHEWTON HILL
✝ PH
HIGH ST
CHURCH LA
DUMPER'S LA
COLE'S LA

53 BELL A
Buddle's Wood
MEARN'S CROSS
Burges's Combe
Grig's Pit
Sage's Farm
Manor House
BACK LA
ORCHARD LA
The Folly
DRIALS LA

6 Bendell's Grove
YORK'S LA
Cole's Farm
Rookery Farm
Riding Stables
WILLET'S LA
SAGE'S LA
Priory Farm
Chewton Cheese Dairy
Westend Farm
CHEDDAR RD
Sperring's Green
🚐 ⛺
Bathway
PUPPY LA
Cutler's Green Farm

Preston's Wood
BROAD ST
CLAY LA
Sperring's Green Farm
B3114
CHAPEL HILL
PUPPY CROSS WAYS
DUDWELL LA

5 Eaker Hill Wood
Pedler's Paddock
BA3
PO
Franklyn's Farm
Cutler's Green Farm

Tor Hole
East End LA
Cutler's Green
HONEYWELL LA
Franklyn's Farm

52 Bishop's Ponds
TORHOLE BOTTOM
NEDGE LA
Bathway Farm
B3114

4 Long Wrangle Plantation
Everard's Farm
NEDGE CNR
East End Farm
East End
EAST END LA
Hippisley Farm
MANNING'S LA

3 Island Plantation
Nedge Farm
Nedge Hill

51 Rookery Farm
B3135

2 **BA5**
Newlands Farm
Shooter's Bottom
Mendip Farm
Shooter's Bottom Farm

1 Gold Batch
Pinelea Farm
PH
GREEN ORE EST
Green Ore
A39
B3135
Works

50 Green Ore Farm

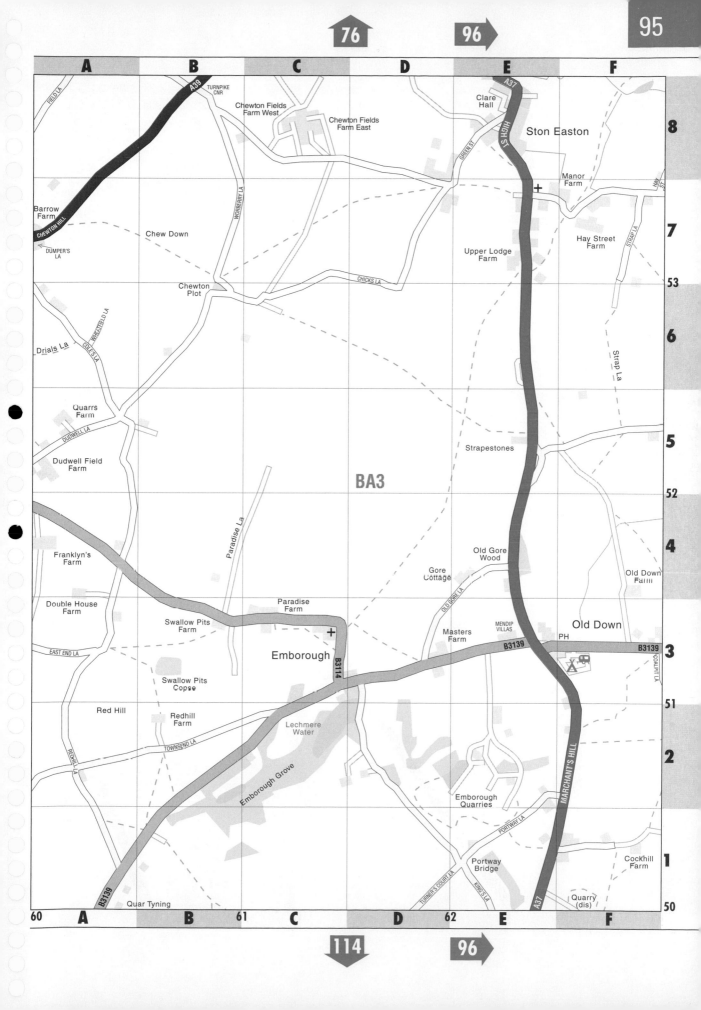

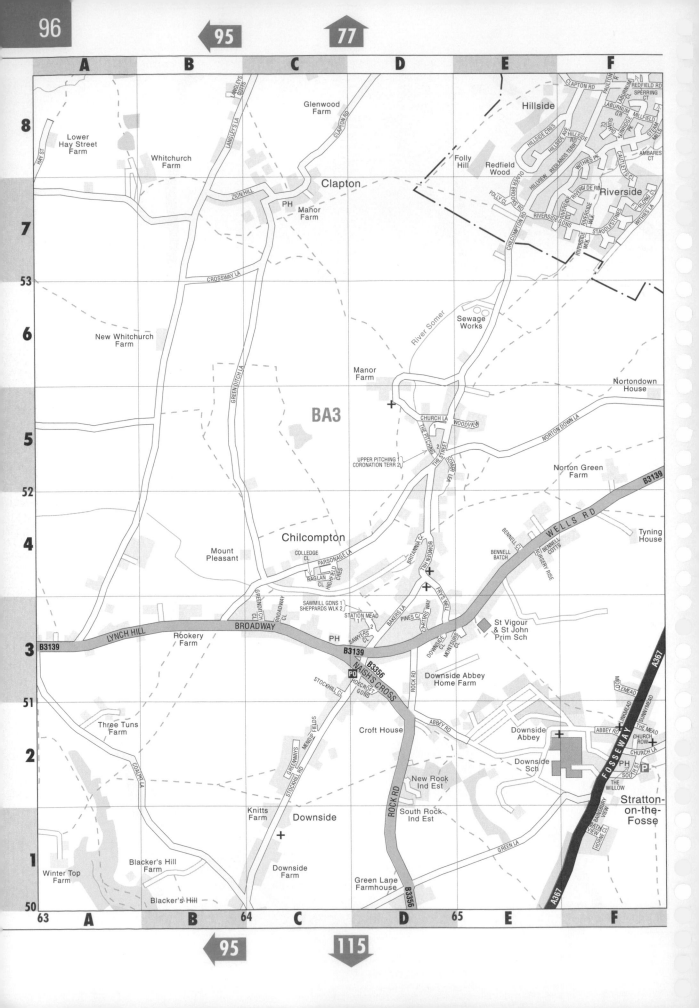

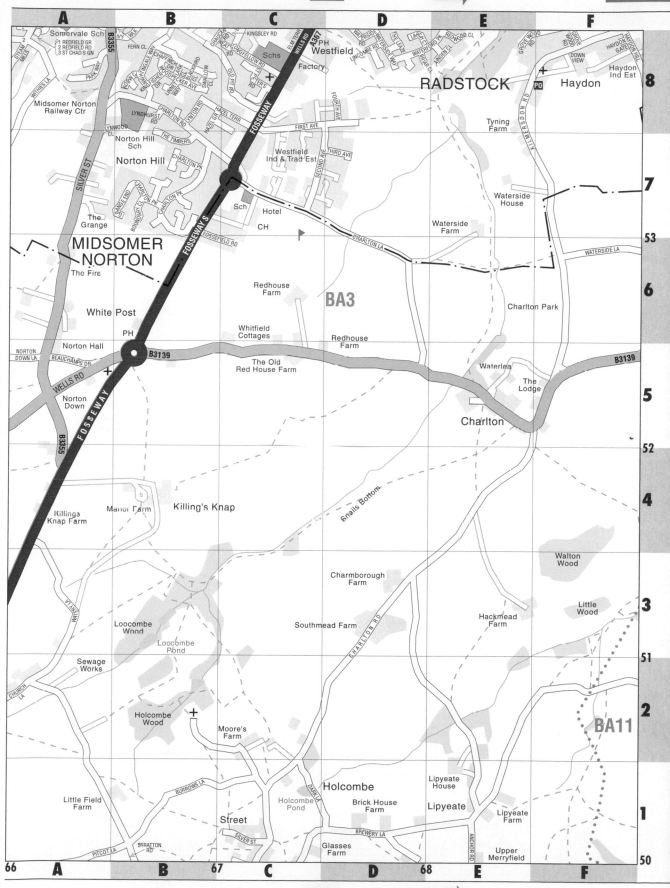

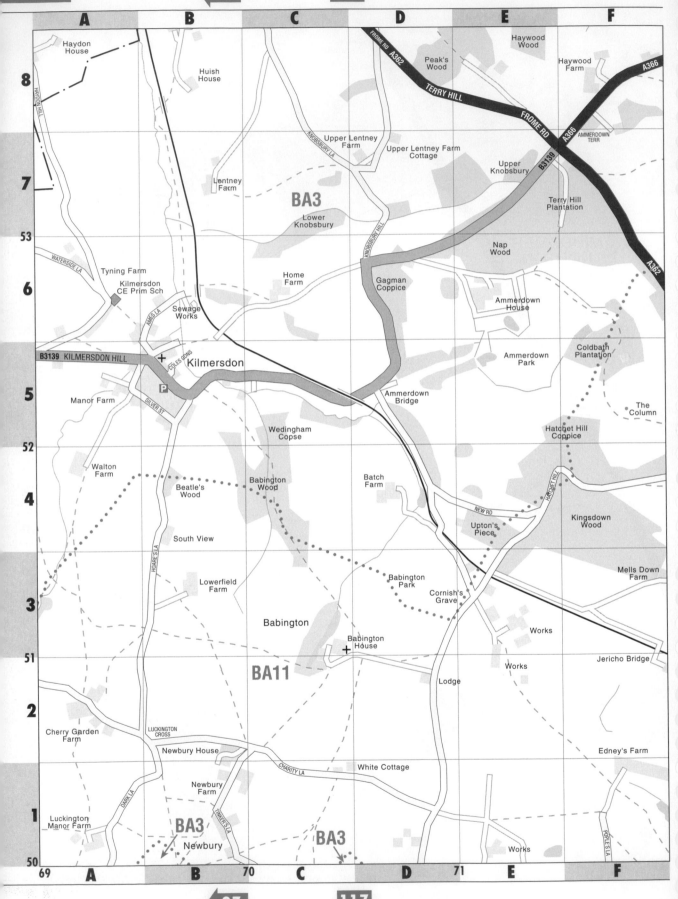

A B C D E F

Haydon House

Huish House

8

HAYDON HILL

Huish House

FROME RD A362
Peak's Wood
Haywood Wood
Haywood Farm
A366

TERRY HILL

FROME RD
A366
AMMERDOWN TERR

B3139

KNOBSBURY LA
Upper Lentney Farm
Upper Lentney Farm Cottage

Lentney Farm

7

BA3
Lower Knobsbury
Upper Knobsbury
Terry Hill Plantation

53

Nap Wood

WATERSIDE LA
Home Farm
KNOBSBURY HILL
Gagman Coppice

A362

Tyning Farm
Kilmersdon CE Prim Sch
Ammerdown House

6

AMES LA
Sewage Works
Ammerdown Park
Coldbath Plantation

B3139 KILMERSDON HILL
COLES GDNS
Kilmersdon
Ammerdown Bridge

The Column

Manor Farm
P
SILVER ST
Wedingham Copse
Hatchet Hill Coppice

5

52

Walton Farm
Beatle's Wood
Babington Wood
Batch Farm
HATCHET HILL
Kingsdown Wood

HOARE'S LA
South View
NEW RD
Upton's Piece

4

Mells Down Farm

Lowerfield Farm
Babington Park
Cornish's Grave

3

Babington
Works

Babington House
Works

51
BA11
Lodge
Jericho Bridge

2

Cherry Garden Farm
LUCKINGTON CROSS
Newbury House
Works

DARK LA
Newbury Farm
CHARITY LA
White Cottage
Edney's Farm

INNER'S LA

1

Luckington Manor Farm
BA3
Newbury
BA3
Works

POPLE'S LA

50
69 A B 70 C D 71 E F

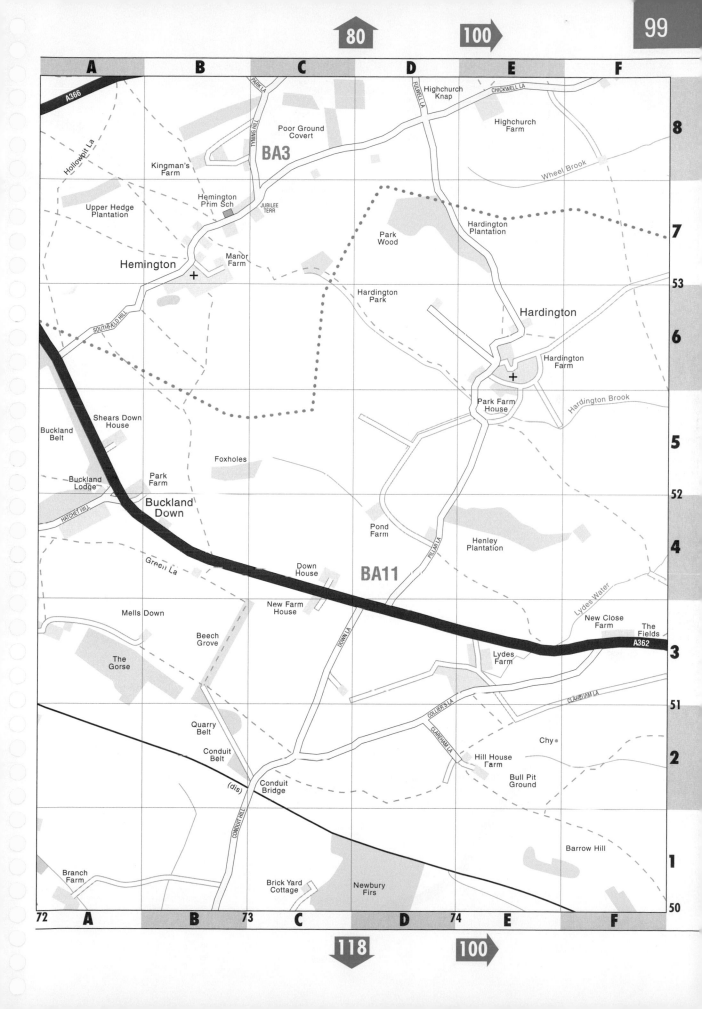

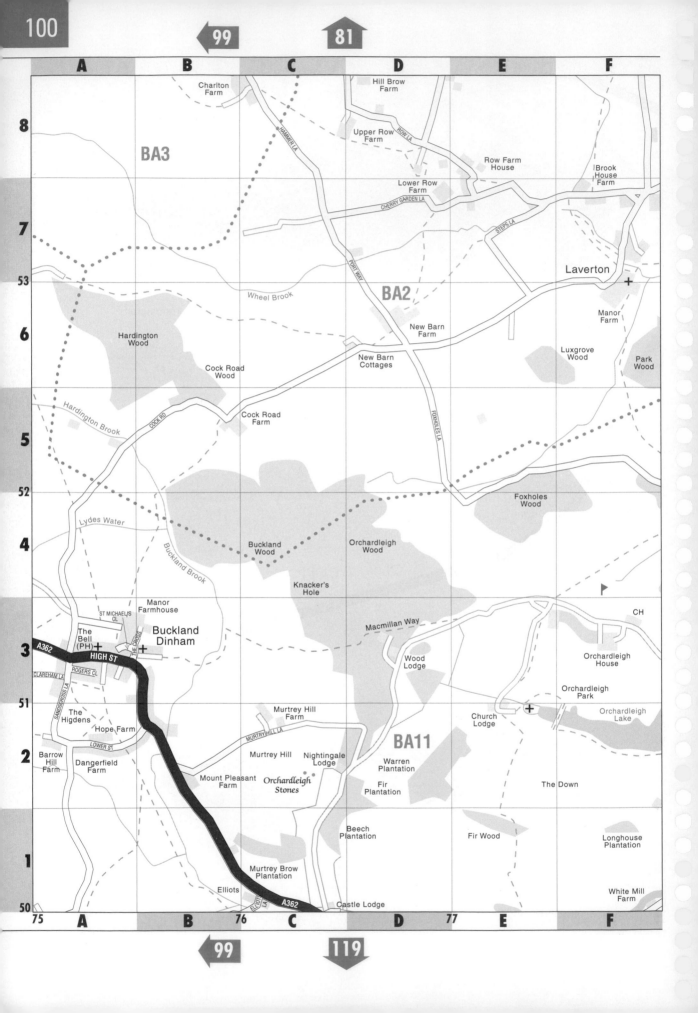

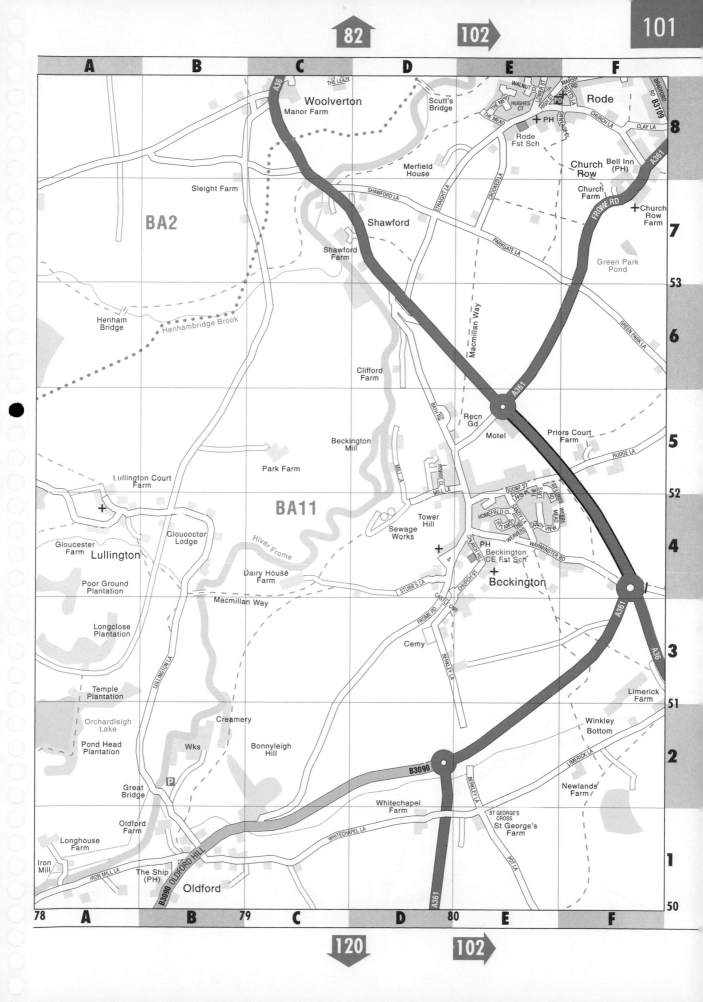

A B C D E F

Woolverton
Manor Farm
THE LEAZE
Scutt's Bridge
THE MEAD
WALNUT CL
LOWER ST
MARSH
HIGH ST
NUTS LA
HUGHES CT
THE MEAD
PO
Rode
BRADFORD RD
B3109

8

PH
Rode Fst Sch
Church La
CLAY LA

Merfield House
SHAWFORD LA
STRAIGHT LA
CROOKED LA
Church Row
Bell Inn (PH)
A361

Sleight Farm

BA2
Shawford
Shawford Farm
PARKGATE LA
Church Farm
FROME RD
Church Row Farm

7

53

Henham Bridge
Henhambridge Brook
Macmillan Way
Green Park Pond
GREEN PARK LA

6

Clifford Farm

A361

Beckington Mill
Recn Gd
Motel
Priors Court Farm
RUDGE LA

5

Park Farm
BATH RD
MILL LA

52

BA11
Lullington Court Farm
Sewage Works
Tower Hill
HORSE CL
MILL LA
GOOSE ST
LA'S PL
THE LA'S
ST LUKES RD
WEBBS
HOMEFIELD CL
FITZ LANE
THE
SANDY
MEAD
SANDY VIEW
WEAVERS
WARMINSTER RD
A361

4

Gloucester Farm
Lullington
Glouooctor Lodge
River Frome
Dairy House Farm
PH
Beckington CE Fst Sch
Beckington
CHURCH HILL
CHURCH ST

Poor Ground Plantation
Macmillan Way
STUBB'S LA
CASTLE CNR
Cemy
FROME RD
BERKLEY LA

3

Longclose Plantation

A36

Temple Plantation
Limerick Farm

51

Orchardleigh Lake
Creamery
Winkley Bottom
LIMERICK LA

2

Pond Head Plantation
Wks
Bonnyleigh Hill
B3090
BERKLEY LA
Newlands Farm

Great Bridge
P
Whitechapel Farm
ST GEORGE'S CROSS
St George's Farm
POT LA

Oldford Farm

Longhouse Farm
OLDFORD HILL
WHITECHAPEL LA

1

Iron Mill
IRON MILL LA
The Ship (PH)
B3090
Oldford
A361

50

78 A B 79 C D 80 E F

A B C D E F

8

BRADFORD RD
A361
B3109
A361

Parsonage
Farm

Rode Farm

Monkley La

BA14

7

The Devil's
Bed & Bolster

Mount
Pleasant

53

6

Seymour's
Court

GREEN PARK LA

DUCK POOL LA

Duck Pool La

Castley
Farm

CASTLEY LA

Norris Hill
Farm

Overcourt
Farm

RUDGE LA

Duck Pool
Farm

Silver Street
Farm

Woodland
Park

Hazel Wood

FAIRWOOD RD

5

Waterslade

Upper Castley
Farm

RUDGE HILL

Church
Farm

Honeybridge
Farm

Round
Wood

Wiltshire STREET ATLAS

52

Lower
Rudge Hill
Farm

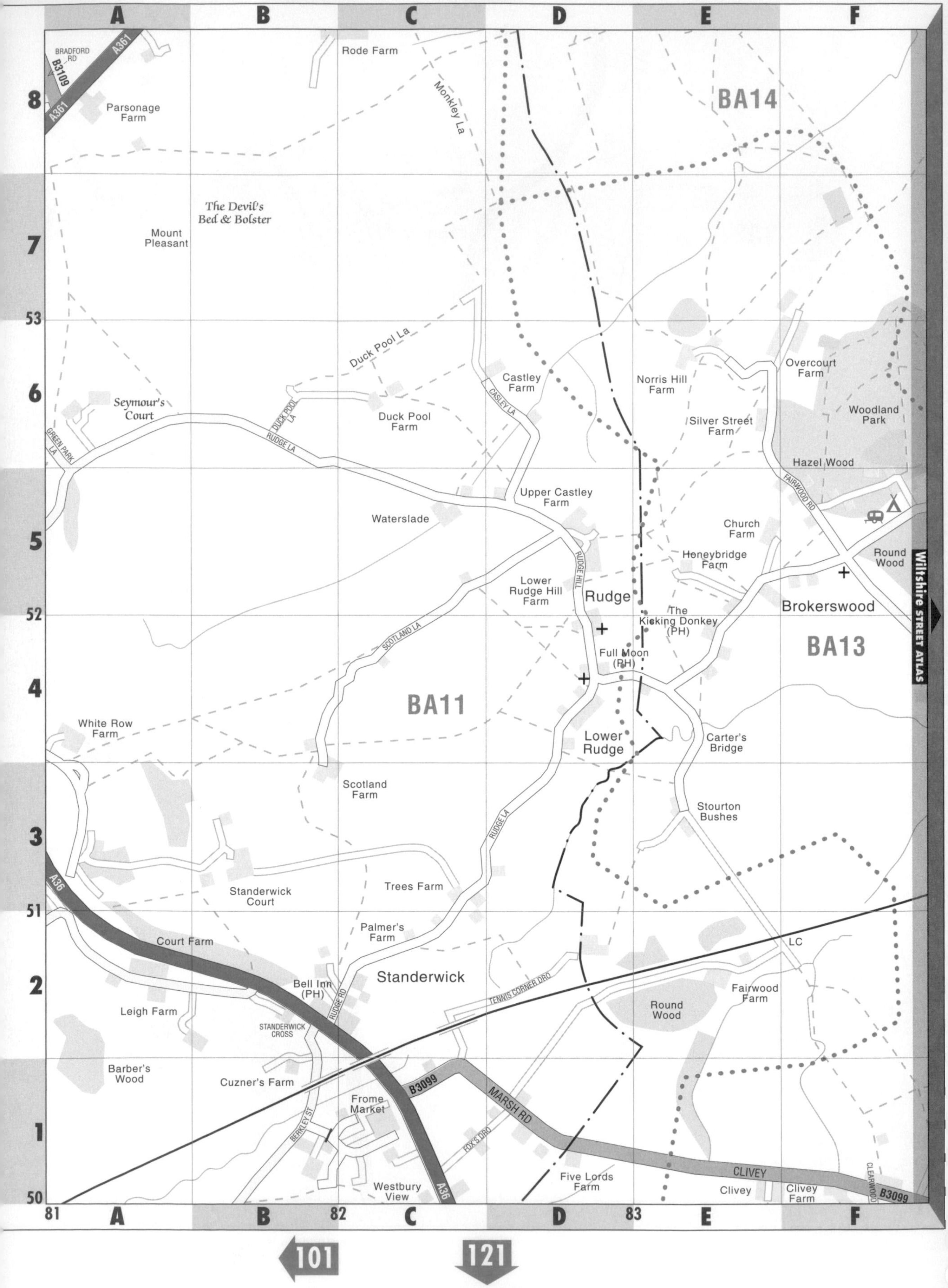

Rudge

The
Kicking Donkey
(PH)

Brokerswood

SCOTLAND LA

Full Moon
(PH)

BA13

4

BA11

Lower
Rudge

Carter's
Bridge

White Row
Farm

Scotland
Farm

RUDGE LA

Stourton
Bushes

3

51

Standerwick
Court

Trees Farm

Palmer's
Farm

LC

A36

Court Farm

Leigh Farm

Bell Inn
(PH)

RUDGE RD

Standerwick

TENNIS CORNER DRO

Round
Wood

Fairwood
Farm

2

STANDERWICK
CROSS

1

Barber's
Wood

Cuzner's Farm

BERKLEY ST

Frome
Market

B3099

MARSH RD

FOX'S DRO

Five Lords
Farm

CLIVEY

Clivey

Clivey
Farm

CLEARWOOD

B3099

Westbury
View

A36

50

81 A B 82 C D 83 E F

A B C D E F

8

7

49

6

Stert Island

5

48

4

3

Stert Point

47

Fenning
Island

2

River Parrett

TA9

Manor
Farm

Cox's
Farm

TA5

Collards
Farm

1

46

27 A B 28 C D 29 E F

103
85

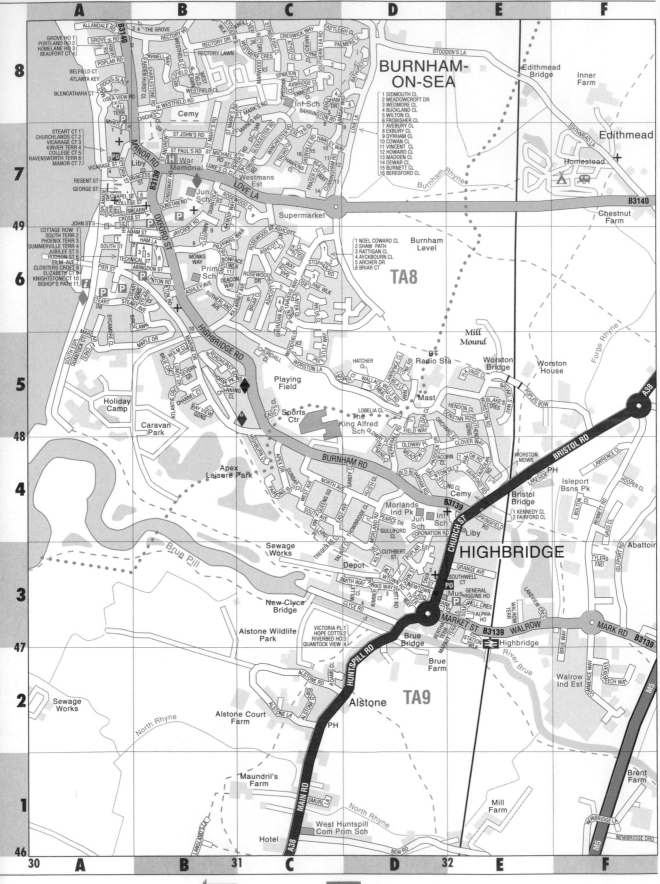

BURNHAM-
ON-SEA

1 SIDMOUTH CL
2 MEADOWCROFT DR
3 WEDMORE CL
4 BUCKLAND CL
5 WILTON CL
6 FROBISHER CL
7 AVEBURY CL
8 EXBURY CL
9 DYRHAM CL
10 COWAN CL
11 VINCENT CL
12 HOWARD CL
13 MADDEN CL
14 DEWAR CL
15 BURNETT CL
16 BERESFORD CL

Edithmead
Bridge

Inner
Farm

Edithmead

Homestead

Chestnut
Farm

TA8

1 NOEL COWARD CL
2 SHAW PATH
3 RATTIGAN CL
4 AYCKBOURN CL
5 ARCHER DR
6 BRIAR CL

Burnham
Level

Mill
Mound

Worston
House

Worston
Bridge

Holiday
Camp

Caravan
Park

Apex
Leisure Park

Playing
Field

Sports
Ctr

The
King Alfred
Sch

Bristol
Bridge

Isleport
Bsns Pk

Abattoir

HIGHBRIDGE

1 KENNEDY CL
2 FAIRFORD CL

Morlands
Ind Pk

Worston
Mdws

Sewage
Works

Depot

Walrow
Ind Est

New Clyce
Bridge

Alstone Wildlife
Park

VICTORIA PL 1
HOPE COTTS 2
RIVERBED HO 3
QUANTOCK VIEW 4

Brue
Bridge

Brue
Farm

Highbridge

Walrow
Ind Est

Sewage
Works

TA9

Alstone Court
Farm

Alstone

Maundril's
Farm

West Huntspill
Com Prim Sch

Hotel

Mill
Farm

Brent
Farm

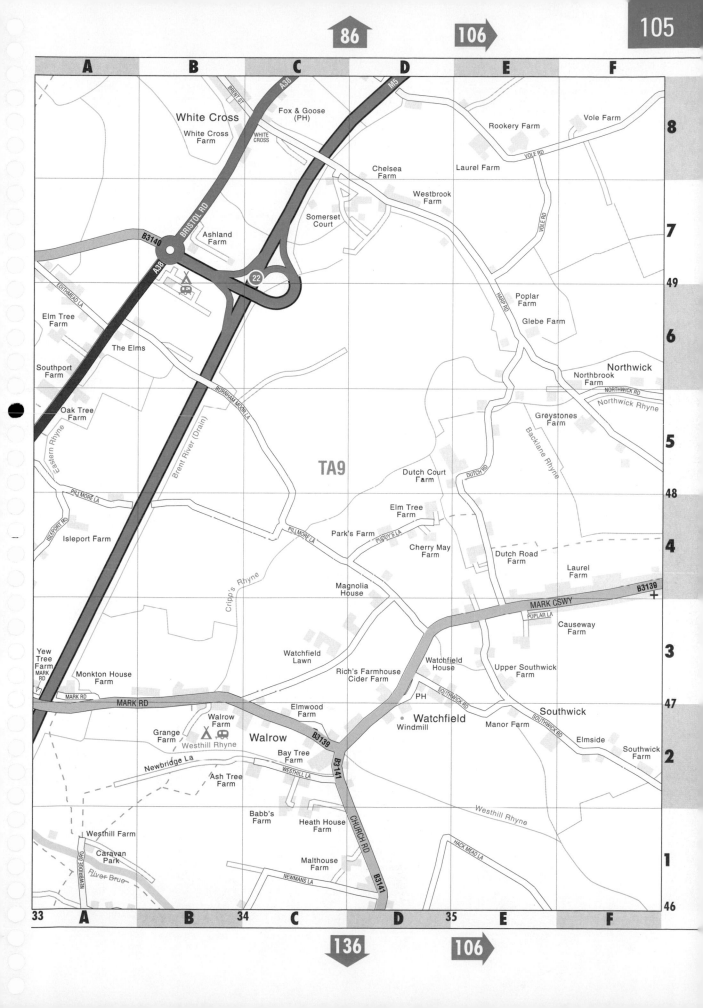

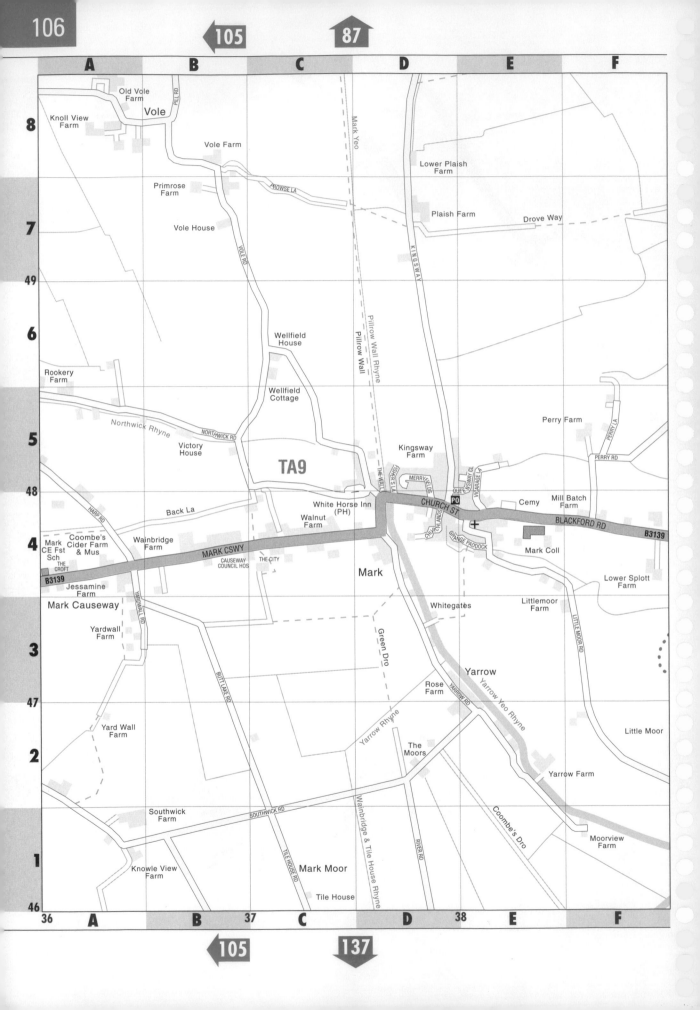

A   B   C   D   E   F

8

Knoll View Farm
Old Vole Farm
Vole

Vole Farm

7

Primrose Farm
PROWSE LA
Mark Yeo

Vole House

Lower Plaish Farm

Plaish Farm

Drove Way

49

VOLE RD

KINGSWAY

6

Wellfield House

Pillrow Wall Rhyne
Pillrow Wall

Rookery Farm

Wellfield Cottage

5

Northwick Rhyne
NORTHWICK RD

Victory House

TA9

Kingsway Farm

Perry Farm

PERRY LA

PERRY RD

48

HARP RD

Back La

White Horse Inn (PH)

Walnut Farm

THE WALL
FISHER'S LA
MERRY FIELDS
QUE...
PO
KINGSWAY CL
VICARAGE
CHURCH ST
CHURCHLANDS

Cemy
Mill Batch Farm

BLACKFORD RD
B3139

4

Mark CE Fst Sch
Coombe's Cider Farm & Mus
THE CROFT

Wainbridge Farm

MARK CSWY
CAUSEWAY COUNCIL HOS
THE CITY

GRANGE PADDOCK

Mark

Mark Coll

Lower Splott Farm

B3139
Jessamine Farm

Mark Causeway

YARDWALL RD

Whitegates

Littlemoor Farm

LITTLE MOOR RD

3

Yardwall Farm

BUTT LAKE RD

Green Dro

Yarrow

Rose Farm

YARROW RD
Yarrow Yeo Rhyne

Little Moor

47

Yard Wall Farm

Yarrow Rhyne

The Moors

Yarrow Farm

2

Southwick Farm

SOUTHWICK RD

Wainbridge & Tile House Rhyne

RIVER RD

Coombe's Dro

Moorview Farm

1

Knowle View Farm

TILE HOUSE RD

Mark Moor

Tile House

46

36   A   B   37   C   D   38   E   F

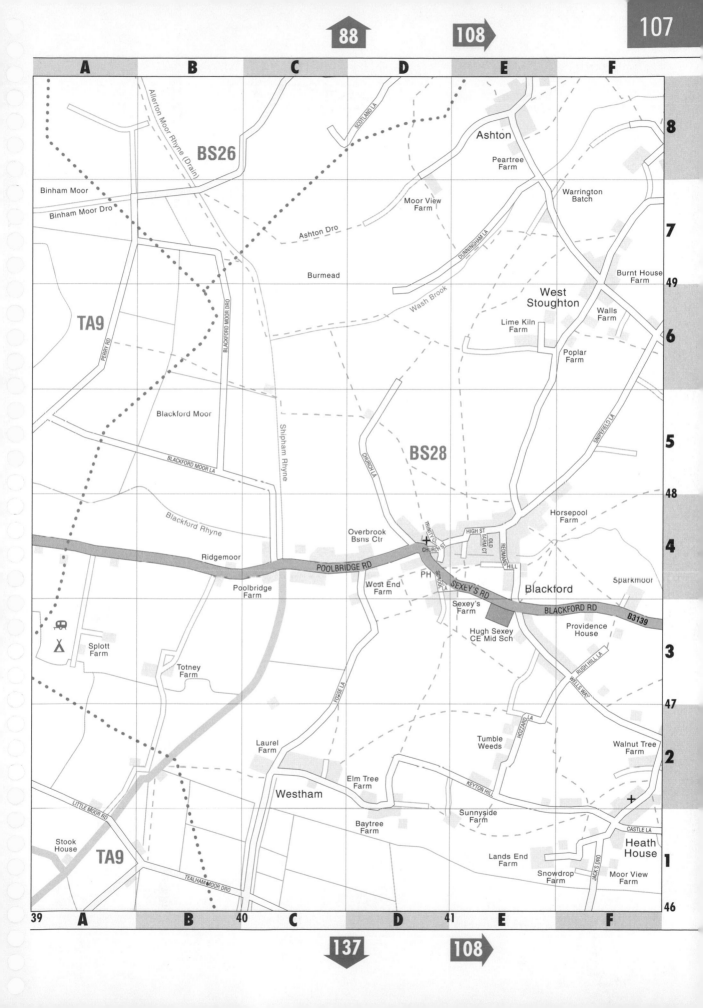

A   B   C   D   E   F

8

Middle
Stoughton

Stoughton
Cross

Yew Tree
Farm
PH

Crickham

Crickham Farm

Crickham La

Bear House
Farm

Walls La

Crib House La

Rughill

B3151

New Rd

Dungeon

Whitehouse
Farm

Maldon
Farm

7

Cocklake

Barrow's Dro

Bartlett's
Bridge

Brook Bank

Nyland Dro

River Axe

Glendale
Farm

49

Snipefield La

Snipefield
Farm

Snipe
Field

Dark La

Riverside
Farm

Landcourse Rhyne

6

Cheddar Rd

Cemy

Wedmore Lowgrounds

Wedmore Moor

Hill
Farm

Pillmead La

Red Hill
Farm

5

Quab La

Lascot Hill

Lascot
Hill

BS28

B3151

Worthington Cl

Wedmore Moor Dro

48

King Alfreds Way 1
St Marys Cl 2

Dane's
Lea

Herwy
Cl

Manor La

Brickyard
Farm

Dunns Ct

St Medard Rd

Donnelly
Dr

Gardiner's
Orch

Church St

The Lerburne

The Borough

Mall

Combe Batch

Southville
Farm

Goosham La

B3139

P O

B3139

Wells Rd

Latcham

4

Quab
La
Cl

Saxon Way 1
2

Pilcorn St

Glanville Rd

Grant's La

Billings
Hill

Combe Batch

Combe La

Mutton La

Wedmore
Fst Sch

West
End

Westover's
Cnr

Goss Orch

Orchard
Cl

Dando's La

B3151

Latcham
Farm

Latcham Dro

West End

Stoneybridge
Farm

B3139

Blackford Rd

Kelson's La

Kelsons
Farm

Birch Cl

Shortland La

Springfield
Dr

Wedmore

Mill La

Maltfield

The Firs

B3139

3

Plud St

Madwomans La

Sand Rd

Apple
Dumpling
Cnr

Greenfield
House

Mudgley Rd

47

Little
Ireland

Heath House
Mill

Townsend
Farm

Hillhead
Farm

Maltfield
Farm

2

Lower
Farm

Sand

Maltfield
Cottage

Castle La

Ash Grove
Farm

Sand
Hall

Sand
House

Oldwood

Mudgley
Cross

Townsend La

MUDGLEY
CROSS ROADS

1

Castle
Farm

Castle

Sand Hill

Mudgley Hill

B3151

Cold Nose

46

42   A   43   B   C   43   D   44   E   F

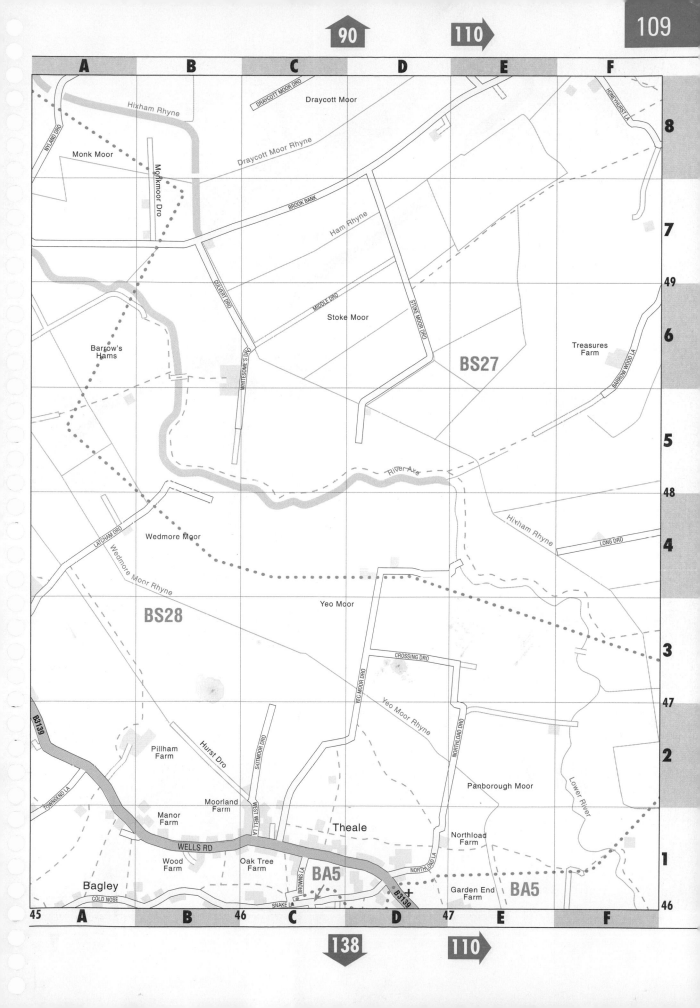

109
91

A B C D E F

8

7

49

6

5

48

4

3

47

2

1

46

48 A B 49 C D 50 E F

HONEYHURST LA
BARROW WOOD LA
BUTTS LA
STOKE ST
Conduit Farm
MILLWAY
WELLS RD
A371
Hill Farm
WESTFIELD LA
BROAD RD
Grove Wood
SLOWLAND LA
Old Ditch Farm
LYNCH LA
STANCOMBE LA
Old Ditch
LONGLANDS LA
LITTLE FIELD LA
Westclose Hill
Broadway Hill
Kites Croft
Meadway
KEX MEAD LA
ROUGHMOOR LA
THE HOLLOW
STOKE RD
BROADWAY LA
BROADWAY
OLD DITCH
BACK LA
KITES CROFT
MARES LA
FIRE HILL
LYNCHCOMBE LA
Croft Lane Farm
CROFT LA
STONLEIGH
STONLEIGH COTTS
SCHOOL HILL
Sch
THE SQUARE
CROW LA
PERCH HILL
PO
Westbury-sub-Mendip
TANHAMS LA
HOME CL
TOP RD
HOMEFIELDS
WELLS RD
BS27
Airstrip
Lodge Hill Ind PK
PRIOR HILL
STATION RD
DUCK LA
BELL CL
ADDMEAD LA
Lodge Hill Farm
Furlong Farm
BA5
Hollybrook Farm
Lodge Hill Wood
Lodge Hill
Windmill Hill
WINDMILL HILL LA
Sewage Works
Holly Brook
Erlong Farm
A371
48
Westbury Moor
LONG DRO
Westbury Straight Rhyne
SHORT DRO
MOOR LA
Court House Farm
ERLON LA
Chalcroft Hill
River Axe
Taylor Paddock Dro
BS28
Knowle Moor Rhyne
Knowle Farm
Knowle Bridge
Eight Acre Dro
KNOWLE MOOR DRO
Knowle Hill
Webby's Rhyne
Barn Rhyne
MOOR SHERD
KNOWLE LA
WETMOOR LA
Marchey Rhyne
Marchey Dro
Knowle Moor
Limbers La

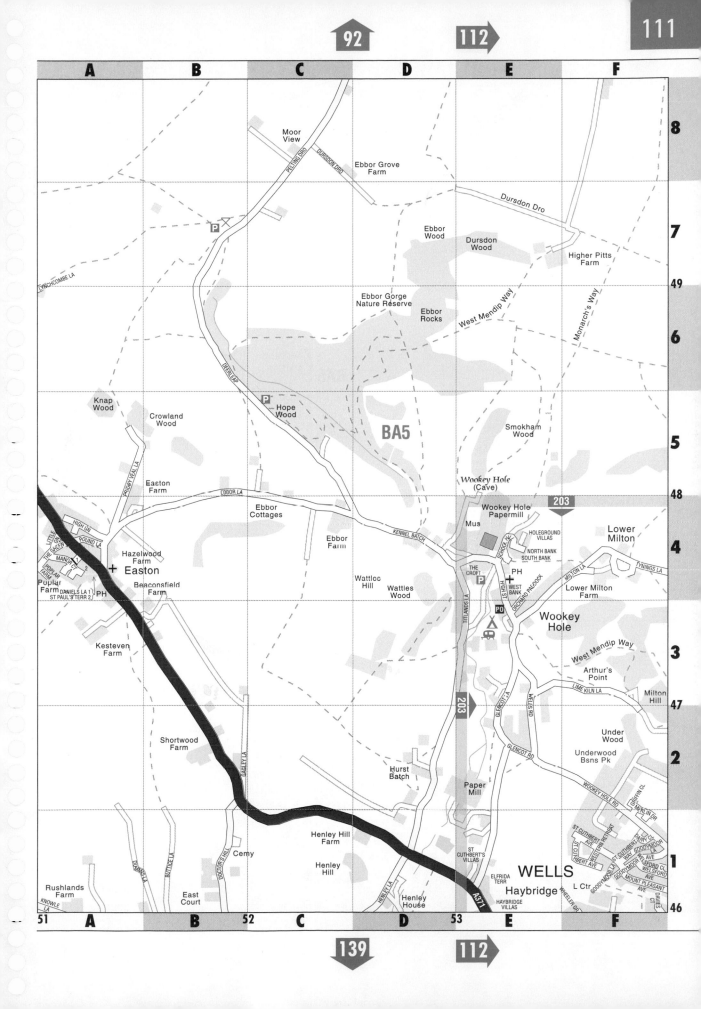

111 93

A B C D E F

8

Southfield Farm

HILLGROVE RD

PRIDDY RD

Rookham House

Drove Cottage

Priddy Road Farm

7

Ores Close Farm

49

BRISTOL RD

6

Mast

OLD BRISTOL RD

DURSDON DRO

Transmitting Sta

Mast Pen Hill

A39

HAYDON DRO

BA5

Rookham

Rookham Wood

The Round Clump

Pen Hill Wood

Pen Hill Farm

Gollege

Big Plantation

5

Ivy Cottage

Vigo Wood

The Wrangle

Prior's Hill

48

203

Walcombe Wood

Gorse Plantation

Biddle Combe

4

TYNINGS LA

Welsh's Green La

Welsh's Green

Nibs Hanging

Dairy House Farm

Manor Farm

Upper Milton

NEW CUT

Walcombe Hanging

BRISTOL HILL

Beryl Wood

3

Model Farm

Milton Lodge Garden

Walcombe

Beryl Hanging

203

Beryl Farm

47

WEST MENDIP WAY

RESERVOIR LA

Milton Lodge

WALCOMBE LA

The Coombe

Beryl

Knapp Hill

2

MILTON LA

WELLS

Stoberry Park

Beryl

B3139

1

HILL SIDE CL

TFR TOR AVE

ORCHARD LEA

ASH GR

ASH LA

MILTON LA

ASH CL

NEW ST

STOBERRY CRES

COLLEGE RD

STOBERRY AVE

St Thomas Terr 1
Old School Pl 2
Lorne Pl 3
St Thomas' Ct 4
St Andrew's Ct 5

Stoberry Park Sch

LITTLE ENTRY

NORTH RD

LENNONS LA

LENNONS AVE

PARAY DR

DRAKE RD

KIDDER BANK

COLLES CL

Knapphill Farm

CHURCHILL CL

CHURCHILL RD E

WEST CT

GILBERT SCOTT RD

46

Cherry Orchard Dr

MARY RD

SINGLETON CT

WOOKEY HOLE RD

SOMERVILLE RD

WALNUT TREE CL

WELSFORD AVE

MOUNT PLEASANT AVE

JK CT HOPE CL

BROOKES

BLAKE RD

SEYMOUR CL

LOVERS WLK

A39 MOUNTERY RD

B3139

THE LIBERTY

Wells Cathedral Sch

MILLERS

SNIDE

ST ANDREW ST

ST THOMAS ST

TOR WOOD VIEW

WOODBURY

BARKHAM CL

WOODBURY AVE

Wells & District

H

MANNING RD

MITCHELL TERR

JOHNSON LA

PLUMPTRE AVE

BROAD CL

HOOPER AVE

ALLENS LA

BEDFORD RD

BEVINTON AVE

FOSTER CL

KING'S CASTLE RD

BATH RD

OLD FROME RD

PO

HERVEY RD

SEALEYS CRES

EVERETT CL

HAMMERS LA

PENN CL

BERYL LA

TEAGLE CL

KIPPAX AVE

54 55 56

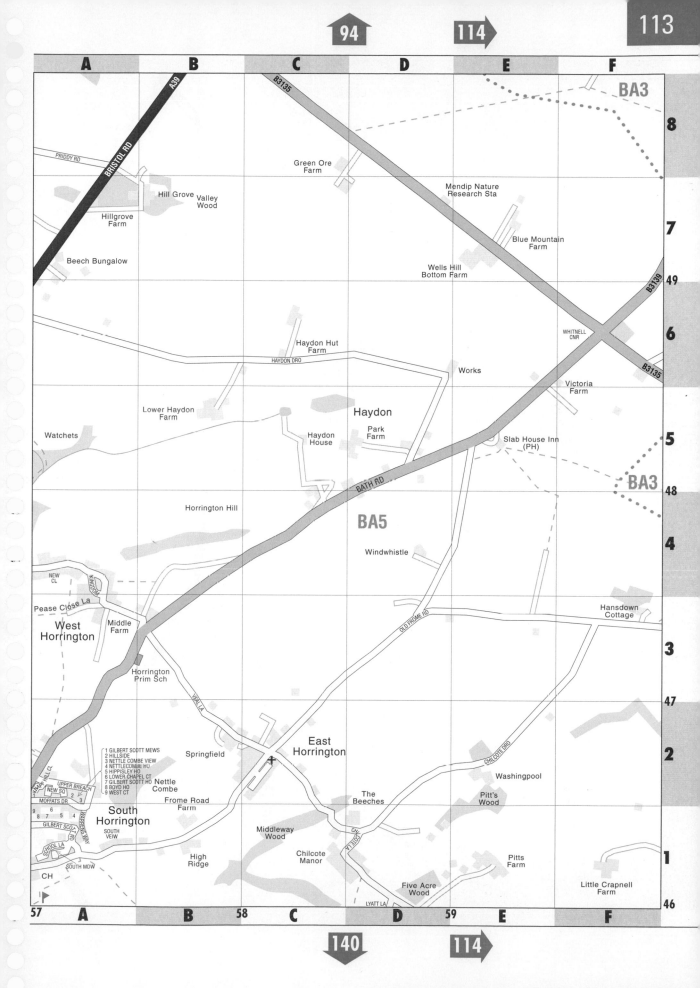

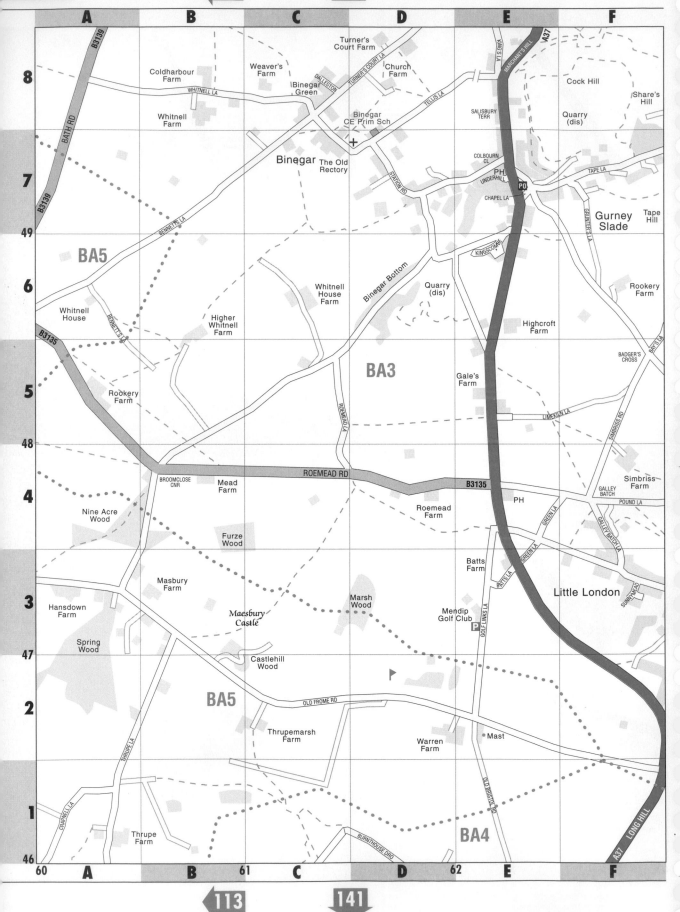

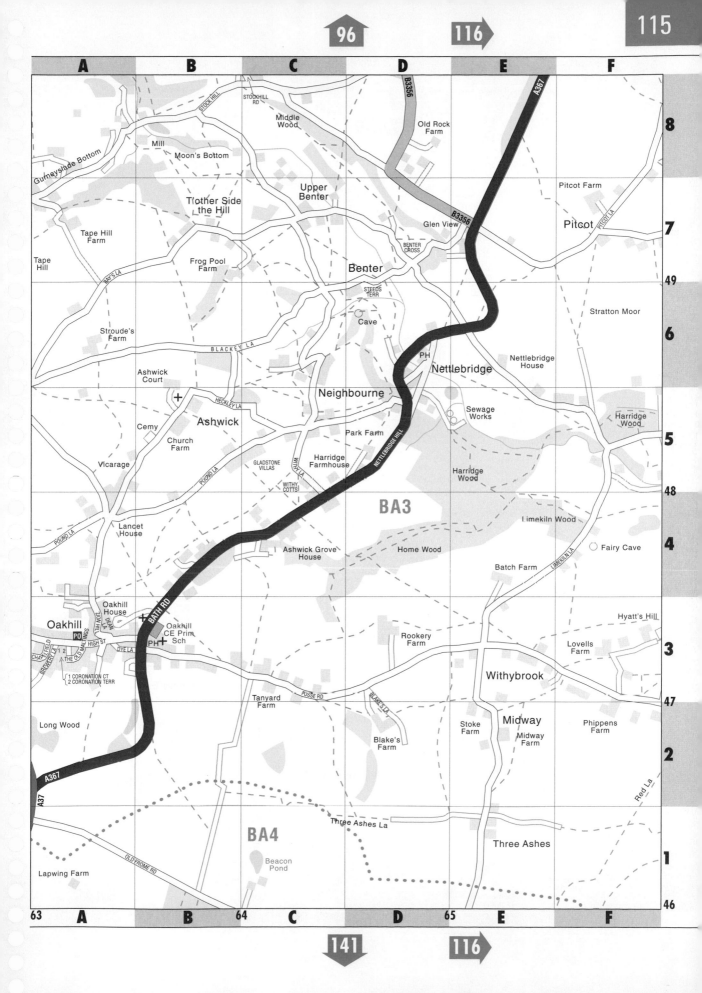

96 116

A B C D E F

8
7
49
6
5
48
4
3
47
2
1
46

Gurneyslade Bottom
Mill
Moon's Bottom
T'other Side the Hill
Tape Hill Farm
Tape Hill
Frog Pool Farm
Stroude's Farm
BAYS LA
BLACKEY LA
Ashwick Court
Cemy
Church Farm
Vicarage
Ashwick
HECKLEY LA
POUND LA
WITHY LA
GLADSTONE VILLAS
WITHY COTTS
Lancet House
POUND LA
Oakhill House
BATH RD
Oakhill
PO
HIGH ST
THE OLD MALTINGS
DYE LA
CHAVEL FIELD
BRIDGE LA
1 CORONATION CT
2 CORONATION TERR
Oakhill CE Prim Sch
PH
Long Wood
A367
A37
BA4
Lapwing Farm
OLD FROME RD
Beacon Pond
Tanyard Farm
PUSSE RD
STOCK HILL
STOCKHILL RD
Middle Wood
Upper Benter
B3356
Old Rock Farm
Glen View
B3356
BENTER CROSS
Benter
STEEDS TERR
Cave
Neighbourne
Park Farm
Harridge Farmhouse
NETTLEBRIDGE HILL
PH
Nettlebridge
Nettlebridge House
Sewage Works
Harridge Wood
BA3
Home Wood
Ashwick Grove House
Limekiln Wood
LIMEKILN LA
Batch Farm
Fairy Cave
Rookery Farm
Withybrook
Midway
Midway Farm
Stoke Farm
Blake's Farm
BLAKES LA
Three Ashes La
Three Ashes
A367
Pitcot Farm
Pitcot
PITCOT LA
Stratton Moor
Harridge Wood
Hyatt's Hill
Lovells Farm
Phippens Farm
Red La

63 64 65

8

7

49

6

5

48

4

3

47

2

1

46

A   B   C   D   E   F

PILCOT LA

Barlake Farm

The Ring o' Roses (PH)

THE MEAD

CROFT RD

CHARLTON RD

BREWERY LA

Holcombe Manor

1 OLD MANOR EST
2 SCOTTS CL

Holcombe

UPPER MERRIFIELD

Ropewalk Farm

RUSH ASH LA

FAIRFIELD

HIGHFIELD

MERRY-FIELD

Manor Farm

STRATTON RD

CAPEL LA

KINGSWAY

KIN CISMEAD

BOUNDARY CL

2

Bishop Henderson CE Prim Sch

FARLEY'S DELL

ANCHOR RD

COAL BARTON

HIGHFIELD

PO

LONGLEAT RD

LONGLEAT LA

HOLCOMBE HILL

JAMES CL

PO

TYNING COTTS

Kilmersdon Common

MENDIP VALE

BEACON VIEW

CROSSWAYS

HARRIS VALE

HIGHBURY ST

MENDIP VIEW

TOP LA

STONES PADDOCK

Flint House

COMMON LA

CAREYS MEAD

PREACHERS VALE

DOUGLAS YATES

LAWRENCE

ROMAN WAY

Barlake House

WOODLANDS LA

Lydford Farm

Spring Farm

Edford

Wks

Coleford

CHURCH ST

WESLEY VILLAS 1
BARTON VILLAS 2
ROCK TERR 3

CHURCH LA

Edford Green

EDFORD HILL

Kilmersdon Common Farm

3

ROSE & CROWN COTTS

2   1

Hippys Farm

THE GREEN

Duke of Cumberland (PH)

BECK'S LA

SPRINGER'S HILL

Bullock's Hill

HIGH ST

Edford Wood

Sewage Works

Ham

HAM HILL

Ham Bridge

Packsaddle Bridge

MARSH LA

Ham Farm

Mells Stream

Whitehole Farm

Dunsford's Farm

GREEN LA

Whitehole Farm

WHITEHOLE HILL

Leigh Wood

Moons Hill Farm

GIDDY LA

Hurdlestone Wood

BA3

Stoke Bottom Farm

MOONS HILL

Folly Wood

Combe Wood

FROG LA

RECTOR LA

Stoke Lane Slocker Hole

Sparks Farm

PITTEN ST

STOCK'S LA

Manor Farm

Stoke St Michael Prim Sch

GOLPIT LA

Somer's Farm

Manor House Farm

Chivers Farm

LEIGH ST

Park Hayes

MOONSHILL COTTS 1
STEEPLE VIEW 2
MILLENNIUM CL 3
TOWER CL 4

RD

1

CLS CL

PRYMAN'S HILL

OAKHILL CT

Town's End

Leigh upon Mendip

FIELD CL

MOONSHILL

BIRCH CL

TOWER HILL

CL

2

3

MILL LA

Cook's Farm

Goldsborough Farm

BLACKER'S LA

SWEETLEAZE

CHURCH ST

THE MEAD

BURNT HOUSE LA

DARK LA

Susanna's Cross

STOKE HILL

PO

Red La

MENDIP RD

Stoke St Michael

SUSANNA'S LA

Grove Shute Farm

Tadhill

Tadhill Farm

East End

TADHILL LA

BA4

Mendip Farm

BURGE'S HILL

BURGE'S LA

Moons Hill Quarry

LONG CROSS BOTTOM

Yellow Marsh Farm

FENFAL LA

OLD WELLS RD

Tadhill House Farm

LUXTON'S LA

BA4

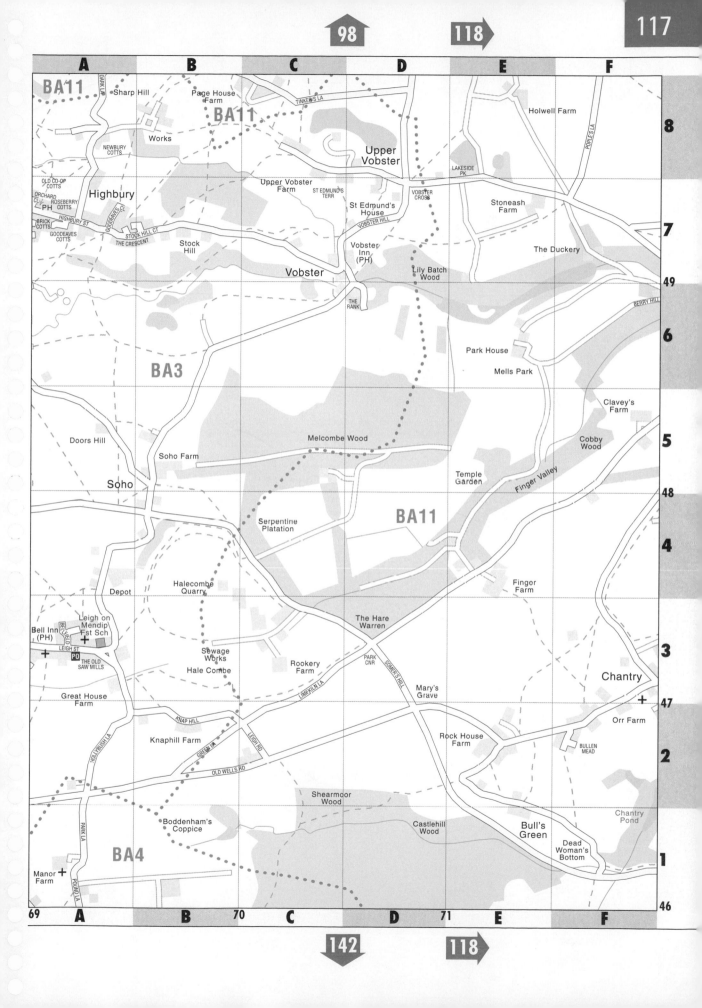

98
118
142
118

BA11

Sharp Hill

Page House Farm

TINKER'S LA

BA11

Works

NEWBURY COTTS

Upper Vobster

Upper Vobster Farm

ST EDMUND'S TERR

Holwell Farm

POPLES LA

LAKESIDE PK

VOBSTER CROSS

Stoneash Farm

OLD CO-OP COTTS

ORCHARD CL

PH

ROSEBERRY COTTS

Highbury

GOODEAVES CL

St Edmund's House

HIGHBURY ST

BRICK COTTS

STOCK HILL CT

GOODEAVES COTTS

THE CRESCENT

Stock Hill

Vobster

VOBSTER HILL

Vobster Inn (PH)

The Duckery

Lily Batch Wood

BERRY HILL

THE RANK

BA3

Park House

Mells Park

Doors Hill

Soho Farm

Melcombe Wood

Clavey's Farm

Cobby Wood

Soho

Temple Garden

Finger Valley

Serpentine Platation

BA11

Depot

Halecombe Quarry

Finger Farm

BELLFIELD

Leigh on Mendip Fst Sch

Bell Inn (PH)

LEIGH ST

PO

THE OLD SAW MILLS

Hale Combe

Sewage Works

The Hare Warren

Rookery Farm

PARK CNR

SOMER'S HILL

Mary's Grave

Chantry

Orr Farm

Great House Farm

KNAP HILL

LIMEKILN LA

Rock House Farm

BULLEN MEAD

HOLLYBUSH LA

Knaphill Farm

GREEN LA

LEIGH RD

OLD WELLS RD

Shearmoor Wood

Bull's Green

Chantry Pond

PARK LA

BA4

Boddenham's Coppice

Castlehill Wood

Dead Woman's Bottom

Manor Farm

POUND LA

DARK LA

49

48

47

46

69

70

71

117

99

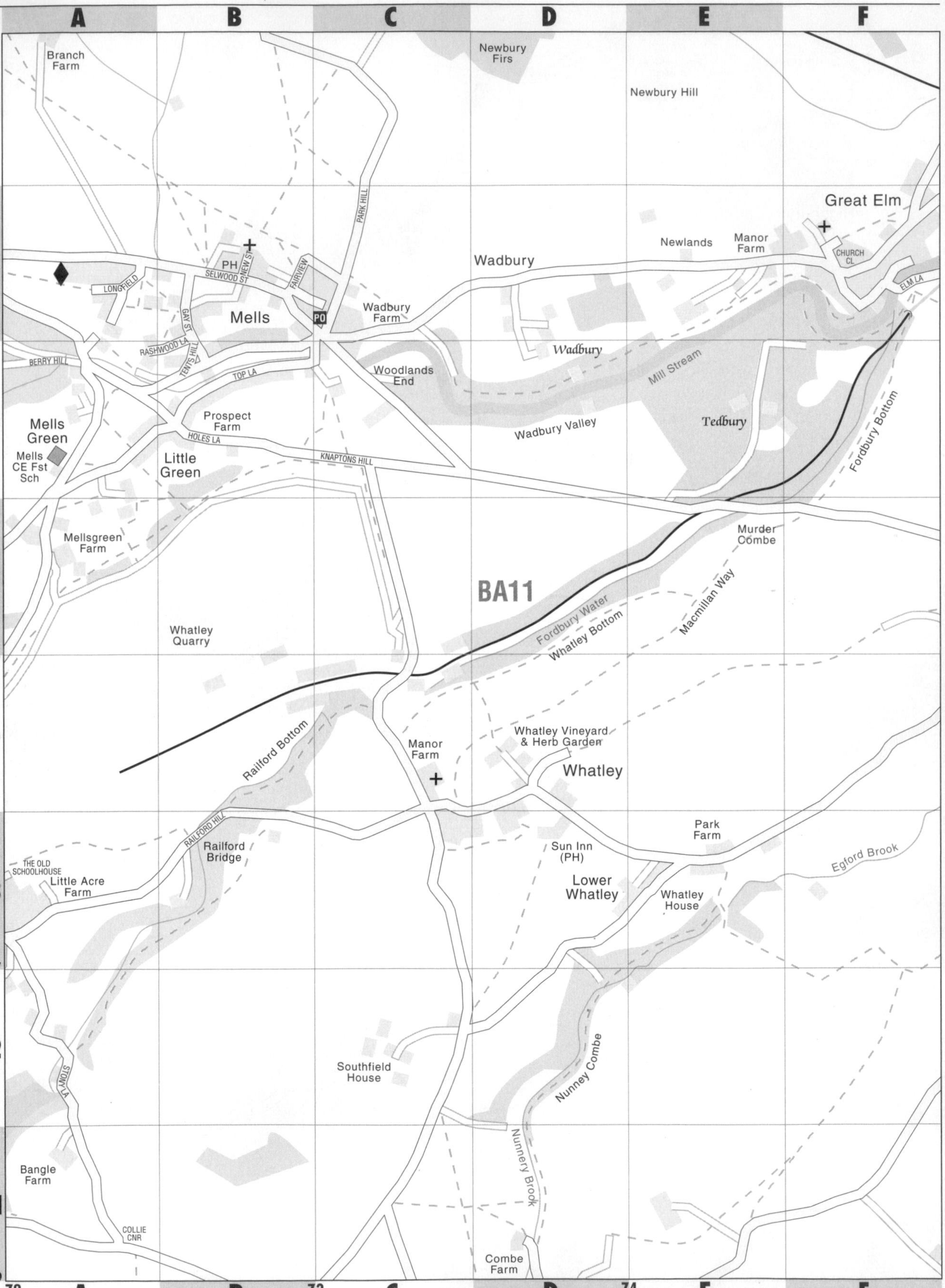

A **B** **C** **D** **E** **F**

8

Branch Farm

Newbury Firs

Newbury Hill

Great Elm

7

PH
SELWOOD ST
NEW ST
FAIRVIEW
PARK HILL
LONGFIELD

Mells

Wadbury Farm

Wadbury

Newlands

Manor Farm

CHURCH CL
ELM LA

49

BERRY HILL
RASHWOOD LA
GAY ST
TENTS HILL
TOP LA

Wadbury

Woodlands End

Mill Stream

PO

6

Mells Green

Mells CE Fst Sch

Prospect Farm

HOLES LA

Little Green

KNAPTONS HILL

Wadbury Valley

Tedbury

Fordbury Bottom

Mellsgreen Farm

Murder Combe

5

BA11

Fordbury Water

Whatley Bottom

Macmillan Way

Whatley Quarry

48

4

Railford Bottom

Manor Farm

Whatley Vineyard & Herb Garden

Whatley

RAILFORD HILL

Sun Inn (PH)

Park Farm

Egford Brook

THE OLD SCHOOLHOUSE

Little Acre Farm

Railford Bridge

Lower Whatley

Whatley House

3

STONEY LA

47

2

Southfield House

Nunney Combe

Nunnery Brook

1

Bangle Farm

COLLIE CNR

Combe Farm

46

72 **A** **B** 73 **C** **D** 74 **E** **F**

117

143

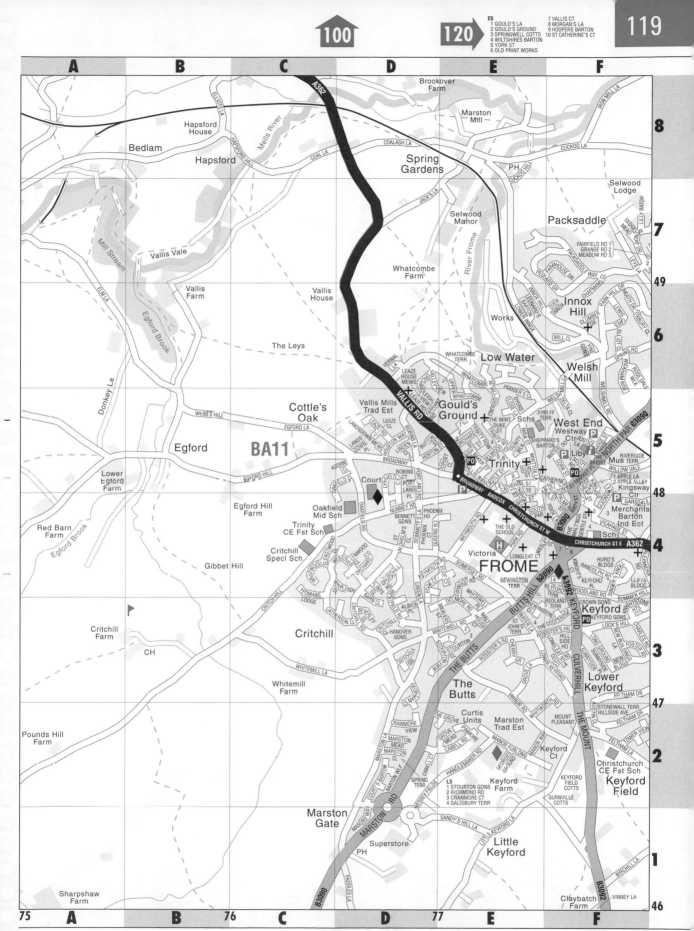

100

120

E5
1 GOULD'S LA
2 GOULD'S GROUND
3 SPRINGWELL COTTS
4 WILTSHIRES BARTON
5 YORK ST
6 OLD PRINT WORKS

7 VALLIS CT
8 MORGAN'S LA
9 HOOPERS BARTON
10 ST CATHERINE'S CT

F4
1 EAGLE LA
2 CHURCH ST
3 MERCHANTS' BARTON
4 BLINDHOUSE LA
5 PLUMBER'S BARTON
6 GOREHEDGE
7 WESLEY SLOPE
8 KEYFORD COTTS

Brookover Farm
Marston Mill
Bedlam
Hapsford House
Hapsford
Hapsford Hill
Mells River
COAL LA
COALASH LA
Spring Gardens
CUCKOO LA
Selwood Lodge
Packsaddle
Vallis Vale
Vallis Farm
Selwood Manor
Whatcombe Farm
River Frome
FAIRFIELD RD 1
GRANGE RD 2
MEADOW RD 3
PACKSADDLE WAY
Innox Hill
ELM LA
Vallis House
The Leys
Works
Low Water
Welsh Mill
Egford Brook
Cottle's Oak
Vallis Mills Trad Est
VALLIS RD
Gould's Ground
West End
Westway Ctr
NORTH PAR B3090
Liby
Mus
Donkey La
WEBB'S HILL
EGFORD LA
Egford
BA11
EGFORD HILL
Court
Trinity
Riverside TERR
Apple La
Kingsway Ctr
Lower Egford Farm
Egford Hill Farm
Oakfield Mid Sch
Trinity CE Fst Sch
Merchants Barton Ind Est
Red Barn Farm
Egford Brook
Critchill Specl Sch
Oakfield Rd
THE OLD SCHOOL
Victoria
LONGLEAT CT
H
HURD'S BLDGS
Gibbet Hill
FROME
Keyford
CULVERHILL
Critchill Farm
CH
CRITCHILL HILL
Critchill
Newington TERR
BUTTS HILL B3090
Lower Keyford
WHITEMILL LA
Whitemill Farm
THE BUTTS
The Butts
Curtis Units
Marston Trad Est
MOUNT PLEASANT
THE MOUNT
STONEWALL TERR
HILLSIDE AVE
Christchurch CE Fst Sch
Keyford Field
Pounds Hill Farm
MARSTON RD
Marston Gate
Keyford Farm
L3
1 STOURTON GDNS
2 RICHMOND RD
3 CRANMORE CT
4 SALISBURY TERR
Keyford Cotts
GURNVILLE COTTS
Superstore
PH
Little Keyford
B3090
B3092
Sharpshaw Farm
Claybatch Farm
VINNEY LA

75 A 76 B C 77 D E F

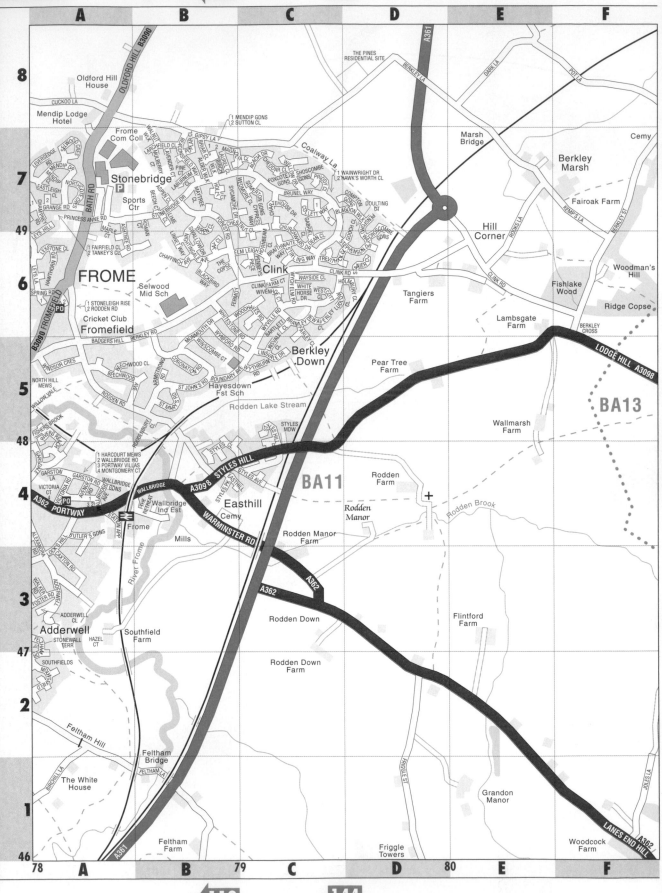

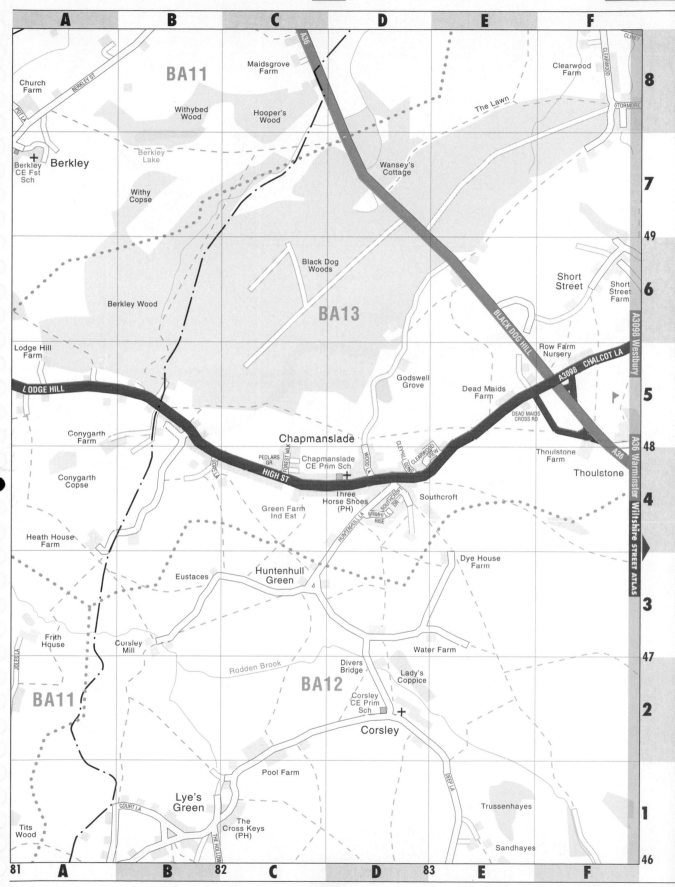

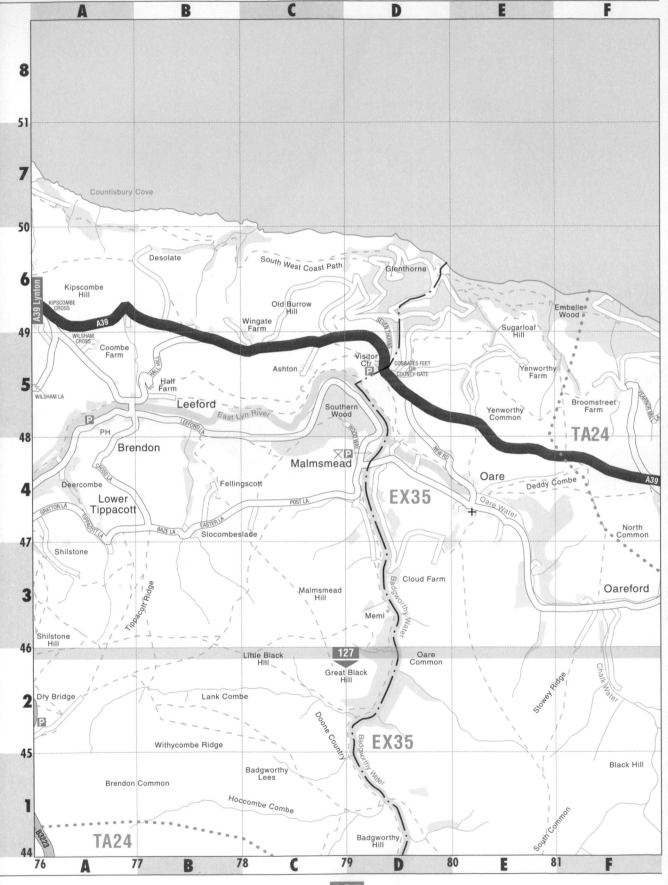

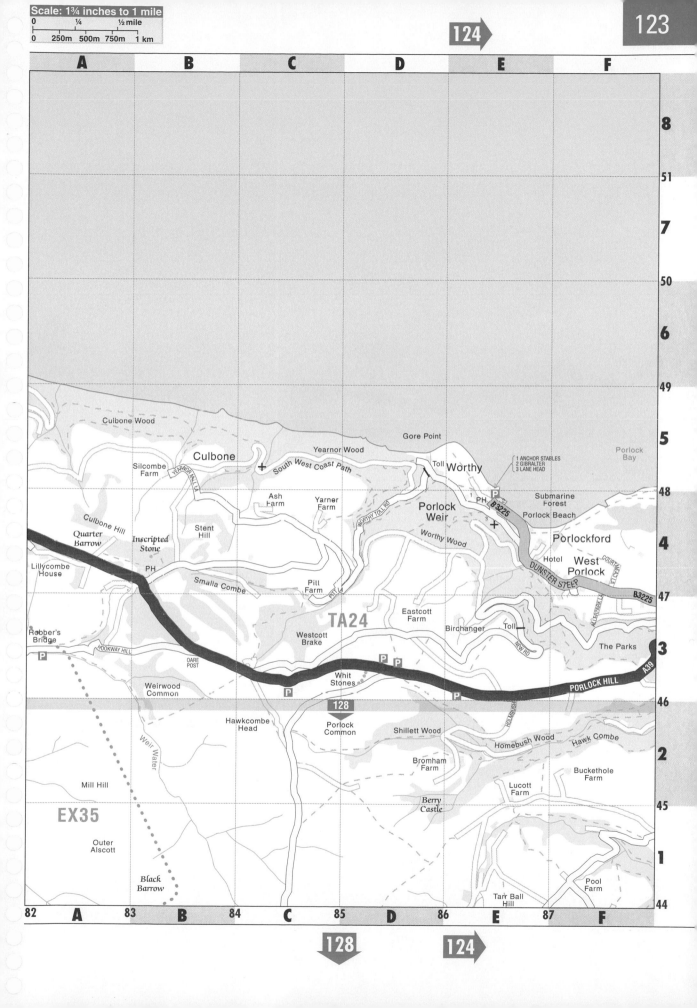

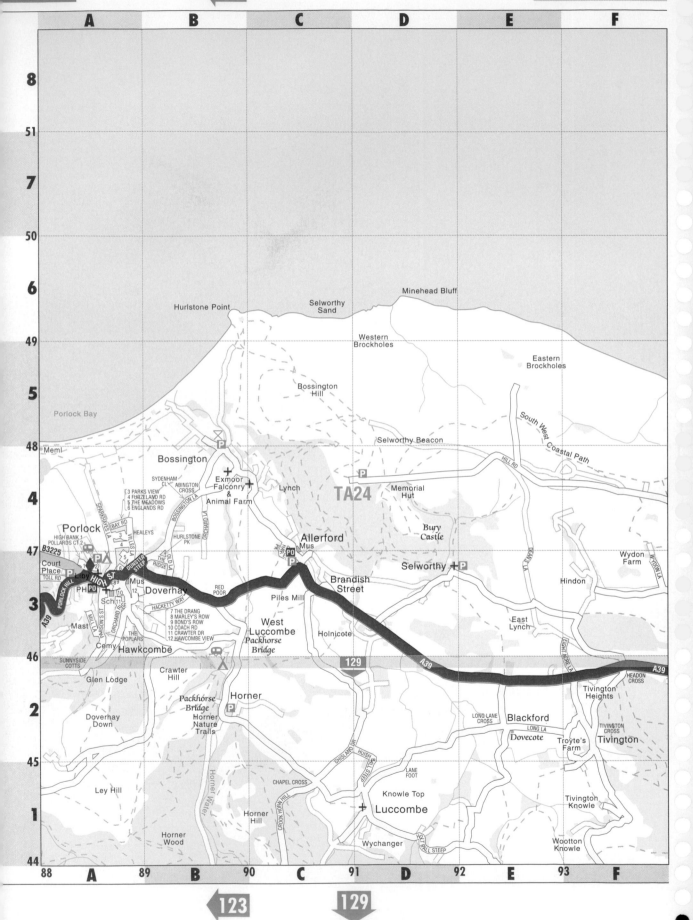

Scale: 1¾ inches to 1 mile

0   ¼   ½ mile
0   250m 500m 750m 1 km

A   B   C   D   E   F

8

51

7

50

6

Minehead Bluff

Hurlstone Point

Selworthy Sand

Western Brockholes

49

Eastern Brockholes

5

Porlock Bay

Bossington Hill

South West Coastal Path

48

Meml

Selworthy Beacon

HILL RD

Bossington

Exmoor Falconry & Animal Farm

Lynch

TA24

Memorial Hut

4

SYDENHAM CL
ABINGTON CROSS

3 PARKS VIEW
4 FURZELAND RD
5 THE MEADOWS
6 ENGLANDS RD

Bury Castle

Porlock

HIGH BANK 1
POLLARDS CT 2

BAY RD

HEALEYS

HURLSTONE PK

BOSSINGTON LA

ORCHARD LA

Allerford

Mus

Wydon Farm

47

B3225

SPARKHAYES LA

VILLES LA

THE RIDGE

OLD LA

PARK LA

PO

Selworthy

P

Hindon

WYDON LA

Court Place

P

Lby

DUNSTER STEEP

ST

Brandish Street

TOLL RD

P

HIGH

Mus

Doverhay

RED POOR

Piles Mill

East Lynch

EIGHT ACRE LA

3

PORLOCK HILL

PH PO

Sch

HACKETTY WAY

7 THE DRANG
8 MARLEY'S ROW
9 BOND'S ROW
10 COACH RD
11 CRAWTER DR
12 HAWCOMBE VIEW

West Luccombe

Holnicote

A39

PARSON'S ST

MILL LA

ORCHARD CRES

THE POPLARS

Packhorse Bridge

Mast

Cemy

Hawkcombe

46

SUNNYSIDE COTTS

Crawter Hill

129

A39

A39

HEADON CROSS

Glen Lodge

Packhorse Bridge

Horner

LONG-LANE CROSS

Tivington Heights

Doverhay Down

Horner Nature Trails

P

LONG LA

Blackford

TIVINGTON CROSS

Tivington

2

Dovecote

Troyte's Farm

45

LANE FOOT

CHISLAND DR

HUISH

BALL STEEP

Ley Hill

CHAPEL CROSS

Knowle Top

Tivington Knowle

CROOK HORN HILL

Luccombe

1

Horner Hill

Wychanger

HT BULL STEEP

Wootton Knowle

Horner Wood

Horner Water

44

88   A   89   B   90   C   91   D   92   E   93   F

Scale: 1¾ inches to 1 mile

0   ¼   ½ mile
0 250m 500m 750m 1 km

A   B   C   D   E   F

8
51
7
50
6
49
5
48
4
47
3
46
2
45
1
44

Burgundy Chapel (remains of)

Greenaleigh Point

North Hill

Greenaleigh Farm

North Hill Woodland Trail

Bratton Ball

Moor Wood

Higher Town

Culvecliffe Ct

North Hill Rd

Beacon

IRB Sta

Harbour

Quay W

200

Woodcombe

St Michael's Rd

Beacon Rd

Vicarage Rd

Moor Rd

Quay St

MINEHEAD

201

Madbrain Sands

Warren Point

Bratton Court

Bratton La

Bratton Mill La

Cemy

Bratton

Whitecross La

The Parks

Sainsbury Rd

Hillview Rd

Periton La

Lower Pk

Sch

Park St

Holloway

TH

Liby

Martlet Rd

Quay La

The Avenue

Minehead

Irnham Rd

The Strand

Warren Rd

CH

LC

Porlock Rd

Whitworth Rd

Periton Way

South Pk

Parkhouse Rd

Regents Way

Old Farm Way

West St

Poundfield Rd

Paganel Rd

Chor

Whitegate Rd

Bampton St

Townsend Rd

130

Sch

Cher

Cats La

Old Pk

Holloway

Benedict Rd

Townsend Rd

Marsh Rd

Martlet Rd

Vulcan Rd

Seaward Way

West Somerset Rly

Holiday Village

A39

200

Periton Rd

Hopcott Rd

Periton

Higher Hopcott

TA24

Hotel

Great Headon Plantation

Periton Hill

Macmillan Way West

Hopcott Common

Callins

Staunton La

Hayfield Rd

Sch

Alcombe Rd

Sch

Staunton Rd

Manor Rd

Quarry Ct

Spring Gdns

Church St

Marshfield

Alcombe

Coll

Millard Rd

Bircham Rd

Conyard Rd

Ellicombe La

Penny Hill

Hagley

Alcombe Common

Aldersmead

Staunton Plantation

Ellicombe

Drift Rd

Works

Dean La

Conygar Tower

A39

Marsh Street

Station Rd

Marsh La

Marsh St

Sea La

The Old Manor

Dunster

LC

LC

Bridges Mead

Loxhole Bridge

201

94   95   96   97   98   99

130   131   For full street detail of the highlighted areas see pages 200 and 201.

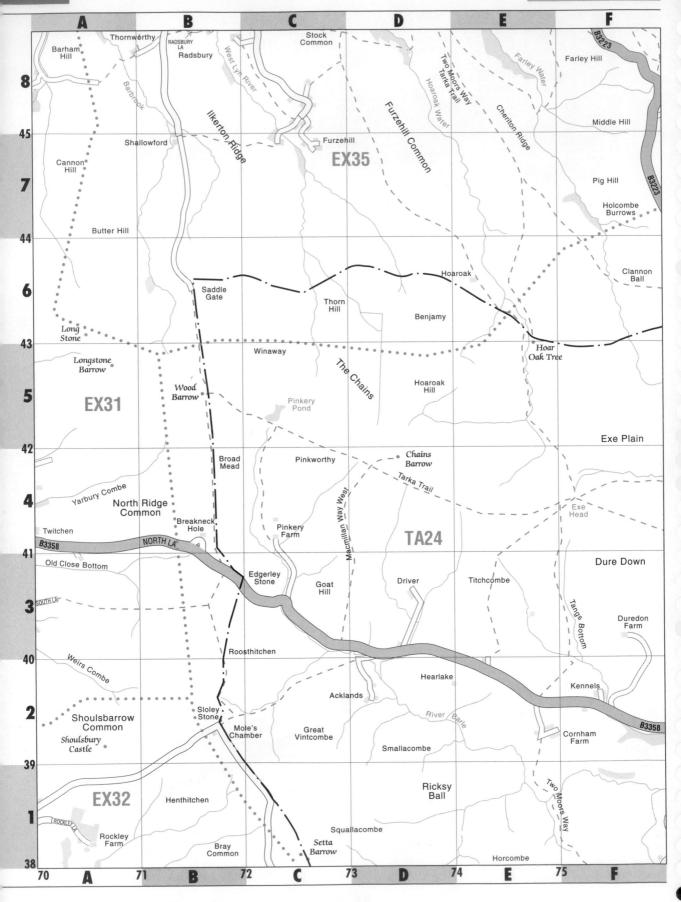

Scale: 1¾ inches to 1 mile

0   ¼   ½ mile
0 250m 500m 750m 1 km

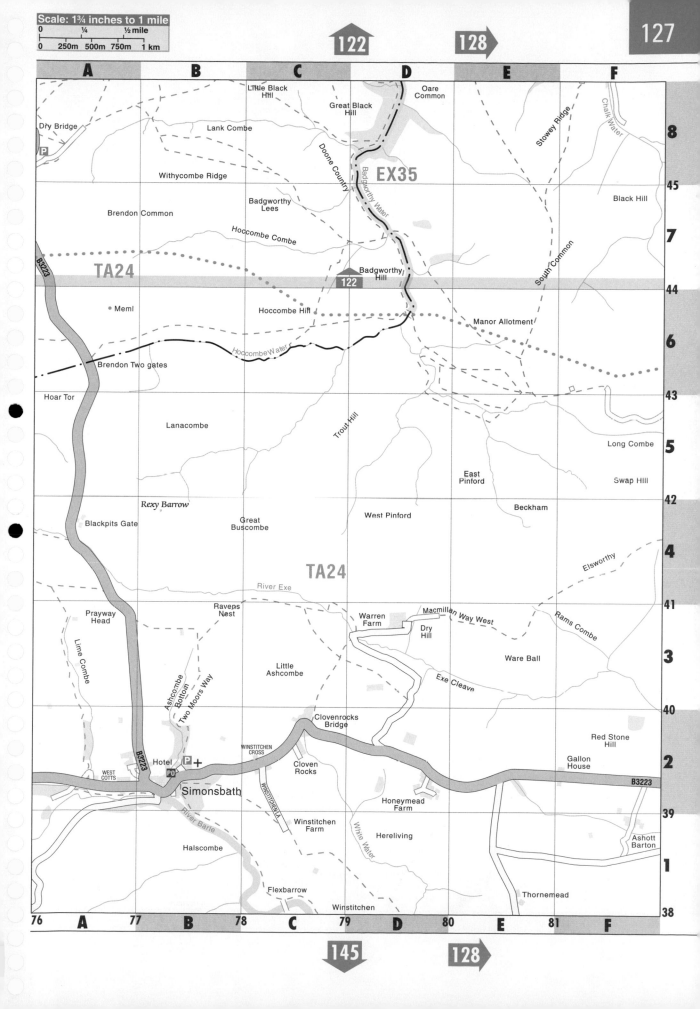

Scale: 1¾ inches to 1 mile
0   ¼   ½ mile
0 250m 500m 750m 1 km

122
128

145
128

8
45
7
44
6
43
5
42
4
41
3
40
2
39
1
38

A   B   C   D   E   F

Little Black Hill
Great Black Hill
Oare Common
Stowey Ridge
Chalk Water

Dry Bridge
Lank Combe
P

Withycombe Ridge
Doone Country
Badgworthy Water
EX35
Black Hill

Brendon Common
Badgworthy Lees
South Common

Hoccombe Combe

TA24
122
Badgworthy Hill

Meml
Hoccombe Hill
Manor Allotment

Hoccombe Water

Brendon Two gates

Hoar Tor
Trout Hill
Long Combe

Lanacombe
East Pinford
Swap Hill

Rexy Barrow
West Pinford
Beckham

Blackpits Gate
Great Buscombe

TA24
Elsworthy

River Exe

Prayway Head
Ravens Nest
Warren Farm
Macmillan Way West
Rams Combe

Lime Combe
Dry Hill
Ware Ball

Little Ashcombe
Exe Cleave

Ashcombe Bottom
Two Moors Way

Clovenrocks Bridge
Red Stone Hill

Gallon House

Hotel
P +
WINSTITCHEN CROSS
Cloven Rocks

B3223
PO
WEST COTTS
Simonsbath
WINSTITCHEN LA
Honeymead Farm
B3223

River Barle
Winstitchen Farm
Hereliving
Ashott Barton

Halscombe
White Water
Thornemead

Flexbarrow
Winstitchen

A   B   C   D   E   F
76   77   78   79   80   81

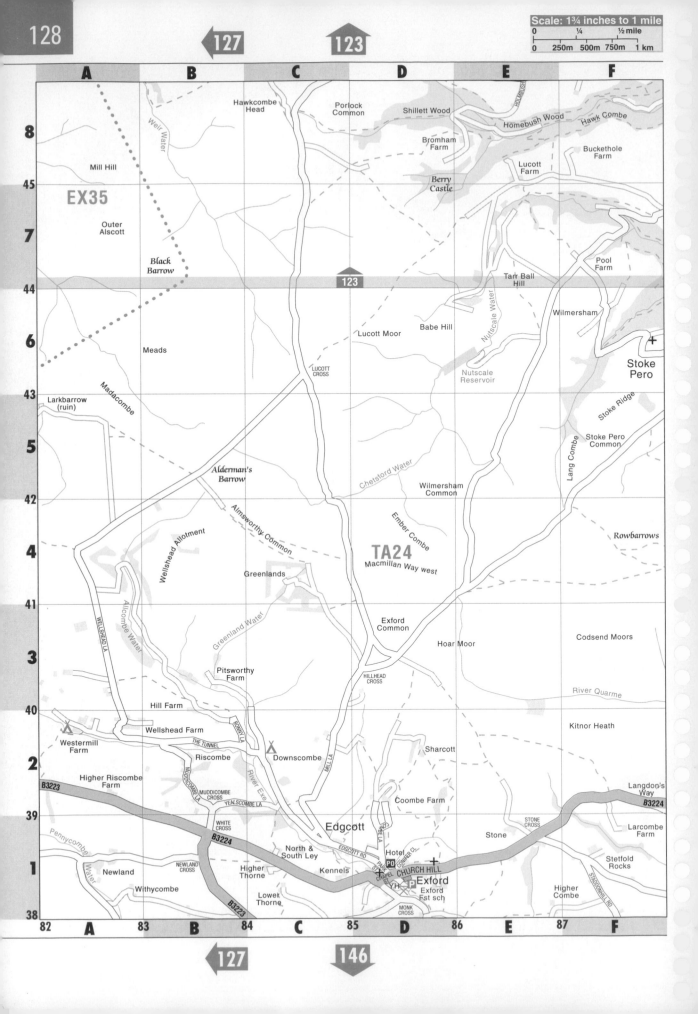

127
123

Scale: 1¾ inches to 1 mile
0   ¼   ½ mile
0 250m 500m 750m 1 km

A   B   C   D   E   F

8

Mill Hill

EX35

45

Outer
Alscott

7

Black
Barrow

44

Meads

6

Larkbarrow
(ruin)

43

Madacombe

Weir Water

Hawkcombe
Head

Porlock
Common

Shillett Wood

Homebush Wood

Hawk Combe

Bromham
Farm

Berry
Castle

Lucott
Farm

Buckethole
Farm

123

Lucott Moor

Babe Hill

Tarr Ball
Hill

Wilmersham

Pool
Farm

Lucott
Cross

Nutscale
Reservoir

Nutscale Water

Stoke
Pero

Stoke Ridge

5

Alderman's
Barrow

42

Wellshead Allotment

Almsworthy Common

4

Greenlands

TA24
Macmillan Way west

41

Chetsford Water

Wilmersham
Common

Ember Combe

Lang Combe

Stoke Pero
Common

Rowbarrows

Exford
Common

Allcombe Water

Greenland Water

3

Pitsworthy
Farm

Hoar Moor

Codsend Moors

River Quarme

WELLSHEAD LA

40

Hill Farm

HILLHEAD
CROSS

Kitnor Heath

Westermill
Farm

Wellshead Farm

THE TUNNEL

BONNY LA

Downscombe

Sharcott

2

Riscombe

MUDDICOMBE LA

River Exe

MILL LA

Coombe Farm

Langdon's
Way

B3223

Higher Riscombe
Farm

Muddicombe
Cross

Yeal-scombe La

B3224

39

White
Cross

Edgcott

Stone
Cross

Stone

Larcombe
Farm

Pennycombe Water

North &
South Ley

EDGCOTT RD

Hotel

B3224

STADDONHILL RD

1

Newland

Newland
Cross

Higher
Thorne

Kennels

PO

CHURCH HILL

Exford
Fst sch

Stetfold
Rocks

Higher
Combe

Withycombe

Lower
Thorne

B3223

MONK
CROSS

38

82   A   83   B   84   C   85   D   86   E   87   F

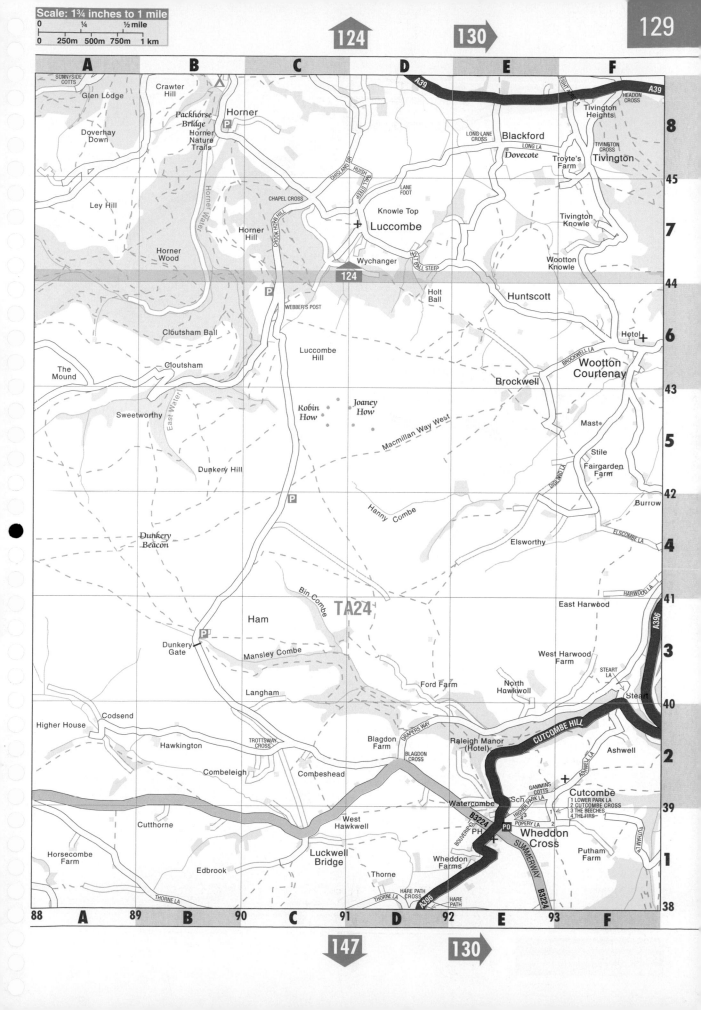

Scale: 1¾ inches to 1 mile

0   ¼   ½ mile
0   250m   500m   750m   1 km

124
130

A39

Sunnyside Cotts
Glen Lodge
Crawter Hill
Packhorse Bridge
Horner
Horner Nature Trails
Doverhay Down
Blackford
Long Lane Cross
Long La
Dovecote
Tivington Heights
Headon Cross
Troyte's Farm
Tivington Cross
Tivington

Ley Hill
Chapel Cross
Lane Foot
Knowle Top
Luccombe
Tivington Knowle

Horner Hill
Crook Horn Hill
Horner Water
Horner Wood
Wychanger
Holt Ball Steep
Hill Steep
Huish
Ghisland Dr
Wootton Knowle

124

Webber's Post
Holt Ball
Huntscott

Cloutsham Ball
Luccombe Hill
Hotel
Brockwell La
Wootton Courtenay

The Mound
Cloutsham
Brockwell
East Water
Robin How
Joaney How
Sweetworthy
Macmillan Way West
Mast
Dicks End La
Digland La
Stile
Fairgarden Farm
Burrow

Dunkery Hill
Hanny Combe
Elscombe La
Elsworthy

Dunkery Beacon
Harwood La

Bin Combe
TA24
East Harwood
A396

Ham
West Harwood Farm
Steart La
Dunkery Gate
Mansley Combe
Ford Farm
North Hawkwoll
Steart

Langham
Cutcombe Hill
Codsend
Higher House
Hawkington
Trottsway Cross
Blagdon Farm
Drapers Way
Raleigh Manor (Hotel)
Ashwell La
Ashwell

Combeleigh
Blagdon Cross
Combeshead
Gammins Cotts
Cutcombe
1 Lower Park La
2 Cutcombe Cross
3 The Beeches
4 The Firs
Sch
Higher Park La

Cutthorne
West Hawkwoll
Watercombe
B3224
PO
Popery La
Wheddon Cross
Putham La

Horsecombe Farm
Luckwell Bridge
Thorne
Bouverie Cl
PH
Wheddon Farms
Summerway
Putham Farm

Edbrook
Thorne La
Hare Path Cross
A396
Hare Path
B3224

Scale: 1¾ inches to 1 mile

0   ¼   ½ mile
0   250m   500m   750m   1 km

A39
PORLOCK RD
PERITON LA
PERITON WAY
PARKHOUSE RD
REGENTS WAY
Periton
PERITON RD
HOPCOTT RD
PERITON WEST
POUNDFIELD RD
PAGANEL RD
SOUTH RD
OLD FARM RD
BAMPTON ST
CHER
WHITEGATE RD
Sch
TOWNSEND RD
PONSFORD RD
CATS LA
MART RD
MART RD
Sch
HAYFIELD RD
MARSFIELD RD
ALCOMBE RD
PO
SEAWARD WAY
WILLARD RD
Holiday Village
West Somerset Rly
Hotel
Higher Hopcott
Alcombe
Coll
BIRCHAM RD
The Old Manor
Works
Great Headon Plantation
STAUNTON RD
CHURCH ST
QUARRY LA
MANOR RD
SPRING GDNS
ELLICOMBE LA
CUMBELAND RD
Marsh Street
LC
Dunster
LC
DRIFT RD
STATION RD
SEA LA
MARSH LA
MARSH
BRIDGES MEAD
Periton Hill
Penny Hill
Ellicombe
Hopcott Common
STAUNTON LA
Hagley
A396
DUNSTER STEEP
Conygar Tower
Loxhole Bridge
Tivington Common
200
201
Macmillan Way West
Staunton Plantation
125
Alcombel Common
Aldersmead
Macmillan Way West
Grabbist Hill
St Leonards Well
CASTLE HILL
Sch
WEST CL
ST GEORGE'S ST
PRIORY GN
Cemy
Butter Cross
PO
Yarn Market
CHURCH ST
Dunster
Wootton Common
Knowle Hill
Burnells
TA24
Aville Farm
KNOWLE LA WEST ST
MILL LA
PARK ST
Mill
Dunster Castle
Gallox Bridge
The Lawns
Dunkery Vineyard
Ranscombe
Kennels
200
Knowle
KNOWLE LA
River Avill
BONNITON NEW RD
201
Vinegar Hill
BONNITON LA
Dunster Park
Black Ball
Cowbridge
MEADOW VIEW
VIGARAGE CT
BEMBERRY BANK
Totterdown Farm
KITSWALL LA
Whits Wood
Bat's Castle
PARK LA
Well Farm
WELL LA
ORCHARD WAY
GREAT HOUSE ST
CHURCH ST
WILLOWBANK
PO
THE GLEBE
Bickham
Timberscombe
WHITSWOOD STEEP
BROADWOOD RD
P
Hur Wood
WITHYCOMBE HILL GATE
Aller Hill
WITHYCOMBE HILL
HORSEPARK LA
WAYDOWN CROSS
WAYDOWN LA
ELSCOMBE LA
HARWOOD CROSS
HARWOOD LA
A396
Pitt Bridge
Broadwood Farm
Gupworthy Farm
STARLING LA
BOWDEN LA
Bowden
OAK LA
Oaktrow Wood
Slade
Slade Lane
Beasley
Croydon House
Croydon Hill
Withycombe Scruffets
Black Hill
40
A39
GUTCOMBE HILL
Sully
Allercott
Well
Rodhuish Common
Oaktrow Farm
TA23
Stowey Farm
PUTHAM LA
KERSHAM LA
Kersham
COUPLE CROSS
Nurcott Farm
Monkham Hill
Slowley Farm
Old Stowey
BEECH TREE
Churchtown
FINLEY LA
STOUT'S WAY LA
Slowley Wood
STOUT'S WAY LA
Kersham Hill

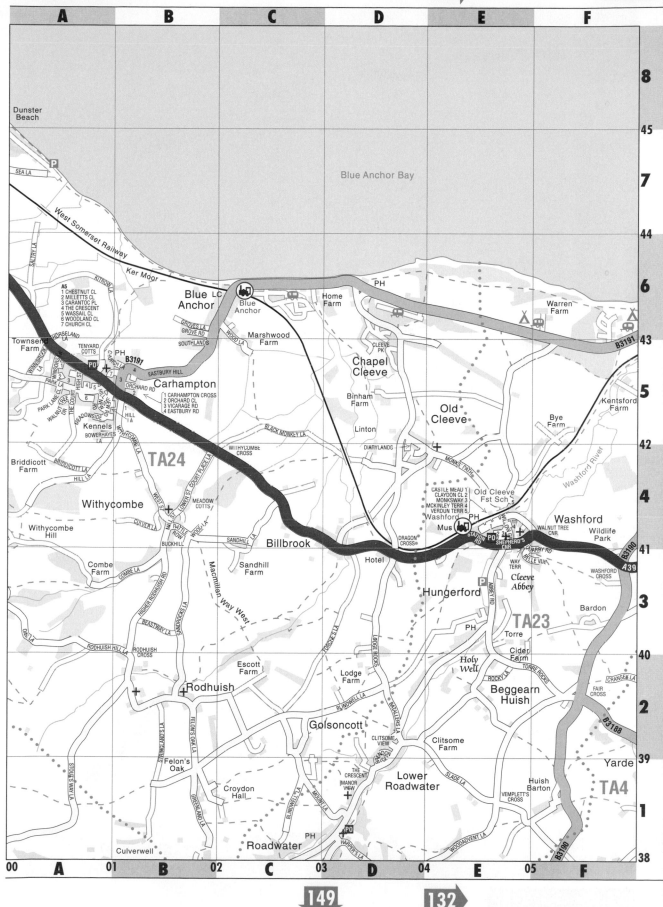

132

Scale: 1¾ inches to 1 mile

0   ¼   ½ mile
0   250m 500m 750m 1 km

A   **B**   **C**   **D**   **E**   **F**

8

45

Dunster
Beach

7

Blue Anchor Bay

SEA LA

West Somerset Railway

44

SALTRY LA

Ker Moor

PH

6

KITROW LA

Blue
Anchor

LC

Blue Anchor

Home
Farm

Warren
Farm

A5
1 CHESTNUT CL
2 MILLETTS CL
3 CARANTOC PL
4 THE CRESCENT
5 WASSAIL CL
6 WOODLAND CL
7 CHURCH CL

HORSELAND LA

GROVES LA

GROVE RD

WOOD LA

CLEEVE PK

B3191

43

Townsend
Farm

TENYARD
COTTS

PH

B3191

SOUTHLANDS

Marshwood
Farm

Chapel
Cleeve

Kentsford
Farm

WINNIBROOK LA

PARK LA

PO

CHURCH LA

EASTBURY HILL

Carhampton

HIGH ST

Binham
Farm

Old
Cleeve

Bye
Farm

5

PARK LANE CL

WALNUT TREE DR

THE COURT

ORCHARD RD

1 CARHAMPTON CROSS
2 ORCHARD CL
3 VICARAGE RD
4 EASTBURY RD

MEADOWSIDE

HILL A

Linton

DAIRYLANDS

MONKS PATH

42

Kennels

BOWERHAYES LA

WITHYCOMBE LA

COURT PLACE LA

Briddicott
Farm

BRIDDICOTT LA

HILL LA

WITHYCOMBE
CROSS

TA24

BLACK MONKEY LA

+

CASTLE MEAD 1
CLAYDON CL 2
MONKSWAY 3
McKINLEY TERR 4
VERDUN TERR 5.

Old Cleeve
Fst Sch

4

Withycombe

WEST ST

MEADOW
COTTS

Washford

PH

Washford

Wildlife
Park

Withycombe
Hill

WELL ST

BATTLE
ROW

CULVER LA

WOOL LA

SANDHILL

MONKSWAY

STATION RD

PO

WALNUT TREE
CNR

B3190

BUCKHILL

Billbrook

Sandhill
Farm

SHEPHERD'S
CNR

QUARRY RD

A39

41

Combe
Farm

COMBE LA

Macmillan Way West

Hotel

DRAGON
CROSS

P

BELLE VUE

Hungerford

Cleeve
Abbey

WAY
TERR

WASHFORD
CROSS

3

HIGHER RODHUISH RD

SANDROCKS LA

ABBEY RD

Bardon

TA23

BEASTWAY LA

TORGLES LA

PH

Torre

RODHUISH HILL LA

Rodhuish

Escott
Farm

Lodge
Farm

LODGE ROCKS

Holy
Well

Cider
Farm

TORRE ROCKS

40

OAK LA

RODHUISH
CROSS

+

ROCKY LA

Beggearn
Huish

FAIR
CROSS

CRANSEY LA

2

FELON'S OAK LA

BLINDWELL LA

Golsoncott

CLITSOME
VIEW

Clitsome
Farm

B3188

STOUTS WAY LA

Felon's
Oak

BAKER'S LA

BRANDON LA

THE
CRESCENT

Lower
Roadwater

SLADE LA

Huish
Barton

Yarde

39

GREENLAND LA

BLINDWELL LA

MOUNT LA

MANOR
VIEW

+

VEMPLETT'S
CROSS

TA4

Croydon
Hall

WOODADVENT LA

B3190

1

Culverwell

PH

PO

Roadwater

HARPER'S LA

38

149

132

Scale: 1¾ inches to 1 mile

0   ¼   ½ mile

0   250m   500m   750m   1 km

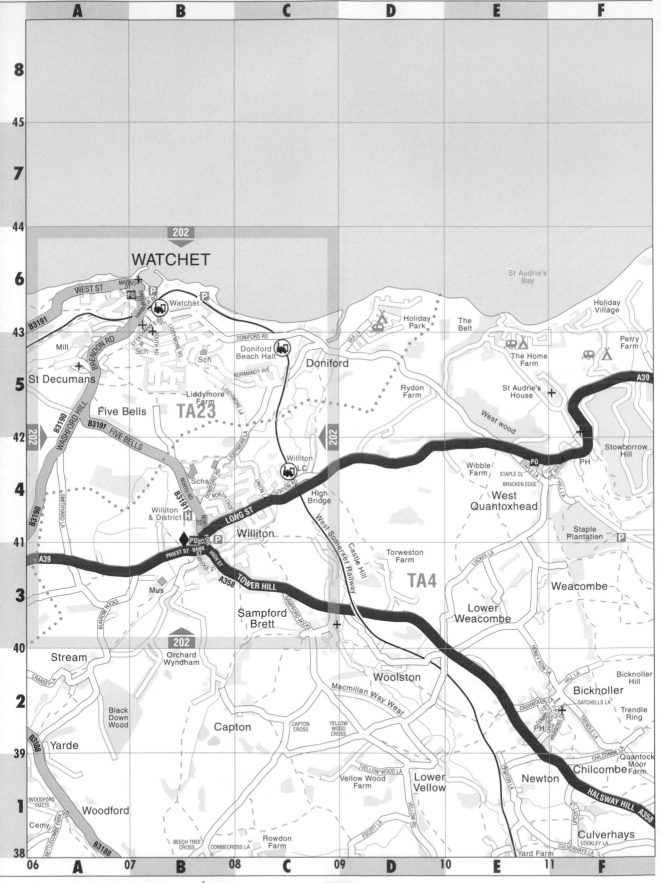

202

WATCHET

WEST ST

St Decumans

Mill

Five Bells

TA23

Liddymore Farm

B3191

B3190

202

WASHFORD HILL

B3191 FIVE BELLS

SMITHYARD LA

Williton & District

NORTH RD

DONIFORD RD

B3191

LONG ST

Williton

PRIEST ST

BANK

HIGH ST

A39

Mus

A358 TOWER HILL

SAMPFORD ROCKS

Sampford Brett

Stream

202

Orchard Wyndham

Black Down Wood

Capton

CAPTON CROSS

CRANSEY LA

B3188

Yarde

B3188

Woodford

NETTLECOMBE PARK RD

Cemy

WOODFORD COITS

BEECH TREE CROSS

COMBECROSS LA

Rowdon Farm

DONIFORD RD

Doniford Beach Halt

NORMANDY AVE

Doniford

LIDDYMORE LA

LIDDYMORE LA

Williton LC

STATION RD

UNION L

Schs

High Bridge

West Somerset Railway

Macmillan Way West

YELLOW WOOD CROSS

Yellow Wood Farm

YELLOW WOOD LA

Lower Vellow

VELLOW RD

ESCOTT LA

SEA LA

Holiday Park

Rydon Farm

Castle Hill

Torweston Farm

Woolston

202

St Audrie's Bay

The Belt

West wood

Wibble Farm

STAPLE CL

BRACKEN EDGE

West Quantoxhead

TA4

LUCKES LA

HONEY PION LA

Lower Weacombe

HILL LA

The Home Farm

St Audrie's House

PO

STAPLE LA

THE AVENUE

HILL LA

PH

Holiday Village

Perry Farm

A39

Stowborrow Hill

Staple Plantation

P

Weacombe

Bicknoller Hill

Bicknoller

GATCHELLS LA

Trendle Ring

DASHWOODS LA

PARSONS LA

COMBE LA

PH

TRENDLE LA

Newton

HALSWAY HILL A358

NEYTON LA

Chilcombe

COOKLEY LA

Quantock Moor Farm

CHILCOMBE LA

Culverhays

CULVERHAYS LA

Yard Farm

8

45

7

44

6

43

5

42

202

4

41

3

40

2

39

1

38

A   06   B   07   C   08   D   09   E   10   F   11

For full street detail of the highlighted area see page 202.

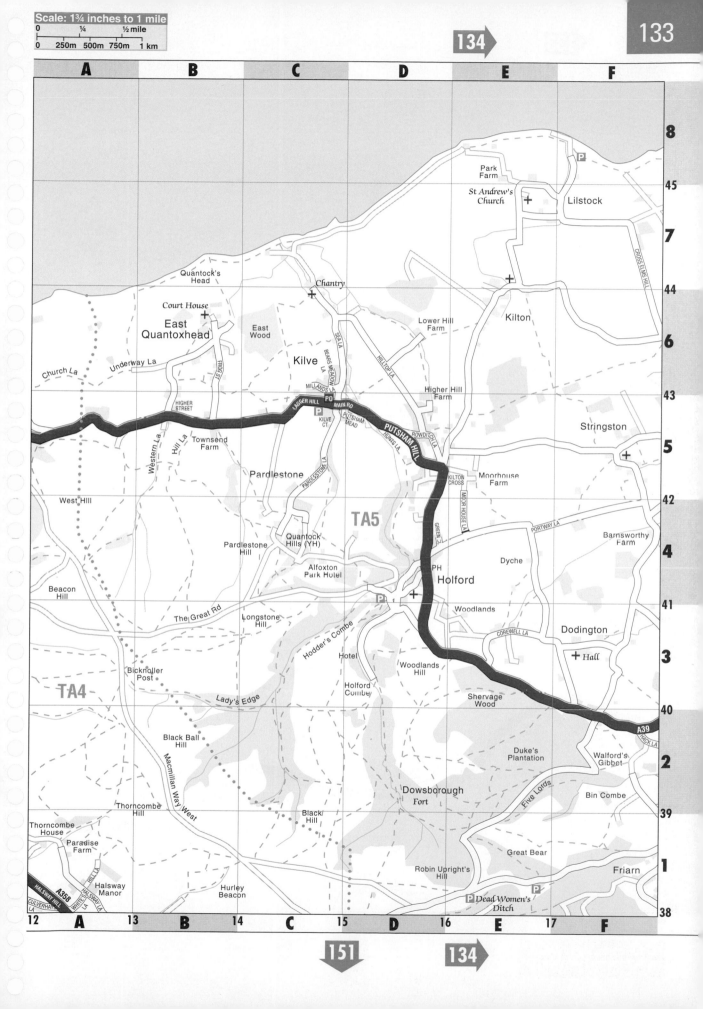

Scale: 1¾ inches to 1 mile

0   ¼   ½ mile
0   250m 500m 750m 1 km

134

A   B   C   D   E   F

8

Park
Farm

45

St Andrew's
Church
✝   Lilstock

7

Quantock's
Head   Chantry   44

CROSS ELMS HILL

Court House
✝   Kilton
East Quantoxhead   East
Wood   ✝

6

Church La   Underway La   Kilve   Lower Hill
Farm

SEA LA
BEARS MEADOW LA
FROG ST

HILLTOP LA

Higher Hill   43
Farm

Higher
Street   MILLANDS LA
LAGGER HILL   PO MAIN RD
P
Western La   Hill La   Townsend   KILVE   PUTSHAM
Farm   CT.   MEAD
PUTSHAM HILL   ROWDITCH LA

Stringston
✝

5

West Hill   Pardlestone   TUNTS LA
PARDLESTONE LA
KILTON
CROSS   Moorhouse
Farm

42

TA5

GREEN LA
MOOR HOUSE LA

PORTWAY LA   Barnsworthy
Farm

4

Pardlestone   Quantock
Hill   Hills (YH)

Dyche

Beacon
Hill   Alfoxton
Park Hotel   PH   Holford

41

The Great Rd   Longstone
Hill   P   ✝   Woodlands
Dodington

CORDWELL LA

Hodder's Combe   Hotel   Woodlands   ✝ Hall   3

Bicknoller
Post   Hill

TA4   Holford   Shervage
Lady's Edge   Combe   Woods
Wood

40

A39

HACK LA

Black Ball
Hill   Duke's
Plantation   Walford's
Gibbet   2

Macmillan Way West

Thorncombe
Hill   Black
Hill   Dowsborough   Five Lords   Bin Combe
Fort

39

Thorncombe
House   Hurley   Great Bear
Paradise   Beacon
Farm

Robin Upright's   Friarn   1

HALSWAY HILL
A358
HALSWAY LA
WHITE LA   Halsway Manor
CULVERHAYS LA   Hill La

P Dead Women's
Ditch   P

38

12   A   13   B   14   C   15   D   16   E   17   F

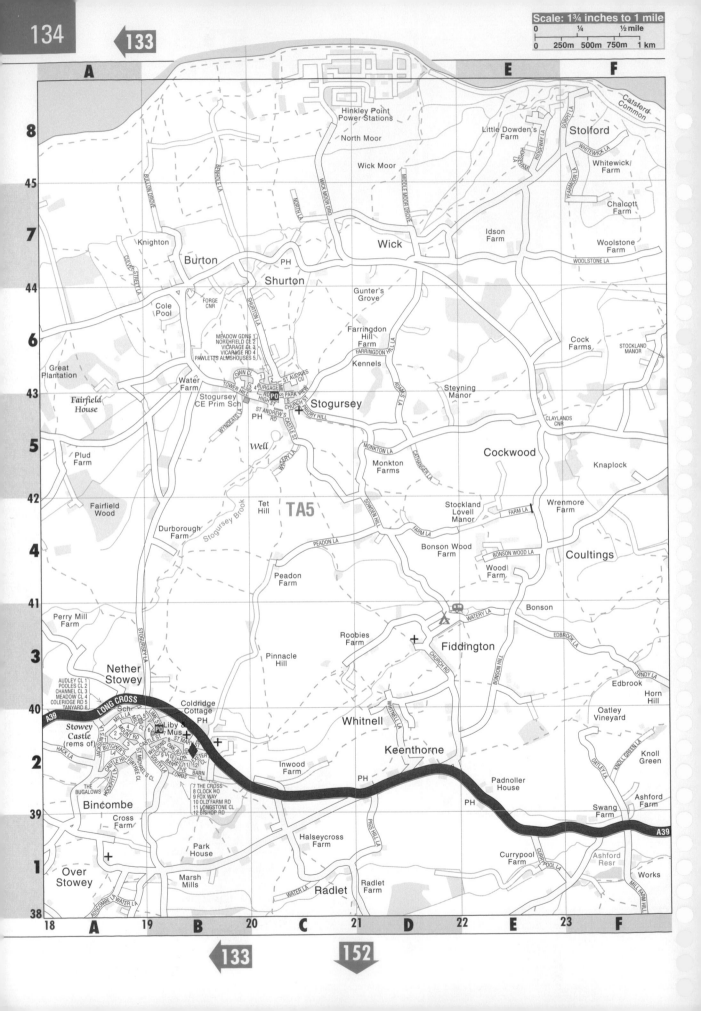

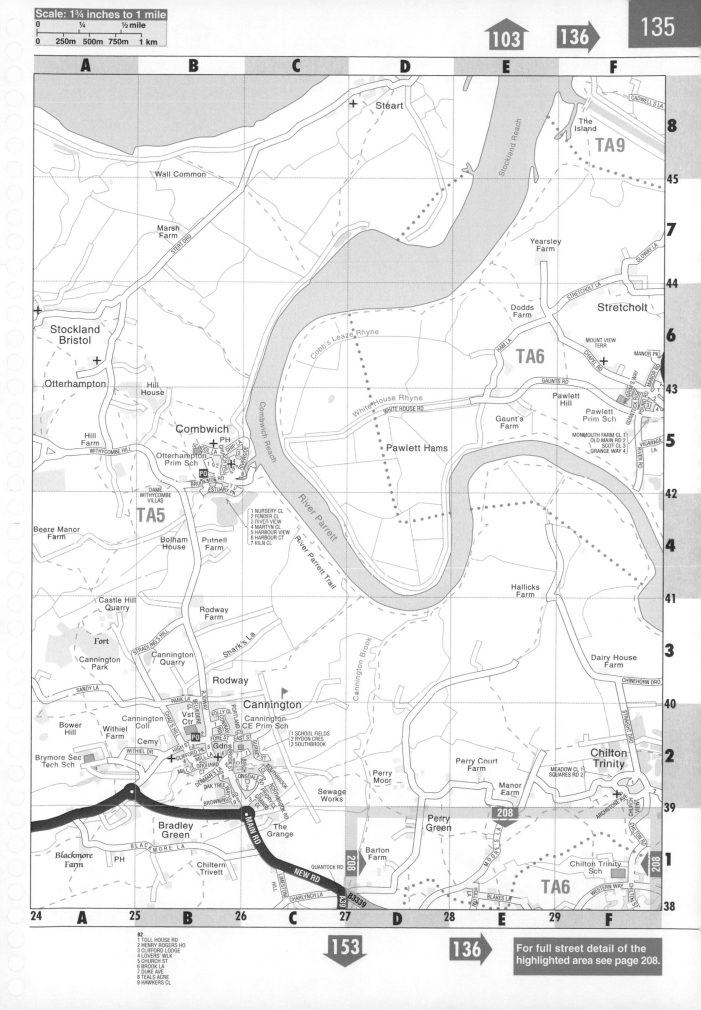

Scale: 1¾ inches to 1 mile

0   ¼   ½ mile
0   250m 500m 750m 1 km

CADWELL'S LA

The Island

TA9

Steart

Wall Common

Stockland Reach

Marsh Farm

STERT DRO

Yearsley Farm

SLOWAY LA

STRETCHOLT LA

Dodds Farm

Stretcholt

Stockland Bristol

HAM LA

TA6

MOUNT VIEW TERR

CHAPEL RD

MANOR PK

Otterhampton

Cobb's Leaze Rhyne

Hill House

GAUNTS RD

Pawlett Hill

PILGRIM'S WAY

MANOR RD

White House Rhyne

WHITE HOUSE RD

Pawlett Prim Sch

Hill Farm

WITHYCOMBE HILL

Combwich Reach

Combwich

PH

SHIP LA

SCHOOL LA

CHURCH HILL

RIVERSIDE

Gaunt's Farm

Pawlett Hams

MONMOUTH FARM CL 1
OLD MAIN RD 2
SCOT CL 3
GRANGE WAY 4

VICARAGE LA

RIVER RD

Otterhampton Prim Sch

PO

BROOKSIDE RD

ESTUARY PK

DAME WITHYCOMBE VILLAS

1 NURSERY CL
2 FENDER CL
3 RIVER VIEW
4 MARTYN CL
5 HARBOUR VIEW
6 HARBOUR CT
7 KILN CL

TA5

River Parrett

Beere Manor Farm

Bolham House

Putnell Farm

River Parrett Trail

Hallicks Farm

Castle Hill Quarry

Rodway Farm

Cannington Brook

Dairy House Farm

Fort

STRADLING'S HILL

Cannington Quarry

Shark's La

CHINEHORN DRO

Cannington Park

Rodway

STRAIGHT DRO

Cannington

SANDY LA

PARK LA

RODWAY

BELVEDERE CL

VST Ctr

Cannington CE Prim Sch

1 SCHOOL FIELDS
2 RYDON CRES
3 SOUTHBROOK

Chilton Trinity

Bower Hill

Cannington Coll

CHAD'S HILL

PO

FOLLY CL

PORTLAND CL

CONWAY RD

Perry Court Farm

MEADOW CL 1
SQUARES RD 2

Withiel Farm

Cemy

HIGH ST

FORE ST

EAST ST

GURNEY ST

Manor Farm

208

ARCHSTONE AVE

CHILTON ST

WITHIEL DR

CLIFFORD PK

MILL CL

ORCHARD

BRICK

SOUTHBROOK

Perry Moor

CHILTON RD

Brymore Sec Tech Sch

DENMAN'S LA

Gdns

LONSDALE CL

OAK TREE WAY

RUSTHOOK RD

PENRYN CL

Perry Green

HOLLOW LA

MOORE'S LA

Chilton Trinity Sch

WESTERN WAY

208

MAIN RD

Bradley Green

The Grange

Sewage Works

Barton Farm

TA6

BLACKMORE LA

Blackmore Farm

PH

Chiltern Trivett

QUANTOCK RD

208

NEW RD

LIMESTONE HILL

CHARLYNCH LA

B3339

BLAKES LA

B2
1 TOLL HOUSE RD
2 HENRY ROGERS HO
3 CLIFFORD LODGE
4 LOVERS' WLK
5 CHURCH ST
6 BROOK LA
7 DUKE AVE
8 TEALS ACRE
9 HAWKERS CL

For full street detail of the highlighted area see page 208.

A   B   C   D   E   F

8

45

7

44

6

43

5

42

4

41

3

40

2

39

1

38

Huntspill

Cadwell's La
Grange Rd
Millgreen Rd
Church Rd
Grove Rd
Silver St
Swell Cl
Ilex Cl
Sealey's Cl
Ringstone
Main Rd
A38
PO

1 Plymor Rd
2 Chapel Forge Cl
3 Sunny Cl
4 Greenwood Cl

Laburnum Lodges

Bleak Bridge

West Huntspill

Old Pawlett Rd
Pawlett Rd
Straight Dro
Rugg's Dro
Hardy Mead Dro

Newbridge La

Huntspill Level

Withy Rd

LC

Withy Gr

Withy Grove Farm

Withy Farm

Huntspill River

TA9

Black Ditch

Catherine St
New Rd
West Cornmoor Dro

East Huntspill Prim Sch
Hackness
PO
B3141
Factory La
Brue Bsns Pk
Moor Row
Hack Mead La
Mead Cl
Orchard Cl
Chapel La
Hackness Ter
Combe Ter
Merry La
Church La
Mill La
Church La
PH
Cornmoor Cres
1 Nut Tree Cl
2 Church Cl
3 Willow Cl
East Huntspill
Cote
White House La
Burtle Rd
Cote Cnr
Cornmoor Farm
Cornmoor La
Huntspill Moor
Gold Corner Dro

Causeway

Pyde Dro
Middle Moor Dro

Pawlett

Old Main Rd
PO
Vicars La
North Farm
Puriton Rd
Pawlett Mead Dro
Bannock Dro
Landfill Site
LC

Parsonage Ct 1
Court Gr 2
Pool Cl 3
Rookery Cl 4
Purewell 5
Walnut Cl 6

Batch Rd
North Mead Dro
Factory
Puriton Level

Moormead Dro
Woolavington Level

Walpole
Motte & Baileys
Downend Terr
Downend Rd
Downend Cres
Church Field La
Batch
Rye
Middle Cl
Cann's La
Waterloo
Waterloo Cl
Puriton
PO
Riverton Rd
Rowlands Rise
Hillside Rise
Cypress Dr
Maple Cl
Puriton La
West Approach Rd
Woolavington Rd
East Approach Rd

7 Hillside Dr
8 Hillside Cres
9 Rowan Cl
10 Birch Ave
11 Maple Cl
12 Manse La
13 Spring Rise
14 Elm Lea Cl

Puriton Prim Sch

Mortimer
Hectors Stones
Crockers La
Lower Rd
Higher Rd
Cherry
Kinder La
Causeway Cl
Cl
School La
Reeds Dro
Elm La
Lockswell
Chilpitts
Dawbins Dr
1 The Drive
2 Church St
3 Vicarage Rd
Woolavington

Woolavington Village Prim Sch

Combe La

Bawden
Highcroft
Mount Pleasant
Meadway
Kinglake
Well Way
Holly Cl
Sedgemoor Rd
Highfield
Southend
Cossington La
Woolavington Hill
Tor View
4 Crossmead
5 Clark Cl
6 Broadlawn
7 Mount View
8 Hillsboro
9 Orchard Way
Brent Rd
Park Cres
Manor Cl
St Mary's Cl
Station Rd
Perip
Millmoot
Millmoot La
Middle Rd

23

A38
A39
A39
Bristol Rd
Station Rd
Webbers Way
Puriton Hill
Puriton Hill

Down End
Ind Est
Factory
Dunball

TA6
River Parrett
Chinefd
Horsey Pill

The Polden Bsns Ctr

TA5
Squares Rd

Sewage Works
Ind Est
209

Crypton Tech Bsns Pk
Wylds Rd
Works
A38

The Wireworks Est
Sedgemount Ind Pk
209
Bower La
Whitrow Rd
A39
M5

Horsey La

Manor Farm
Horsey Level
Horsey
Marsh La

Knowle Hall
Knowle
Crandon Bridge
A39
Bath Rd
PH

TA7

BRIDGWATER
Side La
Gredoy La
Slape Cross
209
Bradney La
West End Ct
Bradney
Peasey Farm

Martland Cl 10
Polden Wlk 11
Windmill Cres 12
Bitham Wlk 13
Mill Wlk 14
B3141
Maple Tree Ct 1
The Copse 2
Walnut La 3

Cossington
Cossington Prim Sch
Manor Rd
PO

New Rd
Little Wall La
Greenfield Rd
Church Wlk
St Michaels Ct
Bawdrip La
Church Wlk
South View
Stone Dro
Kingsmoor Prim Sch
Bawdrip
Bawdrip Level
Brook La
Eastside La
King's Farm
Thistledoo Vine
A39
Pendon Hill
Wood La

A   B   C   D   E   F
30   31   32   33   34   35

For full street detail of the highlighted area see page 209.

135   154

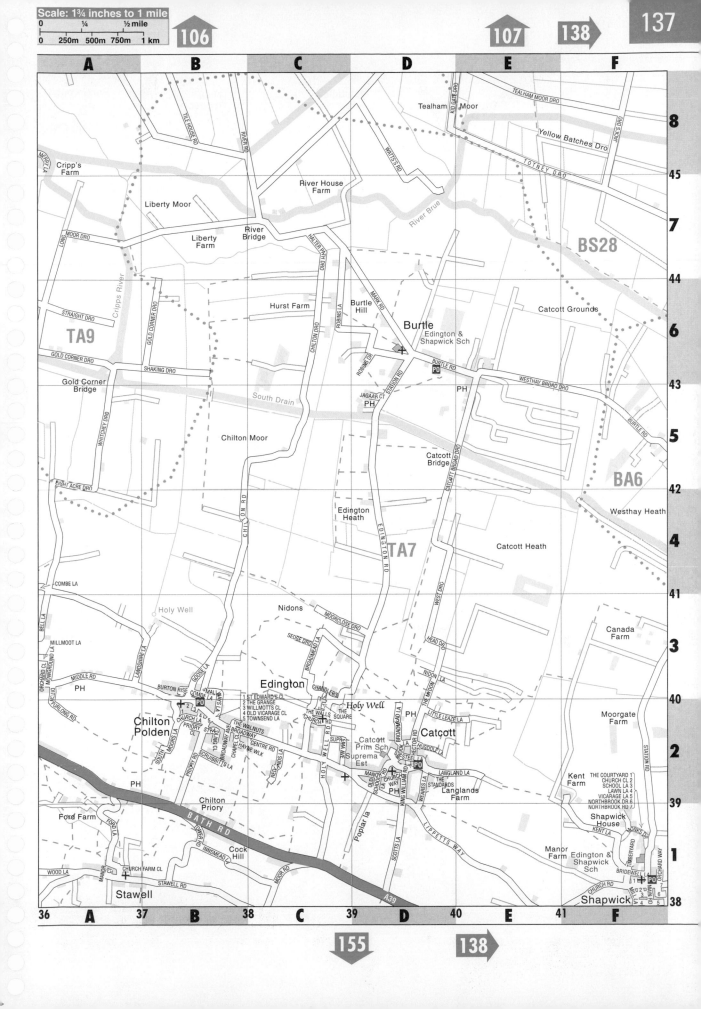

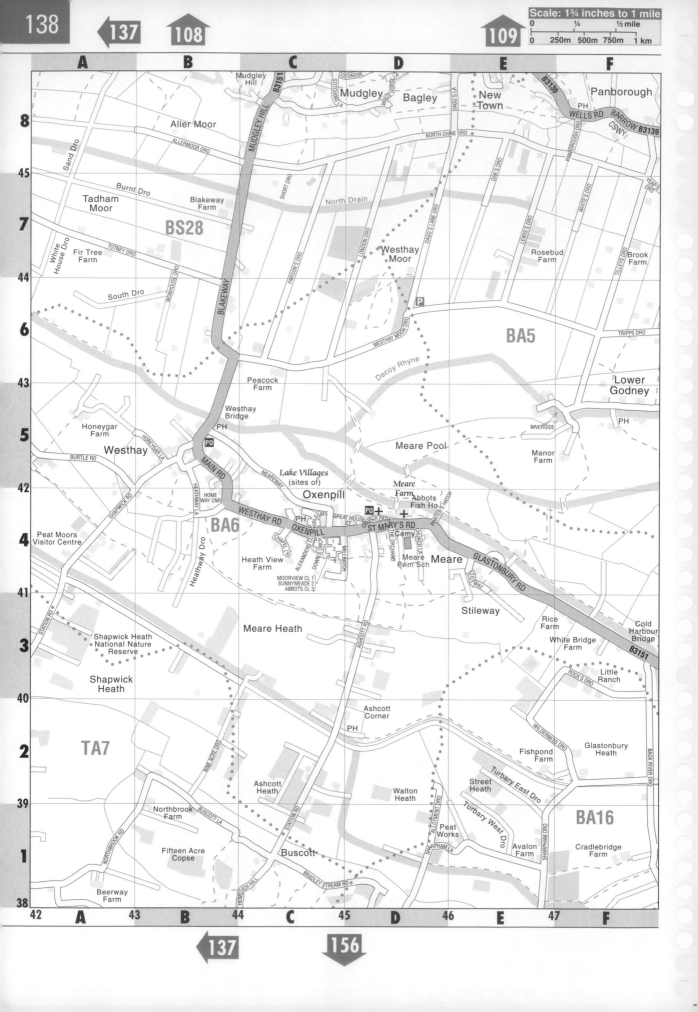

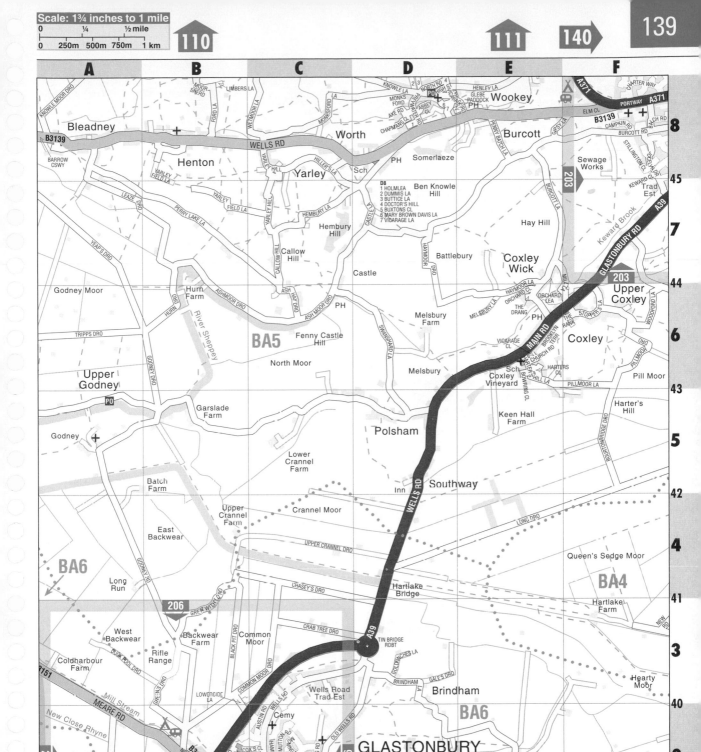

B3139 Bleadney

Henton

Worth

Wookey

PORTWAY A371

Burcott

Sewage Works

Trad Est

45

Yarley

Somerlaeze

Hiller's La

Sch

PH

Ben Knowle Hill

D8
1 HOLMLEA
2 DUMMIS LA
3 BUTTICE LA
4 DOCTOR'S HILL
5 BUXTONS CL
6 MARY BROWN DAVIS LA
7 VICARAGE LA

Hay Hill

7

Hembury Hill

Callow Hill

Castle

Battlebury

Coxley Wick

Hurn Farm

Melsbury Farm

The Drang

PH

Upper Coxley

203

44

Godney Moor

BA5

Fenny Castle Hill

North Moor

Melsbury

Coxley Vineyard

Coxley

Pill Moor

6

MAIN RD

Pillmoor La

43

Upper Godney

PO

Garslade Farm

Polsham

Keen Hall Farm

Harter's Hill

Godney

Lower Crannel Farm

Southway

Inn

WELLS RD

5

Batch Farm

Upper Crannel Farm

Crannel Moor

42

BA6

East Backwear

UPPER CRANNEL DRO

Queen's Sedge Moor

BA4

4

Long Run

206

Hartlake Bridge

Hartlake Farm

41

West Backwear

Backwear Farm

Common Moor

CRAB TREE DRO

A39

Tin Bridge RDBT

Brindham

Hearty Moor

3

Coldharbour Farm

Rifle Range

Wells Road Trad Est

Brindham

BA6

40

MEARE RD

B3751

Cemy

Old Wells Rd

GLASTONBURY

Wick

Norwood Park

2

206

Lower New Close

Higher New Close

Schs

PO

206

Stone Down Hill

39

BA16

New Close Farm

Liby Mus

Schs

PO

Bove Town

Glastonbury Tor

East Street La

Beckery

Sch

TH

Abbey

Chalice Well

East Street

1

Cradle Bridge

A39

STREET RD

BERE LA

CHILKWELL ST

COURSING BATCH

Mus

Edgarley

Sewage Works

Northover

A361

EDGARLEY RD

A361

38

48   A   49   B   50   C   51   D   52   E   53   F

For full street detail of the highlighted areas see pages 203 and 206.

157   140

140

139   112   113

Scale: 1¾ inches to 1 mile
0   ¼   ½ mile
0   250m   500m   750m   1 km

A   B   C   D   E   F

8

Schs
A39
PORTWAY
A371
STRAWBERRY WAY
A39
BURCOTT RD
CHAMBERLAIN ST
CATHEDRAL GN
TOR ST
HIGH ST
CHESTER ST
SILVER ST
Liby
Cath
Palace
Mus
B3139
TORHILL LA
BEKYNTON
KING'S CASTLE RD
Cemy
1 ALLENS LA
2 KEN CL
3 CREIGHTON CL
4 KINGS RD
Lyatt
CHILCOTE LA
CRAPNELL LA
Crapnell Farm

H
Sch
GLASTONBURY RD
A371
EAST SOMERSET WAY
WELLS
The Park
Park Wood
203
King's Castle
BA5
Sharcombe Park
Dinder Wood
LYATT LA
204
WESTLA
SLEIGHT LA
TRUFLE LA

45

A39
Keward
Monarch's Way
BISHOPS PARK WAY
203
Dulcote
B3139
Dinder
CHURCH LA
THE ROOKERY
LONG LA
RIVERSIDE
Croscombe
FAYRE WAY
PO
Sch
SHEPTON RD
A371
HAM LA

7

River Sheppey
203
Dulcote Hill
Dulcote Quarry
SHEPTON OLD RD
Church Hill
OLD WELLS RD
LONG ST
JACK LA
OLD ST

44

Woodford
WOODFORD RD
Wellesley Farm
Dungeon Farm
DUNGEON LA
STUMP CROSS
KNOWLE LA

6

Hill House Farm
LAUNCHERLEY CROSS
Twinhills Wood
RIDGE LA

43

Pill Moor
Launcherley
LAUNCHERLEY RD
Launcherley Hill
Worminster
Worminster Sleight
204
Knowle Farm
Knowle Hill

5

LONG DRO
North Wootton Vineyard
North Town
WORMINSTER BATCH
MILL LA
DARK LA
BACK LA
WES
COMPTON LA
West Compton

42

Greenacres
BARROW LA
Quaish Farm
QUAISH LA
MIDDLE LA
HIGH ST
STOCK'S LA
TANYARD LA
NORTHTOWN RD
North Wootton
BA4
Pilton Wood
SUMMERS HILL LA
WINTER LA
Burford

4

NEW RD
Barrow
SLOUGH LA
Edwicke Farm
CHURCH VIEW
CHESSELL LA
PH
PILTON HILL
Hearne House
Upper Westholme
HIGHER WESTHOLME RD
SLOURDY LA
BURFORD CROSS
BOWERMEAD LA
Pilton
A361
Cemy
NEAT LA

41

Hearty Gate Farm
Redlake Farm
Mead Lane
Lower Westholme
TANYARD LA
204
WHITSTONE HILL
POTTERDOWN LA
TOP ST
COPSE LA
PLATTERWELL LA

3

BROAD DRO
PENNARD LA
Westholme Lane
LOWER WESTHOLME RD
Whitelake
Perridge House
PERRIDGE HILL
PARK HILL
Pilton Manor Vineyard
MOUNT PLEASANT
HITCHEN LA
PYLLE RD
LOWER ST
Worthy Farm

1 PARSON'S BATCH
2 SHOP LA
3 CUMHILL HILL
4 WEIR LA
5 ST MARY'S LA
6 ABBOTS WAY
7 SHUTWELL LA
8 BARROW STILE
9 BAKERY LA
10 JOHN BEALES HILL
11 CULVERWELL COTTS
12 OATHILL COTTS

40

Hearty Moor
MEAD LA
PH
Steanbow
Pilton Park
WORTHY LA
COCKMILL LA

2

BA6
STOCKBRIDGE LA
PAGE LA
Laverley Cotts
SWIFT LA
Laverley
Monarch's Way
HOLT LA
Holt Farm
Manor Farm
STRADDLE LA
Steanbow Park Dairy Unit
King's Hill
Ford

39

LAUREL ST
EAST STREET LA
Piltown
MULBERRY FARM
COTTLES LA
STICKLINCH RD
Sticklinch
Stickleball Hill
COCKMILL LA

1

A361
PH
West Pennard
NEWTOWN LA
CHURCH LA
West Pennard CE Prim Sch
HILLSIDE
Southtown
WINDMILL LA
CASTLE LA
WORTHY LA
DOWN LA
Pennard Hill

38

BREECH LA
SOUTHTOWN LA

54   A   55   B   56   C   57   D   58   E   59   F

139   158

For full street detail of the highlighted area see pages 203 and 204.

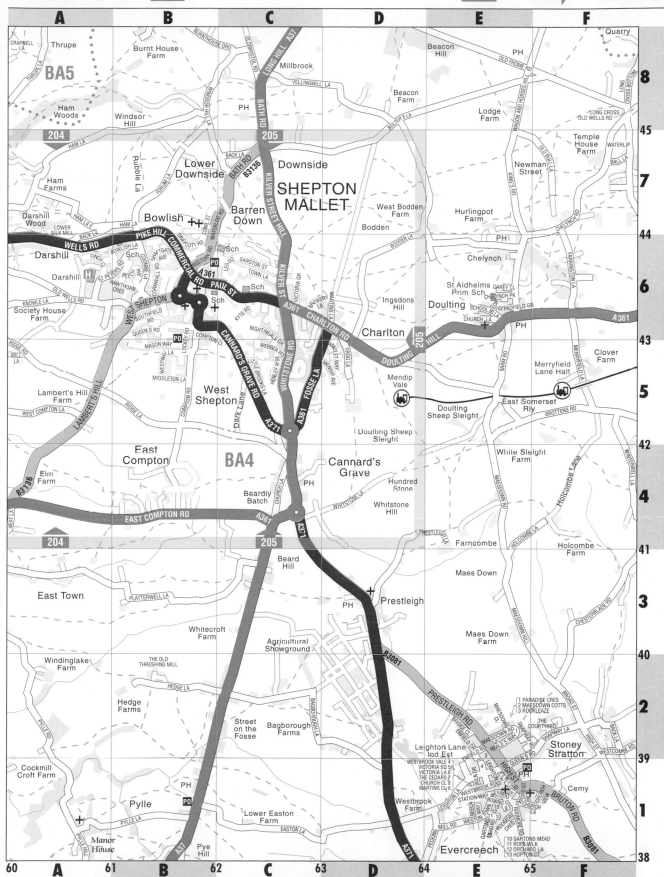

▼ 159   ▼ 142

For full street detail of the highlighted area see pages 204 and 205.

Scale: 1¾ inches to 1 mile
0   ¼   ½ mile
0   250m   500m   750m   1 km

BA3
LONG CROSS BOTTOM
Moons Hill Quarry
FENTAL LA
Downhead
LUXTON'S LA
POUND LA
Asham Wood
Westdown Quarry

OLD WELLS RD
Funtle La
Green Farm
Lodge Hill Farm
Asham Quarry
TUNSCOMBE LA

Cranmore Twr
Heale
Works
Tunscombe La
Heale Ladder

Waterlip
DALLIMORE LA
Merehead Quarry
Steart's La
A361
BA11

Dean Farm
THE ROCKS
Dean
FURZECLOSE LA
SLAIT HILL

Dean Bottom
PAWELSKI CL
TURNPIKE LA
East Cranmore
Works
BACK ST
Leighton

CASTLE LA
TANSEY
MARTINS PADDOCK
COOK'S LA
CRANE COTTS
V.S
PIERS RD
All Hallows Prep Sch
Larkleaze Hanging
Works
CHOVEL LA
Beans Land Farm

A361
OLD DOWN LA
Cranmore
LC
LONG LA
A359

East Somerset Rly
Cranmore West
Southill Ho
Monk Wood
Coldharbour
Mitchells Elm Farm
COVEYHILL LA

Home Farm
WITHY WOOD LA
BRICKYARD LA

BROTERS RD
Southill Farm
Harwood Farm
NEW RD
Weston Town
LOWER LA

WINTERWELL LA
Brickhouse Farm
BREACH LA
CHURCH ST
THE STREET
1 FROG LA
2 ST MARYS PL
3 WESLEY CL
4 CORONATION CL
5 STUDLEY MDWS

Chesterblade
BA4
Higher Alham
Lodge Farm
Breach Wood
LC
TOWER VIEW
MEAD LA
BRIDGE HILL
STUDLEY LA
PH
Wanstrow

CHESTERBLADE RD
Sleight Farm
STATION RD
Studley Farm

Small Down Knoll
Lower Alham Farm
Horsehill Farm
HORSEHILL LA
KNOLL LA
BURT'S HILL
STUDLEY LA

Small Down Farm
SMALL DOWN LA
GREEN LA
Lower Eastcombe Farm
EASTCOMBE LA
BULL'S LA
DARK LA
Wet La
Upton Noble

Westcombe
WESTCOMBE HILL
Walter's Hill
COCKPIT LA
Fry's La
KALE ST
LINCH
MILLARD'S HILL
HINCOMBE HILL
GUNNING'S LA
PO
CHURCH ST
TOP LOWER ST
PH
CHAPEL
BRUTON LA

WESTCOMBE RD
BAILEY'S LA
BACK LA
PH
GOLD HILL
MILL LA
Kale Street Cotts
Upton Noble Prim Sch
STRAP LA

Fosscombe
SPARGROVE LA
HOLLOW LA
Batcombe
SEAT LA
GOOD HILL
Folly Farm
BA10
Brewhamfield Farm

Hillview Farm
Rockwells Farm
Saite Farm
MOOR LA

CROW'S HILL
PORTWAY HILL
Portway Farm
A359
HASSOCK'S LA

River Alham
Spargrove

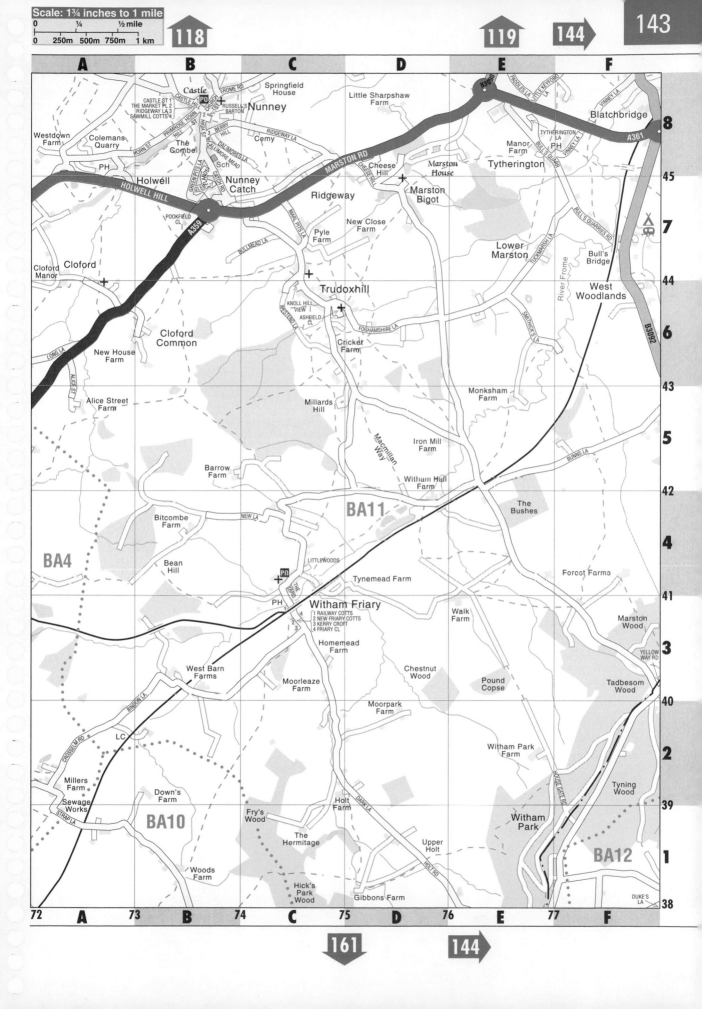

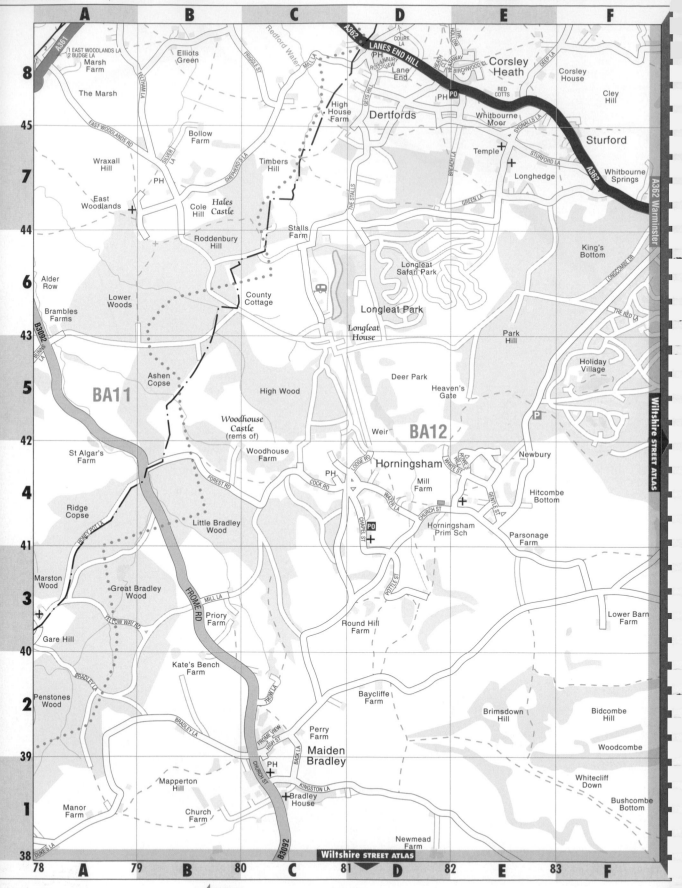

Scale: 1¾ inches to 1 mile
0   ¼   ½ mile
0 250m 500m 750m 1 km

A **B** **C** **D** **E** **F**

A362

1 EAST WOODLANDS LA
2 BUDGE LA
Marsh Farm

Elliots Green

LANES END HILL

COURT LA

THE HOLLOW

Corsley Heath

Corsley House

Cley Hill

8

The Marsh

FELTHAM LA

Redford Water

FRIGGLE ST

MILL LA

High House Farm

Dertfords

PH

GEE'S HILL

KENBURY VIEW

Lane End

PH
PO
RED COTTS

Whitbourne Moor

SYDNALLS LA

45

EAST WOODLANDS RD

Bollow Farm

SHEPHERD'S LA

Timbers Hill

Temple

Longhedge

STURFORD LA

Sturford

A362

Whitbourne Springs

7

Wraxall Hill

SILVER LA

PH

Cole Hill

Hales Castle

Stalls Farm

THE STALLS

BREACH LA

GREEN LA

A362 Warminster

44

East Woodlands

Roddenbury Hill

County Cottage

Longleat Safari Park

King's Bottom

Wiltshire STREET ATLAS

6

Alder Row

Lower Woods

Longleat Park

Longleat House

Park Hill

THE RED LA

LONGCOMBE DR

Brambles Farms

B3092

BURNS LA

43

Ashen Copse

Deer Park

Heaven's Gate

Holiday Village

5

BA11

High Wood

Weir

BA12

P

42

St Algar's Farm

Woodhouse Castle (rems of)

Woodhouse Farm

FOREST RD

COCK RD

PH

LODGE RD

Horningsham

WHITE ST

ROWE'S
Newbury

Hitcombe Bottom

Mill Farm

4

Ridge Copse

HONEYCOTT LA

Little Bradley Wood

WATER LA

CHURCH ST

PO

Horningsham Prim Sch

GENTLE ST

Parsonage Farm

41

Marston Wood

Great Bradley Wood

FELLOW WAY RD

FROME RD

MILL LA

Priory Farm

Round Hill Farm

Lower Barn Farm

3

BRADLEY LA

Gare Hill

Kate's Bench Farm

40

Penstones Wood

BRADLEY LA

Baycliffe Farm

Brimsdown Hill

Bidcombe Hill

2

ROW LA

FROME VIEW

HIGH ST

BACK LA

Perry Farm

Woodcombe

39

Mapperton Hill

CHURCH ST

PH

Maiden Bradley

KINGSTON LA

Whitecliff Down

1

Manor Farm

Church Farm

Bradley House

Newmead Farm

Bushcombe Bottom

DUKE'S LA

B3092

38

A 78 **B** 79 80 **C** 81 **D** 82 **E** 83 **F**

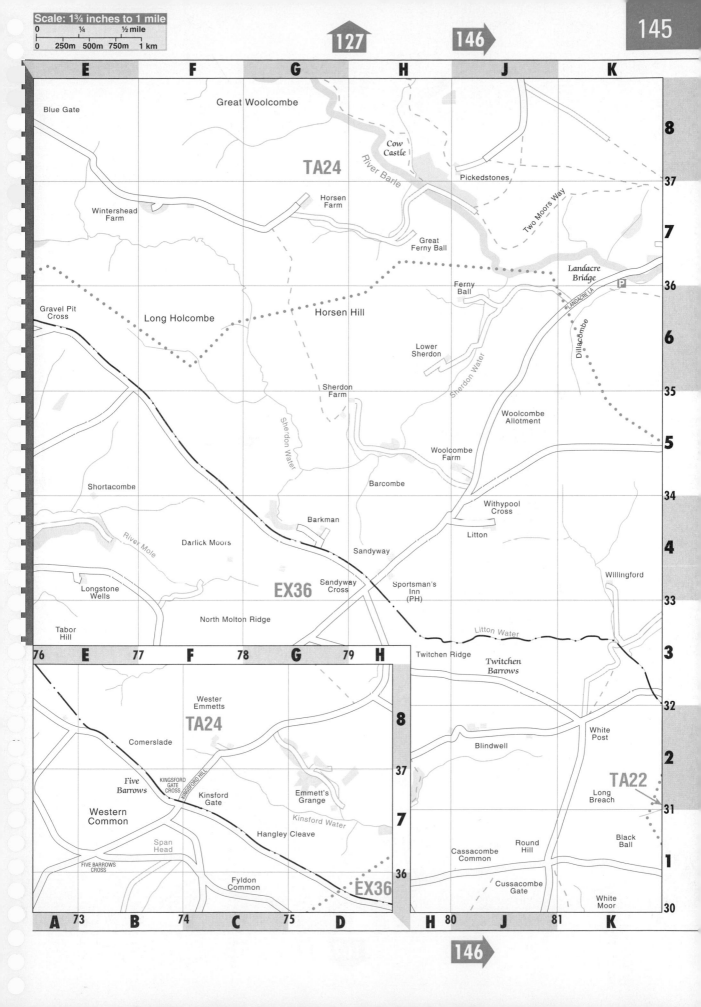

Scale: 1¾ inches to 1 mile
0   ¼   ½ mile
0   250m 500m 750m 1 km

127   146

E   F   G   H   J   K

Blue Gate

Great Woolcombe

8

Cow
Castle

TA24

River Barle

37

Pickedstones

Two Moors Way

7

Horsen
Farm

Wintershead
Farm

Great
Ferny Ball

Landacre
Bridge

P

36

Ferny
Ball

LANDACRE LA.

Gravel Pit
Cross

Long Holcombe

Horsen Hill

Dillacombe

6

Lower
Sherdon

Sherdon Water

35

Sherdon
Farm

Woolcombe
Allotment

5

Sherdon Water

Woolcombe
Farm

Shortacombe

Barcombe

34

Withypool
Cross

Barkman

River Mole

Darlick Moors

Litton

4

Sandyway

EX36

Sandyway
Cross

Sportsman's
Inn
(PH)

Willingford

33

Longstone
Wells

North Molton Ridge

Litton Water

Tabor
Hill

3

76   E   77   F   78   G   79   H

Twitchen Ridge

Twitchen
Barrows

32

Wester
Emmetts

White
Post

TA24

8

2

Comerslade

Blindwell

37

TA22

Five
Barrows

KINGSFORD
GATE
CROSS

Kinsford
Gate

KINGSFORD HILL

Emmett's
Grange

Long
Breach

31

Western
Common

7

Kinsford Water

Span
Head

Hangley Cleave

Round
Hill

Black
Ball

1

Cassacombe
Common

FIVE BARROWS
CROSS

36

Fyldon
Common

EX36

Cussacombe
Gate

White
Moor

30

A   73   B   74   C   75   D   H   80   J   81   K

146

Scale: 1¾ inches to 1 mile

0 ¼ ½ mile
0 250m 500m 750m 1 km

A B C D E F

8

Pennycombe Water

Chibbet
CHIBBET HILL
Chibbet Post
B3223
Court Farm

Buckworthy

37

Road Castle
Lyncombe

SHADDON HILL RD

Herne's Barrow

Halsgrove Farm

Blacklands

ROOM HILL RD

Road Hill

7 TA24

Lanacre
Hillway

LANACRE LA

WOOLPIT LA

SPARROW LA

Weatherslade
Foxwitchen

Room Hill

Nethercote

KITRIDGE LA

36

Brightworthy

Withypool

Newland
PH

Comer's Cross
ASH LA

Great Ash

6

Knighton

PO

King's Farm

Uppington

Comer's Gate

Waterhouse Farm

MOORFIELD GDN

South Hill

35

Withypool Common

Withypool Hill

Winsford

Knigthon Combe

Stone Circle

Batsom Farm

Wambarrows
B3223

5

Great Bradley

34

Worth Hill

West Water

Two Moors Way

River Barle

Two Moors Way

4

EX36

Porchester Post

WORTH LA

Worth
Westwater Farm

Knaplock

Liscombe

Westwater Allotment

33

Humber's Ball

Parsonage Down

Tarr Farm

P Little River

3

Hawkridge Plain

Old Barrow

Hill Farm

Parsonage Farm

Tarr Steps
Hotel

STONY LA

32

Clogg's Down

Hawkridge Common

MARSH LANE HILL

Ashway Side

2

Moorhouse Ridge

Cloggs Farm

TA22

Ashway

31

Lyshwell Farm

Shircombe Farm

HAWKRIDGE CROSS

Hawkridge
PO

Hawkridge Ridge

Slade

1

BROAD LANE HEAD

SLADE LA

BROAD LA

Hollowcombe

Dane's Brook

YENFORD HILL

Eve Valley Way

30

82 A 83 B 84 C 85 D 86 E 87 F

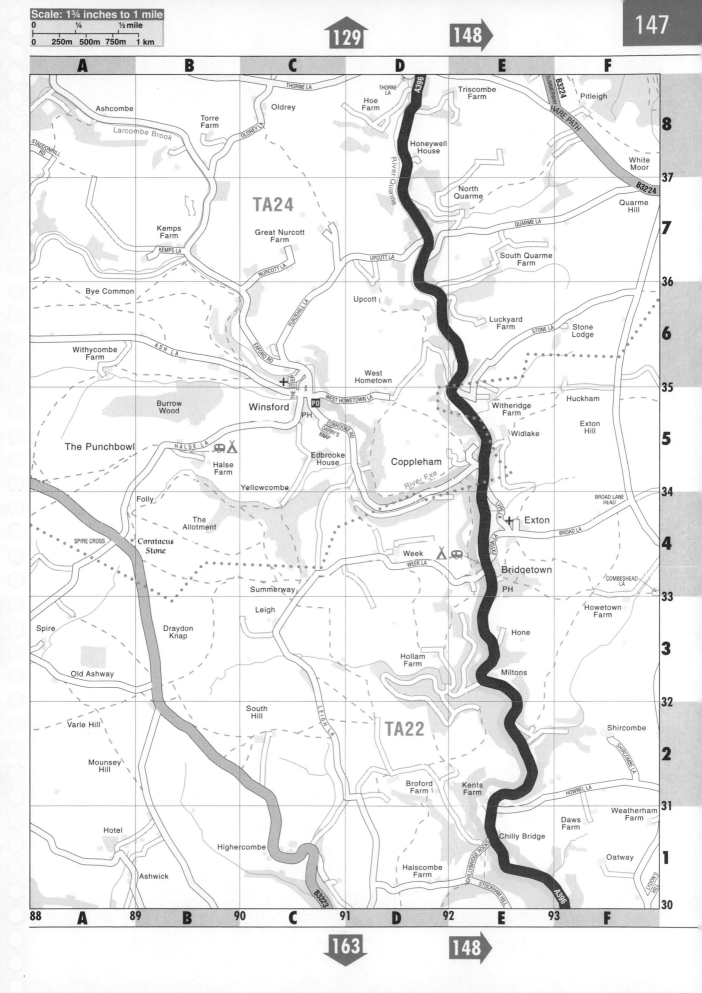

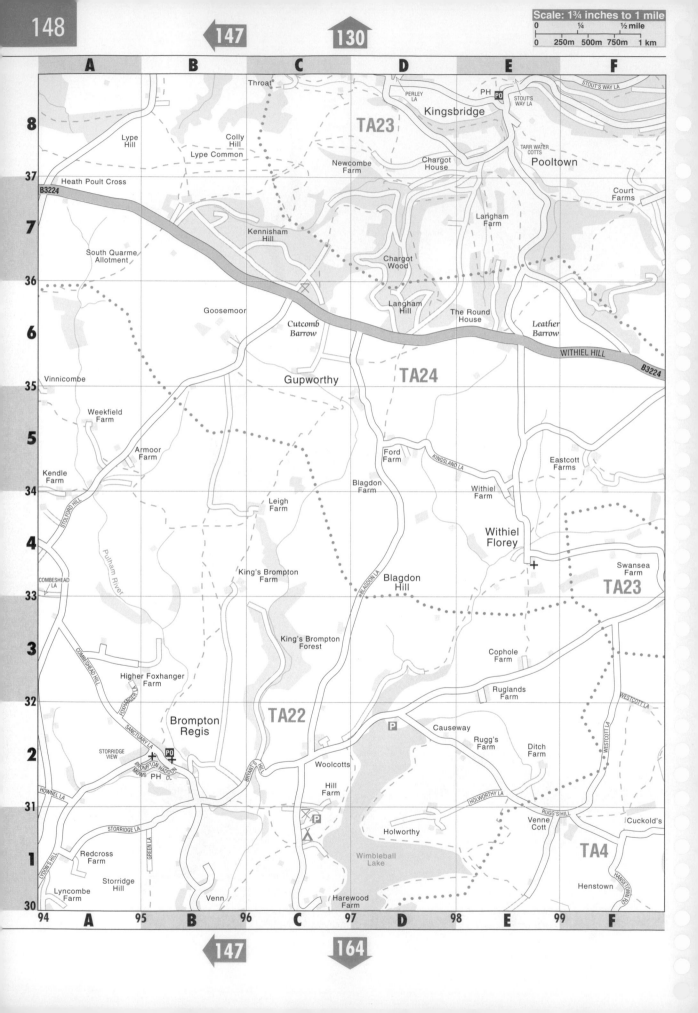

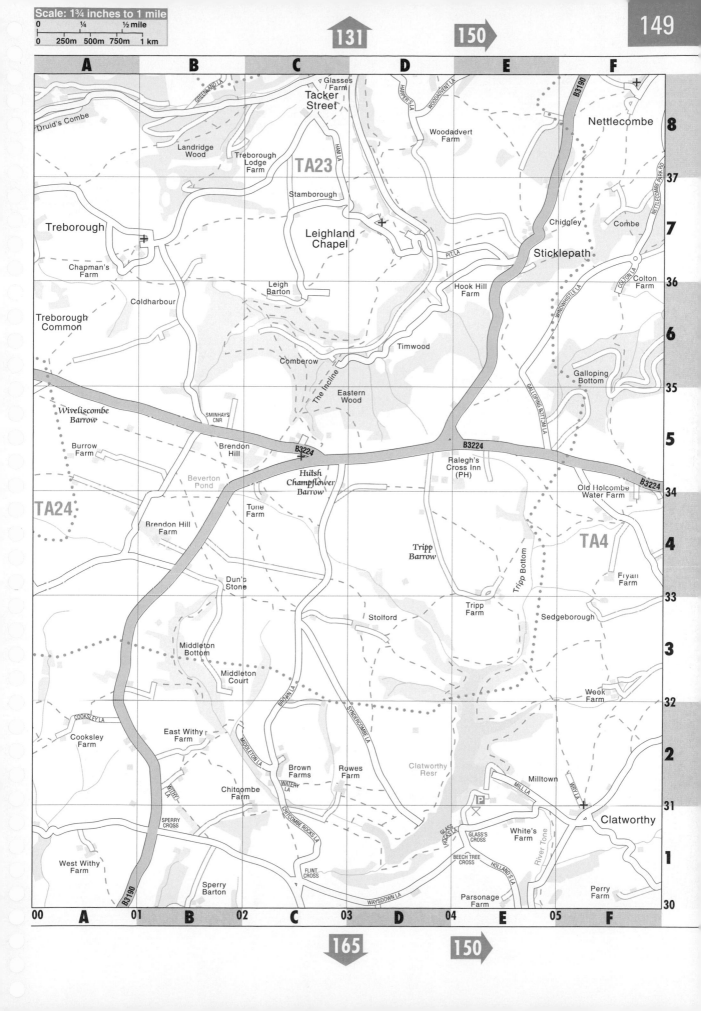

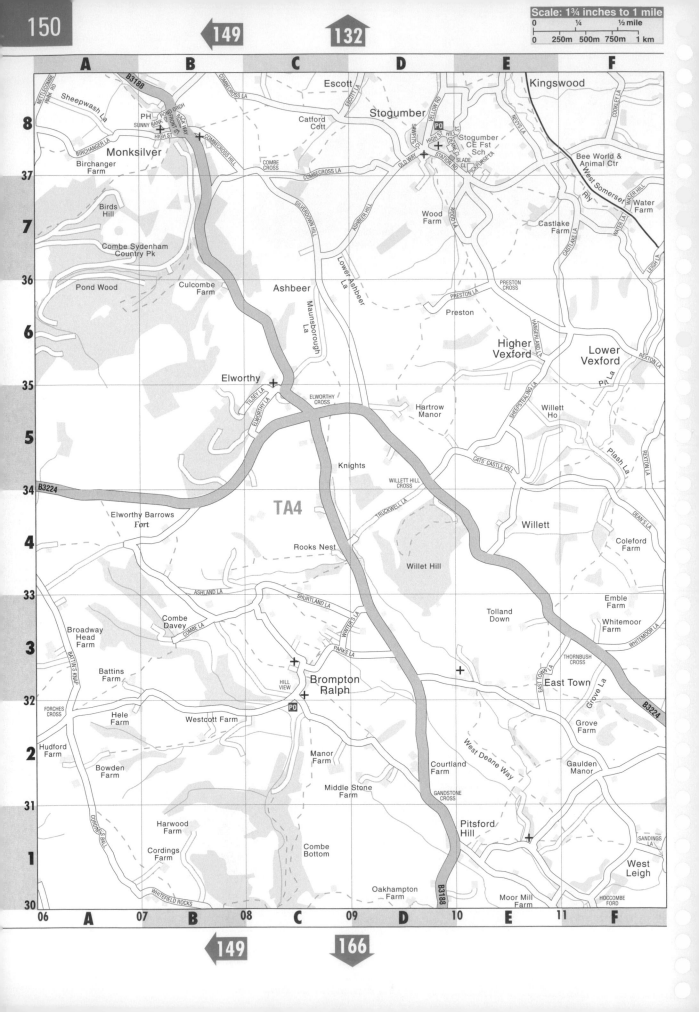

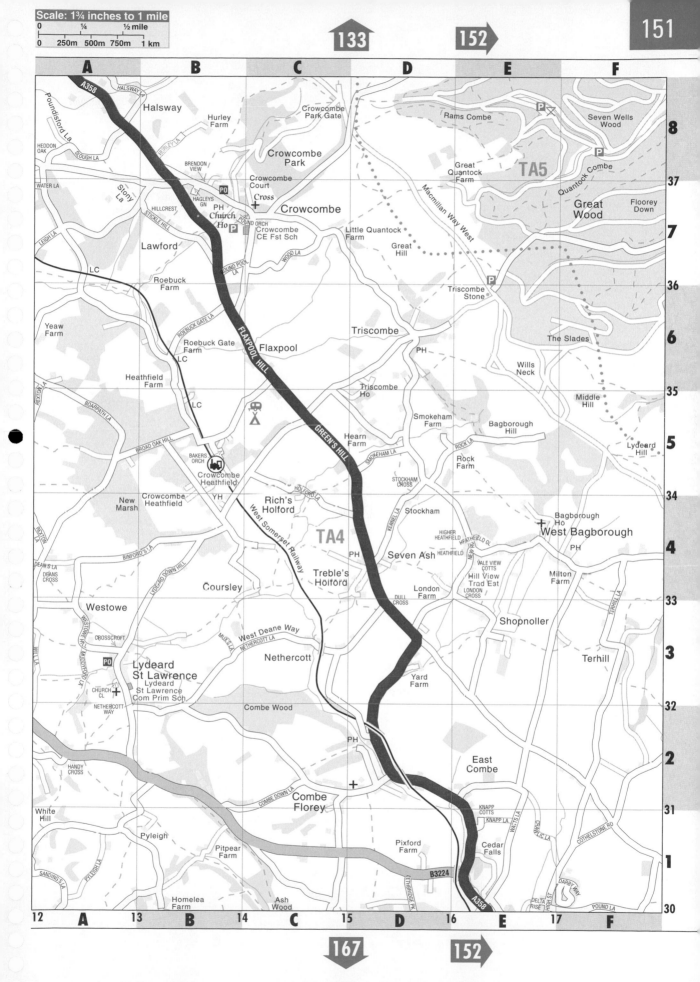

151
134

Scale: 1¾ inches to 1 mile

0   ¼   ½ mile
0   250m 500m 750m 1 km

A **B** **C** **D** **E** **F**

8

Aley
Adscombe
ADSCOMBE LA
Quantock Lodge
Pepper Hill
Rowdens Farm
Radlet Common
The Gables
CUCKOLD'S ROW
Splatt
Spaxton
Charlyneh
MILL FARM HILL
CHARLYNCH HILL

37

Tuxwell Farm
Ebsley Farm
PEARTWATER HILL
PEARTWATER LA
CHURCH RD
SPLATT LA
Spaxton CE Prim Sch
HIGH ST
FOUR FORKS LA
BARFORD CL
PH
Holmes Farm
Four Forks
Postridge Farm
CHARLYNCH RD

7

Round Hill
Plainsfield
PARSONS LA
BROOMFIELD HILL / BROOMYLAND HILL
Hawkridge Resr
LAWYER'S HILL
TWINELL LA
BUSH RD
VICTORIA WAY
Bush
Stephens Farm
Tutton's Farm
PIGHTLEY RD
Durleigh Brook
BARFORD RD

36

Aisholt Wood
Hawkridge Common
BEECH TREE HILL
MERRIDGE HILL
BUSH LA
Pightley
PIGHTLEY LA
Barford House

6

Aisholt Common
Aisholt
Durborough Farm
Lower Aisholt
ELWS LA
BLACKMOOR LA
Enmore Castle

35

Luxborough Farm
GOOD'S LA
PARISH LAND LA
Holwell Combe
NO PLACE LA
Enmore CE Prim Sch
ENMORE RD

5

Bishpool Farm
Good's Farm
Lower Merridge
Merridge
Great Holwell
Smocombe House
Wind Down
Broomfield Hall
Higher Heathcombe Farm

34

BIRCHES CNR
Gib Hill
THREE HORSE SHOES HILL
Tudball
Courtway
TA5
Ruborough Camp
WATERY LA

4

Kenley Bottom
Park End
PH
Rockhouse Farm

33

Twenty Acre Plantation
Merridge Hill
Timbercombe
Broomfield Hill
LYDEARD CROSS
Lydeard Farm
Bolts
SELBY LA
SHELTHORNE

3

COTHELSTONE RD
Cothelstone Hill
TA4
Buncombe Wood
BUNCOMBE HILL
Westleigh Farm
Ducks' Pool
Lydeard Farm
Somerset Wildlife Trust
Fyne Court

32

Badger Copse
Holy Well
Ball Covert
MACMILLAN WAY WEST
BALL LA
Raswell Farm
Broomfield
Rose Hill
ROSE HILL
Wort Wood
Owls Hill Farm

2

Cothelstone Farm
Toulton
WEST DEAN WAY
CUSHUISH LA
Ivyton Farm
Row's Farm

31

Cothelstone
Cushuish
Beech Copse
Tanyard
Cheddon Down
Kingston Beacon
Yards

1

Middlebrooks
FENNINGTON LA
Tetton House
Tetton Farm
TA2
LODES LA
VOLIS CROSS
VOLIS HILL

30

18 **A** 19 **B** 20 **C** 21 **D** 22 **E** 23 **F**

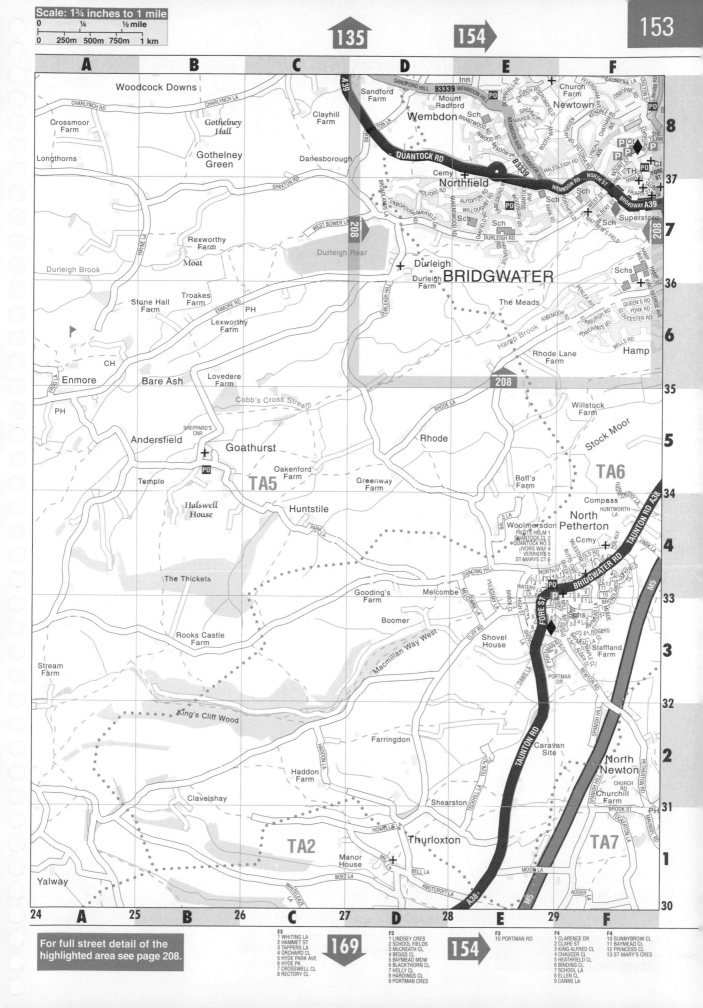

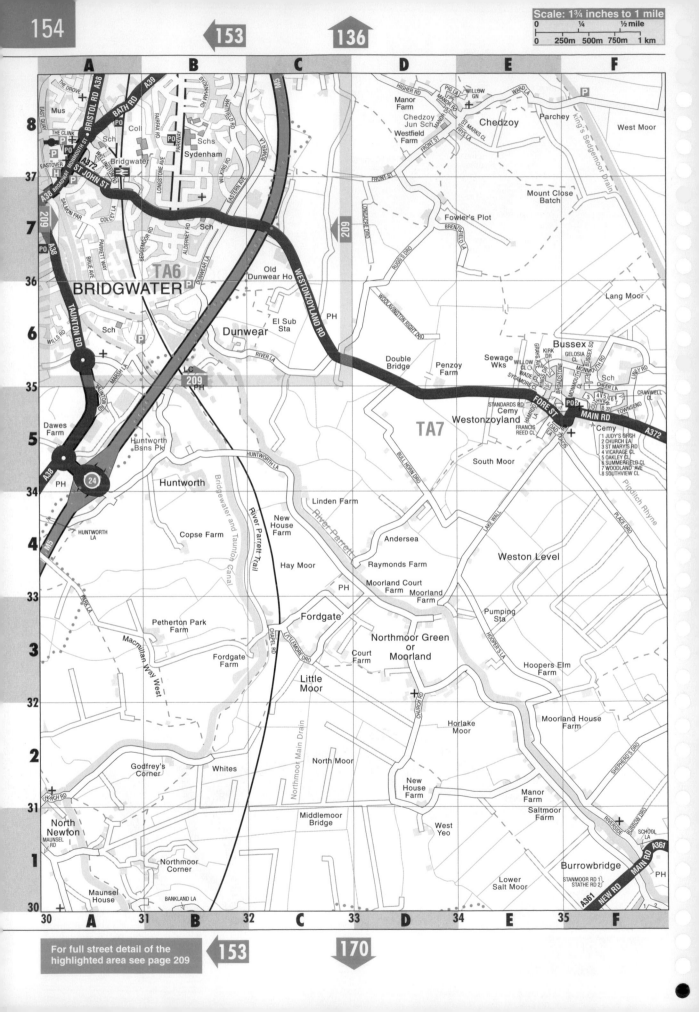

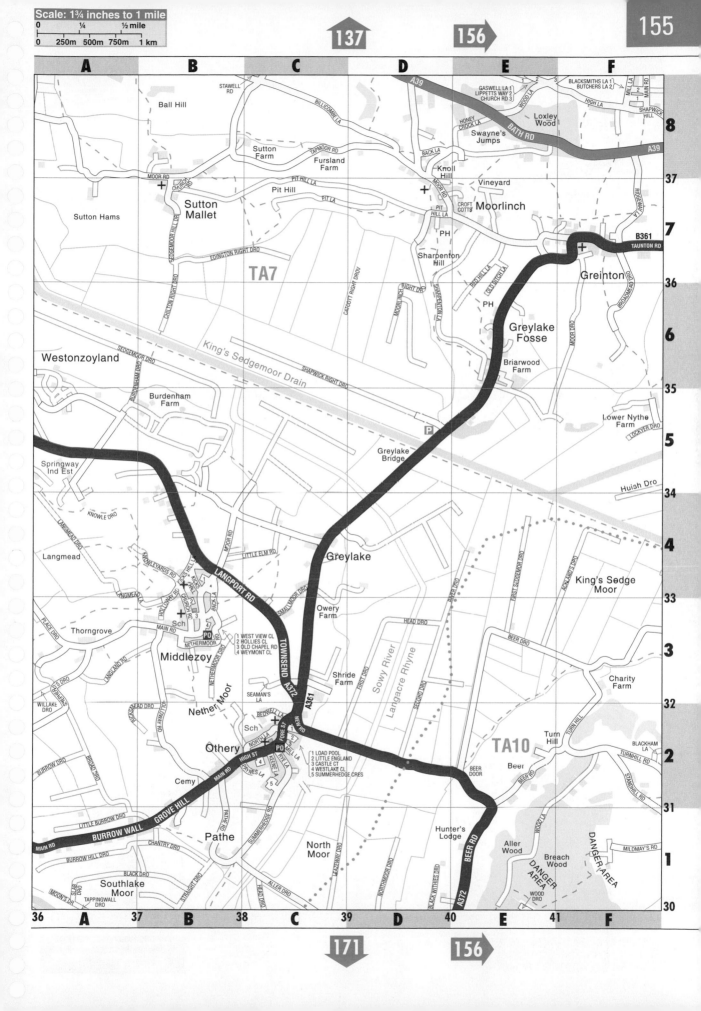

Scale: 1¾ inches to 1 mile

0   ¼   ½ mile
0   250m 500m 750m 1 km

137   156→

| A | B | C | D | E | F |

STAWELL RD

Ball Hill

Sutton Farm

BILLICOMBE LA

BACK LA

A39

GASWELL LA 1
LIPPETTS WAY 2
CHURCH RD 3

BLACKSMITHS LA 1
BUTCHERS LA 2

HONEY CROCK LA

BATH RD

Loxley Wood

HIGH LA

MILL LA
MAIN RD

SHAPWICK HILL

WOOD LA

Swayne's Jumps

A39

8

TAPMOOR RD

Sutton Farm

Fursland Farm

Knoll Hill

37

MOOR RD
CHURCH RD

PIT LA

MOOR RD

Vineyard

Moorlinch

RIDGEWAY LA

Sutton Mallet

Pit Hill

PIT LA

PIT HILL LA

CROFT COTTS

B361
TAUNTON RD

Sutton Hams

SEDGEMOOR HILL DRO

EDINGTON RIGHT DRO

Sharpenton Hill

PH

BRD HILL LA

OLD DUTCH LA

Greinton

7

TA7

CHILTON RIGHT DRO

CARDOTT RIGHT DROV

MOORLINCH RIGHT DRO

SHARPENTON LA

PH

DRO ORCHARD

BROADMEAD DRO

36

Greylake Fosse

6

Westonzoyland

SEDGEMOOR DRO

King's Sedgemoor Drain

SHAPWICK RIGHT DRO

Briarwood Farm

MOOR DRO

35

Burdenham Farm

BURDENHAM DRO

Lower Nythe Farm

LOCKYER DRO

Springway Ind Est

P

Greylake Bridge

Huish Dro

34

KNOWLE DRO

LITTLE ELM RD

ERST SEDGEMOOR DRO

ACKLAND'S DRO

4

LANGMEAD DRO

Langmead

MACKLEYARDS RD

MOOR RD

Greylake

RIVER DRO

King's Sedge Moor

33

LANGMEAD DRO

KINGS HILL LA

CHURCH RD

BACK LA

LANGPORT RD

SMALLMOOR DRO

Owery Farm

HEAD DRO

3

PLACE DRO

HOLLOWAY RD

Sch

1 WEST VIEW CL
2 HOLLIES CL
3 OLD CHAPEL RD
4 WEYMONT CL

Shride Farm

FIRST DRO

Sowy River

Langacre Rhyne

SECOND DRO

Charity Farm

32

Thorngrove

MAIN RD

NETHERMOOR

Middlezoy

NETHERMOOR DRO

TOWNSEND

A372

SEAMAN'S LA

TA10

Turn Hill

TURNHILL RD

BLACKHAM LA

2

CIDERS DRO

WILLAKE DRO

BLACKSMEAD DRO

Nether Moor

Sch

NORTH LA

A361

BEDNELL LA

NEW RD

Beer

Beer Door

STANHILL RD

Othery

FORE ST

PO

1 LOAD POOL
2 LITTLE ENGLAND
3 CASTLE CT
4 WESTLAKE CL
5 SUMMERHEDGE CRES

BEER DRO

WOOL LA

31

BROAD DRO

ENGLAND RD

Cemy

MAIN RD

HIGH ST

FIVE LA

KEENE LA

PAYNES LA

Pathe

PATHE RD

SUMMERHEDGE RD

BURROW WALL

GROVE HILL

North Moor

LEAZEWAY DRO

Hunter's Lodge

BEER RD

Aller Wood

Breach Wood

DANGER AREA

MILDMAY'S RD

DANGER AREA

1

LITTLE BURROW DRO

BURROW HILL DRO

CHANTRY DRO

HEAD DRO

ALLER DRO

NORTHMOOR DRO

BLACK WITHIES DRO

A372

WOOD DRO

SLAB DRO

BLACK DRO

Southlake Moor

STRAIGHT DRO

MOON'S DRO

TAPPINGWALL DRO

MAIN RD

30

| 36 | A | 37 | B | 38 | C | 39 | D | 40 | E | 41 | F |

Scale: 1¾ inches to 1 mile

0 ¼ ½ mile
0 250m 500m 750m 1 km

207
BA6

LOXLEY BATCH
SNAPWICK HILL
A39
PH
THE SPINNEY
Ashcott Prim Sch
CHESTNUT LA
RIDGEWAY
KINGS LA
SCHOOL HILL
Ashcott
Millslade Farm
STATION RD
STAGMAN LA
BRADLEY STREAM RD
West Park Farm
SHARPHAM LA
Park End Farm
SHARPHAM DRO
Sharpham Park
Cemy
CEMETERY LA
PORTLAND RD
PEDWELL LA
PH
PEDWELL HILL
BATH RD
PO MID
LINKHAM CL
GLEBELAND CL
HIGH ST
BRADLEY LA
WHITLEY RD
Whitley Farm
Asney
SMALL MOOR LA
Walton CE Prim Sch
ASNEY DRO
COLWOOD DRO
Superstore
WESTWAY A39
Ind Pk
Pedwell
1 OLD SCHOOL CL
2 HIGH VIEW DR
3 HURMANS CL
4 WEST ST
5 THE BATCH
6 BLAKE GN
A361
TAUNTON RD
A361
Lockhill Hall
BERHILL
LITTLE MOOR LA
MEADOW LA
BROUGHTON CL
SMALL DRO
CRACKS LA
HEMPITTS RD
MILDRED RD
WEST END
PO
STONEHILL
HIGH ST
TA7
Pedwell Hill
COMBE HILL LA
TEIGN CT 1
CHANCELLOR CL 2
MAIN ST
PO
Walton House
QUARRY BATCH
EAST MEAD LA
207
Redlands Farm
Priest Hill
Huckham Farm
BRAMBLE HILL
LONG LA
SOUTH CL
CHANCELLOR RD
Walton
BA16
Eastmead Farm
Brookside Prim Sch
BROOKFIELD WAY
Avalon Sch
MIDDLE BROOKS
SUTTON LA
Little Huckham Farm
Walton Hill
IVEL LA
BUTLEIGH DRO
Nythe Bridge
LOCKYER DRO
Butleigh Moor
Fisher Dro
WALTON DRO
BUTLEIGH DRO
COCKROD
Middle Ivy Thorn Farm
IVY THORN LA
IVY LA
STREET DRO
207
Huish Dro
NYTHE RD
PEDWELL DRO
SUTTONMOOR DRO
Eighteen Feet Rhyne
Street Dro
Dundon Hayes
MIDDLE DRO
Blackhole Dro
Cradle Bridge
HAYES RD
PEAK LA
BEER DRO
HENLEY CORNER DRO
Henley Corner
LOW HAM DRO
Peddie's Barn Dr
Dundon
MOOR DRO
HENLEY RD
Henley
TA10
Low Ham Bridge
River Cary
Pitney Straight Dro
Red Lake
Hayes Farm
HAYES LA
TA11
PH
ST ANDREW'S CL
HIM HILL
COOKE'S LA
HAWTHORN CL
High Ham
High Ham CE Prim Sch
Stout
Broadacre
Somerton Moor
SOMERTON DRO
211
TURNEY RD
STANDHILL RD
FIELD RD
BURFS LA
BREACH FURLONG LA
WINDMILL RD
LOXHAMS
MORTON'S LA
Pitney Steart Bridge
STEART DRO
LIVER MOOR RD
SOMERTON DOOR DRO
211
LUGSHORN LA
Cemy
MILDMAY'S RD
Sedgemoor Hill
Stembridge Tower Mill
LONG ST
STEMBRIDGE RD
LEAZEMOOR LA
Park
PARK LA
TOUCH RD

For full street detail of the highlighted area see pages 207 and 211.

42 A 43 B 44 C 45 D 46 E 47 F

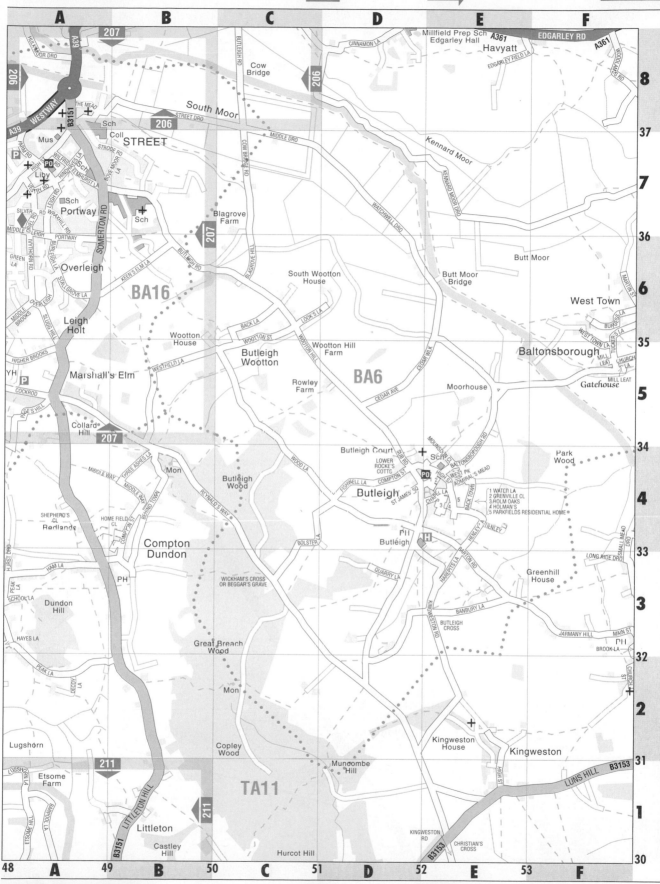

A   B   C   D   E   F

207
206   207
WESTWAY
A39
A39
206
207
THE MEAD
B3151
South Moor
STREET DRO
206
Sch
Coll
STREET
Mus
P
PO
Liby
High
SILVER ST
Portway
Sch
CINNAMON LA
Cow Bridge
COW BRIDGE RD
MIDDLE DRO
Millfield Prep Sch
Edgarley Hall
Havyatt
A361
EDGARLEY RD
A361
EDGARLEY FIELD LA
WOODLANDS RD

8
37
7
36

Blagrove Farm
207
BUTLEIGH RD
BLAGROVE DRO
Overleigh
GREEN LA
IVYTHORN RD
MIDDLE OVERLEIGH
SOMERTON RD
BA16
KEEN'S ELM LA
South Wootton House
WATCHWELL DRO
Kennard Moor
KENNARD MOOR DRO
Butt Moor
Butt Moor Bridge
West Town
BURTLE SS LA
MARTIN'S LA

6
35

Leigh Holt
MIDDLE BROOKS
HIGHER BROOKS
SLUGG HILL
Marshall's Elm
WESTFIELD LA
Wootton House
BACK LA
WOOTTON ST
LOOK'S LA
Butleigh Wootton
WOOTTON HILL
Wootton Hill Farm
CEDAR WLK
BA6
Moorhouse
WEST TOWN LA
TUCKER LA
MILL LEAL
Baltonsborough
CHURCH LA
MILL LEAT
Gatehouse

YH
P
COCKROD
PAGE'S HILL
Rowley Farm
CEDAR AVE

5
34

Collard Hill
207
MIDDLE WAY
THREE ASHES LA
Mon
REYNALD'S WAY
Butleigh Wood
WOOD LA
Butleigh Court
LOWER ROCKE'S COTTS
FISHWELL LA
COMPTON DRO
SUB RD
BALTONSBOROUGH RD
MOUNSEY CL
Sch
PO
WEST PK
High St
ADMIRAL'S MEAD
Park Wood
1 WATER LA
2 GRENVILLE CL
3 HOLM OAKS
4 HOLMAN'S
5 PARKFIELDS RESIDENTIAL HOME

4
33

SHEPHERD'S CL
Redlands
HOME FIELD CL
COMPTON ST
BEHIND TOWN
Compton Dundon
PH
Butleigh
ST JAMES SD
BACK TOWN
HEMERY LA
HENLEY
PH
Butleigh
H

3

HAM LA
PEAK LA
SCHOOL LA
Dundon Hill
HAYES LA
PEAK LA
Wickham's Cross or Beggar's Grave
BOLSTER
QUARRY LA
HARPITS LA
BARTON RD
Greenhill House
BANBURY LA
Butleigh Cross
KINGWESTON RD
JARMANY HILL
LONG RIDE DRO
SMALL MEAD DRO
MAIN ST
PH
BROOK LA
CHURCH ST

32
2

DECOY LA
Lugshorn
Great Breach Wood
Mon
Copley Wood
Kingweston House
Kingweston
LUNS HILL
B3153

211
ETSOME THORN LA
BORROPOT LA
Etsome Farm
LUGSHORN LA
211
B3151
LITTLETON HILL
Littleton
Castley Hill
Muncombe Hill
Hurcot Hill
TA11
KINGWESTON RD
HIGH ST
Christian's Cross
B3153

31
1
30

48   A   49   B   50   C   51   D   52   E   53   F

For full street detail of the highlighted area see pages 206 207 and 211.

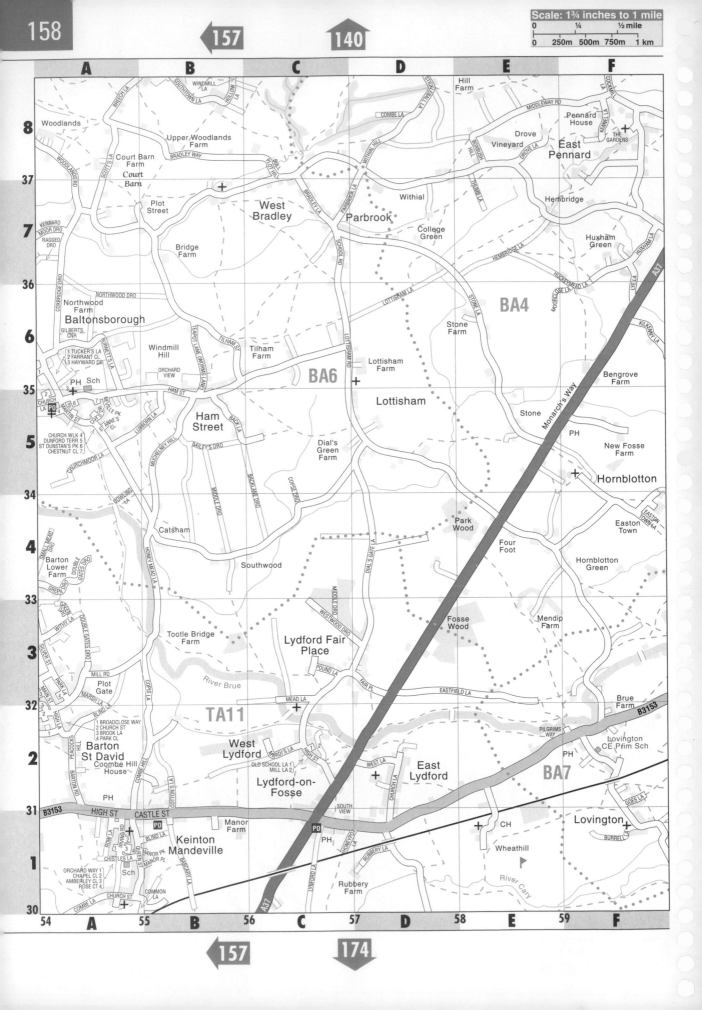

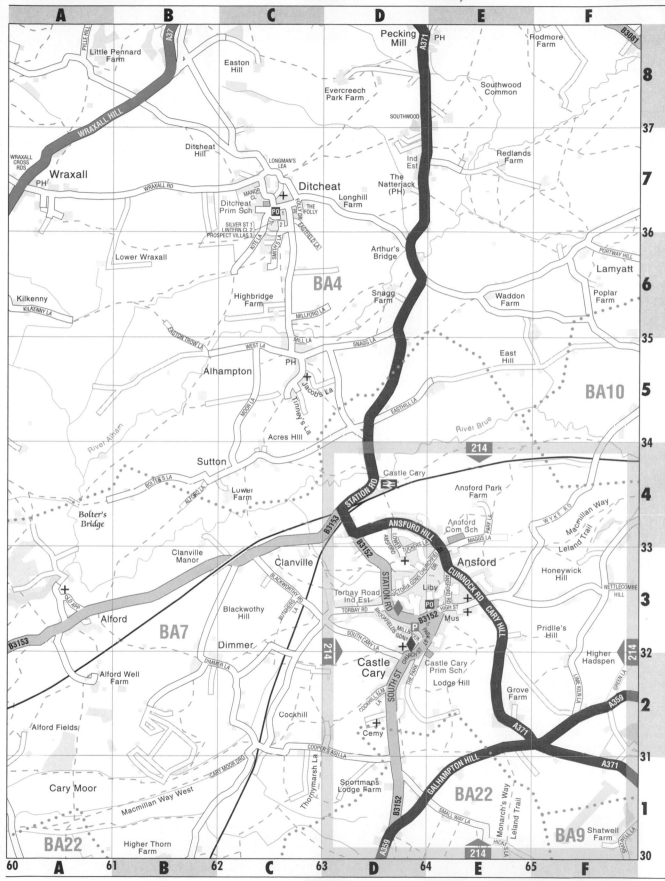

141
160
175
160

For full street detail of the highlighted area see page 214.

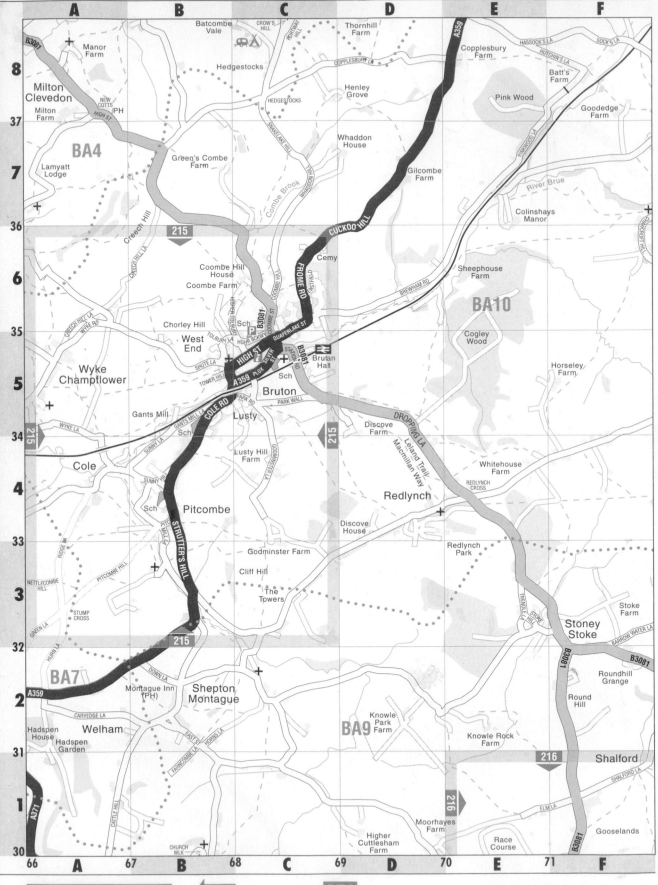

Scale: 1¾ inches to 1 mile

0   ¼   ½ mile
0   250m   500m   750m   1 km

8

37

7

36

6

35

5

34

4

33

3

32

2

31

1

30

A   66   B   67   C   68   D   69   E   70   F   71

B3081

Milton Clevedon
Manor Farm
Milton Farm
NEW COTTS PH
HIGH ST
BA4
Lamyatt Lodge
Batcombe Vale
CROW'S HILL
Hedgestocks
Hedgestocks
PORTWAY HILL
Thornhill Farm
COPPLESBURY LA
Copplesbury Farm
HASSOCK'S LA
HUTCHIN'S LA
SOCK'S LA
Batt's Farm
Pink Wood
Goodedge Farm
PINKWOOD LA
CHARCROFT HILL

Green's Combe Farm
SNAKE LAKE HILL
COMBE HILL
Henley Grove
Whaddon House
WHADDON HILL
Gilcombe Farm
A359
River Brue
Colinshays Manor
Creech Hill
Combe Brook
215
CREECH HILL LA
Coombe Hill House
Coombe Farm
Chorley Hill
HIGHER TOLBURY
Sch
B3081
Cemy
CUCKOO HILL
FROME RD
WESTFIELD
BREWHAM RD
Sheephouse Farm
BA10
WYKE RD
West End
TOLBURY LA
HIGH ST
SILVER ST
QUAPERLAKE ST
COOMBE ST
STATION RD
Bruton Halt
Cogley Wood
Horseley Farm
Wyke Champflower
SHUTE LA
TOWER HILL
A359
PLOX
Sch
Bruton
B3081
215
Gants Mill
PARK RD
GANTS MILL LA
COLE RD
Lusty
PARK WALL
Discove Farm
DROPPING LA
Leland Trail Macmillan Way
Whitehouse Farm
215
WYKE LA
Sch
SUNNY LA
Lusty Hill Farm
GODMINSTER LA
Redlynch
REDLYNCH CROSS
Cole
SUNNY HILL
Sch
Pitcombe
PITCOMBE HILL
STRUTTER'S HILL
Godminster Farm
Cliff Hill
Discove House
Redlynch Park
RIDGE DR
NETTLECOMBE HILL
PITCOMBE HILL
The Towers
STOKE HILL
TRENDLE LA
Stoney Stoke
Stoke Farm
GREEN LA
STUMP CROSS
215
Montague Inn (PH)
DOWN LA
Shepton Montague
B3081
Roundhill Grange
B3081
BA7
A359
CARYEDGE LA
Welham
EAST ST
FARNCOMBE LA
HORNS LA
BA9
Knowle Park Farm
Round Hill
Shalford
216
SHALFORD LA
Hadspen House
Hadspen Garden
CATTLE HILL
HUNN LA
Knowle Rock Farm
216
ELM LA
A371
CHURCH WLK
Higher Cuttlesham Farm
Moorhayes Farm
Race Course
B3081
Gooselands

For full street detail of the highlighted area see pages 215 and 216.

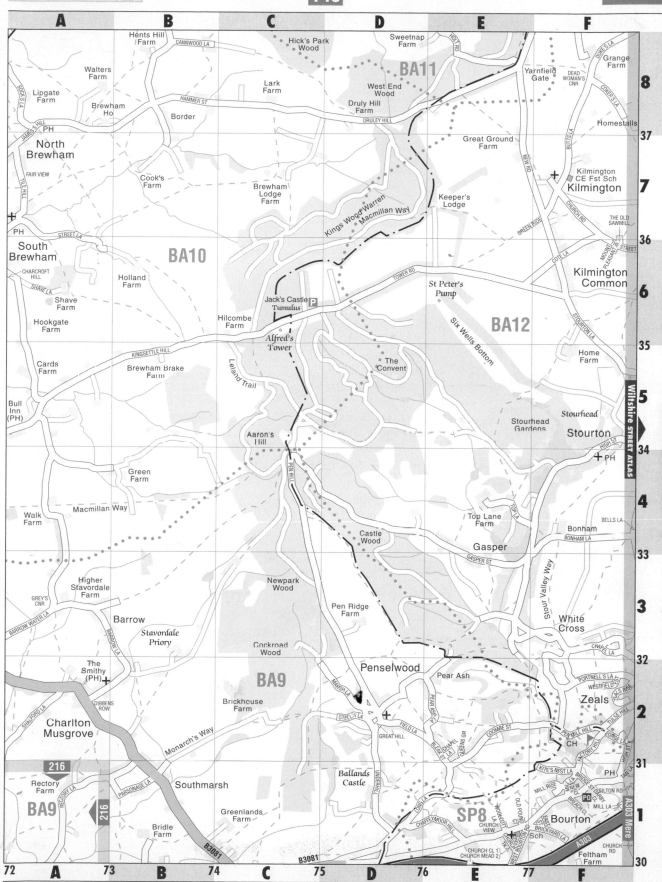

177

For full street detail of the
highlighted area see page 216.

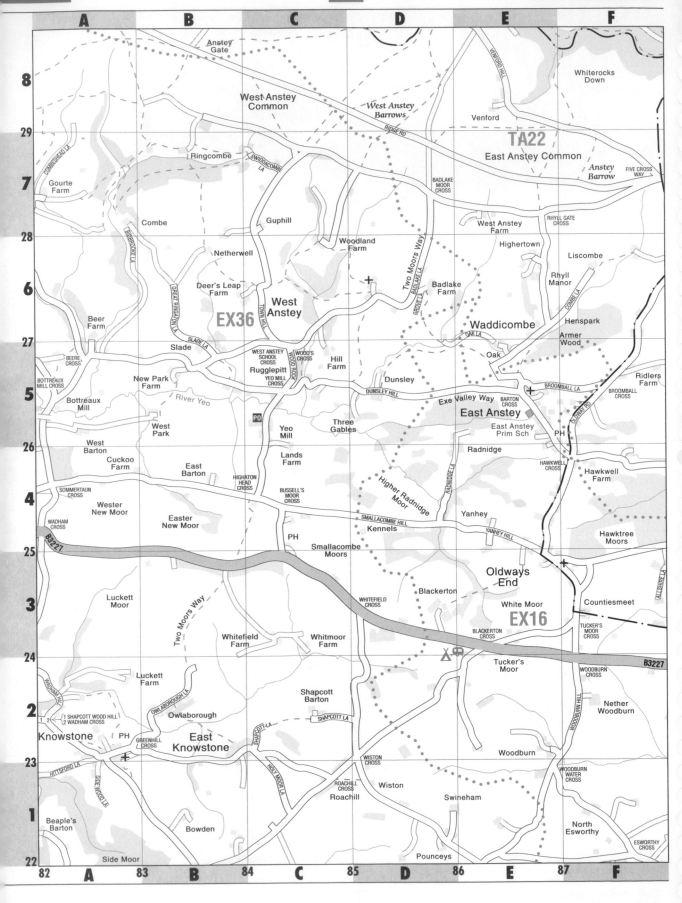

Scale: 1¾ inches to 1 mile

0   ¼   ½ mile
0 250m 500m 750m 1 km

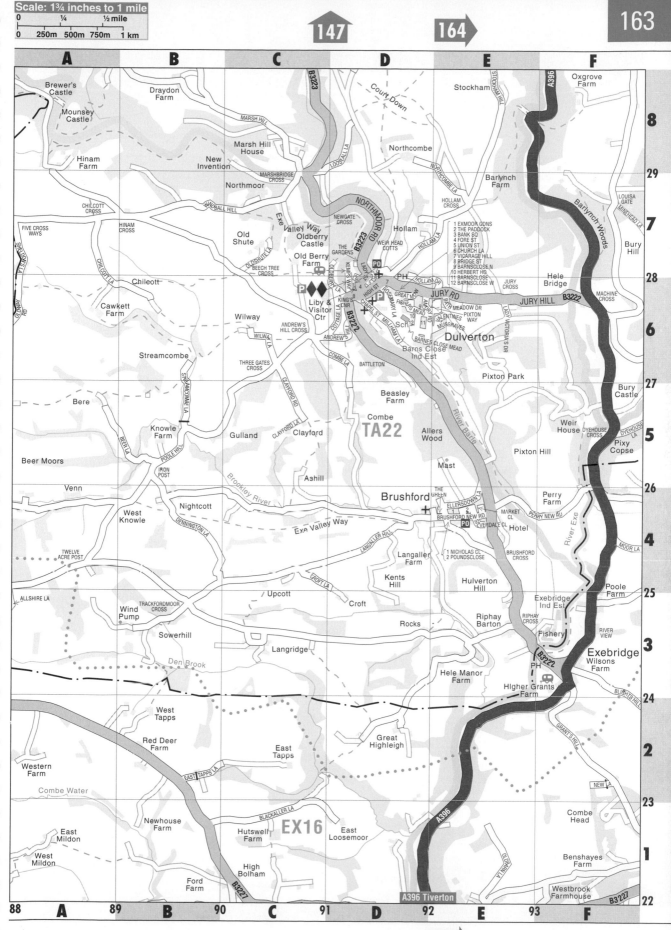

Scale: 1¾ inches to 1 mile

0   ¼   ½ mile
0   250m 500m 750m   1 km

A   B   C   D   E   F

147   164

8
29
7
28
6
27
5
26
4
25
3
24
2
23
1
22

Brewer's Castle
Mounsey Castle
Draydon Farm
Court Down
Stockham
Oxgrove Farm
Hinam Farm
Marsh Hill
Marsh Hill House
Northcombe
New Invention
Barlynch Farm
Northmoor
MARSHBRIDGE CROSS
NORTHCOMBE LA
Louisa Gate
MINEHEAD LA
Five Cross Ways
Chilcott Cross
Hinam Cross
Newgate Cross
Hollam Cross
Bury Hill
WALL HILL
Exe Valley Way
Oldberry Castle
Old Berry Farm
Weir Head Cotts
Hollam
1 EXMOOR GDNS
2 THE PADDOCK
3 BANK SQ
4 FORE ST
5 UNION ST
6 CHURCH LA
7 VICARAGE HILL
8 BRIDGE ST
9 BARNSCLOSE.N
10 HERBERT RD
11 BARNSCLOSE
12 BARNSCLOSE W
Hele Bridge
Old Shute
THE GARDENS
KEMPS WAY
Barlynch Woods
Chilcott
Beech Tree Cross
PH
HOLLAM DR
JURY CROSS
Cawkett Farm
Liby & Visitor Ctr
Wilway
King's Cnr
Andrew's Hill Cross
JURY RD
JURY HILL
B3222
Machine Cross
Dulverton
Streamcombe
Three Gates Cross
ANDREW'S
COMBE LA
Battleton
Pixton Way
Barnes Close Ind Est
Pixton Park
Bury Castle
Bere
Knowle Farm
Gulland
Clayford
Beasley Farm
Combe
TA22
Allers Wood
River Barle
Weir House
DYEHOUSE CROSS
Pixy Copse
DYEHOUSE LA
Beer Moors
IRON POST
Ashill
Mast
Pixton Hill
Venn
West Knowle
Nightcott
Brockley River
Exe Valley Way
Brushford
THE GREEN
Perry Farm
River Exe
TWELVE ACRE POST
DENNINGTON LA
Langaller Farm
Brushford New Rd
PO
VERDALE CL
MARKET CL
PERRY NEW RD
MOOR LA
ALLSHIRE LA
CROFT LA
Langaller Hill
Kents Hill
Hulverton Hill
1 NICHOLAS CL
2 POUNDSCLOSE
Brushford Cross
Exebridge Ind Est
Poole Farm
Wind Pump
TRACKFORDMOOR CROSS
Upcott
Croft
Rocks
Riphay Barton
Riphay Cross
RIVER VIEW
Sowerhill
Langridge
Hele Manor Farm
Fishery
B3222
Exebridge
Wilsons Farm
Den Brook
PH
BLIGHTS HILL
West Tapps
Higher Grants Farm
GRANT'S HILL
Red Deer Farm
East Tapps
Great Highleigh
NEW LA
Western Farm
Combe Water
EAST TAPPS LA
Combe Head
BLACKALLER LA
EX16
Newhouse Farm
Hutswell Farm
East Loosemoor
East Mildon
High Bolham
A396
Benshayes Farm
West Mildon
Ford Farm
B3227
A396 Tiverton
Westbrook Farmhouse
B3227

88   89   90   91   92   93

Scale: 1¾ inches to 1 mile

0   ¼   ½ mile
0   250m   500m   750m   1 km

A   B   C   D   E   F

Lyncombe Farm
Hartford Bottom
Hartford
Lady Harriet Acland's Dr
River Haddeo
West Hill Wood
Wimbleball Lake
Upton Farm
St James Church (rems of)
Hayne Farm
Upton
Eastmoor La
Hahnstown Rd
B3190
Clammer
Hadborough
Lady Harriet Acland's Dr
Haddon Hill
Minehead La
P
TA4
Haddon Farm
HADDON LA
Chapple Farm
Frogwell Farm
Surridge Farm
Blindwell Farm
BLINDWE LA
POST LA
South Haddon
WINDWAY HILL
Frogwell Cross
Bury
DYEHOUSE CNR
HADDON LA
Leigh Barton
CHANGE LA
Skilgate
PITSHAM LA
CROFT LA
GAMBLYN CROSS
DYEHOUSE LA
TA22
Withywine Farm
WITHYWINE LA
Skilgate Wood
CHALCOMBE ROOKS LA
Gamblyn Farm
PORT LA
Combeland
Brockhole Farm
Haynes Down Farm
HONE CROSS
Gamblyn Cross
COMBELAND LA
Willishayes
HAYNE CROSS
Timewell
Morebath Manor
Coombe
East Combe
QUARTLEY HILL
Warmore
Hayne Farm
TIMEWELL HILL
East Holcombe
Burston
MOOR LA
BURSTON LA
MORRELL'S CROSS
Claypits
COURT LA
Court
COMBE CROSS
Quartley Farm
East Holcombe
ASHTOWN CROSS
EX16
HOOPERS CROSS
Eastwoods
Shillingford Fst Sch
B3227
Ashtown Farm
VALLEY VIEW
Morebath
Ben Brook
Loyton
Westwoods
BOWDENS LA
Hayne Barton
Lower Rill
Great Rill Farm
Surridge Farm
Moore Farm
Keens
FIRWAY CROSS
HUKELEY HEAD CROSS
PH
SAWYERS HILL
BANFIELDS
BLIGHTS HILL
BONNY CROSS
Shillingford
Blight's Farm
LOWER LODFIN
CHILTERN CROSS
Hukeley Farm
RIDGEWAY LA
Chapel (rems of)
Doddiscombe
Coldharbour Farm
Exe Valley Way
Lodfin Farm
Holwell Farm
South Hayne Farm
ROWS LA
Rows Farm
Birchdown
B3190
FROG ST
River Batherm
FORD RD
FORDMILL CROSS
Sunderleigh
Borough House
Zeal Farm
HIGH CROSS
Gumbland
HIGH ST
SOUTH MOLTON RD
Liby
BACK CASTLE ST
PH
PO
Bampton
OLD TIVERTON RD
Pipshayne
B3227
Bampton Prim Sch
SCHOOL
WES
BRIDGE
TERR

94   95   96   97   98   99

A   B   C   D   E   F

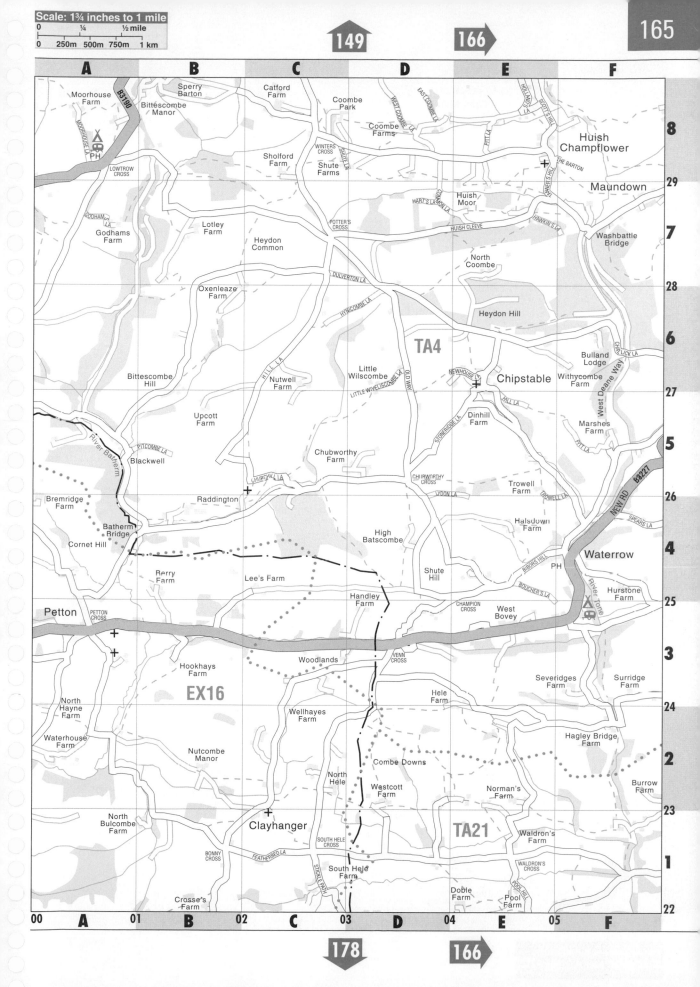

← 165   150

A B C D E F

210

Chorley's
WHITEFIELD ROCKS
Whitefield
Billy Farm
Oakhampton Farm
Burrow Hill Farm

8

Works
PH
Langley Marsh
Langley
Northgate
Ford
Brewers Farm
Knight's Farm
Fitzhead
CHURCH RD

29

7

Maundown Hill
Greenway Farm
GREENWAY LA
Wiveliscombe
West Deane Way
HEATHSTOCK HILL
RIDGE HILL
Castle Hill fort
Castle
CASTLE LA
Croford House
Cat's Ash
Car's Ash La
BEACH TREE CROSS

28

210
Sch
STYLE RD
BURGES LA
FORD RD
PO
P
JEWS LA
SILVER ST
P
CROFT WAY
CHURCH ST
TAUNTON RD
B3188
210
Croford
CROFORD HILL

6

Challick Farm
CHALLICK LA
COATE TURN
COLLEYHAY LA
Coate Farm
Hartswell
HARTSWELL LA
SOUTH ST
Sch
Manor Farm
TA4
Slape Moor
River's Farm

27

Fleed Farm
FLEED CROSS
NEW RD
B3227
PYNCOMBE LA
North Down Farm
Dunnington Park Farm
Westbrook Farm
Fry's Farm
B3187
B3227

5

210
Holm Moor
QUAKINGHOUSE LA
Quaking House
FAIRFIELD TERR
HIGH ST
WOOD ST
B3187

26

WALRIDGE CROSS
SPEARS LA
BICKING'S CLOSE LA
Pyncombe Farm
Sharps Farm
MANWORTHY CROSS
Farthing's Farm
Milverton
WOODBARTON
SAND ST
BUTTS WAY
Sch
B3187

4

Gummer Cleeve La
HELLING'S CROSS
Hellings Farm
Ridge Farm
Screedy
Auton Dolwells
COURTFIELD WAY
HUNTASH LA

25

Hawthorn Farm
ROAD HILL
Woodlands Farm
Cobhay Farm
STONE HILL LA
Spring Grove House
Lower Lovelynch
Higher Lovelynch Farm
BURN HILL

3

RIDGE HIGHWAY
Yeancott Farm
Bathealton Court
Stone Hill La
Leigh Farm
Bindon Budville

24

GIPSY CROSS
Kittisford Farm
Bathealton
BULLOCK FIELD HILL
WATERY LA
Stone Hill
Greenvale Farm
CARVER'S LA
Langford Heathfield
Chipley

2

Stawley Wood Farm
Kittisford Barton
Poleshill
TA21
Stancombe Farm
Langford Budville
CHORNELLA LA
BUTTS LA
Sch SWIFTS
Langford Gate
Langford La
West Deane Way
B3187

23

Stawley
HAM HILL
Kittisford
WATERY LA
COCKLAND HILL
River Tone
PH

1

22

06 A 07 B 08 C 09 D 10 E 11 F

For full street detail of the highlighted area see page 210.

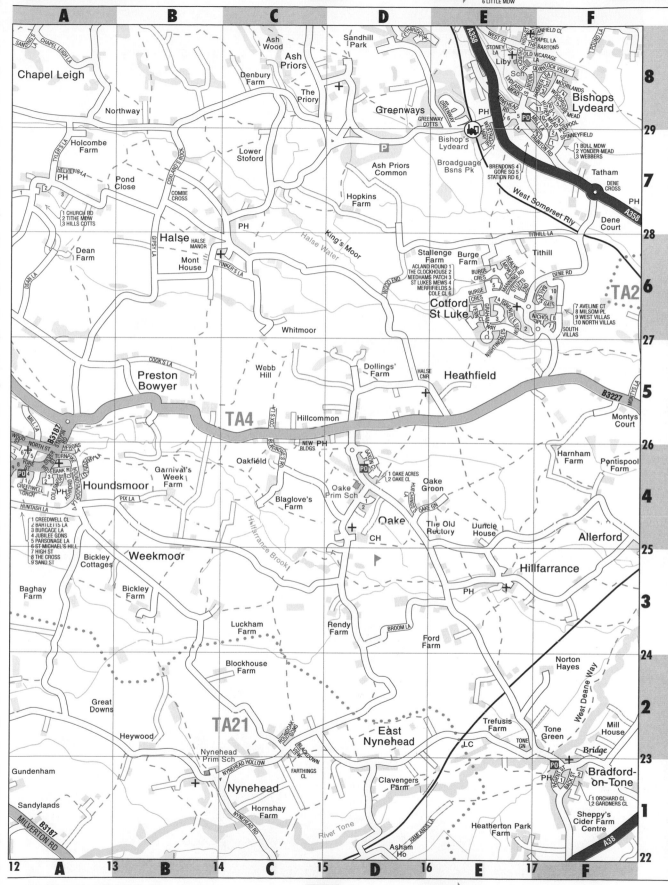

Scale: 1¾ inches to 1 mile

0   ¼   ½ mile
0   250m 500m 750m 1 km

151

168

167

F8
1 FOUR ACRE MEAD
2 BARTON HEY
3 FIVE YARDS
4 SNATHE LEA
5 OXLEAZE
6 LITTLE MDW

7 HOBBS MEAD
8 THE LEAT
9 GROATS
10 WHEATSTONES
11 MILLERS WAY

A   B   C   D   E   F

Chapel Leigh
CHAPEL LEIGH LA
SAXONS LA
TYLER'S LA
Northway
Holcombe Farm
HELVIER'S LA
PH
1 CHURCH RD
2 TITHE MDW
3 HILLS COTTS
Pond Close
COMBE CROSS
CONLAND'S ROCK
Dean Farm
DEAN LA
Halse
HALSE MANOR
Mont House
GIPSY LA
TINKER'S LA
PH
WOOD END

Ash Wood
Ash Priors
Denbury Farm
The Priory
Lower Stoford
Whitmoor

Sandhill Park
Greenways
LETHBRIDGE LA
GREENWAY
Greenway Cotts
Ash Priors Common
PH
Hopkins Farm
King's Moor
Halse Water
Halse CNR
Dollings' Farm
Webb Hill

Bishop's Lydeard
Broadguage Bsns Pk
A358
WEST SOMERSET RLY
West Somerset Rly
Stallenge Farm
Burge Farm
HEALS MDW
MANNING RD
BURGE CRES
BURGE CRES
ACLAND ROUND 1
THE CLOCKHOUSE 2
NEEDHAMS PATCH 3
ST LUKES MEWS 4
MERRIFIELDS 5
COLE CL 6
Cotford St Luke
GRAHAM WAY
GRENVILLE VIEW
STUTTS END
PENN
NICHOL PL
NIGHTINGALES
SOUTH VILLAS

Bishops Lydeard
WEST ST
GLANFIELD CL
THE BARTONS
STONEY LA
Liby
Sch
WEST ST
MOORLANDS
1 BULL MDW
2 YONDER MEAD
3 WEBBERS
Tatham
DENE CROSS
Dene Court
PH
A358
DENE RD
TITHILL LA
Tithill
TA2
7 AVELINE CT
8 MILSOM PL
9 WEST VILLAS
10 NORTH VILLAS

8
29
7
28
6
27

Preston Bowyer
COOK'S LA
TA4
Houndsmoor
B3187
HERONS LA
MILL LA
WOOD ST
NORTH ST
FORE ST
PO
CREEDWELL ORCH
PH
TURNPIKE
BEACON RD
MOUNDSMOOR LA
CHAY LA
PIX LA
HUNTASH LA
1 CREEDWELL CL
2 BARTLETTS LA
3 BURGAGE LA
4 JUBILEE GDNS
5 PARSONAGE LA
6 ST MICHAEL'S HILL
7 HIGH ST
8 THE CROSS
9 SAND ST
Weekmoor
Bickley Cottages
Bickley Farm
Baghay Farm
Great Downs
Heywood
TA21
Gundenham
Sandylands
MILVERTON RD
B3187

Garnival's Week Farm
Oakfield
COX'S LA
BLAGROVE'S RD
Blaglove's Farm
Hillfarrance Brook
Luckham Farm
Blockhouse Farm
Nynehead Prim Sch
NYNEHEAD HOLLOW
ROCKBDAK SIDINGS
BLACKDOWN
Nynehead
NYNEHEAD RD
Hornshay Farm

Hillcommon
NEW BLDGS
PH
Oake Prim Sch
PO
SAXON ST
1 OAKE ACRES
2 OAKE CL
Oake
CH
Oake Green
HUTCHINGS LA
OAKE GN
The Old Rectory
Rendy Farm
BROOM LA
Ford Farm
East Nynehead
HARLANDS LA
Clavengers Farm
River Tone
Asham Ho
LC

Heathfield
B3227
Harnham Farm
MONTYS LA
Montys Court
Pontispool Farm
Duncle House
Allerford
Hillfarrance
PH
Norton Hayes
WEST DEANE WAY
Trefusis Farm
Tone Green
TONE GN
Mill House
Bridge
PO
REGENTS CL
BACK ST
PH
Bradford-on-Tone
1 ORCHARD CL
2 GARDNERS CL
Heatherton Park Farm
Sheppy's Cider Farm Centre
A38

5
26
4
25
3
24
2
23
1
22

Scale: 1¾ inches to 1 mile

0   ¼   ½ mile
0   250m   500m   750m   1 km

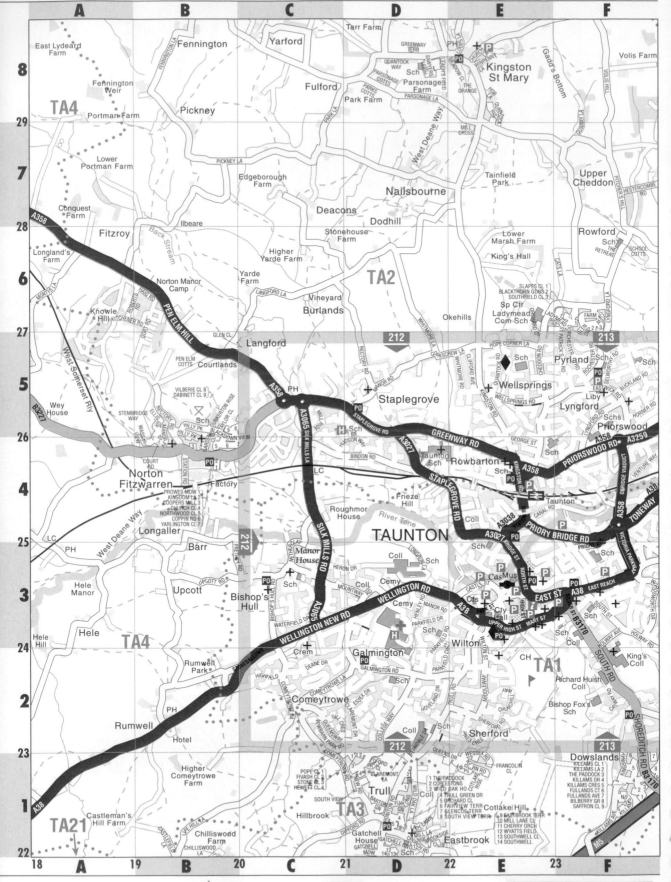

Tarr Farm
East Lydeard Farm
Fennington
Yarford
GREENWAY TERR
PH
Church
P
WIMPENNY
Volis Farm
Kingston St Mary
Gadd's Bottom
QUANTOCK WAY
PARSONAGE COTTS
Parsonage Farm
THE GRANGE
PARSONAGE LA
HOB
QUANTOCK RISE
VOLIS HILL
SNAPPERS LA
LADY'S FIELD
Fennington Weir
TA4
Portman Farm
Pickney
Fulford
Park Farm
PARK LA
PARKS COTTS
MILL CROSS
West Deane Way
Lower Portman Farm
PICKNEY LA
Edgeborough Farm
Nailsbourne
Tainfield Park
Upper Cheddon
HESTERCOMBE LA
PITCHER'S HILL
Conquest Farm
A358
Fitzroy
Ilbeare
Back Stream
Deacons
Dodhill
Stonehouse Farm
TA2
Lower Marsh Farm
King's Hall
Rowford
Sch
THE RETREAT
SCHOOL COTTS
CATS LA
Longland's Farm
MONT'S LA
Higher Yarde Farm
Norton Manor Camp
Yarde Farm
LANGFORD LA
Vineyard
Burlands
Okehills
WHITMORE LA
SLAPES CL 1
BLACKTHORN GDNS 2
SOUTHFIELD CL 3
Sp Ctr
Ladymead Com Sch
LADYMEAD RD
DORCHESTER RD
FARM LA
B3227
West Somerset Rly
Wey House
Knowle Hill
KITCHENER RD
CRAIG RD
ROBERTS RD
PEN ELM HILL
GLEN CL
Langford
212
HOPE CORNER LA
Sch
Wellsprings
QUANTOCK RD
ST PATRICK'S RD
Pyrland
213
ROCHESTER RD
Sch
Sch
SELWORTHY RD
PEN ELM COTTS
Courtlands
VILBERIE CL 8
DABINETT CL 9
A358
PH
RECTORY RD
MANOR RD
Staplegrove
WELLSPRINGS RD
KINGSTON RD
P
EAST WICK RD
Liby
BUCKLAND RD
Lyngford
HORNER RD
Schs
Priorswood
Wey House
STEMBRIDGE WAY
ELLIS RD
WASSAL
RECTORY RD
BLACKDOWN VIEW
A3065 SILK MILLS LA
STAPLEGROVE RD
HUDSON WAY
BINDON RD
GREENWAY RD
GEORGE ST
Sch
A358
A3259
VENTURE WAY
Sch
STATION RD
PO
LC
A3027
Taunton Sch
Rowbarton
KINGSTON RD
P
PRIORSWOOD RD
OXBRIDGE RD
COURT RD
Norton Fitzwarren
PROWES MDW 1
KINGDON 2
COOPERS MILL 3
CHURCH CL 4
NORTHWOOD CL 5
COPPIN RD 6
YARLINGTON CL 7
Factory
LC
Roughmor House
River Tone
Frieze Hill
Coll
STAPLEGROVE RD
A3038
Taunton
STREET
CANAL RD
A358
TONEWAY
A38
West Deane Way
Longaller
Barr
Upcott
UPCOTT RD
SILK MILLS RD
TAUNTON
LONGRUN LA
Coll
Sch
A3027 BRIDGE ST
PRIORY BRIDGE RD
VICTORIA PARKWAY
Sch
LC
PH
Hele Manor
Hele
212
FRETHEY RD
Manor House
WETHERCLAP
HERON DR
Coll
Cemy
HEL RUN LA
CasMus
P
P
NORTH ST
P
P
EAST ST
A38
East Reach
WORDSWORTH DR
Hele Hill
TA4
Bishop's Hull
BISHOP'S HULL RD
Sch
MOUNTWAY
Cemy
HENLEY MANOR RD
PARKFIELD DR
Sch
A38
PARK ST
Cty Hall
HIGH ST
MARY ST
UPPER HIGH ST
PO
B3170
Coll
Sch
HOLWAY AVE
HOLWAY RD
Rumwell Park
A3065
WELLINGTON NEW RD
WATERFIELD DR
Crem
Galmington
GALMINGTON RD
PO
Sch
PARKFIELD RD
H
Wilton
CH
Richard Huish Coll
Bishop Fox's Sch
TA1
SOUTH RD
King's Coll
STONEGALLOWS
Rumwell
PH
WELLINGTON RD
Comeytrowe
COMEYTROWE LA
HIGHFIELD
DEANE DR
COMEYTROWE RD
GILES CL
PEMBROKE
QUEENSWAY
CLAREMONT DR
ESSEX DR
College Way
Coll
SHERFORD RD
TRULL RD
HONEYLANDS RD
AMMETT DOWN
SHERFORD CRES
Sherford
Hotel
PEMBROKE CL
Higher Comeytrowe Farm
QUEENS DR
WESSEX RD
FRANCOLIN CL
212
Dowslands
213
SHOREDITCH RD
B3170
POPE CL 1
FIVASH CL 2
STONE CL 3
HEWETT CL 4
Coll
ORCH DR
CLAREMONT CL
WILD OAK HO
1 THE PADDOCK
2 COPLESTONS
3 WILD OAK HO
4 TRULL GREEN DR
5 ORCHARD CL
6 FAIRVIEW TERR
7 GLENCOE TERR
8 SOUTH VIEW TERR
KILLAMS CL 1
KILLAMS LA 2
THE PADDOCK 3
KILLAMS DR 4
KILLAMS CRES 5
FULLANDS CT 6
FULLANDS AVE 7
BILBERRY GR 8
SAFFRON CL 9
SOUTH VIEW
Trull
TA3
Hillbrook
Cotlake Hill
9 EASTBROOK TERR
10 MILL LANE CL
11 CHERRY ORCH
12 WYATTS FIELD
13 SOUTHWELL CL
14 SOUTHWELL
A38
TA21
Castleman's Hill Farm
Chilliswood Farm
CHILLISWOOD LA
SPIE HILL LA
CASTLE RD
DIPFORD RD
BARTON GN
SOUTH VIEW
STATION RD
MILL LA
BROOKSIDE
Gatchell House
GATCHELL MDW
Sch
Eastbrook
M5
KILLAMS LA
B3170

For full street detail of the highlighted area see pages 212 and 213.

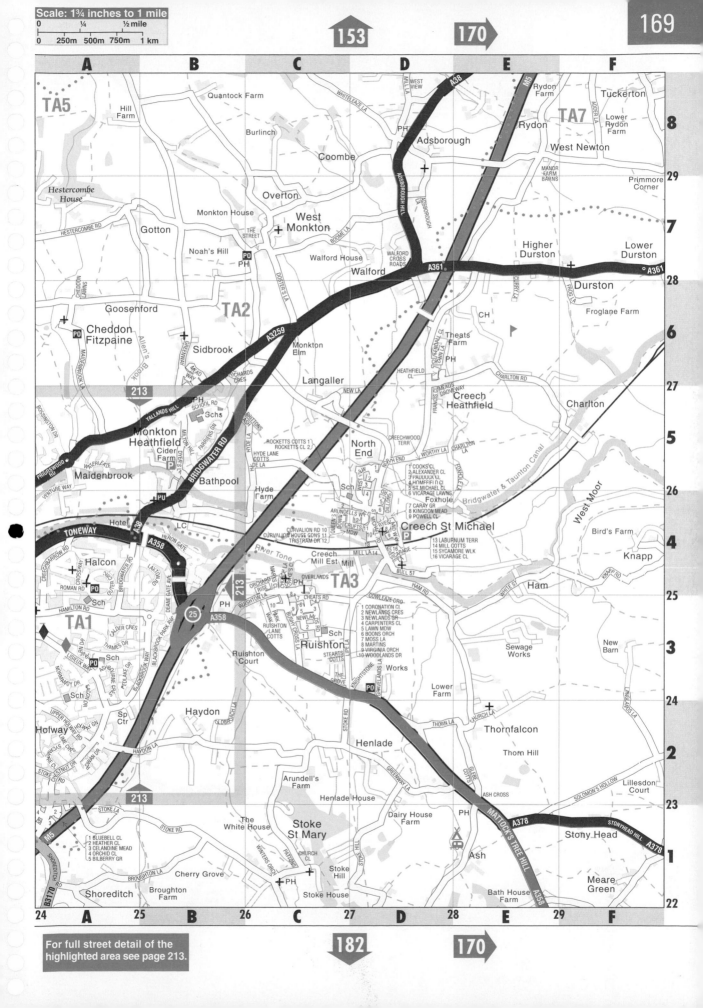

Scale: 1¾ inches to 1 mile

0   ¼   ½ mile
0   250m   500m   750m   1 km

A   **B**   **C**   **D**   **E**   **F**

Bankland

TA7

Bankland Dro

Bankland Bridge

Hedging

HEDGING LA

Starsland Farm

LC

Hitchings

Lyng Dro

East Lyng

PHILLIP'S DRO

HECTORS LA

TA3

NEW RD

A361

Athelney Hill

Mon

Stan Moor

TA7

8

29

Outwood

Outwood House

Lyng

Parsonage Farm

HILL VIEW TERR

NORTH CURRY

LOCKETTS BARTON

LC

Athelney

STANMOOR RD

7

West Lyng

HITCHINGS LA

MAIN RD

Lyng Moor

STREAKED LA

Turkey Cottage

Hook Bridge

Athelney

Stanmoor Mead Dro

PH Curload

Stanmoor Mead

STANMOOR DRO

WOODHILL TERR

28

A361

Cogload Farm

Old Rhyne

NEW RD

Currymoor Dro

Stoke Dro

Curry Moor

River Tone

Cames Meads

Stoke St Gregory

Windmill Hill

PO

COLLISHIRE LA

CHURCH CL

WILLEY RD

Slough Court

SLOUGH LA

Dykes Farm

DARK LA

POC

FIELD

PH

Woodhill

Pound Dro

6

27

New Bridge

Hay Moor

Moredon

Haymoor Old Rhyne

Frog Lane Farm

FROG LA

River Parrett Trail

Meare Green

HUNTHAM LA

SHARPHAM LA

PH

Sch

HUNTHAM CL

WINDMILL

Park Meads

5

Knapp Bridge

HAYMOOR DRO

Haymoor End

Knapp

WEST LA

PH

COMBE LA

MOOR LANE CL

LOWWELL'S ORCH

MOOR LA

North Curry

THE FOSSE

STOKE RD

BROAD LA

HUNTHAM RD

Huntham

ARCH LA

Sedgemoor Old Rhyne

North Dro

TA10

26

KNAPP RD

THE TRIANGLE

KNAPP LA

QUEEN SQ

THE SHAMBLES

PH

PO

CHURCH RD

CANTERBURY

THE

SPINNEY

Broad Lane Farm

HELLAND LA

TA3

4

Borough Farm

HORSECROFT

CHAPEL LA

TOWN CL

PAVEMENT

NINE ACRE LA

OLD FIELD

OVERLANDS

Helland

BARTON WAY

HELLAND HILL

WESTFIELD LA

25

Borough Post

WINDMILL HILL

SH. MAMS

GREENWAY

Sch

Cricket Cotts

OVERLAND LA

PONDCLOSE LA

Helland Meads

WEST SEDGEMOOR RD

3

OXEN LA

24

Lillesdon

WINDMILL HILL

LILLESDON TERR

NEWPORT HILL

Nythe Farm

South Dro

SOUTH DRO

Eastwood Farm

Fivehead Hill

2

Sedgemoor Coll

Newport

SEDGEMOOR DRO

Listock

JUNCTION RD

SOUTH DRO

Smith's Farm

Upper Fivehead

Fivehead

A378

Angel Row

ORCHARD RISE

PO

23

Hammonds Farm

CROFT DITCH

Rock Hill

Rock

Cathanger

CATHANGER LA

GREEN LA

SILVER ST

GRANGE'S HILL

BUTCHER'S LA

PH

Langford

LANGFORD LA

LANGFORD CL

ST MARTIN'S CL

MILLERS ORCH

1

Wrantage

NORTHMEAD DRO

PH

BARCROFT CRES

STONYHEAD HILL

PESTLEFIELD LA

ROCKWAY

MARSHWAY

BERRY LA

Stowey Farm

STOWEY RD

STOWEY LA

St Albans Farm

THE GLEBE

Stillbrook Farm

Cemy

A378

PO

OLDWAY LA

22

30   **A**   **31**   **B**   **32**   **C**   **33**   **D**   **34**   **E**   **35**   **F**

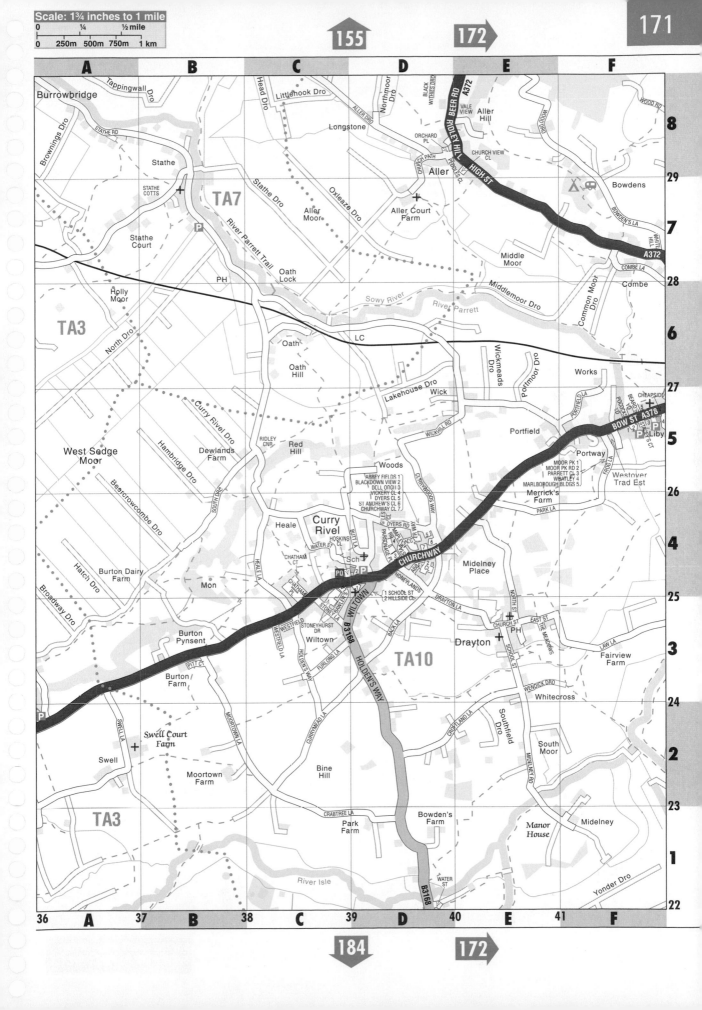

Scale: 1¾ inches to 1 mile
0   ¼   ½ mile
0   250m 500m 750m 1 km

A   B   C   D   E   F

8

Bramwell

Low Ham

Pitney Wood

Park Farm

West Wood

PARK LA

Somerton Door Dro

Bradley Hill

WOOD RD

FIELD RD

LONG ST

Woodbirds Hill

MORTON'S LA

UNDERWOOD LA

Whiscombe Hill

Bancombe Hill

BRADLEY HILL LA

29

Hext Hill

Pitney House

Western Gate

Middle Gate

Somertonfield Rd

Westcombe

Somertonfield Rd

BANCOMBE RD

LEAZEMOOR LA

WOODBIRDS HILL LA

MIDDLEGATE RD

STONEY RD

7

Paradise

Wearne

BOWDEN'S LA

ONE ELM

Pict's Hill

CULVER HILL

GORE LA

Rectory Hill

Pitney

MARSH LA

Somerton Hill

Somerton Hill

LANGPORT RD   B3153

211

TA11

RICKSEY LA

28

WHITE SWALLOW

COMBE LA

NEW WAY

FLIPPITS LA

PH

HERMITAGE RD

SLIPPERY BATCH

BRADLEY HILL LA

6

A372

NEWTOWN RD

WALNUT DR

SYCAMORE DR

B3153

SOMERTON RD

MAPLE RD

MEADOW CL

NEWTOWN PK

Pict's Hill

WILLOW

BROOKLAND RD

UNION DRO

Hamdown House

Pitney Hill

Tengore Farm

HERMITAGE RD

DOWNSLADE LA

SUTTON RD

B3165

WINDMILL LA

211

27

A378

MORT'S LA

PAULL'S CL

KENNEL

GARDEN CITY

BEECHES

BARRYMORE CL

TENGORE LA

ROWMARSH LA

LONG FURLONG LA

8 THE EMBANKMENT
9 EASTOVER CL
10 THE FIRS
11 BISHOPS DR
12 PARSONAGE CL
13 ST MARY'S PK

WAGG DRO

Wagg

Upton

MONDAY'S COURT LA

WINBRIDGE LA

HARDING'S HILL

PO

Sch

THE HILL

EASTOVER

1/3

2

11

12

Sch

POUNSELL LA

PORTLAND RD

Rose Cottage Farm

LIMEPITS LA

BURNT HOUSE LA

Manor House Lane

5

Whatley La 1
Whatley 2
Bush Pl 3
St Gilda's Cl 4
Bonds Pool 5
Orchard Vale 6
St Gildes Ct 7

TANYARD LA

SNAPS LANE

COURT FIELD

P

DUCKS HILL

Huish Episcopi

LANGPORT

Horsey Farm

Pibsbury

LEVEL VIEW

BLAKE LA

GAINSBRAKE LA

BATT'S LA

PEDAL DRO

LANDMOOR LA

LITTLEFIELD LA

LANGPORT RD

STEPHEN'S

WEST VIEW

B3165

Sch

PH

A372

B3165

26

Bicknell's Bridge

Muchelney Level

TA10

Ablake

HELE LA

HAYMOOR LA

CR2
DS LA

ORCHARD CL

PO

Long Sutton

PARSONS CL

KNIGHT LAIDS LA

KNOLE CSWY

4

River Parrett

River Parrett Trail

HORSEY LA

Macmillan Way West

Hay Moor

NEW ST

MARTOCK RD

CHURCH WLK

WITHMOOR DRO

SUTTON CROSS

Sutton LA

ILCHESTER LA

25

Priest's House

LAW LA

Muchelney Abbey

Muchelney

THE ROW

POUND WAY

River Yeo

Lame Hill

CH

3

Westover Farm

Thorneymoor La

SILVER ST

Whit Moor

Wet Moor

Little Load

King's Moor

24

Thorney Moor

Muchelney Ham

WETMOOR LA

CHURCH LA

Load Bridge

Crown Inn (PH)

MILTON LEAZE

2

River Parrett Trail

River Parrett

COOMBE LA

Long Load

College Cl

23

Thorney

Witcombe Bottom

THE COUNCIL HOS

B3165

1

TA12

Stapleton Mead Farm

TOWN TREE LA

TA12

Witcombe La 1
Thornhill Dro 2

New Witcombe Farm

22

42   A   43   B   44   C   45   D   46   E   47   F

For full street detail of the highlighted area see page 211.

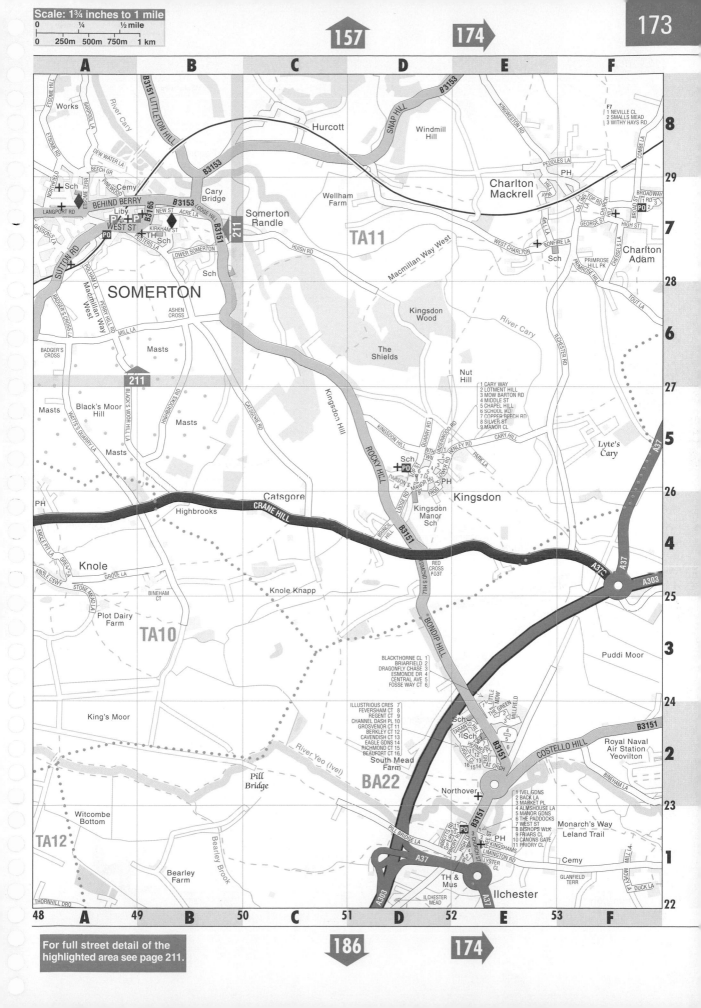

Scale: 1¾ inches to 1 mile

0   ¼   ½ mile
0   250m   500m   750m   1 km

157
174

A   B   C   D   E   F

Works
River Cary
B3151 LITTLETON HILL
ETSOME HILL
BARPOOL LA
DEW WATER LA
BEECH GR
PINEWOOD
B3153
Cemy
Behind Berry
Hurcott
SNAP HILL
Windmill Hill
B3153
KINGWESTON RD
F7
1 NEVILLE CL
2 SMALLS MEAD
3 WITHY HAYS RD
8
PEDDLES LA
PH
29
NORTHFIELD
Sch
ETSOME TERR
Cary Bridge
Somerton Randle
Wellham Farm
Charlton Mackrell
COMBE LA
BROADWAY
PO
LANGPORT RD
Liby
B3765
B3153
LODGE HILL
ACRE LA
Macmillan Way West
WEST CHARLTON
AVN
COLLINS
TOP RD
CHURCH
HIGH ST
Charlton Adam
GASSON'S LA
PO
WEST ST
NEW ST
211
HUISH RD
TA11
GEORGE ST
CHISSEL LA
7
SUTTON RD
TH
KIRKHAM'S ST
Sch
LOWER SOMERTON
Sch
BONFIRE LA
Sch
PRIMROSE HILL PK
PRIMROSE HILL
TOUT LA
28
SOMERTON
POLHAM LA
PERRY HILL RD
ASHEN CROSS
Kingsdon Wood
River Cary
ILCHESTER RD
MILL LA
BADGER'S CROSS
Masts
The Shields
6
BADGER'S CROSS
Macmillan Way West
Nut Hill
1 CARY WAY
2 LOTMENT HILL
3 MOW BARTON RD
4 MIDDLE ST
5 CHAPEL HILL
6 SCHOOL RD
7 COPPER BEECH RD
8 SILVER ST
9 MANOR CL
211
Black's Moor Hill
BLACK'S MOOR HILL LA
HIGHBROOKS RD
CATSGORE RD
Kingsdon Hill
27
Masts
WATTS QUARRY LA
Masts
Masts
ROCKY HILL
QUARRY RD
UNDERWOOD RD
HENLEY RD
CARY HILL
PARK LA
Lyte's Cary
A37
5
Catsgore
CRANE HILL
Highbrooks
NTH
TWN
Sch
PO
ANSON'S LA
FROB
MANOR RD
PH
Kingsdon
26
PH
LODGE RD
BRINCL HILL
B3151
Kingsdon Manor Sch
A37
4
Knole
GROVE LA
KNIGLE PIT LA
GREY LA
STONE MEAD LA
KNOLE CSWY
Bineham CT
EDMONDS HILL
RED CROSS POST
A372
A37
A303
25
Plot Dairy Farm
Knole Knapp
BONDIP HILL
Puddi Moor
3
TA10
BLACKTHORNE CL 1
BRIARFIELD 2
DRAGONFLY CHASE 3
ESMONDE DR 4
CENTRAL AVE 5
FOSSE WAY CT 6
LITTLE MDW
THE GREEN
MILLFIELD
24
King's Moor
ILLUSTRIOUS CRES 7
FEVERSHAM CT 8
REGENT CT 9
CHANNEL DASH PL 10
GROSVENOR CT 11
BERKLEY CT 12
CAVENDISH CT 13
EAGLE GDNS 14
RICHMOND CT 15
BEAUFORT CT 16
Sch
TARRANT RD
Sch
EAGLE
HERMES
GT ORCH
B3151
B3151
COSTELLO HILL
Royal Naval Air Station Yeovilton
BINEHAM LA
2
River Yeo (Ivel)
South Mead Farm
BA22
Northover
1 IVEL GDNS
2 BACK LA
3 MARKET PL
4 ALMSHOUSE LA
5 MANOR GDNS
6 THE PADDOCKS
7 WEST ST
8 BISHOPS WLK
9 FRIARS CL
10 CANONS GATE
11 PRIORY CL
23
Pill Bridge
Witcombe Bottom
PILL BRIDGE LA
Bearley Brook
PO
B3151
PH
ABBOTS LA
PRIORY RIGHT
KINGSHAMS
LIMINGTON RD
LYSTER CL
Monarch's Way
Leland Trail
MILL LA
Cemy
1
TA12
Bearley Farm
A37
A303
A37
TH & Mus
ILCHESTER MEAD
Ilchester
GLANFIELD TERR
DUCK LA
THORNHILL DRO
22

48   A   49   B   50   C   51   D   52   E   53   F

186
174

For full street detail of the highlighted area see page 211.

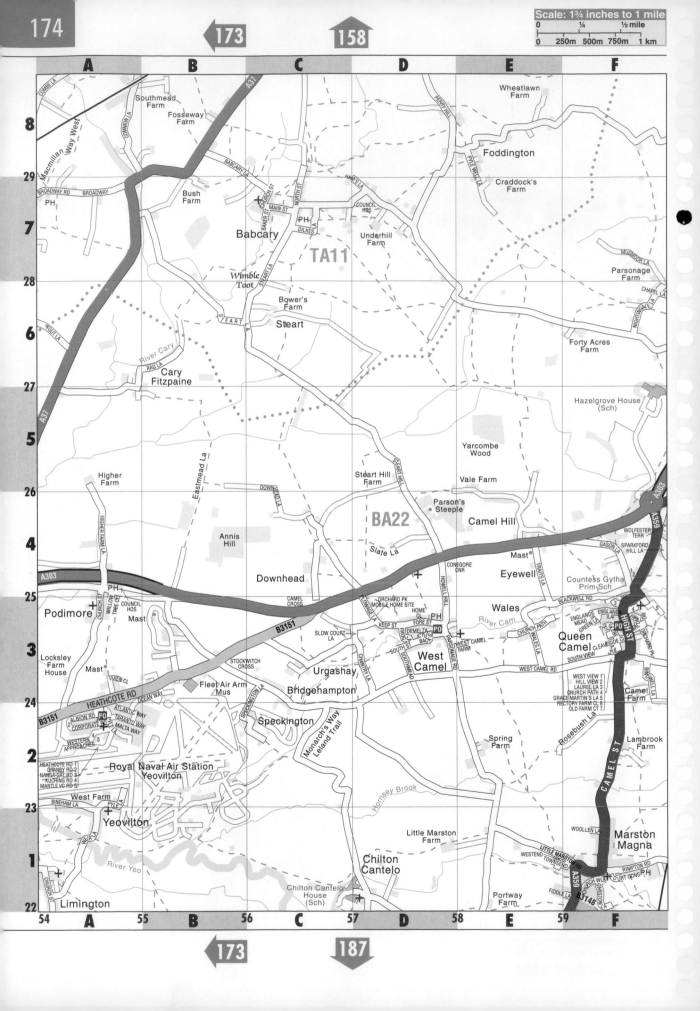

173 158

Scale: 1¾ inches to 1 mile

0   ¼   ½ mile
0   250m 500m 750m 1 km

A **B** **C** **D** **E** **F**

8

29

7

28

6

27

5

26

4

25

3

24

2

23

1

22

54   A   55   B   56   C   57   D   58   E   59   F

COMBE LA
Way West
MACMILLAN
Southmead Farm
Fosseway Farm
COMMON LA
BABCARY LA
BROADWAY RD   BROADWAY
PH
Bush Farm
Babcary
TA11
North St
Main St
PH
DILKES
Church St
Baker St
HAM'S LA
Council Hos
Underhill Farm
PERRY HILL
PYLE WELL LA
Wheatlawn Farm
Foddington
Craddock's Farm
MUSMOOR LA
Parsonage Farm
CHAPEL LA
NIGHTINGALE LA
Wimble Toot
Steart
Bower's Farm
STEART LA
TOUT LA
River Cary
RAG LA
Cary Fitzpaine
Forty Acres Farm
A37
Higher Farm
Eastmead La
DOWNHEAD LA
Annis Hill
Steart Hill Farm
STEART HILL
Yarcombe Wood
Parson's Steeple
Vale Farm
BA22
Camel Hill
Hazelgrove House (Sch)
A303
Slate La
CONEGORE CNR
HOWELL HILL
Mast
Eyewell
TRAITS LA
WOLFESTER TERR
GASON LA
SPARKFORD HILL LA
A359
A303
Podimore
PH
WILLOW TREE CL
Council Hos
Mast
Downhead
CAMEL CROSS
B3151
ORCHARD PK MOBILE HOME SITE
HOME CL
FORE ST
KEEP ST
PH
PO
DEMELZA
River Cam
CHURCH PATH
Countess Gytha Prim Sch
BLACKWELL RD
Wales
ENGLANDS MEAD
ENGLANDS LA
GREEN LA
PO
HIGH ST
ORCHARD PK
Queen Camel
CLEVEMEDE CL
SOUTH VIEW
Camel Farm
Locksley Farm House
Mast
VIXEN CL
Fleet Air Arm Mus
STOCKWITCH CROSS
SLOW COURT LA
Urgashay
Bridgehampton
CHANTRY LA
SOUTH ST
FROG LA
BACK LA
WEST CAMEL
PARSONAGE RD
W CAMEL FARM
WEST CAMEL RD
WALES LA
SOUTH VIEW
WEST VIEW 1
HILL VIEW 2
LAUREL LA 3
CHURCH PATH 4
GRACE MARTIN'S LA 5
RECTORY FARM CL 6
OLD FARM CT 7
HEATHCOTE RD
OCEAN WAY
SPECKINGTON LA
ATLANTIC WAY
TARANTO WAY
MALTA WAY
ALBION RD
CORPORATE RD
PO
WESTERN APPROACHES
B3151
Speckington
Monarch's Way
Leland Trail
Spring Farm
Rosebush La
Lambrook Farm
HEATHCOTE RD 1
GRANBY RD 2
NANGA-GAT RD 3
KUCHING RD 4
MANTLE VC RD 5
Royal Naval Air Station Yeovilton
West Farm
BINEHAM LA
PYLE
Yeovilton
River Yeo
Little Marston Farm
Hornsey Brook
WOOLLEN LA
CAMEL ST
Marston Magna
CHURCH ST
Limington
Chilton Cantelo
Chilton Cantelo House (Sch)
Portway Farm
LITTLE MARSTON RD
WESTEND
TOWNSEND
A359
FIDDLE LA
RIMPTON RD
CURT GDNS
CHURCH WLK
PH
B3148

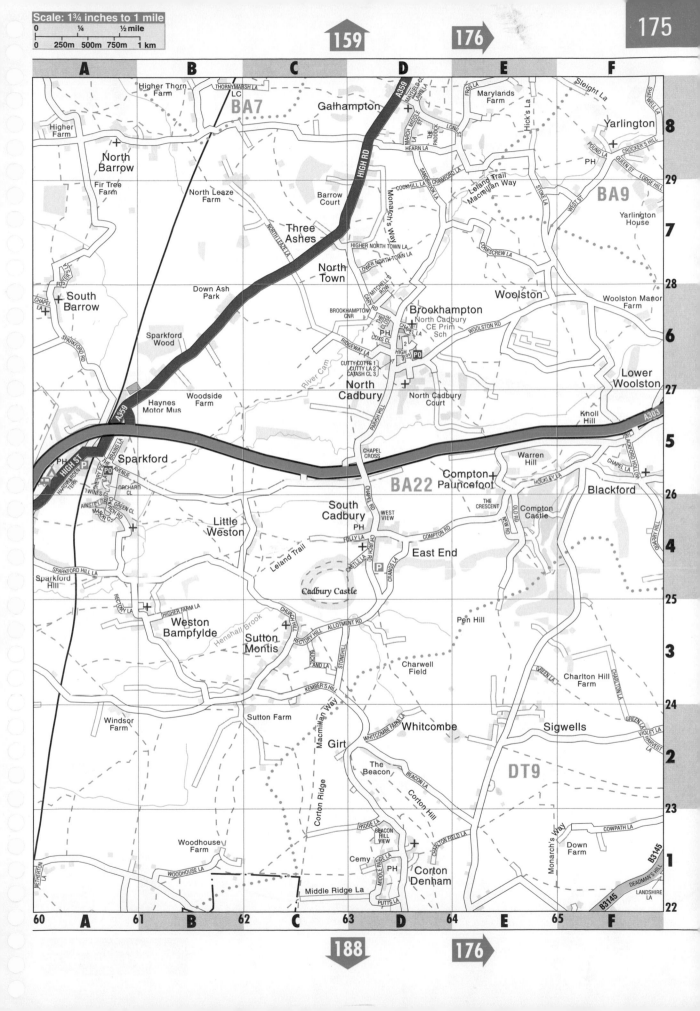

Scale: 1¾ inches to 1 mile
0   ¼   ½ mile
0   250m 500m 750m 1 km

A B C D E F

8

29

7

28

6

27

5

26

4

25

3

24

2

23

1

22

A371
God's Hill
CATTLE HILL
Bratton Hill
Bratton Seymour
UPLANDS 1
BRATTON HO 2
JACK WHITE'S GIBBET
Higher Holbrook Farm
Westleaze Farm
Suddon Grange
Race Course
CH
B3081
Windmill Hill
RECTORY LA
Eastwood Farm
LODGE HILL
Verrington
VERRINGTON LA
Hospl
H
West Hill
Liby
Mus
Sch
BA8
GRANTS LA
BAYFORD HILL
Higher Clapton Farm
Hunger Hill
Holbrook House Hotel
Sch
DANCING LA
SPRINGER RD
WEST HILL
NORTH ST
HIGH ST
SILVER ST
MILL ST
PO
Sch
STATION RD
SOUTH ST
COMMON RD
WINCANTON
Cemy
B3081
SOUTHGATE
A303
BA9
Hook Valley Farm
A371
Lawrence Hill
MOOR LA
Higher Holton
ANCHOR CNR
A357
Hatherleigh Farms
Works
Brains Farm
River Cale
A303
GIBB RD
HOLTON CROSS
HOLTON ST
PH
Holton
Lattiford Farm
Lattiford
SLOPERS LA
216
DANCING CROSS
CLAPTON LA
GIBBET RD
HOOK LA
Maperton
SHEPHERDS CROSS
Marchant-Holliday Sch
B3145
GROVE LA
Grove Farm
BA22
HARDING'S LA
LOWER CHERITON LA
Maltkin Hill Farm
North Cheriton
LANDSEER
WOOD LA
South Cheriton
Monarch's Way
MARSH LA
Horsington Marsh
BLACKACRE HILL
BARRART CL
CHERITON ST
BEHIND HAYES
PH
BROOKSIDE
Cemy
LOWER RD
Horsington CE Prim Sch
Horsington Marsh
BATCHPOOL LA
Marshbarn Farm
CHARLTON HILL
Charlton Hill
Silver Knap
BLACKFORD WAY
GREEN LA
DEV'S LA
HULL LA
Hull Farm
GOATHILL LA
CABBAGE LA
Darkharbour Farm
HIGHER RD
TOWER VIEW
COLDHILLS LA
HOUND HILL
PH
RECTORY LA
WHITE OAK COTTS
DUCK LA
BROADMOOR LA
Combe Throop
Windmill Hill
MAPERTON RD
LESTER LA
NORTH END
HARVEST LA
GUNVILLE LA
VIOLET LA
CATHOLE LA
SOUTHDOWN
HORSE LA
PH
PO
Sch
1 CLEEVEWAYS
2 WARREN CL
3 MANOR CL
4 BRAMLEY CL
5 ORCHARD WAY
Kennels
Charlton Horethorne
BA8
MANOR CT
Horsington
TOWER HILL
HISCOCK'S LA
SLADES HILL
Abbas Combe
THE HAMLET
THROOP RD
Abbas & Templecombe CE Prim Sch
TEMPLE LA
COMPATH LA
CENTENARY COTTS
DEADMAN'S LA
B3145
LANDSHIRE LA
MOUNT LA
DT9
HANGLANDS LA
Wilkinthroop
STOWELL HILL
WATERY LA
North Side Wood
Stowell
WESTWOOD COTTS
LILY LA
CHURCH HILL
SCHOOL LA
HIGH ST
PO
STATION RD
PH
EAST ST
Templecombe
HILLCREST
BOC LA
WEST COMBE
A357
1 YARNBARTON
2 THE KNAP
3 TEMPLARS PL
4 CORONATION VILLAS
5 BRINES ORCH
6 WEST CT
7 TEMPLARS BARTON
8 MERTHYR GUEST CL
9 KINGTON VIEW
WATERLOO CRES

66 67 68 69 70 71

For full street detail of the highlighted area see page 216.

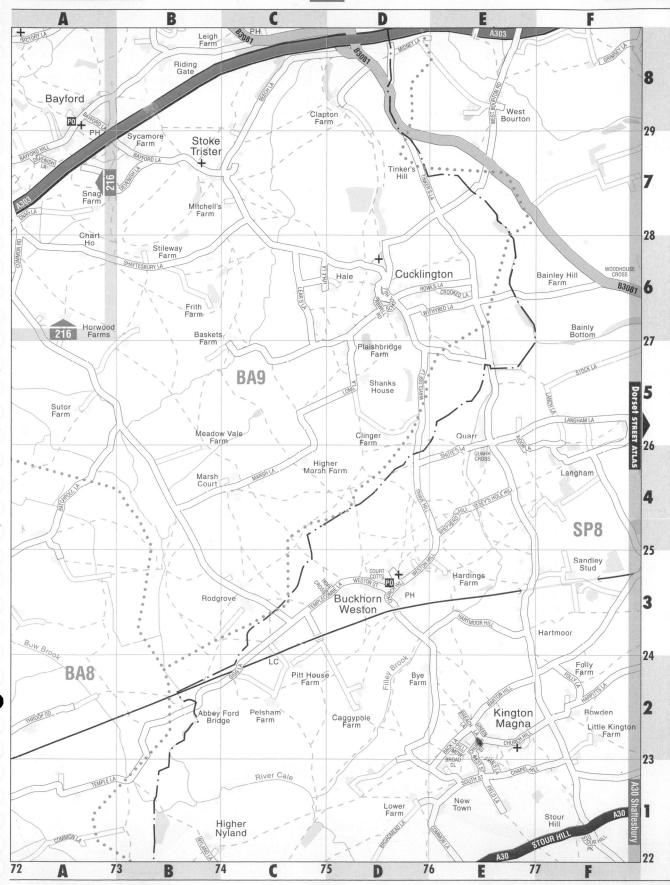

190

For full street detail of the
highlighted area see page 216.

Dorset STREET ATLAS

A303
B3081
Leigh Farm
PH
Riding Gate
Bayford
PO
PH
BAYFORD LA
DEVENISH LA
Sycamore Farm
BAYFORD LA
Stoke Trister
Clapton Farm
MIDNEY LA
A303
West Bourton
WEST BOURTON RD
Snag Farm
216
SNAG LA
Mitchell's Farm
Tinker's Hill
TINKER'S LA
Chart Ho
Stileway Farm
SHAFTESBURY LA
COMMON RD
Hale
HINE LA
Cucklington
Bainley Hill Farm
WOODHOUSE CROSS
B3081
ROWLS LA
CROOKED LA
SCHOOL RD
CHAPEL RD
Frith Farm
LEAR'S LA
WITHYBED LA
Bainly Bottom
Horwood Farms
216
Baskets Farm
Plaishbridge Farm
STOCK LA
BA9
Shanks House
LONG LA
LANGHAM LA
LANCH LA
Sutor Farm
Meadow Vale Farm
Clinger Farm
Quarr
ACRE LA
Langham
BATCHPOOL LA
MARSH LA
Marsh Court
Higher Marsh Farm
SHUTE'S LA
QUARR CROSS
SNAKE HILL
VESEY'S HOLE HILL
SP8
Sandley Stud
SHEPTON HILL
Rodgrove
Court Cotts
WESTON ST
PO
WESTON HILL
Hardings Farm
TEMPLECOMBE CROSSING
INGPEN
CHURCH LA
Buckhorn Weston
PH
HARTMOOR HILL
Hartmoor
Buw Brook
GIGG LA
LC
Pitt House Farm
Filley Brook
Bye Farm
BARTON HILL
Folly Farm
FOLLY LA
HARPITTS LA
BA8
THROOP RD
Abbey Ford Bridge
Pelsham Farm
Caggypole Farm
Kington Magna
Rowden
Little Kington Farm
BREACH LA
CHURCH GREEN
CHURCH HILL
BACK LA
PILL
MDW
BROAD CL
WEST LA
JUBB'S LA
CHAPEL HILL
TEMPLE LA
River Cale
SOUTH ST
FIELD LA
Higher Nyland
NYLAND LA
Lower Farm
BROADMEAD LA
New Town
COMMON LA
Stour Hill
A30
STOUR HILL
STOUR PK
COMMON LA
A30
STOUR HILL
A30 Shaftesbury

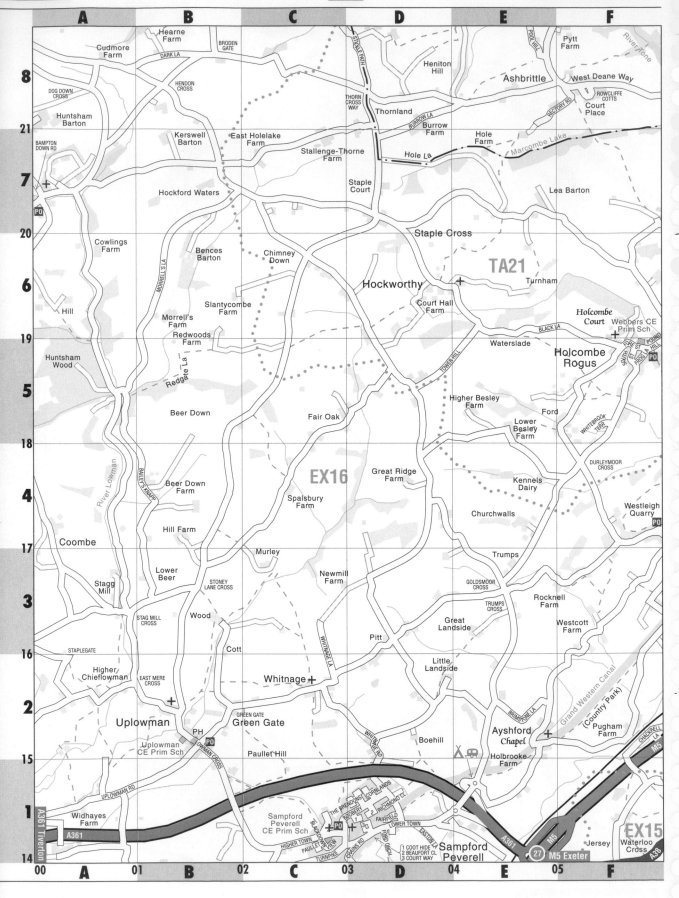

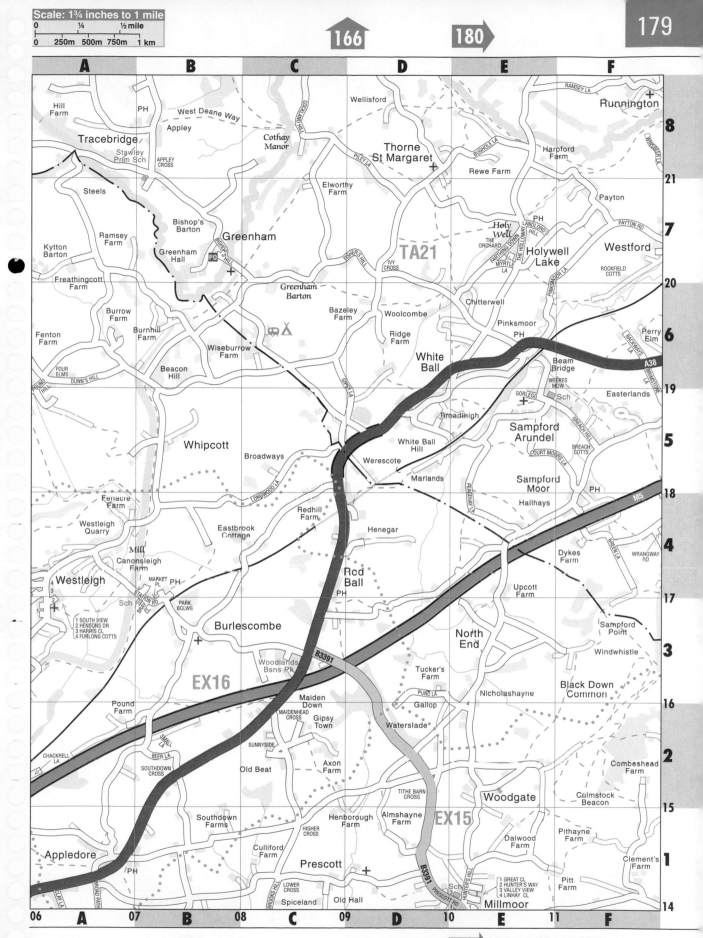

Scale: 1¾ inches to 1 mile

0 ¼ ½ mile
0 250m 500m 750m 1 km

A B C D E F

8

Tone
River Tone
B3187 Ind Ests
Crosslands
MILVERTON RD
Wks
RICHARDS CL
West Deane Way
Pool Farm
Wks
Pool
Ham
TA4 A38
PH
PH
Silver Street
Hockholler

Tonedale
Longforth Farm
BRENDON RD
HOWARD RD
PARKLANDS PL
TAUNTON RD
Cade's Farm
Bsns Pk
SUMMERFIELD AVE
HAM RD
COB CASTLE
CASTLE COTTS
KNIGHTS
Hockholler Green
SILVER ST
POLLARD

21

BURCHILL HILL
CORAMS RD
VICTORIA ST
WATERLOO RD
HIGH ST
PRIORY
GAY CL
Chelston
B3187
A38
CHELSTON TERR
CHELSTON HEATHFIELD
ORCHARD GDNS 1
COBURG CL 2
CHURCH DR 3
CROWN MEWS 4
CROWN HILL 5
BARBERS LA
DYERS
COCKS CL

7

Lower Westford
Sports Ctr
Sch
Rockwell Green
BEECH GR
P
Liby
Mus
SCOTT'S LA
WELLINGTON
Park Farm
Sawyer's Hill
West Buckland
STOFORD LA
Sch
PAYTON RD
NORTH SC
MANTLE ST
BULFORD
Sch
Sch
Jurston Farm
WEST BUCKLAND RD
A38
M5

20

222
EXETER RD
PD
Cemy
WELLESLEY PK
Sch
222
Haywards Water
26
Five Cross Way
WILDMOOR LA

TA21
Bagley Green
FOXDOWN HILL
SWAINS LA
WELLESLEY PK
HOYLES LA
MONUMENT RD
Burts House
Ford St
GERBESTONE LA
Manley's Farm
BUDGETTS
BUDGETT'S CROSS

6

Nurseries
BAGLEY RD
POPE'S LA
NOWERS LA
OLDWAY RD
MIDDLE GREEN
Gerbestone Manor
Hopkin's Farm

STALLARDS
Middle Green
WELLINGTON HILL
Gillard's Farm
TA21
Blackmoor
Perry Farm

19

Stallards
LITTLE SILVER LA
Legglands
Ford Street
Gortnell Farm

Pleamore Cross
Bryant's Farm
Leyland's Farm
Calway's Farm

5

Woodford
Long Wood
222
Voxmoor
Gortnell Common
Buckland Hill

M5
Higher Woodford
PARK LA
BEACON LA

18

Wrangway
Park Farm
Beacon Lane Farm
Quarts Farm
Wiltown

4

WRAGGCOMBE LA
WHATCOMBE RD
Wellington Mon
Scottsdale
SMEATHY LA

WRANGWAY RD
P
Wellington Hill
P
Blackdown Visitors Ctr
Heazle Farm
RED LA
WILTOWN LA
Wiltown Valley

17

P
Hill Farm
BARPARK CNR
APPLEHAYES LA

3

Mast
P
EX15
Simonsburrow
Garlandhayes
GARLANDHAYES LA
RINGDOWN LA

16

Whitehams
Blackaller Farm
Clayhidon
Woodgate's Farm

2

Culm Davy Hill
COMBE HILL
ASHCULM HILL
Brownheath
Clayhidon Turbary
PH
CLAYHIDON CROSSWAY
Lear's Farm

15

Culm Davy
Ashculme
BLACK LA
Gollick Park
SHEPHERD'S LA
HUEWOOD
TA3

Pen Cross
Culm Pyne Barton
GRAY'S LA
GRE'S HILL
NICK RD'S LA
BATTLE ST
Rosemary Lane
PD
Clayhidon Hill
ROSEMARYLANE CROSS
CALLER'S LA

1

Whitehall
WITHY LA
Millhayes
Byes Farm
Gladhayes Farm
BRIDGEHOUSE CROSS
River Culm
Brimley Hill
BRIMLEY CROSS

14

Hemyock
HIGHER MILLHAYES

12 A 13 B 14 C 15 D 16 E 17 F

For full street detail of the highlighted area see page 222

179
191

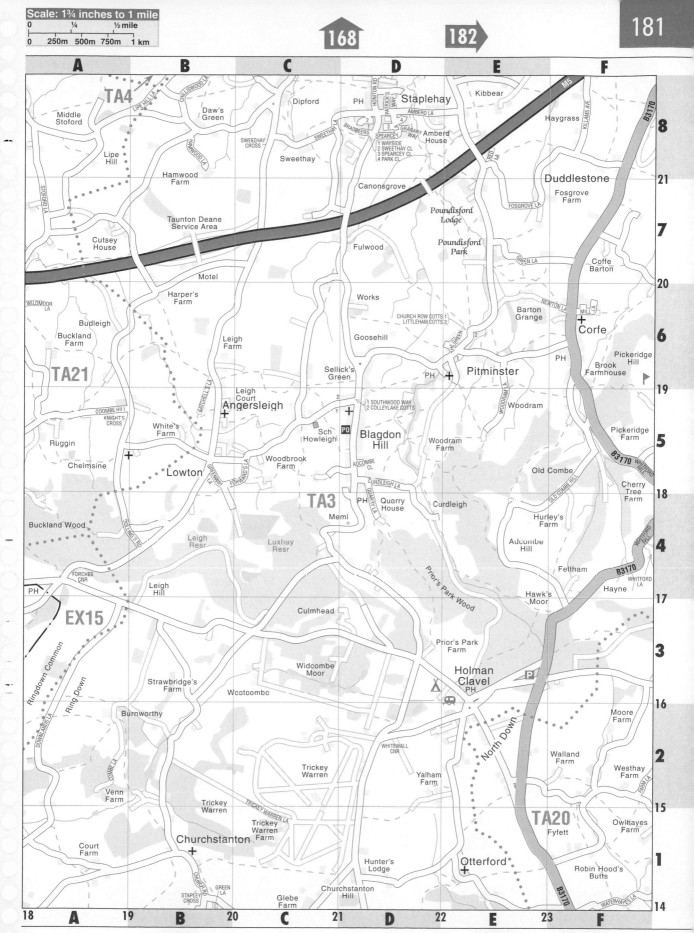

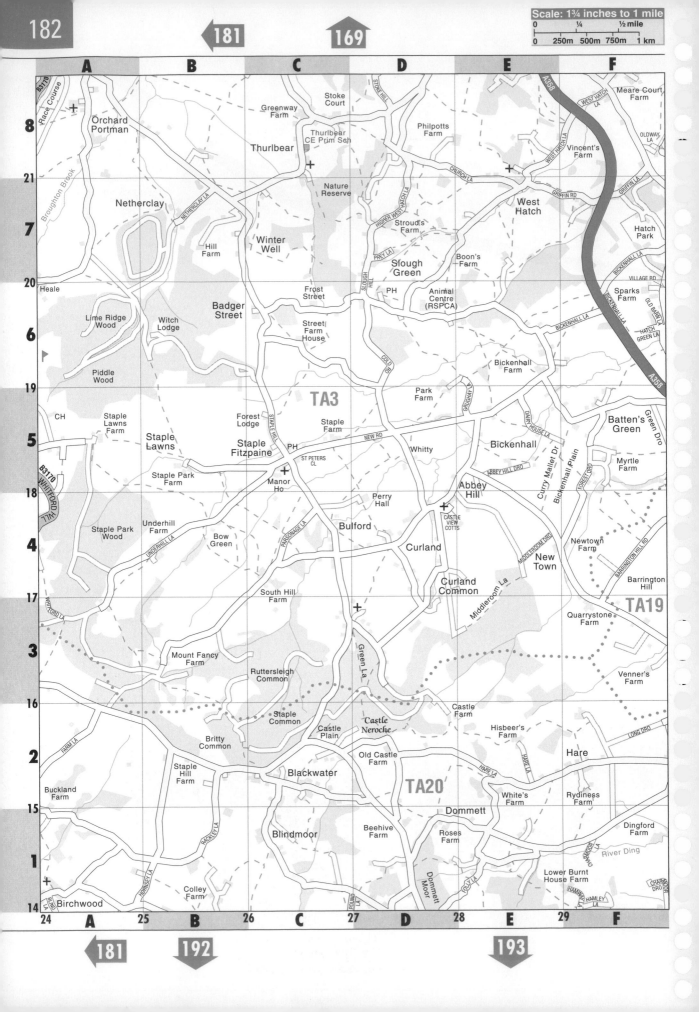

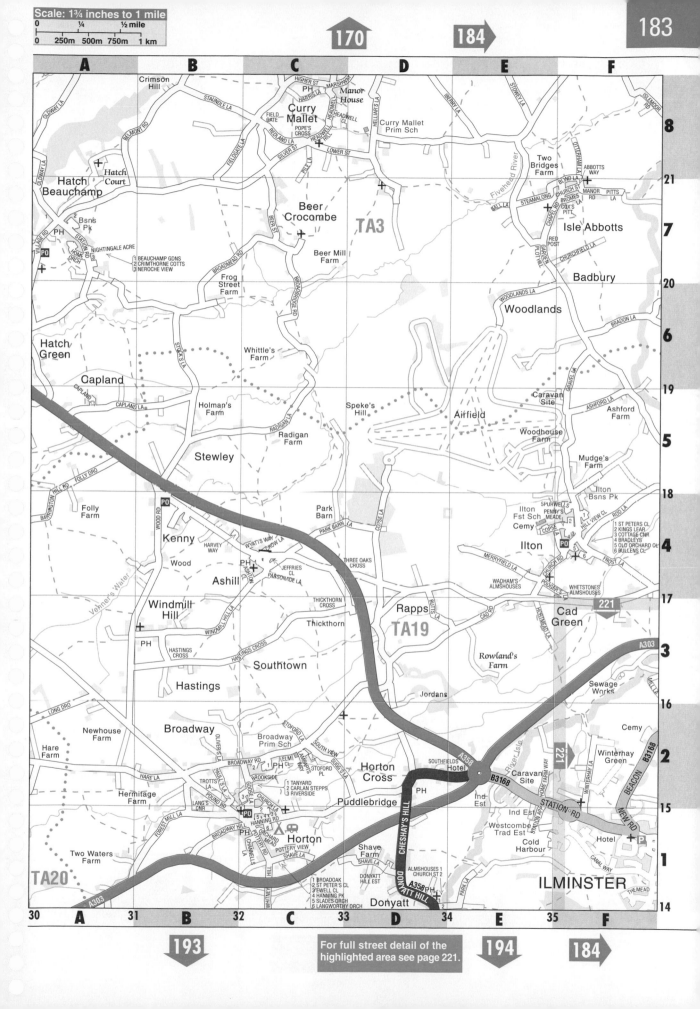

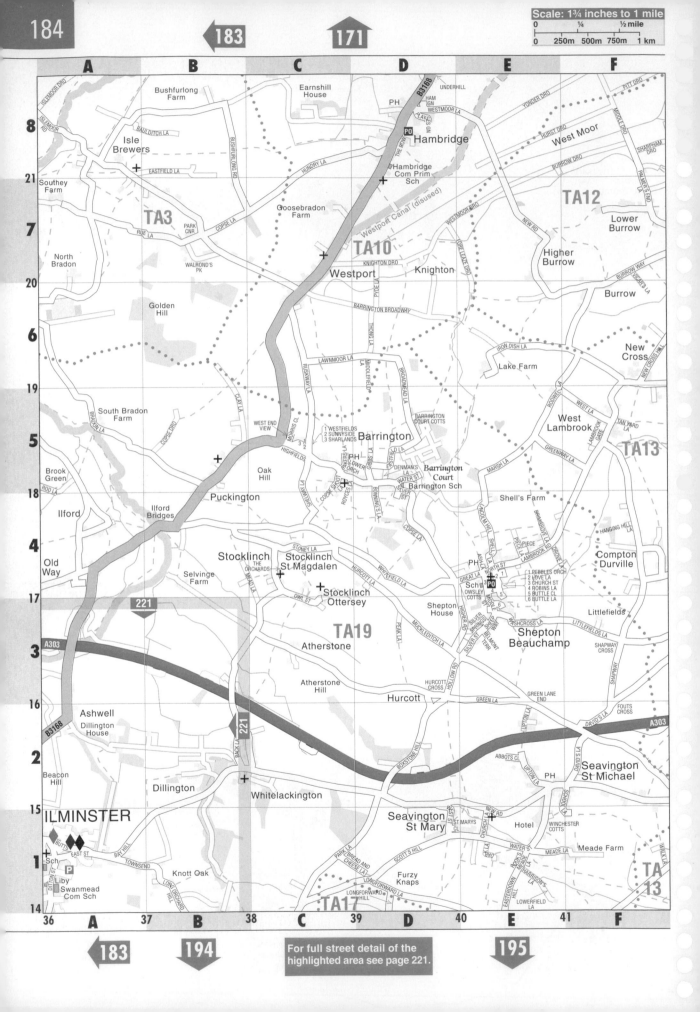

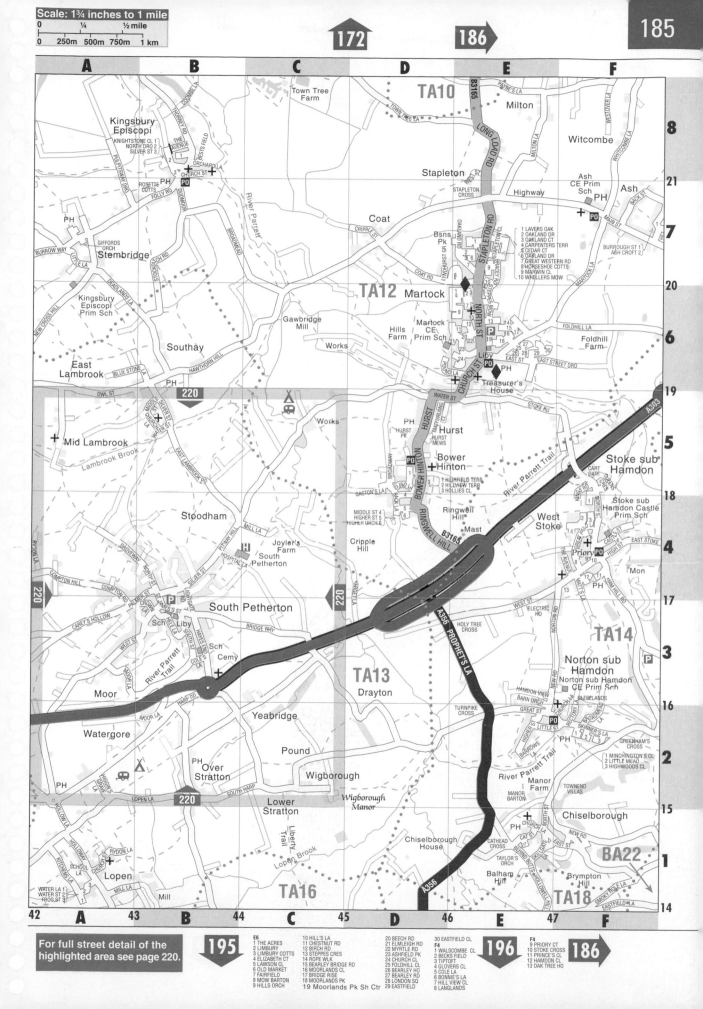

Scale: 1¾ inches to 1 mile

0   ¼   ½ mile
0   250m 500m 750m 1 km

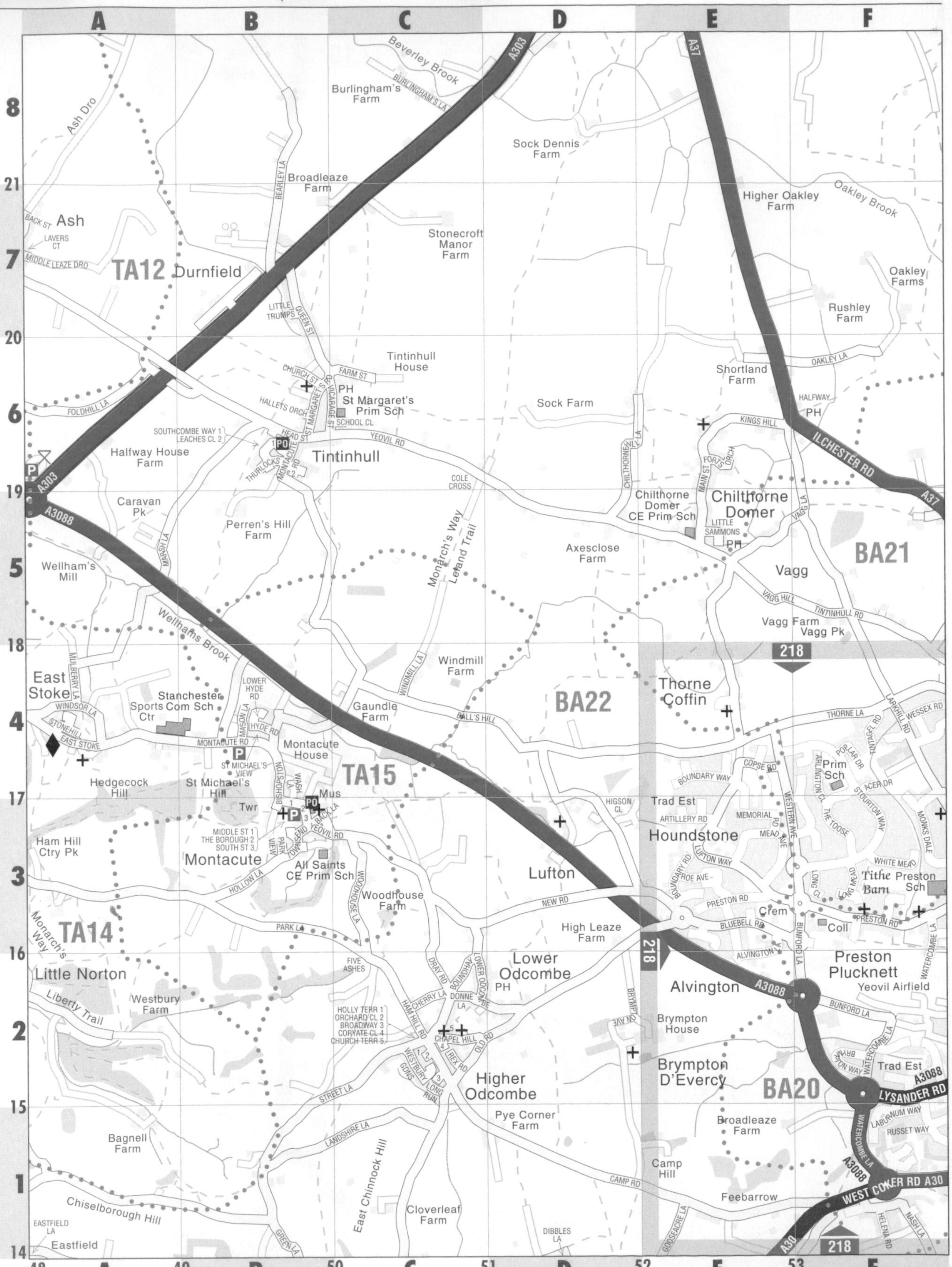

Grid columns: A B C D E F

Ash Dro

8

21

BACK ST

Ash

LAVERS CT

MIDDLE LEAZE DRO

7 **TA12** Durnfield

Beverley Brook

Burlingham's Farm

BURLINGHAM'S LA

A303

Sock Dennis Farm

Higher Oakley Farm

Oakley Brook

A37

Broadleaze Farm

BEARLEY LA

Stonecroft Manor Farm

Rushley Farm

Oakley Farms

20

LITTLE TRUMPS

QUEEN ST

OAKLEY LA

Shortland Farm

Tintinhull House

FARM ST

CHURCH ST

6

FOLDHILL LA

CHURCH ST
VICARAGE

PH St Margaret's Prim Sch

SCHOOL CL

Sock Farm

Halfway PH

ILCHESTER RD

KINGS HILL

HALLETS ORCH

SOUTHCOMBE WAY 1
LEACHES CL 2

HEAD LA

THURLOCKS MD

MONKS RD

PO

YEOVIL RD

Tintinhull

COLE CROSS

CHILTHORNE LA

MAIN ST

FORD

Chilthorne Domer CE Prim Sch

Chilthorne Domer

A37

19

P
A303

A3088

Halfway House Farm

MARSHALL'S LA

Caravan Pk

Perren's Hill Farm

Monarch's Way

Leland Trail

LITTLE SAMMONS PH

VAGG LA

BA21

5

Wellham's Mill

Wellhams Brook

Axesclose Farm

Vagg

VAGG HILL

Vagg Farm Vagg Pk

TINTINHULL RD

18

East Stoke

MILLBERRY LA

WINDSOR LA

LOWER HYDE RD

MASON LA

HYDE RD

Stanchester Sports Com Sch

Gaundle Farm

BALL'S HILL

WINDMILL LA

Windmill Farm

BA22

Thorne Coffin

218

THORNE LA

LARGHILL RD

WESSEX RD

Prim Sch

4

STONEHILL
EAST STOKE

MONTACUTE RD

ST MICHAEL'S VIEW

P

Montacute House

WISH LA

TA15

HIGSON CL

Trad Est

BOUNDARY WAY

COPSE RD

ARLINGTON CL

ACER DR

POLAR DR

STOURTON WAY

17

Hedgecock Hill

St Michael's Hill

Twr

Mus

PO
P
3

MIDDLE ST 1
THE BOROUGH 2
SOUTH ST 3

PARK VIEW

VICARAGE LA

YEOVIL RD

ARTILLERY RD

MEMORIAL
AVE

WESTERN AVE

THE TOOSE

MONKS DALE

Tithe Barn

Preston Sch

Ham Hill Ctry Pk

Montacute

HOLLOW LA

WOODHOUSE LA

All Saints CE Prim Sch

Woodhouse Farm

Lufton

LUFTON WAY

MONROE AVE

Houndstone

BOUNDARY RD

PRESTON RD

WHITE MEAD

LONG CL

BLUEBELL RD

BUNFORD LA

Cfem

Coll

PRESTON RD

WATERCOMBE LA

3

TA14

Monarch's Way

PARK LA

NEW RD

High Leaze Farm

218

ALVINGTON LA

Preston Plucknett

16

Little Norton

Liberty Trail

Westbury Farm

FIVE ASHES

DRAY RD

LOWER ODCOMBE LA

CHERRY LA

DONNE LA

Lower Odcombe PH

A3088

Alvington

BRYMPTON WAY

Yeovil Airfield

BUNFORD LA

15

Bagnell Farm

STREET LA

LANDSHIRE LA

HOLLY TERR 1
ORCHARD CL 2
BROADWAY 3
CORYATE CL 4
CHURCH TERR 5

HAM HILL RD

WESTBURY GDNS

CHAPEL HILL

OLD RD

LONG FURL

REX LA

Higher Odcombe

Pye Corner Farm

Brympton House

Brympton D'Evercy

BA20

WATERCOMBE LA

LYSANDER RD

LABURNUM WAY

A3088

MAGNUM WAY

RUSSET WAY

Trad Est

A3088

1

Chiselborough Hill

EASTFIELD LA

Eastfield

GREEN LA

East Chinnock Hill

Cloverleaf Farm

DIBBLES LA

CAMP RD

Camp Hill

GRASSACRE LA

Feebarrow

A30

WEST COKER RD A30

HELENA RD

NASH LA

A3088

218

14

For full street detail of the highlighted area see page 218.

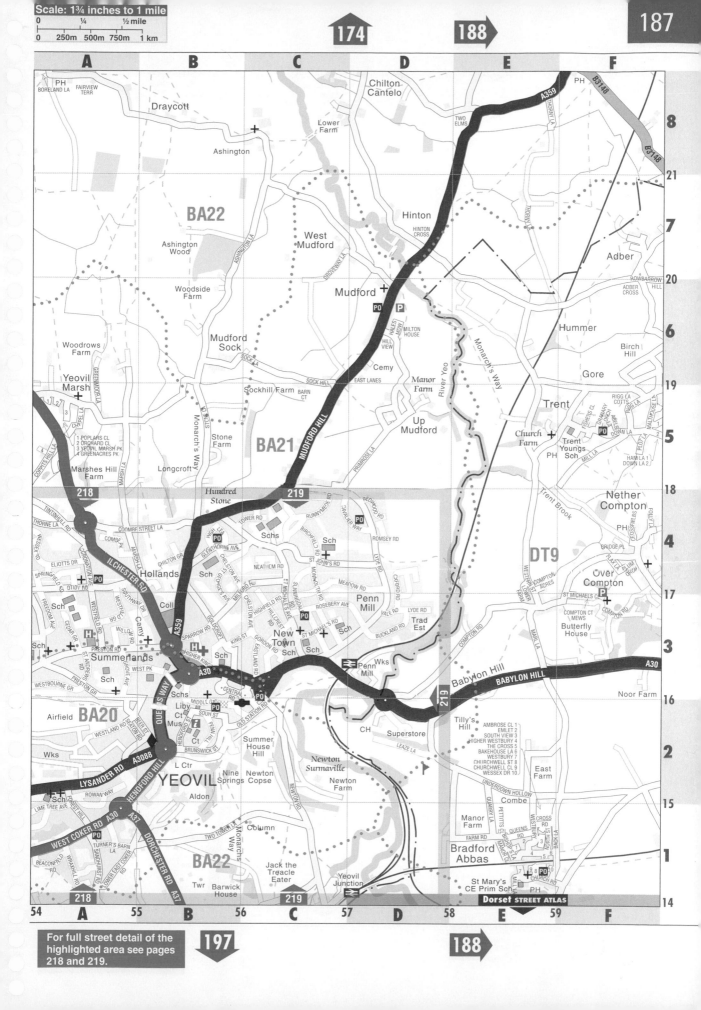

Scale: 1¾ inches to 1 mile

0   ¼   ½ mile
0   250m 500m 750m 1 km

174   188

A   B   C   D   E   F

8
21
7
20
6
19
18
4
17
3
16
2
15
1
14

PH
BORELAND LA   FAIRVIEW TERR
Draycott

Ashington

BA22

Ashington Wood

Lower Farm

Chilton Cantelo

TWO ELMS

A359

THORNY LA

PH B3148

B3148

Woodside Farm

West Mudford

Hinton

HINTON CROSS

Adber

ROWBARROW HILL
ADBER CROSS

Woodrows Farm

Mudford Sock

SOCK LA

Mudford
PO P

HILL VIEW

HALES MDW

MILTON HOUSE

River Yeo

Monarch's Way

Hummer

Birch Hill

Gore

Yeovil Marsh

GREENMOOR LA
CARPEL LA
1 2
3

Sockhill Farm

SOCK HILL

EAST LANES
Cemy

East Lanes

Manor Farm

Up Mudford

Trent

RIGG LA COTTS
RIGG LA
FISHER'S CL
PRIMARY
ABEL'S DOWN LA
MALTHOUSE LA

Church Farm
PH

Trent Youngs Sch
PO

HAM LA 1
DOWN LA 2

1 POPLARS CL
2 ORCHARD CL
3 YEOVIL MARSH PK
4 GREENACRES PK

MARSH LA
MONARCH'S WAY

Stone Farm

BA21

MUDFORD HILL

PRIMROSE LA

Trent Brook

Nether Compton

PH

FOLLY LA
CROSSHILL LA

Marshes Hill Farm

Longcroft

Hundred Stone

218   219

DT9

Over Compton

WESTERN ST
COMPTON ACRES
COMPTON ST
St Michaels C

BRIDGE PL

FLAT LA
PLUM ORCH

TINTINHULL RD
THORNE LA

COOMBE STREET LA

TONER RD
PO
Schs

RUNNYMEDE RD

CAVALIER WAY
PO

REDWOOD RD

ROMSEY RD

Compton Rd

MARL LA

Butterfly House
P
COMPTON CT MEWS

WESSEX RD
WESSEX DR

ILCHESTER RD

COMBE

HIGH LEA
PO
GLENTHORNE AVE
CHELSTON AVE

ST GEORGE'S AVE

BIRCHFIELD RD

ST JOHN'S RD

Sch

MEADOW RD

LYDE RD
OXFORD RD

Penn Mill

LYDE RD
Trad Est

Babylon Hill
BABYLON HILL
A30

Noor Farm

Tilly's Hill

AMBROSE CL 1
EMLET 2
SOUTH VIEW 3
HIGHER WESTBURY 4
THE CROSS 5
BAKEHOUSE LA 6
WESTBURY 7
CHURCHWELL ST 8
CHURCHWELL CL 9
WESSEX DR 10.

WESSEX RD
SPRINGFIELD
ELIOTTS DR
OTIDY RD
PO

Hollands

Sch

CHILTON GR

NEATHEM RD

MILWARD RD
HIGHFIELD RD

SUMMERLEAZE PK
MONMOUTH RD
RUNNYMEDE RD

ROSEBERY AVE

VALE RD
BUCKLAND RD

COMPTON RD

219

FREEDOM AVE
CEDAR GR
Sch

Coll

A359

SPARROW RD

HIGHER KING ST

KING ST
GORDON RD

ST MICHAEL'S AVE
HILLCREST RD

New Town Sch
St Michael's Rd

Sch

Penn Mill

Wks

WILLOW RD
Camy
PRESTON RD

H

H

Sch

WEST PK

Sch

EASTLAND RD

219

Superstore

Manor Farm

East Farm

Sch

WESTBOURNE GR
PRESTON GR
ST ANDREWS RD
GROVE AVE

A30

Schs
LIBY
CT
Mus

CENTRAL RD
PO

PEWTER

MIDDLE ST

SOUTH ST

OLD STATION RD

CH

LEAZE LA

Combe

UNDERDOWN HOLLOW

QUARRY LA
FARM RD

Airfield

BA20

WESTLAND RD
BEREST
STATION RD

Wks

L Ctr

YEOVIL

Summer House Hill

Newton Surmaville

QUEEN'S WAY

HENFORD HILL
BRUNSWICK ST

Nine Springs
Aldon

Newton Copse

Newton Farm

MANOR FARM
PETTITS CL
BISHOP RD
WESTBURY RD
NORTH ST
MILLS
QUEENS

Bradford Abbas

WRANHILL RD
SANDHILLS RD

LYSANDER RD A3088

A37

West Coker Rd A30

HENDFORD HILL

DORCHESTER RD

PO
TURNER'S BARN LA
LOWER EAST COKER RD

BA22

LIME TREE AVE
Sch

ROWAN WAY

Column

TWO TOWER LA
Monarchs Way

Jack the Treacle Eater

Yeovil Junction

St Mary's CE Prim Sch
PO
PH

Twr
Barwick House

218   219

197   188

For full street detail of the highlighted area see pages 218 and 219.

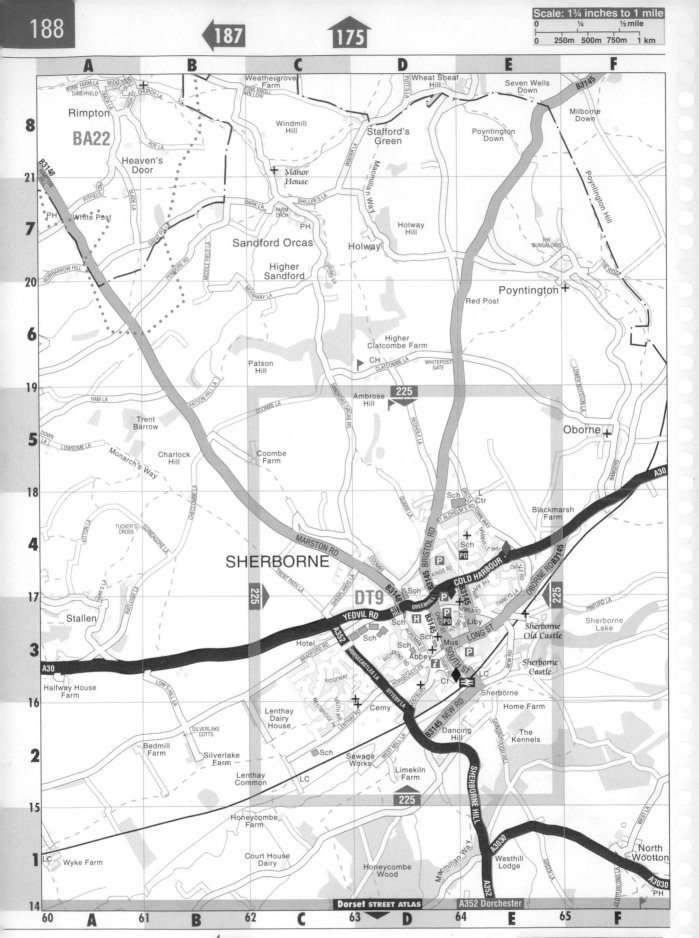

Scale: 1¾ inches to 1 mile

0   ¼   ½ mile
0   250m 500m 750m 1 km

Rimpton

BA22

Heaven's Door

Home Farm La
Daisyfield
Mid La
Mill La
Back La
High St
Church La
Roe La

White Post

PH

B3148
Rimpton

Bombarrow Hill

Pitfield

Slade La

Great Pit La

Penmore Rd

Middle Field La

Weathergrove Farm

Pink Knoll Hollow

Windmill Hill

Putts La

Wheat Sheaf Hill

Seven Wells Down

B3145

Milborne Down

Stafford's Green

Poyntington Down

Manor House

Shiller's La

Winter La

Dark La

Farm Orch

PH

Sandford Orcas

Higher Sandford

Holway Hill

Holway

Macmillan Way

The Bungalows

The Ridge

Poyntington Hill

Poyntington

Spring La

Motway La

Red Post

Ham La

Patson Hill La

Coombe La

Higher Clatcombe Farm

CH

Clatcombe La

Whitepost Gate

Lower Boyston La

Trent Barrow

Down La

Lowsome La

Monarch's Way

Charlock Hill

Patson Hill

Coombe Farm

Sandford Orcas Rd

Ambrose Hill

225

Oborne

Kitton La

Tucker's Cross

Guinagore La

Checcombe La

Marston Rd

Coombe La

Quarr La

Bristol Rd

St Aldhelm's Rd

Town End

Castle Town Way

Granville Way

Sch

PO

Blackmarsh Farm

A30

SHERBORNE

Trent Path La

225

Sch

Kings Rd

P

COLD HARBOUR

Oborne Rd B3145

225

Pinford La

Sherborne Lake

Stallen

Hart's La

Ratleigh La

Sheeplands La

Hitt Hill

B3148

Greenhill

DT9

YEOVIL RD

A352

Hotel

Bradford Rd

Sch

Acreman St

Richmond Rd

Sch

H

P
PO

Sch

Sch

B3145

Cheap St

Mus

Abbey

i

Ct

SOUTH ST

LONG ST

Newland

Liby

The Avenue

Tinney's La

P

New Rd

Sherborne Old Castle

Sherborne Castle

Sherborne

A30

Halfway House Farm

Low's Hill La

Silverlake Cotts

Silverlake Farm

Bedmill Farm

Lenthay Common

Lenthay Dairy House

Westbridge Pk

South Ave

Lenthay Rd

Sch

LC

Ridgeway

Horsecastles La

Horsecastles

Ottery La

Cemy

Westbury

West Mill La

Sewage Works

Limekiln Farm

B3145 NEW RD

Dancing Hill

Gainsborough Hill

Home Farm

The Kennels

LC

Sherborne Hill

225

Honeycombe Farm

Court House Dairy

Honeycombe Wood

Macmillan Way

A3030

A352

Westhill Lodge

Green La

West La

North Wootton

A3030

PH

LC

Wyke Farm

Clotfurlong La

For full street detail of the highlighted area see page 225.

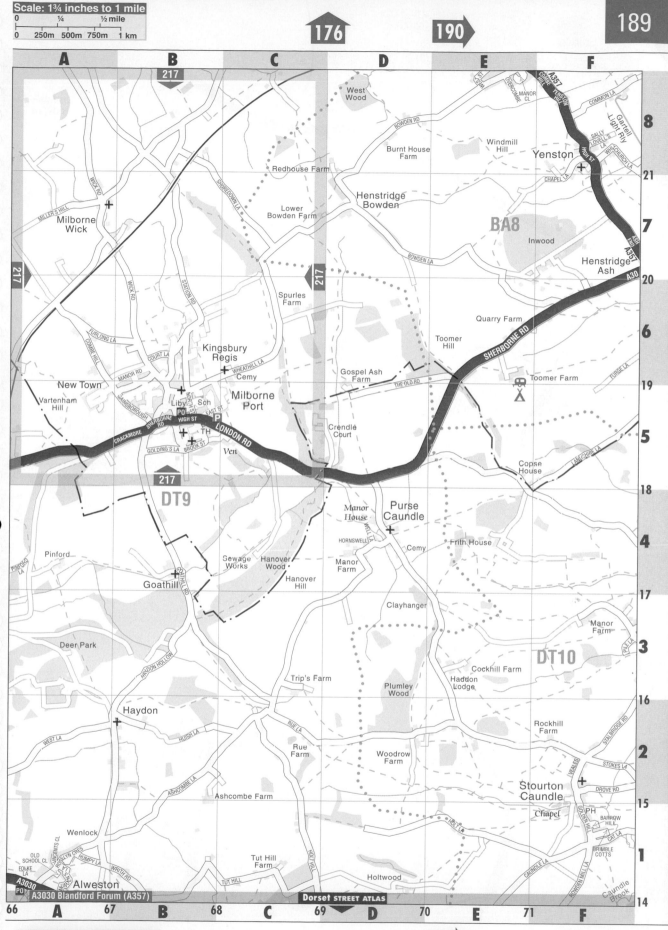

Scale: 1¾ inches to 1 mile

0   ¼   ½ mile
0 250m 500m 750m 1 km

176

190

A   B   C   D   E   F

West Wood

BOWDEN RD

Burnt House Farm

Windmill Hill

MANOR CL

OVERCOMBE

COMBE HILL

A357

COMMON LA

Garell Light Riv

SALLY LOVELL'S LA

WH LA

Yenston

CHAPEL LA

HIGH ST

CHURCH LA

8

21

217

Redhouse Farm

Lower Bowden Farm

Henstridge Bowden

BA8

Inwood

A357

A30

Henstridge Ash

7

20

SHERIDOWN RD

STATION RD

Spurles Farm

217

Quarry Farm

SHERBORNE RD

Toomer Hill

Toomer Farm

TURGE LA

6

19

Miller's Hill

Milborne Wick

WICK RD

COMBE HILL

FURLONG LA

COURT LA

MANOR RD

WICK RD

Kingsbury Regis

WHEATHILL LA

Cemy

Gospel Ash Farm

THE OLD RD

New Town

GAINSBOROUGH

Libry Sch
PO
NORTH ST
EAST ST
HIGH ST
Milborne Port

Crendle Court

LANCHPLE LA

Copse House

5

18

Vartenham Hill

CRACKMORE

SHERBORNE RD

GOLDING'S LA
BROOK ST
TH

LONDON RD

Ven

217

DT9

Manor House

HORNSWELL LA

Purse Caundle

Cemy

Frith House

4

17

Pinford

PINFORD LA

GOATHILL RD

Sewage Works

Hanover Wood

Hanover Hill

Manor Farm

Clayhanger

Manor Farm

PYE LA

DT10

Goathill

Deer Park

HAYDON HOLLOW

Trip's Farm

Plumley Wood

Cockhill Farm

Haddon Lodge

STALBRIDGE RD

Rockhill Farm

3

16

Haydon

WEST LA

HUISH LA

RUE LA

Rue Farm

Woodrow Farm

HOLT LA

STOKES LA

VEAL'S LA

Stourton Caundle

DROVE RD

2

15

ASHCOMBE LA

Ashcombe Farm

Wenlock

Chapel

GOLDEN HILL

BARROW HILL

PH

CAT LA

BRIMBLE COTTS

1

OLD SCHOOL CL
FOLKE LA
ROSELYN CRES
VINCENTS CL
HUMPY LA
WRITH RD

A3030
PO
Alweston

Tut Hill Farm

TUT HILL

HOLT HILL

Holtwood

ROWDEN MILL LA

CAUNDLE LA

Caundle Brook

14

A3030 Blandford Forum (A357)

Dorset STREET ATLAS

190

66 A 67 B 68 C 69 D 70 E 71 F

For full street detail of the highlighted area see page 217.

190

A6
1 VIRGINIA CL
2 PLAYFIELD CL
3 BROOKLAND WAY
4 ST NICHOLAS CL
5 POND CL
6 BLACKMOOR LA

7 BROOK LA
8 CHURCH ST
9 THE CROSS
10 TOWNSEND GN
11 BUGLE CT
12 WOODHAYES HO
13 COTTON CNR

14 VICTORIA TERR
15 VICTORIA GDNS
16 ELIZABETH GDNS
17 WINDSOR TERR

189

177

Scale: 1¾ inches to 1 mile
0   ¼   ½ mile
0 250m 500m 750m 1 km

Fifehead Magdalen

SP8
BA8
DT10

Mohuns Park
Whitchurch
Henstridge Ash
Henstridge
Towns End
Stalbridge
Marnhull
Hains
Strangways Farm

Lower Nyland
Lower Marsh
Hacktthorne Farm
Henstridge Marsh
Higher Marsh
Syles Farm
Airfield
Henstridge Trad Est
Coking Farm
Five Bridges
Factory Farm
Manor Farm

Gibbs Marsh Trad Est
Gibbs Marsh Farm
Landshire Bridge
West Mill
Marnhull Ham
West Mill
Prior's Down
Triangle Farm
Gray's Farm
Gomershay Farm
Works
Pleck
Yardgrove Farm
Mounters

Prim Sch
Station Road Bsns Pk
The Sidings
Bibberne Farm
Hewletts Farm
Bungays Farm
King's Mill Bridge
Stalbrigde Common
Poolestown
Marsh Farm
Ryalls Farm
Manor House
Bagber Bridge
Cook's Farm
Obelisk
Holtham Plantation
Sturt Farm
Stalbridge Weston
Brunsell Knap Farm
Thornhill House
Hargrove Farm
Mullins Farm
Pleak House
Bagber Common
Warr Bridge
Caundle Brook
River Lydden
River Stour

Bagber Cross Rds
King's Mill Rd

Dorset STREET ATLAS

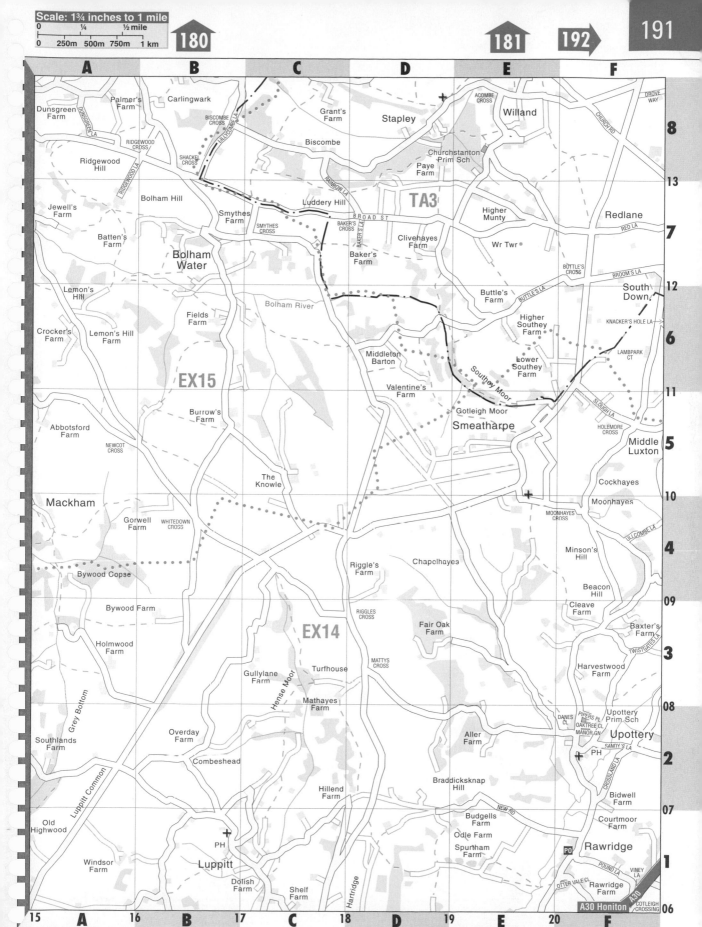

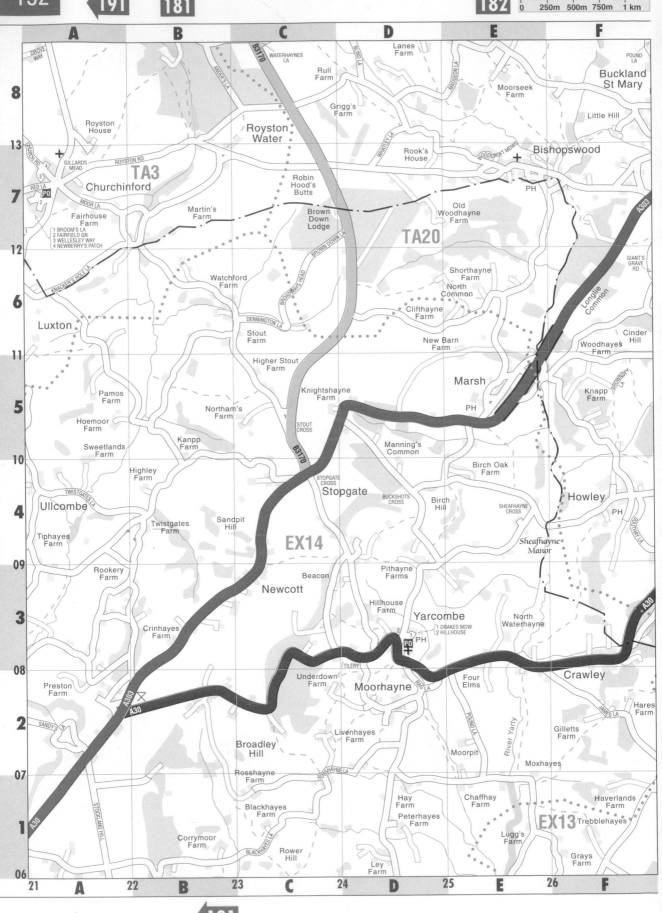

Scale: 1¾ inches to 1 mile

0   ¼   ½ mile
0   250m 500m 750m 1 km

A   B   C   D   E   F

8

DROVE WAY

Royston House

WATERHAYNES LA

B3170

Rull Farm

Grigg's Farm

Lanes Farm

BLIND LA

Moorseek Farm

POUND LA

Buckland St Mary

Little Hill

13

Royston Water

TA3

GILLARDS MEAD

ROYSTON RD

Churchinford

7

CHURCH RD

RED LA

PO

Robin Hood's Butts

Brown Down Lodge

Rook's House

WHATLEY LA

MADGEON LA

Old Woodhayne Farm

WOODCROFT MDWS

Bishopswood

PH

A303

Fairhouse Farm

1 BROOM'S LA
2 FAIRFIELD GN
3 WELLESLEY WAY
4 NEWBERRY'S PATCH

MOOR LA

Martin's Farm

BROWN DOWN LA

TA20

12

KNACKER'S HOLE LA

Luxton

Watchford Farm

BROADWAYS HEAD

DENNINGTON LA

Stout Farm

Shorthayne Farm

North Common

Clifthayne Farm

GIANT'S GRAVE RD

Longlie Common

Cinder Hill

Woodhayes Farm

6

Pamos Farm

Northam's Farm

Higher Stout Farm

New Barn Farm

Marsh

PH

Knapp Farm

BROWNSEY LA

11

Hoemoor Farm

Sweetlands Farm

Kanpp Farm

Knightshayne Farm

STOUT CROSS

B3170

Manning's Common

Birch Oak Farm

5

TWISTGATES LA

Highley Farm

STOPGATE CROSS

Stopgate

BUCKSHOTS CROSS

Birch Hill

SHEAFHAYNE CROSS

Howley

PH

STOUTLA LA

Ullcombe

Twistgates Farm

Sandpit Hill

EX14

Beacon

Pithayne Farms

Sheafhayne Manor

4

Tiphayes Farm

Newcott

Hillhouse Farm

North Waterhayne

A30

09

Rookery Farm

Yarcombe

1 DRAKES MDW
2 HILLHOUSE

PO PH

3

Crinhayes Farm

Moorhayne

RAIL LA

Four Elms

Crawley

POUND LA

Hares Farm

JAMES LA

08

Preston Farm

A303

A30

Underdown Farm

TILERY

River Yarty

Gilletts Farm

2

SANDY'S LA

Broadley Hill

Livenhayes Farm

Moorpit

Moxhayes

07

Rosshayne Farm

ROSSHAYNE LA

Hay Farm

Chaffhay Farm

Haverlands Farm

STOCKLAND HILL

Blackhayes Farm

Peterhayes Farm

EX13

Trebblehayes

1

A30

Corrymoor Farm

BLACKHAYES LA

Rower Hill

Ley Farm

Lugg's Farm

Grays Farm

06

21   A   22   B   23   C   24   D   25   E   26   F

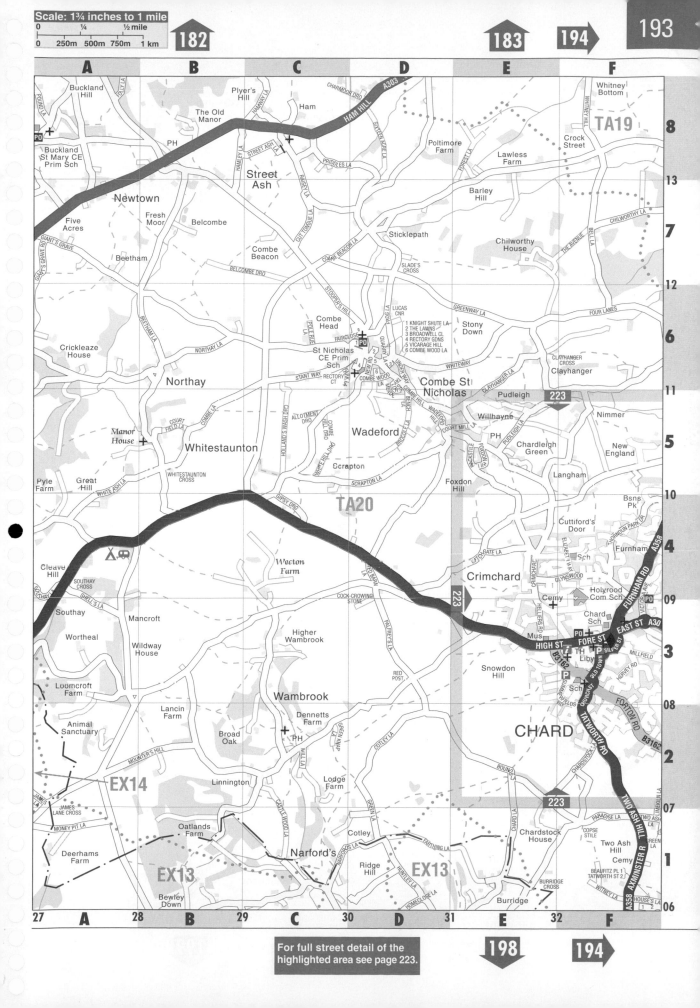

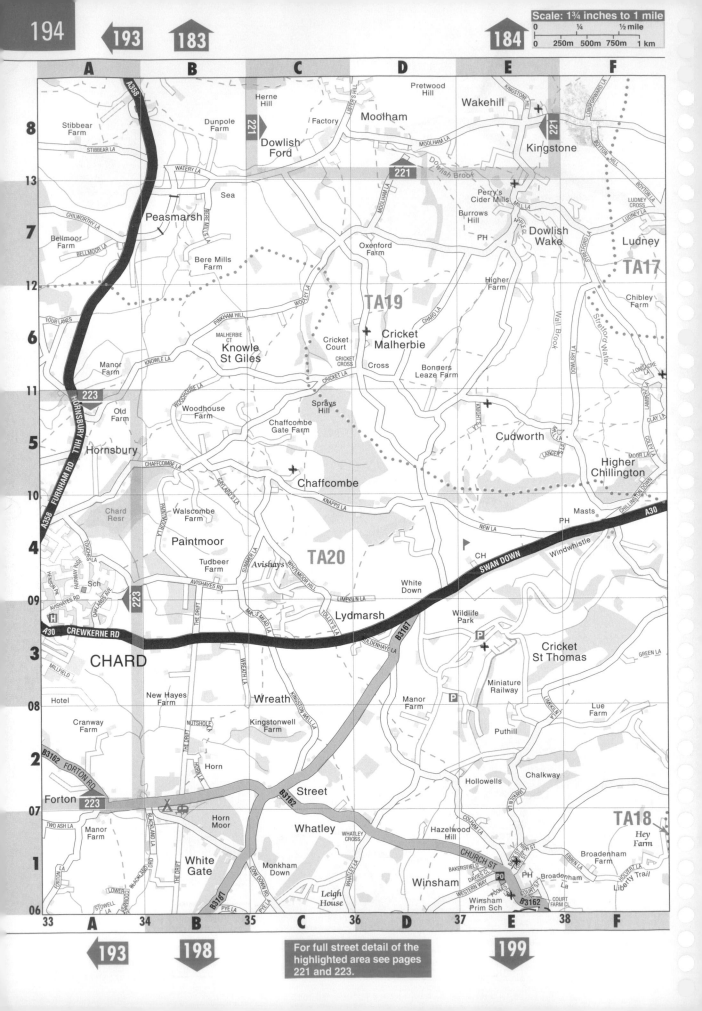

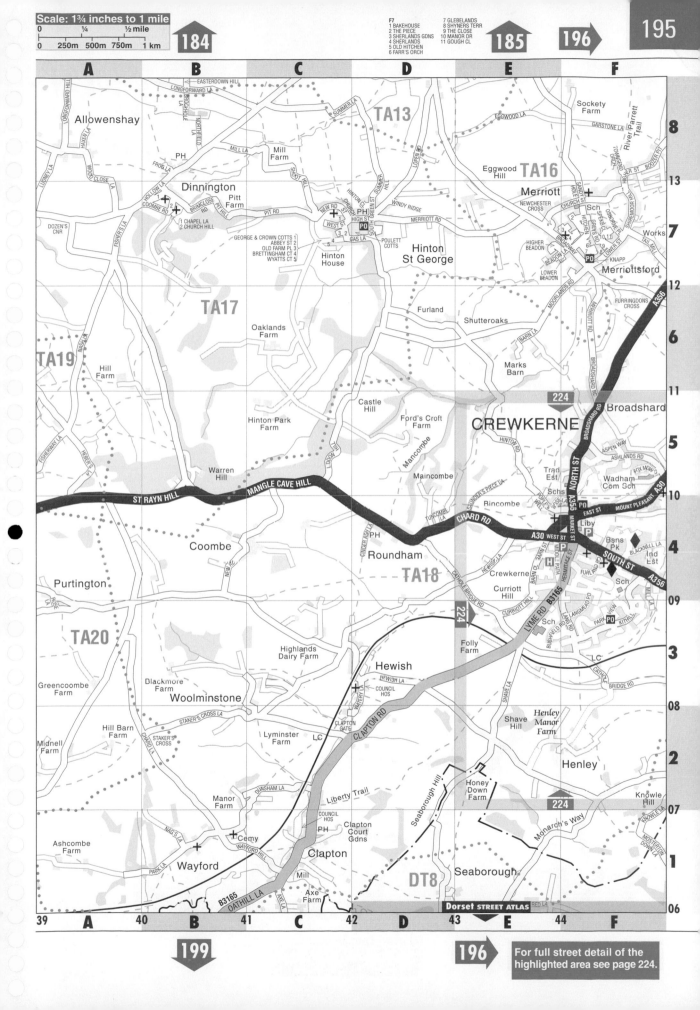

195 185 186

Scale: 1¾ inches to 1 mile

0 ¼ ½ mile
0 250m 500m 750m 1 km

A B C D E F

8

MIDDLEFIELD LA
WALL DITCH LA
A356
Bow Barn Farm
HUT GATE
West Chinnock CE Prim Sch
West Chinnock
LAYNE TERR
NEW COTTS
HIGHER
PH
HOLLOWELL HILL
LEAZE LA
LOWER ST
POOP HILL
1 HAUNTS
2 SMITHS HILL
POOP HILL LA
EASTFIELD LA
BROADWAY
East Chinnock
GREEN LA
COLLARWAY LA
A30
Mast
RIDGE LA

13

BOOZER PIT
TA16
BOW GATE
Snails Hill
SCOTTS WAY
DUCKPOOL LA
1 2 3 4 5
EAST LA
Middle Chinnock
BROADSTONE LA
Chinnock Brook
WEST WAYS
WESTON CL 1
BARROWS CT 2
WESTON CT
FORE LA
PARTMAN CT
WEST COKER HILL
3 BACK LA
4 ODCOMBE HOLLOW
CHINNOCK HOLLOW
HIGH ST
FORDHAY
PO
PH
SPRINGFIELD YARD
FORDHAY TERR

7

TAIL MILL
A356
HIGHFIELD 1
RIDGWAY 2
HILL VIEW CL 3
RICKHAY RISE 4
CHURCH CL 5
LONG
West Chinnock Hill
Monarch's Way
North Down Farm
FOXWELL LA
ELLIOTT'S HILL
COD LA
Barrows Hill
BROAD LA
Cott Farm
BROAD HILL
PARTWAY LA
WAMBROUGH LA
BARRY LA
BROADSTONE LA

12

6

Lower Severalls Farm
Haselbury Bridge
224
Rushy Wood Farm
GLOBE ORCH
A3066 NORTH ST
NEW LA
Haselbury Plucknett
DOWNEY
FIELD LA
Broad Hill Farm
Broad River
Bridge Close Farm
HILL CROSS
BA22
Hill End
COLD HARBOUR LA

11

YEOVIL RD
A30
HIGHER EASTHAMS LA
Lower Easthams Farm
River Parrett Trail
Manor Farm
NEW CL
WINTERFIELD
CHURCH LA
SWAN HILL
PO
FROG LA 1
BRAMBLE LA
Sch
CLAY CASTLE LA
CLAY CASTLE
2
1 PEGGY'S LA
2 CASTLETON
STONAGE LA
NEW RD
East Lease Farm
New Plantation
Hewingbere Farm
Monarch's Way
COMMON LA

5

Cemy
Liberty Trail
NORTH PERROTT RD
WILLIS'S LA
TRINGLEWELL LA
PILL HEAD LA
COMMON LA
TA18
Cowcroft Farm
Hardington Marsh
Marsh Farm
SHORTMARSH LA

10

Sewage Works
Perrott Hill Sch
MANOR BLDGS
CHURCH LA
NEW ST
MIDDLE ST
North Perrott
PH
EASTFIELD LA
1 SYMES CL
2 EAST ST
Kingswood Farm

4

CREWKERNE
Hellings Farm
224
A356
STATION RD
PH
Crewkerne
Misterton
Grey Abbey Farm
DOWNCLOSE LA
Downclose Farm
Haselbury Park Farm
Knowle Hill
Ashland Hill
Whitevine Farm

09

3

MILL LA
ROSE LA
PARK VIEW
1 PACKERS WAY
2 TURNPIKE CL
3 TURNPIKE GN
River Parrett

08

PO
MIDDLE ST
SILVER ST
SCHOOL LA
1 2 3
Sch
PH Cemy
Well Spring Farm
PIPPLEPEN LA
Pipplepen Farm
DT8
Cheddington Woods
Wyke Farm

2

KNOWLE LA
Knowle Farm
TURNPIKE CROSS
LECHER LA

07

224
Bluntsmoor Farm
A3066
PH
SCHOOL HILL
Sockety
CH
HOLT LA
Crook Hill

1

MOSTERTON DOWN LA
Chapel Court Farm
Mohun Castle
PARRETT MEAD
PICKET LA
MANOR CL
Orchard Farm
South Perrott
Manor Farm
A356
Winyard's Gap
STATION LA
DT2

06

A3066 Beaminster
Dorset STREET ATLAS
A356 Dorchester (A37)

45 A 46 B 47 C 48 D 49 E 50 F

For full street detail of the highlighted area see page 224.
195

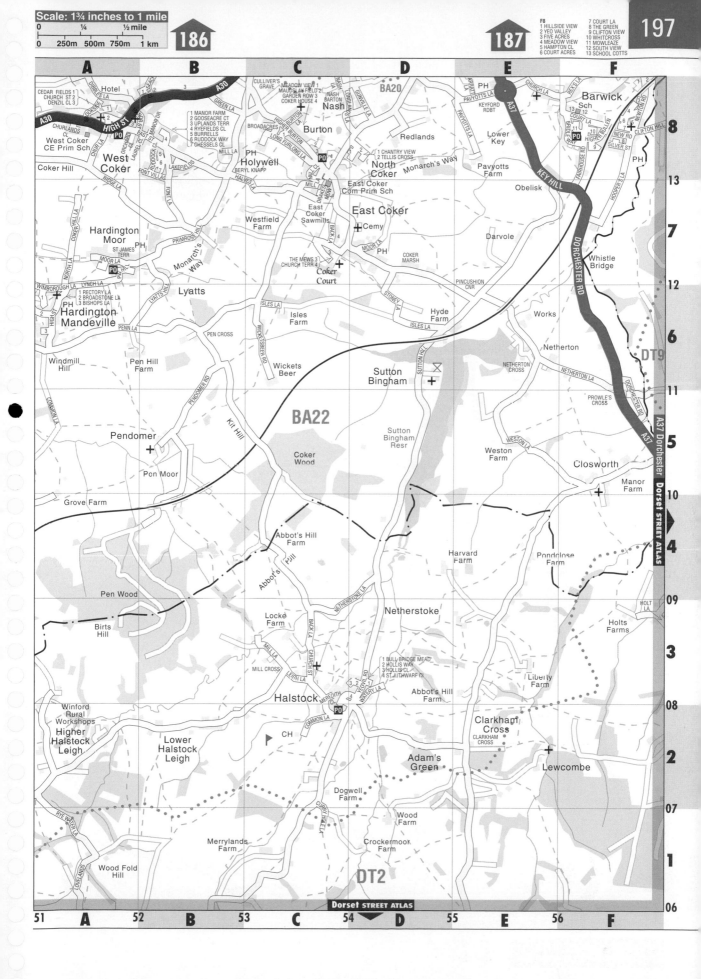

Scale: 1¾ inches to 1 mile

0   ¼   ½ mile
0   250m   500m   750m   1 km

186

187

197

F8
1 HILLSIDE VIEW
2 YEO VALLEY
3 FIVE ACRES
4 MEADOW VIEW
5 HAMPTON CL
6 COURT ACRES
7 COURT LA
8 THE GREEN
9 CLIFTON VIEW
10 WHITCROSS
11 MOWLEAZE
12 SOUTH VIEW
13 SCHOOL COTTS

BA20

Barwick

West Coker

West Coker CE Prim Sch

Coker Hill

Hotel

CEDAR FIELDS 1
CHURCH ST 2
DENZIL CL 3

CHURLANDS

HIGH ST

1 MANOR FARM
2 GOOSEACRE CT
3 UPLANDS TERR
4 RYEFIELDS CL
5 BURRELLS
6 RUDDOCK WAY
7 CHESSELS CL

Holywell

PH
BERYL KNAPP

LAKEFIELDS

CULLIVER'S GRAVE

MEADOW VIEW 1
MAUDS LA FIELD 2
GARDEN ROW 3
COKER HOUSE 4

Nash

Burton

NASH BARTON

Broadacres

HIGHER BURTON

LONG FURLONG LA

North Coker

1 CHANTRY VIEW
2 TELLIS CROSS

East Coker Com Prim Sch

Redlands

Monarch's Way

Lower Key

Pavyotts Farm

KEYFORD RDBT

PAVYOTTS LA

PH

CHURCH LA

REXS LA

Sch

NEW RD

CLIFTON HILL

SILVER ST

PH

Hardington Moor

PH
ST JAMES TERR

MOOR LA

Monarch's Way

PRIMROSE HILL

Westfield Farm

East Coker Sawmills

East Coker

Cemy

MOOR LA

PH

COKER MARSH

Darvole

Obelisk

KEY HILL

DORCHESTER RD

Whistle Bridge

DT9

Hardington Mandeville

PH

WIMBOROUGH LA

NORTH LA

COKER HILL LA

RIDGE LA

LYNCH LA

1 RECTORY LA
2 BROADSTONE LA
3 BISHOPS LA

PENN LA

Lyatts

LYATTS HILL

THE MEWS 3
CHURCH TERR 4

Coker Court

ISLES LA

Isles Farm

ISLES LA

STONEY LA

Hyde Farm

PINCUSHION CNR

Works

Netherton

NETHERTON CROSS

NETHERTON LA

DORCHESTER RD

A37

PROWLE'S CROSS

Windmill Hill

Pen Hill Farm

PEN CROSS

Wickets Beer

WICKETSBEER RD

SUTTON HILL

Sutton Bingham

PENDOMER RD

Kit Hill

BA22

Pendomer

Coker Wood

Sutton Bingham Resr

Weston Farm

WESTON LA

Closworth

Manor Farm

COMMON LA

Pen Moor

Grove Farm

Abbot's Hill Farm

Abbot's Hill

Harvard Farm

Pondclose Farm

Birts Hill

Pen Wood

NETHERSTOKE LA

Locke Farm

BACK LA

Netherstoke

Holts Farms

HOLT LA

Liberty Farm

MILL LA

MILL CROSS

CHURCH ST

LEIGH LA

Halstock

MEREDITH

YEOVIL RD

MONTREY LA

1 BULL BRIDGE MEAD
2 HOLLIS WAY
3 HOLLIS CL
4 ST JUTHWARF CL

Abbot's Hill Farm

Clarkham Cross

CLARKHAM CROSS

Winford Rural Workshops

Higher Halstock Leigh

Lower Halstock Leigh

CH

PO

COMMON LA

Adam's Green

Lewcombe

RYE WATER LA

COVELANDS

Wood Fold Hill

Merrylands Farm

CURRY HOLE LA

Dogwell Farm

Wood Farm

Crockermoor Farm

DT2

Dorset STREET ATLAS

A   B   C   D   E   F

51   52   53   54   55   56

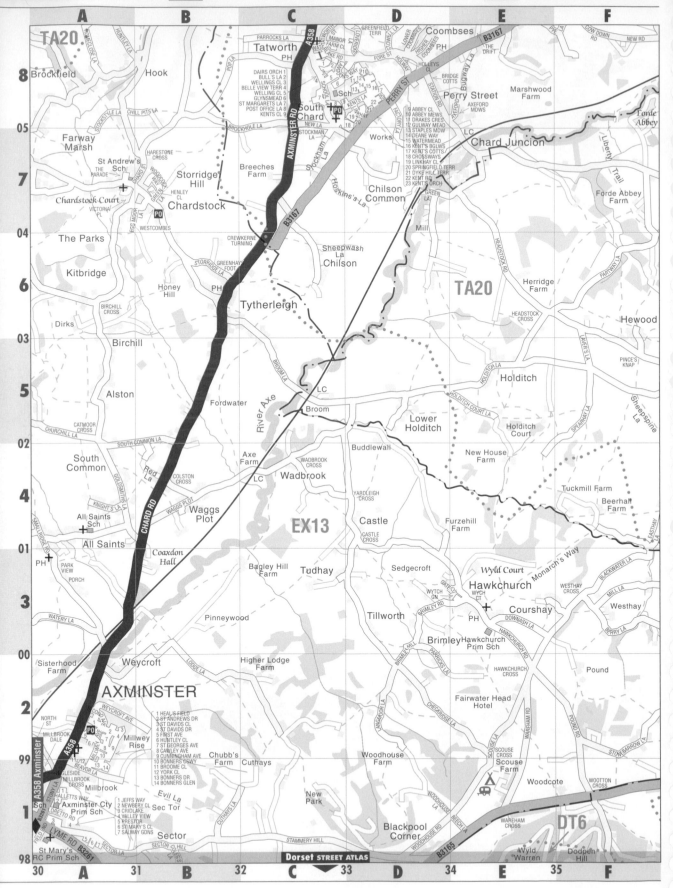

TA20

Brockfield
Hook
Farway Marsh
St Andrew's Sch
THE PARADE
Storridge Hill
Chardstock
Chardstock Court
VICTORIA PL
PO
WESTCOMBES
The Parks
Kitbridge
Honey Hill
Dirks
Birchill
BIRCHILL CROSS
Alston
Fordwater
CATMOOR CROSS
CHURCHILL LA
South Common
SOUTH COMMON LA
All Saints Sch
All Saints
PH
PARK VIEW
PORCH
Coaxdon Hall
Sisterhood Farm
Weycroft
LODGE LA
AXMINSTER
WATERY LA
NORTH ST
Millwee Rise
Millbrook Dale
PO
Axminster Cty Prim Sch
Millbrook
HALLETTS WAY
ORETTO RD
Evil La
A358 Axminster
FIELD RD
B3261
St Mary's RC Prim Sch
Sector
LYME RD

PARROCKS LA
Tatworth PH
DAIRS ORCH 1
BULL'S LA 2
WELLINGS CL 3
BELLE VIEW TERR 4
WELLING CL 5
GLYNSMEAD 6
St MARGARETS 7
POST OFFICE LA 8
KENTS CL 9
South Chard
PO
NEW LA
STOCKMAN LA
Breeches Farm
Storridge Foot
GREENHAYS FOOT
PH
CREWKERNE TURNING
Tytherleigh
BROOM LA
River Axe
Broom
LC
Fordwater
Axe Farm
LC
Wadbrook
WADBROOK CROSS
COLSTON CROSS
Red La
CHARD RD
Waggs Plot
WAGGS PLOT
KNIGHT'S LA
GOLDSMITHS LA
EX13
Bagley Hill Farm
Tudhay
Pinneywood
Higher Lodge Farm
WEYCROFT AVE
1 HEAL'S FIELD
2 St ANDREWS DR
3 St DAVIDS CL
4 St DAVIDS DR
5 FIRST AVE
6 HUNTLEY CL
7 St GEORGES AVE
8 CAWLEY AVE
9 CUNNINGHAM AVE
10 BONNERS GSWY
11 BROOME CL
12 YORK CL
13 BONNERS DR
14 BONNERS GLEN
Chubb's Farm
Cuthays
New Park
1 JEFFS WAY
2 NEWBERRY CL
3 CRIDLAKE
4 VALLEY VIEW
5 PRESTOR
6 St MARY'S CL
7 SALWAY GDNS
CUTHAYS LA
STAMMERY HILL
SECTOR CROSS

GREENFIELD TERR
LOWER COOMBSES
Coombses PH
HIGHER COOMBSES
B3167
The Drift
COW DOWN RD
NEW RD
MANOR FARM CL
PERRY ST
Perry Street
Marshwood Farm
AXEFORD MDWS
Forde Abbey
Chard Junction
LC
9 ABBEY CL
10 ABBEY MEWS
11 DRAKES CRES
12 GULWAY MEAD
13 STAPLES MDW
14 DEANE WAY
15 WATERMEAD
16 KENT'S BGLWS
17 KENT'S COTTS
18 CROSSWAYS
19 LINKHAY CL
20 SPRINGFIELD TERR
21 DYKE HILL TERR
22 KENT RD
23 KENT'S ORCH
Chilson Common
Sheepwash La
Chilson
Mill
GREEN LA
Forde Abbey Farm
Liberty Trail
TA20
Herridge Farm
HEADSTOCK RD
HEADSTOCK CROSS
Hewood
Holditch
PINCE'S KNAP
LAVER'S LA
Lower Holditch
HOLDITCH LA
HOLDITCH COURT LA
Holditch Court
SPEARWAY LA
Sheepspine La
New House Farm
Buddlewall
YARDLEIGH CROSS
Castle
CASTLE CROSS
Furzehill Farm
Tuckmill Farm
Beerhall Farm
EASTHAY LA
Sedgecroft
Wyld Court
WYCH CT
Hawkchurch
PH
Courshay
WESTHAY CROSS
WESTHAY LA
MILL LA
BERRY LA
Westhay
WYTCH GN
BRIMLEY RD
Tillworth
BRIMLEY HILL
Brimley Hawkchurch Prim Sch
HAWKCHURCH RD
DOWNASH LA
Monarch's Way
BLACKWATER LA
GATE CL
CANCAGROR LA
PARROCKS LA
Woodhouse Farm
Fairwater Head Hotel
HAWKCHURCH CROSS
Pound
WAREHAM RD
POUND RD
STONEBARROW LA
WOODHOUSE RD
SCOUSE CROSS
Scouse Farm
Woodcote
WOOTTON CROSS
BEECH LA
CHECKRIDGE LA
Blackpool Corner
WOODHOUSE RD
WAREHAM CROSS
B3165
DT6
Wyld Warren
Dodpen Hill

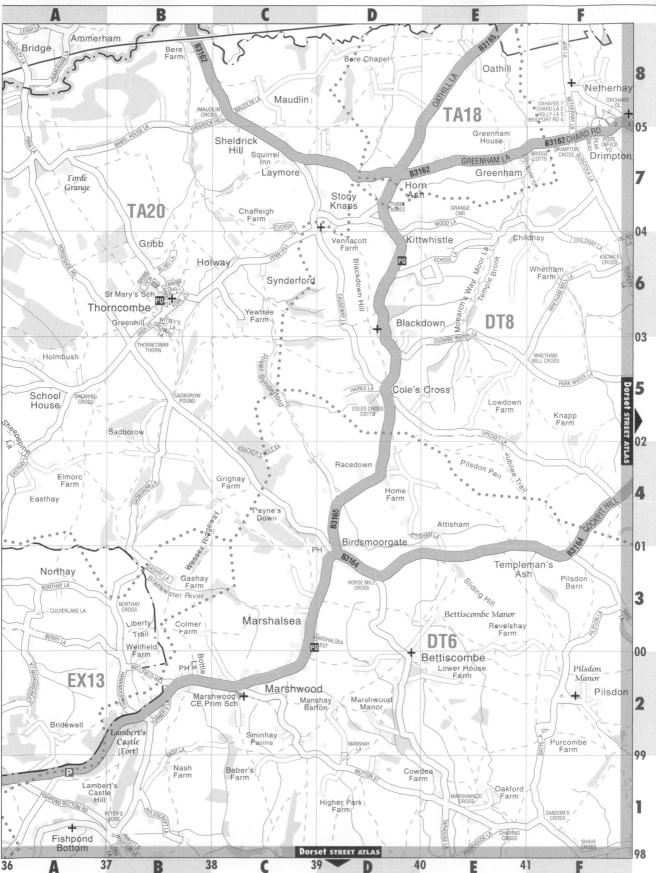

Scale: 1¾ inches to 1 mile

0   ¼   ½ mile

0   250m 500m 750m 1 km

194

195

199

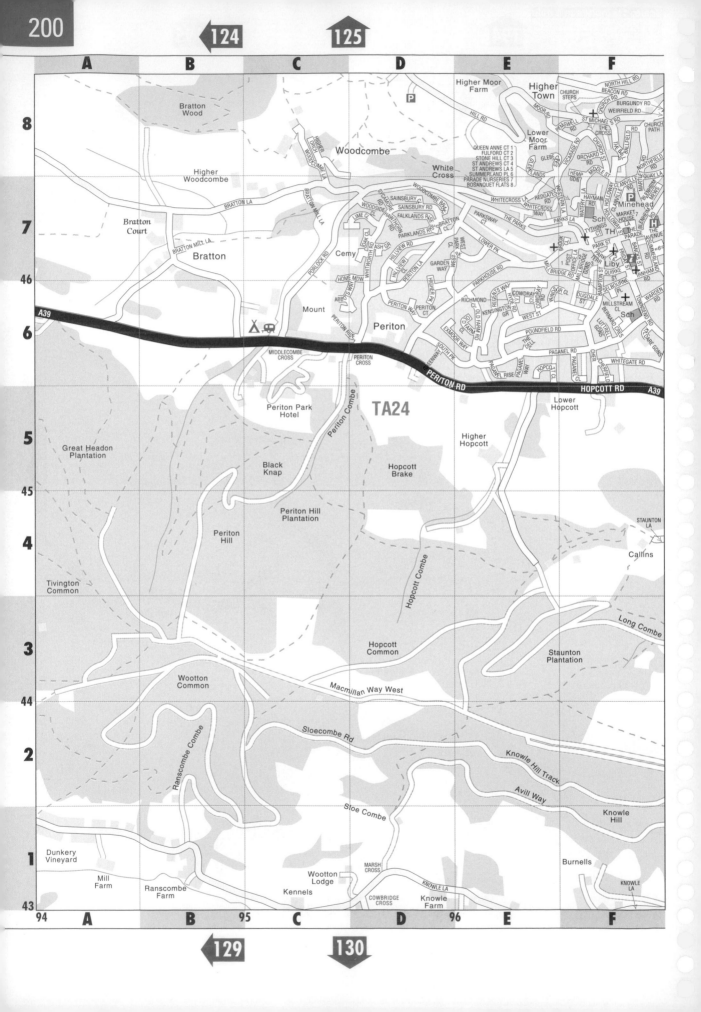

124
125

A B C D E F

8

Bratton
Wood

Higher
Woodcombe

Woodcombe

White
Cross

Higher Moor
Farm

Higher
Town

NORTH HILL RD
BEACON RD
BURGUNDY RD
WEIRFIELD RD
CHURCH
PATH

Lower
Moor
Farm

7

BRATTON LA

Bratton
Court

Higher
Woodcombe

BRATTON MILL LA

Bratton

PORLOCK RD

Cemy

Mount

SAINSBURY

Sainsbury RD

Falklands RD

LIME CL

ASH GR

HILLVIEW RD

PERITON LA

HOME MDW

WHITWORTH

Periton

BRATTON
CL

GARDEN
WAY

Higher PK

PARKSWAY
CT

THE PARKS

LOWER PK

WEST
PARK
CL

PARKHOUSE RD

Richmond
CL

Parkhouse Gdns

QUEEN ANNE CT 1
FULFORD CT 2
STONE HILL CT 3
ST ANDREWS CT 4
ST ANDREWS LA 5
SUMMERLAND PL 6
PARADE NURSERIES 7
BOSANQUET FLATS 8

WHITECROSS

WHITECROSS RD

PARKS LA

Kensington
GR

OLD FARM
CL

COWDRAY
CL

WEST ST

ST MICHAEL S RD
THE
CROSS

HEMP
GDN

ORCHARD
RD

Minehead

Sch
TH
Liby

Sch

46

A39

Middlecombe
Cross

Periton
Cross

PERITON RD

POUNDFIELD RD

THE DELL

PAGANEL RD

HOPCOTT RD

A39

6

Periton Park
Hotel

Periton Combe

Periton
Cross

TA24

Lower
Hopcott

5

Great Headon
Plantation

Black
Knap

Hopcott
Brake

Higher
Hopcott

STAUNTON
LA

45

Periton Hill
Plantation

Callins

4

Tivington
Common

Periton
Hill

Hopcott Combe

Long Combe

3

Hopcott
Common

Staunton
Plantation

Wootton
Common

Macmillan Way West

44

Ransombe Combe

Sloecombe Rd

Knowle Hill Track

2

Stoe Combe

Avill Way

Knowle
Hill

1

Dunkery
Vineyard

Mill
Farm

Ranscombe
Farm

Wootton
Lodge

Kennels

MARSH
CROSS

COWBRIDGE
CROSS

Knowle
Farm

KNOWLE LA

Burnells

KNOWLE
LA

43

94 A B 95 C D 96 E F

129
130

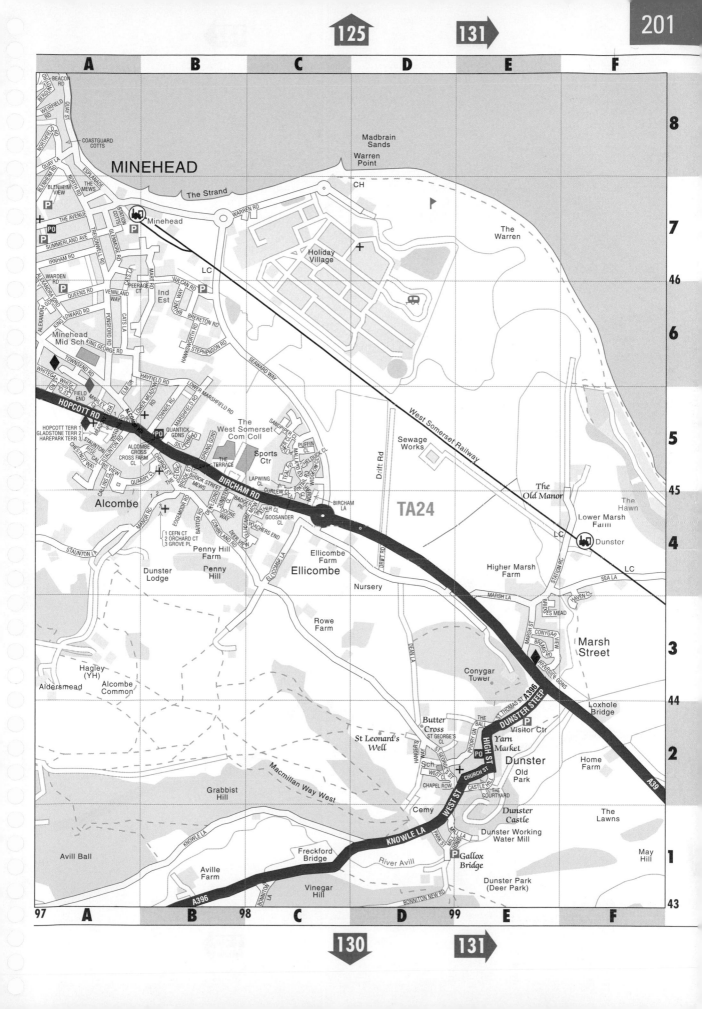

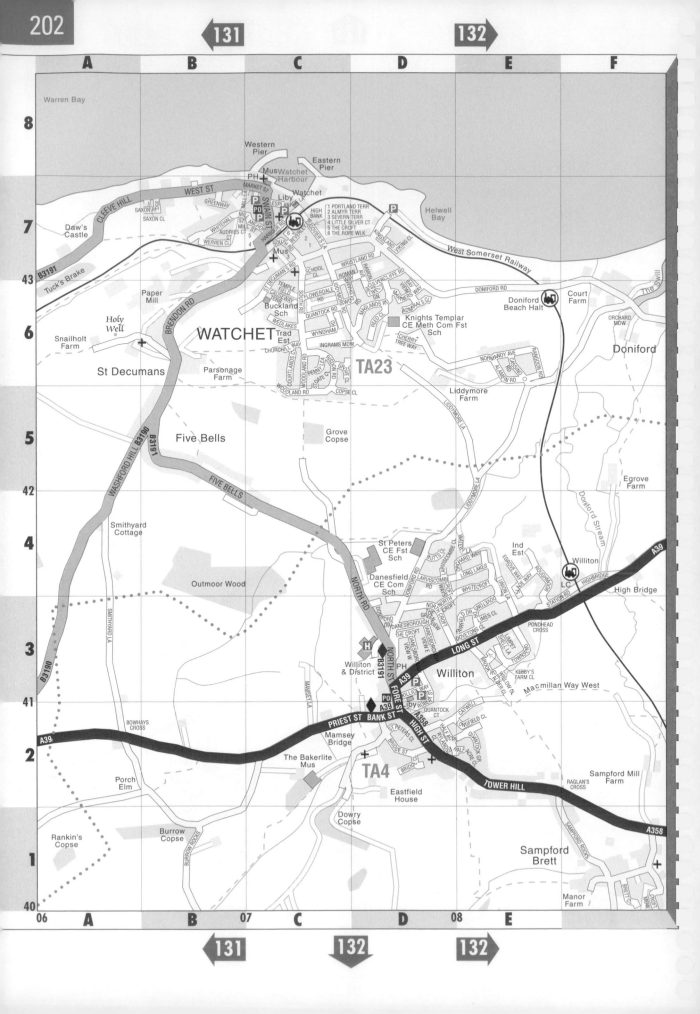

A B C D E F

8

Warren Bay

Western Pier

Eastern Pier

Watchet Harbour

Mus PH Liby Watchet

7

WEST ST CLEEVE HILL

MARKET ST

SAXON RD SAXON CL

GREENWAY

WHITEHALL AUDRIES CT WERREN CL

MILL ST

SWAIN ST

HARBOUR RD

ESPLANADE LA

BECKERLEYS

DOVERS LA

HIGH BANK

1 PORTLAND TERR
2 ALMYR TERR
3 SEVERN TERR
4 LITTLE SILVER CT
5 THE CROFT
6 THE ROPE WLK

P

Helwell Bay

Daw's Castle

43

B3191 Tuck's Brake

Mus

ST DECUMAN'S RD

SCHOOL CL

ROMAN

WRISTLAND RD

BANONS AVE

CULVERCLIFFE RD

GN

BANK VIEW WAY

MAGLANDS RD

MATTNERS CL

KINGSLAND

VIKING CL

ADMIRALS CL

West Somerset Railway

Doniford Beach Halt

Court Farm

DONIFORD RD

The Swill

Paper Mill

BRENDON RD

6

Snailholt Farm

Holy Well

St Decumans

WATCHET

Trad Est

TEMPLE FIELD CAUSEWAY

FLOWERDALE RD

QUANTOCK RD

WEDLAKES

CHURCHILL

COURTLANDS

WOODLAND RD

GROVE CL

SLATE CL

PENNY LA

WYNDHAM

INGRAMS MDW

COPSE CL

TA23

Knights Templar CE Meth Com Fst Sch

CHERRY TREE WAY

NORMANDY AVE

ALAMEIN RD

CASSINO RD

RANGOON RD

Doniford

ORCHARD MDW

Parsonage Farm

Buckland Sch

Liddymore Farm

Liddymore La

Egrove Farm

5

Five Bells

WASHFORD HILL B3190

B3191

FIVE BELLS

Grove Copse

Doniford Stream

42

Smithyard Cottage

4

Outmoor Wood

NORTH RD

St Peters CE Fst Sch

Danesfield CE Com Sch

BUTTS

LANSCOMBE CL

LARVISCOMBE RD

ORCHARD WAY

NO 2 NORTH CROFT

GRACE MDW

Ind Est

EGROVE WAY

STATION RD

LC

Williton

HIGHBRIDGE

A39

High Bridge

SMITHYARD LA

WHITECROFT

LONG LAKES

ROUGHMOOR

UNION LA

LIMES CL

Pondhead Cross

B3190

3

H

Williton & District

NORTH ST

B3191

PH

FORE ST

DANESBOROUGH RD

THE CROFT

DANESBOROUGH VIEW W

DANESBOROUGH VIEW E

KILLICK WAY

DRUSE WAY

LONG ST

DOVETONS DR

SHELLA

TOWNS

LIMPET

BROOK RD

PEVERIL RD

KEBBY'S FARM CL

Williton

Macmillan Way West

41

BOWHAYS CROSS

MARKET LA

P PO Liby A39

PRIEST ST BANK ST

QUANTOCK CT

ST ROBERTS

CATWELL

LONGFIELD CL

2

A39

Mamsey Bridge

The Bakerlite Mus

ST PETERS CL

BRIDGE ST

HIGH ST

A358

TA4

Eastfield House

QUANTOCK GR

VALE VIEW

PYLANDS CL

HALF ACRE

A358

RAGLAN'S CROSS

Sampford Mill Farm

Porch Elm

Dowry Copse

TOWER HILL

SAMPFORD ROCKS

1

Rankin's Copse

Burrow Copse

BURROW ROCKS

Sampford Brett

Manor Farm

BRETT CL

CROFT

40

06 A 07 B C 07 D 08 E F

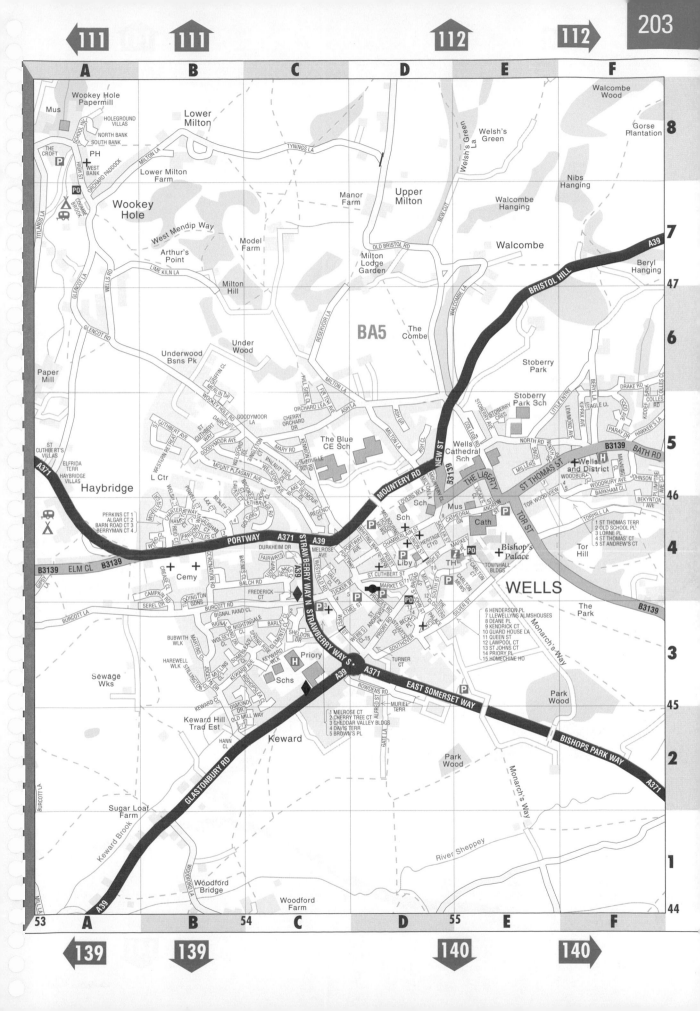

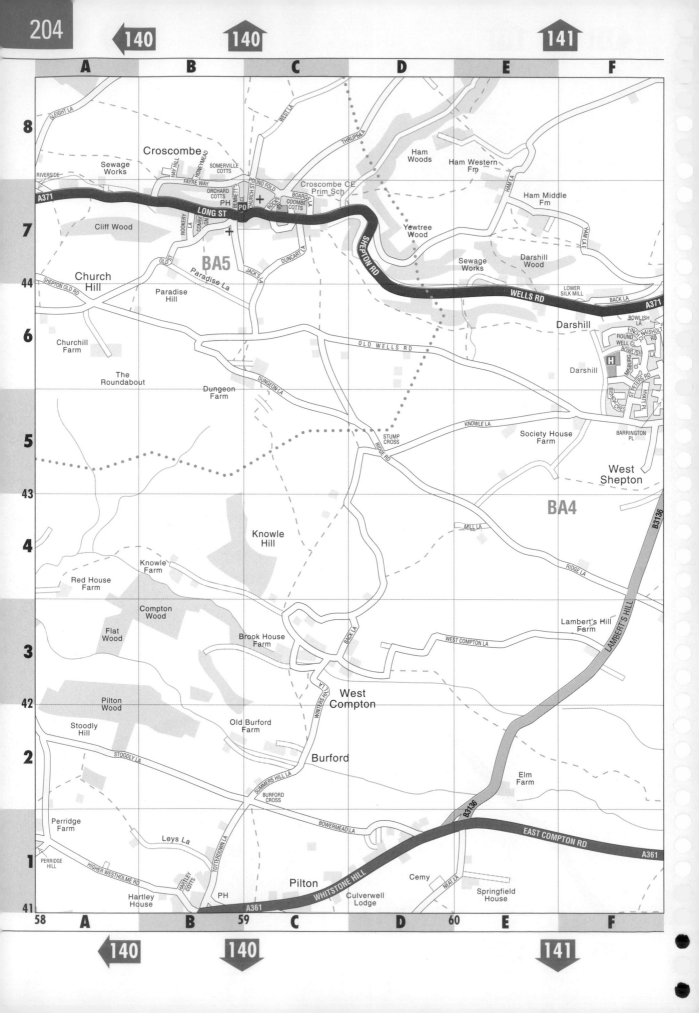

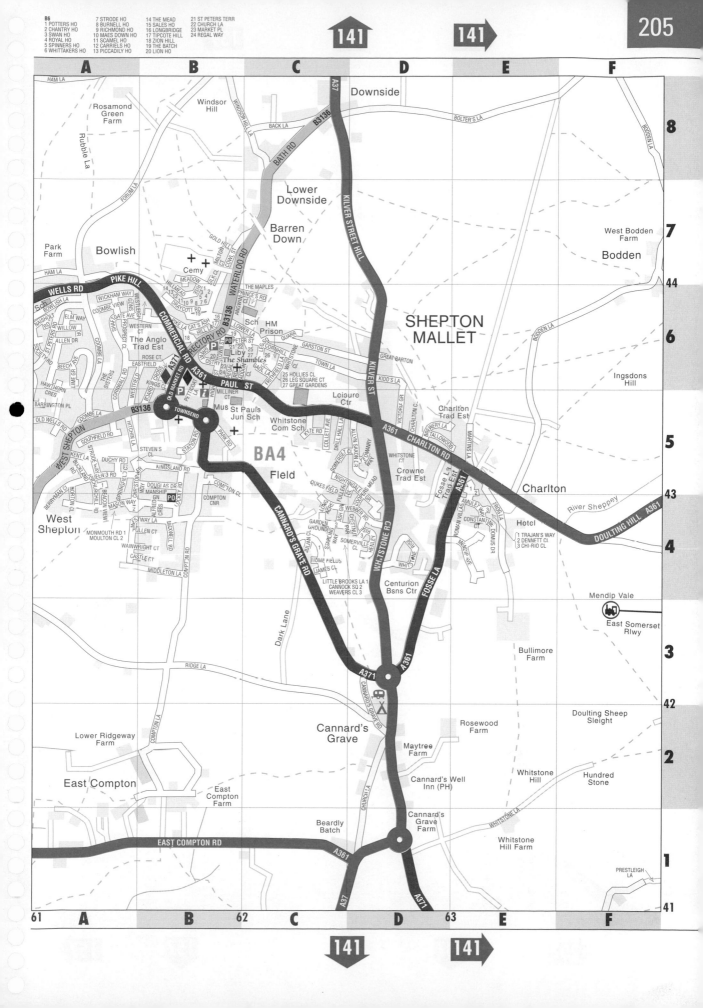

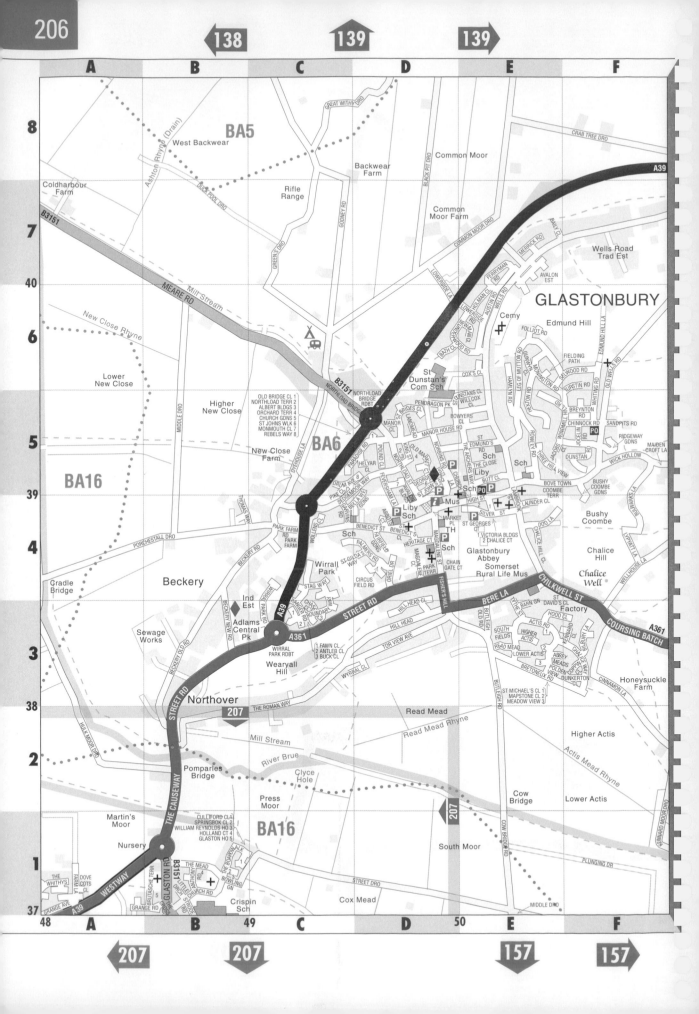

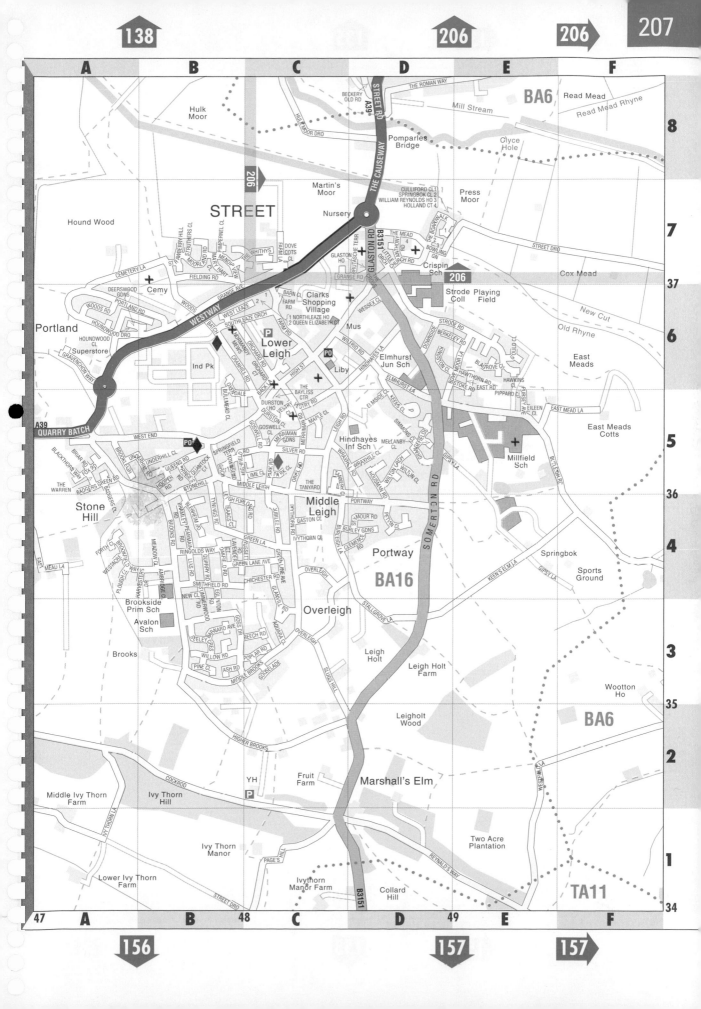

← 135 135

Grid columns: A B C D E F
Grid rows: 8, 7, 38, 6, 5, 37, 4, 3, 36, 2, 1, 35

Perrycroft
Perry Green
Perry Green Farm
Perrymoor Brook
Manor Lodge
Barton Farm
Grabhams Cottage
Grabhams Farm
Moores
Wembdon Farm
Blakes Farm
Blakes La
Moore's La
Chilton Trinity Sch
Sports Ctr
Chilton Park
Richmond Cl
B3339
SANDFORD HILL
Sandford Farm
Inn
Wembdon
WEMBDON HILL
Mount Radford
Cokerhurst Farm
St George's Prim Sch
Church Farm
Newtown
Kidsbury Farm
THE PIPPINS
River Parrett Trail
A39
Greenway Farm
Skimmerton La
QUANTOCK RD
Cemy
WEMBDON RISE
Marina
Dock
Admirals
Quayside
THE CLINK
WEST QUAY
FORE ST
York Ct
BLDGS
Collingwood
Anson Way
B3339
WEMBDON RD
Cemy
NORTH ST
BROADWAY
A39
TA5
Queenswood Farm
Merridge Cl
Westercombe Cl
Northfield
St Joseph's RC Prim Sch
Wembdon Prim Sch
St Matthew's Field
Penrose Sch
River Parrett Trail
Bridgwater & Taunton Canal
Superstore
Charter Cl
Friarn Lawn
George William Ct
Browne's Pond
Durleigh Elms
St Mary's CE Prim Sch
Haygrove Sch
THE PARKS
Durleigh Cl
TA6
BRIDGWATER
Durleigh Brook Farm
Haygrove House
Haygrove Farm
DURLEIGH RD
ROMAN LA
SPRINGFIELD AVE
Durleigh Reservoir
Durleigh
Durleigh Farm
ENMORE RD
DURLEIGH HILL
The Blake Sch
Hamp Inf Sch
Hamp Com Jun Sch
Elmwood Sch
Elmwood
Elmside Ho
The Green
Sunnybank
The Meads
Hamp Brook Way
Hamp
GLOUCESTER RD
QUEEN'S RD
YORK RD
PARKSTONE AVE
Dukes Mead
Rhode La
Hamp Brook
Broadmeadow Farm
South Lea
Rhode Lane Farm
RHODE LA
Poultry Farm
Shortlands Farm
RHODE LA

Grid columns (bottom): A B C D E F
Grid numbers (bottom): 27, 28, 29

← 153 153

F4
1 ST MARY'S CT
2 BLAKE ST
3 OLD TAUNTON RD
4 GREEN DRAGON CT

F5
1 CHALICE MEWS
2 HOMECASTLE HO
3 THE AVENUE
4 CHURCH PASS
5 COURT ST
6 ANGEL PLACE SH CTR
7 BRIDGWATER ENT CTR
8 MARKET CT

SOUTHBOURNE HO 1
WEST BOW HO 2
WESTFIELD HO 3
ALBERT CT 4
ELEVEN CT 5

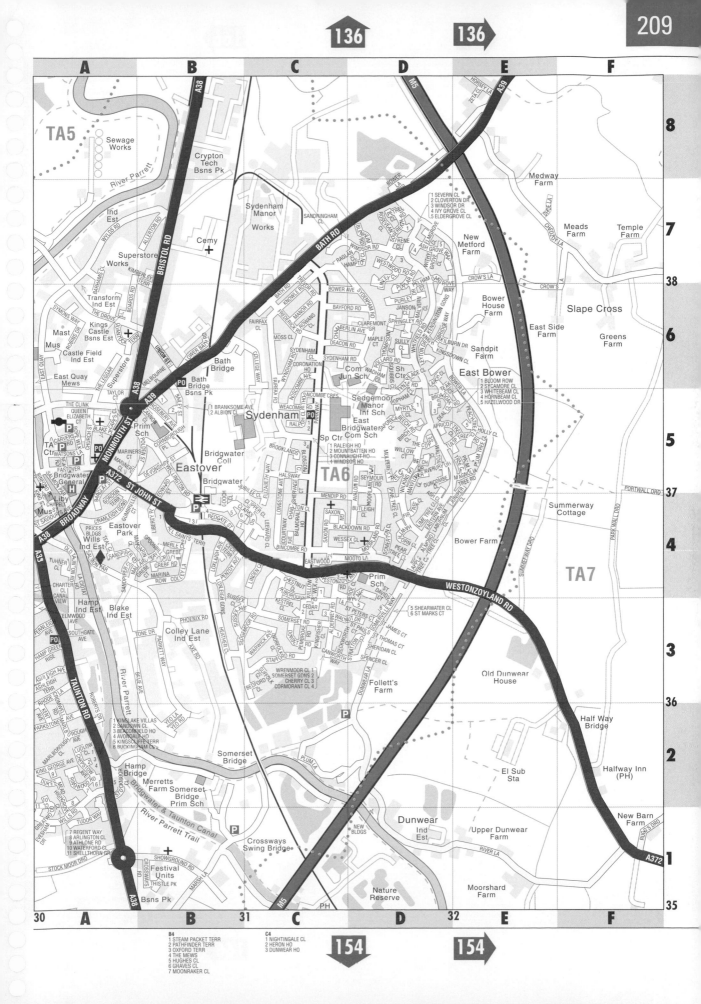

TA5

Sewage Works

River Parrett

Crypton Tech Bsns Pk

Ind Est

Cemy

Sydenham Manor Works

SANDRINGHAM CL

BATH RD

WYLDS RD
ALLERTON RD

Superstore Works

Transform Ind Est

Kings Castle Bsns Est

BARHAMS RD

BRISTOL RD

KIMBERLEY TERR

BOARDS RD

THE DROVE

SYMONS WAY

Mast Mus

ROBINS DR

DIAMOND TERR

Castle Field Ind Est

East Quay Mews

THE LEGGAR

Superstore

UNION ST

TOWER BATH

Bath Bridge

College Way

Bath Bridge Bsns Pk

Bath Bridge

WINDSOR RD

Windsor RD

RAGLAN
HAMPT CL

BOWER AVE

BAYFORD RD

FAIRFAX CL

MOSS CL

FREDERICK RD

MANOR RD

ROWANS

SYDENHAM

CLAREMONT 'GR'

DEACON RD

SULLY
CL

BERLIN AVE
MAPLE CL

1 SEVERN CL
2 CLOVERTON DR
3 WINDSOR DR
4 IVY GROVE CL
5 ELDERGROVE CL

New Metford Farm

Medway Farm

SHOE LA

Meads Farm

Temple Farm

CHEDZOY LA

New Metford Farm

Bower House Farm

Slape Cross

Greens Farm

CROW'S LA

CROW'S

East Side Farm

Sandpit Farm

East Bower

1 BLOOM ROW
2 SYCAMORE CL
3 WHITEBEAM CL
4 HORNBEAM CL
5 HAZELWOOD DR

BATH RD

BATH RD

PO

Bridgwater Coll

Bridgwater

Eastover

Sydenham

SYDENHAM RD

CORONATION HO

Com WAHAM RD

Com Jun Sch

Sedgemoor Manor Inf Sch

East Bridgwater Com Sch

Sp Ctr

PO

BLOSSOM

WILLOW
CT

THE COPE

HOLLY CL

1 RALEIGH HO
2 MOUNTBATTEN CL
3 CONNAUGHT HO
4 WINDSOR HO

TA6

PO

Queen Elizabeth CT

TA Ctr

CARVERS RD

Bridgwater General

H

Libr Mus

BROADWAY

A38

A33

A372

ST JOHN ST

MONMOUTH ST

A38

A39

Mariners CT

Prim Sch

CORNBOARD PL

ROSSBERRY AVE

BAILEY ST

CHILTON ST

Eastover Park

Wills Ind Est

Prices Bldgs

Eastover

Bridgwater

JUBILEE CT

REDGATE ST

ALL SAINTS TERR

MERLE CL

GREBE RD

Marina

COLLEY LA

PHOENIX RD

Colley Lane Ind Est

Blake Ind Est

Hamp Ind Est

ELMWOOD AVE

SOUTHGATE AVE

TONE DR

PARRETT WAY

AXE RD

SUSSEX AVE

CHESTNUT

WILLOW

WALNUT DR

ESTONZOY

Prim Sch

ST PETERS CL

ST PAULS

ST THOMAS CL

SHERIDAN CL

JAMES CT

5 SHEARWATER CL
6 ST MARKS CT

Bower Farm

WESTONZOYLAND RD

Summerway Cottage

PORTWALL DRO

PARK WALL DRO

TA7

SUMMERWAY DRO

Old Dunwear House

Half Way Bridge

RUSH'S DRO

FERNLEIGH AVE

HAMP GREEN RISE

PO

ASHLEIGH TERR

RHODE RD

CHARTER CL

CANAL VIEW

TAUNTON RD

River Parrett

BLUE AVE

YEO RD

YEO LA

1 KINSLAKE VILLAS
2 SANDOWN CL
3 BEACONFIELD HO
4 AVONDALE HO
5 KINGSCLIFFE TERR
6 BUCKINGHAM CL

Bedford CL

Somerset Bridge

WRENMOOR CL 1
SOMERSET GDNS 2
CHERRY CL 3
CORMORANT CL 4

Follett's Farm

PLUM LA

Old Dunwear House

El Sub Sta

Halfway Inn (PH)

MARLBOROUGH AVE

KING GEORGE AVE

DUKES CL

TUDOR WAY

WILLS RD

HOLM

Hamp Bridge

Merretts Farm

Somerset Bridge Prim Sch

STOCKMOOR DRO

ROBERTS DR

Bridgwater & Taunton Canal

Somerset Bridge

River Parrett Trail

P

NEW BLDGS

Dunwear

Dunwear Ind Est

Upper Dunwear Farm

New Barn Farm

A372

7 REGENT WAY
8 ARLINGTON CL
9 ATHLONE RD
10 WATERFORD CL
11 SHELLTHORN GR

STOCK MOOR DRO

SHOWGROUND RD

Festival Units

THISTLE PK

CROSSWAYS RD

MARSH LA

Crossways Swing Bridge

Bsns Pk

A38

M5

PH

Nature Reserve

RIVER LA

Moorshard Farm

B4
1 STEAM PACKET TERR
2 PATHFINDER TERR
3 OXFORD TERR
4 THE MEWS
5 HUGHES CL
6 GRAVES CL
7 MOONRAKER CL

C4
1 NIGHTINGALE CL
2 HERON HO
3 DUNWEAR HO

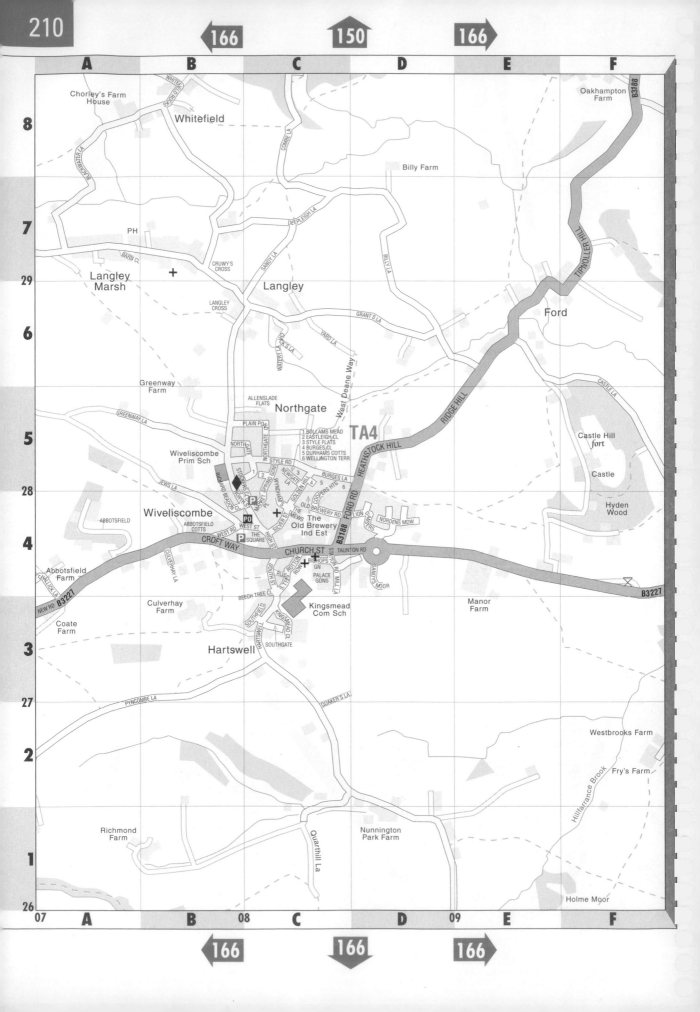

8

Chorley's Farm House

Whitefield

Oakhampton Farm

B3188

Billy Farm

7

PH

BARN CL

CRUWY'S CROSS

DEEPLEIGH LA

SANDY LA

BILLY LA

TIPWOLLER HILL

29

Langley Marsh

LANGLEY CROSS

Langley

GRANT'S LA

Ford

6

Greenway Farm

WATERY LA

YARD LA

West Deane Way

RIDGE HILL

CASTLE LA

5

GREENWAY LA

ALLENSLADE FLATS

PLAIN PO

Northgate

TA4

HEATHSTOCK HILL

Castle Hill fort

Castle

Wiveliscombe Prim Sch

NORTH GATE

NORTHGATE

STYLE RD

NEWGATE

BURGES LA

COOPERS HTS

1 BOLLAMS MEAD
2 EASTLEIGH CL
3 STYLE FLATS
4 BURGES CL
5 DURHAMS COTTS
6 WELLINGTON TERR

28

JEWS LA

RICHARD BEADON CL

STODDENS COURT

MARKET SPRING GDNS

GOLDEN HAY

P

THE OLD BREWERY RD

FORD RD

B3188

LION

Hyden Wood

NORDENS MDW

4

Abbotsfield Farm

CAVALLIER LA

NEW RD B3227

ABBOTSFIELD

ABBOTSFIELD COTTS

WEST RD

CROFT WAY

WEST ST

THE SQUARE

P

HIGH ST

SILVER ST

THE MEWS

CHURCH ST

The Old Brewery Ind Est

BISHOPS GN

PALACE GDNS

ROTTON ROW

RUSS ST

STATION RD

MILL LA

TAUNTON RD

SANDY'S MOOR

Manor Farm

B3227

CULVERHAY LA

Culverhay Farm

BEECH TREE CL

SOUTH ST

SOUTHFIELD

HARTSWELL

KINGSMEAD

Kingsmead Com Sch

3

Coate Farm

Hartswell

SOUTHGATE

27

PYNCOMBE LA

QUAKER'S LA

Westbrooks Farm

2

Hillfarrance Brook

Fry's Farm

1

Richmond Farm

QUARTHILL LA

Nunnington Park Farm

Holme Moor

26

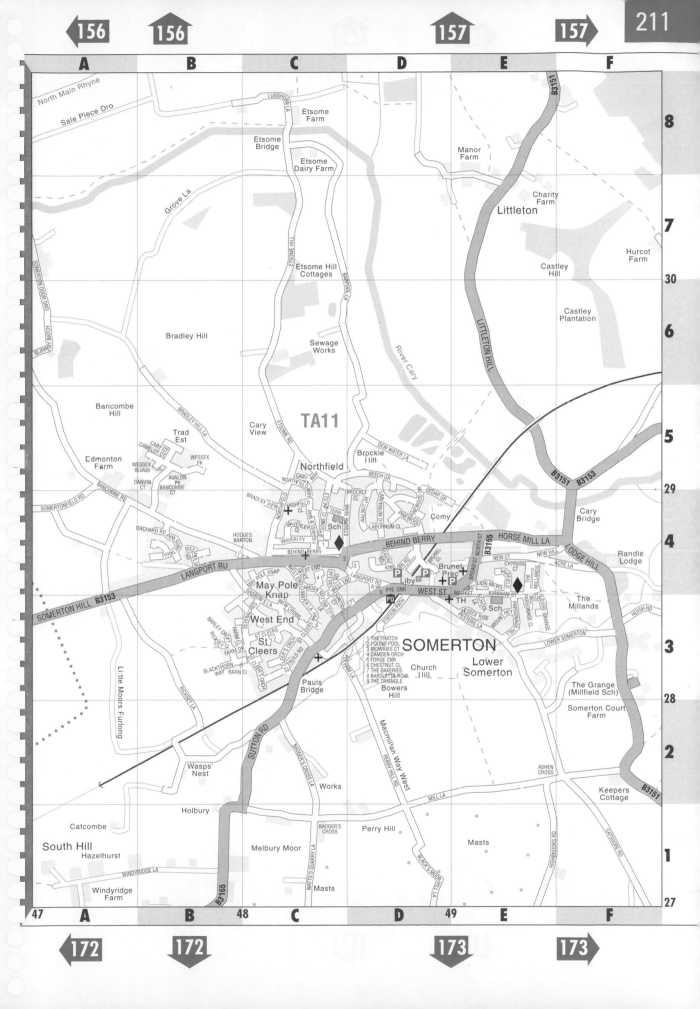

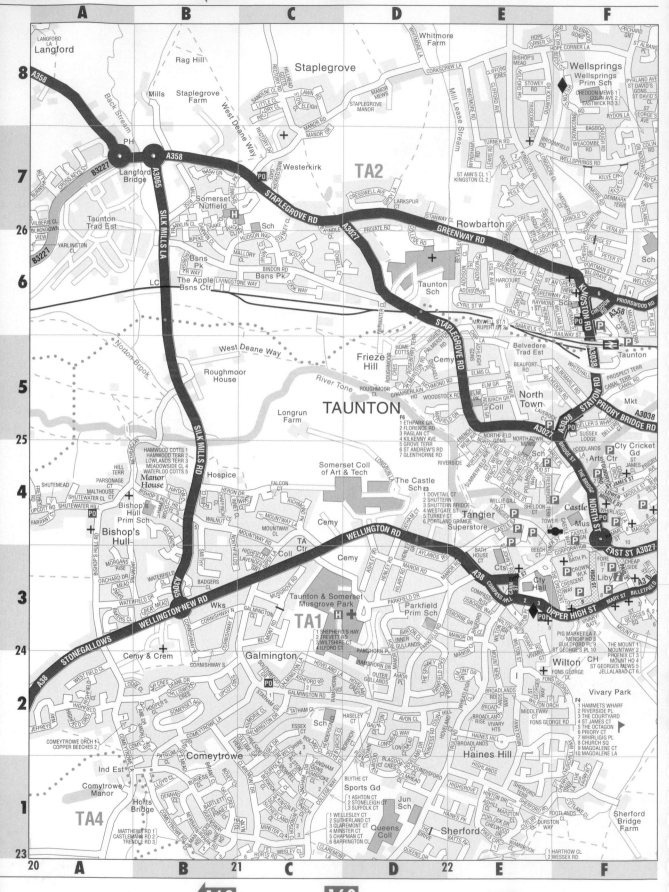

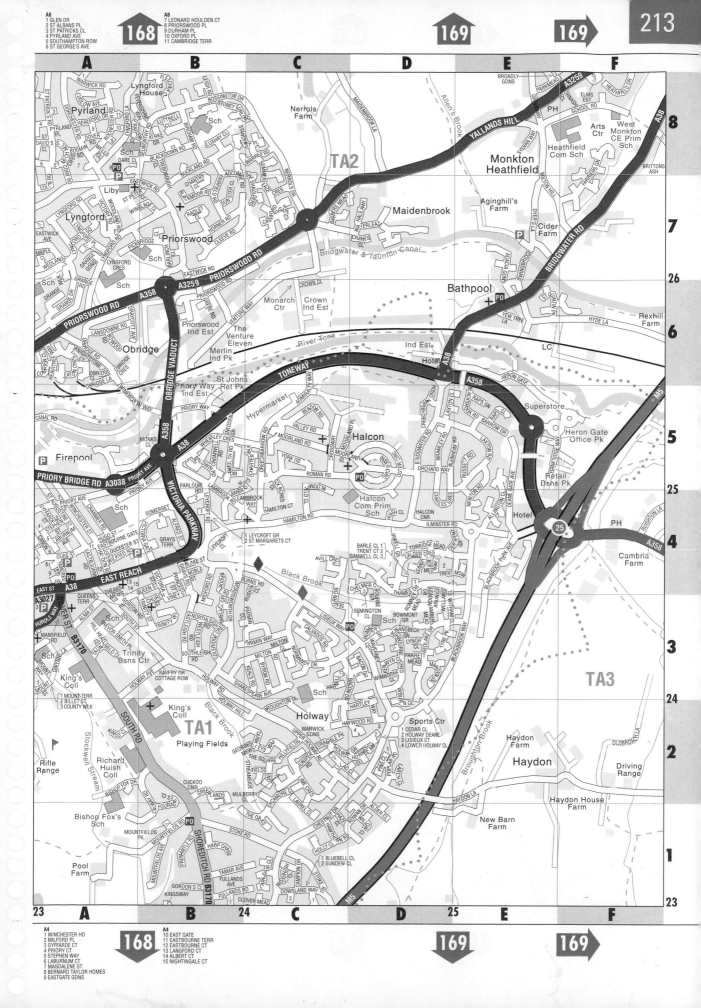

159 159

A B C D E F

River Brue

BA10

8

Ansford Bridge
Castle Cary
STATION RD
A371

Ansford Park Farm

7

A371
Hillcrest Farm
ANSFORD HILL
PARSONS GATE
Ansford Com Sch
WYKE RD
Leland Trail
Macmillan Way
Bottom Barn Farm

B3153

33

B3152
ELMS CL
ORCHARD
HALLETT RD
LOWER ANSFORD
TUCKERS LA
MULLINS WAY
PARSONAGE CRES
CHURCHFIELDS DR
PARK LA
MAGGS LA
YEABSLEYS WAY
BROCK CT
Ansford

Wayside Farm

6
CLOTHER ROWS
FLORIDA FIELDS
VICTORIA GDNS
WEST PK
PRIORY VIEW
CHURCHFIELDS RD
GREENWAY
CATHERINES CL
BARNES CL
COOMBE CL
ANSFORD RD
JUBILEE CT
CUMNOCK RD
NEWCASTLE AVE
ANCASTLE TERR
FOURWAYS CL
CUMNOCK TERR
Sunnydene Farm
Honeywick Hill
NETTLECOMBE HILL
Hadspen

Torbay Road Ind Est
STATION RD
TORBAY CL
Torbay Villas
TORBAY RD
SALISBURY TERR
PRIORYGATE CT
FLORIDA ST
VICTORIA CT
KINGSACRE
NORTH SIDE
CUMNOCK CRES
MOUNT PLEASANT
NORTH ST
Knapp Farm

Liby
PO
Mus
KNIGHTS YD
UPPER HIGH ST
HIGH ST
HANOVER CT
CHAPEL
Mus

5
BROCKFIELDS
BDGERS
VICTORIA RD
VICTORIA TERR
B3152
WOODCOCK ST
FORE ST
FORE ST
CASTLE RISE
1 VICTORIA MEWS
2 MONTAGUE GDNS
3 PRIORY PATH
4 BAILEY HILL
5 MARKET PL
6 LOWER WOODCOCK ST
CARY HILL
BA7
Priddle's Hill

FOLLY
REMALARD CT
DONNES TERR 1
BRIDGWATER BLDGS 2
SOUTH CARY LA
MILLBROOK GDNS
PARK ST
Castle Cary

32
Castle Cary
CHURCH ST
THE PARK
PARK PL
Castle Cary Prim Sch
Hadspen Farm
Higher Hadspen

4
Sewage Works
ANNANDALE
The Countryman Inn
SOUTH ST
CHAPEL YD
Castle Cary Park
Lodge Hill
Hell Ladder La
LINE KILN LA
Farm Hill
A359
GREBLA

COCKHILL ELM LA
SOUTH BANK PARK AVE
Monarch's Way
Grove Farm

3
Higher Cockhill Farm
Cemy
Manor Farm
Mast
Grove Mead
A371
Hadspen Wood

Abbey Gardens
BROADWAY LA
COOPER'S ASH LA

31
Hadspen House
A371

GALHAMPTON HILL
Tor View Farm

2
Macmillan Way
Leland Trail

Sportsman's Lodge Farm
BA22
Small Way
SMALL WAY LA

1
Ferndale Farm
B3152
Redlands Farm
Mount Pleasant Farm
HICKS'S LA
Sleight La
BA9
Shatwell Farm
SHATWELL LA

A359

30

63 A B 64 C D 65 E F

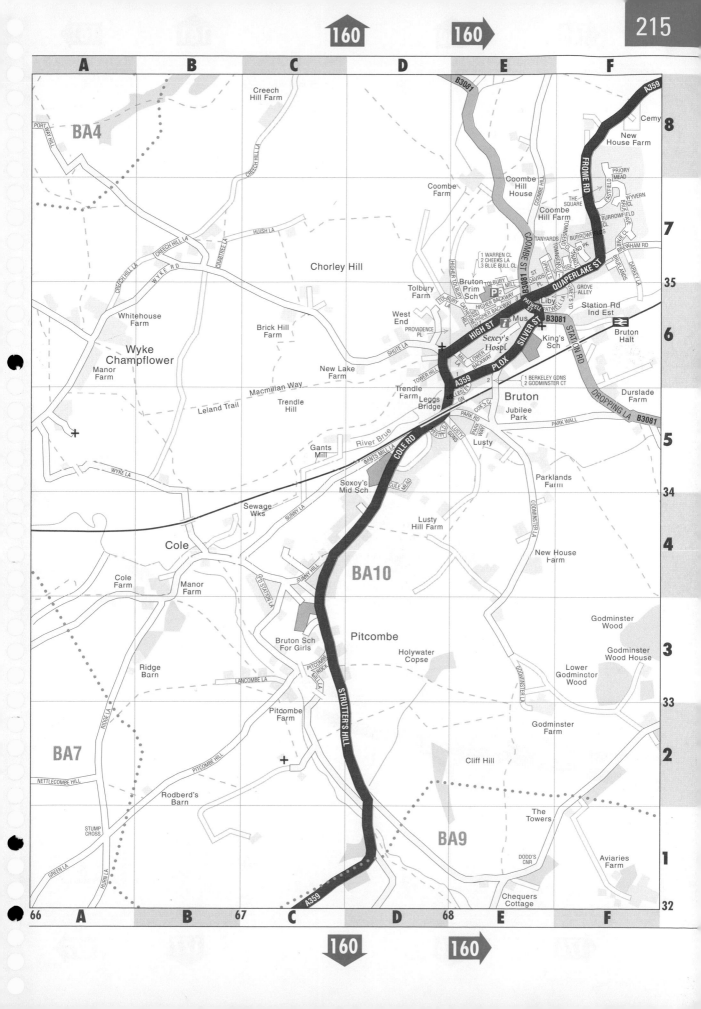

160   160

A   B   C   D   E   F

BA4

Creech
Hill Farm

PORT WAY HILL

CREECH HILL LA

CRABTREE LA

HUISH LA

WYKE RD

Whitehouse
Farm

Wyke
Champflower

Manor
Farm

Chorley Hill

Brick Hill
Farm

New Lake
Farm

Coombe
Farm

Coombe
Hill House

Coombe
Hill Farm

B3081

COOMBE ST

FROME RD

Cemy

New
House Farm

THE
SQUARE

PRIORY
MEAD

WYVERN
CL

ENFIELD

BURROWFIELD

A359

8

7

35

TANYARDS

TOWNSEND
RISE

BRADLEY CL

BRUELANDS

BREWHAM RD

1 WARREN CL
2 CHEEKS LA
3 BLUE BULL CL

Tolbury
Farm

Bruton
Prim Sch

HIGHER TOLBURY

HIGHER BACKWAY

TOLBURY LA

CATHERINE HILL

MILL

ST
DAVIDS

UPHILLS

QUAPERLAKE ST

GROVE
ALLEY

Liby

Mus

KING'S
SCH

Station Rd
Ind Est

Bruton
Halt

Durslade
Farm

B3081

DROPPING LA

6

West
End

PROVIDENCE
PL

SHUTE LA

HIGH ST

LOWER
BACKWAY

TOWER HILL

PLOX

SILVER ST

PATWELL

A359

Sexey's
Hospl

Bruton

Lusty

1 BERKELEY GDNS
2 GODMINSTER CT

Jubilee
Park

PARK RD

PARK WALL

Parklands
Farm

Macmillan Way

Trendle
Hill

Leland Trail

Trendle
Farm

Leggs
Bridge

Gants
Mill

River Brue

COLE RD

BANTS MILL LA

HERCULE MEAD

SUNNY LA

Soxey's
Mid Sch

PARK WAY

Lusty
Hill Farm

GODMINSTER LA

New House
Farm

34

5

Sewage
Wks

Cole

Cole
Farm

Manor
Farm

OLD STATION LA

SUNNY HILL

BA10

Bruton Sch
For Girls

PITCOMBE ROCK

PITCOMBE HILL LA

Pitcombe

Holywater
Copse

GODMINSTER LA

Godminster
Wood

Godminster
Wood House

Lower
Godminster
Wood

4

3

33

Ridge
Barn

RIDGE LA

LANCOMBE LA

PITCOMBE HILL

Pitcombe
Farm

STRUTTER'S HILL

Godminster
Farm

BA7

NETTLECOMBE HILL

Rodberd's
Barn

Cliff Hill

BA9

The
Towers

2

STUMP
CROSS

GREEN LA

HURN LA

A359

DODD'S
CNR

Chequers
Cottage

Aviaries
Farm

1

32

66   A   B   67   C   D   68   E   F

160   160

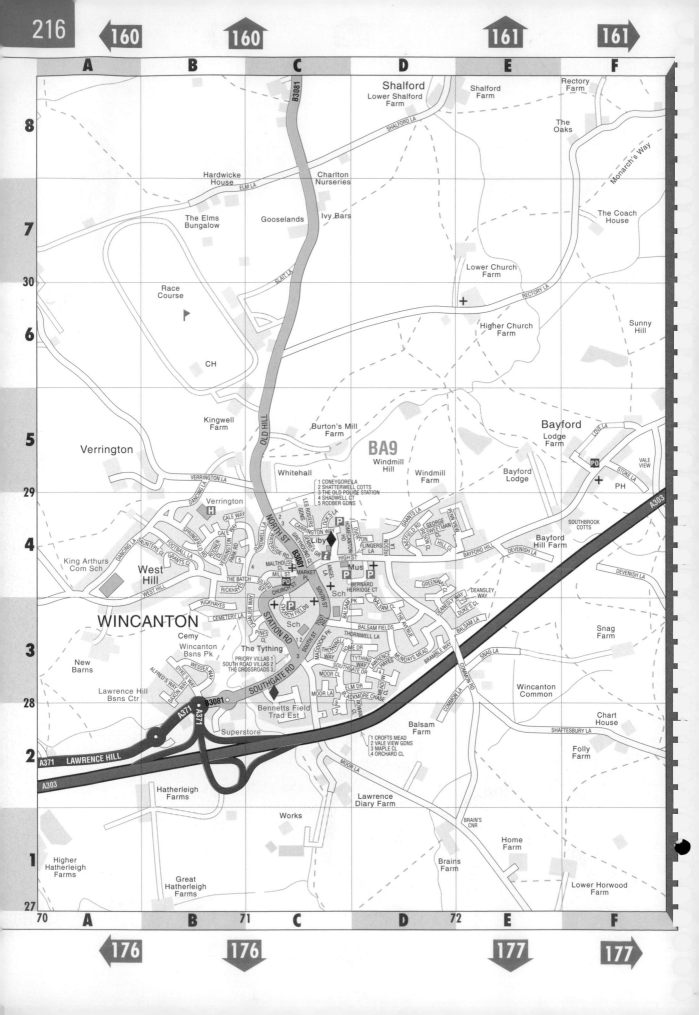

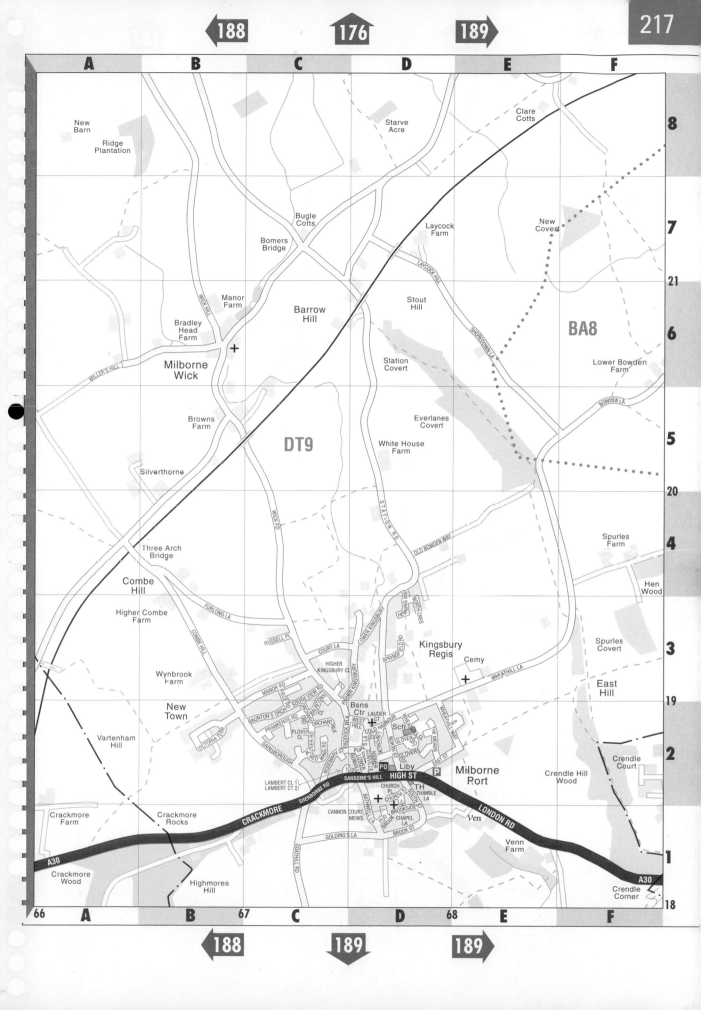

A   B   C   D   E   F

8
7
21
6
5
20
4
19
3
2
1
18

New Barn
Ridge Plantation
Starve Acre
Clare Cotts
New Covert
Bugle Cotts
Laycock Farm
Bomers Bridge
Manor Farm
Barrow Hill
Stout Hill
BA8
Bradley Head Farm
Milborne Wick
Station Covert
Lower Bowden Farm
MILLER'S HILL
WICK HILL
Browns Farm
Everlanes Covert
LAYCOCK HILL
SHOREDOWN LA
BOWDEN LA
DT9
White House Farm
Silverthorne
WICK RD
Three Arch Bridge
Spurles Farm
Combe Hill
OLD BOWDEN WAY
STATION RD
Hen Wood
Higher Combe Farm
FURLONG LA
Kingsbury Regis
Spurles Covert
COMBE HILL
RUSSELL PL
HIGHER KINGSBURY CL
COURT LA
LOWER KINGSBURY
NORTH CRES
SPRINGFIELD RD
NEW SWING
Cemy
WHEATHILL LA
East Hill
Wynbrook Farm
MANOR RD
HIGHER KINGSBURY
SOUTH VIEW RD
PICKETS RD
ORCHARD CL
BALTONS CL
ORCHARD WALK
PADDOCK WALK
Bsns Ctr
LAUDER CT
Sch
WHEATHILL WAY
New Town
VICTORIA TER
BAUNTON'S ORCHD
PRANKERDS RD
PLOVER CL
RED WING RD
PLOVER CL
ROSEMARY ST
WEST HILL
COLD HARBOUR
GLOVERS
THE MEADS
EAST ST
Vartenham Hill
GAINSBOROUGH
PUP
LOWER
GUNVIL
HIGHER GUNVIL
PUDDING LA
NORTH ST
GLOVERS
CHURCH ST
Liby
P
PO
HIGH ST
P
Milborne Port
Crendle Court
Crackmore Farm
Crackmore Rocks
SANSOME'S HILL
LAMBERT CL 1
LAMBERT CT 2
SHERBORNE RD
BATHWELL LA
CHURCH PL
THIMBLE LA
Crendle Hill Wood
CRACKMORE
CANNON COURT MEWS
BROOKSIDE
PUD BROOK
CHAPEL LA
BROOK ST
LONDON RD
Venn
A30
GOATHILL RD
GOLDING'S LA
Venn Farm
Crackmore Wood
Highmores Hill
Crendle Corner
A30

66   A   B   67   C   D   68   E   F   18

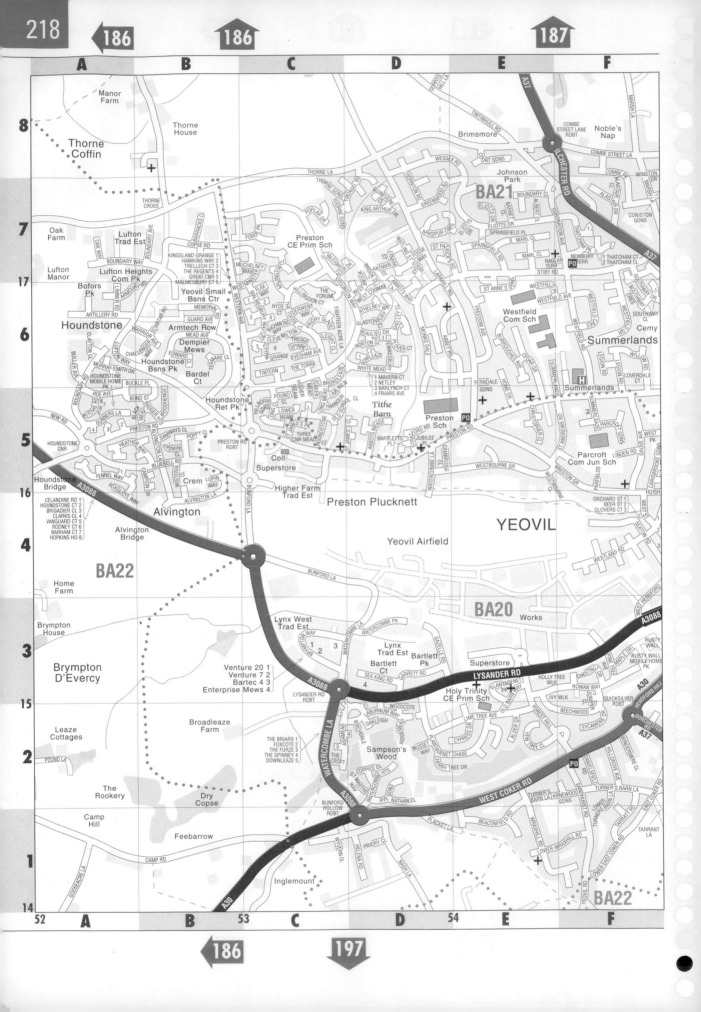

187 187

A B C D E F

YEOVIL

Longcroft
Hundred Stone
Fairmead Sch
Heronsmead
Lower Fairmead Rd
Falconsmead Wlk
Bucklers Mead Wlk
1 Corton Cl
2 Adber Cl
3 Compton Cl
4 Broadlands Cl

Combe Street La
Stone La
Mudford Rd
Hordstone Cl
High Lea
Lea Cl
Bicknell Gdns
Tower Rd
Sports Ctr
Bucklers Mead Sch
St Mary's Cres
Runnymede Rd
Cavalier Cl
Cavalier Way
Constable Cl
Gainsborough Way
Saddlewood Cl
Redwood Rd
Turner Cl
Wilton Cl

Winston Dr
Coniston Gdns
Chilton Gr
Ashford Dr
Glenthorne Ave
Elmhurst Ave
Allingham Rd
Woodstock Rd
The Hollies
Neatham Rd
Northbrook Rd
Cavalier Way
Bedford Rd
Hertford Rd
Romsey Rd
Lyde Rd

Marsh La
Picketta
Yeovil Recn Ctr
Folly Fields
Milford Jun & Inf Schs
BA21
Wingate Ave
Winchester Gdns
Greenhill Rd
Johnson Flats
St John's Rd
Welbeck Rd
Montrose Rd
Lowther Rd
Babylon View
Birchfield Prim Sch
Chatsworth Rd
Number 15
Marksview Bsns Ctr
Bartlett Mews
Yeovil Bsns Ctr

Hollands
Ilchester Rd
Coll
Kingston A37
A359
Mount Pleasant
Crofton Park
Elizabeth Flats
Hillcrest
Highfield Trad Est
St Michael's Ave
Charles Rd
Mayfield Rd
Derwent Gdns
Rosebery Ave
Pen Mill
Meadow Rd
Woburn Rd
Wentworth Rd
Marlborough Rd
Belvedere Rd
Vale Rd
Lyde La
Sewage Works

17

Blackdown 1
Brandon Ho 2
Orchard Ho 3
Pearson Ho 4
Cemy
Fiveways Rdbt
Preston Rd
Crofton Park
New Town
Roman Rd
Grass Royal
Pattinson Ct
St Michael's Rd
St Aldhelms
Pen Mill Marine Sch
Goar Knapp
Charlton Cl
Camborne Pl
Pen Mill Trad Est

6

Huish
Huish Prim Sch
Yeovil District
Higher Kingston
Hospital Rdbt
Crofton Pk Sch
Kiddles
Ryalls Ct
Old School
Perry Sch
Pen Mill Marine Sch
Great Western Terr
Wyndham Ho
Beaumont Ho
Wyndham Hill
Sherborne Rd
Pen Mill
Sewage Works
Yeovil Bridge
Underdown

5

West Pk
Sandown Cl
Osborne Rd
Carisbrooke Gdns
Reckleford
A30
A30
Hillside Terr
Babylon Hill
A30

Queensway
Pen Hill
Mus
Pen Hill Pk
Mill Lane Trad Est
Superstore
CH
Little Covert

16

Hendford Hill
A3088
Horsey Rdbt
Brunswick St
Alcondale Gdns
Summer House Hill
Newton Surmaville
Potters Leaze Plantation

L Ctr
Somerset Pl
1 Seaton Rd
2 Seaton Ct
3 Richmond Ho
4 Orchard St
5 Swift Lodge
6 Wellington Flats
7 Clarkes Ct
8 Tudor Ct
9 Homeville Ho

Aldon
Nine Springs
Monarchs Way
Newton Copse
Newton Farm
BA20
Constitution Hill

East Coker Rd
BA22
The Fish Tower
Two Tower La
Newton Rd
Leaze La

15

DT9

The Rose Tower
Barwick Ho
Jack The Treacle Eater
Lake Mews
Rex's La
Hillside View
Yeo Valley
Yeovil Junction

Tarratta La
Dorchester Rd
A37

55 A B 56 C D 57 E F

B4
1 Flowers Ho
2 King George St
3 The Borough
4 Tabernacle La
5 Fredrick Pl
6 Vicarage St
7 Yeovil Trinity Foyer
8 Clarence Terr
9 Broad Oak
10 Harfield Terr
11 Addlewell La
12 Taunustein Way
13 Trinity Ct
14 Belmont Ho
15 Townrise
16 Marsh Pottinson Ho

B5
1 Cheverton Ho
2 Church Path
3 St Johns Ho
4 Church Terr
5 Vincent St

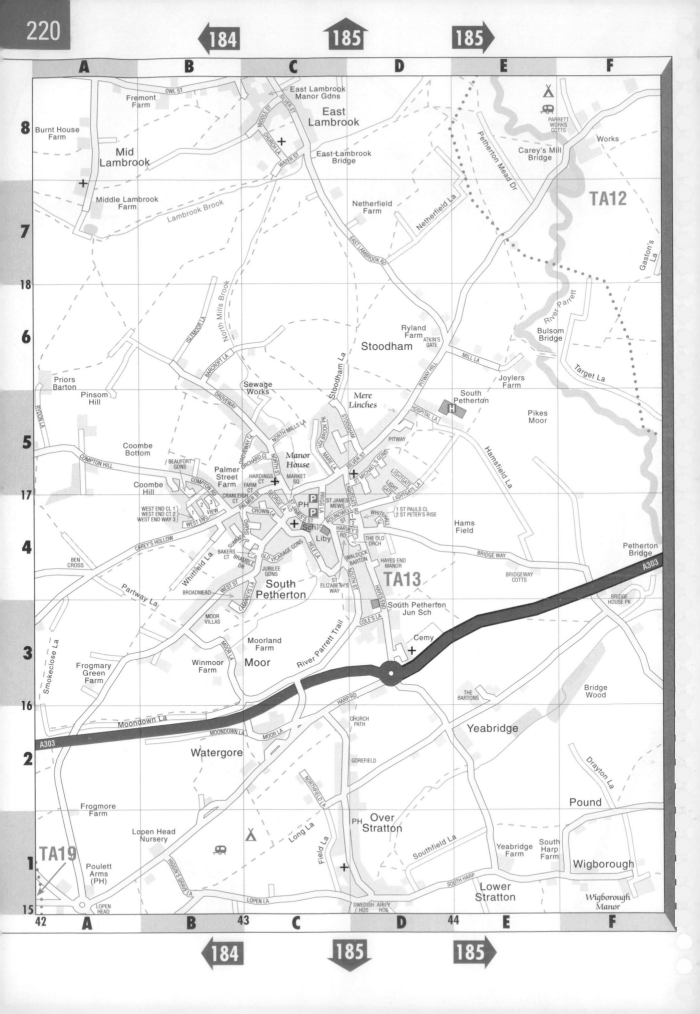

A   B   C   D   E   F

8 Burnt House Farm   Fremont Farm   OWL ST   MIDDLE ST   SILVER ST   East Lambrook Manor Gdns   East Lambrook

Mid Lambrook   CHURCH LA   WATER ST   East Lambrook Bridge

TA12

7 Middle Lambrook Farm   Lambrook Brook   Netherfield Farm   Netherfield La   Carey's Mill Bridge   Works

PARRETT WORKS COTTS

Gaston's La

18   North Mills Brook   EAST LAMBROOK RD   Petherton Mead Dr

6 Priors Barton   Pinsom Hill   BARCROFT LA   Sewage Works   Ryland Farm   ATKIN'S GATE   Stoodham   MILL LA   Joylers Farm   River Parrett   Bulsom Bridge

Target La

DROVEWAY   Stoodham La   PITWAY HILL

Coombe Bottom   GLEEMOOR LA   Mere Linches   HOSPITAL LA   South Petherton   H   Pikes Moor

5 COMPTON HILL   ORCHARD CL   NORTH MILLS LA   Manor House   MARE LA   STOODHAM   SILVER ST   PITWAY   Hamsfield La

Coombe Hill   BEAUFORT GDNS   Palmer Street Farm   HARDINGS CT   MARKET SQ   ST MICHAEL'S GDNS   LIGHTGATE LA

17   COMPTON RD   CRANLEIGH CT   FARM CT   GEORGE LA   P   ST JAMES MEWS   LIGHT GATE   LIGHTGATE LA

Hams Field

WEST END CL 1   WEST END CT 2   WEST END WAY 3   1   2   3   VIEW   PALMER ST   PH   P   ST JAMES ST   ROUNDWELL ST   1 ST PAULS CL   2 ST PETER'S RISE   THE OLD ORCH

4 BEN CROSS   CAREY'S HOLLOW   WHITFIELD LA   CROWN LA   SUMMER LANE   OLD VICARAGE GDNS   Sch   Liby   HARVEY'S RD   WHITEHALL   BRIDGE WAY   Petherton Bridge

BAKERS CT   BRAMBLE DR   HELE LA   WALDOCK BARTON   HAYES END MANOR   BRIDGEWAY COTTS   A303

Partway La   BROADMEAD   WEST ST   JUBILEE GDNS   South Petherton   ST ELIZABETH'S WAY   SOUTH ST   TA13   BRIDGE HOUSE PK

3 Smokeclose La   MOOR LA   MOOR VILLAS   Moorland Farm   River Parrett Trail   South Petherton Jun Sch   THE BARTONS   Bridge Wood

Frogmary Green Farm   Winmoor Farm   Moor   COLE'S LA   Cemy   Yeabridge

16   Moondown La   HARP RD   CHURCH PATH

2 A303   MOONDOWN LA   MOOR LA   Watergore   GOREFIELD   Drayton La   Pound

1 Frogmore Farm   Lopen Head Nursery   Long La   FIELD LA   PH   Over Stratton   Southfield La   Yeabridge Farm   South Harp Farm   Wigborough

TA19   HIGGIN'S GRAVE LA   NORTHFIELD LA   SOUTH HARP   Lower Stratton   Wigborough Manor

Poulett Arms (PH)

15   LOPEN LA   LOPEN LA   SWEDISH HOS   AIREY HOS

LOPEN HEAD

42   A   43   B   C   43   D   44   E   F

A   B   C   D   E   F

8

7

16

6

15

5

4

3

14

2

1

13

CAD RD

Burleaze
Farm

B3168

Cocks
Bridge

Kails

Sewage
Works

Eames
Mill

MILL LA

Ashwell
Farm

Parsonage
Barn

A303

River Isle

Binell's
Copse

A303

Cemy

Ashwell

Dillington
House

Dairy
House

Whitelackington

Abrahams
Farm

Manor
Farm

BACK LA

HANNING CL

Green La

Winterhay
Green

BEACON

Old Road

Beacon
Hill

Dillington
Park

Dillington

WINTERHAY LA

Works

Beacon Lane

B3168

STATION RD

SPRINGFIELD
BGLW

THE HEIGHTS

BEACON
SPEKE CT

SPEKE CL

HILL VIEW TERR

HIGHER BEACON

ILMINSTER

TA19

NEW RD

MADHAM CL

PIPER'S
ALLEY

Strawberry
Bank

LETHAM
CT

Blackdown View

Hotel

HAZELWELL LA

FAIRFIELD

RILEY CT
GREENDALE

PARK DR

WEST ST

BREWERY

HIGH ST

Butts
Castle

BUTTS

HARES CL

ADAMS MD

HITHER HO

REC STR

BGLW

SUMMERLANDS PARK CL

ASHCOMBE CT

SUMMERLANDS PARK AVE

COURT
BARTON

SILVER ST

NORTH ST

ILE CT

QUANTOCK
CT

EAST ST

BAY HILL

Knott Oak
House

West
Wood

CANAL WAY

BREOWEN CL

LADYMEADE

ABBOTS CL

CHURCH WLK 1
VICTORIA CT 2
CHURCH LA 3

SWAN
PREC

DITTON ST

LOVE LA

TOWNSEND

Knott
Oak

MUCHELNEY
HO

WHARF LA

Sch

Liby

SHUDRICK LA

Knott Oak
Dairy

CARPENTERS HO 1
ADAMS HO 2
DUKE HO 3
TAYLOR HO 4
STREET HO 5

ORCHARD VALE

APLINS CL

INCLINE MD

HIGHER MD

Swanmead
Com Sch

Cross Farm
House

Townsend
Farm

LONG ORCHARD HILL

KINGSTONE HILL

THE
CROSS

CROSS

Pretwood Hill

Wakehill

HILL-73-03-HILL

HERNE RISE

WALROND
CT

LISTER'S HILL

PRETWOOD CL

LISTERCOMBE CL

Kingstone

Herne Hill

WEST CRES

THE CRESCENT

SPRINGFIELD

LITTLE LESTER WAY

HERON WAY

LONG CL

EAMES ORCH

KINGSTONE
CROSS

MILL LA

Factory

Moolham

Headstock Hill

Sea Dairy
Farm

NEW
BLDGS

MOOLHAM LA

Dowlish
Ford

Dowlish Brook

Sewage
Works

Greenway

35   A   B   36   C   D   37   E   F

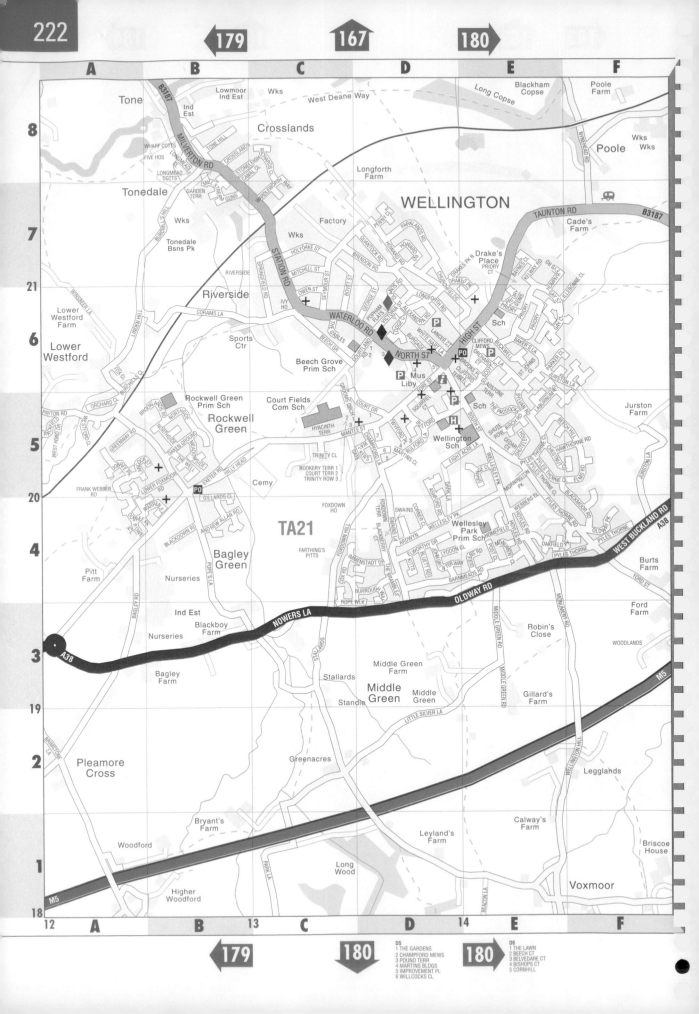

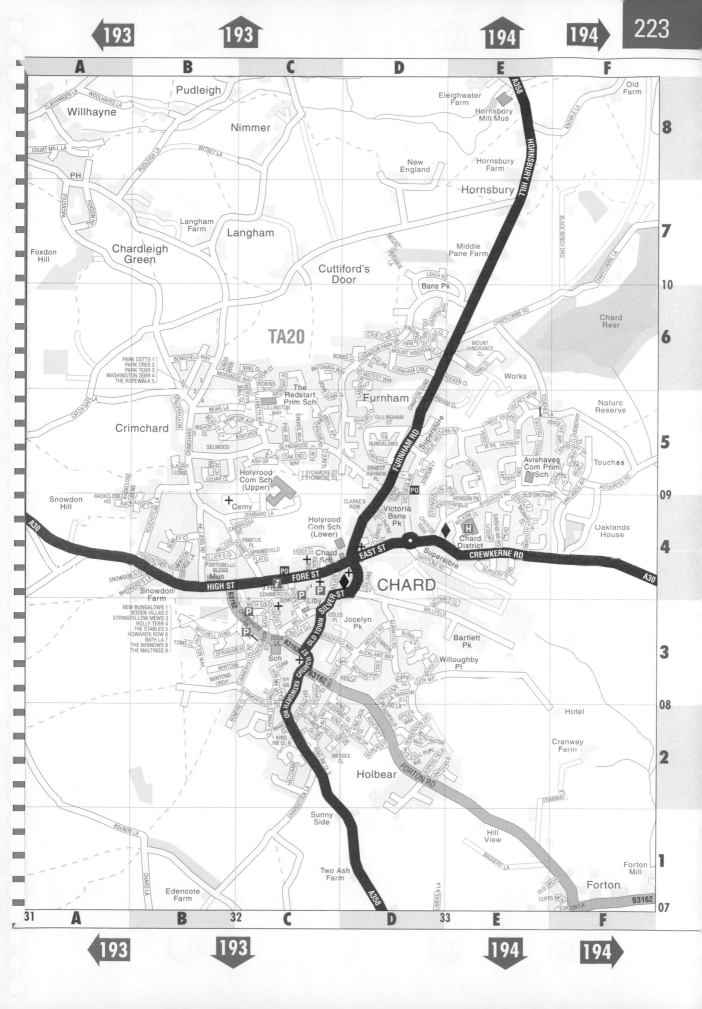

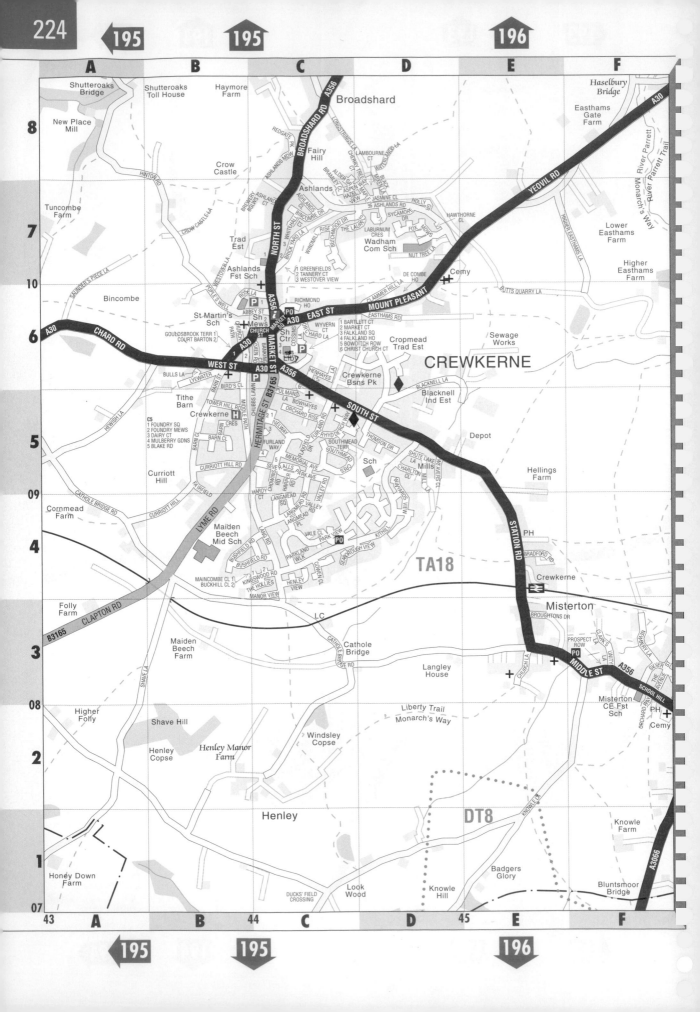

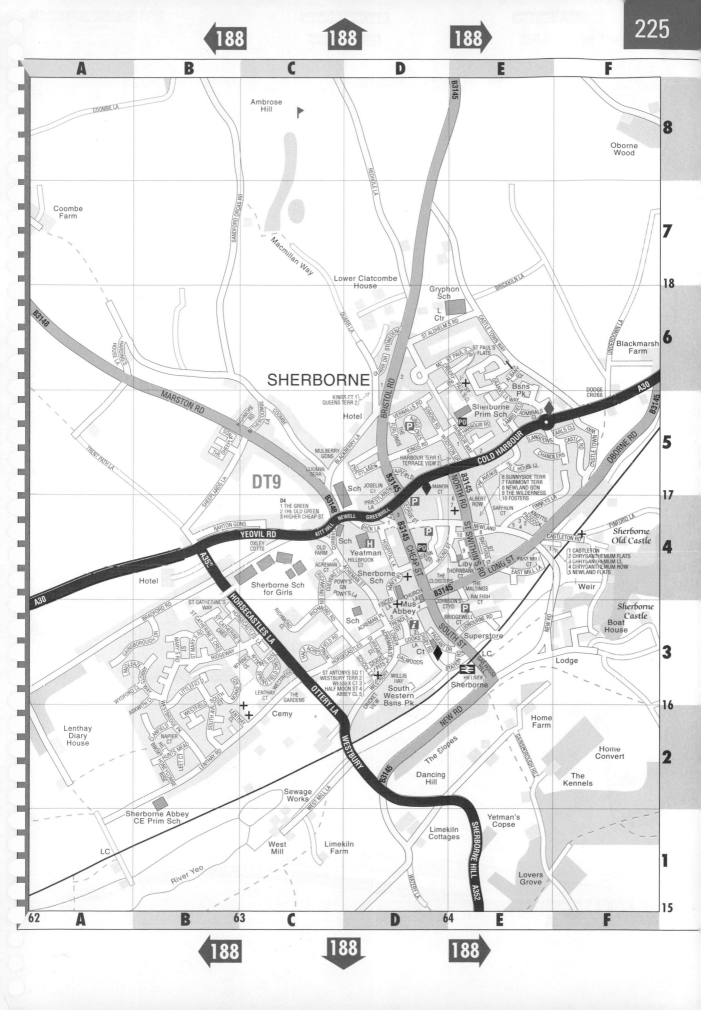

188 ◀ 188 188 ▶

A B C D E F

8

COOMBE LA

Ambrose Hill

Oborne Wood

7

Coombe Farm

SANDFORD ORCAS RD

REIGHOLE LA

Macmillan Way

Lower Clatcombe House

18

B3148

HARDING'S
HOUSE LA

DUARR LA

B3145

Gryphon Sch

L Ctr

BRICKKILN LA

UNDERDOWN LA

6

Blackmarsh Farm

ST ALDHELM'S RD

MC CREERY RD

ST PAUL'S FLATS

CASTLE TOWN WAY

A30

MARSTON RD

HIGHMORE RD

COOMBE LA

NETHERCOOMBE LA

THE CHEAP

BRISTOL RD

QUARR DR STONEGENE

SHERBORNE

KINGS CT 1
QUEENS TERR 2

Hotel

VERNALLS RD

KINGS CRES

SIMONS RD

ST PAUL'S RD

GRANVILLE WAY

Bsns Pk

Sherborne Prim Sch

ALBANY CL

ADMIRALS CT

DODGE CROSS

B3145

OBORNE RD

5

TRENT PATH LA

SHERBARDS LA

DT9

BARTON GDNS

KITT HILL

NEWELL

GREENHILL

MULBERRY GDNS

COOMBE TERR

BLACKBERRY LA

THE FURLONGS

P

HARBOUR RD

WOOTTON GR

KINGS RD

COLD HARBOUR

PO

HILL HOUSE CL

HARBOUR TERR 1
TERRACE VIEW 2

CASTLANDS

Sch

FAIRFIELD

JOSELIN CT

PRIESTLANDS

NORTH RD

THE AVENUE

ALBANY CL

LANGDONS

EARLS CL

CASTLE RD

CHANDLERS

CASTLE TOWN WAY

17

D4
1 THE GREEN
2 THE OLD GREEN
3 HIGHER CHEAP ST

YEOVIL RD

A352

B3148

GEORGE ST

MANOR CT

ALBERT RD

SAFFRON ROW

NEWLAND

6 SUNNYSIDE TERR
7 FAIRMONT TERR
8 NEWLAND GDN
9 THE WILDERNESS
10 FOSTERS

TIMNEYS LA

PINNOTTS LA

PADDOCK

PINFORD LA

CASTLETON RD

Sherborne Old Castle

A30

OXLEY COTTS

OLD FARM

Sch

H

Yeatman

HILLBROOK CT

B3145 CHEAP ST

SWAN YD

ST SWITHIN'S RD

LONG ST

MOUND RD

FAST MILL LA

EAST MILL LA

1 CASTLETON
2 CHRYSANTHEMUM FLATS
3 CHRYSANTHEMUM CL
4 CHRYSANTHEMUM ROW
5 NEWLAND FLATS

4

Hotel

Sherborne Sch for Girls

BRADFORD RD

ST CATHERINE'S WAY

HORSECASTLES LA

RICHMOND CT

ACREMAN CT

ACREMAN ST

POWYS
GN

POWY'S LA

Sherborne Sch

ABBEY

THORNBANK CT

THE CLOISTERS

Liby

THE MALTINGS

RALEIGH

RICHMOND RD

Sch

ACREMAN PL

CHURCH LA

Mus

Abbey

FINGER LA

TRENDLE ST

JOHNSON'S CTYD

BRIDGEWELL

P

LUDBOURNE RD

RAL

Weir

Sherborne Castle Boat House

3

Lenthay Diary House

GAINSBOROUGH DR

MACKLEAZE

ABBOTS WAY

WYOFORD CL

ST MARY'S RD

ST CATHERINE'S CRES

RIDGEWAY

ST CATHERINE'S CRES

WYNNES RISE

WYNNES CL

SPRINGFIELD CRES

WESTBRIDGE

LITTLEFIELD

THE GARDENS

HALF ACRE

ACRESMEAD

SCHOOL LA

HORSECASTLES

DURRANT

GRAVEL
PITS

DALWOODS

COOKS
Ct

DIGBY RD

OLD RD

PAGEANT GDNS

SOUTH ST

Superstore

GAS HOUSE

LC

Lodge

NEW RD

16

ASKWITH CL

WESTBURY

SOUTH AVE

CLANFIELD

WESTFIELD

NAPIER CT

LENTHAY CT

LENTHAY

Cemy

OTTERY LA

ST ANTONYS SQ 1
WESTBURY TERR 2
WESSEX CT 3
HALF MOON ST 4
ABBEY CL 5

CRICKET VIEW

Willis Hay

South Western Bsns Pk

HK'SIDE

Sherborne

NEW RD

Home Farm

GAINSBOROUGH HILL

2

MOORE CL

HUNTS MEAD

BRIT

HINE TCOMBE

LEET CL

RISE

LENTHAY RD

Sherborne Abbey CE Prim Sch

WEST MILL LA

Sewage Works

WESTBURY

B3145

The Slopes

Dancing Hill

Home Convert

The Kennels

1

LC

West Mill

River Yeo

Limekiln Farm

WATER LA

SHERBORNE HILL
A352

Limekiln Cottages

Yetman's Copse

Lovers Grove

15

62 A B 63 C D 64 E F

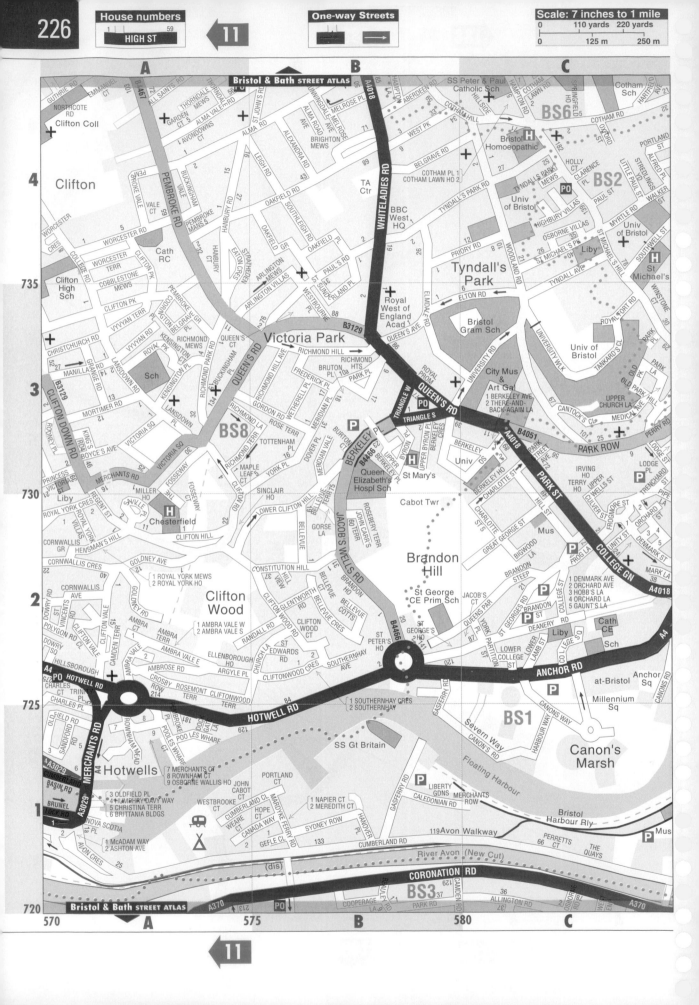

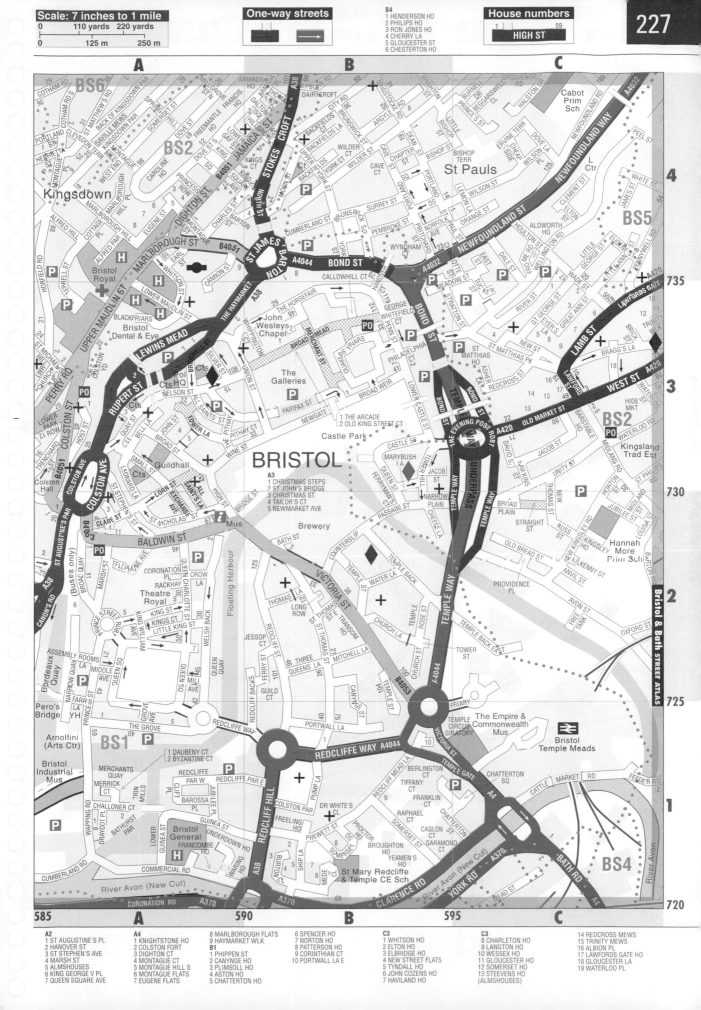

BS6

BS2

Kingsdown

St Pauls

BS5

BRISTOL

Bristol
Temple Meads

BS2

BS1

BS4

Floating Harbour

River Avon (New Cut)

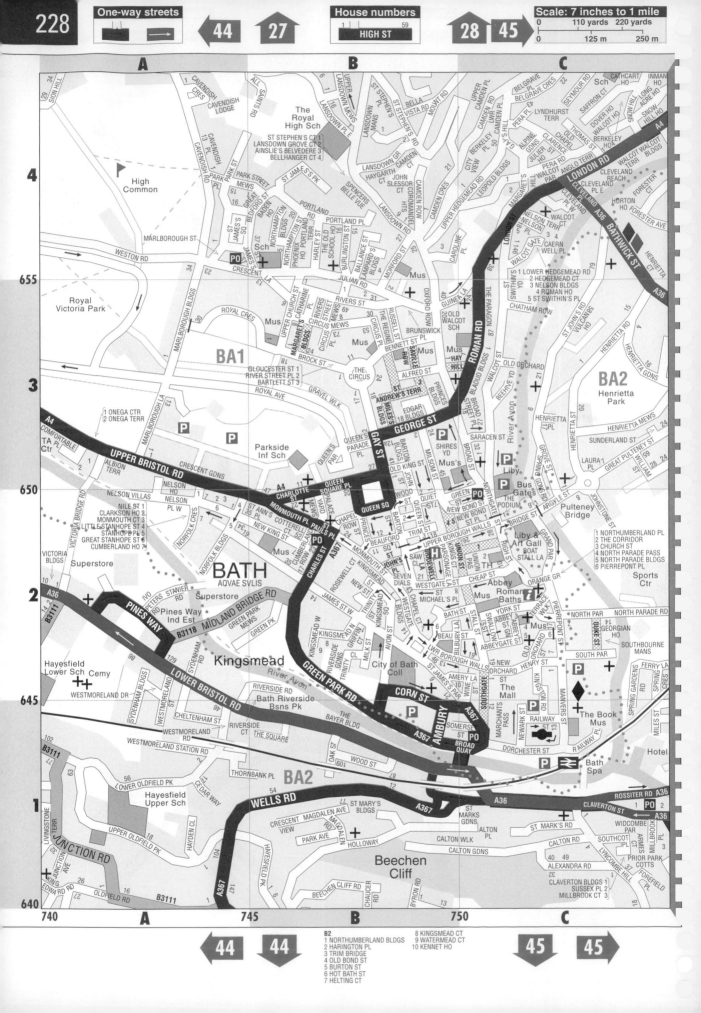

Church Rd 6 Beckenham BR2..........**53** C6

Place name	Location number	Locality, town or village	Postcode district	Page and grid square
May be abbreviated on the map	Present when a number indicates the place's position in a crowded area of mapping	Shown when more than one place has the same name	District for the indexed place	Page number and grid reference for the standard mapping

Public and commercial buildings are highlighted in **magenta**   **Places of interest** are highlighted in blue with a star★

Abbreviations used in the index

Acad	Academy	Comm	Common	Gd	Ground	L	Leisure	Prom	Promenade
App	Approach	Cott	Cottage	Gdn	Garden	La	Lane	Rd	Road
Arc	Arcade	Cres	Crescent	Gn	Green	Lby	Library	Recn	Recreation
Ave	Avenue	Cswy	Causeway	Gr	Grove	Mdw	Meadow	Ret	Retail
Bglw	Bungalow	Ct	Court	H	Hall	Meml	Memorial	Sh	Shopping
Bldg	Building	Ctr	Centre	Ho	House	Mkt	Market	Sq	Square
Bsns, Bus	Business	Ctry	Country	Hospl	Hospital	Mus	Museum	St	Street
Bvd	Boulevard	Cty	County	HQ	Headquarters	Orch	Orchard	Sta	Station
Cath	Cathedral	Dr	Drive	Hts	Heights	Pal	Palace	Terr	Terrace
Cir	Circus	Dro	Drove	Ind	Industrial	Par	Parade	TH	Town Hall
Cl	Close	Ed	Education	Inst	Institute	Pas	Passage	Univ	University
Cnr	Corner	Emb	Embankment	Int	International	Pk	Park	Wk, Wlk	Walk
Coll	College	Est	Estate	Intc	Interchange	Pl	Place	Wr	Water
Com	Community	Ex	Exhibition	Junc	Junction	Prec	Precinct	Yd	Yard

Index of localities, towns and villages

A

Abbots Leigh 11 A8
Alhampton 159 C5
Aller 171 D8
Allerford 124 C4
Alweston 189 A1
Angersleigh 181 C5
Ash 185 F7
Ashbrittle 178 E8
Ashcott 156 B8
Ashill 183 B4
Avonmouth 4 B8
Axbridge 70 B1
Axminster 198 B2

B

Babcary 174 C7
Backwell 19 B6
Baltonsborough 158 A6
Bampton 163 C1
Banwell 51 B3
Barrington 184 D5
Barrow Gurney 20 E5
Barton St David 158 A2
Barwick 197 F8
Batcombe 142 D1
Bath 44 E8
Bath 228 A2
Bathampton 28 F1
Batheaston 28 F4
Bathford 29 C1
Bawdrip 136 E2

Beckington 101 E4
Berkley 121 A7
Berrow 84 E5
Bicknoller 132 F2
Biddisham 87 E8
Binegar 114 C7
Bishop Sutton 57 D3
Bishops Lydeard 167 F8
Bitton 25 E8
Blagdon 54 E2
Blagdon Hill 181 D5
Blatchbridge 143 F8
Bleadney 139 A8
Bleadon 67 C7
Blue Anchor 131 B6
Bourton 161 F1
Bradford Abbas 187 E1
Bradford on Tone 167 F1
Bratton Seymour 176 C8
Brean 65 F5
Brendon 122 A4
Brent Knoll 86 A1
Bridgwater 154 A6
Bridgwater 208 E3
Bristol 22 E6
Bristol 227 B3
Broadway 183 B2
Brockley 18 C2
Brompton Ralph 150 C3
Brompton Regis 148 B2
Brushford 163 D4
Bruton 160 C5
Bruton 215 E8
Buckhorn Weston 177 D3
Buckland Dinham 100 B3
Buckland St Mary 182 F8
Burcott 139 E8

Burlescombe 179 B3
Burnham-on-Sea 104 D8
Burrington 53 F3
Burrowbridge 154 F1
Burtle 137 D6
Butleigh 157 D4

C

Camerton 78 E8
Cannington 135 C2
Carhampton 131 B5
Castle Cary 159 D2
Castle Cary 214 B5
Catcott 137 D2
Chantry 117 F3
Chapel Leigh 167 A8
Chapmanslade 121 C5
Chard 193 E2
Chard 223 D4
Chard Junction 198 E7
Chardstock 198 B7
Charlcombe 27 E3
Charlton Adam 173 F7
Charlton Horethorne 176 B2
Charlton Mackrell 173 E7
Cheddar 90 D8
Chedzoy 154 E8
Chesterblade 142 A4
Chew Magna 39 C4
Chew Stoke 56 D8
Chewton Mendip 94 E7
Chilcompton 96 C4
Chilthorne Domer 186 E5

Chilton Polden 137 B2
Chilton Trinity 135 F2
Chipstable 165 E6
Chiselborough 185 F1
Churchill 52 F5
Churchill Green 52 D5
Churchinford 192 A7
Churchstanton 181 B1
Clapton 195 C1
Clapton In Gordano 8 F8
Clatworthy 149 F1
Claverham 17 C1
Clayhanger 165 C1
Cleeve 35 C8
Clevedon 6 B3
Clutton 58 E3
Cold Ashton 12 F6
Coleford 116 F7
Colerne 29 F8
Combe St Nicholas 193 D6
Combwich 135 B5
Compton Bishop 69 A3
Compton Dando 41 D6
Compton Dundon 157 B4
Compton Martin 74 A7
Congresbury 34 E4
Corfe 181 F6
Corsley Heath 144 E8
Corston 43 B7
Cossington 136 F3
Cotford St Luke 167 E6
Coultings 134 F4
Coxley 139 F6
Cranmore 142 B6
Creech St Michael 169 D4
Crewkerne 195 E5
Crewkerne 224 D6

Cricket St Thomas 194 E3
Croscombe 140 E7
Croscombe 204 B8
Crowcombe 151 C7
Cucklington 177 D6
Culverhays 132 F1
Curland 182 D4
Curry Mallet 183 C8
Curry Rivel 171 C4

D

Dinder 140 D7
Dinnington 195 B7
Ditcheat 159 C7
Donyatt 183 D1
Doulting 141 E6
Downhead 142 C8
Doynton 12 A8
Draycott 90 E2
Drayton 171 E3
Drimpton 199 F7
Dulverton 163 E6
Dundry 21 D2
Dunkerton 61 E4
Dunster 130 F6
Dunster 201 E2

E

East Anstey 162 E5
East Brent 86 D5
East Chinnock 196 E8

5

5c Bsns Ctr BS21 . . . 6 B1

A

Abbas & Templecombe CE Prim Sch BA8 . . . 176 E1
Abbey Cl Curry Rivel TA10 . . . 171 D4
Keynsham BS31 . . . 24 F6
Sherborne DT9 . . . 225 D3
Tatworth TA20 . . . 198 D8
Wookey BA5 . . . 139 D8
Abbey Ct BA2 . . . 45 B7
Abbey Fields TA10 . . . 171 D4
Abbey Gn BA1 . . . 228 C2
Abbey Hill Dro TA3 . . . 182 E5
Abbey La BA3 . . . 64 A4
Abbey Meads BA6 . . . 206 E3
Abbey Mews TA20 . . . 198 D8
Abbey Pk BS31 . . . 24 F6
Abbey Rd Bristol BS9 . . . 5 F7
Chilcompton BA3 . . . 96 D2
Sherborne DT9 . . . 225 D4
Stratton-on-the-Fosse BA3 . . . 96 F2
Washford TA23 . . . 131 E3
Yeovil BA21 . . . 218 D6
Abbey St Bath BA1 . . . 228 C2
Crewkerne TA18 . . . 224 C6
Hinton St George TA17 . . . 195 C7
Abbey View Bath BA2 . . . 45 B5
Radstock BA3 . . . 79 A3
Abbey View Gdns BA2 . . . 45 B5
Abbeygate St BA1 . . . 228 C2
Abbeywood Dr BS9 . . . 5 C5
Abbot's Cl BS22 . . . 32 A3
Abbots Cl Bristol BS14 . . . 23 A3
Burnham-On-Sea TA8 . . . 104 B6
Ilminster TA19 . . . 221 B3
Oxenpill BA6 . . . 138 C4
Seavington TA19 . . . 184 E2
Abbots Ct BA6 . . . 206 D4
Abbots Fish Ho* BA6 . . . 138 D4
Abbots Horn BS48 . . . 8 D2
Abbots Leigh Rd BS8 . . . 11 C7
Abbots Meade BA21 . . . 218 D5
Abbots Way
Minehead TA24 . . . 200 C6
Pilton BA4 . . . 140 E3
Sherborne DT9 . . . 225 B3
Yeovil BA21 . . . 218 D6
Abbotsbury Rd BS48 . . . 8 D1
Abbotsfield TA4 . . . 210 A4
Abbotsfield Cotts TA4 . . . 210 B4
Abbott La TA16 . . . 196 A8
Abbott's Wootton La DT6 . . . 199 B1
Abbotts Farm Cl BS39 . . . 77 D5
Abbotts Rd BA22 . . . 173 D1
Abbotts Way TA3 . . . 183 F7
Abels La DT9 . . . 187 F5
Aberdeen Rd BS6 . . . 226 B4
Abingdon Gdns BA2 . . . 62 D8
Abingdon St TA8 . . . 104 B6
Abington Cross TA24 . . . 124 B4
Ablake La TA10 . . . 172 C5
Ableton Wlk BS9 . . . 5 C5
Abon Ho BS9 . . . 5 C4
Acacia Ave BS23 . . . 49 B8
Acacia Ct BS31 . . . 24 C4
Acacia Dr BA11 . . . 120 C7
Acacia Gdns TA2 . . . 213 E7
Acacia Gr BA2 . . . 44 C3
Acacia Rd BA3 . . . 78 E1
Accommodation Rd BS24 . . . 66 E6
Acer Dr BA21 . . . 218 C7
Ackland's Dro TA10 . . . 155 F4
Acland Round TA4 . . . 167 E6
Acombe Cross TA3 . . . 191 E8
Aconite Cl BS22 . . . 32 B5
Acorn Cl Frome BA11 . . . 119 D5
Highbridge TA9 . . . 104 D4
Acorn Gr BS13 . . . 21 E6
Acre La TA11 . . . 211 F4
Acreman Ct DT9 . . . 225 C4
Acreman Pl DT9 . . . 225 D3
Acreman St DT9 . . . 225 D4
Acres Ct BA22 . . . 197 F8
Acres The 1 TA12 . . . 185 E6
Acresbush Cl BS13 . . . 22 A5
Actis Rd BA6 . . . 206 E3
Adam St TA8 . . . 104 B6
Adam's La TA5 . . . 134 D6
Adams Cl Highbridge TA9 . . . 104 C2
Peasedown St John BA2 . . . 79 D8
Adams Ct 5 BS8 . . . 11 F6
Adams Ho TA19 . . . 221 B3
Adams Mdw TA19 . . . 221 A4
Adastral Rd BS24 . . . 50 D4
Adber Cl BA21 . . . 219 E8
Adber Cross DT9 . . . 187 F6
Adcombe Cl TA3 . . . 181 D5
Adcombe Rd TA2 . . . 213 B8
Adder La TA7 . . . 169 F8
Adderwell BA11 . . . 120 A3
Adderwell Cl BA11 . . . 120 A3
Addicott Rd BS23 . . . 48 E6
Addiscombe Rd
Bristol BS14 . . . 23 B5
Weston-Super-Mare BS23 . . . 48 E4
Addison Gr TA2 . . . 212 E6
Addlewell La 11 BA20 . . . 219 B4
Adlams Central Pk BA6 . . . 206 B3
Admiral Blake Mus* TA6 . . . 209 A4
Admiral's Mead BA6 . . . 157 E4
Admiral's Wlk BS20 . . . 2 B5
Admirals Cl
Sherborne DT9 . . . 225 E5
Watchet TA23 . . . 202 D6
Admirals Ct TA6 . . . 208 F5
Admiralty Way TA1 . . . 213 C5
Adsborough Hill TA2 . . . 169 D7
Adsborough La TA2 . . . 169 D7
Adscombe Ave TA6 . . . 209 C6
Adscombe La TA5 . . . 134 A1
Aelfric Mdw BS20 . . . 2 F4
Ainslie's Belvedere BA1 . . . 228 B4
Ainstey Dr BA22 . . . 175 A4
Airey Hos TA13 . . . 220 D1
Airport Rd BS14 . . . 23 A8
Airport Rdbt BS24 . . . 49 E7
Aisecome Way BS22 . . . 49 C6
Akeman Cl BA21 . . . 218 D7
Akeman Way BS11 . . . 4 C8
Alamein Rd TA23 . . . 202 E6
Alard Rd BS4 . . . 22 F7
Alastair Cl BA21 . . . 218 F7
Alastair Dr BA21 . . . 218 F7
Albany BS23 . . . 30 F1
Albany Cl DT9 . . . 225 E6
Albany Rd BA2 . . . 44 C6
Albemarle Rd TA1 . . . 212 F5
Albermarle Row 9 BS8 . . . 11 F6
Albert Ave
Peasedown St John BA2 . . . 79 C7
Weston-Super-Mare BS23 . . . 48 E6
Albert Bldgs BA6 . . . 206 D5
Albert Cl BA21 . . . 218 E7
Albert Ct Bridgwater TA6 . . . 208 E4
14 Taunton TA1 . . . 213 A4
Weston-Super-Mare BS23 . . . 48 E6
Albert Pl Bath BA2 . . . 45 C1
Portishead BS20 . . . 2 D4
Albert Quadrant BS23 . . . 48 E8
Albert Rd Clevedon BS21 . . . 6 C3
Keynsham BS31 . . . 24 E5
Portishead BS20 . . . 2 D5
Weston-Super-Mare BS23 . . . 48 E6
Albert Row DT9 . . . 225 E4
Albert St TA6 . . . 208 E4
Albert Terr BA2 . . . 44 C6
Albion Cl TA6 . . . 209 B5
Albion Pl 10 Bristol BS2 . . . 227 C3
Frome BA11 . . . 119 D3
Albion Rd BA22 . . . 174 A2
Albion Terr BA1 . . . 228 A3
Alburys BS40 . . . 35 D3
Alcombe Cross TA24 . . . 201 B5
Alcombe Rd TA24 . . . 201 A5
Aldeburgh Pl BA14 . . . 83 F6
Alder Cl
North Petherton TA6 . . . 153 F3
Taunton TA1 . . . 213 D1
Williton TA4 . . . 202 E3
Alder Gr Crewkerne TA18 . . . 224 C7
Yeovil BA20 . . . 218 E2
Alder Terr BA3 . . . 78 E2
Alder Way BA2 . . . 62 D8
Alder Wlk BA11 . . . 120 B7
Aldercombe Rd BS9 . . . 5 C8
Alderdown Cl BS11 . . . 5 A8
Alderley Rd BA2 . . . 44 B4
Alderney Rd TA6 . . . 209 C3
Aldondale Gdns BA20 . . . 219 B3
Aldwick Ave BS13 . . . 22 C3
Aldwick La BS40 . . . 54 C7
Aldworth Ho BS2 . . . 227 C4
Alec Ricketts Cl BA2 . . . 43 F5
Alexander Bldgs 12 BA1 . . . 28 B1
Alexander Cl TA3 . . . 169 D5
Alexander Ho 5 BS23 . . . 48 F4
Alexander Mews BS23 . . . 48 E7
Alexander Pl BA3 . . . 64 C6
Alexander Way BS49 . . . 34 B7
Alexanders Cl BA6 . . . 138 C4
Alexandra Ct BS21 . . . 6 C4
Alexandra Gdns TA24 . . . 201 A6
Alexandra Par BS23 . . . 48 E7
Alexandra Pk BS39 . . . 77 E5
Alexandra Pl BA2 . . . 45 C1
Alexandra Rd Bath BA2 . . . 228 C1
Bridgwater TA6 . . . 208 E5
Bristol BS8 . . . 226 B4
Bristol, Highridge BS13 . . . 21 F7
Clevedon BS21 . . . 6 C4
Frome BA11 . . . 119 F4
Minehead TA24 . . . 201 A6
Wellington TA21 . . . 222 D6
Yeovil BA21 . . . 219 D6
Alexandra Terr BS39 . . . 77 E5
Alford La BA4,BA7 . . . 159 B4
Alfoxton Rd TA6 . . . 208 C4
Alfred Cres BA4 . . . 205 B4
Alfred Ct BS23 . . . 48 E7
Alfred Hill BS2 . . . 227 A4
Alfred Par BS2 . . . 227 A4
Alfred Pl BS2 . . . 226 C4
Alfred St Bath BA1 . . . 228 B3
Taunton TA1 . . . 213 B4
Wells BA5 . . . 203 D3
Weston-Super-Mare BS23 . . . 48 E8
Alfred's Twr* BA10 . . . 161 C6
Alfred's Way BA9 . . . 216 B3
Algar Ct BA5 . . . 203 B4
Alice St BA11 . . . 143 A6
Alison Gdns BS48 . . . 19 A7
All Hallows Prep Sch BA4 . . . 142 C6
All Saints CE Prim Sch TA15 . . . 186 B3
All Saints East Clevedon CE Prim Sch BS21 . . . 6 F4
All Saints La BS21 . . . 6 F4
All Saints Rd BA1 . . . 228 B4
All Saints Sch EX13 . . . 198 A4
All Saints' La BS1 . . . 227 A2
All Saints' Rd Bristol BS8 . . . 226 A4
Weston-Super-Mare BS23 . . . 30 E1
All Saints' St BS1 . . . 227 A3
All Saints' Terr TA6 . . . 209 B4
Allandale Rd TA8 . . . 104 A8
Allanmead Rd BS14 . . . 23 B8
Allen Dr BA4 . . . 205 A6
Allen Rd TA6 . . . 208 F1
Allens La Shipham BS25 . . . 70 F8
Wells BA5 . . . 112 E1
Allenslade Flats TA4 . . . 210 C5
Aller BS24 . . . 49 B2
Aller Dro Aller TA10 . . . 171 D8
NonRoady TA7 . . . 155 C1
Aller Par BS24 . . . 49 B2
Allermoor Dro BS28 . . . 138 B8
Allerpark La TA24 . . . 123 F3
Allerton Cres BS14 . . . 23 B4
Allerton Gdns BS14 . . . 23 B5
Allerton Rd
Bridgwater TA6 . . . 209 B7
Bristol BS14 . . . 23 B4
Allingham Rd BA21 . . . 219 C7
Allington Cl TA1 . . . 213 E4
Allington Gdns BS48 . . . 18 C8
Allington Rd BS3 . . . 226 C1
Allotment Dro
Combe St Nicholas TA20 . . . 193 C5
Glastonbury BA16 . . . 138 D1
Allotment Rd BA22 . . . 175 C3
Allshire La EX16 . . . 162 F3
Allyn Saxon Dr BA4 . . . 205 D5
Alma Rd BS8 . . . 226 B4
Alma Road Ave BS8 . . . 226 B4
Alma St Taunton TA1 . . . 213 A3
Weston-Super-Mare BS23 . . . 48 E7
Alma Vale Rd BS8 . . . 226 A4
Almond Cl BS22 . . . 32 A1
Almond Tree Cl TA6 . . . 209 D4
Almshouse La BA22 . . . 173 E1
Almshouses
5 Bristol BS1 . . . 227 A2
Donyatt TA19 . . . 183 D1
Marshfield SN14 . . . 13 E8
Almyr Terr TA23 . . . 202 C7
Alpha Ho TA9 . . . 104 E3
Alpine Cl BS39 . . . 77 F4
Alpine Gdns BA1 . . . 228 C4
Alpine Rd BS39 . . . 77 F4
Alston Cl TA1 . . . 212 C1
Alston Sutton Rd BS26 . . . 88 F4
Alstone Gdns TA9 . . . 104 C2
Alstone La TA9 . . . 104 C2
Alstone Rd TA9 . . . 104 C2
Alstone Wildlife Pk* TA9 . . . 104 C3
Alton Pl BA2 . . . 228 C1
Alverstoke BS14 . . . 22 F7
Alveston Wlk BS9 . . . 5 B7
Alvington La BA22 . . . 218 B5
Alweston DT9 . . . 189 A1
Ambares Ct BA3 . . . 96 F8
Amber Mead TA1 . . . 213 D3
Amberd La TA3 . . . 181 D8
Amberey Rd BS23 . . . 48 F5
Amberlands Cl BS48 . . . 19 A7
Amberley Cl
Keinton Mandeville TA11 . . . 158 A1
Keynsham BS31 . . . 24 E4
Amberley Gdns 3 BS48 . . . 8 D1
Ambleside Rd BA2 . . . 44 C2
Ambra Ct BS8 . . . 226 A2
Ambra Terr BS8 . . . 226 A2
Ambra Vale BS8 . . . 226 A2
Ambra Vale E BS8 . . . 226 A2
Ambra Vale S BS8 . . . 226 A2
Ambra Vale W BS8 . . . 226 A2
Ambridge BA16 . . . 207 B4
Ambrose Cl DT9 . . . 187 E1
Ambrose Rd BS8 . . . 226 A2
Ambury BA1 . . . 228 B1
Amercombe Wlk BS14 . . . 23 D7
American Mus in Britain* BA2 . . . 46 A5
Amery La BA1 . . . 228 C2
Ames La BA3 . . . 98 B6
Amesbury Dr BS24 . . . 67 B6
Ammerdown Terr BA3 . . . 98 F7
Ammerham La TA20 . . . 199 A8
Amor Pl TA1 . . . 212 D2
Amory Rd TA22 . . . 163 D6
Amulet Way BA4 . . . 205 E4
Ancastle Ave BA7 . . . 214 D6
Ancastle Terr BA7 . . . 214 C6
Anchor Cl BA3 . . . 116 E8
Anchor Cnr BA9 . . . 176 D6
Anchor Hill BA9 . . . 176 D6
Anchor Rd Bathford BA1 . . . 27 B1
Bristol BS1 . . . 226 C2
Coleford BA3 . . . 116 E8
Anchor Sq BS1 . . . 226 C2
Anchor St TA23 . . . 202 C7
Anchor Stables TA24 . . . 123 E4
Anchor Way BS20 . . . 4 D4
Ancliff Sq BA15 . . . 64 E4
Ander's La TA3 . . . 192 B8
Andereach Cl BS14 . . . 23 B8
Andersfield Cl TA6 . . . 208 A4
Andrew Allan Rd TA21 . . . 222 B4
Andrew's Hill TA22 . . . 163 D6
Andrew's Hill Cross TA22 . . . 163 C6
Andruss Dr BS41 . . . 21 D2
Angel Cres TA6 . . . 208 F5
Angel La BA9 . . . 216 C4
Angel Place Sh Ctr 6 TA6 . . . 208 F5
Angel Row TA3 . . . 170 F2
Angela Cl TA1 . . . 212 D2
Anglesey Cotts DT10 . . . 190 B4
Anglo Terr BA1 . . . 228 C4
Anglo Trad Est The BA4 . . . 205 B6
Angwin Cl BA4 . . . 205 B6
Animal Farm Ctry Pk* TA8 . . . 66 B2
Annaly Rd BS27 . . . 90 A7
Annandale BA7 . . . 214 B4
Annandale Ave BS22 . . . 31 E1
Ansford Com Sch BA7 . . . 214 C7
Ansford Hill BA7 . . . 214 B7
Ansford Rd BA7 . . . 214 C6
Anson Cl BS31 . . . 25 D2
Anson Rd Locking BS24 . . . 50 B5
Weston-Super-Mare BS22 . . . 31 D4
Anson Way TA6 . . . 208 F5
Anthony Rd BA16 . . . 207 D7
Antler Cl BA6 . . . 206 C3
Antona Ct BS11 . . . 4 D7
Antona Dr BS11 . . . 4 D7
Anvil Rd BS49 . . . 17 F1
Anvil St BS2 . . . 227 C2
Apex Dr TA9 . . . 104 C4
Aplins Cl TA19 . . . 221 B3
Apple Alley BA11 . . . 119 F5
Apple Bsns Ctr The TA2 . . . 212 B6
Apple Cl TA19 . . . 194 E7
Apple Dumpling Cnr BS28 . . . 108 C3
Apple La BA11 . . . 119 F5
Apple Tree Cl TA6 . . . 209 D4
Apple Tree Dr BS25 . . . 70 A8
Appleby Wlk BS4 . . . 22 D7
Applecroft BA2 . . . 79 E6
Appledore 4 BS22 . . . 31 F2
Appledore Cl BS14 . . . 23 B8
Applehayes La EX15 . . . 180 F2
Appletree Ct BS22 . . . 32 B2
Appletree Mews BS22 . . . 32 B2
Appley Cross TA21 . . . 179 B8
Appsley Cl BS22 . . . 31 C1
Apricot Tree Cl TA6 . . . 209 D5
Apsley Rd BA1 . . . 44 A7
Aquara Cl BA16 . . . 207 C3
Arbutus Dr BS9 . . . 5 C8
Arcade The 2 BS1 . . . 227 B3
Arch Cl BS41 . . . 10 F1
Arch La TA3 . . . 170 E4
Archbishop Cranmer CE Com Prim Sch TA1 . . . 213 A4
Archer Ct BS21 . . . 6 D4
Archer Dr TA8 . . . 104 C6
Archer Wlk BS14 . . . 23 D4
Archers Way The BA6 . . . 206 E5
Arches The BA2 . . . 44 A6
Archgrove BS41 . . . 10 F1
Archstone Ave TA5 . . . 135 F2
Archway St BA2 . . . 45 B5
Arden Cl BS22 . . . 31 F3
Ardern Cl BS9 . . . 5 B8
Ardmore BS8 . . . 11 D7
Ardwyn TA21 . . . 222 D4
Argyle Ave BS23 . . . 48 F4
Argyle Pl BS8 . . . 226 A2
Argyle Rd Bristol BS2 . . . 227 B4
Clevedon BS21 . . . 6 D6
Argyle St BA2 . . . 228 C2
Argyle Terr BA2 . . . 44 C6
Arlington Cl
Bridgwater TA6 . . . 209 A2
Yeovil BA21 . . . 218 C7
Arlington Mans BS8 . . . 226 B4
Arlington Rd BA2 . . . 44 D5
Arlington Villas BS8 . . . 226 B3
Armada Ho BS2 . . . 227 A4
Armada Pl BS1 . . . 227 B4
Armada Rd BS14 . . . 23 A6
Armes Ct BA2 . . . 228 C1
Armoury Rd BA22 . . . 218 A6
Armstrong Rd BA11 . . . 120 B5
Armtech Row BA22 . . . 218 B6
Arnewood Gdns BA20 . . . 218 F2
Arnold Cl TA2 . . . 212 F7
Arnold Noad Cnr BA14 . . . 83 E3
Arnold's Way BS49 . . . 17 A2
Arnolfini (Arts Ctr) BS1 . . . 227 A1
Arnor Cl BS22 . . . 32 A4
Arrowfield Cl BS14 . . . 23 A2
Artemesia Ave BS22 . . . 49 E8
Arthurswood Rd BS13 . . . 22 A4
Artillery Rd BA22 . . . 218 A6
Arun Gr TA1 . . . 213 D4
Arundel Cl BS13 . . . 22 B5
Arundel Rd Bath BA1 . . . 28 A1
Clevedon BS21 . . . 6 D3
Yeovil BA21 . . . 219 E6
Arundel Wlk BS31 . . . 24 D5
Arundell Ct BS23 . . . 48 E8
Arundell Rd BS23 . . . 30 E1
Arundells Way TA3 . . . 169 D4
Ascension Ho BA2 . . . 44 D4
Ash Brook BS39 . . . 59 D1
Ash CE Prim Sch TA12 . . . 185 F7
Ash Cl Bridgwater TA6 . . . 209 D4
Wells BA5 . . . 203 D5
Winscombe BS25 . . . 52 A1
Ash Cres TA1 . . . 212 B2
Ash Croft TA12 . . . 185 F7
Ash Cross TA3 . . . 169 E2
Ash Ct BS14 . . . 23 A6
Ash End BA8 . . . 189 F7
Ash Gr Bath BA2 . . . 44 C4
Chard TA20 . . . 223 C5
Clevedon BS21 . . . 6 E4
Ash Gr *continued*
Minehead TA24 . . . 200 D7
Shepton Mallet BA4 . . . 205 C4
Wells BA5 . . . 203 D5
Weston-Super-Mare BS23 . . . 48 E2
Ash Grove Way TA6 . . . 209 D7
Ash Hay Dro BA5 . . . 139 C6
Ash Hayes Dr BS48 . . . 8 E1
Ash Hayes Rd BS48 . . . 8 F1
Ash Ho TA8 . . . 65 F2
Ash La
Shepton Beauchamp TA19 . . . 184 E4
Wells BA5 . . . 203 C5
Winsford TA24 . . . 147 B6
Ash Moor Dro BA5 . . . 139 C6
Ash Rd Banwell BS29 . . . 50 E4
Street BA16 . . . 207 B3
Ash Tree Cl Bleadon BS24 . . . 67 C6
Burnham-On-Sea TA8 . . . 85 A3
Ash Tree Cres TA8 . . . 85 A3
Ash Tree Ct BA3 . . . 78 E1
Ash Tree Pl TA8 . . . 85 A3
Ash Tree Rd TA8 . . . 85 A3
Ash Trees TA9 . . . 86 C5
Ash Wlk BA8 . . . 190 A6
Ashbeer Hill TA4 . . . 150 D7
Ashbourne Cres TA1 . . . 213 D3
Ashbrooke House Sch BS23 . . . 48 D6
Ashbury Dr BS22 . . . 31 B2
Ashcombe Ct
Ilminster TA19 . . . 221 B4
Weston-Super-Mare BS23 . . . 48 F7
Ashcombe Gdns BS23 . . . 49 A8
Ashcombe La
Alweston DT9 . . . 189 B2
Ilminster TA19 . . . 221 B4
Ashcombe Park Rd BS23 . . . 31 A1
Ashcombe Prim Sch BS23 . . . 49 A7
Ashcombe Rd BS23 . . . 48 F7
Ashcott BS14 . . . 22 F7
Ashcott Cl TA8 . . . 104 C6
Ashcott Dr TA8 . . . 104 C6
Ashcott Pl TA8 . . . 104 C6
Ashcott Prim Sch TA7 . . . 156 B8
Ashcott Rd BA6 . . . 138 D3
Ashcroft Chard TA20 . . . 223 D2
Weston-Super-Mare BS24 . . . 49 B2
Ashcroft Ave BS31 . . . 24 D5
Ashcroft Rd BS9 . . . 5 C7
Ashculm Hill EX15 . . . 180 C2
Ashdene Rd BS23 . . . 49 A8
Ashdown Ct BS9 . . . 5 F8
Ashdown Rd BS20 . . . 2 A6
Ashel's Batch BA3 . . . 94 C8
Ashen Cross TA11 . . . 211 E2
Asher La BS2 . . . 227 C3
Ashes La BA3 . . . 64 A4
Ashey La Burrington BS40 . . . 54 A5
Cheddar BS27 . . . 90 B8
Ashfield TA20 . . . 223 D2
Ashfield Cl BA11 . . . 143 C6
Ashfield Pk 23 TA12 . . . 185 E6
Ashford Cl
Bridgwater TA6 . . . 208 E2
Milverton TA4 . . . 167 A4
Ashford Dr BS24 . . . 49 A1
Ashford Gr BA21 . . . 219 B7
Ashford La TA19 . . . 183 F5
Ashford Rd Bath BA2 . . . 44 D4
Redhill BS40 . . . 36 E4
Taunton TA1 . . . 212 C2
Wellington TA21 . . . 222 D4
Ashgrove BA2 . . . 79 D8
Ashgrove Ave BS8 . . . 11 B7
Ashgrove Ct BA2 . . . 79 D8
Ashill Cl TA1 . . . 212 E1
Ashington La BA21 . . . 187 B7
Ashland Ct TA18 . . . 224 C7
Ashland La TA4 . . . 150 B4
Ashland Rd BS13 . . . 22 A4
Ashlands Cl TA18 . . . 224 C7
Ashlands Fst Sch TA18 . . . 224 C7
Ashlands Mdw TA18 . . . 224 C8
Ashlands Rd TA18 . . . 224 D7
Ashlea Pk TA9 . . . 136 E8
Ashleigh Ave TA6 . . . 209 A3
Ashleigh Cl Paulton BS39 . . . 77 E6
Weston-Super-Mare BS23 . . . 49 A8
Ashleigh Cres BS49 . . . 34 B8
Ashleigh Gdns TA1 . . . 212 E5
Ashleigh Rd
Weston-Super-Mare BS23 . . . 49 A8
Yatton BS49 . . . 34 B8
Ashleigh Terr TA6 . . . 209 A3
Ashley Ave Bath BA1 . . . 44 C7
Burnham-On-Sea TA8 . . . 104 B6
Ashley Cl BS25 . . . 70 A7
Ashley La BA15 . . . 64 F7
Ashley Rd Bathford BA1 . . . 29 E3
Clevedon BS21 . . . 6 B1
Taunton TA1 . . . 212 D3
Ashley Terr BA1 . . . 44 C7
Ashman Way TA6 . . . 208 D4
Ashmans Ct BA1 . . . 44 B6
Ashmans Gate BS39 . . . 77 E5
Ashmans Yd BA1 . . . 44 B6
Ashmead
Temple Cloud BS39 . . . 58 E1
Yeovil BA20 . . . 218 C2
Ashmead Rd BS31 . . . 25 B5
Ashmead Road Ind Est BS31 . . . 25 B5
Ashmead Way 8 BS1 . . . 11 F5

Barton Way TA3 170 C4
Barton Wlk BA11 119 D2
Bartons The
Bishops Lydeard TA4 167 E8
South Petherton TA13 220 E3
Barwick & Stoford Com Prim Sch BA22 197 E8
Barwick Ho BS11 4 E7
Basketfield La BA6 139 D1
Bat Alley DT10 190 F5
Batallers La TA23 131 D2
Batch Bsns Pk BS24 66 F2
Batch Cl TA7 136 C4
Batch La Clutton BS39 58 F3
Lympsham BS24 66 F3
Batch Rd TA7 136 B5
Batch The Ashcott TA7 156 B7
Backwell BS48 19 D1
Batheaston BA1 28 F3
Blagdon BS40 55 B8
Burrington BS40 54 B3
Chew Magna BS40 39 B3
Churchill BS25 52 F4
Draycott BS27 90 F2
Farmborough BA2 60 A6
Hinton Charterhouse BA2 63 E1
Saltford BS31 25 F3
19 Shepton Mallet BA4 205 B6
Wincanton BA9 216 B4
Yatton BS49 34 B7
Batchpool La BA8 176 F3
Bath Abbey* BA1 228 C2
Bath Bridge Bsns Pk TA6 209 B6
Bath Cl BA6 206 D6
Bath Foyer The BA2 44 A6
Bath Hill Keynsham BS31 24 F5
Wellow BA2 62 D2
Bath House Ct TA1 212 E3
Bath La TA20 223 C5
Bath Meadow Dr TA22 163 E6
Bath New Rd BA3 78 F4
Bath Old Rd BA3 78 F4
Bath Pl TA1 212 F3
Bath Postal Mus* BA1 228 C3
Bath Race Course* BA1 26 F6
Bath Rd Ashcott TA7 156 B7
Bawdrip TA7 136 D2
Beckington BA11 101 D5
Bitton BA1,BA2,BS30 25 F7
Bitton BS30 25 D8
Blagdon BS40 55 B1
Bridgwater TA6 209 C7
Bristol BS2 227 C1
Farmborough BA2 59 E5
Frome BA11 120 A7
Horrington BA3,BA5 113 D5
Kingsdown SN13 29 F5
Moorlinch TA7 155 E8
Norton St Philip BA2 81 E5
Oakhill BA3 115 B3
Paulton BS39 77 F6
Peasedown St John BA2 79 C7
Saltford BS31 25 D3
Shepton Mallet BA4 141 C8
Stawell TA7 137 B1
Wells BA5 112 E1
Bath Riverside Bsns Pk BA2 228 B1
Bath Small Sch BA1 28 C2
Bath Spa Sta BA1 228 C1
Bath Spa Univ Coll BA1 27 E1
Bath Spa University Coll BA2 43 B5
Bath Sq TA20 223 C3
Bath St Bath BA1 228 C2
Bristol BS1 227 B2
Chard TA20 223 C3
Cheddar BS27 90 B7
Frome BA11 119 F4
Bath View BA3 96 F1
Bathampton La BA2 28 E1
Bathampton Prim Sch BA2 28 F2
Batheaston CE Prim Sch BA1 28 F4
Bathford Hill Bathford BA1 29 B2
Compton Dando BS39 41 E5
Bathford Prim Sch BA1 29 C2
Bathurst Cl TA8 104 D8
Bathurst Par BS1 227 A1
Bathurst Rd BS22 49 C8
Bathwell La DT9 217 D1
Bathwick Hill BA2 45 C6
Bathwick Rise BA2 45 B7
Bathwick St BA1,BA2 228 C4
Batstone Cl BA1 28 B2
Batt's La TA10 172 D5
Battery La BS20 2 D7
Battery Rd BS20 2 D6
Battin's Knap TA4 150 A3
Battle La BS40 39 A3
Battle St EX15 180 E1
Battleborough La TA9 86 B1
Battleton TA22 163 D6
Batts La Marshwood DT6 199 F2
Oakhill BA3 114 E3
Batts Pk TA1 212 E1
Battson Rd BS14 23 E4
Baulditch La TA3 184 B8
Baunton's Orch DT9 217 C2
Bauntons Cl DT9 217 C2
Bawden Cl TA7 136 E4
Bawdrip La TA7 136 E2
Bawler's La TA10 171 C3
Bay Hill TA19 221 D4
Bay La BS27 90 F2
Bay Rd Clevedon BS21 6 D6
Bay Rd *continued*
Porlock TA24 124 A4
Bay Tree Rd Bath BA1 28 B2
Clevedon BS21 6 E1
Bay Tree View BS22 31 D1
Bay View TA23 202 D6
Bay View Gdns TA8 104 B5
Bay's La BA3 115 A7
Bayer Bldg The BA2 228 B1
Bayford Hill BA9 216 E4
Bayford La BA9 177 B7
Bayford Rd TA6 209 C6
Bayliss Ctr The BA16 207 C5
Baymead Cl 11 TA6 153 F4
Baymead La TA6 153 F3
Baymead Mdw 5 TA6 153 F3
Baynes Cl TA21 222 E7
Bays The BS27 90 C8
Baytree Ct BS22 31 D1
Baytree Rd BS22 31 C1
Baytree Sch BS22 49 C8
Baytree View BS22 31 D1
Baze La EX35 122 B4
Bazelands Hill BA8 190 B7
Beach Ave BS21 6 C2
Beach Ct BS23 48 D6
Beach End Rd BS23 48 C2
Beach Hill BS20 2 C6
Beach Mews BS21 6 C4
Beach Rd
Weston-Super-Mare BS22 31 A5
Weston-Super-Mare BS23 48 D6
Beach Rd E BS20 2 D6
Beach Rd W BS20 2 C6
Beach The BS21 6 C4
Beach Tree Cross TA4 166 F6
Beachley Wlk BS11 4 D7
Beacon TA19 221 B5
Beacon Hill View DT9 175 D1
Beacon La
Charlton Horethorne DT9 175 D2
Wellington TA21 180 C4
Beacon Rd Bath BA1 28 A1
Minehead TA24 200 F8
Beacon View
Coleford BA3 116 E7
Shepton Mallet BA4 205 A4
Beaconfield Ho TA6 209 A2
Beaconsfield Rd BA20 218 E1
Beaconsfield Rd
Clevedon BS21 6 E3
Weston-Super-Mare BS23 48 E7
Beaconsfield Way BA11 120 B7
Beadon La TA16 195 F7
Beadon Rd TA1 213 C5
Beale Cl BS14 23 E6
Beale Way TA8 104 D5
Bean Acre The BS11 4 D8
Bearbridge Rd BS13 21 F4
Beard's Yd TA10 171 F5
Bearley Bridge Rd 15 TA12 185 E6
Bearley Ho 26 TA12 185 E6
Bearley La BA22 186 B7
Bearley Rd 27 TA12 185 E6
Bears Meadow La TA5 133 C6
Beasley Ct TA20 223 B5
Beastway La TA24 131 B3
Beatty Way TA8 104 C7
Beau St BA1 228 B2
Beauchamp Gdns TA3 183 A7
Beauchamps Dr BA3 97 A5
Beaufitz Pl TA20 193 F1
Beauford Sq BA1 228 B2
Beaufort Ave BA3 78 A2
Beaufort Bldgs 7 BS8 11 F7
Beaufort Cl Locking BS24 50 C3
Sampford Peverell EX16 178 D1
Beaufort Ct
Burnham-On-Sea TA8 85 A1
Clevedon BS21 6 C5
Ilchester BA22 173 E2
Beaufort E BA1 28 C1
Beaufort Gdns
2 Nailsea BS48 8 D1
South Petherton TA13 220 B5
Beaufort Mews 3 BA1 28 C1
Beaufort Pl BA1 28 C1
Beaufort Rd Taunton TA1 212 E5
Weston-Super-Mare BS23 48 F7
Beaufort Villas 8 BA1 28 B1
Beaufort W 11 BA1 28 B1
Beauley Rd BS3 226 B1
Beaulieu Dr BA21 218 D6
Beaumont Cl BS23 48 F4
Beaumont Ho BA21 219 D5
Beavor La EX13 198 A1
Beck's La BA3 116 D6
Beckery New Rd BA6 206 B3
Beckery Old Rd BA6 206 B3
Beckery Rd BA6 206 B4
Becket Dr BS22 32 A3
Becket Pl BA5 203 D3
Becket Prim Sch BS22 32 A2
Becket Rd BS22 32 A4
Becket's La BS48 18 E8
Beckford Ct BA2 45 B7
Beckford Gdns Bath BA2 45 B8
Bristol BS14 23 A3
Beckford Rd BA2 45 B7
Beckford's Twr* BA1 27 D4
Beckhampton Rd BA2 44 D5
Beckington BS24 49 A2
Beckington CE Fst Sch BA11 101 E4
Beckington Cres TA20 223 D3
Becks Bsns Pk BS23 49 A6
Becks Field 2 TA14 185 F4
Beckworth Cl TA6 209 C3
Bector La BA3 116 C4
Bedford Cl TA6 209 C3
Bedford Ct BA1 45 B8
Bedford Rd Wells BA5 112 E1
Weston-Super-Mare BS23 48 E4
Yeovil BA21 219 D8
Bedford St BA1 45 B8
Bedminster Down Sch BS13 21 F7
Bedwell La TA7 155 C2
Bedwin Cl BS20 1 F4
Bee World & Animal Ctr* TA4 150 F8
Beech Ave Bath BA2 45 E5
Shepton Mallet BA4 205 A6
Beech Cl Doulting BA4 141 E6
Shipham BS25 70 F8
Taunton TA2 212 F8
Beech Ct Bristol BS14 23 A5
Frome BA11 120 B7
Taunton TA1 212 E3
2 Wellington TA21 222 D6
Beech Dr Bridgwater TA6 209 D5
Nailsea BS48 9 A3
Shipham BS25 70 E8
Beech Gr Bath BA2 44 D4
Somerton TA11 211 D5
Wellington TA21 222 C6
Beech Grove Prim Sch TA21 222 C6
Beech Hill TA21 222 F5
Beech La Axminster EX13 198 E1
Stoke Trister BA9 177 C8
Beech Rd
Bridgwater TA6 209 D5
20 Martock TA12 185 E6
Saltford BS31 25 E3
Shipham BS25 70 F8
Street BA16 207 C3
Yatton BS49 34 C8
Beech Terr BA3 78 E1
Beech Tree TA23 130 D1
Beech Tree Cl TA4 210 C4
Beech Tree Cross
Clatworthy TA4 149 E1
Dulverton TA22 163 C7
Monksilver TA4 132 B1
Beech Tree Hill TA5 152 C6
Beech Way BA4 141 E1
Beechcroft BS41 21 D2
Beechen Cliff Boys' Sch BA2 45 A4
Beechen Cliff Rd BA2 228 B1
Beeches The Bath BA2 44 D1
Langport TA10 172 A6
Sandford BS25 52 B4
Wheddon Cross TA24 129 E1
Beechfield Cl BS41 11 C2
Beechfield Gr BS9 5 C8
Beechfield Inf Sch TA9 104 D4
Beeching Cl TA20 223 E6
Beechmont Cl BS24 48 F1
Beechmont Dr BS24 49 A1
Beechmount Ct BS14 23 B8
Beechmount Gr BS14 23 B8
Beechwood
Bridgwater TA6 208 E2
Yeovil BA20 218 F2
Beechwood Ave
Frome BA11 120 A5
Locking BS24 50 A5
Beechwood Cl
Bristol BS14 23 C8
Frome BA11 120 A5
Beechwood Dr
Crewkerne TA18 224 C7
Portishead BS20 1 E5
Beechwood Rd Bath BA2 45 B1
Easton-in-G BS20 4 A4
Nailsea BS48 8 D2
Portishead BS20 1 E5
Beehive Yd BA1 228 C3
Beek's La SN14, BA1 13 D5
Beer Door TA10 155 E2
Beer Dro TA10 155 E3
Beer La
Burlescombe EX16 179 B2
Dulverton TA22 163 B5
Beer Rd TA10 155 E1
Beer St Curry Mallet TA3 183 C7
Yeovil BA20 219 A4
Beere Cross EX36 162 A5
Bees Ho BS21 6 C2
Beetham La TA20 193 B6
Beggar Bush La BS8 11 B6
Beggarswell Cl BS2 227 C4
Beggs Cl 4 TA6 153 F3
Behind Berry TA11 211 D4
Behind Butts TA14 185 E1
Behind Hayes BA8 176 D3
Behind Town TA11 157 B4
Bekynton Ave BA5 203 F4
Belcombe Dro TA20 193 B7
Belfast Wlk BS4 22 E8
Belfield Ct TA8 104 A8
Belgrave Cres BA1 228 C4
Belgrave Pl Bath BA1 228 C4
Bristol BS8 226 A3
Taunton TA2 212 F6
Belgrave Rd Bath BA1 28 B1
Bristol BS8 226 B4
Weston-Super-Mare BS22 49 B8
Belgrave Terr 2 BA1 28 A1
Bell Barn Rd BS9 5 D6
Bell Cl Bridgwater TA6 208 F6
Farmborough BA2 59 F6
Westbury Sub Mendip BA5 110 E6
Bell Hill
Chewton Mendip BA3 94 B7
Norton St Philip BA2 81 E4
Bell La Bristol BS1 227 A3
Chard TA19,TA20 193 F7
Chewton Mendip BA3 94 B7
Cossington TA7 137 A3
Thurloxton TA2 153 D1
Bell Orch TA10 171 D4
Bell Sq BS40 54 E3
Bell Wlk BS40 35 E2
Bella View Gdns BA6 206 D4
Bella Vista Rd BA1 228 B4
Bellamy Ave BS13 22 C4
Belland Dr BS14 22 F4
Belle View BA3 78 B3
Belle View Terr TA20 198 C8
Belle Vue TA23 131 E3
Bellevue BS8 226 B2
Bellevue Cotts BS8 226 B2
Bellevue Cres BS8 226 B2
Bellevue Ct Bristol BS8 226 B2
Clevedon BS21 6 D4
Bellevue Mans BS21 6 D4
Bellevue Rd BS21 6 D4
Bellevue Terr BS8 226 B2
Bellfield BA3 117 A3
Bellhanger Ct BA1 228 B4
Bellhorse La BS40 74 C5
Bellifants BA2 60 A6
Bellman's Cross BA8 190 B7
Bellmoor La TA19 194 A7
Bellotts Rd BA2 44 C6
Belluton La BS39 40 D5
Belluton Terr BS39 40 D5
Belmont Cl TA6 208 B4
Belmont Dr Failand BS8 10 B3
Taunton TA1 212 E2
Belmont Hill BS48 10 B1
Belmont Ho 14 BA20 219 B4
Belmont Rd Bath BA2 45 C1
Hatch Beauchamp TA3 183 A8
Taunton TA1 212 C3
Winscombe BS25 70 A8
Belmont Terr TA19 184 E3
Belmore Gdns BA2 44 A3
Belstone Wlk BS4 22 C8
Belton Ct BA1 27 B2
Belton Rd BS20 2 A5
Belvedare Ct 3 TA21 222 D6
Belvedere Cl TA5 135 B2
Belvedere Cres BS22 31 C1
Belvedere Grange TA11 211 E3
Belvedere Rd
Taunton TA1 212 F5
Yeovil BA21 219 E7
Belvedere Trad Est TA1 212 E5
Belvoir Rd BA2 44 D5
Bemberry Bank TA24 130 B5
Ben Cross TA13 220 A4
Ben Travers Way TA8 104 C6
Bences Cl SN14 13 F8
Bench La TA20 193 D5
Benches La BS40 37 D3
Benedict St BA6 206 D4
Benhole La TA5 134 B8
Bennell Batch BA3 96 E4
Bennell Cl BA3 96 E4
Bennell Cotts BA3 96 E4
Bennett Gdns BA11 119 D4
Bennett La BA1 28 A1
Bennett Rd TA9 104 E4
Bennett St BA1 228 B3
Bennett Way BS1,BS8 11 F5
Bennett's Cl BA5 204 B7
Bennett's Rd BA1 28 C3
Bennetts Field Trad Est BA9 216 C2
Bennetts La BA3,BA5 114 B7
Bennetts Way BS21 6 E5
Benter Cross BA3 115 D7
Bentley Cl BS14 22 F3
Bentley Rd BS22 32 B3
Benville Ave BS9 5 C8
Bere La BA6 206 E4
Bere Mills La TA19 194 B7
Beresford Cl
Burnham-On-Sea TA8 104 C7
Saltford BS31 25 E2
Beresford Gdns BA1 27 A3
Berhill TA7 156 C7
Berkeley Ave Bristol BS8 226 C3
Midsomer Norton BA3 78 A2
Berkeley Cres
Bristol BS8 226 B3
Weston-Super-Mare BS23 48 C2
Berkeley Ct BA2 45 C6
Berkeley Gdns
Bruton BA10 215 E6
Keynsham BS31 24 E4
Berkeley Ho Bath BA1 228 C4
Bristol BS1 226 C3
Berkeley Pl Bath BA1 228 C4
Bristol BS8 226 B3
Berkeley Rd Street BA16 207 E6
Yeovil BA20 219 A4
Berkeley Sq BS8 226 B3
Berkley Ave BS8 226 B3
Berkley CE Fst Sch BA11 121 A7
Berkley Cross BA11 120 F6
Berkley Ct BA22 173 E2
Berkley La
Beckington BA11 101 D3
Frome BA11 120 D8
Berkley Rd BA11 120 B6
Berkley St BA11 121 A8
Berlington Ct BS1 227 B1
Bernard Cres TA24 200 F6
Bernard Herridge Ct BA9 216 D4
Bernard Ireland Ho BA1 27 B1
Bernard Taylor Homes 8 TA1 213 A4
Berners Cl BS4 22 D7
Berrow CE Prim Sch TA8 84 F4
Berrow Lodge 7 BS23 48 E5
Berrow Rd TA8 85 A2
Berry Cl TA6 208 E2
Berry Hill Mells BA11 118 A6
Nunney BA11 143 B8
Berry La EX13 198 F3
Berrydale Ave TA6 208 F6
Berryman Cl BA4 205 A5
Berryman Ct BA5 203 B4
Bertha Terr TA9 104 D3
Berwick Cl TA1 212 C1
Beryl Gr BS14 23 C8
Beryl Knapp BA22 197 B8
Beryl La BA5 203 F6
Besley Ct BA5 203 B4
Bests Field TA12 185 B8
Beverley Cl Frome BA11 119 D3
Taunton TA2 212 E6
Beverley Dr TA23 202 C7
Beverley Gdns BS9 5 D7
Bewdley Rd BA2 45 B4
Bewley Ct TA20 223 B4
Bews La TA20 223 B5
Bibors Hill TA4 165 E4
Bibury Cl BS48 9 A1
Bibury Ho BA1 27 B2
Bickenhall La TA3 182 F6
Bickfield La BS40 74 B8
Bicking's Close La TA4 166 A4
Bicknell Gdns BA21 219 B8
Bidbrooke La EX36 162 A6
Biddiscombe Cl TA6 208 E1
Biddisham Cl 6 BS48 8 E1
Biddisham La BS26 87 E7
Biddle St BS49 34 B7
Bideford Cres BS4 22 F8
Bideford Rd BS22 31 F2
Bifield Cl BS14 23 F5
Bifield Gdns BS14 23 E5
Bifield Rd BS14 23 F5
Big Tree Cl BS26 69 C3
Bignal Rand Cl BA5 203 B3
Bignal Rand Dr BA5 203 B3
Bignell Cl BS25 69 F8
Bigwood La BS1 226 C2
Bilberry Cl BS9 5 C8
Bilberry Gr TA1 168 F1
Bilbie Cl BS40 56 E8
Bilbie Rd Chew Stoke BS40 56 E8
Weston-Super-Mare BS22 32 B3
Bilbury La Bath BA1 228 B2
Glastonbury BA6 206 F3
Billand Cl BS13 21 E3
Billet St TA1 212 F3
Billetfield TA1 212 F3
Billicombe La TA7 155 C8
Billing's Hill BS28 108 C4
Billy La TA4 210 D7
Bince's Lodge La BA3 78 B3
Binces La BA2 42 E3
Bincombe Dr TA18 224 C7
Bincombe Rd TA6 209 C4
Binding Cl 6 TA6 153 F4
Bindon La BA11 143 B2
Bindon Rd TA2 212 C6
Bindwell La BA22 174 F3
Binegar CE Prim Sch BA3 114 D8
Bineham Ct TA10 173 B4
Bineham La
Ilchester BA22 173 F2
Yeovilton BA22 174 A2
Binford Pl TA6 209 A5
Binford's La TA4 151 A4
Binhay Rd BS49 34 C7
Binley Gr BS14 23 D5
Binmead Gdns BS13 22 B4
Binnings The BS27 90 F3
Birbeck Rd BS9 5 E5
Birch Ave Bleadon BS24 67 C6
Clevedon BS21 6 E4
Puriton TA7 136 C4
Birch Cl Bridgwater TA6 209 D5
Cannington TA5 135 B2
Cheddar BS27 90 C8
Locking BS24 50 B4
Wedmore BS28 108 C3
Birch Croft BS14 23 A3
Birch Ct BS31 24 C4
Birch Dene BS48 9 A2
Birch Dr BS40 53 A5
Birch Gr Portishead BS20 2 C4
Taunton TA1 212 E5
Birch Hill BS27 90 C8
Birch Ho TA8 65 F2
Birch Lawn TA8 104 B6
Birch Rd
12 Martock TA12 185 E6
Radstock BA3 78 E1
Wellington TA21 222 E5
Birch Wlk BA11 120 B7
Bircham Cl TA6 208 C4
Bircham La TA24 201 C4
Bircham Rd
Minehead TA24 201 B5
Taunton TA2 213 B8
Birchanger La TA4 150 A8

Clevedon Rd
Midsomer Norton BA3 ... 78 A2
Nailsea BS21 ... 8 B4
Portishead BS20 ... 2 D3
Weston-Super-Mare BS23 ... 48 E6
Wraxall BS48 ... 9 B4
Wraxall BS48 ... 9 D6
Wraxall, Flax Bourton BS48 ... 9 F2
Clevedon Terr BS6 ... 227 A4
Clevedon Wlk 2 BS48 ... 8 E2
Cleveland Ct BA2 ... 45 C6
Cleveland Pl BA1 ... 228 C4
Cleveland Pl E BA1 ... 228 C4
Cleveland Pl W BA1 ... 228 C4
Cleveland Reach BA1 ... 228 C4
Cleveland Row BA1 ... 45 B8
Cleveland St TA1 ... 212 E4
Cleveland Wlk BA2 ... 45 C6
Clewson Rise BS14 ... 22 F3
Cleyhill Gdns BA13 ... 121 D4
Cliff Rd Cheddar BS27 ... 71 E1
North Petherton TA6 ... 153 E3
Weston-Super-Mare BS22 ... 31 A2
Cliff St BS27 ... 90 C8
Cliffe Dr BA3 ... 64 A6
Clifford Ave TA2 ... 212 E8
Clifford Cres TA2 ... 212 E8
Clifford Gdns BS11 ... 4 E6
Clifford Lodge 3 TA5 ... 135 B2
Clifford Mews TA21 ... 222 E6
Clifford Pk TA5 ... 135 B2
Clifford Terr TA21 ... 222 E6
Cliffs The BS27 ... 90 C8
Clift House Rd BS3 ... 11 F4
Clift House Spur BS3 ... 11 F4
Clift Pl BS1 ... 227 A1
Clifton Ave BS23 ... 48 E5
Clifton Cl 1 Bristol BS8 ... 11 F7
Yeovil BA21 ... 219 E6
Clifton Coll BS8 ... 226 A4
Clifton College Prep Sch
BS8 ... 5 F1
Clifton Ct 11 BS21 ... 6 C2
Clifton Down BS8 ... 11 F7
Clifton Down Rd BS8 ... 226 A3
Clifton High Gr BS9 ... 5 E5
Clifton High Sch BS8 ... 226 A4
Clifton Hill Barwick BA22 197 F8
Bristol BS8 ... 226 A2
Clifton Park Rd BS8 ... 11 F8
Clifton Pk BS8 ... 226 A3
Clifton Rd Bristol BS8 ... 226 A2
Weston-Super-Mare BS23 ... 48 E5
Clifton St BS20 ... 2 C2
Clifton Suspension Bridge*
BS8 ... 11 E7
Clifton Vale BS8 ... 226 A2
Clifton Vale Cl BS8 ... 226 A2
Clifton View 9 BA22 ... 197 F8
Clifton Wood Ct BS8 ... 226 B2
Clifton Wood Rd BS8 ... 226 B2
Cliftonwood Cres BS8 ... 226 B2
Cliftonwood Terr BS8 ... 226 A2
Clifts Bldgs BA11 ... 119 F4
Clink Farm Ct BA11 ... 120 C6
Clink Rd BA11 ... 120 D6
Clink The TA6 ... 209 A5
Clipper Cl TA6 ... 209 C4
Clitsome View TA23 ... 131 D2
Clive Rd BS14 ... 23 C8
Clivey BA13 ... 102 E1
Clock Ho TA5 ... 134 B2
Clockhouse Mews BS20 ... 2 D6
Clockhouse The TA4 ... 167 E6
Cloister The DT9 ... 225 D4
Cloisters Croft TA8 ... 104 B6
Cloisters The BA5 ... 203 D3
Close The
Glastonbury BA6 ... 206 E5
9 Merriott TA16 ... 195 F7
Minehead TA24 ... 201 B5
North Cadbury BA22 ... 175 D6
Portishead BS20 ... 1 F1
Closemead BS21 ... 6 D1
Clotfurlong La DT9 ... 188 F1
Clothier Mdws BA7 ... 214 B6
Cloud Hill Ind Est BS39 ... 77 A8
Cloudberry Cl TA20 ... 223 F5
Clovelly Rd BS22 ... 32 A2
Clover Cl Clevedon BS21 ... 6 F3
Paulton BS39 ... 77 E4
Clover Ct BS22 ... 49 D7
Clover Mead TA1 ... 213 C1
Clover Rd BS22 ... 32 A6
Clover Way TA9 ... 104 E4
Cloverton Dr TA6 ... 209 D7
Clumber Dr BA11 ... 119 F6
Clutton Hill BS39 ... 59 B4
Clutton Prim Sch BS39 ... 58 E3
Clyce Rd TA9 ... 104 D3
Clyde Ave BS31 ... 24 F4
Clyde Gdns BA2 ... 44 B6
Clydesdale Cl BS14 ... 23 A6
Clynder Gr BS21 ... 6 E6
Coach House Mews
BS23 ... 30 D1
Coach Rd TA24 ... 124 A3
Coal Barton BA3 ... 116 E8
Coal La BA11 ... 119 C8
Coal Orch TA1 ... 212 F4
Coalash La BA11 ... 119 D8
Coalbridge Cl BS22 ... 31 F2
Coaley Rd BS11 ... 4 D5
Coalpit La
Chilcompton BA3 ... 96 A2
Stoke St Michael BA3 ... 116 B3
Coalpit Rd BA1 ... 29 A4
Coape Rd BS14 ... 23 F5
Coast Rd TA8 ... 84 F7
Coastguard Cotts TA24 ... 201 A8
Coat Rd TA12 ... 185 D7
Coate Turn TA4 ... 166 A6
Coates Est BS48 ... 8 F3
Coates Gr BS48 ... 9 A2
Coates Wlk BS4 ... 22 D6
Cob Castle TA21 ... 180 D8
Cobblestone Mews BS8 226 A4
Cobhorn Dr BS13 ... 21 F4
Cobley Croft BS21 ... 16 C8
Cobthorn Way BS49 ... 34 E5
Coburg Cl TA21 ... 180 F7
Coburg Villas 11 BA1 ... 28 A1
Cock & Yew Tree Hill
BS40 ... 38 A2
Cock Rd
Buckland Dinham BA2,
BA11 ... 100 B5
Horningsham BA12 ... 144 C4
Cock-Crowing Stone
TA20 ... 193 D4
Cockers Hill BS39 ... 41 C5
Cockhill Elm La BA7 ... 214 B4
Cockhill La BA22 ... 175 D7
Cockland Hill
Holywell Lake TA21 ... 179 C8
Langford Budville TA21 ... 166 C1
Cockmill La BA4 ... 140 F1
Cockpit Hill DT6,DT8 ... 199 F4
Cockpit La BA4 ... 142 C2
Cockrod BA16 ... 207 B2
Cod La BA22 ... 196 D7
Codrington Pl BS8 ... 226 A3
Cogsall Rd BS14 ... 23 F6
Coker Hill BA22 ... 196 F8
Coker Hill La BA22 ... 197 A7
Coker Ho BA22 ... 197 C8
Coker Marsh BA22 ... 197 D7
Coker Rd BS22 ... 32 B2
Coker's La BA12 ... 161 F8
Colbourn Cl BA3 ... 114 E7
Colbourne Rd BA2 ... 44 D1
Colchester Cres BS4 ... 22 D7
Cold Harbour
Milborne Port DT9 ... 217 D2
Sherborne DT9 ... 225 E5
Cold Harbour La BA22 ... 196 F6
Cold Nose BS28 ... 138 D8
Cold Rd TA3 ... 182 D6
Coldharbour Bsns Pk
DT9 ... 225 E6
Coldharbour La BS23 ... 48 D3
Coldhills La BA8 ... 176 D2
Coldpark Gdns BS13 ... 21 E5
Coldpark Rd BS13 ... 21 E5
Coldrick Cl BS14 ... 22 F3
Coldridge Cottage*
TA5 ... 134 B2
Cole Cl TA4 ... 167 E6
Cole Cross BA22 ... 186 C6
Cole La 5 TA14 ... 185 F4
Cole Mead BA10 ... 215 D5
Cole Rd BA10 ... 215 D5
Cole's La
Chewton Mendip BA3 ... 95 A6
South Petherton TA13 ... 220 D3
Colehouse La BS21 ... 16 C8
Colemead BS13 ... 22 B5
Coleridge Cres TA1 ... 213 B3
Coleridge Gdns TA8 ... 85 B2
Coleridge Gn TA6 ... 208 E5
Coleridge Rd
Bridgwater TA6 ... 208 E6
Clevedon BS21 ... 6 C3
Nether Stowey TA5 ... 134 A2
Weston-Super-Mare BS23 ... 49 A4
Coleridge Sq TA6 ... 208 E6
Coleridge Vale Rd E 1
BS21 ... 6 D2
Coleridge Vale Rd N BS21 ... 6 C2
Coleridge Vale Rd S BS21 ... 6 D2
Coleridge Vale Rd W 3
BS21 ... 6 C2
Coles Cross Cotts DT8 ... 199 D5
Coles Gdns BA3 ... 98 B5
Coles Pl TA20 ... 223 C3
Coles's La EX13 ... 198 B1
Coleshill Dr BS13 ... 22 B5
Colesmore TA4 ... 167 A4
Coley La TA19 ... 194 F5
Coley Rd BS40 ... 75 B4
Colham La TA20 ... 194 E1
Colin Ave TA2 ... 212 F7
Colin Rd TA2 ... 213 A7
Collarway La BA22 ... 196 F8
Colledge Cl BA3 ... 96 C4
College BA22 ... 196 E8
College Cl TA10 ... 172 E2
College Ct TA8 ... 104 A7
College Fields BS8 ... 11 F8
College Gn Bristol BS1 ... 226 C2
Yeovil BA21 ... 219 B6
College Rd Bath BA1 ... 27 E1
Bristol, Clifton BS8 ... 11 F8
Taunton TA2 ... 212 D6
Wells BA5 ... 203 E5
College Sq BS1 ... 226 C2
College St Bristol BS1 ... 226 C2
Burnham-On-Sea TA8 ... 104 A7
College View
Taunton TA1 ... 212 C2
18 Bath BA1 ... 28 A1
College Way
Bridgwater TA6 ... 209 C6
Taunton TA1 ... 212 C1
Colles Cl BA5 ... 203 F5
Colles Rd BA5 ... 203 F5
Collett Ave BA4 ... 205 C5
Collett Cl BS22 ... 32 C4
Collett Way BA11 ... 120 C7
Colley La TA6 ... 209 B4
Colley Lane Ind Est TA6 209 B3
Colleylake Cotts TA3 ... 181 C5
Collickshire La TA3 ... 170 E6
Collie Cnr BA11 ... 118 A1
Collier's La BA11 ... 99 D2
Colliers Cl BA2 ... 78 D8
Colliers La BA1 ... 27 F4
Colliers Rise BA3 ... 79 A3
Colliers Wlk 4 BS48 ... 8 E2
Collingwood Cl
Saltford BS31 ... 25 E2
Weston-Super-Mare BS22 ... 31 E4
Collingwood Ct TA6 ... 208 F5
Collins St BS11 ... 4 B8
Collins' La TA11 ... 173 F7
Collinson Rd BS13 ... 22 B5
Collum La BS22 ... 31 E6
Colman Rd TA1 ... 212 B1
Colmer Rd
Bridgwater TA6 ... 208 F7
Yeovil BA21 ... 219 B6
Colne Gn BS31 ... 25 A4
Colombo Cres BS23 ... 48 E3
Colston Ave BS1 ... 227 A2
Colston Cross EX13 ... 198 B4
Colston Fort 2 BS2 ... 227 A4
Colston Par BS1 ... 227 B1
Colston St BS1 ... 227 A3
Colston Yd BS1 ... 227 A3
Colton La TA4 ... 149 F7
Columbus Ho BA2 ... 45 D8
Colyton 11 BS22 ... 32 A2
Combe Ave BS20 ... 2 C6
Combe Batch BS28 ... 108 D4
Combe Batch Rise
BS28 ... 108 D4
Combe Beacon La TA20 193 C7
Combe Cl Bicknoller TA4 ... 132 E2
Yeovil BA21 ... 219 A8
Combe Cross Halse TA4 ... 167 B7
Monksilver TA4 ... 150 C8
Shillingford EX16 ... 164 D4
Combe Cross Wlk BS13 ... 22 B3
Combe Down La TA4 ... 151 C2
Combe Down Prim Sch
BA2 ... 45 B1
Combe Fields BS20 ... 2 C6
Combe Gn BA5 ... 204 B7
Combe Gr BA1 ... 44 B8
Combe Hay La BA2 ... 62 B6
Combe Hill
Barton St David TA11 ... 158 A2
Combe St Nicholas TA20 ... 193 D5
Hemyock EX15 ... 180 C2
Milborne Port DT9 ... 217 B3
Templecombe BA8 ... 176 E1
Yenston BA8 ... 189 F8
Combe Hill Dro TA20 ... 193 C5
Combe Hill La TA7 ... 156 B7
Combe La
Brompton Ralph TA4 ... 150 B3
Charlton Adam TA11 ... 173 F8
Chilton Polden TA7 ... 137 B3
Churchstanton TA3 ... 181 A2
Combe St Nicholas TA20 ... 193 B5
Dulverton TA22 ... 163 D6
East Anstey TA22 ... 162 F6
Exford TA24 ... 128 D1
Langport TA10 ... 171 F7
North Curry TA3 ... 170 A4
Parbrook BA4 ... 158 D8
Paulton BS39 ... 77 B6
Rodhuish TA24 ... 131 B3
Wedmore BS28 ... 108 D4
Wiveliscombe TA4 ... 210 C8
Woolavington TA7 ... 136 F4
Combe Pk Bath BA1 ... 44 C8
Yeovil BA21 ... 218 F8
Combe Rd Bath BA2 ... 45 B1
Portishead BS20 ... 2 D5
Combe Road Cl BA2 ... 45 B1
Combe Side BS48 ... 19 A7
Combe St TA20 ... 223 C4
Combe Street La BA21 ... 219 A8
Combe Street Lane Rdbt
BA21 ... 218 F8
Combe Sydenham Country
Pk* TA4 ... 150 A7
Combe Terr TA9 ... 136 E8
Combe The BS40 ... 53 F2
Combecross Hill TA4 ... 150 B8
Combecross La
Monksilver TA4 ... 150 B8
Stogumber TA4 ... 150 C8
Combeland La TA22 ... 164 A5
Combeland Rd TA24 ... 201 B4
Combeshead Hill TA22 ... 148 A3
Combeshead La
Brompton Regis TA22 ... 148 A4
West Anstey EX36 ... 162 A7
Combeside BA2 ... 45 A3
Comer Rd BS27 ... 90 A7
Comer's Cross TA24 ... 146 E6
Comeytrowe La TA1,TA4 212 A2
Comeytrowe Orch TA1 ... 212 A2
Comeytrowe Rd TA1 ... 212 B1
Comeytrowe Rise TA1 ... 212 B2
Comfortable Pl BA1 ... 228 A3
Commerce Way TA9 ... 104 F2
Commercial Rd
Bristol BS1 ... 227 A1
Shepton Mallet BA4 ... 205 B6
Commercial Row TA20 ... 223 C4
Common La
Charlton Adam TA11 ... 174 A8
Churchill Green BS25 ... 52 B5
Easton-in-G BS20 ... 4 B2
Halstock BA22 ... 197 C2
Hardington Mandeville
BA22 ... 197 A5
Holcombe BA3 ... 116 D7
Huish Champflower TA4 ... 165 D7
Kington Magna SP8 ... 177 E1
Marnhull DT10 ... 190 E4
North Perrott TA18 ... 196 D4
Templecombe BA8 ... 177 A1
Wincanton BA9 ... 216 D3
Yenston BA8 ... 189 F8
Common Moor Dro BA6 206 E7
Common Rd BA9 ... 216 E3
Compass Hill TA1 ... 212 E3
Compass Rise TA1 ... 212 E3
Compton Acres DT9 ... 187 E4
Compton Cl
Shepton Mallet BA4 ... 205 B5
Taunton TA2 ... 213 A6
Yeovil BA21 ... 219 E8
Compton Cnr BA4 ... 205 B5
Compton Ct Mews DT9 ... 187 F3
Compton Dr BS9 ... 5 C7
Compton Flats BA21 ... 219 C6
Compton Gdns BA11 ... 120 D7
Compton Gn BS31 ... 24 E4
Compton Hill TA13 ... 220 A5
Compton La BA4 ... 205 B2
Compton Rd
Shepton Mallet BA4 ... 205 B4
South Cadbury BA22 ... 175 D4
South Petherton TA13 ... 220 B5
Yeovil BA21 ... 187 E3
Compton St Butleigh BA6 157 D4
Compton Dundon TA11 ... 157 B4
Comrade Ave BS25 ... 70 E8
Concorde Dr BS21 ... 6 B1
Condell Cl TA6 ... 208 F7
Condor Cl BS22 ... 49 D8
Conduit Hill BA11 ... 99 B1
Conegore Cnr BA22 ... 174 D4
Coneygree BS13 ... 21 F6
Conference Ave BS20 ... 2 F5
Conference Cl BS20 ... 2 F4
Conifer Cl TA24 ... 128 D1
Conifer Way BS24 ... 49 E5
Coniston Ave BS9 ... 5 E6
Coniston Cres BS23 ... 48 F4
Coniston Gdns BA21 ... 219 A7
Connaught Ho TA6 ... 209 C5
Connaught Pl BS23 ... 48 D8
Connaught Rd BS4 ... 22 E8
Connection Rd BA2 ... 44 A6
Connelly Dr BS28 ... 108 C4
Constable Cl
Keynsham BS31 ... 24 F6
Yeovil BA21 ... 219 E8
Constable Dr BS22 ... 31 F3
Constantine Ct BA4 ... 205 E4
Constitution Hill
Bristol BS8 ... 226 B2
Wells BA5 ... 140 C8
Convocation Ave BA2 ... 45 F5
Conway Cres TA8 ... 85 C1
Conway Gn BS31 ... 25 A3
Conway Rd TA5 ... 135 B2
Conygar Cl BS21 ... 6 F5
Conygar View TA24 ... 201 E3
Conygre Gn BA2 ... 60 B2
Conygre Rise BA2 ... 59 F6
Cook Ave TA20 ... 223 D3
Cook St BS11 ... 4 C8
Cook Way TA2 ... 212 C6
Cook's Folly Rd BS9 ... 5 D3
Cook's La Banwell BS29 ... 51 A4
Clevedon BS21 ... 7 B2
Cranmore BA4 ... 142 A6
Milverton TA4 ... 167 B5
Stalbridge DT10 ... 190 B2
Cooke's La TA10 ... 156 B2
Cookley La TA4 ... 150 F8
Cooks Bridle Path BS48 ... 36 D8
Cooks Cl TA3 ... 169 D5
Cooks Gdns BS48 ... 9 A2
Cooks La DT9 ... 225 D3
Cooksley La TA4 ... 149 A2
Coomb End BA3 ... 78 F3
Coomb Rocke BS9 ... 5 D6
Coomband Ho BA3 ... 78 F3
Coombe DT9 ... 225 C5
Coombe Bridge Ave BS9 ... 5 D6
Coombe Brook BA5 ... 203 A7
Coombe Cl BA7 ... 214 C6
Coombe Cotts BA5 ... 204 C7
Coombe Dale
Backwell BS48 ... 37 A8
Bristol BS9 ... 5 C6
Coombe Gdns BS9 ... 5 E6
Coombe Hill
Angersleigh TA21 ... 181 A5
Bruton BA10 ... 215 E7
Coombe La Bristol BS9 ... 5 E6
Compton Bishop BS26 ... 69 B4
East Harptree BS40 ... 74 E4
Easton-in-G BS8 ... 4 A1
Kingsbury Episcopi TA12 ... 185 B8
Shepton Mallet BA4 ... 205 A6
Coombe Lodge (Coll)
BS40 ... 54 D3
Coombe Rd
Dinnington TA17 ... 195 B7
Nailsea BS48 ... 8 E1
Weston-Super-Mare BS23 ... 30 E1
Coombe Side TA9 ... 86 B2
Coombe St Bruton BA10 ... 215 E7
Penselwood BA9 ... 161 E2
Coombe Terr
Glastonbury BA6 ... 206 E5
Sherborne DT9 ... 225 C5
Coombe The
Blagdon BS40 ... 54 C3
Compton Martin BS40 ... 74 A6
Coombe View BA4 ... 205 A6
Coombe Water La DT8 ... 199 E5
Coombe's Cider Farm &
Mus* TA9 ... 106 A4
Coombe's Way BS26 ... 87 E8
Cooper Rd BS9 ... 5 F7
Cooper's Ash La BA7,
BA22 ... 214 A2
Cooperage La BS3 ... 226 B1
Cooperage The BA11 ... 119 F3
Coopers Hts TA4 ... 210 C4
Coopers Mead BA4 ... 205 D4
Coopers Mill TA2 ... 168 B4
Coot Hide EX16 ... 178 D1
Coots The BS14 ... 23 E6
Copeland Dr BS14 ... 23 B5
Copford La BS41 ... 11 B1
Copis La TA11 ... 158 B3
Coplestons TA3 ... 168 D1
Copley Gdns BS22 ... 31 F2
Coppack Ho 7 BS21 ... 6 C2
Copper Beech Rd TA11 ... 173 D5
Copper Beeches TA1 ... 212 A2
Copper Cl BS27 ... 90 A8
Copperfield Dr BS22 ... 31 F4
Coppern Way DT10 ... 190 B4
Coppice Cl BA20 ... 218 D2
Coppice End Cnr BS24 ... 67 C2
Coppice The BS13 ... 21 E4
Coppin Cl BA6 ... 206 F3
Coppin Rd TA2 ... 168 B4
Coppits Hill La
Yeovil BA21 ... 218 D8
Yeovil Marsh BA21 ... 187 A5
Copplesbury La BA4,
BA10 ... 160 D8
Copse Cl Watchet TA23 ... 202 C5
Weston-Super-Mare BS24 ... 49 A1
Copse Cnr BS24 ... 67 C2
Copse Dro
Baltonsborough BA6 ... 158 C5
Barrington TA19 ... 184 B5
Copse End BS25 ... 51 F2
Copse La Ashill TA19 ... 183 D4
Barrington TA19 ... 184 D4
Hambridge TA3 ... 184 B7
Ilton TA19 ... 183 F4
Pilton BA4 ... 140 F3
Copse Rd Clevedon BS21 ... 6 C4
Houndstone BA22 ... 218 B7
Keynsham BS31 ... 25 C4
Copse Shoot La TA19 ... 184 C5
Copse Stile TA20 ... 193 F1
Copse The
Bridgwater TA6 ... 209 D5
Cossington TA7 ... 136 F3
Frome BA11 ... 120 B6
Copseland BA2 ... 45 D5
Copsewood La BS26 ... 88 B2
Copthorne Cl BS14 ... 23 B5
Coralberry Dr BS22 ... 31 F1
Corams La TA21 ... 222 B6
Cording's Ball TA4 ... 150 A1
Corewell La TA5 ... 133 E3
Corfe Cl BS48 ... 8 D1
Corfe Cres BS31 ... 24 E4
Corfe Rd BS4 ... 22 D7
Corinthian Ct 9 BS1 ... 227 B1
Cork Pl BA1 ... 44 D7
Cork St Bath BA1 ... 44 D7
Frome BA11 ... 119 F5
Cork Terr BA1 ... 44 D7
Corkscrew La
North Cadbury BA22 ... 175 E7
Staplegrove TA2 ... 212 D8
Cormorant Cl
Bridgwater TA6 ... 209 C3
Weston-Super-Mare BS22 ... 31 F1
Corn St Bath BA1 ... 228 B2
Bristol BS1 ... 227 A3
Cornborough Pl TA6 ... 209 B5
Corner Cl TA21 ... 222 D4
Corner Croft BS21 ... 6 D1
Cornfields The BS22 ... 31 F5
Cornhill Bridgwater TA6 ... 208 F5
Shepton Mallet BA4 ... 205 C6
Sherborne DT9 ... 225 C4
5 Wellington TA21 ... 222 D6
Cornhill Dr BS14 ... 23 A7
Cornish Gr BS14 ... 23 E6
Cornish Rd BS14 ... 23 E6
Cornish Wlk BS14 ... 23 E6
Cornishway E TA1 ... 212 B3
Cornishway N TA1 ... 212 B3
Cornishway S TA1 ... 212 B2
Cornishway W TA1 ... 212 B3
Cornlands EX16 ... 178 D1
Cornleaze BS13 ... 22 A5
Cornmoor Cres TA9 ... 136 E7
Cornmoor La TA9 ... 136 E7
Cornwall Rd BA4 ... 205 A6
Cornwallis Ave
Bristol BS8 ... 226 A2
Weston-Super-Mare BS22 ... 31 F4
Cornwallis Cres BS8 ... 11 F6
Cornwallis Gr BS8 ... 226 A2
Coromandel Hts BA1 ... 228 B4

Daghole BS27 90 C8
Daglands The BA2 78 E8
Dairs Orch TA20 198 C8
Dairy Cl BA5 203 B5
Dairy Ct 3 TA18 224 C5
Dairy Hill BA2 80 B5
Dairy House La TA3 182 E5
Dairycroft BS2 227 B4
Dairylands TA24 131 D4
Daisey Bank BA2 45 B4
Daisyfield BA22 188 A8
Dakota Dr BS14 23 A4
Dale La BA5 92 C3
Dale St BS2 227 C4
Daley Cl BS22 32 B3
Dalimores La BA11 143 B8
Dalleston BA3 114 C8
Dallimore Mead BA11 143 B8
Dalton Sq BS2 227 B4
Dalwood 12 BS22 32 A2
Dalwoods DT9 225 D3
Dame Court Cl BS22 31 F4
Dame Withycombe Villas TA5 135 B5
Dampier Pl BA21 219 C5
Dampier St BA21 219 C5
Dampiet St TA6 208 F4
Damson Rd BS22 49 E7
Dancey Mead BS13 21 F6
Dancing Cross BA9 176 B5
Dancing Hill TA6 153 E4
Dancing La BA9 216 A4
DandO's La BS28 108 C4
Dandy's Mdw BS20 2 E4
Dane Cl BA15 64 E7
Dane Rise BA15 64 E7
Dane's Lea BS28 108 C4
Daneacre Rd BA3 79 A3
Danes Cl EX14 191 F2
Danesboro Rd TA6 208 C4
Danesborough View TA4 202 D3
Danesborough View E TA4 202 D3
Danesborough View W TA4 202 D3
Danesfield CE Com Sch TA4 202 D4
Dangerfield Ave BS13 21 F6
Daniel Cl BS21 6 F3
Daniel Mews BA2 45 B7
Daniel St BA2 45 B7
Daniels La BA5 111 A4
Danielsfield Rd BA20 218 F2
Dano View Gdns BS20 2 C5
Dapps Hill BS31 24 F5
Dapwell La BS14,BS31 24 A1
Darby Cl SP8 161 F1
Darby Way TA4 151 F1
Darby's Knap TA24 147 C5
Dare Cl TA2 213 A8
Dark La Backwell BS48 19 B5
Banwell BS29 51 C2
Berkley BA11 120 E8
Blagdon BS40 54 E3
Chew Magna BS40 38 F3
Freshford BA3 64 B5
Hockworthy EX16 178 B8
Holcombe BA3 97 C1
Kilmersdon BA11 98 A1
North Wootton BA4 140 C5
Sandford Orcas DT9 188 C7
Seavington TA19 184 E1
Stoke St Gregory TA3 170 F6
Stoke St Michael BA3 116 C2
Upton Noble BA4 142 F2
Wellington TA21 222 D5
Witham Friary BA11 143 D2
Darkey La BA10 215 F7
Darkfield Way TA7 136 E3
Darlington Mews BA2 45 B7
Darlington Pl BA2 45 B6
Darlington Rd BA2 45 B8
Darlington St BA2 45 B7
Darmead BS24 32 B1
Darshill Hospl BA4 204 F6
Dart Rd BS21 6 D1
Dartmouth Ave BA2 44 C5
Dartmouth Cl BS22 32 A2
Dartmouth Wlk BS31 24 D4
Darwin Cl TA2 212 B6
Dashwoods La TA4 132 E2
Daubeny Ct BS1 227 A1
Daunton Cl TA9 104 D4
David St BS2 227 C3
David's La TA19 184 F2
David's Rd BS14 23 C6
Davies Cl Bridgwater TA6 208 F2
Winsham TA20 194 E1
Davies Ct BA5 203 B4
Davin Cres BS20 4 C3
Davis La BS21 16 F8
Davis St BS11 4 B8
Davis Terr BA5 203 C4
Daw's La DT9 176 A3
Dawbins Dr TA7 136 E4
Dawes Cl BS21 6 D1
Dawes Ct 2 BS8 11 F6
Daws Cl TA6 208 E2
Daws La TA6 153 E3
Daws Mead TA1 212 A3
Day Cres BA2 43 F6
De Combe Ho TA18 224 D6
Deacon Rd TA6 209 C6
Deacon Way TA8 104 B6
Deacons Cl BS22 31 E2
Deacons Ct BS22 31 C1
Dead Maids Cross Rd BA13 121 E5
Dead Woman's Cnr BA12 161 F8
Deadlands La TA12,TA13 185 A6
Deadman's Hill DT9 176 A1
Deadmill La BA1 28 C3
Deal Cl TA6 209 D5
Dean Cl Frome BA11 120 C6
Weston-Super-Mare BS22 32 B3
Dean La Dunster TA24 201 D3
Milverton TA4 167 A6
Oakhill BA3 115 A3
Dean St BS2 227 B4
Dean's Cross TA24 124 E3
Dean's La Allerford TA24 124 E3
Brompton Ralph TA4 150 F4
Deane Cl TA4 150 D8
Deane Dr TA1 212 B2
Deane Gate Ave TA1 213 E5
Deane Pl BA5 203 D4
Deane Way TA20 198 D8
Deanery Rd BS1 226 C2
Deanery Wlk BA3 64 C6
Deanesly Way BA9 216 D3
Deanhill La BA1 27 A2
Deans Cross TA4 151 A4
Deans Mead BS11 5 A8
Deans The BS20 2 B4
Deansley Way BA9 216 E3
Debecca's La BS20 4 B4
Decoy La TA11 157 A2
Deep La BA12 121 E1
Deepleigh La TA4 210 C7
Deer Mead BS21 6 B1
Deer View TA24 201 C4
Deerleap Easton BA5 111 B6
Shipham BS25 70 F8
Deerswood Gdns BA16 207 A6
Delapre Rd BS23 48 D3
Delhorn La BS24 86 C7
Delius Gr BS4 22 D7
Dell The
Bristol, Westbury on Trym BS9 5 F5
Minehead TA24 200 E6
Nailsea BS48 8 D2
Weston-Super-Mare BS22 31 E4
Deller's Wharf TA1 212 F5
Dellers Ct TA1 212 F5
Dellshore Cl TA20 223 D4
Delmore Rd BA11 119 E3
Delta Cl BA11 119 F5
Delta Rise TA4 151 E1
Demelza Ct BA22 174 D3
Dempier Mews BA22 218 B6
Dene Cl BS31 24 F3
Dene Cross TA4 167 F7
Dene Gdns TA24 201 B4
Dene Rd
Cotford St Luke TA4 167 F6
Whitchurch BS14 23 C4
Dening Cl TA20 223 C6
Denleigh Cl BS14 23 A4
Denman's La TA19 184 D5
Denman's La TA5 135 B2
Denmark Ave BS1 226 C2
Denmark Rd BA2 44 D6
Denmark St BS1 226 C2
Denmark Terr TA2 212 F7
Dennett Cl BA4 205 E4
Denning Cl TA1 212 B1
Denning Ct BS22 32 B4
Dennington La
Churchinford EX14 192 C6
Dulverton TA22 163 B4
Dennor Pk BS14 23 B7
Denny Cl BS20 2 A5
Denny La BS40 39 B1
Denny View BS20 2 A5
Dennyview Rd BS8 10 F8
Denston Dr BS20 2 E4
Denston Wlk BS13 22 A7
Dentwood Gr BS9 5 B8
Denvale Trad Pk BS4 22 E7
Denzil Cl BA22 197 A8
Derham Cl BS49 34 B8
Derham Ct BS49 34 B8
Derham Pk BS49 34 B8
Derham Rd BS13 22 A5
Derricke Rd BS14 23 F6
Dertfords BA12 144 D8
Derwent Gdns BA21 219 D6
Derwent Gr
Keynsham BS31 25 A5
Taunton TA1 213 E4
Derwent Rd BS23 49 A5
Derwent Way BA21 218 C6
Devenish La BA9 216 F4
Deveron Gr BS31 25 A4
Devonshire Bldgs BA2 44 F4
Devonshire Ct BS23 48 E4
Devonshire Dr BS20 1 F5
Devonshire Pl BA2 44 F4
Devonshire Rd
Bathampton BA2 28 E1
Weston-Super-Mare BS23 48 E4
Devonshire St TA6 209 B5
Devonshire Villas BA2 44 F3
Dew Water La TA11 211 D5
Dewar Cl TA8 104 C7
Dial Hill Rd BS21 6 D4
Dial La BS40 20 D1
Dial's Gate La BA6,TA11 158 D4
Diamond Batch BS24 32 B1
Dibbens Row BA9 161 A2
Dibbles La BA22 197 A8
Dickenson Rd BS23 48 E6
Dickenson's Gr BS49 34 E3
Digby Rd DT9 225 D3
Dighton Ct 3 BS2 227 A4
Dighton St BS2 227 A4
Digland La TA24 129 F5
Dilkes La TA11 174 C7
Dillons Rd TA3 169 D4
Dimmer La BA7 159 B2
Dinder Cl BS48 18 E8
Dinghurst Rd BS25 52 E4
Dingle Cl BS9 5 C6
Dingle Ct BS13 21 F7
Dingle Rd BS9 5 D7
Dingle The BS9 5 D7
Dingle View BS9 5 C7
Dinglewood Cl BS9 5 D7
Dinhay DT10 190 F6
Dipford Rd TA3 168 D1
Dipland Gr BS40 54 F2
Disraeli Pl TA1 212 D5
Ditch Furlong Rd TA7 137 A2
Ditcheat Prim Sch BA4 159 C7
Ditton St TA19 221 C3
Dixon Gdns BA1 27 F1
Dobree Pk TA21 222 A4
Dock Gate La BS8 226 A1
Doctor's Hill BA5 111 B1
Dod La BA6 206 E4
Dodd Ave BA5 203 F5
Dodge Cross DT9 225 F5
Dog Down Cross EX16 178 A8
Doleberrow BS25 52 F3
Dolemead La BS27 90 E2
Dolemoor La
Congresbury BS49 34 A4
Congresbury BS49 34 C3
Dolling Cl TA20 223 D6
Dolling's Rd TA3 181 B4
Dominion Rd BA2 44 A6
Dominy Cl TA20 223 D3
Dommett's La BA11 119 D4
Domus Dr BA4 205 E4
Donald Rd BS13 21 F7
Doniford Beach Halt TA23 202 E6
Doniford Dr TA4 202 D3
Doniford Rd
Watchet TA23 202 E6
Williton TA4 202 D4
Donne La BA22 186 C2
Donnes Terr BA7 214 B5
Donnington Wlk BS31 24 D4
Donstan Rd TA9 104 E5
Donyatt Hill TA19 183 D1
Donyatt Hill Est TA19 183 D1
Doone Way TA24 201 B4
Dorchester Cl 6 BS48 8 D1
Dorchester Rd
Barwick BA22 197 F7
East Coker BA22 197 F5
Taunton TA2 213 A8
Yeovil BA22 219 A1
Dorchester St BA1 228 C1
Dorset Cl Bath BA2 44 D6
Frome BA11 119 E5
Dorset Ho BA2 44 D3
Dorset Rd TA6 209 C3
Dorset St BA2 44 D6
Doster's La TA2 169 C6
Double Gates Dro TA11 158 A3
Douglas Ct BS23 48 F5
Douglas Dr BA4 205 B5
Douglas Rd BS23 48 F5
Douglas Yates Ct BA3 116 F7
Doulting BA4 141 E6
Doulting Ct BA11 120 D7
Doulting Hill BA4 205 F4
Doulton Way BS14 23 B5
Dove Cots Cl BA16 207 C7
Dove La BS2 227 C4
Dove St BS2 227 A4
Dove St S BS2 227 A4
Dover Ho BA1 228 C4
Dover Pl 6 Bath BA1 28 A1
Bristol BS8 226 B3
Dover Rd TA2 213 A8
Dovers La BA1 29 C2
Dovers Pk BA1 29 C2
Dovery Manor Mus★ TA24 124 A3
Doveswell Gr BS13 22 A4
Dovetail Ct 1 TA1 212 E3
Dovetail Dr BS23 49 A7
Dovetons Cl TA4 202 E3
Dovetons Dr TA4 202 E3
Dowding Rd BA1 28 B1
Dowell Cl TA2 212 C6
Dowland 13 BS22 32 A2
Dowling La BA6 158 A5
Dowling Rd BS13 22 D3
Dowlish La TA19 194 F5
Down Ave BA2 45 A1
Down Cl BS20 1 F4
Down La Bathampton BA2 28 F1
Buckland Dinham BA11 99 C3
Shepton Montague BA9 160 B2
Sherborne DT9 188 A5
Trent DT9 187 F5
West Pennard BA4,BA6 140 C1
Down Rd BS20 1 F4
Down View BA3 97 F8
Down's Orch BA6 138 C4
Downash La EX13 198 E3
Downclose La TA18 196 C3
Downend Cres TA6 136 B4
Downend Rd TA6 136 B4
Downend Terr TA6 136 B4
Downey Field La TA18 196 D6
Downfield Bristol BS9 5 C7
Keynsham BS31 24 D5
Downhall Dr TA6 208 D6
Downhead La BA22 174 C5
Downland Cl Bristol BS4 22 D6
5 Nailsea BS48 8 D1
Downlands La TA3 181 A2
Downleaze
Bristol, Stoke Bishop BS9 5 F3
Portishead BS20 2 A5
Yeovil BA20 218 D2
Downleaze Rd BS9 5 F3
Downs Cl BS22 31 F1
Downs Cote Ave BS9 5 F6
Downs Cote Dr BS9 5 F6
Downs Rd BS41 21 D2
Downs Sch The BS48 9 C8
Downs The BS20 2 B4
Downside Portishead BS20 2 C5
Street BA16 207 D6
Downside Abbey★ BA3 96 F2
Downside Cl
Bathampton BA2 28 F1
Chilcompton BA3 96 D3
Downside Rd
Backwell BS48 36 E8
Weston-Super-Mare BS23 48 F4
Downside Sch BA3 96 F2
Downslade La TA10 172 D5
Downsway BS39 77 D6
Downton Rd BS13 22 D8
Dowry Pl 3 BS8 11 F5
Dowry Rd BS8 226 A2
Dowry Sq BS8 226 A2
Dowsland Way TA1 213 C1
Dozen's Cnr TA17 195 A7
Dr White's Cl BS1 227 B1
Dragon Cross TA24 131 D3
Dragonfly Chase BA22 173 E2
Dragons Hill Cl BS31 24 F5
Dragons Hill Ct BS31 24 F5
Dragons Hill Gdns BS31 24 F5
Drake Ave BA2 44 F2
Drake Cl Saltford BS31 25 D2
Staplegrove TA2 212 B7
Weston-Super-Mare BS22 31 F4
Drake Rd BA5 203 F6
Drake's Cl TA3 169 C4
Drakes Cl TA6 208 F5
Drakes Cres TA20 198 D8
Drakes Mdw
East Coker BA22 197 C7
Yarcombe EX14 192 D3
Drakes Pk TA21 222 D7
Drakes Pk N TA21 222 D7
Drakes Way BS20 2 D5
Drang The Coxley BA5 139 E6
Porlock TA24 124 A3
Dransfield Way BA2 44 C4
Drapers Way TA24 129 D2
Dray Rd BA22 186 C2
Draycot Pl BS1 227 A1
Draycott & Rodney Stoke CE First Sch BS27 90 F3
Draycott Ave TA2 213 A6
Draycott Moor Dro BS27 90 D1
Draycott Rd Cheddar BS27 90 D5
Shepton Mallet BA4 205 B6
Draydon Rd BS4 22 D8
Drayton BS24 49 A2
Drayton Cl BS14 23 B8
Drayton La TA10 171 D3
Drayton Rd BS9 5 C8
Drew's La DT10 190 B5
Drials La BA3 94 F6
Drift Rd TA24 201 D4
Drift The TA20 194 B3
Drill Hall La BA4 205 C5
Drimpton Cross DT8 199 F7
Dring The BA3 78 E2
Drive The
Bristol, Hengrove BS14 23 C6
Burnham-On-Sea TA8 85 A2
Churchill BS25 52 E4
Shipham BS25 70 E8
Stanton Drew BS39 39 F1
Taunton TA1 212 D1
Weston-Super-Mare BS23 48 F8
Woolavington TA7 136 E4
Dropping La BA10 160 D5
Drove Ct BS48 8 E3
Drove La
East Pennard BA4 158 E8
Shepton Beauchamp TA19 184 E4
Drove Rd
Stourton Caundle DT10 189 F2
Weston-Super-Mare BS23 48 F5
Drove Road Hospl BS23 48 F5
Drove The
Bridgwater TA6 209 A6
Portbury BS20 3 D6
Drove Way
Churchinford TA3 191 F8
Sandford BS24,BS25 51 E7
Droveway TA13 220 B5
Droveway Cl TA13 220 C5
Droveway La BA21 187 C7
Druid Cl BS9 5 E5
Druid Hill BS9 5 E5
Druid Rd BS9 5 D4
Druid Stoke Ave BS9 5 D5
Druid Woods BS9 5 C5
Druids Wlk TA20 223 C5
Druley Hill BA10 161 D8
Drum Ave BA6 206 C5
Drumhead Way The BS25 70 E8
Dryleaze BS31 24 E7
Drysdale Cl BS22 31 D1
Duchy Cl BA3 78 E5
Duchy Rd Radstock BA3 78 E5
Shepton Mallet BA4 205 A5
Duck La Chard TA20 223 C3
Horsington BA8 176 E2
Ilchester BA22 173 F1
Kenn BS21 17 A6
Langford BS40 53 A8
Stalbridge DT10 190 B5
Westbury Sub Mendip BA5 110 E6
Duck Pool Dro BA6 206 B7
Duck Pool La BA11 102 B6
Duck St BS25 52 C5
Duckpool La TA18 196 B8
Ducks Hill TA10 172 B5
Ducks' Field Crossing TA18 224 C1
Dudley Cl BS31 24 E4
Dudmoor TA12 185 B7
Dudwell La BA3 95 A5
Dugdale St TA24 200 F6
Duke Ave 7 TA5 135 B2
Duke Ho TA19 221 B3
Duke St Bath BA2 228 C2
Frome BA11 119 E5
Taunton TA1 213 A4
Duke's Cl BA9 216 E3
Duke's La
Horningsham BA12 144 A1
Kilmington BA12 161 F8
Dukes Field BA4 205 C5
Dukes Mead TA6 209 A2
Dull Cross TA4 151 D3
Dulverton Com Sch TA22 163 D6
Dulverton La TA4 165 D7
Dumfries Pl BS23 48 E5
Dummis La BA5 111 A1
Dumper's La BA3 94 F7
Dumpers La BS40 39 B2
Dunbar Cl TA9 104 C4
Duncan Gdns BA1 27 A3
Duncart La BA5 204 C7
Duncliffe Cl DT10 190 B4
Duncombe Cl TA6 209 D5
Dundry CE Prim Sch BS41 21 D2
Dundry La Dundry BS41 21 C3
Winford BS40 38 A7
Dunedin Way BS22 32 C4
Dunford Terr BA6 158 A5
Dungeon BS28 108 D7
Dungeon La BA5 204 C6
Dunkerry Rd BS26 88 C4
Dunkerton Cl BA6 206 F3
Dunkerton Hill BA2 61 E2
Dunkerton Rise TA2 168 B5
Dunkery Cl BS48 8 E1
Dunkery Rd
Bridgwater TA6 208 D4
Weston-Super-Mare BS23 30 F1
Dunkery Vineyard★ TA24 200 A1
Dunkleys Way TA1 213 C2
Dunn's Hill TA21 179 A6
Dunningham La BS28 107 E7
Dunns Cl BS28 108 C4
Dunsford Pl BA2 45 B6
Dunsgreen La EX15 191 A8
Dunsham La TA18 195 C2
Dunsley Hill EX16,EX36 162 D5
Dunstan Rd
Burnham-On-Sea TA8 104 B7
Glastonbury BA6 206 F5
Dunstan Way BS27 90 B6
Dunster Castle★ TA24 201 E1
Dunster Cl
Minehead TA24 201 B4
Taunton TA2 213 B7
Dunster Cres BS24 49 A2
Dunster Ct BS25 70 A8
Dunster Fst Sch TA24 201 D2
Dunster Gdns 5 BS48 8 E1
Dunster Ho BA2 45 A2
Dunster Rd Bristol BS4 22 F8
Keynsham BS31 24 E4
Dunster Sta★ TA24 201 F4
Dunster Steep
Dunster TA24 201 E2
Porlock TA24 123 F4
Porlock TA24 124 A3
Dunster Visitor Ctr★ TA24 201 E2
Dunster Working Water Mill★ TA24 201 E1
Dunsters Rd BS49 17 F1
Dunwear Ho 3 TA6 209 C4
Dunwear La TA6 209 D3
Durban Way BS49 17 B1
Durbin Park Rd BS21 6 D5
Durcott Rd BA2 78 D8
Durham Gr BS31 24 D4
Durham Pl 9 TA2 213 A8
Durhams Cotts TA4 210 C5
Durkheim Dr BA5 203 C4
Durleigh Cl
Bridgwater TA6 208 D3
Bristol BS13 22 A7
Durleigh Hill TA5 208 A2
Durleigh Rd TA6 208 C3
Durley Hill BS31 24 C7
Durley La BS31 24 D7
Durley Pk BA2 45 B2
Durleymoor Cross EX16 178 F4

Granby Hill BS8 11 F6
Granby Rd BA22 174 A2
Grand Par BA2 228 C2
Grand Pier★ BS23 48 D7
Grand Western Canal (Country Pk)★ EX16 178 F2
Grange (Millfield Sch) The TA11 211 F3
Grange Ave
Highbridge TA9 104 E3
Street BA16 207 B6
Grange Cl
Cannington TA5 135 C2
Wellington TA21 222 E5
Weston-Super-Mare BS23 48 E1
Grange Cnr DT8 199 E7
Grange Dr
Bridgwater TA6 208 D4
Taunton TA2 213 A6
Grange End BA3 97 B7
Grange Gdns TA2 213 A7
Grange Paddock TA9 106 E4
Grange Rd Bristol BS8 226 A3
Bristol, Bishopsworth BS13 22 A5
Frome BA11 120 A7
Saltford BS31 25 C3
Street BA16 207 D7
Taunton TA2 213 A6
West Huntspill TA9 136 A8
Weston-Super-Mare BS23 48 E1
Grange The Bristol BS9 5 D7
Chilton Polden TA7 137 B2
Flax Bourton BS48 19 F7
Kingston St Mary TA2 168 E8
Grange Way TA6 135 F5
Grange Wlk TA2 213 A6
Grangefields BA16 207 D5
Grant's Hill EX16,TA22 163 F2
Grant's La
Wedmore BS28 108 D4
Wiveliscombe TA4 210 D6
Grants Cl BA9 216 B4
Grants La BA9 216 D4
Granville Chapel 5 BS8 11 F5
Granville Rd BA1 27 E4
Granville Way DT9 225 E6
Grasmere TA6 208 C5
Grasmere Dr BS23 48 F4
Grass Meers Dr BS14 23 A4
Grass Rd TA8 65 F4
Grass Royal BA21 219 C6
Grass Royal Jun Sch BA21 219 C6
Grassmere Rd BS49 34 B8
Gratton La EX35 122 A4
Gravel Hill BS40 56 B7
Gravel La TA3,TA19 183 F6
Gravel Pits DT9 225 D3
Gravel Wlk BA1 228 B3
Gravelands La TA3 169 D3
Gravenchon Way BA16 207 A6
Graves Cl 6 TA6 209 B4
Gray Hollow BS40 74 F4
Gray's Hill EX15 180 D1
Gray's La EX15 180 D1
Grayling Ho BS9 5 F7
Grays Ave TA7 154 E6
Grays Hill BA2 80 B5
Grays Rd TA1 213 B4
Grays Terr TA1 213 B4
Great Ann St BS2 227 C3
Great Barton BA4 205 D6
Great Bedford St BA1 228 B4
Great Brockeridge BS9 5 F6
Great Cl EX15 179 E1
Great Cnr BA21 218 C6
Great Field La TA14 185 F4
Great Gdns BA4 205 C6
Great George St
Bristol BS1 226 C2
Bristol BS2 227 C3
Great Hayles Rd BS14 23 A6
Great Hill BA9 161 D2
Great House Ct BA6 138 D4
Great House St TA24 130 B5
Great La Knole TA10 173 A4
Shepton Beauchamp TA19 184 E4
Great Mdw TA22 163 D6
Great Mead TA1 212 B3
Great Orch BA22 173 E2
Great Ostry BA4 205 B6
Great Pit La BA22,DT9 188 B7
Great Pulteney St BA2 228 C3
Great Ringaton La EX36 162 B6
Great St TA14 185 E2
Great Stanhope St BA1 228 A2
Great Western Rd
Chard TA20 223 D5
Clevedon BS21 6 D2
Martock TA12 185 E7
Great Western Terr BA21 219 D5
Great Withy Dro BA5 206 C8
Greatstone La BS40 37 F5
Greatwood Cl TA6 209 A2
Grebe Cl TA6 209 B4
Grebe Ct TA6 209 B4
Grebe Rd Bridgwater TA6 209 B4
Taunton TA2 213 B6
Green Cl Holford TA5 133 D4
Paulton BS39 77 E6
Sparkford BA22 175 A4
Green Cotts BA2 45 C2
Green Ditch La BA3 96 B6
Green Dragon Ct 4 TA6 208 F4
Green Dro TA11 158 A4
Green Farm Ind Est BA13 121 C4
Green Gate EX16 178 C2
Green Knap La TA20 193 C2
Green La Blagdon BS40 55 A7
Brompton Regis TA22 148 B1
Castle Cary BA7 214 F4
Chard TA20 193 F1
Chard Junction TA20 198 D7
Chardstock EX13 198 B7
Charlton Horethorne DT9 175 F2
Charlton Horethorne DT9 176 A2
Corfe TA3 181 E7
Corsley Heath BA12 144 E7
Cricket St Thomas TA20 194 F3
East Chinnock BA22 186 B1
East Chinnock BA22 196 E8
East Coker BA22 197 B8
Failand BS8 10 C4
Farrington Gurney BS39 76 F6
Felton BS40 37 C3
Fivehead TA3 170 E2
Freshford BA3 64 B2
Frome BA11 119 D4
Hinton Charterhouse BA2 63 E1
Kington Magna SP8 177 E2
Leigh upon Mendip BA3, BA11 117 B2
Marshfield SN14 13 E8
Oakhill BA3 114 E4
Pitcombe BA7 215 A1
Priddy BS40 73 B7
Queen Camel BA22 174 F3
Sampford Arundel TA21 179 F4
Shepton Beauchamp TA19 184 E3
Sherborne DT9 188 E1
Southwick BA14 83 D2
Stoke St Michael BA3 116 B5
Stratton-on-the-Fosse BA3 96 E1
Street BA16 207 C4
Tatworth TA20 193 D1
Winsley BA15 64 F6
Green Lane Ave BA16 207 C4
Green Lane End TA19 184 E3
Green Lane Gate BA9 176 A8
Green Mead BA21 218 C5
Green Ore Est BA5 94 B1
Green Park La BA11 101 F6
Green Park Mews BA1 228 A2
Green Park Rd BA1 228 B2
Green Parlor Rd BA3 79 D1
Green Pastures Rd BS48 9 B2
Green Pits La BA11 143 B7
Green Pk BA1 228 B2
Green Ride BA12 161 F7
Green St Bath BA1 228 C2
Hinton St George TA17 195 D7
Peasedown St John BA2 79 E5
Ston Easton BA3 95 E8
Green The Backwell BS48 19 A5
Bath BA2 44 D1
Bridgwater TA6 208 E2
Brushford TA22 163 E4
Coleford BA3 116 F6
8 East Coker BA22 197 E8
Easton BA5 111 A4
Hinton Charterhouse BA2 63 F1
Ilchester BA22 173 E2
Locking BS24 50 A4
Pill BS20 4 D4
Pitminster TA3 181 E6
1 Sherborne DT9 225 D4
Williton TA4 202 D3
Winscombe BS25 70 A7
Green Tree Rd BA3 78 B3
Green's Dro BA6 206 C7
Green's Hill TA4 151 C5
Greenacre
Wembdon TA6 208 D6
Weston-Super-Mare BS22 31 B2
Greenacre Rd BS14 23 A3
Greenacres Bath BA1 27 B3
Bristol BS9 5 E7
Midsomer Norton BA3 77 E1
Greenacres Pk BA21 187 A5
Greenbank Gdns BA1 27 B1
Greenbrook Terr TA1 212 E4
Greendale TA19 221 B3
Greenditch Ave BS13 22 C5
Greenditch Cl BA3 96 C3
Greendown Pl BA2 45 A1
Greenfield Cres BS48 8 E3
Greenfield La TA7 136 D2
Greenfield Pk BS20 2 C3
Greenfield Pl BS23 48 C8
Greenfield Terr TA20 198 D8
Greenfields TA18 224 C7
Greenfields Ave BS29 51 A3
Greenfylde CE First Sch TA19 221 C3
Greengage Cl BS22 49 E8
Greenham La TA18 199 E7
Greenham Yd TA18 199 E7
Greenham's Cross TA14 185 F2
Greenhayes BS27 90 B8
Greenhays Foot EX13 198 B6
Greenhill DT9 225 D4
Greenhill Cl Nailsea BS48 8 D2
Weston-Super-Mare BS22 32 A3
Greenhill Cross EX36 162 B2
Greenhill La
Axbridge BS26 88 E5
Sandford BS25 52 B4
Greenhill Pl BA3 78 A3
Greenhill Rd
Midsomer Norton BA3 78 A3
Sandford BS25 52 B4
Greenhill Rd continued
Yeovil BA21 219 D7
Greenland La TA24 131 B1
Greenland Rd BS22 31 D1
Greenlands TA1 213 B2
Greenlands Rd BA2 79 C8
Greenmoor La BA21 187 A5
Greenridge BS39 58 F3
Greenridge Cl BS13 21 E4
Greenslade Gdns BS48 8 D3
Greenslade Inf Sch BS48 8 D3
Greenvale Cl BA2 60 B1
Greenvale Dr BA2 60 B1
Greenvale Rd BS39 77 D5
Greenway
Bishops Lydeard TA4 167 E8
Faulkland BA3 80 C1
Minehead TA24 200 D6
Monkton Heathfield TA2 169 B6
North Curry TA3 170 B3
Watchet TA23 202 B7
Greenway Ave TA2 212 E6
Greenway Cl BA9 216 D4
Greenway Cotts TA4 167 E8
Greenway Cres TA2 212 E7
Greenway Ct BA2 44 F4
Greenway La
Angersleigh TA3 181 B5
Barrington TA13 184 E5
Bath BA2 45 A4
Cold Ashton SN14 12 D5
Combe St Nicholas TA20 193 E6
Stoke St Mary TA3 169 D2
Wiveliscombe TA4 210 A5
Greenway Pk 3 BS21 6 F3
Greenway Rd
Castle Cary BA7 214 B6
Rockwell Green TA21 222 A5
Taunton TA2 212 E6
Greenway Terr TA2 168 D8
Greenways BA3 96 C2
Greenwell La BS40 53 C7
Greenwood Cl TA9 136 B8
Greenwood Rd
Weston-Super-Mare BS22 31 E2
Yeovil BA21 218 D7
Gregory Mead BS49 17 A1
Gregorys Gr BA2 62 D8
Gregorys Tyning BS39 77 F6
Greinton BS24 49 A2
Grenville Ave BS24 50 A4
Grenville Cl BA6 157 E4
Grenville Ho TA6 208 F2
Grenville Pl 7 BS1 11 F5
Grenville Rd TA8 104 C7
Grenville View TA4 167 E6
Grey's Cnr BA9 161 A3
Greyfield Comm BS39 59 C2
Greyfield Rd BS39 59 C2
Greyfield View BS39 58 F1
Greyhound Cl BA9 216 C4
Greylands Rd BS13 21 F7
Greys Rd TA16 195 F7
Grib La BS40 54 F2
Gribb View TA20 199 B6
Griffin Cl Wells BA5 203 B6
Weston-Super-Mare BS22 32 B2
Griffin Ct BA1 228 B2
Griffin La TA3 182 F7
Griffin Rd Clevedon BS21 6 E3
Hatch Beauchamp TA3 182 F7
Griggfield Wlk BS14 23 A7
Grimsey La SP8 177 F8
Grinfield Ave BS13 22 C4
Grinfield Cl BS13 22 C4
Grinfield Ct BS13 22 C4
Groats 9 TA4 167 F8
Grooms Orch TA21 222 C5
Grosvenor Bridge Rd BA1 28 C1
Grosvenor Ct BA22 173 E2
Grosvenor High Sch BA1 28 B1
Grosvenor Pk BA1 28 C1
Grosvenor Pl BA1 28 C1
Grosvenor Rd
Bristol BS2 227 C4
Stalbridge DT10 190 B4
Grosvenor Terr BA1 28 C2
Grosvenor Villas 9 BA1 28 B1
Grove Alley BA10 215 E6
Grove Ave Bristol BS1 227 A1
Bristol, Coombe Dingle BS9 5 C7
Yeovil BA20 218 F5
Grove Cl TA23 202 C6
Grove Ct BS9 5 E5
Grove Dr Taunton TA2 212 F8
Weston-Super-Mare BS22 31 C1
Grove Hill TA7 155 B1
Grove Ho TA8 104 A8
Grove Jun Sch BS48 18 D8
Grove La Faulkland BA3 80 D2
Frome BA11 119 E3
Knole TA10 173 A4
South Cheriton BA8 176 E5
Stalbridge DT10 190 B4
West Anstey EX36 162 D6
Weston-Super-Mare BS23 48 D8
Grove Lane Cl DT10 190 B4
Grove Leaze BS11 4 D6
Grove Mead BA11 119 E2
Grove Orch BS40 54 E2
Grove Park Ct BS23 30 D1
Grove Park Rd BS23 30 D1
Grove Pl TA24 201 B4
Grove Rd Banwell BS29 50 E4
Blue Anchor TA24 131 B6
Bristol, Coombe Dingle BS9 5 D8
Burnham-On-Sea TA8 104 A8
Grove Rd continued
West Huntspill TA9 136 A8
Weston-Super-Mare BS22 31 C1
Weston-Super-Mare BS23 48 D8
Grove St BA2 228 C3
Grove Terr 5 TA2 212 F6
Grove The Bath BA1 27 C1
Bristol BS1 227 A1
Burnham-On-Sea TA8 85 B1
Frome BA11 119 E2
Paulton BS39 77 B7
Ruishton TA3 169 C3
Winscombe BS25 51 F1
Wraxall BS48 9 C3
Grove Wood Rd BA3 78 F1
Groves La TA24 131 B6
Groves The BS13 22 D4
Grughay La TA3 182 E5
Grunter's La BA3 114 F7
Gryphon Sch DT9 225 E6
Guard Ave BA22 218 B6
Guard House La BA5 203 D4
Gug The BS39 59 C2
Guild Ct BS1 227 B2
Guildford Pl TA1 212 F3
Guildhall La BS28 108 C4
Guinea La BA1 228 C3
Guinea St BS1 227 A1
Guineagore La DT9 188 B4
Guinevere Cl BA21 218 D7
Gullen BA2 80 A6
Gulliford Cl TA9 104 D1
Gulliford's Bank BS21 6 F2
Gullimores Gdns BS13 22 B4
Gullock Tyning BA3 78 B1
Gullon Wlk BS13 21 F5
Gullons Cl BS13 22 A6
Gulway Mead TA20 198 D8
Gumbrells Ct TA6 209 A4
Gunners La BA22 218 A5
Gunning's La BA4 142 F2
Gunville La
Charlton Horethorne DT9 176 A2
East Coker BA22 197 D8
Gunwyn Cl BA6 206 E6
Gurney St TA5 135 C2
Gurnville Cotts BA11 119 F2
Guthrie Rd BS8 226 A4
Gwynne La TA1 213 A3
Gyffarde Ct 3 TA1 213 A4
Gyffarde St TA1 213 A4
Gypsy La Axbridge BS28 89 D6
Keynsham BS31 42 B8
Marshfield SN14 13 F7

H

Haberfield Hill BS8 4 E2
Haberfield Ho 1 BS8 11 F6
Hack La Holford TA5 133 F2
Nether Stowey TA5 134 A2
Hack Mead La TA9 105 E1
Hacketty Way TA24 124 B3
Hackness Rd TA9 136 E8
Haddon Cl TA22 148 B2
Haddon La
Brompton Regis TA4 164 C7
North Petherton TA6 153 C2
Stalbridge DT10 190 C5
Hadley Rd BA2 45 B2
Hadrian Cl BS9 5 C4
Hadspen Gdn★ BA7 160 A2
Hadworthy La TA6 153 F4
Hagget Cl TA6 208 F1
Hagleys Gn TA4 151 B7
Haig Cl BS9 5 B7
Haig Rd TA2 168 B6
Haines Hill TA1 212 E2
Haines La DT8 199 D5
Haines Pk TA1 212 E1
Hains La DT10 190 F7
Halcombe TA20 223 C2
Halcon Cnr TA1 213 D4
Halcon Com Prim Sch TA1 213 D4
Hale La BA9 177 C6
Hale Way TA2 213 D7
Hales Mdw BA21 187 D6
Halesleigh Rd TA6 208 E5
Half Acre TA4 202 D2
Half Acre Cl TA4 202 D2
Half Acres DT9 225 C3
Half Moon St DT9 225 D3
Half Yd BS40 53 D8
Halfacre Cl BS14 23 A3
Halfacre La BS14 23 B4
Halfpenny Row BA11 82 E1
Halfway BA22 186 F6
Hall Hill EX35 122 B5
Hall La BA1 12 B3
Hall Sch The BS25 70 B8
Hall Terr TA8 104 A8
Hallam Ct BS21 6 C4
Hallam Rd BS21 6 C4
Hallards Cl BS11 4 F8
Hallatrow Rd BS39 77 C6
Hallen Dr BS9 5 C7
Hallet Gdns BA20 219 A4
Hallets Orch BA22 186 B6
Hallett Rd BA7 214 B7
Halletts Way
Axminster EX13 198 A1
Portishead BS20 2 D5
Halliwell Rd BS20 1 D4
Halse Cnr TA4 167 D5
Halse La TA24 147 B5
Halse Manor TA4 167 B6
Halston Dr BS2 227 C4
Halsway TA6 209 C5
Halsway Hill TA4 132 F1
Halsway La
Bicknoller TA4 133 A1
Crowcombe TA4 151 A8
Halswell Cl TA6 208 E4
Halswell Gdns BS13 22 B4
Halswell Rd BS21 6 D1
Halt End BS14 23 C3
Halter Path Dro TA7 137 C7
Halves La BA22 197 C7
Halwyn Cl BS9 5 D5
Ham Cl BS39 58 F1
Ham Gn Hambridge TA10 184 D8
Pill BS20 4 D3
Ham Gr BS39 77 E5
Ham Green Hospl BS20 4 E4
Ham Hill Coleford BA3 116 D6
Combe St Nicholas TA20 193 D8
High Ham TA10 156 A2
Langford Budville TA21 166 A1
Ham Hill Ctry Pk★ TA14 186 A3
Ham Hill Rd
Higher Odcombe BA22 186 C2
Stoke sub Hamdon TA14 185 F4
Ham La Bishop Sutton BS39 57 C5
Burnham-On-Sea TA8 104 B6
Compton Dundon TA11 157 A3
Croscombe BA4,BA5 204 E7
Dundry BS41 21 D3
Farrington Gurney BS39 76 F5
Kingston Seymour BS21 16 B2
Marnhull DT10 190 F6
North End BS49 17 A3
Paulton BS39 77 E5
Pawlett TA6 135 E6
Rodhuish TA23 149 C8
Shepton Mallet BA4 141 A7
Shepton Mallet BA4 205 A7
Sherborne DT9 188 A5
Trent DT9 187 F5
Wraxall BS48 9 B4
Yatton BS49 17 A3
Ham La E BA4 204 F7
Ham Link BS40 53 F3
Ham Mdw DT10 190 E6
Ham Rd Brean BS24,TA8 66 B3
Burnham-On-Sea TA9 85 E4
Creech St Michael TA3 169 D4
Wellington TA21 180 D8
Ham St BA6 158 B5
Ham Wood Cl BS24 49 B2
Ham's La TA11 174 D7
Hamber Lea TA4 167 F8
Hambledon Rd BS22 32 C4
Hambridge Com Prim Sch TA10 184 D8
Hamdon Cl 12 TA14 185 F4
Hamdon View TA14 185 E3
Hamilton Ct Taunton TA1 213 C4
Wells BA5 203 B4
Hamilton Rd Bath BA1 27 E2
Taunton TA1 213 C4
Weston-Super-Mare BS23 30 C1
Hamilton Terr BA2 79 F5
Hamlands La TA21 167 D1
Hamlet The Nailsea BS48 9 A3
Templecombe BA8 176 E1
Hamley La
Buckland St Mary TA20 193 B8
Combe St Nicholas TA20 182 F1
Hamlyn Cl TA1 212 C1
Hamlyn Rd BA6 206 E6
Hammer La BA2,BA3 100 C8
Hammer St BA10 161 B8
Hammet St
2 North Petherton TA6 153 E3
Taunton TA1 212 F4
Hammets Wharf 1 TA1 212 F4
Hammond Gdns BS9 5 E7
Hamp Ave TA6 208 F3
Hamp Brook Way TA6 208 E2
Hamp Com Jun Sch TA6 208 F3
Hamp Green Rise TA6 209 A3
Hamp Ind Est TA6 209 A3
Hamp Inf Sch TA6 208 F3
Hamp St TA6 208 F3
Hampden Rd BS22 31 E2
Hampton Cl
5 Barwick BA22 197 F8
Bridgwater TA6 209 D7
Hampton Cnr BS11 4 E6
Hampton Ho 10 BA1 28 C1
Hampton La BS8 226 B4
Hampton Rd BS6 226 C4
Hampton Row BA2 45 B8
Hampton View BA1 28 B1
Hamrod La TA7 154 E5
Hams La BS26 68 C3
Hams Rd BS31 24 F7
Hamway La TA20 193 C8
Hamwood TA1 212 B4
Hamwood Cotts TA1 212 B4
Hamwood La TA3 181 B8
Hamwood Terr TA1 212 B4
Hanbury Ct BS8 226 A4
Hanbury Rd BS8 226 A4
Handel Rd BS31 24 E5
Handlemaker Rd BA11 119 E2
Handy Cross TA4 151 A2
Hanford Ct BS14 23 D7
Hang Hill BA2 80 A6

High St continued
Bristol, Shirehampton BS11 4 E6
Bruton BA10 215 E6
Buckland Dinham BA11 100 A3
Burnham-On-Sea TA8 104 A6
Butleigh BA6 157 E4
Cannington TA5 135 B2
Carhampton TA24 131 A5
Castle Cary BA7 214 C5
Chapmanslade BA13 121 C4
Chard TA20 223 B4
Charlton Adam TA11 173 F7
Chew Magna BS40 39 A3
Chewton Mendip BA3 94 F7
Claverham BS49 17 F1
Coleford BA3 116 F6
Congresbury BS49 34 D4
Dulverton TA22 163 D6
Dunster TA24 201 E2
East Chinnock BA22 196 E8
East Harptree BS40 74 F5
Evercreech BA4 141 E1
Faulkland BA3 80 D1
Freshford BA3 64 B5
Frome BA11 119 E5
Glastonbury BA6 206 E4
Hardington Mandeville
BA22 197 A6
Henstridge BA8 190 A6
High Littleton BS39 59 D1
Hinton Charterhouse BA2 63 E1
Hinton St George TA17 195 D7
Ilchester BA22 173 E1
Ilminster TA19 221 B4
Keinton Mandeville TA11 158 A1
Keynsham BS31 24 E6
Kingweston BA6 157 E1
Lynford-on-Fosse TA11 158 C2
Maiden Bradley BA12 144 C2
Marshfield SN14 13 F8
Midsomer Norton BA3 78 B1
Milborne Port DT9 217 D2
Milton Clevedon BA4 160 A8
Milverton TA4 166 F5
Monksilver TA4 150 B8
Nailsea BS48 8 F3
North Cadbury BA22 175 D6
North Petherton TA6 153 F4
North Wootton BA4 140 C4
Norton St Philip BA2 81 E4
Nunney BA11 143 B8
Oakhill BA3 115 A3
NonRoady TA7 155 C2
Paulton BS39 77 E5
Paulton, Plummer's Hill
BS39 77 E6
Pensford BS39 40 E4
Porlock TA24 124 A3
Portbury BS20 3 E3
Portishead BS20 2 D5
Queen Camel BA22 174 F3
Rimpton BA22 188 A8
Rode BA11 101 E8
Saltford BS31 25 F3
Shepton Mallet BA4 205 B5
Sparkford BA22 175 A5
Spaxton TA5 152 E7
Stalbridge DT10 190 B5
Stogumber TA4 150 D8
Stogursey TA5 134 C5
Stoke sub Hamdon TA14 185 F4
Ston Easton BA3 95 E8
Stoney Stratton BA4 141 F2
Stourton BA12 161 F5
Street BA16 207 C6
Taunton TA1 212 F3
Templecombe BA8 176 E1
Thorncombe TA20 199 B6
Timsbury BA2 60 B2
Wedmore BS28 107 E4
Wellington TA21 222 E6
Wellow BA2 62 D1
Wells BA5 203 D4
West Coker BA22 197 A8
Weston-Super-Mare BS22 31 E2
Weston-Super-Mare BS23 48 D8
Williton TA4 202 D2
Wincanton BA9 216 C4
Winford BS40 38 A7
Winsham TA20 194 E1
Wiveliscombe TA4 210 C4
Wookey BA5 139 D8
Wookey Hole BA5 203 A8
Woolley BA1 27 F6
Wrington BS40 35 D2
Yatton BS49 34 C8
Yenston BA8 189 F8
Yeovil BA20 219 B4
High View BS20 2 A4
High View Dr TA7 156 B8
Highaton Head Cross
EX36 162 C4
Highbridge TA4 202 F4
Highbridge Rd TA8 104 B5
Highbridge Sta TA9 104 E3
Highbrooks Rd TA11 173 B5
Highburn Cl TA8 104 C4
Highbury Cotts [8] BA1 28 A1
Highbury Par BS23 30 C1
Highbury Pl BA1 28 A1
Highbury Rd Paulton BS39 77 B7
Weston-Super-Mare BS23 30 C1
Highbury St BA3 117 A7
Highbury Terr [10] BA1 28 A1
Highbury Villas
[9] Bath BA1 28 A1
Bristol BS2 226 C4
Highcroft
Weston-Super-Mare BS23 30 F1
Woolavington TA7 136 E4
Highdale Ave BS21 6 E3
Highdale Cl BS14 23 B4
Highdale Rd BS21 6 E3
Higher Actis BA6 206 E3
Higher Backway BA10 215 E6
Higher Beacon TA19 221 B4
Higher Beadon TA16 195 E7
Higher Brooks BA16 207 C2
Higher Bullen BA22 197 F8
Higher Burton BA22 197 C8
Higher Cheap St [3]
DT9 225 D4
Higher Coombses TA20 198 D8
Higher Cross EX15 179 C1
Higher Easthams La
TA18 224 F7
Higher Farm La
Podimore BA22 174 A4
Sparkford BA22 175 B3
Higher Farm Trad Est
BA20 218 C5
Higher Gunville DT9 217 D2
Higher Heathfield TA4 151 E4
Higher Kingsbury DT9 217 D3
Higher Kingsbury Cl
DT9 217 C3
Higher Kingston BA21 219 B5
Higher Mead TA19 221 B3
Higher Millhayes EX15 180 B1
Higher North Town La
BA22 175 D7
Higher Orch
Martock TA12 185 D4
Minehead TA24 200 C8
Higher Palmerston Rd
TA2 212 D6
Higher Park La TA24 129 E2
Higher Pk TA24 200 D6
Higher Rd Chedzoy TA7 154 D8
Horsington BA8 176 D3
Shepton Beauchamp TA19 184 E3
Woolavington TA7 136 E4
Higher Ream BA21 218 C6
Higher Rodhuish Rd
TA24 131 B3
Higher St
Curry Mallet TA3 183 C8
East Quantoxhead TA5 133 B5
Martock TA12 185 D4
Merriott TA16 195 F8
Norton Sub Hamdon TA14 185 E2
West Chinnock TA18 196 B8
Higher Tolbury BA10 215 E6
Higher Town EX16 178 C1
Higher West Hatch La
TA3 182 D7
Higher Westbury DT9 187 E1
Higher Westholme Rd
North Wootton BA4 140 D4
Pilton BA4 204 A1
Highfield Coleford BA3 116 E8
Ilminster TA19 221 B4
Taunton TA1 212 A2
Taunton TA1 212 C3
West Chinnock TA18 196 B8
Highfield Cl Bath BA2 44 B5
Somerton TA11 211 C4
Taunton TA1 212 A2
Highfield Cres
Chilcompton BA3 96 C4
Taunton TA1 212 A2
Highfield Dr BS20 1 E3
Highfield La
Compton Martin BS40 74 B6
East Harptree BS40 75 A3
Highfield Rd
Keynsham BS31 24 F2
Peasedown St John BA2 79 C8
Street BA16 207 B5
Weston-Super-Mare BS24 49 A1
Yeovil BA21 219 C6
Highfield Terr TA12 185 D5
Highfield Trad Est BA21 219 C6
Highfield View BA3 116 E8
Highfield Way TA11 211 C4
Highfields
Barrington TA19 184 C5
Midsomer Norton BA3 78 D2
Radstock BA3 78 E4
Stanton Drew BS39 39 F1
Highgrove TA1 212 E1
Highgrove Cl TA6 209 A2
Highland Cl BS22 31 B2
Highland Ct BA21 219 C6
Highland Rd BA2 44 B5
Highland Terr BA2 44 D6
Highlands TA1 212 E1
Highlands La BS24 50 A8
Highlands Rd
Long Ashton BS41 11 A2
Portishead BS20 2 B5
Highmead Gdns BS13 21 E4
Highmore Rd DT9 225 C5
Highridge Cres BS13 21 F5
Highridge Gn BS13 21 E6
Highridge Inf Sch BS13 21 F6
Highridge Pk BS13 21 F6
Highridge Rd BS13,BS41 21 E4
Highridge Wlk BS13 21 E7
Highwall La BS14,BS31 23 F1
Highwoods Cl TA14 185 F2
Higson Cl BA22 186 D3
Hilary Rd TA1 212 D3
Hildesham Bridge BS23 48 F7
Hildesheim Cl BS23 48 F6
Hildeshiem Ct BS23 48 E7
Hilhouse BS9 5 C6
Hill Ave BA2 44 F1
Hill Brow DT9 225 B2
Hill Cl BA9 216 D4
Hill Crest Rd BA21 219 C6
Hill Cross BA22 196 F6
Hill Ct BS39 77 E6
Hill Dr BS8 10 C3
Hill Gay Cl BS20 1 F4
Hill Ground BA11 119 E5
Hill Head BA6 206 D3
Hill Head Cl
Glastonbury BA6 206 D3
Taunton TA1 213 A3
Hill House Cl DT9 225 E5
Hill La Bicknoller TA4 132 F2
Brent Knoll TA9 86 B3
Carhampton TA24 131 A4
Chipstable TA4 165 C6
Clevedon BS21 7 C4
Culverhays TA4 133 A1
Draycott BS27 90 C2
Portishead BS20 1 F1
Rodney Stoke BS27 91 B2
Rowberrow BS25 53 A1
Shepton Mallet BA4 205 B6
Waterrow TA4 165 E5
West Quantoxhead TA4 132 F4
Hill Lea Gdns BS27 90 B8
Hill Moor BS21 6 E2
Hill Pk BS49 34 E5
Hill Rd Allerford TA24 124 E4
Clevedon BS21 6 D4
Dundry BS41 21 D2
Minehead TA24 125 B4
Sandford BS25 52 A3
Weston-Super-Mare BS22 31 E2
Weston-Super-Mare BS23 48 F8
Hill Rd E BS22 31 E2
Hill Side Cl BA5 203 C5
Hill St Bristol BS1 226 C2
Stogumber TA4 150 D8
Hill Terr TA1 212 A4
Hill The Freshford BA3 64 C5
Langport TA10 172 A5
Hill Top BS20 2 A4
Hill View Brean TA8 65 F2
Bristol BS8 226 B2
Brompton Ralph TA4 150 C3
Farrington Gurney BS39 77 B3
Marksbury BA2 42 B1
Priston BA2 61 A5
Yeovil BA21 219 C5
Yeovil, Mudford BA21 187 D6
Hill View Cl Ilton TA19 183 F4
[7] Stoke sub Hamdon
TA14 185 F4
West Chinnock TA18 196 B8
Hill View Ct BS22 49 D8
Hill View Park Homes
BS22 49 D8
Hill View Rd Bath BA1 28 B2
Bristol BS13 22 A8
Carhampton TA24 131 A5
Weston-Super-Mare BS23 49 A7
Hill View Terr
Ilminster TA19 221 B4
Lyng TA3 170 C7
Hill View Trad Est TA4 151 E4
Hill's La [10] TA12 185 E6
Hillborne Gdns BA21 218 C5
Hillbrook Ct DT9 225 D4
Hillclose La TA19 221 F2
Hillcote Est BS24 67 B8
Hillcrest Crowcombe TA4 151 B7
Peasedown St John BA2 79 C7
Pensford BS39 40 E3
Hillcrest Cl Nailsea BS48 8 E1
Yeovil BA21 219 C7
Hillcrest Dr BA2 44 C4
Hillcrest Rd Nailsea BS48 8 E1
Portishead BS20 1 E4
Templecombe BA8 176 E1
Hillcroft Cl BS22 31 A2
Hilldale Rd BS48 19 B5
Hiller's La BA5 139 C8
Hillfield BS27 90 B7
Hillgrove Ave BA20 218 F2
Hillgrove Cl TA6 208 E5
Hillgrove Rd BA5 93 C1
Hillgrove St BS2 227 B4
Hillgrove St N BS2 227 A4
Hillgrove Terr BS23 48 D1
Hillhead Cotts TA2 212 C8
Hillhead Cross TA24 128 D3
Hillhouse EX14 192 D3
Hillier's La BS25 52 D4
Hillingdon Ct BA21 218 C6
Hillmead Langford BS40 53 A5
Shepton Mallet BA4 205 B6
Hillmer Rise BS29 50 F3
Hillpath BS29 51 B2
Hills Cl BS31 25 A5
Hills Cotts TA4 167 A7
Hills Orch [9] TA12 185 E6
Hillsboro TA7 136 E4
Hillsborough BS8 226 A2
Hillsborough Gdns TA8 85 B1
Hillsborough Ho BS23 49 A4
Hillsdon Rd BS9 5 F8
Hillside Bristol BS6 226 C4
Chard TA20 223 B4
Horrington BA5 113 A2
Portbury BS20 3 E3
Puriton TA7 136 C4
Sherborne DT9 225 E3
West Pennard BA6 140 B1
Hillside Ave Frome BA11 119 F2
Midsomer Norton BA3 96 F8
Hillside Cl
Curry Rivel TA10 171 D4
Paulton BS39 77 F6
Hillside Cres
Midsomer Norton BA3 96 E8
Puriton TA7 136 C4
Hillside Dr TA7 136 C4
Hillside Fst Sch BS22 31 E2
Hillside Gdns
Bishop Sutton BS39 57 C3
Weston-Super-Mare BS22 31 B1
Hillside Gr TA1 212 C1
Hillside Ho BA11 119 F3
Hillside Rd Backwell BS48 19 A4
Bath BA2 44 D4
Bleadon BS24 67 B8
Clevedon BS21 6 D3
Long Ashton BS41 11 B2
Midsomer Norton BA3 96 F8
Portishead BS20 1 D4
Hillside Terr BA21 219 C5
Hillside View
[1] Barwick BA22 197 F8
Midsomer Norton BA3 78 A3
Peasedown St John BA2 79 C8
Yeovil BA22 219 D1
Hillside W BS24 49 F2
Hilltop La TA5 133 D6
Hillview
Midsomer Norton BA3 96 E7
Queen Camel BA22 174 F4
Timsbury BA2 60 B1
Hillview Ave BS21 6 D2
Hillview Cl TA24 200 D7
Hillview Gdns BS40 37 C8
Hillview Rd Loxton BS26 68 C4
Minehead TA24 200 D7
Hillview Terr TA12 185 D5
Hillway TA11 173 E7
Hilly Head TA21 222 B5
Hilly Pk TA2 168 B5
Hillyfield Rd BS13 22 A6
Hillyfields Taunton TA1 213 C2
Winscombe BS25 70 B8
Hillyfields Way BS25 70 A8
Hinam Cross TA22 163 B7
Hinckley Cl BS22 32 C4
Hincombe Hill BA4 142 E2
Hind Pitts BS25 70 F7
Hindhayes Inf Sch BA16 207 D5
Hindhayes La BA16 207 D6
Hine Rd TA1 212 B1
Hinton BS24 49 A2
Hinton Cl Bath BA2 43 F6
Hinton St George TA17 195 D7
Saltford BS31 25 E3
Hinton Cross BA22 187 D7
Hinton Dr TA1 212 E1
Hinton Hill BA2,BA3 63 A1
Hinton La [12] BS8 11 F6
Hinton Rd TA18 224 B8
Hippisley Dr BS26 70 D2
Hippisley Ho BA5 113 A1
Hiscocks Dr BA2 44 E4
Hiscocks La BA8 176 E2
Hitchen TA16 195 F7
Hitchen Cl SN14 13 F8
Hitchen Hill BA4 140 F3
Hitchin La BA4 205 A5
Hitchings La TA3 170 B7
Hither Acre TA19 221 A4
Hither Gn BS21 6 F2
Hither Green Ind Est BS21 6 F2
Hither Mead TA4 167 F8
Hittsford La EX36 162 A1
Hoare's La BA11 98 B3
Hob La TA2 168 E8
Hobart Rd BS23 48 F3
Hobb's La BS1 226 C2
Hobbiton Rd BS22 32 A4
Hobbs Ct BS48 8 F2
Hobbs La BS48 20 E3
Hobbs Mead [7] TA4 167 F8
Hobwell La BS41 11 C2
Hoccombe Ford TA4 150 F1
Hocken Cl TA20 223 D6
Hockley Ct BA1 27 D1
Hockley La BA22 175 E5
Hockpitt La TA5 134 A2
Hodder's Cl BA11 119 E5
Hodges Barton TA11 211 C4
Hodshill BA2 62 F6
Hoecroft Gdns BA3 96 D3
Hogarth Mews BS22 32 A3
Hogarth Wlk BS22 32 A3
Hoggington La BA14 83 E3
Hogues Wlk BS13 22 B4
Holbeach Way BS14 23 A2
Holbrook Cres BS13 22 D4
Holbrook Pk TA13 220 C5
Holburne Mus & Crafts Study
Ctr BA2 45 B7
Holcombe BS14 23 A5
Holcombe Cl BA2 28 F1
Holcombe Gn BA1 27 B2
Holcombe Gr BS31 24 D5
Holcombe Hill BA3 116 C7
Holcombe La
Bathampton BA2 28 F1
Doulting BA4 141 E4
Holcombe Vale BA2 28 F1
Holden's Way TA10 171 C3
Holden's Way TA10 171 D3
Holders Wlk BS41 20 F8
Holditch Court La TA20 198 E5
Holditch La EX13,TA20 198 E5
Holdscroft La DT6 199 B1
Holeground Villas BA5 203 A8
Holemore Cross EX14 191 F5
Holes La BA11 118 B6
Holford Cl BS48 8 E1
Holford Ct BS14 23 B5
Holford La TA4 151 C5
Holford Rd
Bridgwater TA6 208 B4
Taunton TA2 212 E8
Hollam Cross TA22 163 E7
Hollam Dr TA22 163 D6
Hollam La TA22 163 D7
Holland Ct BA16 207 D7
Holland Rd Bath BA1 28 B1
Clevedon BS21 6 B1
Holland St BS23 49 A8
Holland's La
Clatworthy TA4 149 E1
Huish Champflower TA4 165 E8
Holland's Wash Dro
TA20 193 C5
Holleys Cl TA20 198 D8
Hollies Cl Martock TA12 185 D5
Middlezoy TA7 155 B3
Shepton Mallet BA4 205 C6
Hollies La BA1 29 A6
Hollies The
Crewkerne TA18 224 C4
Midsomer Norton BA3 78 A1
Yeovil BA21 219 C7
Hollis Ave BS20 2 C3
Hollis Cl Halstock BA22 197 D3
Long Ashton BS41 21 A8
Hollis Cres BS20 2 C3
Hollis Way
Halstock BA22 197 D3
Southwick BA14 83 F3
Hollister's Dr BS13 22 D4
Hollow La
Baltonsborough BA6 158 B8
Dinnington TA17 195 B7
Lopen TA13 185 A1
Montacute TA15 186 B3
Wembdon TA5,TA6 208 C7
Weston-Super-Mare BS22 31 F3
Hollow Marsh La BA3,
BS39 76 B4
Hollow Rd
Shepton Beauchamp TA19 184 D3
Shipham BS25 70 F8
Hollow The Bath BA2 44 B4
Corsley Heath BA12 144 E8
Peasedown St John BA2 61 D4
Westbury Sub Mendip
BA5 110 D7
Holloway Bath BA2 228 B1
Lopen TA13 185 A1
Minehead TA24 200 F7
Holloway Rd TA7 155 B2
Holloway St TA24 200 F7
Holloway The TA21 179 E7
Hollowbrook La BS39,
BS40 57 D6
Hollowell Hill
Norton Sub Hamdon TA14,
TA18 185 E1
West Chinnock TA18 196 B8
Hollowmead BS49 34 E8
Hollowmead Cl BS49 34 F8
Hollway Cl BS14 23 E5
Hollway Rd BS14 23 E5
Holly Cl Bridgwater TA6 209 E5
Nailsea BS48 9 A3
[7] North Petherton TA6 153 F3
Taunton TA1 213 C1
Weston-Super-Mare BS22 32 A1
Holly Ct Bristol BS2 226 C4
Frome BA11 120 B7
Holly Dr BA2 62 D8
Holly Gr TA18 224 D7
Holly Hill BA4 142 C1
Holly La Clevedon BS21 6 F6
Drimpton DT8 199 F8
Holly Ridge BS20 2 A5
Holly Terr Chard TA20 223 C4
Higher Odcombe BA22 186 C2
Holly Tree Wlk BA20 218 E3
Holly Wlk Keynsham BS31 24 D4
Radstock BA3 78 E1
Hollybush Cl BA15 64 E7
Hollybush La Bristol BS9 5 E5
Bristol BS9 5 F4
Leigh upon Mendip BA3 117 A2
Hollyman Wlk [5] BS21 6 F3
Hollymead La BS9 5 E4
Hollyridge BS14 23 C6
Holm Cl TA8 104 B5
Holm Oaks BA6 157 E4
Holm Rd BS24 49 E2
Holman Cl BA6 206 E6
Holman's BA6 157 E4
Holmbury Cl BA11 120 D6
Holmbush TA24 128 E8
Holmlea Portishead BS20 2 F5
[1] Wookey BA5 139 D8
Holmoak Rd BS31 24 C4
Holms Rd BS23 49 A5
Holsom Cl BS14 23 F6
Holsom Rd BS14 23 F6
Holst Gdns BS4 22 D7
Holt Ball Steep TA24 129 D7
Holt Hill DT9 189 C1
Holt La Halstock BA22 197 F3
South Perrott DT8 196 D1

I

J

Laburnum Ct *continued*
Weston-Super-Mare BS23 49 B7
Laburnum Dr TA11 211 D4
Laburnum Gr BA3 96 F8
Laburnum Lodges TA9 136 A8
Laburnum Rd
Wellington TA21 222 E5
Weston-Super-Mare BS23 49 B7
Laburnum Terr TA3 169 D4
Laburnum Way BA20 218 D2
Laburnum Wlk BS31 24 C3
Lacey Rd BS14 23 F6
Ladd Cl TA9 104 D3
Ladies Mile BS8 5 F1
Ladman Gr BS14 23 E6
Ladman Rd BS14 23 E5
Lady Harriet Acland's Dr TA22 164 A8
Lady Lawn TA3 168 D1
Lady St TA22 163 D7
Lady Victoria's Dr TA22 163 E6
Ladycroft 4 BS21 6 B1
Ladye Bay BS21 6 D7
Ladye Wake BS22 31 F4
Ladymead BS20 2 F5
Ladymead Cl TA6 208 B4
Ladymead Com Sch TA2 168 E6
Ladymead La BS40 52 F5
Ladymead Rd TA2 168 F6
Ladymeade Backwell BS48 19 A7
Ilminster TA19 221 B3
Ladywell BS40 35 D2
Laggan Gdns BA1 27 E1
Lagger Hill TA5 133 C5
Lahs Pl BA11 101 E4
Lake Mews BA22 219 B1
Lake Rd BS20 2 D7
Lake Wall TA7 154 E4
Lakefields BA22 197 B8
Lakemead Gdns BS13 21 F4
Lakemead Gr BS13 21 F6
Lakeside TA9 104 E4
Lakeside Cl BS40 55 D5
Lakeside Pk BA11 117 E8
Lakeview Cres TA9 104 E3
Lamb La TA6 208 F4
Lamb St BS2 227 C3
Lambert Cl DT9 217 C2
Lambert Ct DT9 217 D2
Lambert La TA19 194 F5
Lambert Pl BS4 22 D6
Lambert's Hill BA4 204 F3
Lamberts Marsh BA14 83 E2
Lambourn Rd BS31 25 A4
Lambourne Ct TA18 224 D7
Lambourne Way BS20 2 F5
Lambpark Ct TA3 191 F6
Lambridge 6 BA1 28 C1
Lambridge Bldgs 1 BA1 28 C1
Lambridge Mews 5 BA1 28 C1
Lambridge Pl BA1 28 C1
Lambridge St BA1 28 C1
Lambrok Cl BA14 83 F6
Lambrok Rd BA14 83 F6
Lambrook Cl TA1 213 B4
Lambrook Gate TA13 184 F5
Lambrook Rd
Shepton Beauchamp TA19 184 E4
Taunton TA1 213 B4
Lambrook St BA6 206 E4
Lambrook Way TA1 213 C4
Lambs Field DT9 225 E5
Lamont Ho 7 BA1 28 C1
Lampard's Bldgs BA1 228 B4
Lamparts Way TA19 183 C2
Lampley Rd BS21 16 D2
Lampreys La TA13 220 C3
Lampton Ave BS13 22 E3
Lampton Gr BS13 22 E3
Lampton Rd BS41 10 F1
Lancaster House Sch BS23 48 F8
Lancer Ct TA21 222 D6
Lanch La SP8 177 F5
Lancock St TA21 222 A5
Lancombe La BA10 215 C3
Landacre La TA24 146 A7
Landemann Cir BS23 30 E1
Landemann Path 2 BS23 48 E8
Landford Budville CE Prim Sch TA21 166 F1
Landlord's Hill TA21 179 E7
Landmead BA6 206 D5
Landmoor La TA10 172 D4
Landsdown Mews BA11 119 D5
Landsdown Pl BA11 119 D5
Landsdown View BA3 80 D1
Landseer BA8 176 D4
Landseer Cl BS22 31 F3
Landseer Rd BA2 44 B6
Landshire La
Charlton Horethorne DT9 176 A1
Chilton Polden TA7 137 A3
Henstridge BA8 190 C6
Higher Odcombe BA22 186 C1
Lane End BA12 144 D8
Lane Foot TA24 129 D7
Lane Head TA24 123 E4
Lanes End Hill BA11, BA12 144 D8
Lanesborough Rise BS14 23 D7
Laneys Dro BS24 49 E5
Lang Rd TA18 224 C4
Lang's Cnr TA19 183 B1
Langaller Hill TA22 163 D4
Langdon Cl TA20 223 D6
Langdon Rd BA2 44 B4
Langdons DT9 225 E5
Langdons Way TA20 198 C8
Langdown Ct BS14 23 E5
Langer's La TA19 194 E5
Langford Cl TA3 170 F1
Langford Ct 13 TA1 213 A4
Langford Gate TA4 166 F2
Langford House Sch of Vet Science BS40 53 B6
Langford La
Fivehead TA3 170 F2
Langford BS40 53 E5
Norton Fitzwarren TA2 168 C6
Langford Rd Bristol BS13 21 F8
Langford BS40 53 C6
Weston-Super-Mare BS23 49 A6
Langford's La BS39 59 D1
Langfords La BS39 77 C8
Langham Dr TA1 212 C1
Langham Gdns TA1 212 C1
Langham La SP8 177 F5
Langham Pl BA11 82 F1
Langhill Ave BS4 22 D7
Langland La TA7 137 D2
Langland's La TA9 104 B1
Langlands 8 TA14 185 F4
Langlands La TA3 169 F2
Langley Cres BS3 11 E1
Langley Cross TA4 210 B6
Langley's La BA3, BS39 77 C1
Langleys Cotts BA3 96 D7
Langmead Dro
Middlezoy TA7 155 A4
Westonzoyland TA7 154 F5
Langmead La TA7 155 A4
Langmead Pl TA18 224 C4
Langmead Rd TA18 224 C4
Langmead Sq TA18 224 C4
Langmoor La EX13 198 D2
Langport Gdns BS48 18 E8
Langport Rd
Long Sutton TA10 172 E5
Middlezoy TA7 155 B4
Somerton TA11 211 B4
Weston-Super-Mare BS23 48 E5
Langridge La BA1 27 D8
Langton Ho 9 BS2 227 C3
Langworthy Orch TA19 183 C1
Lansdown Cres Bath BA1 27 F1
Timsbury BA2 60 C2
Lansdown Ct BS23 48 F8
Lansdown Gdns BS22 32 B5
Lansdown Gr BA1 228 B4
Lansdown Grove Ct BA1 228 B4
Lansdown Hts BA1 27 F1
Lansdown La Bath BA1 27 B4
Upton Cheyney BS30 26 D8
Lansdown Mans BA1 228 B4
Lansdown Pk BA1 27 E3
Lansdown Pl Bristol BS8 226 A3
High Littleton BS39 59 D1
Lansdown Pl E BA1 228 B4
Lansdown Pl W BA1 27 F1
Lansdown Rd Bath BA1 27 E2
Bristol BS8 226 A3
Saltford BS31 25 E3
Lansdown View Bath BA2 44 C5
Timsbury BA2 60 C2
Lansdowne Rd TA2 213 A6
Lanthony Cl BS24 50 A8
Lapwing Cl TA24 201 C5
Lapwing Gdns BS22 31 F1
Larch Ave TA20 223 B5
Larch Cl Bridgwater TA6 209 D6
Langford BS40 53 A5
Nailsea BS48 9 A2
Taunton TA1 213 D2
Larch Ct BA3 97 D8
Larches The BS22 32 A3
Larchfield Cl BA11 120 B7
Larchgrove Cres BS22 31 F1
Larchgrove Wlk BS22 31 F1
Lark Cl BA3 97 B8
Lark Pl BA1 44 D7
Lark Rd BS22 31 F1
Larkhall Pl BA1 28 C2
Larkhall Terr BA1 28 C2
Larkhill Rd Locking BS24 50 B6
Yeovil BA21 218 D7
Larks Mdw DT10 190 C4
Larkspur Cl TA1 213 C1
Larkspur Cres BA21 218 D7
Larkspur Ct TA2 212 D7
Larviscombe Cl TA4 202 D4
Larviscombe Rd TA4 202 D4
Lasbury Gr BS13 22 C5
Lascot Hill BS28 108 C5
Latcham Dro BS27,BS28 109 A4
Latches La BS27 90 D3
Latchmoor Ho BS13 22 A8
Late Broads BA15 64 D7
Lauder Ct DT9 217 D2
Launcherley Cross BA5 140 A6
Launcherley Rd BA4,BA5 140 B5
Launder Cl BA6 206 E4
Laura Pl BA2 228 C3
Laurel Ave TA9 86 A2
Laurel Cl
East Coker BA22 197 B8
Frome BA11 120 B7
Taunton TA1 213 C1
Laurel Dr Nailsea BS48 8 F2
Paulton BS39 77 E5
Laurel Dr *continued*
Weston-Super-Mare BS23 48 E2
Laurel Gdns Chard TA20 223 B5
Yatton BS49 17 B1
Laurel La BA22 174 F3
Laurel St BA6 140 A1
Laurel Terr BS49 17 B1
Laurels The
Crewkerne TA18 224 D7
Wembdon TA6 208 C6
Weston-Super-Mare BS23 48 E2
Westwood BA15 64 F3
Lavender Cl BS22 32 A5
Lavender Ct Frome BA11 120 B7
Street BA16 207 B4
Lavender Gr TA1 212 C3
Laver's La TA20 198 F5
Laverley Cotts BA6 140 C2
Laverock Ct TA1 212 E5
Lavers Ct TA12 186 A7
Lavers Oak TA12 185 E7
Lavington Cl BS21 6 B1
Law La Drayton TA10 171 F3
Langport TA10 172 A3
Lawford St BS2 227 C3
Lawfords Gate BS2 227 C3
Lawfords Gate Ho 17 BS2 227 C3
Lawn La
Galhampton BA22 175 D8
Shapwick TA7 137 F1
Lawn Mdw TA3 169 C3
Lawn Rd TA2 212 C8
Lawn The 1 TA21 222 D6
Lawnmoor La TA10 184 C6
Lawns The Bristol BS11 4 E7
Combe St Nicholas TA20 193 D6
Weston-Super-Mare BS22 32 B3
Yatton BS49 17 A1
Lawnside BS48 19 B5
Lawpool Ct BA5 203 D4
Lawrence Cl
Burnham-On-Sea TA8 104 D5
Highbridge TA9 104 F4
Lawrence Hayes BA9 216 D3
Lawrence Hill BA9 216 A2
Lawrence Hill Bsns Ctr BA9 216 A3
Lawrence Mews BS22 31 E2
Lawrence Rd
Coleford BA3 116 F7
Weston-Super-Mare BS22 31 E2
Wrington BS40 35 E2
Lawson Cl
5 Martock TA12 185 E6
Saltford BS31 25 C2
Lawyer's Hill TA5 152 C7
Lax Ct BA5 203 B4
Laxton Cl TA1 213 D5
Laxton Rd TA1 213 E5
Laxton Way BA2 79 D7
Laycock Hill DT9 217 D7
Layfield La TA3 170 C3
Layne Terr TA18 196 B8
Lays Bsns Ctr BS31 24 C4
Lays Dr BS31 24 C5
Lays La BS40 54 D4
Lays The BA11 101 E5
Lea Cl BA21 219 B8
Lea Croft BS13 22 A4
Lea Grove Rd BS21 6 C4
Leach Cl BS21 6 D1
Leach Rd TA20 223 D7
Leach's Field TA2 168 D8
Leaches Cl BA22 186 B6
Leadon Gr TA1 213 D4
Leafy Way BS24 50 B4
Leaholme Gdns BS14 23 A3
Lear's La BA9 177 C6
Leat The 8 TA4 167 F8
Leawood Ct BS23 30 C1
Leaze Cl BA11 119 D5
Leaze Dro BA5 139 A7
Leaze Ho BA11 119 D5
Leaze House Mews BA11 119 D5
Leaze La Blagdon BS40 72 E8
West Chinnock TA18 196 B8
Yeovil BA21 219 F4
Leaze Rd BA11 119 D5
Leaze The Radstock BA3 97 D8
Rode BA2 82 C1
Leazemoor La TA10 172 B8
Leazeway Dro TA7 155 C1
Lecher La DT8,TA18 196 B1
Leda Ave BS14 23 A7
Lee Pk TA21 180 F7
Leedham Rd BS24 50 C5
Leeford La EX35 122 B5
Leeming Way BS11 4 C8
Leeside BS20 2 C5
Leet Ct DT9 225 B2
Leeward Cl TA6 209 C4
Leewood Rd BS23 30 F1
Leg La BS40 54 B3
Leg Of Mutton Rd BA6 206 E6
Leg Sq BA4 205 C6
Leg Square Ct BA4 205 C6
Leggar The TA6 209 A6
Legion Rd BA21 218 F6
Leigh Cl BA1 28 A2
Leigh Court Bsns Ctr BS8 5 A2
Leigh Furlong Rd BA16 207 B4
Leigh La Cold Ashton BA1 13 B3
Crowcombe TA4 151 A7
Halstock BA22 197 C3
Winsford TA22 147 C2
Winsham TA20 199 A8
Leigh on Mendip Fst Sch BA3 117 A3
Leigh Rd Bristol BS8 226 B4
Leigh upon Mendip BA11 117 C2
Street BA16 207 C5
Taunton TA2 213 B8
Leigh St BA3 116 F3
Leigh View Rd BS20 2 E7
Leigh Woods Forest Walks★ BS8 5 C1
Leighton Cl BA4 141 E1
Leighton Cres BS24 67 A8
Leighton La BA4 141 E1
Leighton Lane Ind Est BA4 141 E2
Leighton Rd BA1 27 A3
Leighwood Dr BS48 8 B1
Leinster Ave BS4 22 D8
Lemon La BS2 227 C4
Lenover Gdns BS13 22 B4
Lenthay Cl DT9 225 C2
Lenthay Ct DT9 225 C3
Lenthay Rd DT9 225 B2
Leonard Houlden Ct 7 TA2 213 A8
Leonard La BS1 227 A3
Leonard's Barton BA11 119 E6
Leopold Bldgs BA1 228 C4
Lerburne The BS28 108 D4
Les Rosiers Gdns BA9 216 C4
Leslie Ave TA2 212 E6
Leslie Rise BA15 64 F3
Lester Dr BS22 32 A3
Lester La DT9 176 A2
Letham Ct TA19 221 B4
Lethbridge Pk TA4 151 D1
Lethbridge Rd BA5 203 C4
Level La DT9 176 A2
Level View TA10 172 C5
Leversedge Rd BA11 120 A7
Lewins Mead BS1 227 A3
Lewis Cres BA11 119 F6
Lewis Rd Bristol BS13 22 A8
Taunton TA2 212 E7
Lewis's Dro BA5 138 E7
Lewisham Gr BS23 49 A8
Lewmond Ave BA5 203 F5
Leycroft Cl TA1 213 B4
Leycroft Gr TA1 213 B4
Leycroft Rd TA1 213 B4
Leyland Wlk BS13 21 F4
Leys Hill BA11 120 A6
Leys La BA11 119 F7
Leys The BS21 6 B1
Leystone Cl BA11 120 A6
Leyton Dr TA6 209 D6
Lias Rd BA16 207 B4
Liberty Gdns BS1 226 B1
Liberty La BS40 54 E2
Liberty Pl TA6 209 B4
Liberty The BA5 203 E5
Liddon Hill TA18 195 C5
Liddymore La
Watchet TA23 202 D5
Williton TA4,TA23 202 E4
Liddymore Rd TA23 202 C6
Lightgate TA13 220 D5
Lightgate La TA13 220 D4
Lightgate Rd TA13 220 D4
Lilac Cl TA1 213 C2
Lilac Ct BS31 24 C4
Lilac Terr BA3 78 C2
Lilac Way BS22 32 A5
Lilian Terr BS39 77 E5
Lillebonne Cl TA21 222 F6
Lillesdon Terr TA3 170 A2
Lillington Cl BA3 79 B2
Lillington Rd BA3 79 B2
Lillington Way TA20 223 C5
Lilly Batch BA11 119 F7
Lillycombe La TA3 EX15 191 B8
Lillypool Cheese & Cider Farm★ BS25 70 F6
Lily La BA8 176 E1
Limber Rd BA22 218 A6
Limbers La BA5 139 B8
Limbury 2 TA12 185 E6
Limbury Cotts 3 TA12 185 E6
Lime Cl Frome BA11 120 B7
Locking BS24 50 B4
Minehead TA24 200 D7
Street BA16 207 C5
Weston-Super-Mare BS22 32 A1
Lime Cres TA1 213 C2
Lime Ct BS31 24 C4
Lime Gr Bath BA2 45 B6
Shepton Mallet BA4 205 A6
Lime Grove Gdns BA2 45 B6
Lime Grove Sch BA2 45 B6
Lime Kiln BA21 218 C5
Lime Kiln La
Castle Cary BA7 214 E4
Clevedon BS21 6 D3
Henstridge BA8 190 A6
Wookey Hole BA5 203 B7
Lime St
Nether Stowey TA5 134 B2
Stogursey TA5 134 C6
Lime Terr BA3 78 D1
Lime Tree Ave BA20 218 E2
Lime Tree Cl TA6 209 D4
Lime Tree Gr BS20 4 D3
Limebreach Wood BS48 8 D3
Limeburn Hill BS40 38 E5
Limekiln La Bath BA2 45 F4
Chard TA20 194 C3
Chard TA20 223 D1
Cricket St Thomas TA20 194 E2
Limekiln La *continued*
Leigh upon Mendip BA11 117 C3
Oakhill BA3 114 E5
Stoke St Michael BA3 115 F4
Tatworth TA20 193 F1
Limekilns Cl BS31 24 F5
Limepits La TA10 172 D5
Limerick Cl DT9 217 D2
Limerick La BA11 101 F2
Limes Cl TA4 202 E3
Limestone Hill TA5 135 C1
Limington Rd BA22 173 E1
Limpetshell La TA4 202 E3
Limpley Stoke Rd BA15 64 D6
Linch La BA4 142 D2
Lincolm Hill TA19 184 E4
Lincoln Cl BS31 24 C4
Lincombe Rd BA3 97 D8
Lincott View BA2 79 C8
Linden Ave BS23 49 B8
Linden Cl Bridgwater TA6 209 C4
Bristol, Stockwood BS14 23 E6
Frome BA11 119 D5
Radstock BA3 97 E8
Linden Ct BS21 6 D4
Linden Gdns BA1 44 D8
Linden Gr TA1 212 E5
Linden Hill TA21 222 A6
Linden Rd Clevedon BS21 6 D4
Yeovil BA20 218 F5
Lindens The BS22 31 E4
Lindisfarne Cl BA15 64 E6
Lindsey Cl BS20 1 F4
Lindsey Cres 1 TA6 153 F3
Linemere Cl BS48 19 D6
Lines Way BS14 23 C3
Liney Rd TA7 154 F6
Lingfield Ave BA21 219 D7
Linham Rd TA6 208 F6
Linhay Cl EX15 179 E1
Link La Burrington BS40 53 F3
Monkton Farleigh BA15 46 F8
Link Rd Nailsea BS48 8 F2
Portishead BS20 2 C5
Link The BS27 90 B8
Linkhay TA20 198 D8
Linkhay Cl TA20 198 D8
Linkmead BA3 96 F2
Links Ct BS23 48 D4
Links Gdns TA8 84 F3
Links Rd BS23 48 C2
Linkside BS21 6 E6
Linley Cl Bath BA2 44 A5
Bridgwater TA6 209 D7
Linleys The BA1 44 C7
Linne Ho BA2 44 A5
Linnet Cl Taunton TA1 212 B4
Weston-Super-Mare BS22 31 E1
Linnet Way Frome BA11 120 B6
Midsomer Norton BA3 97 B8
Linsvale Cl BA11 120 C5
Linsvale Dr BA11 120 C5
Lintern Cl BA4 159 C7
Lion Cl BS48 8 D2
Lion Ho 20 BA4 205 B6
Lion Mews TA11 211 E4
Lipe Hill La TA3,TA4 168 B1
Lipe La TA3 169 C3
Lipgate Pl BS20 2 D3
Lippetts Way TA7 137 D1
Lippiat Hill BA3 80 C3
Lippiatt La Cheddar BS27 90 C7
Shipham BS25 70 F8
Timsbury BA2 60 B3
Lippiatt The BS27 90 C8
Lisieux Ct TA1 213 D2
Lisieux Way TA1 213 C3
Lisle Rd BS22 32 B4
Lister Gr BA15 64 F3
Lister's Hill TA19 221 C2
Listercombe Cl TA19 221 C2
Litfield Pl BS8 11 F7
Litfield Rd BS8 11 F8
Litt Hill BA3 75 F2
Little Ann St BS2, BS5 227 C4
Little Birch Croft BS14 23 A3
Little Bishop St BS2 227 B4
Little Brooks La BA4 205 C4
Little Burrow Dro TA7 155 A1
Little Caroline Pl 4 BS8 11 F5
Little Cl TA2 212 C8
Little Elm Rd TA7 155 C4
Little England TA7 155 C2
Little Entry BA5 203 F5
Little Field La BA5 110 F7
Little George St
Bristol BS2 227 C4
Weston-Super-Mare BS23 48 E7
Little Gn BA5 111 A4
Little Halt BS20 1 E4
Little Ham BS21 16 C8
Little Headley Cl BS13 22 B7
Little Keyford La BA11 119 E1
Little King St BS1 227 A2
Little La Farmborough BA2 60 A6
Kingsbury Episcopi TA12 185 A7
Little Leaze La TA7 137 D2
Little Lester TA19 221 C2
Little Marston Rd BA22 174 F1
Little Mdw
6 Bishops Lydeard TA4 167 F8
Ilchester BA22 173 E2
Little Mead TA14 185 F2
Little Mead Cl BS24 49 E3
Little Meadow End BS48 18 E8
Little Moor Rd TA9 106 F3
Little Orch Cheddar BS27 90 C8
Street BA16 207 D7

Meadway *continued*
Temple Cloud BS39 ... 58 E1
Woolavington TA7 ... 136 E4
Meadway Ave BS48 ... 8 D2
Mearcombe La BS24 ... 67 F6
Meardon Rd BS14 ... 23 E6
Meare BS24 ... 48 F2
Meare Prim Sch BA6 ... 138 D4
Meare Rd Bath BA2 ... 45 A2
Glastonbury BA6 ... 206 B6
Meareway BA6 ... 138 C5
Mearn's Cross BA3 ... 94 B6
Mede Cl BS1 ... 227 B1
Medical Ave BS2, BS8 ... 226 C3
Medway Cl
Keynsham BS31 ... 25 A3
Taunton TA1 ... 213 D4
Medway Dr BS31 ... 25 A3
Meetinghouse La BS49 ... 18 A1
Melbourne House Mews
BA5 ... 203 D4
Melbourne Pl TA6 ... 209 B6
Melbourne Terr 2 BS21 ... 6 D2
Melcombe Ct BA2 ... 44 D4
Melcombe La TA6 ... 153 E3
Melcombe Rd BA2 ... 44 D4
Mellanby Cl BA16 ... 207 D5
Mellent Ave BS13 ... 22 C3
Mells CE Fst Sch BA11 ... 118 A6
Mells Cl BS31 ... 25 A2
Mells La BA3 ... 79 B1
Melrose Ave Bristol BS8 ... 226 B4
Wells BA5 ... 203 C4
Melrose Ct BA5 ... 203 C4
Melrose Gr BA2 ... 44 B3
Melrose Pl BS8 ... 226 B4
Melrose Rd BA21 ... 219 B6
Melrose Terr BA1 ... 28 A2
Melsbury La BA5 ... 139 E6
Memorial Ave TA18 ... 224 C5
Memorial Rd
Houndstone BA22 ... 218 B6
Wrington BS40 ... 35 E2
Mendip Ave
Shepton Mallet BA4 ... 205 E4
Weston-Super-Mare BS22 ... 31 F2
Mendip Centre (Coll) The
BS40 ... 54 D2
Mendip Cl Axbridge BS26 ... 70 D2
Frome BA11 ... 120 A7
Keynsham BS31 ... 24 D5
3 Nailsea BS48 ... 8 E1
Paulton BS39 ... 77 E4
Yatton BS49 ... 34 B7
Mendip Dr BA11 ... 120 A7
Mendip Edge BS24 ... 66 F8
Mendip Fields BA3 ... 96 C2
Mendip Gdns Bath BA2 ... 62 D8
Frome BA11 ... 120 B7
Yatton BS49 ... 34 B7
Mendip Green Fst Sch
BS22 ... 31 E1
Mendip Ho TA1 ... 212 F3
Mendip Lea Cl BS27 ... 90 F2
Mendip Lodge BS25 ... 70 A8
Mendip Rd
Bridgwater TA6 ... 209 C4
Locking BS24 ... 50 D4
Portishead BS20 ... 2 D5
Rooksbridge BS26 ... 87 A6
Stoke St Michael BA3 ... 116 A2
Weston-Super-Mare BS23 ... 49 A7
Yatton BS49 ... 34 B7
Mendip Rise BS24 ... 50 B4
Mendip Vale BA3 ... 116 E7
Mendip Vale Sta★ BA4 ... 205 F3
Mendip Vale Trad Est
BS27 ... 90 A7
Mendip View
Coleford BA3 ... 116 F7
Street BA16 ... 207 B7
Mendip Villas
Cheddar BS27 ... 71 A1
Compton Martin BS40 ... 73 F7
Emborough BA3 ... 95 E3
Mendip Way
Burnham-On-Sea TA8 ... 104 B7
Radstock BA3 ... 78 F3
Menlea BS40 ... 54 D3
Mercer Ct BS14 ... 23 B8
Merchant St BS1 ... 227 B3
Merchants Barton Ind Est
BA11 ... 119 F4
Merchants Ct BS8 ... 226 A1
Merchants Quay BS1 ... 227 A1
Merchants Rd
Bristol BS8 ... 226 A3
Bristol, Hotwells BS8 ... 226 A1
Merchants Row BS1 ... 226 C1
Merchants' Barton 3
BA11 ... 119 F4
Meredith Cl BA22 ... 197 C3
Meredith Ct BS1 ... 226 A1
Meriden BA1 ... 44 D8
Meridian Pl BS8 ... 226 B3
Meridian Vale BS8 ... 226 B3
Meriet Ave BS13 ... 22 B4
Merle Cl TA6 ... 209 B4
Merlin Cl Bristol BS9 ... 5 F8
Weston-Super-Mare BS22 ... 49 E8
Merlin Dr BA5 ... 203 B5
Merlin Ind Pk TA2 ... 213 B6
Merlin Pk BS20 ... 2 A4
Merrick Ct BS1 ... 227 A1
Merrick Rd BA6 ... 206 E7
Merridge Cl TA6 ... 208 A4
Merridge Hill TA5 ... 152 D6
Merrifields TA4 ... 167 E6
Merriman Gdns BA16 ... 207 C5
Merriman Rd BA16 ... 207 C5
Merrimans Rd BS11 ... 4 D8
Merriott Fst Sch TA16 ... 195 F7
Merriott Rd
Hinton St George TA17 ... 195 D7
Merriott TA16 ... 195 F6
Merry La TA9 ... 136 F8
Merry-field BA3 ... 116 E8
Merryfield La
Doulting BA4 ... 141 F5
Ilton TA19 ... 183 E4
Merryfield Rd BS24 ... 50 B6
Merryfields TA9 ... 106 D5
Merthyr Guest Cl BA8 ... 176 E1
Merton Dr BS24 ... 50 A8
Mervyn Ball Cl TA20 ... 223 C5
Methwyn Cl BS22 ... 49 C7
Mews The Bath BA1 ... 44 A8
4 Bridgwater TA6 ... 209 B4
East Coker BA22 ... 197 C7
Minehead TA24 ... 201 A7
Wiveliscombe TA4 ... 210 C4
Mewswell Dr BS27 ... 71 B1
Michaels Mead BA1 ... 27 B2
Middle Ave BS1 ... 227 A2
Middle Brooks BA16 ... 207 C3
Middle Dro
Baltonsborough BA6 ... 158 B4
Compton Dundon TA11 ... 156 F3
Glastonbury BA6 ... 206 B5
Hambridge TA10,TA12 ... 184 F8
Lydford-on-Fosse TA11 ... 158 C3
Rodney Stoke BS27 ... 109 C6
Street BA6 ... 157 C7
Middle Field La DT9 ... 188 B7
Middle Gate TA10 ... 172 D8
Middle Green Rd TA21 ... 222 E3
Middle La Bath BA1 ... 28 B1
Kingston Seymour BS21 ... 15 F4
Middle Leaze Dro TA12 ... 185 F7
Middle Leigh BA16 ... 207 C5
Middle Moor Dro TA5 ... 134 D7
Middle Moor La BS27 ... 89 E7
Middle Path TA18 ... 224 B5
Middle Rd TA7 ... 137 A3
Middle Ridge La DT9 ... 175 D1
Middle St Ashcott TA7 ... 156 B7
Burnham-On-Sea TA9 ... 85 E5
Crewkerne TA18 ... 224 F3
East Harptree BS40 ... 74 F4
East Lambrook TA13 ... 220 C8
Galhampton BA22 ... 175 D8
Kingsdon TA11 ... 173 D5
Martock TA12 ... 185 D4
Minehead TA24 ... 200 F8
Montacute TA15 ... 186 B3
North Perrott TA18 ... 196 C4
Puriton TA7 ... 136 C4
Rimpton BA22 ... 188 A8
Shepton Beauchamp TA19 ... 184 E3
Taunton TA1 ... 212 F4
Yeovil BA20 ... 219 B4
Middle Stoke BA3 ... 64 A6
Middle Touches TA20 ... 223 E5
Middle Way TA11 ... 157 B4
Middle Yeo Gn BS48 ... 8 D3
Middle's La BA4 ... 140 C4
Middlecombe Cross
TA24 ... 200 C6
Middlefield La TA10 ... 184 D6
Middlefield Rd TA10 ... 172 C7
Middleford Ho BS13 ... 22 C4
Middlegate Rd TA10 ... 172 C7
Middlemead BA3 ... 96 F3
Middlepiece La BA2,BS31 ... 42 B7
Middleroom Dro TA3 ... 182 E4
Middlestream Cl TA6 ... 208 D2
Middleton La
Clatworthy TA4 ... 149 C2
Shepton Mallet BA4 ... 205 B4
Middleton Rd BS11 ... 4 F8
Middleway TA1 ... 212 E2
Middleway Ct TA1 ... 212 E2
Middleway Rd BA4 ... 158 E8
Middlezoy Prim Sch
TA7 ... 155 B3
Midelney Rd TA10 ... 171 E2
Midford BS24 ... 48 F2
Midford Hill BA2,BA3 ... 63 C5
Midford La BA2,BA3 ... 63 E7
Midford Rd
Southstoke BA2 ... 63 B7
Taunton TA1 ... 213 B4
Midhaven Rise BS22 ... 31 E4
Midland Bridge Rd BA1,
BA2 ... 228 A2
Midland Rd Bath BA1 ... 44 D7
Bristol BS2 ... 227 C3
Midland St BS2 ... 227 C2
Midleaze DT9 ... 225 A3
Midney La BA9 ... 177 D8
Midsomer Ent Pk BA3 ... 78 C2
Midsomer Norton Prim Sch
BA3 ... 78 B1
Midsomer Norton Railway
Ctr★ BA3 ... 97 A8
Midsummer Bldgs BA1 ... 28 B2
Milborne Port Bsns Ctr
DT9 ... 217 D2
Milborne Port Prim Sch
DT9 ... 217 D2
Milbourne Cl BA15 ... 64 D7
Milburn Rd BS23 ... 48 F7
Milbury Gdns BS22 ... 31 C2
Mildmay Dr BA22 ... 174 F3
Mildmay's Rd TA10 ... 155 F1
Mildred Rd BA16 ... 156 E7
Mile Wlk BS14 ... 23 A6
Miles St BA2 ... 228 C1
Miles's Bldgs BA1 ... 228 B3
Milestone Cl TA6 ... 153 F4
Milestone Ct BS22 ... 32 D2
Milford Inf Sch BA21 ... 219 B7
Milford Jun Sch BA21 ... 219 B7
Milford Pl 2 TA1 ... 213 A4
Milford Rd BA21 ... 219 C7
Milk St Bath BA1 ... 228 B2
Frome BA11 ... 119 E5
Milking La BS27 ... 90 E2
Mill Ave BS1 ... 227 A2
Mill Batch Farm Ind Est
TA9 ... 86 F4
Mill Cl Cannington TA5 ... 135 B2
East Coker BA22 ... 197 C8
Frome BA11 ... 119 F6
Nether Stowey TA5 ... 134 A2
Portbury BS20 ... 3 D2
Mill Cotts TA3 ... 169 D4
Mill Cross Halstock BA22 ... 197 C3
Kingston St Mary TA2 ... 168 E7
Mill Ct TA23 ... 202 B7
Mill Farm Hill TA5 ... 134 F1
Mill Gdns TA24 ... 201 D1
Mill Hill BA2 ... 62 E1
Mill La Alhampton BA4 ... 159 C5
Axbridge BS26 ... 88 D4
Axminster EX13 ... 198 F3
Batcombe BA4 ... 142 C1
Bath BA2 ... 44 B6
Bathampton BA2 ... 28 F2
Beckington BA11 ... 101 D5
Bishops Lydeard TA4 ... 167 F8
Bitton BS30 ... 25 E8
Bourton SP8 ... 161 F1
Bradford Abbas DT9 ... 187 E1
Bruton BA10 ... 215 E6
Cannington TA5 ... 135 B2
Chard TA20 ... 223 C3
Chard, Wambrook TA20 ... 193 C2
Charlton Mackrell TA11 ... 173 E7
Chew Stoke BS40 ... 56 D8
Clatworthy TA4 ... 149 E2
Compton Martin BS40 ... 74 A7
Congresbury BS49 ... 34 D4
Corfe TA3 ... 181 F6
Corsley Heath BA11,BA12 ... 144 C8
Creech St Michael TA3 ... 169 D4
Crewkerne TA18 ... 224 D5
Crewkerne, Misterton
TA18 ... 196 B3
Dinnington TA17 ... 195 B8
Dunster TA24 ... 201 D1
East Coker BA22 ... 197 B8
East Coker BA22 ... 197 C7
East Huntspill TA9 ... 136 D8
Exford TA24 ... 128 C2
Halstock BA22 ... 197 C3
Higher Chillington TA19 ... 194 E5
Ilchester BA22 ... 173 F1
Ilminster TA19 ... 221 B7
Ilminster, Dowlish Wake
TA19 ... 194 E7
Ilminster, Kingstone TA19 ... 221 F1
Lopen TA13 ... 185 A1
Lynford-on-Fosse TA11 ... 158 C2
Maiden Bradley BA12 ... 144 D3
Marnhull DT10 ... 190 F6
Milverton TA4 ... 167 A5
Monkton Combe BA2 ... 63 E8
Nether Stowey TA5 ... 134 A2
North Wootton BA4 ... 140 D5
NonRoady TA7 ... 155 C2
Pitcombe BA10 ... 215 C3
Porlock TA24 ... 124 A3
Portbury BS20 ... 3 E3
Priston BA2 ... 61 A7
Redhill BS40 ... 55 A8
Shapwick TA7 ... 155 F8
Shepton Mallet BA4 ... 204 E4
Somerton TA11 ... 211 D2
South Petherton TA13 ... 220 E6
Stoke St Michael BA3 ... 116 B3
Taunton TA3 ... 168 D1
Thurloxton TA2 ... 153 D1
Timsbury BA2 ... 60 B1
Trent DT9 ... 187 F5
Watchet TA23 ... 202 C7
Wedmore BS28 ... 108 E3
Wells BA5 ... 203 A1
West Monkton TA2 ... 169 D8
Wiveliscombe TA4 ... 210 C4
Wrington BS40 ... 53 F8
Yeovil BA20 ... 219 B4
Mill La Trad Est BA20 ... 219 C4
Mill Lane Cl TA3 ... 168 D1
Mill Leat BA6 ... 157 F5
Mill Leg BS49 ... 34 D4
Mill Rd
Barton St David TA11 ... 158 A3
Radstock BA3 ... 79 B2
Mill Rise Bourton SP8 ... 161 F1
Staplegrove TA2 ... 212 B7
Mill Road Ind Est BA3 ... 79 B3
Mill St Carhampton TA24 ... 131 B5
North Petherton TA6 ... 153 F3
Rimpton BA22 ... 188 A8
Watchet TA23 ... 202 C7
Wells BA5 ... 203 D4
Wincanton BA9 ... 216 C4
Mill Stream Cl BS26 ... 70 C1
Mill Stream Gdns TA21 ... 222 B7
Mill Wlk TA7 ... 136 E3
Millands La TA5 ... 133 C6
Millands The TA11 ... 211 E4
Millard's Hill
Batcombe BA4 ... 142 D2
Midsomer Norton BA3 ... 78 C3
Millards Ct BA3 ... 78 B3
Millards Hill BA3 ... 78 B3
Millbatch BA6 ... 138 C4
Millbourne Rd BS27 ... 90 C7
Millbridge Gdns TA24 ... 200 F7
Millbridge Rd TA24 ... 200 E7
Millbrook BA20 ... 219 A4
Millbrook Cross EX13 ... 198 A1
Millbrook Ct BA2 ... 228 C1
Millbrook Dale EX13 ... 198 A1
Millbrook Gdns BA7 ... 214 B5
Millbrook Pl BA2 ... 228 C1
Millcross BS21 ... 16 C8
Millennium Cl BA3 ... 116 A3
Millennium Sq BS1 ... 226 C2
Miller Cl BS23 ... 48 F8
Miller Ho BS8 ... 226 A2
Miller Wlk BA2 ... 28 F1
Miller's Hill DT9 ... 217 A5
Millers Cl BS20 ... 4 C4
Millers Gdns BA5 ... 203 E5
Millers Orch TA3 ... 170 F1
Millers Rise BS22 ... 32 A4
Millers Way 11 TA4 ... 167 F8
Milletts Cl 2 TA24 ... 131 A5
Millfield Chard TA20 ... 223 D3
Ilchester BA22 ... 173 E2
Midsomer Norton BA3 ... 96 F8
Millfield Cl TA20 ... 223 D3
Millfield Pre Prep Sch
BA6 ... 206 D4
Millfield Prep Sch Edgerley
Hall BA6 ... 139 D1
Millfield Sch
Glastonbury BA6 ... 206 E5
Street BA16 ... 207 E5
Millfield Sch (Chindit Ho)
BA6 ... 206 E5
Millford La BA4 ... 159 C6
Millgreen Cl TA9 ... 136 B8
Millground Rd BS13 ... 21 F5
Millham La TA22 ... 163 D6
Millier Rd BS49 ... 35 B8
Milliman Cl BS13 ... 22 C5
Milliner Ct BA4 ... 205 B5
Millmead Ho BS13 ... 22 C4
Millmead Rd BA2 ... 44 C5
Millmoot La TA7 ... 136 F3
Millstream Cl TA24 ... 200 F6
Millward Terr BS39 ... 77 E6
Millway BS27 ... 110 B8
Millwey Ave EX13 ... 198 A2
Millwood Cl TA6 ... 208 E2
Milne Cl TA6 ... 208 F2
Milsom Pl TA4 ... 167 F6
Milsom St BA1 ... 228 B3
Milton Ave Bath BA2 ... 44 F4
Weston-Super-Mare BS23 ... 49 A8
Milton Brow BS22 ... 31 B2
Milton Cl Nailsea BS48 ... 8 E3
Taunton TA1 ... 213 C3
Yeovil BA21 ... 218 C6
Milton Ct BA4 ... 205 B7
Milton Gn BS22 ... 31 C1
Milton Hill
Monkton Heathfield TA2 ... 213 E7
Weston-Super-Mare BS22 ... 31 B2
Milton Ho BA21 ... 187 D6
Milton Jun & Inf Schs
BS22 ... 31 C1
Milton La Martock TA12 ... 185 E8
Wells BA5 ... 203 D5
Wookey Hole BA5 ... 203 B8
Milton Leaze TA10 ... 172 E2
Milton Lodge Gdn★
BA5 ... 203 D7
Milton Park Rd BS22 ... 31 C1
Milton Pl TA6 ... 208 E4
Milton Rd Radstock BA3 ... 78 C1
Taunton TA1 ... 213 C3
Weston-Super-Mare BS22,
BS23 ... 49 B8
Milton Rise BS22 ... 31 C1
Miltons Cl BS13 ... 22 D4
Milverton BS24 ... 48 F2
Milverton Com Prim Sch
TA4 ... 166 F4
Milverton Rd TA21 ... 222 B8
Milward Rd BS31 ... 24 E6
Minchington's Cl TA14 ... 185 F2
Minehead First Sch
TA24 ... 200 F6
Minehead Hospl TA24 ... 200 F7
Minehead La TA22 ... 164 A7
Minehead Mid Sch
TA24 ... 201 A6
Minehead Rd
Bishops Lydeard TA4 ... 167 E8
Bristol, Hengrove BS14 ... 23 A8
Minehead Sta★ TA24 ... 201 B7
Miners Cl BS41 ... 10 F2
Minerva Gdns BA2 ... 44 C4
Minnows The TA20 ... 223 C3
Minsmere Rd BS31 ... 25 A4
Minster Cl TA1 ... 212 C1
Minster Ct TA1 ... 212 C1
Minster Way BA2 ... 45 C8
Mint The BA11 ... 119 E5
Minton Cl BS14 ... 23 B5
Mintons TA20 ... 223 B3
Mintons Orch TA20 ... 223 B3
Misburg Cl BA4 ... 204 F6
Misterton CE Fst Sch
TA18 ... 224 F3
Mitchell Gdns TA20 ... 223 B3
Mitchell La BS1 ... 227 B2
Mitchell St TA21 ... 222 C7
Mitchell Terr BA5 ... 112 E1
Mitchell's Row BA22 ... 175 D6
Mitchelmore Rd BA21 ... 219 B5
Mitford-Slade Ct BS49 ... 34 C7
Mizzymead Cl 1 BS48 ... 8 D1
Mizzymead Rd BS48 ... 8 E1
Mizzymead Rise BS48 ... 8 E1
Moffats Dr BA5 ... 113 A2
Molesworth Cl BS13 ... 22 A4
Molesworth Dr BS13 ... 22 A4
Molly Cl BS39 ... 76 E8
Monarch Ctr TA2 ... 213 C6
Monday's Court La
TA10 ... 172 E5
Money Pit La EX13 ... 193 A1
Monger Cotts BS39 ... 77 F4
Monger La
Midsomer Norton BA3 ... 78 A3
Paulton BS39 ... 78 A4
Monington Rd BA6 ... 206 E6
Monk Cross TA24 ... 128 D1
Monkley La BA11 ... 83 C1
Monks Cl
Rooksbridge BS26 ... 87 B5
Taunton TA1 ... 213 B5
Monks Dale BA21 ... 218 D6
Monks Dr TA7 ... 137 F1
Monks Ford BA5 ... 139 D8
Monks Hill BS22 ... 31 B3
Monks Way TA8 ... 104 B6
Monks' Path TA23,TA24 ... 131 E4
Monksdale Rd BA2 ... 44 D4
Monksford La BA5 ... 139 C8
Monkstone Dr TA8 ... 84 F5
Monksway TA23 ... 131 E4
Monkton Ave BS24 ... 49 A2
Monkton Combe Jun Sch
BA2 ... 45 C1
Monkton Combe Jun Sch
(Pre-Prep) BA2 ... 45 C1
Monkton Combe Senior Sch
BA2 ... 45 E1
Monkton Farleigh Prim Sch
BA15 ... 46 E7
Monkton La TA5 ... 134 D5
Monmouth Cl
Chard TA20 ... 223 E4
Glastonbury BA6 ... 206 D5
Portishead BS20 ... 1 F4
Westonzoyland TA7 ... 154 F6
Monmouth Ct Bath BA1 ... 228 A2
Chard TA20 ... 223 C4
Monmouth Dr BA11 ... 120 B6
Monmouth Farm Cl TA6 ... 135 F5
Monmouth Paddock BA2 ... 81 E5
Monmouth Pl BA1 ... 228 B2
Monmouth Rd
Keynsham BS31 ... 24 D5
Pill BS20 ... 4 C5
Shepton Mallet BA4 ... 205 A5
Taunton TA1 ... 213 B5
Westonzoyland TA7 ... 154 F6
Yeovil BA21 ... 219 D7
Monmouth St Bath BA1 ... 228 B2
Bridgwater TA6 ... 209 A5
Montacute Ho★ TA15 ... 186 B4
Montacute Rd
Montacute TA14,TA15 ... 186 B4
Tintinhull BA22 ... 186 B6
Montague Ct 4 BS2 ... 227 A4
Montague Flats 6 BS2 ... 227 A4
Montague Gdns BA7 ... 214 B5
Montague Hill BS2 ... 227 A4
Montague Hill S 5 BS2 ... 227 A4
Montague Ho 8 BA1 ... 28 C1
Montague Pl BS6 ... 227 A4
Montague Rd
Peasedown St John BA2 ... 79 E5
Saltford BS31 ... 25 D2
Montague St BS1 ... 227 A4
Montague Way TA20 ... 223 C3
Monteclefe CE Jun Sch
TA11 ... 211 E3
Montepelier BS23 ... 48 F8
Montgomery Ct BA11 ... 120 A4
Montpelier E BS23 ... 30 F1
Montrose Rd BA21 ... 219 E7
Montrose Villas BS27 ... 90 C7
Montsurs Cl BA3 ... 96 E3
Monument Cl TA21 ... 222 E4
Monument Rd TA21 ... 222 E3
Moolham La
Ilminster TA19 ... 221 D1
Ilminster, Moolham TA19 ... 194 D7
Moon La TA7 ... 153 E1
Moon St BS2 ... 227 B4
Moon's Dro TA7 ... 155 A1
Moondown La TA13 ... 220 B2
Moonhayes Cross EX14 ... 191 F4
Moonraker Cl 7 TA6 ... 209 B4
Moons Hill BA3 ... 116 B4
Moonshill Cl BA3 ... 116 A3
Moonshill Cotts BA3 ... 116 A3
Moonshill Rd BA3 ... 116 A3
Moor Cl
Compton Dundon TA11 ... 156 F2
Langport TA10 ... 172 A6
Wincanton BA9 ... 216 C3
Moor Croft Rd BS24 ... 49 E3
Moor Dro TA7 ... 155 F6
Moor End Spout BS48 ... 8 D2
Moor Gn BS26 ... 70 C1
Moor Gr BS11 ... 5 A8

Moor House La TA5 . . . .133 E4
Moor La Alhampton BA4 .159 C5
Backwell BS48 . . . . .18 F6
Batcombe BA4 . . . . .142 D1
Brushford TA22 . . . . .163 F4
Churchinford TA3 . . . . . . .192 A7
Clapton In Gordano BS20 . . .2 E1
Clevedon BS21 . . . . .6 E2
Clevedon BS21 . . . . .7 A2
Cucklington SP8 . . . . .177 E5
Draycott BS27 . . . . .90 F1
East Coker BA22 . . . . . . .197 D7
Hardington Mandeville
BA22 . . . . .197 A7
Higher Chillington TA20 . . .194 F5
Hutton BS24 . . . . .49 D3
North Curry TA3 . . . . .170 B4
South Petherton TA13 . . . .220 B3
Tickenham BS21 . . . . .7 F4
Westbury Sub Mendip BA5 110 C5
Weston-Super-Mare BS24 . .49 F7
Wincanton BA9 . . . . .216 C2
Moor Lane Cl TA3 . . . . . .170 B4
Moor Park Rd TA10 . . . .171 F5
Moor Pk Clevedon BS21 . . . .6 E2
Langport TA10 . . . . .171 F5
Moor Rd Banwell BS29 . . . .51 B5
Bridgwater TA7 . . . . .154 F8
Middlezoy TA7 . . . . .155 B4
Minehead TA24 . . . . .200 E8
Moorlinch TA7 . . . . .155 D7
Sutton Mallet TA7 . . . . . . .155 B8
Yatton BS49 . . . . .17 B2
Moor Sherd BS28 . . . . . .110 C1
Moor Villas TA13 . . . . . .220 B3
Moorclose Dro TA7 . . . .137 C3
Moorclose La BA4 . . . . .158 E6
Moore's La TA5,TA6 . . . .208 C7
Moorend Gdns BS11 . . . . . .4 F7
Moores Yd BA14 . . . . .83 C6
Moorfield Gdn TA24 . . . .146 C6
Moorfield Rd BS48 . . . . . .19 A6
Moorfields Cl BA2 . . . . . .44 D3
Moorfields Ct BS48 . . . . . . .8 D2
Moorfields Ho BS48 . . . . . .8 D2
Moorfields Rd Bath BA2 . .44 D4
Nailsea BS48 . . . . .8 D2
Moorgrove Ho BS9 . . . . . . .5 C7
Moorham Rd BS25 . . . . . .52 A1
Moorhouse La TA4 . . . . .165 A8
Moorings The BS20 . . . . . . .4 C4
Moorland Cl TA1 . . . . . .213 C5
Moorland Cotts BS26 . . . .69 F2
Moorland Pl TA1 . . . . . .213 C5
Moorland Rd Bath BA2 . . .44 D5
Bridgwater TA6 . . . . .209 D4
Street BA16 . . . . .207 B7
Taunton TA1 . . . . .213 C5
Weston-Super-Mare BS23 . .48 E4
Moorland St BS26 . . . . . .70 C1
Moorland Way TA6 . . . . .209 D5
Moorlands TA4 . . . . . . .167 F8
Moorlands Cl
16 Martock TA12 . . . . .185 E6
Nailsea BS48 . . . . .8 D2
Moorlands Dr BA3 . . . . . .64 B6
Moorlands Inf Sch BA2 . .44 D4
Moorlands Jun Sch BA2 .44 D3
Moorlands Pk 18 TA12 . .185 E6
Moorlands Pk Sh Ctr 19
TA12 . . . . .185 E6
Moorlands Rd TA16 . . . .195 E6
Moorledge La BS39,BS40 .57 F7
Moorledge Rd BS40 . . . . .39 B1
Moorlinch Right Dro
TA7 . . . . .155 D6
Moorside BS49 . . . . .17 B1
Moorside Ct BS21 . . . . .6 E2
Moorside Villas BS21 . . . . .6 E2
Moortown La TA10 . . . . .171 B2
Moorview Cl BA6 . . . . . .138 C4
Moorway La DT9 . . . . . .188 C6
Moots La TA6 . . . . .209 D4
Morangis Way TA20 . . . .223 B6
Morden Wlk BS14 . . . . . . .23 D7
Moreton Cl BS14 . . . . . . .23 A4
Moreton La BS40 . . . . . . .56 E2
Morford St BA1 . . . . . . .228 B4
Morgan Cl Saltford BS31 . .25 D2
Weston-Super-Mare BS24 . .50 B8
Morgan Way BA2 . . . . . . .79 E7
Morgan's La
East Harptree BS40 . . . . . . .74 F2
8 Frome BA11 . . . . .119 E5
Morgans Bldgs BS20 . . . . . .8 F8
Morgans Hill Cl BS48 . . . .18 D8
Morgans Rise TA1 . . . . .212 A3
Morland Rd TA9 . . . . . . .104 D4
Morlands Ind Pk TA9 . . .104 D4
Morley Terr Bath BA2 . . . .44 D6
Radstock BA3 . . . . .79 A3
Mornington Pk TA21 . . .222 E5
Morpeth Rd BS4 . . . . .22 D8
Morrell's Cross EX16 . . .164 B4
Morrell's La EX16 . . . . . .178 B6
Morris Cl TA19 . . . . .184 C5
Morris La BA1 . . . . .29 B3
Mortimer Cl Bath BA1 . . . .27 B2
Woolavington TA7 . . . . . . .136 E4
Mortimer Rd BS8 . . . . . .226 A3
Morton's La TA10 . . . . . .156 C1
Moseley Gr BS23 . . . . . . .48 E2
Moss Cl TA6 . . . . .209 C6
Moss La TA3 . . . . .169 C3
Mosterton Down La
DT8 . . . . .196 A1
Moulton Cl BA4 . . . . . . .205 A4
Mounsdon Cl BA6 . . . . . .157 E4
Mount Beacon Row 1
BA1 . . . . .28 A1
Mount Gr BA2 . . . . .44 B3
Mount Hey TA11 . . . . . . .211 E3
Mount Hindrance Cl
TA20 . . . . .223 D6
Mount Hindrance La
TA20 . . . . .223 D6
Mount Ho TA1 . . . . .212 F3
Mount La
Charlton Horethorne DT9 .176 A1
Golsoncott TA23,TA24 . . . .131 C1
Mount Nebo TA1 . . . . . . .212 E2
Mount Pleasant Bath BA2 45 D1
Castle Cary BA7 . . . . .214 C5
Crewkerne TA18 . . . . .224 D6
Frome BA11 . . . . .119 F2
Kilmington BA12 . . . . .161 F6
Pill BS20 . . . . .4 D4
Pilton BA4 . . . . .140 F3
Radstock BA3 . . . . .79 B2
Yeovil BA21 . . . . .219 C5
Mount Pleasant Ave
BA5 . . . . .203 B5
Mount Rd Bath BA1 . . . .228 B4
Nether Stowey TA5 . . . . . .134 A2
Mount St
Bishops Lydeard TA4 . . . . .167 E8
Bridgwater TA6 . . . . .208 F5
Taunton TA1 . . . . .212 F3
Mount Terr TA1 . . . . . . .213 A3
Mount The Frome BA11 . . .119 F2
Taunton TA1 . . . . .212 F3
Yatton BS49 . . . . .34 C8
Mount View Bath BA1 . . . .28 A1
Bath BA2 . . . . .44 B3
Woolavington TA7 . . . . . . .136 E4
Mount View Terr TA6 . . .135 F6
Mountain Ash BA1 . . . . . .27 D1
Mountain Wood BA1 . . . .29 C2
Mountain's La BA2 . . . . . .59 E6
Mountbatten Cl
Burnham-On-Sea TA8 . . . . .85 A1
Weston-Super-Mare BS22 . .31 E4
Mountbatten Ho TA6 . . . .209 C5
Mounter's Hill EX13,
TA20 . . . . .193 B2
Mounters Cl DT10 . . . . . .190 F5
Mountery Cl BA5 . . . . . .203 D5
Mountery Rd BA5 . . . . . .203 D5
Mountfields Ave TA1 . . .213 B1
Mountfields Pk TA1 . . . .213 B1
Mountfields Rd TA1 . . . .213 B1
Mountsfield BA11 . . . . . .120 A2
Mountway TA1 . . . . .213 A3
Mountway Cl TA1 . . . . . .212 C4
Mountway La TA1 . . . . . .212 C4
Mountway Rd TA1 . . . . . .212 C4
Movey La BA22 . . . . .173 F1
Mow Barton Bristol BS13 . .21 F6
8 Martock TA12 . . . . .185 E6
Mow Barton Rd TA11 . . .173 D5
Mowbray Rd BS14 . . . . . . .23 C7
Mowcroft Rd BS13 . . . . . .22 D4
Mowes La DT10 . . . . . . .190 F4
Mowground La TA7 . . . . .137 A3
Mowleaze 11 BA22 . . . . .197 F8
Mowries Ct TA11 . . . . . .211 D4
Moxham Dr BS13 . . . . . . .22 C4
Muchelney Abbey★
TA10 . . . . .172 A3
Muchelney Hill BA6 . . . .158 B5
Muchelney Ho TA19 . . . .221 B3
Muchelney Way BA21 . . .218 C7
Muckleditch La TA19 . . .184 D3
Mud La BS49 . . . . .17 D2
Muddicombe Cross
TA24 . . . . .128 B2
Muddicombe La TA24 . . .128 B2
Muddy La BS22 . . . . .32 A8
Muddyford La TA4 . . . . .151 A3
Mudford Hill BA21 . . . . .187 C5
Mudford Rd BA21 . . . . . .219 B8
Mudgley Cross Roads
BS28 . . . . .108 F1
Mudgley Hill BS28 . . . .108 E1
Mudgley Rd
Rooksbridge BS26 . . . . .87 A4
Wedmore BS28 . . . . .108 E3
Mulberry Ave BS20 . . . . . .2 E5
Mulberry Cl
Backwell BS48 . . . . .19 A6
Portishead BS20 . . . . .2 F5
Taunton TA1 . . . . .213 C2
Weston-Super-Mare BS22 . .32 A1
Mulberry Ct BA11 . . . . . .120 B7
Mulberry Farm BA6 . . . .140 B1
Mulberry Gdns
4 Crewkerne TA18 . . . . . .224 C5
Sherborne DT9 . . . . .225 C5
Mulberry La Bleadon BS24 67 C6
Stoke Sub Hamdon TA14 . .186 A4
Mulberry Rd BS49 . . . . . .34 E3
Mulberry Tree Cl TA6 . . .209 D5
Mulberry Wlk BS9 . . . . . . .5 C8
Mullins Cl BA5 . . . . .203 B3
Mullins Way BA7 . . . . . .214 B6
Mundays Mead BA9 . . . .216 D3
Munden's La DT9 . . . . . .189 A1
Murford Ave BS13 . . . . . .22 B4
Murford Wlk BS13 . . . . . .22 B4
Murhill BA3 . . . . .64 C6
Muriel Terr BA5 . . . . . . .203 D3
Murray-Smith Dr BA22 .218 A6
Murtry Hill La BA11 . . . .100 C2
Mus of Bath at Work★
BA1 . . . . .228 B4
Mus Of Costume★ BA1 .228 B3
Mus of East Asian Art★
BA1 . . . . .228 B3
Musbury Cl DT10 . . . . . .190 F6
Musbury La DT10 . . . . . .190 F6
Museum Of South
Somerset★ BA20 . . . . .219 B4
Musgraves TA22 . . . . . . .163 E6
Musgrove Rd TA1 . . . . . .212 C3
Musmoor La BA22 . . . . . .174 F7
Mutton La BS28 . . . . . . .108 D4
Mutton St DT6 . . . . .199 D1
Mux's La TA4 . . . . .151 B3
Myrtle Cl TA6 . . . . .209 D5
Myrtle Dr Bristol BS11 . . . . .4 E5
Burnham-On-Sea TA8 . . . . .104 A7
Myrtle Gdns BS49 . . . . . . .34 C8
Myrtle Hill BS20 . . . . .4 C5
Myrtle La TA21 . . . . .179 E7
Myrtle Rd Bristol BS2 . . .226 C4
22 Martock TA12 . . . . .185 E6
Myrtle Tree Cres BS22 . . .31 A6
Myrtleberry Mead BS22 . .32 A5
Myrtles The BS24 . . . . . . .49 D2

N

Nag's La TA18 . . . . .195 B1
Nailsea & Backwell Sta
BS48 . . . . .18 F7
Nailsea Cl BS13 . . . . .22 A7
Nailsea Com Sch BS48 . . . .8 E1
Nailsea Moor La BS48 . . .17 F7
Nailsea Pk BS48 . . . . .8 F2
Nailsea Wall BS21 . . . . . .17 C8
Nailsea Wall La BS48 . . . .17 E7
Naish Hill BS20 . . . . .2 F1
Naish Ho BA2 . . . . .44 A6
Naish La BS48 . . . . .20 D3
Naish Rd TA8 . . . . .85 A3
Naish's Cross BA3 . . . . . .96 D3
Naish's St BA11 . . . . . . .119 E5
Naishes Ave BA2 . . . . .79 D7
Naisholt Rd BA4 . . . . . . .204 F6
Nanga-gat Rd BA22 . . . .174 A2
Nanny Hurn's La BS39 . . .58 A1
Napier Ct Bristol BS1 . . .226 B1
Sherborne DT9 . . . . .225 B2
Napier Miles Rd BS11 . . . . .5 A8
Napier Rd BA1 . . . . .27 A3
Narfords La TA20 . . . . . .193 C1
Narrow Plain BS2 . . . . . .227 B2
Narrow Quay BS1 . . . . . .227 A2
Nash Barton BA22 . . . . . .197 C8
Nash Cl BS31 . . . . .25 A5
Nash Gn TA2 . . . . .212 B7
Nash La
Dinnington TA17,TA19 . . . .195 A6
East Coker BA22 . . . . .197 C8
Marshwood DT6 . . . . .199 B2
Yeovil BA20 . . . . .218 D1
Nates La BS40 . . . . .35 F1
Nathan Cl BA20 . . . . . . .218 D2
Naunton Way BS22 . . . . . .31 B2
Neale's Way BA4 . . . . . .141 E2
Neat La BA4 . . . . .204 D1
Neathem Rd BA21 . . . . .219 C7
Nedge Cnr BA3 . . . . .94 D4
Nedge La BA3 . . . . .94 C4
Needhams Patch TA4 . . .167 E6
Nelson Bldgs BA1 . . . . .228 C4
Nelson Ct Bridgwater TA6 208 F5
Weston-Super-Mare BS22 . .31 E4
Nelson Ho BA1 . . . . .228 A3
Nelson Pl BA1 . . . . .228 C4
Nelson Pl W BA1 . . . . . .228 A2
Nelson St BS1 . . . . .227 A3
Nelson Terr BA1 . . . . . . .228 C4
Nelson Villas BA1 . . . . . .228 A2
Nempnett St BS40 . . . . . .55 D5
Neroche View TA3 . . . . .183 A7
Nerrols Dr TA2 . . . . .213 C7
Neston Wlk BS4 . . . . .22 F8
Nether Stowey CE Prim Sch
TA5 . . . . .134 A2
Netherclay TA1 . . . . .212 A4
Netherclay La TA3 . . . . .182 B7
Nethercoombe La DT9 . .225 C5
Nethercott La TA4 . . . . .151 C3
Nethercott Way TA4 . . . .151 A3
Netherhay La DT8 . . . . .199 F8
Nethermoor Rd TA7 . . . .155 B3
Netherstoke La BA22 . . .197 C3
Netherton Cross BA22 . .197 E6
Netherton La
East Coker BA22 . . . . .197 F6
Marston Magna BA22 . . . .175 A1
Netherton Rd BA21 . . . . .219 D7
Netherton Wood La BS48 18 A6
Netherways BS21 . . . . .6 B1
Netley BA21 . . . . .218 D6
Nettle Combe View
BA5 . . . . .113 A2
Nettlebridge Hill BA3 . .115 D5
Nettlecombe Hill
Castle Cary BA7 . . . . .214 F6
Pitcombe BA7 . . . . .215 A2
Nettlecombe Ho BA5 . . .113 A1
Nettlecombe Park Rd
Monksilver TA4 . . . . .132 A1
Sticklepath TA4 . . . . .149 F7
Neva Rd BS23 . . . . .48 E6
Neville Cl 1 TA11 . . . . . .173 F7
Neville Pk BA6 . . . . .158 A5
Nevys La TA4 . . . . .150 E8
New Bglws TA20 . . . . . .223 C3
New Bldgs
Bampton EX16 . . . . .164 C1
Bridgwater TA7 . . . . .209 D1
Frome BA11 . . . . .119 F3
Ilminster TA19 . . . . .221 B1
Oake TA4 . . . . .167 C4
New Bond St BA1 . . . . . .228 C2
New Bond Street Pl
BA1 . . . . .228 C2
New Bristol Rd BS22 . . . .31 E1
New Buildings La BA11 . .119 F3
New Church Rd BS23 . . . .48 D2
New Cl Bourton SP8 . . . . .161 F1
Haselbury Plucknett TA18 .196 B5
Horrington BA5 . . . . .113 A4
Street BA16 . . . . .207 B4
New Cotts
Milton Clevedon BA4 . . . . .160 A8
West Chinnock TA18 . . . . .196 B8
New Cross TA11 . . . . . . .211 C3
New Cross Hill
Barrington TA12,TA13 . . . .184 F6
Kingsbury Episcopi TA12 . .185 A6
New Cut BA5 . . . . .203 D7
New Cut Bow BS21 . . . . . .16 A6
New Fosseway Rd BS14 .23 B6
New Fosseway Sch BS14 23 B6
New Friary Cotts BA11 .143 C3
New Hill TA11 . . . . .211 E4
New King St BA1 . . . . . .228 B2
New Kingsley Rd BS2 . .227 C2
New La Bampton EX16 . . .163 F2
Charlton Horethorne DT9 .176 A1
Creech St Michael TA3 . . .169 D5
Cricket St Thomas TA20 . .194 E4
Haselbury Plucknett TA18 .196 C6
Tatworth TA20 . . . . .198 C8
Witham Friary BA11 . . . . .143 C4
New Orchard St BA1 . . .228 C2
New Park Ho BS21 . . . . . . .6 D5
New Pit Cotts BA2 . . . . . .60 F1
New Rd Axbridge BS26 . . .88 C2
Banwell BS29 . . . . .50 E4
Barwick BA22 . . . . .197 F8
Bathford BA1 . . . . .29 D2
Bawdrip TA7 . . . . .136 D2
Brendon EX35 . . . . .122 D4
Bridgwater TA6 . . . . .209 A5
Burrowbridge TA3,TA7 . . . .170 E8
Burrowbridge TA7 . . . . . . .154 F1
Cannington TA5 . . . . .135 C1
Carhampton TA24 . . . . . . .131 A5
Chard Junction TA20 . . . . .198 F8
Churchill BS25 . . . . .52 F4
Clevedon BS21 . . . . .6 D2
Combe St Nicholas TA20 . .193 D6
Crewkerne TA18 . . . . .195 B4
Draycott BS27 . . . . .91 C3
East Huntspill TA9 . . . . . .136 D8
Freshford BA3 . . . . .64 B5
Hambridge TA12 . . . . .184 E7
Haselbury Plucknett TA18 .196 E6
High Littleton BS39 . . . . . . .59 C3
Higher Odcombe BA22 . . . .186 D3
Hinton St George TA17 . . .195 C7
Houndstone BA22 . . . . . . .218 A5
Ilminster TA19 . . . . .221 B4
Kilmersdon BA3 . . . . .98 E4
Kilmington BA12 . . . . .161 E7
Lyng TA3 . . . . .170 B6
North Wootton BA4 . . . . . .140 A4
Norton Sub Hamdon TA14 . .185 E3
Norton Sub Hamdon TA14 . .185 F1
NonRoady TA7 . . . . .155 C2
Pensford BS39 . . . . .40 D3
Pill BS20 . . . . .4 C4
Porlock TA24 . . . . .123 E3
Redhill BS40 . . . . .37 A4
Seavington TA19 . . . . .184 E1
Sherborne DT9 . . . . .225 E3
Shipham BS25 . . . . .52 E1
South Cadbury BA22 . . . . .175 E4
Stalbridge DT10 . . . . .190 B4
Staple Fitzpaine TA3 . . . . .182 D5
Taunton TA3 . . . . .168 D1
Upottery EX14 . . . . .191 E1
Wanstrow BA4 . . . . .142 D5
Waterrow TA21 . . . . .165 F4
Wedmore BS28 . . . . .108 D8
West Bagborough TA4 . . . .151 E4
Wiveliscombe TA4 . . . . . . .166 A6
New Rock Ind Est BA3 . . .96 D2
New Sq BA5 . . . . .113 A2
New St Bath BA1 . . . . . .228 B2
Bristol BS2 . . . . .227 C3
Long Sutton TA10 . . . . . . .172 E4
Marnhull DT10 . . . . .190 F5
Mells BA11 . . . . .118 B7
North Perrott TA18 . . . . . .196 C4
Somerton TA11 . . . . .211 E4
Wells BA5 . . . . .203 D5
New Street Flats 4
BS2 . . . . .227 C3
New Thomas St BS2 . . . .227 C2
New Way TA10 . . . . .172 B7
Newark St BA1 . . . . .228 C1
Newbarn Park Rd TA1 . .212 B1
Newberry's Patch TA3 . .192 A7
Newbery Cl EX13 . . . . . .198 A1
Newbery La TA18 . . . . . .224 F3
Newbolt Cl BS23 . . . . . . .49 B4
Newbourne Rd BS22 . . . . .49 C8
Newbridge Ct BA1 . . . . . .44 B7
Newbridge Dro TA9 . . . .105 A1
Newbridge Gdns BA1 . . . .44 A8
Newbridge Hill BA1 . . . . .44 B7
Newbridge Ho BS9 . . . . . . .5 C4
Newbridge Jun Sch BA1 .44 B7
Newbridge La TA9 . . . . .104 F1
Newbridge Rd BA1,BA2 . .44 B7
Newbridge St John's Inf Sch
BA1 . . . . .44 B7
Newbury BA12 . . . . .144 E4
Newbury Cotts BA3 . . . .117 A3
Newbury Terr BA21 . . . .218 F7
Newchester Cross TA16 195 E7
Newclose La BS40 . . . . . .56 D1
Newcombe Dr BS9 . . . . . . .5 C4
Newcombe Rd BS9 . . . . . . .5 F7
Newcot Cross EX15 . . . .191 A5
Newditch La BS40 . . . . . .20 C1
Newell DT9 . . . . .225 C4
Newell House Sch DT9 .225 C4
Newfields BS40 . . . . .72 C8
Newfoundland Rd BS2 .227 C4
Newfoundland St BS2 . .227 C4
Newfoundland Way
BS2 . . . . .227 C4
Newgate BS1 . . . . .227 B3
Newgate Cross TA22 . . .163 D7
Newgate La TA4 . . . . . .210 C5
Newhaven Pl BS20 . . . . . . .1 E4
Newhaven Rd BS20 . . . . . .1 D4
Newhouse La TA4 . . . . .165 E6
Newington Cl BA11 . . . .119 E3
Newington Terr BA11 . .119 E4
Newland DT9 . . . . .225 E4
Newland Cross TA24 . . .128 B1
Newland Dr BS13 . . . . . . .22 A4
Newland Flats DT9 . . . .225 E4
Newland Gdn DT9 . . . . .225 E4
Newland Rd Bristol BS13 .22 A3
Weston-Super-Mare BS23 . .48 F6
Newland Wlk BS13 . . . . . .22 A3
Newlands Cl BS20 . . . . . . .2 C5
Newlands Cres TA3 . . . .169 C3
Newlands Gn BS21 . . . . . . .6 E1
Newlands Gr TA3 . . . . . .169 C3
Newlands Hill BS20 . . . . . .2 C4
Newlands Rd
Keynsham BS31 . . . . .24 D4
Ruishton TA3 . . . . .169 C3
Newlyn Ave BS9 . . . . .5 D5
Newlyn Cres TA7 . . . . . .136 B4
Newman Cl BA6 . . . . . . .206 E6
Newmans La
East Huntspill TA9 . . . . . .105 C1
Timsbury BA2 . . . . .60 B2
Newmarket Ave 5 BS1 .227 A3
Newnham Cl BS14 . . . . . .23 D7
Newport Cl Clevedon BS21 .6 C2
Portishead BS20 . . . . .1 F4
Newport Hill TA3 . . . . . .170 B2
Newport Rd BS20 . . . . .4 C5
Newsome Ave BS20 . . . . . .4 C4
Newton Cl
Burnham-On-Sea TA8 . . . . .85 A2
West Harptree BS40 . . . . . .74 E6
Newton Gn BS48 . . . . . . .18 C8
Newton La Bicknoller TA4 132 E1
Corfe TA3 . . . . .181 F6
Newton Rd Barwick BA22 197 F8
Bath BA2 . . . . .43 F6
North Petherton TA6 . . . . .153 F3
Taunton TA1 . . . . .213 E4
Weston-Super-Mare BS23 . .48 E6
Yeovil BA20 . . . . .219 D3
Newton Sq 8 EX16 . . . . .164 B1
Newton's Rd
Weston-Super-Mare BS22 . .31 E3
Weston-Super-Mare BS22 . .31 E4
Newtown La BA6 . . . . . . .140 A1
Newtown Pk TA10 . . . . .172 A6
Newtown Rd
Highbridge TA9 . . . . .104 D3
Langport TA10 . . . . .172 A6
Nibley Rd BS11 . . . . .4 E5
Nichol Pl TA4 . . . . .167 F6
Nichol's Rd BS20 . . . . .1 F5
Nicholas Cl TA22 . . . . . .163 E4
Nicholls Cl TA6 . . . . . . .208 D4
Nick Reed's La EX15 . . .180 D1
Nidon La TA7 . . . . .137 D3
Nigel Pk BS11 . . . . .4 E7
Nightingale Acre TA3 . .183 A7
Nightingale Ave BA11 . .120 B6
Nightingale Cl
1 Bridgwater TA6 . . . . . . .209 C4
Burnham-On-Sea TA8 . . . . .85 B1
Wells BA5 . . . . .203 B3
Weston-Super-Mare BS22 . .31 E1
Nightingale Ct 15 TA1 . .213 A4
Nightingale Gdns BS48 . . .8 D2
Nightingale Gr BA4 . . . .205 D5
Nightingale La BA22 . . .174 F6
Nightingale Rise BS20 . . . .1 F3
Nightingale Way BA3 . . . .97 B8
Nightingales TA4 . . . . . .167 E6
Nile St BA1 . . . . .228 A2
Nine Acre Dro TA7 . . . . .138 B2
Nine Acre La TA3 . . . . . .170 B3
Nine Barrows La BA5 . . . .92 E4
Nippors Way BS25 . . . . . .69 F8
Nithsdale Rd BS23 . . . . . .48 E4
Nixon Trad Units BS24 . . .49 A3
No 1 Royal Cres Mus★
BA1 . . . . .228 B3
No Place La TA5 . . . . . .152 E5
Noake Rd DT9 . . . . .225 B3
Noble St TA1 . . . . .213 B4
Noel Coward Cl TA8 . . .104 C6
Nomis Pk BS49 . . . . .34 E2
Norbins Rd BA6 . . . . . . .206 D5
Nordens Mdw TA4 . . . . .210 D4

Oldway Rd
East Anstey TA22 162 F5
Wellington TA21 222 E4
Oliver Brooks Rd BA3 96 E7
Oliver's La TA19 183 B2
Olivier Cl TA8 104 C6
One Elm TA10 172 B7
Onega Ctr BA1 228 A3
Onega Terr BA1 228 A3
Oolite Gr BA2 44 D1
Oolite Rd BA2 44 D1
Orange Gr BA1 228 C2
Orange St BS2 227 C4
Orchard Ave Bristol BS1 226 C2
Midsomer Norton BA3 77 F1
Portishead BS21 7 E4
Orchard Cl Banwell BS29 51 B3
Bishop Sutton BS39 57 C3
Bradford On Tone TA4 167 F1
Bristol, Westbury on Trym BS9 5 F5
Carhampton TA24 131 B5
Castle Cary BA7 214 B7
Cheddar BS27 90 B8
Coleford BA3 117 A7
Congresbury BS49 34 D4
Cossington TA7 137 A3
Coxley BA5 139 E6
Drimpton DT8 199 F8
East Brent TA9 86 E4
East Huntspill TA9 136 E8
Felton BS40 37 C8
Flax Bourton BS48 20 A8
Frome BA11 119 D4
Highbridge TA9 104 E4
Higher Odcombe BA22 186 C2
Keynsham BS31 24 D6
Long Sutton TA10 172 E4
4 North Petherton TA6 153 E3
Portishead BS20 2 D5
Rockwell Green TA21 222 A5
South Petherton TA13 220 C5
Sparkford BA22 175 A5
Taunton TA3 168 D1
Wedmore BS28 108 C4
West Coker BA22 197 A8
Weston-Super-Mare, Kewstoke BS22 31 B3
Weston-Super-Mare, Worle BS22 31 F2
Westwood BA15 64 F3
Wincanton BA9 216 D3
Wrington BS40 35 E2
Yeovil Marsh BA21 187 A5
Orchard Cl The BS24 49 F4
Orchard Cotts
Croscombe BA5 204 B7
Timsbury BA2 60 F1
Orchard Cres BS11 4 D7
Orchard Ct
Cannington TA5 135 B2
Claverham BS49 17 F1
Minehead TA24 201 B4
Street BA16 207 C6
Wellington TA21 222 E6
Orchard Dr Sandford BS25 52 A4
Southwick BA14 83 E3
Taunton TA1 212 A3
Orchard End BS40 74 F4
Orchard Gdns
Paulton BS39 77 E6
West Buckland TA21 180 F7
Orchard Gn TA2 212 F8
Orchard Ho BA21 219 A6
Orchard La
Allerford TA24 124 B4
Bristol BS1 226 C2
Chewton Mendip BA3 94 F6
Crewkerne TA18 224 C6
Evercreech BA4 141 E1
Kingsbury Episcopi TA12 185 B8
Thorncombe TA20 199 B6
Wembdon TA6 208 D5
Orchard Lea Coxley BA5 139 E7
Pill BS20 4 D4
Wells BA5 203 C5
Orchard Mdw TA23 202 F6
Orchard Mead TA19 183 C1
Orchard Paddock BA5 203 A7
Orchard Pk Mobile Home Site BA22 174 D3
Orchard Pl Aller TA10 171 D8
Queen Camel BA22 174 F3
Weston-Super-Mare BS23 48 E7
Orchard Rd Axbridge BS26 70 C1
Backwell BS48 19 A6
Carhampton TA24 131 B5
Clevedon BS21 6 D2
Hutton BS24 49 E2
Long Ashton BS41 10 F1
Milborne Port DT9 217 C2
Minehead TA24 200 F8
Nailsea BS48 8 D1
Paulton BS39 77 E6
Somerton TA11 211 B4
Street BA16 207 C6
Orchard Rise
Crewkerne TA18 224 C5
Fivehead TA3 170 F2
Porlock TA24 124 A3
Ruishton TA3 169 C4
Orchard St Bristol BS1 226 C2
Frome BA11 119 E5
Weston-Super-Mare BS23 48 E8
Yeovil BA20 219 A4
Orchard Terr Bath BA2 44 B6
Glastonbury BA6 206 D5
Orchard The
Banwell BS29 51 A3
Bath BA2 45 B1
Freshford BA3 64 C5
Holywell Lake TA21 179 E7
Locking BS24 50 A5
Meare BA6 138 D4
Pensford BS39 40 E4
Pill BS20 4 C4
Stanton Drew BS39 40 A2
Weston-Super-Mare BS24 50 A8
Orchard Vale
Ilminster TA19 221 B3
Langport TA10 172 A5
Midsomer Norton BA3 77 F1
Orchard View
Baltonsborough BA6 158 B6
Haselbury Plucknett TA18 196 C6
Orchard Way
Charlton Horethorne DT9 176 A2
Cheddar BS27 90 B8
Crewkerne TA18 224 F3
Keinton Mandeville TA11 158 A1
Peasedown St John BA2 79 D7
Shapwick TA7 137 F1
Taunton TA1 213 D5
Timberscombe TA24 130 B5
Williton TA4 202 E4
Woolavington TA7 136 E3
Orchard Wlk
Churchill BS25 52 E4
Milborne Port DT9 217 C2
Orchardleigh BA22 196 E8
Orchardleigh View BA11 119 D6
Orchards The
Bristol, Shirehampton BS11 4 E6
Stocklinch TA19 184 C4
Orchid Cl TA1 169 A1
Orchids The TA8 85 A2
Oriel Dr BA6 206 D4
Oriel Gdns BA1 28 C2
Oriel Gr BA2 44 B4
Oriel Rd BA16 207 C5
Orme Dr BS21 6 D5
Ormerod Rd BS9 5 E5
Orneage Cl BA11 101 E8
Orwell Dr BS31 25 A4
Osborne Ave BS23 48 F7
Osborne Gr TA1 212 E3
Osborne Pl TA16 195 F7
Osborne Rd Bath BA1 44 B7
Bridgwater TA6 208 F6
Bristol BS3 226 C1
Weston-Super-Mare BS23 48 F7
Yeovil BA20 219 A5
Osborne Villas BS2 226 C4
Osborne Wallis Ho BS8 226 A1
Osborne Way TA1 212 E3
Osborne Wlk TA8 104 C6
Oslings La BA1 29 B2
Osmond Dr BA5 203 B3
Osprey Ct BS14 22 D5
Osprey Gdns BS22 31 F1
Ostrey Mead BS27 90 B7
Othery Village Prim Sch TA7 155 C2
Ottawa Rd BS23 48 F3
Otter Rd 1 BS21 6 E1
Otter Vale Cl EX14 191 F1
Otterford Cl BS14 23 B5
Otterham La TA3 183 F8
Otterhampton Prim Sch TA5 135 B5
Ottery La DT9 225 C3
Our Lady of Mount Carmel RC Prim Sch BA9 216 C3
Our Lady of the Rosary Cath Prim Sch BS11 5 A8
Outer Circ TA1 213 D5
Outer Gullands TA1 212 D2
Oval The BA2 44 C4
Over Innox BA11 119 F6
Overbrook Bsns Ctr BS28 107 D4
Overcombe BA8 189 E8
Overdale
Peasedown St John BA2 60 F3
Radstock BA3 78 E5
Overhill BS20 4 D4
Overland La TA3 170 C3
Overlands
North Curry TA3 170 C4
Ruishton TA3 169 C4
Overleigh Street BA16 207 C3
Street BA16 207 C4
Overton BA9 216 D4
Owen Dr BS8 10 B4
Owen St TA21 222 C6
Owl St
South Petherton TA13 220 B8
Stocklinch TA19 184 C3
Owlaborough La EX36 162 B2
Owsley Cotts TA19 184 E4
Oxen La TA3 170 B3
Oxen Rd TA18 224 C6
Oxendale BA16 207 B5
Oxenpill BA6 138 C4
Oxford Pl
19 Bristol, Clifton BS8 11 F6
10 Taunton TA2 213 A8
Weston-Super-Mare BS23 48 D7
Oxford Rd BA21 219 E7
Oxford Row BA1 228 B3
Oxford Sq BS24 50 B6
Oxford St Bristol BS2 226 C4
Oxford St *continued*
Bristol BS2 227 C2
Burnham-On-Sea TA8 104 B6
Evercreech BA4 141 E1
Weston-Super-Mare BS23 48 D7
Oxford Terr 3 TA6 209 B4
Oxhayes DT8 199 F8
Oxhouse La Failand BS8 10 B6
Winford BS40 37 D6
Oxleaze
5 Bishops Lydeard TA4 167 F8
Bristol BS13 22 D4
Oxleaze La BS41 21 E3
Oxley Cotts DT9 225 C4
Ozenhay BS39 75 E6

P

Pack Horse La BA2 62 F7
Packers' Way TA18 196 B3
Packsaddle Way BA11 119 F7
Paddles La BA11 119 D1
Paddock Cl TA3 169 D5
Paddock Dr TA9 104 D4
Paddock Gdn BS14 22 F4
Paddock Park Homes BS22 32 B2
Paddock The
Banwell BS29 51 A3
Clevedon BS21 6 D2
Corston BA2 43 B7
Dulverton TA22 163 D6
Galhampton BA22 175 D8
Portishead BS20 2 D4
Taunton, Dowsland TA1 168 F1
Taunton, Trull TA3 168 D1
Paddock Wlk DT9 217 C2
Paddock Woods BA2 45 D2
Paddocks Cvan Pk The BS26 87 A7
Paddocks The Bath BA2 45 B1
Ilchester BA22 173 E1
Sandford BS25 52 C4
Wellington TA21 222 E5
Weston-Super-Mare BS23 48 D2
Padfield Cl BA2 44 B5
Padfield Gn BA4 141 E6
Padleigh Hill BA2 44 B2
Padstow Rd BS4 22 F8
Paganel Cl TA24 200 F6
Paganel Rd TA24 200 F6
Paganel Rise TA24 200 E6
Paganel Way TA24 200 E6
Pagans Hill BS40 38 D2
Page La BA6 140 A2
Page's Ct BS49 34 C8
Page's Hill BA16 207 C1
Pageant Dr DT9 225 D3
Pages Mead BS11 4 C8
Paintmoor La TA20 194 B4
Palace Ct BA5 203 D3
Palace Gdns TA4 210 C4
Palace Yard Mews BA1 228 B2
Palfrey's La TA20 193 D3
Palm Tree Cl TA6 209 E5
Palmer Cl TA6 208 F2
Palmer Row 7 BS23 48 E8
Palmer St Frome BA11 119 F4
South Petherton TA13 220 C4
Weston-Super-Mare BS23 48 E8
Palmer's Elm BS24 33 B4
Palmer's End La TA12 184 F7
Palmer's Way BS24 49 D2
Palmers Cl TA8 104 D8
Palmers Rd BA6 206 D4
Palmerston Rd TA1 212 D5
Panborough Dro BA5 138 F8
Paquet Ho BS20 4 D5
Parade Nurseries TA24 200 F7
Parade The Bath BA2 44 B6
Bristol, Bishopsworth BS13 22 A6
Bristol, Shirehampton BS11 4 E6
Chardstock EX13 198 A7
Minehead TA24 200 F7
Paradise Cres BA4 141 E2
Paradise La
Glastonbury BA6 139 D2
Langport TA10 172 A7
Tatworth TA20 193 F1
Paradise Rd BA6 206 D5
Paradise Row BS39 41 A6
Paragon Ct BS23 30 C1
Paragon Rd BS23 30 C1
Paragon Sch The BA2 45 A3
Paragon The Bath BA1 228 C3
Bristol BS8 11 F6
Paray Dr BA5 203 F5
Parbrook Ct BS14 23 B5
Parbrook La BA6 158 D7
Parcroft Com Jun Sch BA20 218 F5
Parcroft Gdns BA20 218 F5
Pardlestone La TA5 133 C5
Parfields BA20 218 F5
Parish Brook Rd BS48 8 B2
Parish Hill BA22 175 D5
Parish Land La TA5 152 D5
Parish Wharf Est BS20 2 D6
Park Ave Bath BA2 228 B1
Bridgwater TA6 208 D4
Castle Cary BA7 214 B4
Yatton BS49 17 B1
Park Barn La TA19 183 C4
Park Batch BS40 54 F3
Park Bglws EX16 179 B3
Park Cl
Barton St David TA11 158 A3
Park Cl *continued*
Cossington TA7 136 F3
Keynsham BS31 24 D5
Paulton BS39 77 D5
Staplehay TA3 181 D8
Street BA16 207 C5
Park Cnr Hambridge TA3 184 B7
Leigh upon Mendip BA11 117 D3
Park Cotts TA20 223 B5
Park Cres Chard TA20 223 B5
Cossington TA7 136 F3
Park Ct 8 BS23 48 E5
Park End BS29 50 E4
Park Farm BA6 206 C4
Park Farm Rd BA6 206 C4
Park Gdns Bath BA1 44 D8
Yeovil BA20 219 A5
Park Gr DT10 190 B4
Park Hayes BA3 116 F3
Park Hill Bristol BS11 4 F6
Pilton BA4 140 E3
Whatley BA11 118 C7
Park Hill Dr BA11 119 F6
Park Ho BA2 44 E4
Park La
Barton St David TA11 158 A3
Bath BA1 44 D7
Blagdon BS40 54 F3
Bridgwater TA7 154 A3
Bristol BS2 226 C3
Cannington TA5 135 B3
Carhampton TA24 131 A5
Castle Cary BA7 214 D7
Clapton TA18 195 B1
Combe St Nicholas TA20 193 C6
Downhead BA4 117 A1
Faulkland BA3 80 B1
Goathurst TA5 153 C4
Henstridge BA8 190 A8
High Ham TA10 156 D1
Ilminster TA19 183 E1
Kingsdon TA11 173 E5
Kingston St Mary TA2 168 C8
Langport TA10 171 E4
Montacute BA22,TA15 186 B3
North Petherton TA6 153 F4
Seavington TA19 184 C1
Thorncombe TA20 199 A7
Wellington TA21 222 C1
Wellington, Chelston TA21 180 E7
Yenston BA8 189 F8
Park Lane Cl TA24 131 A5
Park Pl Bath BA1 228 A4
Bristol BS2 226 C3
Bristol BS8 226 B3
Castle Cary BA7 214 C5
Weston-Super-Mare BS23 48 D8
Park Prep Sch for Boys BA1 44 C8
Park Rd Bath BA1 44 B7
Bridgwater TA6 208 D4
Bristol BS3 226 B1
Bristol, Shirehampton BS11 4 F6
Bruton BA10 215 E5
Chard TA20 223 C4
Clevedon BS21 6 D4
Congresbury BS49 34 E3
Frome BA11 119 E4
Henstridge BA8 190 A6
Keynsham BS31 24 E4
Paulton BS39 77 D5
Shepton Mallet BA4 205 B5
Stalbridge DT10 190 B4
Street BA16 207 C5
Yeovil BA20 219 B5
Park Row BS1 226 C3
Park Sch The BA20 219 A5
Park St Bath BA1 228 A4
Bristol BS1 226 C3
Castle Cary BA7 214 C5
Dunster TA24 201 D1
Exford TA24 128 D1
Minehead TA24 200 F7
Taunton TA1 212 E3
Yeovil BA20 219 B4
Park Street Ave BS1 226 C3
Park Street Mews BA1 228 A4
Park Terr Chard TA20 223 B6
Glastonbury BA6 206 D4
Minehead TA24 200 F7
Park The Castle Cary BA7 214 B4
Keynsham BS31 24 E6
Portishead BS20 2 F5
Yatton BS49 17 B1
Yeovil BA20 219 A5
Park View
Axminster EX13 198 A3
Bath BA2 44 D6
Crewkerne TA18 224 C4
Crewkerne, Misterton TA18 196 B3
Montacute TA15 186 B3
Stogursey TA5 134 C5
Park Villas BS23 48 D8
Park Wall BA10 215 F5
Park Wall Dro TA7 209 F4
Park Water La DT8 199 F5
Park Way Bruton BA10 215 E5
Midsomer Norton BA3 97 A8
Ruishton TA3 169 C3
Park Wood Cl BS14 22 F4
Parker Cl TA21 222 E6
Parkes Rd BS24 50 C5
Parkfield Cl TA6 153 F4
Parkfield Cres TA1 212 D2
Parkfield Dr TA1 212 D3
Parkfield Gdns BS39 57 D3
Parkfield Prim Sch TA1 212 D3
Parkfield Rd
Axbridge BS26 70 D1
Taunton TA1 212 D3
Parkfields Residential Home BA6 157 E4
Parkgate La BA11 101 E7
Parkhouse La BS31 24 C2
Parkhouse Rd TA24 200 E7
Parkhurst Rd BS23 49 A7
Parkland Wlk TA18 224 C4
Parklands BS39 59 D2
Parklands Ave BS22 32 A4
Parklands Rd Bristol BS3 11 E4
Wellington TA21 222 D7
Parklands Rise TA24 200 D7
Parklands Way TA11 211 B4
Parkmead TA2 213 E8
Parks Cotts TA2 168 D8
Parks La
Brompton Ralph TA4 150 C3
Minehead TA24 200 F7
Parks The
Bridgwater TA6 208 D4
Minehead TA24 200 E7
Parks View TA24 124 A4
Parkside Inf Sch BA1 228 B3
Parkstone Ave TA6 209 A2
Parksway Ct TA24 200 E7
Parkway TA6 209 C5
Parkway La BA2 60 D3
Parlour Ho TA1 213 B5
Parmin Cl TA1 213 C3
Parmin Way TA1 213 C3
Parnell Rd BS21 6 D3
Parnell Way TA8 104 B8
Parrett Cl TA10 171 F5
Parrett Mead
South Perrott DT8 196 C1
Taunton TA1 213 D3
Parrett Way TA6 209 B3
Parrett Works Cotts TA12 220 F8
Parricks La EX13 198 D3
Parrocks La TA20 198 C8
Parry Cl BA2 44 B4
Parry's Cl BS9 5 E5
Parry's La BS9 5 F5
Parrys Gr BS9 5 E5
Parson's Batch BA4 140 E3
Parson's Dro BS28 138 C7
Parson's La TA11 173 D5
Parson's St TA24 124 A3
Parsonage Cl
Langport TA10 172 A5
Somerton TA11 211 E3
Winford BS40 37 F6
Parsonage Cotts TA2 168 D8
Parsonage Cres BA7 214 B6
Parsonage Ct
Puriton TA7 136 B4
Taunton TA1 212 A4
Parsonage Hill TA11 211 E3
Parsonage La
Ashill TA19 183 C4
Axbridge BS26 70 E2
Bath BA1 228 B2
Chilcompton BA3 96 C4
Kingston St Mary TA2 168 D8
Milverton TA4 167 A4
Pensford BS39 40 D6
Staple Fitzpaine TA3 182 C4
Wincanton BA9 161 B1
Winford BS40 37 F6
Parsonage Pl TA10 171 D4
Parsonage Rd Berrow TA8 84 F5
Long Ashton BS41 11 C2
West Camel BA22 174 D3
Parsons Cl Bicknoller TA4 132 F2
Long Sutton TA10 172 F4
Parsons Gate BA7 214 B7
Parsons Gn Clevedon BS21 16 C8
Weston-Super-Mare BS22 32 A3
Parsons Mead BS48 19 F7
Parsons Paddock BS14 23 A7
Parsons Pen BS27 90 B7
Parsons Rd TA9 104 C4
Parsons Way Wells BA5 203 B4
Winscombe BS25 69 E6
Parsons' La TA5 152 A7
Partis Coll BA1 44 A8
Partis Way BA1 44 A8
Partition St BS1 226 C2
Partman's Hill BA3 116 B3
Partridge Cl BS22 31 F1
Partway La
Chard Junction TA20 198 F6
East Chinnock BA22 196 F7
Passage Leaze BS11 4 D6
Passage St BS2 227 B2
Pastures The BA15 64 E3
Patch Croft BS21 16 C8
Pathe Rd TA7 155 B1
Pathfinder Terr 2 TA6 209 B4
Patrick's Way TA3 181 D8
Patrum Cl TA1 212 B1
Patson Hill La DT9 188 B5
Patterson Ho 8 BS1 227 B1
Pattinson Cl BA21 219 D6
Pattons TA3 169 C1
Patwell La BA10 215 E6
Patwell St BA10 215 E6
Paul St Bristol BS2 226 C4
Frome BA11 119 F5
Shepton Mallet BA4 205 B6
Taunton TA1 212 F3
Paul's Cswy BS49 34 D4
Paull's La TA19 183 B2
Paullet EX16 178 C1

Paulls Cl TA10 172 A6
Paulman Gdns BS41 20 F8
Paulmont Rise BS39 58 E1
Pauls Rd TA11 211 C3
Paulto' Hill BA3, BS39 78 B6
Paulton Inf Sch BS39 77 E5
Paulton Jun Sch BS39 77 E5
Paulton La BA2,BA3 78 D7
Paulton Meml Hospl BS39 77 F4
Paulton Rd
Farrington Gurney BS39 77 B4
Midsomer Norton BA3 77 F1
Paulton BS39 77 B7
Paulwood Rd BS39 58 E1
Pavement The TA3 170 B4
Pavey Cl BS13 22 C4
Pavey Rd BS13 22 C4
Pavyotts La BA22 197 E8
Pawelski Cl BA4 142 B7
Pawlett BS24 49 A2
Pawlett Mead Dro TA6 136 A5
Pawlett Prim Sch TA6 135 F5
Pawlett Rd Bristol BS13 22 C3
Puriton TA6 136 B4
West Huntspill TA6,TA9 136 A7
Pawlett Wlk BS13 22 C3
Pawletts Almshouses TA5 134 C5
Paybridge Rd BS13 21 F4
Payne Rd BS24 49 D2
Payne's La TA12 185 E8
Paynes La TA7 155 C2
Payton Rd
Holywell Lake TA21 179 F7
Rockwell Green TA21 222 A5
Peace Cl TA6 209 D6
Peacehay La TA21 179 E4
Peach Tree Cl TA6 209 E5
Peacocks Cl TA21 180 F7
Peacocks Hill TA11 158 A2
Peadon La TA5 134 C4
Peak La
Compton Dundon TA11 157 A2
Shepton Beauchamp TA19 184 D3
Pear Ash La BA9 161 E2
Pear Tree Cl TA6 209 D4
Pear Tree Gdns BS24 67 C6
Pear Tree Ind Est BS40 53 C4
Pearce Dr TA9 104 D4
Pearmain Rd BA16 207 B4
Pearse Cl BS22 32 B5
Pearson Ho BA21 219 A6
Peart Cl BS13 21 E5
Peart Dr BS13 21 E4
Peartree Field BS20 2 F5
Peartwater Hill TA5 152 D8
Peartwater Rd TA5 152 D7
Peasedown St John Prim Sch BA2 79 C7
Peat Moors Visitor Ctr★ BA6 138 A4
Pebbles Orch TA19 184 E4
Pecking Mill Rd BA4 141 E1
Pedder Rd BS21 6 D1
Peddles Cl TA10 171 D8
Peddles La TA11 173 E8
Pedlars Gr
Chapmanslade BA13 121 C4
Frome BA11 119 E7
Pedwell Hill TA7 156 A7
Pedwell La TA7 156 A7
Peel St BS5 227 C4
Peerage Ct TA24 201 A6
Peggy's La TA18 196 C5
Peile Dr TA2 212 E7
Pelham Ct TA6 209 D7
Pelican Cl BS22 49 F8
Pelting Dro BA5 92 C1
Pembroke Ave BS11 4 E6
Pembroke Cl
Burnham-On-Sea TA8 85 B1
Taunton TA1 212 C1
Yeovil BA21 219 E7
Pembroke Ct BS21 6 C4
Pembroke Gr BS8 226 A3
Pembroke Mans BS8 226 A4
Pembroke Pl BS8 226 A1
Pembroke Rd
Bridgwater TA6 209 C3
Bristol BS8 226 A4
Bristol, Shirehampton BS11 4 E6
Portishead BS20 1 E4
Weston-Super-Mare BS23 48 F4
Pembroke St BS2 227 B4
Pembroke Vale BS8 226 A4
Pemswell Rd TA24 200 F8
Pen Cross BA22 197 B6
Pen Elm Cotts TA2 168 B5
Pen Elm Hill TA2 168 B6
Pen Hill BA9 161 C4
Pen Mill Hill SP8,BA12 161 F2
Pen Mill Inf Sch BA21 219 D6
Pen Mill Sta BA21 219 E5
Pen Mill Trad Est BA21 219 F6
Penarth Dr BS24 49 A1
Penarth Rd TA6 208 D4
Pendlesham Gdns BS23 31 A1
Pendomer Rd BA22 197 B5
Pendragon Pk BA6 206 D5
Penel Orlieu TA6 208 F4
Penfield BA21 219 C5
Penlea Ave TA6 208 E2
Penlea Cl TA6 208 E2
Penlea Ct BS11 4 D7
Penmoor Pl TA8 84 F5
Penmoor Rd TA8 84 F5
Penmore Rd BA22,DT9 188 B7
Penn Cl Cheddar BS27 90 C7
Wells BA5 112 E2
Penn Gdns BA1 44 A8
Penn Hill BA20 219 B4
Penn Hill Pk BA20 219 B4
Penn Hill Rd BA1 27 A1
Penn La BA22 197 A6
Penn Lea Ct BA1 44 B8
Penn Lea Rd BA1 44 B8
Penn Rd BS27 90 C7
Penn St BS1 227 B3
Penn View BA9 216 D4
Penn Way BS26 70 C1
Pennard BS24 49 A2
Pennard Ct BS14 23 B5
Pennard Gn BA2 44 A6
Pennard La BA6 140 A2
Penneys Piece BA11 120 C6
Pennine Gdns BS23 31 A1
Pennlea BS13 22 C7
Penns The BS21 6 E2
Penny Batch La BA5 139 E8
Penny Cl TA21 222 D7
Penny Lea TA23 202 C6
Penny's Meade TA19 183 F4
Pennycress BS22 49 D7
Pennyquick BA2 43 D6
Pennyquick View BA2 43 F6
Pennywell Est 3 BS21 6 D2
Pennywell Rd BS2 227 C4
Penpole Ave BS11 4 E6
Penpole Cl BS11 4 D7
Penpole La BS11 4 E7
Penpole Pk BS11 4 E7
Penpole Pl BS11 4 E6
Penrice Cl BS22 31 C2
Penrose BS14 22 F7
Penrose Sch TA6 208 E4
Pensford Ct BS14 23 D5
Pensford Hill BS39 40 D5
Pensford La BS39 40 A3
Pensford Old Rd BS39 40 E3
Pensford Prim Sch BS39 40 D4
Pensford Way BA11 120 D7
Pentagon The BS9 5 B5
Pentire Ave BS13 22 A6
Pentridge La DT10 190 E3
Penzoy Ave TA6 209 B4
Pepperall Rd TA9 104 D4
Peppershells La BS39 41 C6
Pepys Cl BS31 25 D2
Pera Pl BA1 228 C4
Pera Rd BA1 228 C4
Perch Hill BA5 110 E6
Percival Rd BS8 11 F8
Percy Pl 13 BA1 28 B1
Percy Rd BA21 219 D6
Peregrine Cl BS22 31 F1
Perfect View BA1 28 A1
Periton Cross TA24 200 D6
Periton Ct TA24 200 D6
Periton La TA24 200 D7
Periton Rd TA24 200 D6
Periton Rise TA24 200 D6
Periton Way TA24 200 D6
Perkins Ct BA5 203 B4
Perley La TA23 148 D8
Perrett Way BS20 4 E4
Perretts Ct BS1 226 C1
Perridge Hill BA4 140 D4
Perrin Cl BS39 76 E8
Perrings The BS48 18 E8
Perrot Hill Sch TA18 196 B4
Perrow La BS28 89 C2
Perry Court Inf Sch BS14 23 A6
Perry Court Jun Sch BS14 23 A6
Perry Hill TA11 174 D8
Perry Hill Rd TA11 211 D2
Perry La TA9 106 F5
Perry Lake La BA5 139 B7
Perry New Rd TA22 163 F4
Perry Pl BA21 219 C5
Perry Rd Bristol BS1 227 A3
Wedmore TA9 107 A6
Perry St TA20 198 D8
Perry's Cider Mills★ TA19 194 E7
Perry's Cl BS27 90 A7
Perrycroft Ave BS13 22 A6
Perrycroft Rd BS13 22 A6
Perrymead Bath BA2 45 B3
Weston-Super-Mare BS22 32 B5
Perrymead Ct BA2 45 B4
Pesley Cl BS13 22 A4
Pesters La TA11 211 E3
Pestlefield La TA3 170 C1
Peter St
Shepton Mallet BA4 205 B6
Taunton TA2 212 F6
Yeovil BA20 219 B4
Peter's Gore DT6 199 B1
Petercole Dr BS13 22 A6
Peterside BS39 76 E8
Peterson Sq BS13 22 C3
Petherton Gdns BS14 23 B7
Petherton Rd Bristol BS14 23 B7
North Newton TA7 153 F2
Petherton Road Inf Sch BS14 23 B7
Pethick Ho BS4 22 F8
Peto Garden at Iford Manor The★ BA15 64 E3
Petrel Cl TA6 209 D7
Petter's Way BA20 219 B4
Petticoat La BA4 205 B6
Pettitts Cl DT9 187 E1
Petton Cross EX16 165 A3
Petvin Cl BA16 207 D4
Pevensey Wlk BS4 22 D7
Phelps Cl TA20 223 D6
Philadelphia Ct 6 BS1 227 B3
Philippa Cl BS14 23 A7
Philips Ho 2 BS2 227 B4
Phillip Ho TA6 208 F2
Phillip's Dro TA3 170 D7
Phillips Cl TA6 208 D4
Phillips Rd BS23 49 A6
Phillis Hill BS39 77 F4
Phippen St 1 BS1 227 B1
Phoenix Ct Frome BA11 119 D4
Taunton TA1 212 F3
Phoenix Ho Bath BA1 228 B4
Frome BA11 119 D4
Phoenix Rd TA6 209 B3
Phoenix Terr TA8 104 B6
Piccadily Ho 13 BA4 205 B6
Pickeridge Cl TA2 213 B7
Picket La DT8 196 C1
Pickett La BA21 219 A7
Pickney La TA2 168 B7
Pickpurse La TA4 150 E8
Pickwick Rd BA1 28 A2
Piece TA19 184 E4
Piece La TA19 184 E4
Piece Rd DT9 217 C3
Piece The 2 TA16 195 F7
Pier Rd BS20 2 E7
Pier St TA8 104 A6
Pierrepont Pl BA1 228 C2
Pierrepont St BA1 228 C2
Piers Rd BA4 142 A6
Pig Hill BA22 197 A7
Pig La TA7 154 D8
Pig Market La TA1 212 F3
Pigeon House Dr BS13 22 D4
Pigeon La BS40 36 E1
Pightley La TA5 152 F6
Pightley Rd TA5 152 E7
Pigott Ave BS13 22 A4
Pigs Hill La TA5 134 D1
Pike Cl BA6 206 C5
Pike Hill BA4 205 A7
Pike La BA4 205 B6
Pikes Cres TA1 212 E1
Pilcorn St BS28 108 C4
Pile La Curry Mallet TA3 183 C8
Stourton Caundle DT10 189 F3
Piley La TA21 179 D8
Pilgrim's Way TA6 135 F5
Pilgrims Way
Chew Stoke BS40 56 D8
Lovington BA7 158 E2
Shirehampton BS11 4 C7
Weston-Super-Mare BS22 31 E3
Pill Bridge La BA22 173 D1
Pill Head La TA18 196 C4
Pill Mdw SP8 177 E2
Pill Rd Abbots Leigh BS8 4 F1
Pill BS20 4 E2
Rooksbridge BS26,TA9 87 C2
Pill St BS20 4 D4
Pill Way BS21 6 B2
Pillar La BA11 99 D4
Pillmead La BS28 108 D5
Pillmoor Dro BA5 139 F6
Pillmoor La BA5 139 F6
Pillmore La
Highbridge TA9 105 A4
Watchfield TA9 105 C4
Pilots Helm TA6 153 E4
Pilsdon La DT6 199 F3
Pilton Hill BA4 140 C4
Pilton Manor Vineyard★ BA4 140 E3
Pimm's La BS22 31 B2
Pimms La BS22 31 B3
Pimpernel Cl BA16 207 B7
Pince's Knap TA20 198 F5
Pinchay La BS40 38 A4
Pincushion Cnr BA22 197 E6
Pine Ave TA20 223 C5
Pine Cl Street BA16 207 B3
Taunton TA1 213 D2
Weston-Super-Mare BS22 31 D2
Pine Ct Chew Magna BS40 39 B3
Frome BA11 120 B7
Keynsham BS31 24 C4
Radstock BA3 79 A2
Pine Hill BS22 31 D2
Pine Lea BS24 67 B6
Pine Ridge Cl BS9 5 C4
Pine Tree Ave BA20 218 F3
Pine Tree Cl TA6 209 D4
Pine Wlk BA3 78 E1
Pinecroft Bristol BS14 22 F7
Portishead BS20 1 F6
Pines Cl Chilcompton BA3 96 D3
Wincanton BA9 216 C3
Pines Residential Site The BA11 120 D8
Pines Way Bath BA2 228 A2
Radstock BA3 79 A2
Pines Way Ind Est BA2 228 A2
Pinetree Rd BS24 50 D4
Pinewood TA11 211 D4
Pinewood Ave BA3 77 F1
Pinewood Dr TA11 211 D4
Pinewood Gr BA3 77 F1
Pinewood Rd BA3 77 F1
Pinewood Way TA8 65 F3
Pinford La DT9 188 F3
Pinhay Rd BS13 22 B6
Pink Knoll Hollow DT9 188 C8
Pinkham Hill TA20 194 B6
Pinkhams Twist BS14 23 A5
Pinksmoor La TA21 179 E7
Pinkwood La BA10 160 E7
Pinmore BA11 119 E2
Pinney Cl TA1 212 B1
Pinnockscroft TA8 84 F5
Pintail Rd TA24 201 C5
Pinter Cl TA8 104 C6
Pioneer Ave BA2 44 F1
Pipe La BS1 226 C2
Pipehouse La BA2 63 F4
Piper's Alley TA19 221 B4
Pipers Cl BS26 88 E6
Pipers Pl EX14 191 F2
Pippard Cl BA16 207 E5
Pippin Cl BA2 79 D7
Pippins The TA6 208 D6
Pipplepen La DT8,TA18 196 B2
Pit Hill TA17 195 B7
Pit Hill La TA7 155 C7
Pit La Sticklepath TA23 149 D7
Sutton Mallet TA7 155 C7
Ubley BS40 55 F5
Pit Rd Dinnington TA17 195 C7
Midsomer Norton BA3 78 B1
Pitch & Pay La BS9 5 E3
Pitch & Pay Pk BS9 5 E3
Pitchcombe Gdns BS9 5 D7
Pitcher's Hill TA2 168 F7
Pitching The BA3 96 D5
Pitcombe Hill BA10 215 B2
Pitcombe La TA4 165 B5
Pitcombe Rock BA10 215 C3
Pitcot La BA3 115 F7
Pitfield Cnr BA22 188 A7
Pitfour Terr BA2 60 B2
Pithay Ct BS1 227 A3
Pithay The Bristol BS1 227 A3
Paulton BS39 77 E6
Pitman Ct BA1 28 C2
Pitman Ho BA2 44 D4
Pitman Rd BS23 48 E6
Pitminster Prim Sch TA3 181 C5
Pitney Hill TA10 172 C6
Pitsham La TA4 164 E6
Pitt Ct TA10 171 B3
Pitt La
Huish Champflower TA4 165 F8
Porlock TA24 123 C3
Waterrow TA4 165 F5
Pitt's La BS40 39 B1
Pitten St BA3 116 E3
Pitts Cl TA1 212 C1
Pitts La TA3 183 F7
Pitway TA13 220 D5
Pitway Cl BS39 76 F4
Pitway Hill TA13 220 D6
Pitway La BS39 76 E4
Pix La TA4 167 B4
Pixash Bsns Ctr BS31 25 B5
Pixash La BS31 25 C5
Pixton Way TA22 163 E6
Pizey Ave
Burnham-On-Sea TA8 85 A1
Clevedon BS21 6 B2
Pizey Ave Ind Est BS21 6 C2
Pizey Cl BS21 6 B2
Place Dro TA7 154 F4
Placket La BA20 218 D1
Plain Pond TA4 210 C5
Plain The BA2 81 E4
Plais St TA2 212 F6
Plantagenet Chase BA20 218 D2
Plantagenet Pk BA20 218 E3
Platterwell La BA4 141 B3
Players La TA8 85 A1
Playfield Cl 2 BA8 190 A6
Playford Gdns BS11 4 E8
Playses Gn TA10 184 D8
Pleasant Pl BA1 29 D2
Pleshey Cl BS22 31 D2
Plimsoll Ho 3 BS1 227 B1
Plot La DT9 187 F5
Plott La BA8 190 B7
Plough Cl BA16 207 A4
Ploughed Paddock BS48 8 D1
Plover Cl
Milborne Port DT9 217 C2
Minehead TA24 201 C5
Weston-Super-Mare BS22 31 F1
Plover Ct BA21 218 D6
Plover Rd DT9 217 C2
Plovers Rise BA3 79 A3
Plowage La BA22 174 D3
Plox BA10 215 E6
Plud St BS28 108 B3
Plum La TA6 209 C2
Plum Orch DT9 187 F4
Plum Tree Cl TA6 209 E5
Plumber's Barton 5 BA11 119 F4
Plumers Cl 4 BS21 6 E1
Plumley Cres BS24 50 A4
Plumley Ct BS23 48 D4
Plummer's La BA5 92 D5
Plumptre Ave BA5 203 F5
Plumptre Cl BS39 77 E5
Plumptre Rd BS39 77 E5
Plumtree Cl BS25 52 A1
Plumtree Rd BS22 49 E8
Plunder St BS49 35 B7
Plunging Dr BA6 206 F1
Plymor Rd TA9 136 A8
Poachers End TA24 201 C4
Pococks Yd TA10 171 F5
Podger's La TA19 183 F4
Podgers Dr BA1 27 B2
Podium The BA1 228 C2
Polden Bsns Ctr The TA6 136 B2
Polden Cl BS48 8 E1
Polden Rd Portishead BS20 2 B5
Weston-Super-Mare BS23 48 F8
Polden St TA6 209 B5
Polden View BA6 206 E3
Polden Wlk TA7 136 E3
Pole Rue La TA20 193 C6
Polestar Way BS24 50 A8
Polham La TA11 211 D3
Polkes Field TA3 170 F6
Pollard Rd TA6 209 D6
Pollard Way BS22 49 F8
Pollard's La TA21 180 F7
Pollards Ct TA24 124 A3
Pollards Way TA1 212 E4
Polygon Rd BS8 226 A2
Polygon The 15 BS8 11 F6
Pomeroy La BA14 83 B6
Pomfrett Gdns BS14 23 E5
Pond Cl 5 BA8 190 A6
Pond La TA21 179 D3
Pond Orch TA4 150 B8
Pond Wlk DT10 190 B4
Pondhead Cross TA4 202 E3
Pondpool La TA3 170 C3
Ponsford Rd Bristol BS14 23 B8
Minehead TA24 201 A6
Pookfield Cl BA11 143 B7
Pool Cl TA7 136 C4
Pool Hill TA21 165 E1
Pool La BS40 38 A2
Poolbridge Rd BS28 107 C4
Poole Hill TA22 163 B5
Poole Ho BA2 43 F5
Poole St BS11 4 B8
Pooles Cl TA5 134 A2
Pooles La TA20 194 E1
Pooles Wharf BS8 226 A1
Pooles Wharf Ct BS8 226 A1
Poolmead Rd BA2 43 F5
Poop Hill TA18 196 C8
Poop Hill La TA18 196 C8
Poor Hill BA2 59 F6
Poorhouse La DT6 199 E1
Pop La EX13,TA20 198 B8
Pope Cl TA1 168 D1
Pope's La
Milborne Port DT9 217 D2
Rockwell Green TA21 222 B4
Pope's Wlk BA2 45 B3
Popery La TA24 129 E1
Popham Cl
Bridgwater TA6 209 D5
East Brent TA9 86 D5
Popham Flats TA21 222 D6
Poplar Ave BS9 5 D6
Poplar Cl Bath BA2 44 D4
Frome BA11 120 B7
Poplar Dr BA21 218 C7
Poplar Est TA9 104 D3
Poplar Farm BA5 111 A4
Poplar La TA9 105 F3
Poplar Pl 16 BS23 48 E8
Poplar Rd Bath BA2 62 D8
Bridgwater TA6 209 D7
Bristol, Highridge BS13 21 F7
Burnham-On-Sea TA8 104 A8
Street BA16 207 C3
Taunton TA1 213 D2
Poplar Tree La BA14 83 C2
Poplar Wlk BS24 49 E5
Poplars Cl BA21 187 A5
Poplars The
Easton-in-G BS20 4 B4
Porlock TA24 124 A3
Weston-Super-Mare BS22 32 A1
Pople's La BA11 117 F8
Pople's Well TA18 224 B6
Poples Bow TA9 104 E5
Poppy Cl
Houndstone BA22 218 B5
Weston-Super-Mare BS22 32 A5
Porch EX13 198 A3
Porchestall Dro BA6 206 B4
Porlock Cl
3 Clevedon BS21 6 E1
Weston-Super-Mare BS23 48 F2
Porlock Dr TA1 212 E1
Porlock Gdns BS48 8 E1
Porlock Hill TA24 123 F3
Porlock Rd Bath BA2 45 A1
Minehead TA24 200 C7
Port La TA22 164 A5
Port View BS20 4 C5
Port Way BA2 100 D7
Portal Rd BS24 50 D4
Portbury Comm BS20 2 F4
Portbury Gr BS11 4 D6
Portbury Hundred The BS20 3 C4
Portbury La BS20 9 E7
Portbury Way BS20 3 E5
Portbury Wlk BS11 4 D6
Portcullis Rd TA10 172 A6
Porter's Hatch BA6 138 D4
Portfield La TA10 171 F5
Portishead Bsns Pk BS20 2 E5
Portishead Lo BS20 2 D6
Portishead Prim Sch BS20 2 C5
Portishead Rd BS22 32 B4
Portishead Way BS3 11 E3

Rossiter Rd BA2 228 C1
Rossiter's Hill BA11 119 F3
Rossiter's Rd BA11 119 E3
Rosslyn Rd BA1 44 B7
Rotcombe La BS39 59 D2
Rotcombe Vale BS39 59 D2
Rotton Row TA4 210 C4
Roughmoor TA4 202 E4
Roughmoor Cl TA1 212 D5
Roughmoor Cres TA1 212 D5
Roughmoor La BA5 110 C7
Round Oak Gr BS27 90 A8
Round Oak Rd BS27 90 A8
Round Pool La TA4 151 B7
Round Well Cl BA4 204 F6
Roundhill Gr BA2 44 B3
Roundhill Pk BA2 44 A4
Roundmoor Cl BS31 25 D3
Roundmoor Gdns BS14 23 D7
Roundoak Gdns TA21 167 C2
Roundwell St TA13 220 C4
Row La
Keinton Mandeville TA11 158 A1
Laverton BA2 100 D8
Row Of Ashes La BS40 36 F4
Row The
Hambridge TA10 184 D8
Langport TA10 172 B3
Rowacres Bath BA2 44 B3
Bristol BS14 22 F6
Rowan Cl Nailsea BS48 9 A2
Puriton TA7 136 C4
Wincanton BA9 216 D2
Rowan Ct Frome BA11 120 B7
Radstock BA3 78 E1
Rowan Dr TA1 213 D1
Rowan Ho BS13 22 D4
Rowan Pl BS24 32 B1
Rowan Way Langford BS40 53 A5
Yeovil BA20 218 F3
Rowan Wlk BS31 24 C4
Rowans Cl TA6 209 C6
Rowans The BS20 2 C4
Rowbarrow Hill
Rimpton DT9 188 A7
Trent DT9 187 F6
Rowbarton Cl TA2 212 F7
Rowberrow BS14 22 F7
Rowberrow La BS25 70 F8
Rowberrow Way BS48 8 E1
Rowcliffe Cotts TA21 178 F8
Rowden Mill La DT10 189 F1
Rowdens Rd BA5 203 D3
Rowditch La TA5 133 D5
Rowe Cl TA21 222 A4
Rowe's Hill BA12 144 E4
Rowlands Cl BA1 29 B2
Rowlands Rise TA7 136 C4
Rowley Rd BA6 206 E5
Rowls La BA9 177 E6
Rowmarsh La TA10 172 D5
Rownham Cl BS3 11 E4
Rownham Ct BS8 226 A1
Rownham Hill BS8 11 E4
Rownham Mead BS8 226 A1
Rows La EX16 164 A1
Rows The BS22 31 E2
Royal Ave BA1 228 B3
Royal Cl BA21 219 C6
Royal Cres★ Bath BA1 228 A3
Weston-Super-Mare BS23 48 D8
Royal Ct BS23 48 D4
Royal Fort Rd BS2, BS8 226 C3
Royal High Sch The
BA1 228 B4
Royal Ho 4 BA4 205 B6
Royal Hospl for Sick Children
BS2 226 C3
Royal National Hospl for Rheumatic Diseases
BA1 228 B2
Royal Par BS23 48 D8
Royal Photographic Society★
BA1 228 B3
Royal Pk BS8 226 A3
Royal Portbury Dock Rd
BS20 3 E5
Royal Prom BS8 226 B3
Royal Sands BS23 48 D4
Royal Sch The BA1 27 F2
Royal Terr BS20 2 E7
Royal United Hospl BA1 44 B8
Royal West of England Acad
BS8 226 B3
Royal York Cres BS8 11 F6
Royal York Ho BS8 226 A2
Royal York Mews BS8 226 A2
Royal York Villas BS8 226 A2
Royces La TA19 184 C5
Roynon Way BS27 90 B7
Royston Lodge BS23 48 D6
Royston Rd TA3 192 A7
Rubbery La TA11 158 D1
Rubens Cl BS31 25 A5
Ruborough Rd TA6 209 C4
Ruddock Cl BA22 197 B8
Ruddock Way BA22 197 B8
Ruddymead BS21 6 D2
Rudge Hill BA11 102 D5
Rudge La
Beckington BA11 102 B6
Standerwick BA11 102 D3
Rudge Rd BA11 102 B2
Rudgeway Rd BS39 77 E4
Rudgewood Cl BS13 22 D4
Rudgleigh Ave BS20 4 C4
Rudgleigh Rd BS20 4 C4
Rudhall Gn BS22 32 B3
Rudmore Pk BA1 44 A7
Rue La Alweston DT9 189 C2
Hambridge TA3 184 B7
Ruett La BS39 77 B4
Rugg's Dro Chedzoy TA7 154 D7
West Huntspill TA9 136 B7
Rugg's Hill TA4 148 E1
Rughill BS28 108 D8
Rugosa Dr TA8 84 F4
Ruishton CE Sch TA3 169 C3
Ruishton La TA3 169 C3
Ruishton Lane Cotts
TA3 169 C3
Runnymede Rd BA21 219 D8
Rupert St Bristol BS1 227 A3
Taunton TA2 212 E6
Rush Ash La BA3 116 E8
Rush Hill Bath BA2 44 C2
Farrington Gurney BS39 76 F3
Rush Hill La BS28 107 F3
Rusham BS13 21 F4
Rushgrove Gdns BS39 57 C4
Rushmoor BS21 6 A1
Rushmoor Gr BS48 19 A5
Rushmoor La BS48 19 A5
Rushway BS40 53 F4
Ruskin Cl TA1 213 C4
Ruskin Rd BA3 78 C1
Ruskway La TA10 184 C6
Russ La BS21 16 E4
Russ St BS2 227 C2
Russell Cl BS40 38 A6
Russell Pl
Bridgwater TA6 208 F6
Milborne Port DT9 217 C3
Russell Pope Ave TA20 223 D2
Russell Rd Clevedon BS21 6 C3
Locking BS24 50 C6
Russell St BA1 228 B3
Russell's TA4 210 C4
Russell's Barton BA11 143 B8
Russet Way
Peasedown St John BA2 79 D7
Yeovil BA20 218 D2
Russett Cl BS48 19 B6
Russett Gr BS48 18 C8
Russett Rd Street BA16 207 C4
Taunton TA1 213 E5
Russetts Cotts BS48 19 B8
Rusty Wall BA20 218 F3
Rusty Wall Mobile Home Pk
BA20 218 F3
Ruthven Rd BS4 22 E8
Rutland Cl BS22 49 C8
Rutters La TA19 221 B4
Ryalls Ct BA21 219 C5
Ryburn Cl TA1 213 D3
Rydal Ave BS24 50 A4
Rydal Rd BS23 48 F4
Rydon Cres TA5 135 C2
Rydon La Lopen TA13 185 A1
South Petherton TA13 220 A5
Taunton TA2 212 F8
Rye TA7 136 C4
Rye Cl BS13 21 E6
Rye Gdns BA20 218 D2
Rye La TA7 155 C2
Rye Water La DT2 197 A1
Ryecroft Ave BS22 31 E2
Ryecroft Rise BS41 11 B1
Ryefields Cl BA22 197 B8
Ryepool TA4 167 F8
Ryesland Way TA3 169 D4
Rylands BA11 101 E4
Rylands Cl TA4 202 D2
Rylestone Gr BS9 5 F5
Rysdale Rd BS9 5 F6

S

Sabrina Way BS9 5 C4
Sackmore Gn DT10 190 F6
Sackmore La DT10 190 F5
Sadborow La TA20 199 B4
Sadborow Pound TA20 199 B5
Sadbury Cl BS22 32 B4
Sadler St BA5 203 D4
Sadlier Cl BS11 5 A8
Saffron Cl TA1 168 F1
Saffron Ct Bath BA1 228 C4
Sherborne DT9 225 E4
Saffron Ho 10 BS23 48 E8
Saffrons The 7 BS22 32 B4
Sage Cl BS20 1 E4
Sage's La BA3 94 D6
Sainsbury Cl TA24 200 D7
Sainsbury Rd TA24 200 D7
SS Great Britain★ BS1 226 B1
SS Peter & Paul Catholic Sch
BS8 226 C4
SS Peter & Paul RC Cath★
BS8 226 A4
St Agnes Cl BS48 9 A1
St Albans Pl TA2 212 F8
St Aldhelm's Cl BA11 119 D4
St Aldhelm's Rd DT9 225 D6
St Aldhelms CE Prim Sch
BA4 141 E6
St Andrew St BA5 203 E4
St Andrew's CE Jun Sch
BS49 34 C4
St Andrew's CE Prim Sch
Bath BA1 228 B4
Taunton TA2 212 F6
St Andrew's Cl
Curry Rivel TA10 171 D4
High Ham TA10 156 A2
St Andrew's Ct BA5 203 F5
St Andrew's Dr BS21 6 A2
St Andrew's Jun Sch
TA8 104 B7
St Andrew's Par 1 BS23 48 F4
St Andrew's Rd
Burnham-On-Sea TA8 104 B7
Stogursey TA5 134 C5
6 Taunton TA2 212 F6
St Andrew's Sch EX13 198 A7
St Andrew's Terr BA1 228 B3
St Andrews Cl Nailsea BS48 9 A1
Weston-Super-Mare BS22 31 F3
St Andrews Ct TA24 200 F7
St Andrews Dr EX13 198 A2
St Andrews La TA24 200 F7
St Andrews Pk BA5 203 D3
St Andrews Rd
Backwell BS48 19 B5
Cheddar BS27 90 C7
Yeovil BA20 218 F5
St Andrews View TA2 212 F6
St Ann's Cl TA2 212 E7
St Ann's Dr TA8 85 A1
St Ann's Pl BA1 228 B2
St Ann's Way BA2 45 C6
St Anne's Ave BS31 24 D6
St Anne's CE Prim Sch
BS24 33 B5
St Anne's Cl BA6 158 A5
St Anne's Ct BS31 24 D6
St Anne's Gdns BA21 218 E6
St Anthony's Cl BA3 78 A2
St Antonys Sq DT9 225 D3
St Aubyn's Ave BS23 48 D2
St Audries Cl TA5 134 C6
St Augustine of Canterbury
Sec Sch The TA2 213 A7
St Augustine St TA1 213 A4
St Augustine's Par BS1 227 A2
St Augustine's Pl 1
BS1 227 A2
St Austell Cl BS48 19 A8
St Austell Rd BS22 49 B8
St Barnabas CE Prim Sch
BS20 2 B5
St Barnabas Cl BA3 78 B3
St Bartholomew's CE Fst
Sch TA18 224 D5
St Benedict's Cl BA6 206 D4
St Benedict's Jun Sch
BA6 206 D4
St Benedict's RC Prim Sch
BA3 97 C7
St Bernadette RC Prim Sch
BS14 23 B6
St Bernadette RC Sch
BS14 23 B6
St Bernard's RC Sch
BS11 4 E6
St Bernard's Rd BS11 4 E6
St Brandon's Sch BS21 6 B3
St Brides Cl BA6 206 D5
St Bridges Cl BS22 31 A6
St Bridget's Cl TA8 65 F5
St Cadoc Ho BS31 24 F5
St Catherine's Cl BA2 45 C6
St Catherine's Cres DT9 225 B3
St Catherine's Ct 10
BA11 119 E5
St Catherine's Mead BS20 4 D3
St Catherine's Way DT9 225 B3
St Catherines Hill BA10 215 E6
St Chad's Ave BA3 78 A1
St Chad's Gn BA3 97 A8
St Charles Cl BA3 78 A2
St Christopher's Ct BS21 6 C5
St Christopher's Sch
TA8 85 A2
St Christopher's Way
TA8 85 A2
St Christophers Cl BA2 45 C8
St Cleer's Orch TA11 211 C3
St Cleers TA11 211 C3
St Cleers Way TA11 211 C3
St Clements Ct Bath BA1 27 C1
Clevedon BS21 6 C4
Keynsham BS31 24 E4
2 Weston-Super-Mare
BS22 32 A2
St Clements Rd BS31 24 F4
St Cuthbert Ave BA5 203 B5
St Cuthbert St BA5 203 D4
St Cuthbert Way BA5 203 B5
St Cuthbert's CE Inf Sch
BA5 203 C3
St Cuthbert's Villas
BA5 203 A5
St David's Cl BA6 206 E4
St David's Cl
Taunton TA2 213 A8
Weston-Super-Mare BS22 31 B2
St David's Cres BA21 219 B7
St David's Dr EX13 198 A2
St David's Gdns TA2 212 F8
St Davids Cl EX13 198 A2
St Davids Ct TA6 209 D3
St Davids Pl BA10 215 E7
St Decuman's Rd TA23 202 C7
St Dubricius CE Fst Sch
TA24 124 A3
St Dunstan's Com Sch
BA6 206 D5
St Dunstan's Pk BA6 158 A5
St Dunstans Cl BA6 206 D5
St Edmund's Rd BA6 206 D5
St Edmund's Terr BA3 117 C7
St Edmunds's Rd BA6 206 E5
St Edward's Cl TA7 137 B2
St Edward's Rd BS8 226 B2
St Edyth's Rd BS9 5 C6
St Elizabeth's Way TA13 220 C4
St Frances Prim Sch BS48 8 F1
St Francis Rd BS31 24 D6
St George CE Prim Sch
BS1 226 B2
St George's Ave
Taunton TA2 212 F8
Yeovil BA21 219 B7
St George's Cl TA24 201 D2
St George's Cross
BA11 101 E1
St George's Hill Bath BA2 45 D8
Easton-in-G BS20 4 A3
St George's Ho BS8 226 B2
St George's Pl TA1 212 F3
St George's Prim Sch
TA6 208 C6
St George's RC Prim Sch
TA1 213 A3
St George's Rd
Keynsham BS31 24 D6
Portbury BS20 3 E7
St George's St TA24 201 D2
St Georges Ave EX13 198 A2
St Georges CE Sch SP8 161 E1
St Georges Ct BA6 206 E5
St Georges Mews TA1 212 F3
St Georges Rd BS1 226 C2
St Georges Sq TA1 212 F3
St Georges Way TA1 212 E2
St Gilda's Cl TA10 172 A5
St Gilda's Way BA6 206 D4
St Gildas TA20 223 D4
St Gildas RC Prim Sch
BA21 219 B5
St Gildes Ct TA10 172 A5
St Gregory's CE Prim Sch
DT10 190 F5
St Gregory's RC Sch
BA2 62 D8
St Hilary Cl BS9 5 D5
St Ives Cl BS48 9 A1
St Ives Rd BS23 49 A5
St James Cl TA1 212 F4
St James Ct
Bridgwater TA6 209 D3
4 Taunton TA1 212 F4
St James Mews TA13 220 C4
St James St Taunton TA1 212 F4
Weston-Super-Mare BS23 48 D7
St James Terr BA22 197 A7
St James' Barton BS1 227 B4
St James' Sq BA6 157 D4
St James's Cl BA21 218 D5
St James's Par BA1 228 B2
St James's Pk Bath BA1 228 B4
Yeovil BA20 218 C5
St James's Sq BA1 228 A4
St James's St Bath BA1 228 B4
South Petherton TA13 220 C4
St John & St Francis CE Prim
Sch TA6 209 D4
St John St
Bridgwater TA6 209 B4
Wells BA5 203 D4
St John the Evangelist CE
Prim Sch BS21 6 C1
St John's Ave BS21 6 D3
St John's Bridge 2 BS1 227 A3
St John's CE Fst Sch
BA11 119 F4
St John's CE Jun Sch
TA9 104 D4
St John's CE Prim Sch
TA21 222 E6
St John's CE Sch BA3 78 A1
St John's Cl
Peasedown St John BA2 79 B7
Weston-Super-Mare BS23 30 D1
St John's Cres
Midsomer Norton BA3 78 A2
Trowbridge BA14 83 F6
St John's Pl BA1 228 B2
St John's Prim Sch
BS31 24 E5
St John's RC Prim Sch
BA2 45 B6
St John's RC Prim Sch
(Annexe) BA2 44 D4
St John's Rd
Backwell BS48 19 B5
Bath BA1 44 C7
Bath BA2 228 C3
Burnham-On-Sea TA8 104 B7
Clevedon BS21 6 D3
Frome BA11 120 B5
Taunton TA1 212 E3
Yeovil BA21 219 D7
St John's Sq BA6 206 D5
St John's Terr BA11 119 E3
St Johns CE Inf Sch
BA6 206 E5
St Johns Cl TA21 222 E6
St Johns Ct Axbridge BS26 70 B2
Keynsham BS31 24 E6
Wells BA5 203 D3
St Johns Ho 3 BA20 219 B5
St Johns Rd BA2 60 B1
St Johns Ret Pk TA1 213 B5
St Johns Wlk BA6 206 D5
St Joseph & St Teresa's RC
Sch BA5 203 D4
St Joseph's RC Prim Sch
Bridgwater TA6 208 D4
Burnham-On-Sea TA8 104 B6
St Joseph's RC Prim Sch
BS20 2 C6
St Joseph's Rd BS23 30 E1
St Jude's Terr BS22 31 C1
St Julian's CE Prim Sch
BA2 62 E1
St Julian's Rd BA2 79 F5
St Julians Cl BS39 77 E4
St Juthware Cl BA22 197 C3
St Katherine's Ce Prim Sch
BS40 37 A7
St Katherine's Sch BS20 4 E3
St Kenya Ct BS31 24 F5
St Keyna Rd BS31 24 E5
St Kilda's Rd BA2 44 D5
St Ladoc Rd BS31 24 D6
St Laud Cl BS9 5 D5
St Lawrence's CE Prim Sch
BA5 110 E6
St Louis RC Prim Sch
BA11 119 E5
St Luke's Cl TA8 104 B7
St Luke's Rd Bath BA2 44 F3
Midsomer Norton BA3 77 F2
St Lukes Mews TA4 167 E6
St Lukes Rd BA11 101 E5
St Margaret's Cl BS31 24 D6
St Margaret's La BS48 19 A5
St Margaret's Prim Sch
BA22 186 C6
St Margaret's Rd BA22 186 B6
St Margaret's Terr BS23 48 D8
St Margarets Cl BS48 19 A5
St Margarets Ct TA1 213 B4
St Margarets La TA20 198 C8
St Mark's CE Sch BA1 28 B2
St Mark's CE/Methodist
Ecumenical Prim Sch
BS22 31 F4
St Mark's Rd Bath BA2 228 C1
Burnham-On-Sea TA8 104 B8
Midsomer Norton BA3 78 A2
Weston-Super-Mare BS22 32 A3
St Marks Cl Chedzoy TA7 154 E8
Keynsham BS31 24 E6
St Marks Ct TA6 209 D3
St Marks Gdns BA2 228 C1
St Martin's Cl TA3 170 F1
St Martin's Ct BA2 44 E1
St Martin's Garden Prim Sch
BA2 44 D1
St Martin's La SN14 13 F8
St Martin's Pk SN14 13 F8
St Martin's Sch TA18 224 B6
St Martins BS21 6 C5
St Martins CE Jun Sch
BS22 31 D2
St Martins Ct BS22 31 E3
St Martins Hospl BA2 44 E1
St Martins Way BA20 218 D2
St Mary Prim Sch BA2 45 C8
St Mary Redcliffe & Temple
CE Sch BS1 227 B1
St Mary St
Bridgwater TA6 208 F4
Nether Stowey TA5 134 B2
St Mary's Bldgs BA2 228 B1
St Mary's CE Prim Sch
Bradford Abbas DT9 187 E1
Bridgwater TA6 208 C4
St Mary's CE Prim Sch
BA3 79 C1
St Mary's CE Prim Sch
BA2 60 C3
St Mary's Cl
Axminster EX13 198 A1
Bath BA2 45 B6
Chard TA20 223 C2
Cossington TA7 136 F3
Timsbury BA2 60 B2
St Mary's Cres
Chard TA20 223 C3
13 North Petherton TA6 153 F4
Yeovil BA21 219 C8
St Mary's Ct 1 TA6 208 F4
St Mary's Ct BS24 49 A1
St Mary's Gdns BS40 53 B5
St Mary's Gr BS48 18 C8
St Mary's Hospl BS8 226 B3
St Mary's La BA4 140 E3
St Mary's Park Rd BS20 2 C4
St Mary's Pk
Langport TA10 172 A5
Nailsea BS48 18 C8
St Mary's Prim Sch BS20 3 E3
St Mary's RC Prim Sch
Axminster EX13 198 A1
Bath BA1 27 B1
St Mary's Rd Bristol BS11 4 D7
Burnham-On-Sea TA8 104 B7
Frome BA11 120 B5
Hutton BS24 49 D2
Leigh Woods BS8 11 D6
Meare BA6 138 D4
Oxenpill BA6 138 C4
Portishead BS20 2 C4
Sherborne DT9 225 B3
Westonzoyland TA7 154 F5
St Mary's Sch TA20 199 B6
St Mary's St BS26 70 C2
St Mary's Wlk BS11 4 D6
St Marys Cl Hutton BS24 49 D2
Seavington TA19 184 D1
Wedmore BS28 108 C4
St Marys Ct TA6 153 E4

Stoke Mead BA2 . . . . .63 F7
Stoke Moor Dro BS27 . .109 D6
Stoke Paddock Rd BS9 . . .5 D6
Stoke Park Rd BS9 . . . . . . .5 F4
Stoke Park Rd S BS9 . . . . .5 E3
Stoke Rd Bristol BS9 . . . . . .5 F8
Martock TA12 . . . . .185 E5
North Curry TA3 . . . . . . .170 C4
Portishead BS20 . . . . .2 D5
Ruishton TA3 . . . . .169 C2
Stoke St Mary TA3 . . . . . .169 B1
Street BA16 . . . . .207 E6
Taunton TA1 . . . . .213 B1
Westbury Sub Mendip
BA5 . . . . .110 D6
Stoke St BS27 . . . . .110 B8
Stoke St Gregory Prim Sch
TA3 . . . . .170 E6
Stoke St Michael Prim Sch
BA3 . . . . .116 A3
Stoke sub Hamdon Castle
Prim Sch TA14 . . . . .185 F4
Stoke sub Hamdon Priory★
TA14 . . . . .185 F4
Stokeleigh Wlk BS9 . . . . . .5 C5
Stokes Croft BS1 . . . . . .227 B4
Stokes La DT10 . . . . . . .189 F2
Stolford Hill TA22 . . . . . .148 A4
Stonage La TA18 . . . . . .196 C5
Stone Allerton Dro BS26 .88 B2
Stone Cl TA1 . . . . .168 D1
Stone Cross TA24 . . . . . .128 E1
Stone Down La BA6 . . . .139 D1
Stone Hill Ct TA24 . . . . .200 F7
Stone Hill La TA4 . . . . . .166 D3
Stone La
East Pennard BA4 . . . . . . .158 E6
Winsford TA24 . . . . .147 E6
Yeovil BA21 . . . . .187 B5
Stone Mead La TA10 . . . .173 A4
Stone Rd TA8 . . . . .104 D5
Stoneable Rd BA3 . . . . . .79 A3
Stoneage La BA2 . . . . .61 E4
Stonebarrow La EX13 . .198 F2
Stoneberry Rd BS14 . . . . .23 B3
Stonebridge BS21 . . . . .6 D1
Stonebridge Dr BA11 . . .120 B7
Stonebridge Rd BS23 . . . .48 F4
Stonedene DT9 . . . . .225 D6
Stonegallows TA1 . . . . . .212 A3
Stonehenge La BS48 . . . . .8 E4
Stonehill
South Cadbury BA22 . . . . .175 C3
Stoke Sub Hamdon TA14 . .186 A4
Street BA16 . . . . .207 B5
Stonehouse Cl BA2 . . . . . .45 B2
Stonehouse La BA2 . . . . .45 B2
Stoneleigh
Chew Magna BS40 . . . . . . .39 B3
Wellington TA21 . . . . .222 B8
Stoneleigh Cl
Burnham-On-Sea TA8 . . . .104 C8
Staplegrove TA2 . . . . .212 C8
Stoneleigh Ct Bath BA1 . .27 E3
Taunton TA1 . . . . .212 C1
Stoneleigh Rise BA11 . .120 A6
Stoneridge La TA4 . . . . .165 D5
Stones Cross BA3 . . . . . .78 B2
Stones Paddock BA3 . . .116 C7
Stonewall Terr BA11 . . .119 F2
Stonewell Dr BS49 . . . . . .34 D3
Stonewell Gr BS49 . . . . . .34 D3
Stonewell La BS49 . . . . . .34 D3
Stonewell Park Rd BS49 .34 D3
Stoney Furlong TA2 . . . .213 B8
Stoney La
Bishops Lydeard TA4 . . . . .167 E8
Curry Rivel TA10 . . . . . . .171 C3
East Coker BA22 . . . . . . .197 D6
Stocklinch TA19 . . . . .184 C4
Stoney Lane Cross
EX16 . . . . .178 B3
Stoney Steep BS48 . . . . . . .9 A5
Stoneyard La BA3 . . . . . .75 D2
Stoneyfield Cl BS20 . . . . .4 B5
Stoneyfields BS20 . . . . . . .4 B4
Stoneyhurst Dr TA10 . . .171 C3
Stony La Axminster EX13 .198 A1
Hawkridge TA22 . . . . .146 E3
Whatley BA11 . . . . .118 A2
Stony Littleton Long
Barrow★ BA2 . . . . .80 C7
Stony St BA11 . . . . .119 F5
Stonyhead Hill TA3 . . . .169 F1
Stoodham TA13 . . . . . . .220 D5
Stoodly La
North Wootton BA4 . . . . . .140 D4
Pilton BA4 . . . . .204 A2
Stooper's Hill TA20 . . . .193 C6
Stopgate Cross EX14 . . .192 C4
Stoppard Rd TA8 . . . . . .104 C6
Stopper's La BA5 . . . . . .139 F6
Stormont Cl BS23 . . . . . . .48 F3
Stormore BA13 . . . . .121 F8
Storridge La
Axminster EX13 . . . . .198 B6
Brompton Regis TA22 . . . .148 A1
Storridge View TA22 . . .148 A2
Stour Hill SP8 . . . . .177 E1
Stour Hill Pk SP8 . . . . .177 F1
Stourhead★ BA12 . . . . . .161 F5
Stourton Cl BA11 . . . . . .119 E3
Stourton Gdns 1 BA11 .119 E3
Stourton La BA12 . . . . . .161 F6
Stourton View BA11 . . . .119 E3
Stourton Way BA21 . . . .218 D6
Stout Cross EX14 . . . . . .192 C5
Stout's Way La
Kingsbridge TA23 . . . . . . .148 F8
Rodhuish TA24 . . . . .131 A1
Stowborough Cotts BA2 .79 C7
Stowell Hill DT9 . . . . . . .176 C1
Stowell La TA20 . . . . . . .198 D8
Stowey Bottom BS39 . . . .57 E5
Stowey La
Curry Mallet TA3 . . . . . . .183 E8
Fivehead TA3 . . . . .170 E1
Stowey Pk BS49 . . . . .34 D7
Stowey Rd Pitney TA10 . .172 D7
Taunton TA2 . . . . .212 E8
Yatton BS49 . . . . .34 C8
Stradling Ave BS23 . . . . .48 F5
Stradling Cl TA7 . . . . . .137 B2
Stradling's Hill TA5 . . . .135 B3
Straight Dro
Burrowbridge TA7 . . . . . . .155 B1
Chilton Trinity TA5 . . . . . .135 F2
West Huntspill TA9 . . . . . .136 B7
Woolavington TA9 . . . . . . .137 A6
Straight La BA11 . . . . . .101 D7
Straight St BS2 . . . . . . .227 C2
Straightmead BA3 . . . . . .75 F1
Strap La Ston Easton BA3 . .95 F7
Upton Noble BA4,BA10 . . .143 A1
Stratford Cl BS14 . . . . . . .22 F3
Stratford Ct BS9 . . . . .5 F8
Stratford La BS40 . . . . . .56 E1
Stratford Rd BA21 . . . . .218 D5
Stratheden BS8 . . . . . . .226 A4
Stratton Cl TA6 . . . . . . .209 D3
Stratton Rd
Holcombe BA3 . . . . .116 B8
Saltford BS31 . . . . .25 E3
Stratton St BS2 . . . . . . .227 B3
Strawberry Bank TA19 . .221 C4
Strawberry Cl BS48 . . . . . .8 D1
Strawberry Field BS26 . . .70 D2
Strawberry Gdns BS48 . .18 D8
Strawberry Hill
Clevedon BS21 . . . . .6 F4
Street BA16 . . . . .207 B7
Strawberry La BS13,BS41 .21 E3
Strawberry Way N BA5 .203 C4
Strawberry Way S BA5 .203 C3
Streaked La TA3 . . . . . .170 C6
Streamcombe La TA22 .163 B5
Streamcross BS49 . . . . . .17 D1
Streamleaze BS40 . . . . . .39 B3
Streamside
Chew Magna BS40 . . . . . . .39 B3
1 Clevedon BS21 . . . . .6 F3
Taunton TA1 . . . . .213 C2
Stredlings Yd BS2 . . . . .226 C4
Street Ash La TA20 . . . . .193 C8
Street Dro Street BA16 . .207 B1
Street BA16 . . . . .207 E7
Street End BS40 . . . . .54 D2
Street End La BS40 . . . . .54 D2
Street Ho TA19 . . . . . . .221 B3
Street La
Higher Odcombe BA22 . . .186 C2
North Brewham BA10 . . .161 A7
Street Rd
Glastonbury BA6 . . . . . . .206 D3
Street BA6 . . . . .207 D8
Street Shoe Mus★
BA16 . . . . .207 C6
Street The
Bishop Sutton BS39 . . . . . .57 D4
Bishop Sutton, Stowey BS39 57 F4
Chew Stoke BS40 . . . . .56 D8
Chilcompton BA3 . . . . .96 D5
Compton Martin BS40 . . . .74 B7
Draycott BS27 . . . . .90 F2
Farmborough BA2 . . . . . . .59 F6
Kilmington BA12 . . . . . . .161 F6
Radstock BA3 . . . . .78 F2
Ubley BS40 . . . . .55 D1
Wanstrow BA4 . . . . .142 F4
West Monkton TA2 . . . . . .169 C7
Winford BS40 . . . . .37 F1
Stretcholt La TA6 . . . . . .135 F6
Stretford La TA19 . . . . .194 F7
Stringfellow Cres TA20 .223 D5
Stringfellow Mews
TA20 . . . . .223 C3
Stringland's La TA24 . . .131 B2
Strode Coll BA16 . . . . . .207 D6
Strode Ho 7 BA4 . . . . . .205 B6
Strode Rd Clevedon BS21 . .6 C2
Street BA16 . . . . .207 D6
Strode Way Clevedon BS21 .6 B1
Shepton Mallet BA4 . . . . .205 A5
Stroud Rd BS11 . . . . .4 E5
Strowland La BS24 . . . . . .86 F6
Strowlands BS24,TA9 . . . .86 E6
Struthers Cl BA16 . . . . .207 B7
Strutter's Hill BA10 . . . .215 D2
Stuart Pl BA2 . . . . .44 D6
Stuart Rd BS23 . . . . .49 A5
Stuarts Cl BA5 . . . . .203 D3
Stubb's La BA11 . . . . . . .101 D4
Studley La BA4 . . . . .142 F4
Studley Mdws BA4 . . . . .142 F4
Stump Cross
Pitcombe BA7 . . . . .215 A1
Shepton Mallet BA4 . . . . .204 D5
Sturford La BA12 . . . . . .144 E7
Sturmey Way BS20 . . . . . .4 E3
Sturminster Cl BS14 . . . .23 D6
Sturminster Rd BS14 . . . .23 D7
Stutts End TA4 . . . . .167 E6
Style Flats TA4 . . . . .210 C5
Style Rd TA4 . . . . .210 C5
Styles Ave BA11 . . . . . . .120 C4
Styles Cl BA11 . . . . .120 B4
Styles Hill BA11 . . . . . . .120 B4
Styles Mdw BA11 . . . . . .120 C5
Styles Pk BA11 . . . . .120 B4
Sub Rd BA6 . . . . .157 D4
Suffolk Cl TA6 . . . . .209 C3
Suffolk Cres TA1 . . . . . .212 C1
Suffolk Ct TA1 . . . . .212 C1
Sugg's La TA19 . . . . . . .183 C2
Sulis Manor Rd BA2 . . . . .62 D8
Sullivan Cl BS4 . . . . .22 D6
Sully Cl TA6 . . . . .209 D6
Sumerleaze Cres TA2 . .213 C8
Sumerlin Dr BS21 . . . . .6 F3
Summer Hill Frome BA11 119 F3
Hinton St George TA17 . . .195 D7
Summer House Terr
BA20 . . . . .219 B4
Summer La Banwell BS29 .50 E5
Chard TA20 . . . . .194 C4
Hinton St George TA13,
TA17 . . . . .195 C8
Monkton Combe BA2 . . . . . .63 D8
Weston-Super-Mare BS22,
BS24 . . . . .32 B1
Weston-Super-Mare BS29 . .50 D7
Summer La N BS22 . . . . .32 A2
Summer Shard TA13 . . .220 C4
Summerfield BS22 . . . . . .32 A3
Summerfield Ave TA21 .180 D8
Summerfield Cl TA7 . . . .154 F5
Summerfield Ct TA1 . . .212 E4
Summerfield Rd BA1 . . . .28 A1
Summerfield Sch BA1 . . .27 D1
Summerfield Terr BA1 . . .28 A1
Summerfield Way TA21 180 D8
Summerfields BA8 . . . . .190 A7
Summerfields Rd TA20 .223 C3
Summerhedge Cres
TA7 . . . . .155 C2
Summerhedge Rd TA7 .155 C1
Summerhill Rd BA1 . . . . .27 D1
Summerhouse BS21 . . . . . .8 D4
Summerhouse View
BA21 . . . . .219 C6
Summerland Ave TA24 .201 A7
Summerland Pl TA24 . .200 F7
Summerland Rd TA24 . .200 F7
Summerlands
Backwell BS48 . . . . .19 B5
Yeovil BA21 . . . . .218 E6
Summerlands Hospl
BA21 . . . . .218 F6
Summerlands Park Ave
TA19 . . . . .221 B4
Summerlands Park Cl
TA19 . . . . .221 B4
Summerlands Park Dr
TA19 . . . . .221 B4
Summerlands Rd BS23 . .49 B8
Summerlays Ct BA2 . . . . .45 B6
Summerlea BA2 . . . . .61 A5
Summerleaze BS31 . . . . .24 E7
Summerleaze Cres TA2 .213 C7
Summerleaze Pk BA20 .218 F5
Summers Hill La BA4 . .204 C2
Summerville Terr TA8 . .104 B6
Summerway TA24 . . . . .129 E1
Summerway Dro TA7 . . .209 E4
Summerwood Rd BA16 .207 B4
Sun Batch BS27 . . . . .91 A3
Sun St BA11 . . . . .119 E5
Sunderland Pl BS8 . . . .226 B3
Sunderland St BA2 . . . .228 C3
Sundew Cl TA1 . . . . .213 C1
Sunfield Rd BS24 . . . . . . .49 E3
Sunningdale BS8 . . . . . .226 B4
Sunningdale Cl BS48 . . . . .9 A1
Sunningdale Rd
Weston-Super-Mare BS22 . .31 F3
Yeovil BA21 . . . . .219 C6
Sunny Bank TA4 . . . . . . .150 B8
Sunny Bank Way BS24 . . .32 B1
Sunny Cl TA9 . . . . .136 B8
Sunny Hill Bristol BS9 . . . .5 C7
Pitcombe BA10 . . . . .215 C4
Sunny La BA10 . . . . .215 C4
Sunnybank BA2 . . . . .45 B4
Sunnybank Rd TA6 . . . .208 E2
Sunnybrow Cl 10 TA6 . . .153 F4
Sunnyhill Dr BS11 . . . . . . .4 E6
Sunnyhill Ho E BS11 . . . . .4 E6
Sunnyhill Ho W BS11 . . . . .4 E6
Sunnymead
Bridgwater TA6 . . . . .208 E2
Keynsham BS31 . . . . .24 F3
Midsomer Norton BA3 . . . .77 F2
Oakhill BA3 . . . . .114 F3
Stratton-on-the-Fosse BA3 .96 F2
Sunnymeade BA6 . . . . . .138 C4
Sunnymede Rd BS48 . . . . .8 D3
Sunnyside
Barrington TA19 . . . . .184 C5
Bristol BS9 . . . . .5 E5
Burlescombe EX16 . . . . . .179 C2
Clutton BS39 . . . . .59 B4
Farrington Gurney BS39 . . .77 B3
Frome BA11 . . . . .119 F3
Sunnyside Cotts TA24 . .129 A8
Sunnyside Cres BS21 . . . .6 D3
Sunnyside Pl BA11 . . . . .119 F3
Sunnyside Rd
Clevedon BS21 . . . . .6 D3
Weston-Super-Mare BS23 . .48 E5
Sunnyside Rd N BS23 . . .48 E6
Sunnyside Terr DT9 . . . .225 E4
Sunnyside View BA2 . . . . .79 C7
Sunnyvale Clevedon BS21 . .6 B1
Peasedown St John BA2 . . .78 E8
Sunridge Cl BA3 . . . . . . .96 F8
Sunridge Pk BA3 . . . . . . .96 F8
Sunset Cl BA2 . . . . .79 C7
Suprema Ave TA7 . . . . . .137 C2
Suprema Est TA7 . . . . . .137 D2
Surrey St BS2 . . . . .227 B4
Susanna's Cross BA3 . . .116 B2
Susanna's La BA3 . . . . .116 C2
Sussex Ave TA6 . . . . . . .209 B3
Sussex Cl TA6 . . . . .209 B3
Sussex Lodge TA1 . . . . .212 F5
Sussex Pl BA2 . . . . .228 C1
Sutherland Ave TA8 . . . .104 B6
Sutherland Cl TA1 . . . . .212 C1
Sutherland Ct TA1 . . . . .212 C1
Sutherland Dr BS24 . . . . .49 D2
Sutton Cl Frome BA11 . . .120 B7
Weston-Super-Mare BS22 . .49 E8
Sutton Cross TA10 . . . . .172 F4
Sutton Grange BA21 . . .218 C6
Sutton Hill
East Coker BA22 . . . . .197 D6
Long Sutton TA10 . . . . . . .172 E3
Sutton Hill Rd BS39 . . . . .57 D4
Sutton La Redhill BS40 . . . .36 F1
Walton BA16 . . . . .156 D6
Sutton Pk BS39 . . . . .57 D4
Sutton Rd TA11 . . . . . . .211 C2
Sutton St BA2 . . . . .45 B7
Swain St TA23 . . . . .202 C7
Swains TA21 . . . . .222 D4
Swains La TA21 . . . . . . .222 D4
Swainswick BS14 . . . . . . .22 F6
Swainswick Gdns BA1 . . .28 C2
Swainswick La BA1 . . . . .28 D4
Swainswick Prim Sch
BA1 . . . . .28 B5
Swallow Cl BA3 . . . . .97 B8
Swallow Ct BS14 . . . . . . .23 F6
Swallow Dr BA11 . . . . . .120 B6
Swallow Gdns BS22 . . . . .49 E8
Swallow Hill TA10 . . . . .172 A6
Swallow St BA1 . . . . . . .228 C2
Swallowcliffe Ct BA20 . .219 A5
Swallowcliffe Gdns
BA20 . . . . .219 A5
Swallows The BS22 . . . . .49 D7
Swan Cl BS22 . . . . .49 E8
Swan Down TA20 . . . . . .194 E4
Swan Hill TA18 . . . . . . .196 C5
Swan Ho 3 BA4 . . . . . . .205 B6
Swan Prec TA19 . . . . . . .221 C3
Swan Yd DT9 . . . . .225 D4
Swancombe Blagdon BS40 54 E2
Clapton In Gordano BS20 . . .8 E8
Swane Rd BS14 . . . . .23 F6
Swanmead Com Sch
TA19 . . . . .221 C3
Swans La BS27 . . . . .90 F2
Swanshard La BA5 . . . . .139 D6
Swedish Hos TA13 . . . . .220 D1
Sweetgrass Rd BS24 . . . .50 A8
Sweethay Cl TA3 . . . . . .181 D8
Sweethay Cross TA3 . . .181 C8
Sweethay La TA3 . . . . . .181 C8
Sweetleaze BA3 . . . . . . .116 A2
Swell Cl TA9 . . . . .136 B8
Swell La TA3 . . . . .171 A2
Swiddacombe La EX36 .162 C7
Swift Cl BS22 . . . . .31 F1
Swift Lodge BA20 . . . . . .219 A4
Swifts TA21 . . . . .166 F1
Swingbridge TA2 . . . . . .213 E7
Swiss Dr BS3 . . . . .11 F2
Swiss Rd Bristol BS3 . . . . .11 F1
Weston-Super-Mare BS23 . .48 F7
Sycamore Cl
Bridgwater TA6 . . . . .209 D5
Burnham-On-Sea TA8 . . . .104 A5
Nailsea BS48 . . . . .8 E2
Shipham BS25 . . . . .70 E8
Taunton TA1 . . . . .213 C2
Weston-Super-Mare BS23 . .49 A8
Westonzoyland TA7 . . . . . .154 E5
Sycamore Ct TA20 . . . . .223 C5
Sycamore Dr
Crewkerne TA18 . . . . .224 D7
Frome BA11 . . . . .120 B7
Langport TA10 . . . . .172 A6
Yeovil BA20 . . . . .218 F2
Sycamore Rd
Minehead TA24 . . . . .200 D7
Radstock BA3 . . . . .79 B2
Sycamore Sq TA20 . . . . .223 C5
Sycamore Wlk TA3 . . . . .169 D4
Sycamores BS23 . . . . . . .30 E1
Sydenham Bldgs BA2 . .228 A2
Sydenham Cl
Bridgwater TA6 . . . . .209 C6
Porlock TA24 . . . . .124 B4
Sydenham Rd Bath BA2 .228 A2
Bridgwater TA6 . . . . .209 C6
Sydenham Terr BA2 . . . . .45 C1
Sydling Rd BA21 . . . . . .219 D6
Sydnalls La BA12 . . . . . .144 E8
Sydney Bldgs BA2 . . . . . .45 B6
Sydney Ho Bath BA2 . . . . .45 B7
Pill BS20 . . . . .4 D4
Sydney Mews BA2 . . . . . .45 B7
Sydney Pl BA2 . . . . .45 B7
Sydney Rd BA2 . . . . .45 B7
Sydney Row BS1 . . . . . .226 B1
Sydney Wharf BA2 . . . . . .45 B7
Sylvan Rd TA21 . . . . . . .222 E5
Sylvan Way Bristol BS9 . . . .5 B7
Sylvan Way *continued*
Monkton Heathfield TA2 . .213 E8
Symes Ave BS13 . . . . . . .22 C4
Symes Cl TA18 . . . . .196 C4
Symes Pk BA1 . . . . .27 A2
Symons Way
Bridgwater TA6 . . . . .209 A6
Cheddar BS27 . . . . .90 C7
Syndercombe La TA4,
TA23 . . . . .149 D2

T

Tabernacle La 4 BA20 .219 B4
Tacchi Morris Arts Ctr
TA2 . . . . .213 F8
Tadhill La BA3 . . . . .116 D2
Tadwick La BA1 . . . . .28 A6
Tail Mill TA16 . . . . .195 F7
Tailor's Ct 4 BS1 . . . . .227 A3
Talbot Cl TA9 . . . . .104 D3
Tallis Gr BS4 . . . . .22 D6
Tallowood BA4 . . . . . . .205 D5
Tamar Ave TA1 . . . . . . .213 B1
Tamar Dr BS31 . . . . .25 A4
Tamar Rd BS22 . . . . .32 A2
Tamblyn Cl BA3 . . . . .79 A3
Tamsin Ct BS31 . . . . .24 F5
Tamworth Rd BS31 . . . . .24 E4
Tan La SP8 . . . . .161 F1
Tan Yard La TA13 . . . . .184 F5
Tancred St TA1 . . . . . . .213 A4
Tangier TA1 . . . . .212 E4
Tankard's Cl BS8 . . . . .226 C3
Tankey's Cl BA11 . . . . .120 A7
Tanner's Hill TA4 . . . . .165 E7
Tanners La SN14 . . . . . . .13 F8
Tanners Wlk Bath BA2 . . . .43 F5
Marshfield SN14 . . . . .13 F8
Tannery Cl BA16 . . . . . .207 C5
Tannery Ct TA18 . . . . . .224 C7
Tanorth Cl BS14 . . . . . . .23 A3
Tanorth Rd BS14 . . . . . . .22 F3
Tansee Hill TA20 . . . . . .199 B6
Tansey BA4 . . . . .142 A6
Tanyard Broadway TA19 . .183 C2
Nether Stowey TA5 . . . . . .134 B2
Tanyard La
Langport TA10 . . . . .172 A5
North Wootton BA4 . . . . . .140 C4
North Wootton, Lower Westholme
BA4 . . . . .140 D3
Tanyard The BA16 . . . . .207 C5
Tanyards BA10 . . . . . . .215 F7
Tape La BA3 . . . . .114 F7
Taphouse La DT6 . . . . . .199 E1
Tapmoor Rd TA7 . . . . . .155 C8
Tappers La 3 TA6 . . . . .153 E3
Tapps La TA7 . . . . .136 E4
Tapstone Rd TA20 . . . . .223 D4
Taranto Hill BA22 . . . . .173 E2
Taranto Way BA22 . . . . .174 A2
Target La TA12 . . . . . . .185 D4
Tarnock Ave BS14 . . . . . .23 A7
Tarnwell BS39 . . . . .40 A2
Tarr Stps★ TA22 . . . . . .146 E3
Tarr Water Cotts TA23 . .148 E8
Tarrant La BA20 . . . . . . .218 F1
Tarratt La
East Coker BA22 . . . . .197 E8
Yeovil BA20,BA22 . . . . . . .219 A1
Tarratt Rd BA20 . . . . . . .218 F1
Tatham Ct TA1 . . . . . . .212 D4
Tatworth Prim Sch
TA20 . . . . .198 C8
Tatworth Rd TA20 . . . . .223 C2
Tatworth St TA20 . . . . .198 C8
Tauntfield Cl TA1 . . . . .213 A3
Taunton & Somerset Hospl
Musgrove Pk TA1 . . . . . .212 C3
Taunton Rd Ashcott TA7 .156 B7
Bishops Lydeard TA4 . . . . .167 F7
Bridgwater TA6 . . . . .153 F4
Bridgwater TA6 . . . . .209 A3
North Petherton TA6 . . . . .153 E2
Wellington TA21 . . . . .222 E7
Weston-Super-Mare BS22 . .32 B4
Wiveliscombe TA4 . . . . . .210 D4
Taunton Sch TA2 . . . . . .212 D6
Taunton Sta TA1 . . . . . .212 F5
Taunton Trad Est TA2 . .212 A7
Taunusstein Way 12
BA20 . . . . .219 B4
Taveners Wlk BS48 . . . . . .8 F3
Taverner Cl BS4 . . . . . . .22 D7
Tavistock Rd BS22 . . . . .32 A2
Tawny Way BS22 . . . . . . .49 F8
Taylor Cl TA2 . . . . .168 B5
Taylor Ct Bridgwater TA6 .209 A5
Weston-Super-Mare BS22 . .32 B4
Taylor Gdns BS13 . . . . . .21 F4
Taylor Ho TA19 . . . . . . .221 B3
Taylor's Meade TA20 . .193 D6
Taylor's Orch TA14 . . . .185 E1
Tayman Ridge BS30 . . . . .25 D8
Teagle Cl BA5 . . . . .203 F5
Teak Cl TA6 . . . . .209 D6
Teal Cl Bridgwater TA6 . .209 A4
Weston-Super-Mare BS22 . .31 F1
Teal Rd TA24 . . . . .201 C5
Tealham Moor Dro
BS28 . . . . .137 E8
Teals Acre 8 TA5 . . . . . .135 B2
Teapot Lane (Worms Lane)
BA6 . . . . .158 B6
Teasel Wlk BS22 . . . . . . .49 D7
Technical St TA8 . . . . . .104 B6

Teck Hill TA6 153 E2
Teckhill La TA6 153 E2
Teddington Cl BA2 44 C4
Teesdale Cl BS22 49 D8
Teign Ct BA16 156 D7
Teignmouth Rd BS21 6 E3
Telephone Ave BS1 227 A2
Telford Ho BA2 44 D3
Tellis Cross BA22 197 D8
Tellis La BA3 114 D8
Tellisford La BA2 81 F4
Temblett Gn TA6 208 C5
Templars Barton BA8 176 E1
Templars Pl BA8 176 E1
Templars Way BS25 70 E7
Temple Back BS1 227 B2
Temple Back E BS1 227 C2
Temple Circus Giratory
BS1 227 C1
Temple Ct BS31 24 E5
Temple Field TA23 202 C6
Temple Gate BS1 227 B1
Temple Inf Sch BS31 24 F5
Temple Inn La BS39 58 E1
Temple Jun Sch BS31 24 F6
Temple La BA8 176 F1
Temple Rose St BS1 227 B2
Temple St Bristol BS1 227 B2
Keynsham BS31 24 F5
Temple Way BS2 227 B2
Temple Way Underpass
BS2 227 C3
Templecombe La SP8 177 C3
Templecombe Sta BA8 176 E1
Templeland Rd BS13 21 F5
Tenby Rd BS31 24 D4
Tengore La TA10 172 C6
Tennis Corner Dro
BA11 102 D2
Tennis Court Ave BS39 77 D5
Tennis Court Rd BS39 77 D5
Tennyson Ave BS21 6 B2
Tennyson Cl BS31 24 F6
Tennyson Rd Bath BA1 44 D7
Weston-Super-Mare BS23 49 A3
Tenterk Cl BS24 67 B6
Tents Hill BA11 118 B6
Tenyard Cotts TA24 131 A5
Terhill La TA4 151 F3
Termare Cl BA22 218 B6
Terrace The
Minehead TA24 201 A5
Shipham BS25 70 E7
Terrace View DT9 225 E5
Terrace Wlk BA1 228 C2
Terrell St BS2 227 A4
Terry Hill BA3 98 D8
Terry Ho BS1 226 C3
Tetbury Gdns BS48 9 A1
Tetton Cl TA6 208 B4
Teviot Rd BS31 25 A4
Tewkesbury BA21 218 D6
Tewther Rd BS13 22 D3
Teyfant Com Sch BS13 22 E4
Teyfant Rd BS13 22 E4
Teyfant Wlk BS13 22 E4
Thackeray Ave BS21 6 E4
Thackeray Ho BS23 49 A5
Thackeray Rd BS21 6 E4
Thames Dr TA1 213 D4
Thatch The TA11 211 C4
Thatcham Cl BA21 218 F7
Thatcham Ct BA21 218 F7
Thatcham Pk BA21 218 F7
Thatcher Cl BS20 2 D4
Theaks Mews TA1 213 A3
Theatre Royal BS1 227 A2
There-and-Back-Again La
BS1 226 C3
Theynes Croft BS41 11 B1
Thicket Mead BA3 78 A2
Thickthorn Cross TA19 183 C3
Thimble La DT9 217 D2
Third Ave Bath BA2 44 D5
Bristol, Hengrove BS14 23 B7
Radstock BA3 97 D7
Thirlmere Rd BS23 49 A4
Thistle Pk TA6 209 B1
Thistledoo Vine TA7 136 F2
Thomas Cl BS29 51 A3
Thomas La BS1 227 B2
Thomas St Bath BA1 228 C4
Bristol BS2 227 B4
Taunton TA2 212 F6
Thomas Way BA6 206 B4
Thompson Cl TA6 209 D6
Thompson Rd BS14 23 E6
Thomson Dr TA18 224 D5
Thong La TA10 184 D6
Thorn Cl BS22 32 B2
Thorn Cross Way TA21 178 D8
Thorn La TA3 169 D2
Thornash Cl TA2 213 F8
Thornbank Ct DT9 225 E4
Thornbank Pl BA2 228 A1
Thornbury Dr BS23 48 D2
Thornbury Rd BS23 48 C2
Thornbush Cross TA4 150 F3
Thorncombe Cres TA6 209 C5
Thorncombe Thorn
TA20 199 B5
Thorndale BS8 226 A4
Thorndale Cl BS22 49 D8
Thorndale Mews BS8 226 A4
Thorndun Park Dr TA20 223 D6
Thorne Cross BA22 218 B7
Thorne Gdns BA21 218 C7
Thorne La
Wheddon Cross TA24 147 C8
Winsford TA24 147 C8
Yeovil BA21 218 C8
Thorne Pk TA8 104 B5
Thorney Rd TA12 185 B8
Thorneymoor La TA10 172 A3
Thornhill Dro TA12 173 A1
Thornhill Rd DT10 190 B4
Thornton Rd BA21 218 D7
Thornwell La BA9 216 D3
Thornwell Way BA9 216 C3
Thorny La BA21 187 E8
Thornymarsh La BA7 175 B8
Three Ashes DT8 199 D7
Three Ashes La TA11 157 B4
Three Corner Mead
BA21 218 C5
Three Gates Cross
TA22 163 C6
Three Hill View BA6 206 E5
Three Horse Shoes Hill
TA5 152 C4
Three Oaks Cross TA19 183 C4
Three Queens' La BS1 227 B2
Three Wells Rd BS13 21 F4
Thrift Cl DT10 190 C4
Throgmorton Rd BS4 22 F8
Throop Rd BA8 176 F1
Thrubwell La BS40 37 B4
Thrupe La BA5 114 A2
Thrush Cl BS22 49 E8
Thumb La BA4 158 E7
Thurlbear CE Prim Sch
TA3 182 C8
Thurlestone BS14 23 A6
Thurlocks BA22 186 B6
Thynne Cl BS27 90 B6
Tibbott Rd BS14 23 D5
Tibbott Wlk BS14 23 D5
Tichborne Rd BS23 30 E1
Tickenham Hill BS48 8 E4
Tickenham Prim Sch BS21 7 F4
Tickenham Rd BS21 7 A4
Tide Gr BS11 5 A8
Tiffany Ct BS1 227 B1
Tile Hill BA10 161 A7
Tile House Rd
East Huntspill TA7 137 B8
Mark TA9 106 C1
Tiledown BS39 58 E1
Tiledown Cl BS39 58 F1
Tilery EX14 192 D3
Tilham St BA6 158 B6
Tilley Cl Farmborough BA2 60 A5
Keynsham BS31 25 A2
Tilley La BA2 60 A5
Tilleys Dro BA5 138 F7
Tilsey La TA4 150 C5
Timbers The BA3 97 B7
Timberscombe Way
TA6 208 B4
Timberscombe Wlk BS14 23 C5
Timberyard TA7 137 F1
Timewell Hill EX16 164 C4
Timsbury Rd
Farmborough BA2 60 B5
High Littleton BS39 59 D1
Tin Bridge Rdbt BA6 139 D3
Tinker's La
Compton Martin BS40 74 B7
Cucklington BA9 177 D7
Halse TA4 167 C6
Kilmersdon BA11 98 B1
Tinneys La DT9 225 E4
Tintagel Cl BS31 24 D4
Tintagel Rd BA21 218 D7
Tintern BA21 218 C6
Tintinhull Rd Yeovil BA21 186 F5
Yeovil BA21 218 E8
Tipcote Hill 17 BA4 205 B6
Tipnoller Hill TA4 210 F7
Tippacott La EX35 122 A4
Tiptoft 3 TA14 185 F4
Tirley Way BS22 31 B2
Titan Barrow BA1 29 C2
Tithe Barn Cross EX15 179 D2
Tithe Mdw TA4 167 A7
Tithill La TA4 167 F7
Titlands La BA5 203 A7
Tiverton Gdns BS22 32 A2
Tiverton Rd
1 Bampton EX16 164 C1
2 Clevedon BS21 6 E1
Tivington Cross TA24 129 F8
Tivoli Ho BS23 48 E8
Tivoli La BS23 48 E8
Toghill La BS30 12 A8
Tolbury La BA10 215 D6
Tolbury Mill BA10 215 E6
Toll Bridge Rd BA1 28 E3
Toll House Rd 1 TA5 135 B2
Toll Rd Porlock TA24 124 A3
Weston-Super-Mare BS23 66 F8
Tolland BS24 49 A2
Tolley's La TA20 194 C3
Tom Tit's La TA11 211 C3
Toms Cl TA20 223 B3
Tone Dr TA6 209 B3
Tone Gn TA4 167 E2
Tone Hill TA21 222 B8
Tone Rd BS21 6 D1
Tonedale Bsns Pk TA21 222 B7
Toneway TA2 213 C6
Toose The BA21 218 C6
Top Hill BA4 142 F2
Top La Mells BA11 118 B6
Stourton BA12 161 E4
Top Rd
Charlton Adam TA11 173 F7
Cheddar BS27 90 E5
Shipham BS25 70 F7
Westbury Sub Mendip BA5 110 E6
Top St Kingsdon TA11 173 D5
Pilton BA4 140 F3
Top Wood BA3 116 B7
Tor Cl BS22 32 A2
Tor St BA5 203 E4
Tor View Cheddar BS27 90 C7
Woolavington TA7 136 E4
Tor View Ave BA6 206 D3
Tor Wood View BA5 203 E5
Torbay Cl BA7 214 B5
Torbay Rd BA7 214 A5
Torbay Road Ind Est
BA7 214 A5
Torbay Villas BA7 214 A5
Torhill La BA5 203 F4
Torhole Bottom BA3 94 A4
Tormynton Rd BS22 31 E3
Torre Rocks TA23 131 E2
Torre The BA21 218 C6
Torridge Mead TA1 213 D4
Torridge Rd BS31 25 A4
Torrington Ave BS4 22 F8
Torrington Cres BS22 32 A3
Totnes Cl BS22 32 A2
Totney Dro BS28 137 E8
Totshill Dr BS13 22 E4
Totshill Gr BS13 22 E4
Tottenham Pl BS8 226 B3
Totterdown La
Pilton BA4 204 B1
Weston-Super-Mare BS24 49 A1
Totterdown Rd BS23 48 F4
Touch La TA10 156 C1
Touches La TA20 223 E5
Touches Mdw TA20 223 E5
Touching End La SN14 13 F8
Touchstone Cl TA20 223 B4
Touchstone La TA20 223 B4
Tout Hill BA9 216 C3
Tout La BA22TA11 174 A6
Tovey Cl BS22 31 E4
Tower Cl Cheddar BS27 90 B6
Stoke St Michael BA3 116 A3
Tower Hill Bristol BS2 227 B3
Bruton BA10 215 D6
Holcombe Rogus TA21 178 D5
Horsington BA8 176 E2
Locking BS24 50 D4
Stogursey TA5 134 B5
Stoke St Michael BA3 116 A3
Williton TA4 202 E2
Tower Hill Rd TA18 224 B5
Tower House La BS48 9 A4
Tower La Bristol BS1 227 A3
Taunton TA1 212 E4
Tower Rd
Kilmington BA12 161 D6
Portishead BS20 2 A4
Stawell TA7 137 B1
Yeovil BA21 219 C8
Tower St Bristol BS1 227 B2
Taunton TA1 212 E4
Tower View Frome BA11 119 F2
South Cheriton BA8 176 D3
Wanstrow BA4 142 E4
Tower Wlk BS23 30 D1
Towerhead Rd BS29 51 D3
Towerleaze BS9 5 D3
Town Barton BA2 81 F4
Town Cl North Curry TA3 170 B4
Stogursey TA5 134 B6
Town End BA2 81 F4
Town Hill EX36 162 C6
Town La BA4 205 C6
Town St BA4 205 B6
Town Tree La TA10,
TA12 185 D8
Townend Villas TA14 185 F2
Townhall Bldgs BA5 203 E4
Townrise 15 BA20 219 B4
Townsend
East Harptree BS40 75 A5
Ilminster TA19 221 D3
Marston Magna BA22 174 F1
Middlezoy TA7 155 C3
Montacute TA15 186 B3
Shepton Mallet BA4 205 B5
Westonzoyland TA7 154 F5
Williton TA4 202 E3
Townsend Cl Bristol BS14 23 F5
Bruton BA10 215 F7
Townsend Gn 10 BA8 190 A6
Townsend La
Chilton Polden TA7 137 B2
Emborough BA3 95 B2
Theale BS28 109 A2
Townsend Orch
Merriott TA16 195 F8
Street BA16 207 B5
Townsend Pk BA10 215 F7
Townsend Rd Bristol BS14 23 F5
Minehead TA24 201 A6
Townsend Rise BA10 215 F7
Townshend Rd BS22 32 B5
Trackfordmoor Cross
TA22 163 B3
Tracy Cl BS14 22 F7
Trafalgar Rd BA1 27 B1
Traits La BA22 174 E4
Trajan's Way BA4 205 E5
Transform Ind Est TA6 209 A6
Transom Ho BS1 227 B2
Travers Cl BS4 22 D6
Trawden Cl BS23 31 A1
Treasure Ct TA8 85 A1
Treasurer's Ho★ TA12 185 E6
Treborough Cl TA2 213 B8
Treefield Rd BS21 6 D2
Tregarth Rd BS3 11 F1
Tregelles Cl TA9 104 C4
Tregonwell Rd TA24 201 A7
Trelawn Cl BS22 32 D2
Trellech Ct BA21 218 C6
Tremes Cl SN14 13 F8
Tremlett Mews 3 BS22 32 B4
Trenchard Rd
Locking BS24 50 D4
Saltford BS31 25 D3
Trenchard St BS1 226 C3
Trendle La Bicknoller TA4 132 F2
Wincanton BA9 160 E3
Trendle Rd TA1 212 B1
Trendle St DT9 225 D3
Trendlewood Way BS48 9 A1
Trenleigh Dr BS22 32 A2
Trent Cl BA21 219 E8
Trent Ct TA1 213 D4
Trent Gr BS31 25 A4
Trent Mdw TA1 213 E4
Trent Path La DT9 225 A5
Trent Youngs Sch DT9 187 F5
Tresco Spinney BA21 218 C6
Trevanna Rd BS3 11 F1
Trevelyan Rd BS23 48 F7
Trevett Rd TA1 212 C2
Trevithick Cl BA11 120 C6
Trevor Rd TA6 209 C6
Trevor Smith Pl TA1 213 A3
Trewartha Cl BS23 48 F8
Trewartha Pk BS23 48 F8
Trewint Gdns BS4 22 F8
Triangle Ct BA2 44 D5
Triangle Ctr The BS21 6 D3
Triangle E BA2 44 D5
Triangle N BA2 44 D5
Triangle S BS8 226 B3
Triangle The
Clevedon BS21 6 D3
North Curry TA3 170 A4
Somerton TA11 211 D4
Wrington BS40 35 D2
Triangle W Bath BA2 44 D5
Bristol BS8 226 B3
Tribunal & Lake Village
Mus★ BA6 206 D4
Trickey Warren La TA3 181 C1
Trim Bridge 3 BA1 228 B2
Trim St BA1 228 B2
Trin Mills BS1 227 A1
Trinder Rd BS20 4 B4
Trindlewell La TA18 196 C4
Trinity Bsns Ctr TA1 213 A3
Trinity CE Fst Sch BA11 119 C4
Trinity Cl Bath BA1 228 B2
Burnham-On-Sea TA8 85 A1
Wedmore BS28 107 D4
Wellington TA21 222 C5
Trinity Coll BS9 5 E4
Trinity Ct Bridgwater TA6 208 F6
Nailsea BS48 8 C1
10 Yeovil BA20 219 B4
Trinity Mews 15 BS2 227 C3
Trinity Pl Bristol BS8 226 A2
Weston-Super-Mare BS23 30 C1
Trinity Rd Bath BA2 45 B2
Nailsea BS48 8 D1
Taunton TA1 213 B3
Weston-Super-Mare BS23 30 C1
Trinity Rise TA8 85 A1
Trinity Row Frome BA11 119 E5
Wellington TA21 222 C5
Trinity St Bath BA1 228 B2
Frome BA11 119 E5
Taunton TA1 213 B3
Trinity Wlk Bristol BS2 227 C3
Frome BA11 119 E5
Tripps Cnr BS49 34 D7
Tripps Dro BA5 139 A6
Triscombe Ave TA6 208 D4
Triscombe Rd TA2 212 E8
Tristram Dr TA3 169 D4
Tropical Bird Gdn★ TA8 47 F2
Tropicana Leisure Pool★
BS23 48 D6
Trossachs Dr BA2 45 D8
Trotts La TA19 183 B2
Trottsway Cross TA24 129 C2
Trow La BA12 144 C2
Trowbridge Cl TA9 104 D4
Trowell La TA4 165 E4
Truckwell La TA4 150 D4
Trull CE Prim Sch TA3 168 D1
Trull Green Dr TA3 168 D1
Trull Rd TA1 212 E2
Trumps Cross EX16 178 E3
Truro Cl TA8 104 C7
Truro Rd BS48 9 A1
Trym Bank BS9 5 D7
Trym Cross Rd BS9 5 C5
Trym Side BS9 5 C5
Trymleaze BS9 5 C5
Trymwood Par BS9 5 D6
Tucker St Bristol BS2 227 C3
Wells BA5 203 C4
Tucker's Cross DT9 188 A4
Tucker's La
Baltonsborough BA6 157 F6
Compton Martin BS40 73 E8
Tucker's Moor Cross
EX16 162 F3
Tuckers La BA7 214 B7
Tuckerton La TA7 153 F1
Tuckingmill La BS39 41 E5
Tuckmarsh La BA11 143 E7
Tuckmill BS21 6 B1
Tuddington Gdns BA5 203 B4
Tudor Ct Chard TA20 223 C6
Yeovil BA20 219 A4
Tudor Rd Portishead BS20 2 E4
Weston-Super-Mare BS22 32 A4
Tudor Way TA6 209 A1
Tudway Cl BA5 203 C4
Tufton Ave BS11 5 A8
Tugela Rd BS13 21 F7
Tuggy's La BA2 63 E1
Tulip Tree Rd TA6 209 E5
Tulse Hill BA12 161 F2
Tunbridge Cl BS40 39 B2
Tunbridge Rd BS40 39 B2
Tuncombe La TA18 195 D4
Tunley Hill BA2 60 E2
Tunley Rd BA2,BA3 61 D5
Tunnel The TA24 128 B2
Tunscombe La BA4 142 D8
Tunstall Cl BS9 5 E4
Turkey Ct 5 TA1 212 E3
Turn Hill TA10 155 F2
Turnbury Ave BS48 9 A1
Turnbury Cl BS22 31 F3
Turner Cl Bridgwater TA6 209 A4
Keynsham BS31 25 A5
Turner Ct Wells BA5 203 D3
Weston-Super-Mare BS22 31 F3
Turner Rd TA2 212 E7
Turner Way BS21 6 B1
Turner's Barn La BA20 218 F2
Turner's Court La BA3 114 D8
Turner's La DT6 199 B2
Turner's Terr BA3 80 A1
Turnhill Rd TA10 156 A2
Turnpike Milverton TA4 167 A4
Sampford Peverell EX16 178 C1
Turnpike Cl TA18 196 B3
Turnpike Cnr BA3 95 B8
Turnpike Cross TA14 185 E2
Turnpike Gn TA18 196 B3
Turnpike La BA4 142 B6
Turnpike Rd
Axbridge BS26 69 E1
Shipham BS25 70 E8
Turstin Rd BA6 206 F6
Turtlegate Ave BS13 21 E4
Turtlegate Wlk BS13 21 E4
Tut Hill DT9 189 C1
Tutton Way BS21 6 D1
Tuttors Hill BS27 71 C1
Tuxwell La TA5 152 C8
Tweed Rd BS21 6 C1
Tweed Rd Ind Est 2 BS21 6 C1
Tweentown BS27 90 B8
Twelve Acre Post TA22 163 A4
Twerton Farm Cl BA2 44 B6
Twerton Inf Sch BA2 44 A5
Twinell La TA5 152 D7
Twines Cl BA22 175 A5
Twinhoe La BA2 62 E2
Twistgates La EX14 192 A4
Twitchens La BS27 90 F2
Two Acres Cvn Pk BS21 1 B1
Two Acres Rd BS14 23 A7
Two Ash Hill TA20 193 F1
Two Ash La TA20 194 A1
Two Elms BA21 187 E8
Two Tower La BA22 219 B2
Two Trees BS40 72 E8
Twyford Pl TA21 222 D5
Tydeman Rd BS20 2 F5
Tyler Gn 2 BS22 32 B4
Tyler Way TA9 104 D3
Tyler's La TA4 167 A7
Tylers End TA9 104 F3
Tyndall Ave BS8 226 C4
Tyndall Ho 5 BS2 227 C3
Tyndall's Park Rd BS8 226 C4
Tyndalls Park Mews
BS2 226 C4
Tyne Pk TA1 213 D3
Tyning Cl BS14 23 A7
Tyning Cotts BA3 116 C7
Tyning End BA2 45 B5
Tyning Hengrove Jun Sch
BS14 23 A7
Tyning Hill Hemington BA3 99 C8
Radstock BA3 79 B3
Tyning La BA1 28 B1
Tyning Pl BA2 45 C2
Tyning Rd Bath BA2 45 C2
Bathampton BA2 28 F2
Peasedown St John BA2 79 D7
Saltford BS31 25 E2
Winsley BA15 64 E7
Tyning The Bath BA2 45 B5
Freshford BA3 64 B4
Tynings BS39 58 D3
Tynings La BA5 203 C8
Tynings Mews BS23 48 E4
Tynings Rd BA16 207 B4
Tynings The Clevedon BS21 6 A1
Portishead BS20 1 F1
Tynings Way Clutton BS39 58 E3
Westwood BA15 64 F3
Tynning Terr 18 BA1 28 A1
Tynte Ave BS13 22 E3
Tynte Rd TA6 209 D6
Tyntesfield Rd BS13 22 A8
Tyrone Wlk BS4 22 E8

Westcombe Hill BA4 . . .142 C2
Westcombe Rd
Evercreech BA4 . . . . . . .141 F2
Westcombe BA4 . . . . .142 A2
Westcombe Trad Est
TA19 . . . . .183 E1
Westcombes EX13 . . . . .198 B7
Westcott Cl BA11 . . . . . .120 C6
Westcott La TA4 . . . . . .148 F2
Westend BA22 . . . . .174 E1
Westend La BA11 . . . . . .143 C6
Westerkirk Gate TA2 . . .212 C7
Westerleigh Rd Bath BA2 .45 B1
Clevedon BS21 . . . . .6 B2
Western Approaches
BA22 . . . . .174 A2
Western Ave BA21 . . . . .218 B6
Western Ct Clevedon BS21 .6 D3
Shepton Mallet BA4 . . . . .205 B6
Western Dr BS14 . . . . .22 E6
Western Gate TA10 . . . .172 C7
Western La
East Harptree BS40 . . . . . .74 C3
Minehead TA24 . . . . .200 F7
Western Retreat BA5 . . .203 B5
Western St DT9 . . . . .187 E4
Western Way
Bridgwater TA6 . . . . .208 F7
Winsham TA20 . . . . .194 E1
Westex Ho BS23 . . . . .49 B5
Westfield Bruton BA10 . .215 D5
Clevedon BS21 . . . . .16 D8
Curry Rivel TA10 . . . . .171 C3
Shepton Mallet BA4 . . . . .205 A6
Sherborne DT9 . . . . .225 B2
Westfield Ave BA21 . . . .218 E6
Westfield Cl
Backwell BS48 . . . . .19 A6
Bath BA2 . . . . .44 E3
Bridgwater TA6 . . . . .208 E4
Burnham-On-Sea TA8 . . . .104 B8
Keynsham BS31 . . . . .24 C5
Weston-Super-Mare BS23 . .48 D2
Westfield Com Sch
BA21 . . . . .218 E6
Westfield Cres
Banwell BS29 . . . . .51 A3
Yeovil BA21 . . . . .218 F6
Westfield Ct TA8 . . . . . . .104 B8
Westfield Dr
Backwell BS48 . . . . .19 A6
Burnham-On-Sea TA8 . . . .104 B8
Westfield Est BA12 . . . . .161 F2
Westfield Gr BA21 . . . . .218 F6
Westfield Ho Bath BA2 . . .44 E3
Bridgwater TA6 . . . . .208 E4
Westfield Ind & Trad Est
BA3 . . . . .97 C7
Westfield La
Curry Rivel TA10 . . . . .171 C3
Draycott BS27 . . . . .90 E3
North Curry TA3 . . . . .170 C3
Rodney Stoke BS27 . . . . . .110 C8
Street BA6,BA16 . . . . .207 E2
Westfield Pk BA1 . . . . . . .44 A7
Westfield Pk S BA1 . . . . .44 A7
Westfield Pl Bristol BS8 . .11 F7
Yeovil BA21 . . . . .218 E6
Westfield Prim Sch BA3 .97 C8
Westfield Rd
Backwell BS48 . . . . .19 A6
Banwell BS29 . . . . .51 A3
Burnham-On-Sea TA8 . . . .104 B8
Frome BA11 . . . . .119 D3
Wells BA5 . . . . .203 C4
Weston-Super-Mare BS23 . .48 D2
Yeovil BA21 . . . . .218 F6
Westfield Terr BA3 . . . . . .78 D1
Westfields TA19 . . . . . . .184 C5
Westford Cl TA21 . . . . . .222 A5
Westgate Bldgs BA1 . . . .228 B2
Westgate St Bath BA1 . . .228 B2
4 Taunton TA1 . . . . .212 E3
Westhall Rd BA1 . . . . .44 D7
Westhaven Sch BS23 . . . .48 D2
Westhay Broad Dro TA7 137 E6
Westhay Cross EX13 . . .198 F3
Westhay Moor Dro BA5,
BA6 . . . . .138 D6
Westhay Rd BA6 . . . . . . .138 C4
Westhill La TA9 . . . . .105 C2
Westholm Rd TA11 . . . . .211 B4
Westlake Cl TA7 . . . . . . .155 C2
Westland Rd BA20 . . . . .218 F4
Westleigh Gdns BA4 . . . .205 A6
Westleigh Pk BS14 . . . . . .23 B8
Westleigh Rd TA1 . . . . . .213 B3
Westmans Est TA8 . . . . .104 C7
Westmarch Way BS22 . . . .32 A4
Westmead Gdns BA1 . . . .27 A2
Westmere Cres TA8 . . . .104 C8
Westminster BA21 . . . . .218 C7
Westminster Bldgs
DT10 . . . . .190 B4
Westminster Cotts
DT10 . . . . .190 B4
Westminster St BA20 . . .219 A4
Westmoor Dro TA10,
TA12 . . . . .184 E7
Westmoor La TA10 . . . . .184 D8
Westmoreland Dr BA2 .228 A2
Westmoreland Rd BA2 .228 A1
Westmoreland St BA2 . .228 A2
Westmoreland Station Rd
BA2 . . . . .228 A1
Weston All Saints CE Prim
Sch BA1 . . . . .27 A2
Weston Bsns Pk BS24 . . .49 E5
Weston Cl Bristol BS9 . . . . .5 C7
East Chinnock BA22 . . . . .196 E8
Weston Dro BS20 . . . . .7 F8
Weston Euro Pk BS24 . . .49 B4
Weston Express Bsns Pk
BS22 . . . . .49 C6
Weston Farm La BA1 . . . .27 C2
Weston Hill SP8 . . . . . . .177 D3
Weston Ind Est BS24 . . . .49 B2
Weston La Bath BA1 . . . .44 C8
East Coker BA22 . . . . . . .197 E5
Halstock DT2 . . . . .196 F1
Weston Lock Ret BA2 . . .44 C6
Weston Lodge BS23 . . . . .48 D8
Weston Miiature Rly
BS23 . . . . .48 D5
Weston Milton Sta BS22 .49 C7
Weston Park Ct BA1 . . . .27 D1
Weston Park Prim Sch
BS11 . . . . .4 F8
Weston Pk BA1 . . . . .27 C1
Weston Pk E BA1 . . . . . . .27 D1
Weston Pk W BA1 . . . . . . .27 C1
Weston Rd Bath BA1 . . . . .44 D8
Brean TA8 . . . . .66 A5
Congresbury BS49 . . . . . . .34 B5
East Brent BS24,TA9 . . . . .86 D6
Failand BS8 . . . . .10 C3
Long Ashton BS41 . . . . . . .20 D8
Weston Ret Pk BS23 . . . .49 A6
Weston Sixth Form Coll
BS23 . . . . .48 F2
Weston St
Buckhorn Weston SP8 . . . .177 D3
East Chinnock BA22 . . . . .196 E8
Weston Town BA4 . . . . . .141 E1
Weston Way BS24 . . . . . . .49 F2
Weston Wood Rd BS20 . . .2 C3
Weston-Super-Mare Sea Life
Ctr★ BS23 . . . . .48 D6
Weston-Super-Mare Sta
BS23 . . . . .48 E7
Weston-Super-Mare Tech
Coll & Sch of Art BS23 .48 D8
Westonia BS22 . . . . .31 E2
Westonian Ct BS9 . . . . . . .5 C4
Westonzoyland Prim Sch
TA7 . . . . .154 F5
Westonzoyland Rd TA6,
TA7 . . . . .209 E4
Westover BA11 . . . . .119 D4
Westover Gdns BS9 . . . . . .5 F8
Westover Gn TA6 . . . . . .208 E4
Westover Green Prim Sch
TA6 . . . . .208 E4
Westover La
Crewkerne TA18 . . . . .224 B7
Martock TA12 . . . . .185 F8
Westover Rd BS9 . . . . .5 F8
Westover Trad Est TA10 .171 F5
Westover View TA18 . . . .224 C7
Westover's Cnr BS28 . . .108 B4
Westowe Hill TA4 . . . . . .151 A3
Westridge DT9 . . . . .225 C3
Westridge Way TA4 . . . .167 E7
Westview BS39 . . . . .77 C5
Westview Orch BA3 . . . . .64 B5
Westville BA21 . . . . .219 C5
Westward BS41 . . . . .11 B2
Westward Cl BS40 . . . . . .35 D2
Westward Dr BS20 . . . . . . .4 C4
Westward Gdns BS41 . . . .11 B2
Westward Rd BS13 . . . . . .21 F7
Westway Nailsea BS48 . . . . .8 E2
Street BA16 . . . . .207 B6
Westway Ctr BA11 . . . . .119 F5
Westway La BA4 . . . . . . .205 B4
Westwood BA2 . . . . .45 F6
Westwood Ave BS39 . . . . .59 C2
Westwood Cl 2 BS22 . . . .31 F2
Westwood Cotts BA8 . . .176 E1
Westwood Dr BA11 . . . .119 C4
Westwood Dro TA11 . . . .158 C3
Westwood Rd
Bridgwater TA6 . . . . .209 D7
Bristol BS4 . . . . .23 D8
Westwood with Iford Prim
Sch BA15 . . . . .64 F3
Westwoods BA1 . . . . .29 B3
Wet La BS27 . . . . .90 F2
Wetherell Pl BS8 . . . . . .226 B3
Wetlands La BS20 . . . . . . .2 C3
Wetmoor La
Langport TA10 . . . . .172 C2
Westbury Sub Mendip
BA5 . . . . .110 E1
Wexford Rd BS4 . . . . .22 D8
Weycroft Ave EX13 . . . .198 A2
Weymont Cl TA7 . . . . . . .155 B3
Weymouth Ct BA1 . . . . . .45 B8
Weymouth Rd
Evercreech BA4 . . . . .141 E1
Frome BA11 . . . . .119 E4
Weymouth St BA1 . . . . . .45 B8
Whaddon Hill BA10 . . . .160 C7
Wharf Cotts TA21 . . . . .222 B8
Wharf La Ilminster TA19 .221 B3
Portbury BS20 . . . . .3 B5
Wharfside BS24 . . . . .66 E3
Wharnecliffe Cl BS14 . . . .23 B5
Wharnecliffe Gdns BS14 .23 B5
Whatcombe Rd BA11 . . .119 E6
Whatcombe Terr BA11 . .119 E6
Whatley TA10 . . . . .171 F5
Whatley Cross TA20 . . . .194 C1
Whatley La
Buckland St Mary TA20 . . .192 D7
Langport TA10 . . . . .172 A5
Tatworth TA20 . . . . .194 C1
Winsham TA20 . . . . .199 A8
Whatley Vineyard & Herb
Gdn★ BA11 . . . . .118 D4
Wheatfield Dr BS22 . . . . .32 A5
Wheatfield La BA3 . . . . . .95 A6
Wheathill Cl
Keynsham BS31 . . . . .24 D5
Milborne Port DT9 . . . . . .217 D2
Wheathill La DT9 . . . . . .217 E3
Wheathill Way DT9 . . . .217 D2
Wheatleigh Cl TA1 . . . . .212 E2
Wheatley Cres TA1 . . . . .213 B5
Wheatstones 10 TA4 . . . .167 F8
Wheel House La TA20 . .199 B7
Wheeler Gr BA5 . . . . . . .203 B4
Wheelers Cl BA3 . . . . .78 D2
Wheelers Dr BA3 . . . . . . .78 C2
Wheelers Rd BA3 . . . . . . .78 D2
Whellers Mdw TA12 . . . .185 E7
Whetham Mill Cross
DT8 . . . . .199 F5
Whetham Mill La DT8 . .199 F6
Whetstones Almshouses
TA19 . . . . .183 F4
Whippington Ct 1 BS1 .227 B3
Whirligig La TA1 . . . . . .212 F4
Whirligig Pl 7 TA1 . . . . .212 F4
Whistley La BS40 . . . . . . .74 F6
Whitbourne Moor BA12 144 E8
Whitbourne Springs
BA12 . . . . .144 F7
Whitchey Dro TA9 . . . . .137 A5
Whitchurch District Ctr
BS14 . . . . .23 A5
Whitchurch La
Bristol, Bishopsworth BS13 .22 B5
Bristol, Hartcliffe BS13 . . . .22 C5
Bristol, Whitchurch BS14 . . .22 E5
Dundry BS41 . . . . .22 C1
Yenston BA8 . . . . .189 F8
Whitchurch Prim Sch
BS14 . . . . .23 C4
Whitchurch Rd BS13 . . . .22 A6
Whitcombe Farm La
DT9 . . . . .175 D2
Whitcombe La TA12 . . . .185 F8
Whitcross 10 BA22 . . . . .197 F8
White Ash La TA20 . . . . .193 A5
White Cats Cotts BA8 . .176 E3
White Cross
Brent Knoll TA9 . . . . .105 C8
Exford TA24 . . . . .128 B1
White Cross Gate BS39 . .76 F6
White Hart La TA21 . . . .222 D6
White Hill Langport TA10 .172 A7
Peasedown St John BA2 . . .79 F6
White Hill Dro TA20 . . . .193 C5
White Horse Dr BA11 . .120 C6
White Horse La BS28 . . .138 D8
White Horse Rd BA15 . . .64 E7
White House La
East Huntspill TA9 . . . . . . .136 E7
Loxton BS26 . . . . .68 A3
White House Rd
Claverham BS49 . . . . .34 F8
Pawlett TA5,TA6 . . . . .135 D5
White Lodge Pk BS20 . . . .2 D6
White Mead BA21 . . . . . .218 D6
White Ox Mead La BA2 . .61 F1
White St Bristol BS5 . . . .227 C4
Creech St Michael TA3 . . .169 E4
Horningsham BA12 . . . . . .144 E4
North Curry TA3 . . . . .170 C4
White's Dro BA5 . . . . . . .138 F7
White's La TA4 . . . . .133 A1
Whitebeam Cl TA6 . . . . .209 D5
Whitebrook La BA2 . . . . .79 A8
Whitebrook Terr TA21 . .178 F5
Whitechapel La BA11 . . .101 C1
Whitechurch La BA8 . . . .190 A7
Whitecroft TA4 . . . . .202 E4
Whitecross Ave BS14 . . . .23 C6
Whitecross La
Banwell BS29 . . . . .51 A4
Minehead TA24 . . . . .200 E7
Whitecross Rd
East Harptree BS40 . . . . . . .74 F4
Weston-Super-Mare BS23 . .48 E6
Whitecross Way TA24 . . .200 E7
Whitedown Cross EX15 .191 B4
Whitefield Cl BA1 . . . . . . .29 B4
Whitefield Cross EX36 .162 D3
Whitefield La TA19 . . . . .184 D4
Whitefield Rocks TA4 . . .150 B1
Whitegate Cl
Bleadon BS24 . . . . .67 B6
Minehead TA24 . . . . .201 A6
Whitegate Rd TA24 . . . .201 A6
Whitehall Taunton TA1 . . .212 F5
Watchet TA23 . . . . .202 B7
Whitehall Cl TA13 . . . . . .220 D4
Whitehall Ct TA18 . . . . .224 C7
Whitehole Hill BA3 . . . .116 E4
Whitehouse Com Sch
BS13 . . . . .22 C5
Whitehouse La Litton BA3 75 D3
Wraxall BS48 . . . . .9 A6
Whiteladies Rd BS8 . . . .226 B4
Whitelands Hill BA3 . . . .79 B3
Whiteleaze La
Thurloxton TA2 . . . . .153 C1
West Monkton TA2 . . . . . .169 D8
Whitemill La BA11 . . . . .119 C3
Whitemoor Hill TA20 . . .194 C4
Whitemoor La TA4 . . . . .150 F3
Whiteoak Way BS48 . . . . .18 D8
Whitepost Gate DT9 . . .188 D6
Whites Cl TA6 . . . . .208 E2
Whitesfield Ct BS48 . . . . . .8 D2
Whitesfield Rd BS48 . . . . .8 D1
Whitesome's Dro BS27 .109 C6
Whitestaunton Cross
TA20 . . . . .193 B5
Whitestone Rd BA11 . . .120 B6
Whitewall Cnr TA3 . . . . .181 D2
Whiteway TA20 . . . . .193 E6
Whiteway Ave BA2 . . . . . .44 A3
Whiteway Rd BA2 . . . . . .44 A3
Whitewell Pl BA11 . . . . .119 E3
Whitewell Rd BA11 . . . . .119 E3
Whitewells Rd BA1 . . . . .28 A2
Whitewick La TA5 . . . . . .134 F8
Whitfield Rd TA6 . . . . . .209 D6
Whitford Hill Corfe TA3 .182 A4
Pitminster TA3 . . . . .181 F5
Whitford La TA3 . . . . . . .182 A4
Whithys The BA16 . . . . .207 C7
Whiting La 1 TA6 . . . . . .153 E3
Whiting Rd Bristol BS13 . .22 A4
Glastonbury BA6 . . . . . . .206 F5
Whiting Way BA5 . . . . . .203 D4
Whitland Ave BS13 . . . . . .22 B5
Whitland Rd BS13 . . . . . .22 B5
Whitley Rd TA7,BA16 . . .156 C8
Whitling St BS40 . . . . . . .38 A2
Whitmead Gdns BS13 . . .22 C4
Whitmore La TA2 . . . . . .212 D8
Whitmore Rd TA2 . . . . . .212 E8
Whitnage La EX16 . . . . .178 C2
Whitnell Cnr BA5 . . . . . .113 F6
Whitnell La Binegar BA3 .114 B8
Keenthorne TA5 . . . . .134 D2
Whitney Hill TA19 . . . . .193 F8
Whitson Ho 1 BS2 . . . . .227 C3
Whitson St BS1 . . . . .227 A4
Whitstone Cl BA4 . . . . . .205 C6
Whitstone Com Sch
BA4 . . . . .205 C5
Whitstone Ct BA4 . . . . . .205 D5
Whitstone Hill BA4 . . . .204 C1
Whitstone La BA4 . . . . . .205 E1
Whitstone Rd BA4 . . . . .205 D4
Whitstone Rise BA4 . . . .205 D4
Whitswood Steep TA24 .130 D4
Whittakers Ho 6 BA4 . . .205 B6
Whitting Rd BS23 . . . . . . .48 E4
Whittington Dr BS22 . . . .31 D2
Whittock Rd BS14 . . . . . .23 D6
Whittock Sq BS14 . . . . . .23 D7
Whittox La BA11 . . . . . . .119 E5
Whitwell Rd BS14 . . . . . .23 B8
Whitworth Rd
Frome BA11 . . . . .119 F2
Minehead TA24 . . . . .200 D7
Wick Hill
Charlton Horethorne DT9 .176 A1
Milborne Port DT9 . . . . . .217 B6
Wick Hollow BA6 . . . . . .206 F5
Wick House Cl BS31 . . . .25 D3
Wick La
Burnham-On-Sea TA9 . . . . .85 E6
Camerton BA2,BA3 . . . . . . .60 F1
Glastonbury BA6 . . . . . . .139 E2
Lympsham BS24 . . . . .66 E1
Pensford BS39 . . . . .40 D3
Upton Cheyney BS30 . . . . . .26 A8
Wick Moor Dro TA5 . . . .134 C7
Wick Rd
Bishop Sutton BS39 . . . . . .57 C3
Lympsham BS24 . . . . .66 D2
Milborne Port DT9 . . . . . .217 C4
Wicketsbeer Rd BA22 . . .197 C6
Wickfield BS21 . . . . .6 C1
Wickham Ct BS21 . . . . .6 C3
Wickham Rise BA11 . . . .119 F6
Wickham Way
East Brent TA9 . . . . .86 D4
Shepton Mallet BA4 . . . . .205 A6
Wickham's Cross or
Beggar's Grave BA6 . . .157 C3
Wickhill Rd TA10 . . . . . .171 D5
Wicklow Rd BS4 . . . . .22 E8
Widcombe BS14 . . . . .23 A6
Widcombe CE Jun Sch
BA2 . . . . .45 B5
Widcombe Cres BA2 . . . .45 B5
Widcombe Hill BA2 . . . . .45 C4
Widcombe Inf Sch BA2 . .45 B5
Widcombe Par BA2 . . . . .228 C1
Widcombe Rise BA2 . . . . .45 B5
Widcombe Terr BA2 . . . . .45 B5
Wideatts Rd BS27 . . . . . . .90 A7
Widmore Rd BS13 . . . . . . .22 B5
Wigeon Cl TA24 . . . . . . .201 C5
Wigmore Gdns BS22 . . . .31 D2
Wilbye Gr BS4 . . . . .22 D7
Wild Oak Ho TA3 . . . . . .168 D1
Wild Oak La TA3 . . . . . . .168 D1
Wildcountry La BS48 . . . .20 E6
Wilde Cl TA8 . . . . .104 C6
Wilder Ct BS2 . . . . .227 B4
Wilder St BS2 . . . . .227 B4
Wilderness Dro BA16 . . .138 E2
Wilderness The DT9 . . . .225 E4
Wildmoor La TA21 . . . . .181 A6
Wilfred Rd TA1 . . . . .213 A4
Wilfrid Rd BA16 . . . . . . .207 D6
Wilkins Cl TA20 . . . . . . .223 E4
Wilkins Rd TA6 . . . . .209 D5
Will La TA4 . . . . .151 A3
Willcocks Cl 6 TA21 . . . .222 D5
Willcox Cl BA6 . . . . .206 E5
Willet Cl TA9 . . . . .104 D3
Willet's La BA3 . . . . .94 D6
Willett Hill Cross TA4 . .150 E6
Willey Rd TA3 . . . . .170 E6
William Daw Cl BS29 . . . .50 F3
William Herschel Mus★
BA1 . . . . .228 B2
William Reynolds Ho
BA16 . . . . .207 D7
William St Bath BA2 . . . .228 C3
Taunton TA2 . . . . .212 F6
Williamstowe BA2 . . . . . .45 C1
Willie Gill Ct TA1 . . . . . .212 E4
Willinton Rd BS4 . . . . . . .22 F8
Willis Hay DT9 . . . . .225 D3
Willis's La TA18 . . . . . . .196 C4
Williton & District Hospl
TA4 . . . . .202 D3
Williton Cres BS23 . . . . .48 F3
Williton Sta TA4 . . . . . . .202 F4
Willmott Cl BS14 . . . . . . .22 F3
Willmotts Cl TA7 . . . . . .137 B2
Willoughby Cl BS13 . . . . .22 B7
Willoughby Pl TA20 . . . .223 D3
Willoughby Rd TA6 . . . .208 C4
Willow Cl Bath BA2 . . . . .62 E8
Clevedon BS21 . . . . .6 E3
East Huntspill TA9 . . . . . . .136 E7
Langport TA10 . . . . .172 A6
Long Ashton BS41 . . . . . . .10 F1
Portishead BS20 . . . . .2 C4
Radstock BA3 . . . . .78 E2
Taunton TA1 . . . . .213 D1
Weston-Super-Mare BS22 . .32 D2
Weston-Super-Mare BS23 . .48 E2
Westonzoyland TA7 . . . . . .154 E5
Williton TA4 . . . . .202 E3
Willow Ct TA6 . . . . .209 D5
Willow Dr Bleadon BS24 . .67 C6
Hutton BS24 . . . . .49 E2
Shepton Mallet BA4 . . . . .205 A6
Weston-Super-Mare BS24 . .49 E5
Willow Gdns BS22 . . . . . .32 D2
Willow Gn TA7 . . . . .154 D8
Willow Gr TA23 . . . . . . .131 E4
Willow Ho BS13 . . . . .22 D4
Willow La★ EX15 . . . . . .180 F2
Willow Rd Street BA16 . .207 B3
Yeovil BA21 . . . . .218 F6
Willow The BA3 . . . . .96 F2
Willow Tree Cl BA22 . . . .174 A4
Willow Vale BA11 . . . . . .119 F5
Willow Wlk
Bridgwater TA6 . . . . .209 C4
Keynsham BS31 . . . . .24 D4
Willowbank TA24 . . . . . .130 B4
Willowdown BS22 . . . . . . .31 E4
Willowfalls The BA1 . . . . .28 E3
Willows The
Brent Knoll TA9 . . . . .86 A2
Nailsea BS48 . . . . .8 F3
Wills Ind Est TA6 . . . . . .209 A4
Wills Rd TA6 . . . . .208 F1
Willway St BS2 . . . . .227 C3
Wilmots Way BS20 . . . . . . .4 D4
Wilmott Ho BS20 . . . . .4 D4
Wilsham Cross EX35 . . . .122 A5
Wilsham La EX35 . . . . . .122 A5
Wilson Pl BS2 . . . . .227 C4
Wilson St BS2 . . . . .227 C4
Wilsons Cl TA5 . . . . .134 B2
Wilton Cl
Burnham-On-Sea TA8 . . . .104 C8
Street BA16 . . . . .207 D5
Taunton TA1 . . . . .212 E3
Wilton Gdns BS23 . . . . . .48 D7
Wilton Gr TA1 . . . . .212 E3
Wilton Orch Street BA16 207 D5
Taunton TA1 . . . . .212 E2
Wilton Rd BA21 . . . . . . .219 E8
Wilton St TA1 . . . . .212 E3
Wiltons BS40 . . . . .35 D2
Wiltown TA10 . . . . .171 D3
Wiltown La EX15 . . . . . .180 F3
Wiltshire Cl TA1 . . . . . . .212 C2
Wiltshire Ct TA1 . . . . . . .212 C2
Wiltshire Way BA1 . . . . .28 A2
Wiltshires Barton 4
BA11 . . . . .119 E5
Wilway La TA22 . . . . . . .163 C6
Wimblestone Rd BS25 . . .51 F2
Wimborne Cl TA1 . . . . . .213 D3
Wimborough La BA22 . . .196 F6
Winash Cl BS14 . . . . .23 D7
Wincanton Bsns Pk BA9 216 B3
Wincanton Cl BS48 . . . . . . .9 B1
Wincanton Prim Sch
BA9 . . . . .216 C3
Wincanton Town Mus★
BA9 . . . . .216 C4
Winchcombe Cl BS48 . . . .19 A8
Winchester Cotts TA19 .184 E1
Winchester Gdns BA21 .219 C7
Winchester Ho 1 TA1 . . .213 A4
Winchester Rd Bath BA2 .44 D5
Burnham-On-Sea TA8 . . . .104 C7
Winchester St TA1 . . . . .213 A4
Wind Down Cl TA6 . . . . .208 C4
Windball Hill TA22 . . . . .163 B7
Windcliff Cres BS11 . . . . . .4 E7
Windermere Ave BS23 . . .48 F4
Windermere Cl BA20 . . .218 F2
Windmill TA3 . . . . .170 F5
Windmill Cres TA7 . . . . .136 E3
Windmill Hill Hutton BS24 50 A2
Wrantage TA3 . . . . .170 A2
Windmill Hill La
Ashill TA19 . . . . .183 B3

NG	NH	NJ	NK
NM	NN	NO	NP
NR	NS	NT	NU
	NX	NY	NZ
	SC	SD	SE	TA
	SH	SJ	SK	TF	TG
SM	SN	SO	SP	TL	TM
SR	SS	ST	SU	TQ	TR
SW	SX	SY	SZ	TV

Any feature in this atlas can be given a unique reference to help you find the same feature on other Ordnance Survey maps of the area, or to help someone else locate you if they do not have a Street Atlas.

The grid squares in this atlas match the Ordnance Survey National Grid and are at 500 metre intervals. The small figures at the bottom and sides of every other grid line are the National Grid kilometre values (**00** to **99** km) and are repeated across the country every 100 km (see left).

To give a unique National Grid reference you need to locate where in the country you are. The country is divided into 100 km squares with each square given a unique two-letter reference. Use the administrative map to determine in which 100 km square a particular page of this atlas falls.

The bold letters and numbers between each grid line (**A** to **F**, **1** to **8**) are for use within a specific Street Atlas only, and when used with the page number, are a convenient way of referencing these grid squares.

Example   The railway bridge over DARLEY GREEN RD in grid square B1

Step 1: Identify the two-letter reference, in this example the page is in **SP**

Step 2: Identify the 1 km square in which the railway bridge falls. Use the figures in the southwest corner of this square: Eastings **17**, Northings **74**. This gives a unique reference: **SP 17 74**, accurate to 1 km.

Step 3: To give a more precise reference accurate to 100 m you need to estimate how many tenths along and how many tenths up this 1 km square the feature is (to help with this the 1 km square is divided into four 500 m squares). This makes the bridge about **8** tenths along and about **1** tenth up from the southwest corner.

This gives a unique reference: **SP 178 741**, accurate to 100 m.

Eastings (read from left to right along the bottom) come before Northings (read from bottom to top). If you have trouble remembering say to yourself "Along the hall, THEN up the stairs"!

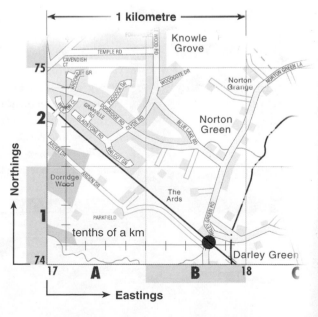